W9-DEU-221

Readers Rave About
Windows 95 SECRETS, 3rd Edition

"If you buy only one Windows book this year, make it this one."
—Edward Mendelson, PC Magazine

"Your SECRETS are pure gold!"
—Marc Julius, Parsippany, NJ

"Down to earth, understandable dialog."
—Ronald Jesser, Orange, CA

"This book saved my butt! I love this book."
—Dave Redic, Chesterland, OH

"Congrats! You have a winner!"
—Joe Gutierrez, Riverside, CA

"It is concise and thorough. I take it wherever I go – it's indispensable!"
—Jeanne Touw, Waterford, CT

"It contained information I couldn't find elsewhere."
—Denise Ryan, Fayetteville, NC

"A five-star lifesaver!"
—Timothy Wallace, Concord, CA

"Of the thousands of authors of technical books, Brian Livingston is far out front."
—Betty Whitson, Monroe, OK

"Excellent book – a must for the Windows 95 user."
—Lee O'Dell, Nashville, TN

"This is by far the best book out on Windows 95 and I've seen them all."
—Robert Long, Fontana, CA

"Mr. Livingston rips the cover off Windows 95 and provides a multitude of useful tips and tricks to make Windows 95 a joy to use."
—Matthew A. Martin, Birmingham, AL

"Sensational! I wish the book would have come my direction some months ago."
—Loy L. Banks, Raymore, MO

"This book should be issued with each copy of Windows 95."
—T. Daniels, Denver, CO

"Please continue to write great books like this one."
—Chad Lane, Bridgeville, DE

"Brian Livingston is a wizard."
—Eugene N. Young , Columbia, MD

"Easy to read – well-suited for beginner to advanced users."
—Johnie P. Gibson, San Diego, CA

"This book is excellent; Brian Livingston is the best!"
—Reid Hackney, Darien, CT

"I could not have mastered Windows 95 without it."
—James L. Birkhimer, Wakeman, OH

Windows® 95
SECRETS®
4th Edition

Windows® 95 SECRETS® 4th Edition

by Brian Livingston
and Davis Straub

IDG Books Worldwide, Inc.
An International Data Group Company

Foster City, CA ♦ Chicago, IL ♦ Indianapolis, IN ♦ Southlake, TX

Windows® 95 SECRETS®, 4th Edition

Published by
IDG Books Worldwide, Inc.
An International Data Group Company
919 E. Hillsdale Blvd.
Suite 400
Foster City, CA 94404
www.idgbooks.com (IDG Books Worldwide Web site)

Library of Congress Catalog Card No.: 96-80029

ISBN: 0-7645-3070-4

Printed in the United States of America

10 9 8 7 6 5 4 3

1B/TQ/RQ/ZX/IN

Distributed in the United States by IDG Books Worldwide, Inc.

Distributed by Macmillan Canada for Canada; by Transworld Publishers Limited in the United Kingdom; by IDG Norge Books for Norway; by IDG Sweden Books for Sweden; by Woodslane Pty. Ltd. for Australia; by Woodslane Enterprises Ltd. for New Zealand; by Longman Singapore Publishers Ltd. for Singapore, Malaysia, Thailand, and Indonesia; by Simron Pty. Ltd. for South Africa; by Toppan Company Ltd. for Japan; by Distribuidora Cuspide for Argentina; by Livraria Cultura for Brazil; by Ediciencia S.A. for Ecuador; by Addison-Wesley Publishing Company for Korea; by Ediciones ZETA S.C.R. Ltda. for Peru; by WS Computer Publishing Corporation, Inc., for the Philippines; by Unalis Corporation for Taiwan; by Contemporanea de Ediciones for Venezuela; by Computer Book & Magazine Store for Puerto Rico; by Express Computer Distributors for the Caribbean and West Indies. Authorized Sales Agent: Anthony Rudkin Associates for the Middle East and North Africa.

For general information on IDG Books Worldwide's books in the U.S., please call our Consumer Customer Service department at 800-762-2974. For reseller information, including discounts and premium sales, please call our Reseller Customer Service department at 800-434-3422.

For information on where to purchase IDG Books Worldwide's books outside the U.S., please contact our International Sales department at 415-655-3200 or fax 415-655-3295.

For information on foreign language translations, please contact our Foreign & Subsidiary Rights department at 415-655-3021 or fax 415-655-3281.

For sales inquiries and special prices for bulk quantities, please contact our Sales department at 415-655-3200 or write to the address above.

For information on using IDG Books Worldwide's books in the classroom or for ordering examination copies, please contact our Educational Sales department at 800-434-2086 or fax 817-251-8174.

For press review copies, author interviews, or other publicity information, please contact our Public Relations department at 415-655-3000 or fax 415-655-3299.

For authorization to photocopy items for corporate, personal, or educational use, please contact Copyright Clearance Center, 222 Rosewood Drive, Danvers, MA 01923, or fax 508-750-4470.

About the Authors

Brian Livingston

Brian Livingston is the author of IDG Books' bestselling *Windows 3 SECRETS; Windows 3.1 SECRETS,* 2nd Edition; *More Windows 3.1 SECRETS;* and coauthor of *Windows Gizmos,* a collection of shareware and freeware tools and games. His books are printed in more than 20 languages. In addition to writing books, Mr. Livingston is a contributing editor of *InfoWorld* and *Windows Sources* magazines, and has been a contributing editor of *PC/Computing, PC World,* and other magazines. He was a recipient of the 1991 Award for Technical Excellence from the National Microcomputer Managers Association.

Davis Straub

Davis Straub has previously worked as a Windows multimedia software and content developer. He is the former president of Generic Software (a successful CAD computer company) and Personal Workstations, Inc. (a successful computer VAR). When not furiously digging for Windows secrets, he spends his time hang gliding.

Publishing History

Windows 3 SECRETS (1st Edition)	Published 1991
Windows 3.1 SECRETS (2nd Edition)	Published 1992
Windows 95 SECRETS (3rd Edition)	Published 1995
Windows 95 SECRETS (4th Edition)	Published 1997

ABOUT IDG BOOKS WORLDWIDE

Welcome to the world of IDG Books Worldwide.

IDG Books Worldwide, Inc., is a subsidiary of International Data Group, the world's largest publisher of computer-related information and the leading global provider of information services on information technology. IDG was founded more than 25 years ago and now employs more than 8,500 people worldwide. IDG publishes more than 275 computer publications in over 75 countries (see listing below). More than 60 million people read one or more IDG publications each month.

Launched in 1990, IDG Books Worldwide is today the #1 publisher of best-selling computer books in the United States. We are proud to have received eight awards from the Computer Press Association in recognition of editorial excellence and three from *Computer Currents*' First Annual Readers' Choice Awards. Our best-selling *...For Dummies*® series has more than 30 million copies in print with translations in 30 languages. IDG Books Worldwide, through a joint venture with IDG's Hi-Tech Beijing, became the first U.S. publisher to publish a computer book in the People's Republic of China. In record time, IDG Books Worldwide has become the first choice for millions of readers around the world who want to learn how to better manage their businesses.

Our mission is simple: Every one of our books is designed to bring extra value and skill-building instructions to the reader. Our books are written by experts who understand and care about our readers. The knowledge base of our editorial staff comes from years of experience in publishing, education, and journalism — experience we use to produce books for the '90s. In short, we care about books, so we attract the best people. We devote special attention to details such as audience, interior design, use of icons, and illustrations. And because we use an efficient process of authoring, editing, and desktop publishing our books electronically, we can spend more time ensuring superior content and spend less time on the technicalities of making books.

You can count on our commitment to deliver high-quality books at competitive prices on topics you want to read about. At IDG Books Worldwide, we continue in the IDG tradition of delivering quality for more than 25 years. You'll find no better book on a subject than one from IDG Books Worldwide.

John J. Kilcullen
John Kilcullen
CEO
IDG Books Worldwide, Inc.

Steven Berkowitz
Steven Berkowitz
President and Publisher
IDG Books Worldwide, Inc.

Eighth Annual Computer Press Awards ≥ 1992

Ninth Annual Computer Press Awards ≥ 1993

Tenth Annual Computer Press Awards ≥ 1994

Eleventh Annual Computer Press Awards ≥ 1995

IDG Books Worldwide, Inc., is a subsidiary of International Data Group, the world's largest publisher of computer-related information and the leading global provider of information services on information technology. International Data Group publishes over 275 computer publications in over 75 countries. Sixty million people read one or more International Data Group publications each month. International Data Group's publications include: **ARGENTINA:** Buyer's Guide, Computerworld Argentina, PC World Argentina; **AUSTRALIA:** Australian Macworld, Australian PC World, Australian Reseller News, Computerworld, IT Casebook, Network World, Publish, Webmaster; **AUSTRIA:** Computerwelt Osterreich, Networks Austria, PC Tip Austria; **BANGLADESH:** PC World Bangladesh; **BELARUS:** PC World Belarus; **BELGIUM:** Data News; **BRAZIL:** Annuário de Informática, Computerworld, Connections, Macworld, PC Player, PC World, Publish, Reseller News, Supergamepower; **BULGARIA:** Computerworld Bulgaria, Network World Bulgaria, PC & MacWorld Bulgaria; **CANADA:** CIO Canada, Client/Server World, ComputerWorld Canada, InfoWorld Canada, NetworkWorld Canada, WebWorld; **CHILE:** Computerworld Chile, PC World Chile; **COLOMBIA:** Computerworld Colombia, PC World Colombia; **COSTA RICA:** PC World Centro America; **THE CZECH AND SLOVAK REPUBLICS:** Computerworld Czechoslovakia, Macworld Czech Republic, PC World Czechoslovakia; **DENMARK:** Communications World Danmark, Computerworld Danmark, Macworld Danmark, PC World Danmark, Techworld Denmark; **DOMINICAN REPUBLIC:** PC World Republica Dominicana; **ECUADOR:** PC World Ecuador; **EGYPT:** Computerworld Middle East, PC World Middle East; **EL SALVADOR:** PC World Centro America; **FINLAND:** MikroPC, Tietoverkko, Tietoviikko; **FRANCE:** Distributique, Hebdo, Info PC, Le Monde Informatique, Macworld, Reseaux & Telecoms, WebMaster France; **GERMANY:** Computer Partner, Computerwoche, Computerwoche Extra, Computerwoche FOCUS, Global Online, Macwelt, PC Welt; **GREECE:** Amiga Computing, GamePro Greece, Multimedia World; **GUATEMALA:** PC World Centro America; **HONDURAS:** PC World Centro America; **HONG KONG:** Computerworld Hong Kong, PC World Hong Kong, Publish in Asia; **HUNGARY:** ABCD CD-ROM, Computerworld Szamitastechnika, Internetto online Magazine, PC World Hungary, PC-X Magazin Hungary; **ICELAND:** Tolvuheimur PC World Island; **INDIA:** Information Communications World, Information Systems Computerworld, PC World India, Publish in Asia; **INDONESIA:** InfoKomputer PC World, Komputek Computerworld, Publish in Asia; **IRELAND:** ComputerScope, PC Live!; **ISRAEL:** Macworld Israel, People & Computers/Computerworld; **ITALY:** Computerworld Italia, Macworld Italia, Networking Italia, PC World Italia; **JAPAN:** DTP World, Macworld Japan, Nikkei Personal Computing, OS/2 World Japan, Windows NT World, Windows World Japan, SunWorld Japan; **KENYA:** PC World East African; **KOREA:** Hi-Tech Information, Macworld Korea, PC World Korea; **MACEDONIA:** PC World Macedonia; **MALAYSIA:** Computerworld Malaysia, PC World Malaysia, Publish in Asia; **MALTA:** PC World Malta; **MEXICO:** Computerworld Mexico, PC World Mexico; **MYANMAR:** PC World Myanmar; **NETHERLANDS:** Computer! Totaal, LAN Internetworking Magazine, LAN World Buyers Guide, Macworld Netherlands, Net, WebWereld; **NEW ZEALAND:** Absolute Beginners Guide and Plain & Simple Series, Computer Buyer, Computer Industry Directory, Computerworld New Zealand, MTB, Network World, PC World New Zealand; **NICARAGUA:** PC World Centro America; **NORWAY:** Computerworld Norge, CW Rapport, Datamagasinet, Financial Rapport, Kursguide Norge, Macworld Norge, Multimediaworld Norge, PC World Ekspress Norge, PC World Nettverk, PC World Norge, PC World ProduktGuide Norge; **PAKISTAN:** Computerworld Pakistan; **PANAMA:** PC World Panama; **PEOPLE'S REPUBLIC OF CHINA:** China Computer Users, China Computerworld, China InfoWorld, China Telecom World Weekly, Computer & Communication, Electronic Design China, Electronics Today, Electronics Weekly, Game Software, PC World China, Popular Computer Week, Software Weekly, Software World, Telecom World; **PERU:** Computerworld Peru, PC World Profesional Peru, PC World SoHo Peru; **PHILIPPINES:** Click!, Computerworld Philippines, PC World Philippines, Publish in Asia; **POLAND:** Computerworld Poland, Computerworld Special Report Poland, Cyber, Macworld Poland, Networld Poland, PC World Komputer; **PORTUGAL:** Cerebro/PC World, Computerworld/Correio Informático, Dealer World Portugal, Mac*In/PC*In Portugal, Multimedia World; **PUERTO RICO:** PC World Puerto Rico; **ROMANIA:** Computerworld Romania, PC World Romania, Telecom Romania; **RUSSIA:** Computerworld Russia, Mir PK, Publish, Seti; **SINGAPORE:** Computerworld Singapore, PC World Singapore, Publish in Asia; **SLOVENIA:** Monitor; **SOUTH AFRICA:** Computing SA, Network World SA, Software World SA; **SPAIN:** Communicaciones World Espana, Computerworld Espana, Dealer World Espana, Macworld Espana, PC World Espana; **SRI LANKA:** Infolink PC World; **SWEDEN:** CAP&Design, Computer Sweden, Corporate Computing Sweden, Internetworld Sweden, it.branschen, Macworld Sweden, MaxiData Sweden, MikroDatorn, Natverk & Kommunikation, PC World Sweden, PCaktiv, Windows World Sweden; **SWITZERLAND:** Computerworld Schweiz, Macworld Schweiz, PCtip; **TAIWAN:** Computerworld Taiwan, NEW ViSiON/Publish, PC World Taiwan, Windows World Taiwan; **THAILAND:** Publish in Asia, Thai Computerworld; **TURKEY:** Computerworld Turkiye, Macworld Turkiye, Network World Turkiye, PC World Turkiye; **UKRAINE:** Computerworld Kiev, Multimedia World Ukraine, PC World Ukraine; **UNITED KINGDOM:** Acorn User UK, Amiga Action UK, Amiga Computing UK, Apple Talk UK, Computing, Macworld, Parents and Computers UK, PC Advisor, PC Home, PSX Pro, The WEB; **UNITED STATES:** Cable in the Classroom, CIO Magazine, Computerworld, DOS World, Federal Computer Week, GamePro Magazine, InfoWorld, I-Way, Macworld, Network World, PC Games, PC World, Publish, Video Event, THE WEB Magazine, and WebMaster; online webzines: JavaWorld, NetscapeWorld, and SunWorld Online; **URUGUAY:** InfoWorld Uruguay; **VENEZUELA:** Computerworld Venezuela, PC World Venezuela; and **VIETNAM:** PC World Vietnam.
3/24/97

This book is dedicated to Margie Livingston and Belinda Boulter.

Credits

**Senior Vice President
and Group Publisher**
Brenda McLaughlin

**Vice President
and Group Publisher**
Walter Bruce

Acquisitions Manager
Gregory Croy

Acquisitions Editor
Ellen L. Camm

Brand Manager
Melisa M. Duffy

Managing Editor
Andy Cummings

Software Acquisitions Editor
Tracy Lehman Cramer

Development Editor
Heidi Steele

Editor
Erik Dafforn

Copy Edit Coordinator
Barry Childs-Helton

Editorial Assistant
Timothy Borek

Technical Reviewers
Beth Slick
Stephen Pedrick
Nathan Pedrick

Production Director
Beth Jenkins

**Supervisor of Project
Coordination, Production
Proofreading, and Indexing**
Cindy L. Phipps

Supervisor of Page Layout
Kathie S. Schutte

**Supervisor of Graphics
and Design**
Shelley Lea

Production Systems Specialist
Debbie J. Gates

Project Coordinator
Regina Snyder

Layout and Graphics
Linda Boyer
Elizabeth Cárdenas-Nelson
J. Tyler Connor
Dominique DeFelice
Angela F. Hunckler
Drew R. Moore
Brent Savage
Michael Sullivan

Proofreaders
Nancy L. Reinhardt
Joel K. Draper
Rachel Garvey
Nancy Price
Dwight Ramsey
Robert Springer
Karen York

Indexer
Sharon Hilgenberg

Production Administration
Tony Augsburger
Todd Klemme
Tom Missler
Jacalyn L. Pennywell
Leslie Popplewell
Theresa Sánchez-Baker
Melissa Stauffer
Bryan Stephenson

Cover Design
Draper and Liew, Inc.

Acknowledgments

No book is the sole work of its authors. While our efforts were focused on writing this work, many others provided the help we needed to complete it. Our editor, Heidi Steele, turned our best efforts into much more readable text. Pat O'Brien and Beth Slick checked our findings to make sure they weren't idiosyncratic.

We spent a considerable amount of time on the Windows 95 beta news group and working over the phone with Microsoft Personal Systems support personnel. Our fellow Windows 95 and Internet Explorer beta testers provided us with crucial assistance and guidance. The beta support people at Microsoft were top-notch and deserve great praise from everyone in the industry for their commitment to quality and their willingness to help make Windows 95 and Internet Explorer better products.

Throughout this book we have mentioned various beta testers, news group participants, and support personnel who were especially helpful and insightful. Without their assistance *Windows 95 Secrets,* 4th Edition, would not be nearly as useful.

(The Publisher would like to give special thanks to Patrick J. McGovern, without whom this book would not have been possible.)

Contents at a Glance

Table of Contents

Part V: Communications **809**

Chapter 28: Calling Your Computer at Work from Your Computer at Home 811

Chapter 1

Read This First

Why Windows 95 Secrets

Windows 95 is a large and complicated piece — actually many pieces — of software with thousands of features and capabilities. Microsoft focused on writing the code for the operating system as its primary task. Documentation was a secondary consideration.

Microsoft has decided that the Windows 95 operating system should be "discoverable" without a manual. Company officials contend that no one reads the manual anyway, so they left you, the user, to figure out how to use Windows 95 on your own. That's where we come in. *Windows 95 Secrets* is a detailed map of the Windows 95 territory. While *Introducing Microsoft Windows 95* (the manual that ships with Windows 95) delivers only a jumping off point, we give you guidance at (almost) every turn in the road.

We give you access to all those helpful features and capabilities that Microsoft didn't take the time or effort to document — or documented in a manner not accessible to mere mortals. *Windows 95 Secrets* exists because there is much that is not obvious in Windows 95 and much that must be coaxed to the surface.

How to Use This Book

If you want an overview of Windows 95 and a summary of its features, check out the next chapter. It is written both for users who are new to Windows and for those familiar with previous versions of Windows.

If you haven't yet installed Windows 95 or need to install additional portions of the operating system to support a network, modem, or printer, turn to Chapter 3 in Part I.

If you want to get a feel for Windows 95 (assuming that it is already installed) turn to Chapters 4 and 5. These chapters provide a quick look at, a basic tutorial on, and an overview of the Windows 95 Desktop.

More detailed information on aspects of the Windows 95 user interface is provided in Part II. Go to the chapter that addresses the aspect you are most interested in.

If you have DOS programs that you continue to use, you will be happy to know that Windows 95 provides a robust DOS environment and lots of services to help you better use these older applications. Turn to Part III to learn (among other secrets) how to customize the DOS environment for each of your DOS applications.

Windows 95 comes with routines to automatically detect the hardware in your computer. This doesn't mean that you won't need to or want to make some changes in how that hardware is configured. Part IV covers virtually all the hardware types that are found in computers today. Turn to Part IV to find the chapter that covers the hardware that interests you.

Windows 95 provides many tools to facilitate communication through dial-in remote network access, faxes, e-mail, connections to online services, local area networking, and direct access to the network of networks — the Internet. Turn to Part V for details on how to configure and use these communications options.

Finally, Part VI provides you with some software help and fun to go with your new operating system.

This Book's Overall Structure

Windows 95 Secrets is organized into six sections:

Part I: Introduction and Installation

This section summarizes the features of Windows 95 and explains how Windows 95 differs from previous versions of Windows. It also details the installation procedures required to get Windows 95 up and working on your computer. If you already have Windows 95 installed, but need to provide additional software drivers for new hardware or a network connection, this is where you will find the information you need.

In addition, Chapters 4 and 5 will familiarize you with the underlying logic of the Windows 95 user interface. If you read and carry out the procedures in these two chapters, it will be that much easier for you to become proficient at using Windows 95.

Part II: The Windows 95 User Interface

Most of us think of the user interface as Windows 95, forgetting all that is going on in the background. This section goes into detail about every aspect of the Windows 95 user interface. We discuss the Internet Explorer (both versions 3.01 and 4.0) and the new Active desktop, providing you with the knowledge you need to use and control Windows 95 and its applications.

Part III: DOS Secrets

This section gives you the complete story on how to continue running DOS applications and take advantage of the DOS services provided by Windows 95. You can run DOS programs in a sizable window using TrueType fonts, or you can run them full screen. You can tailor each DOS virtual machine (the environment surrounding your DOS application) to provide just the right amount of memory and other resources.

Part IV: Plug and Play

This section tells you how to make changes in the Windows 95 configuration of your hardware. We introduce you to the Device Manager, the Fonts and Printers folders, and new characters sets, and we tell you how to set up your display and change your Desktop. Windows 95 comes with some powerful disk and file management tools you'll want to learn about so you can protect your data.

Modems, ports, and the operating system's phone-management capabilities are all covered in this section.

Part V: Communications

Windows 95 provides a wealth of new tools to facilitate communication. Dial-Up Networking gives you a way to hook your portable computer to your Desktop computer or to the Internet, whether your portable is in the office, at home, or on the road. The Windows 95 Briefcase helps you make sure that both of your computers have the latest copies of your files and documents.

You can connect to bulletin boards using HyperTerminal, connect your portable to your office network using Direct Cable Connection, and send e-mail through your local area network or over the Internet. Using Windows 95's advanced networking clients, you can connect your computer to any of the popular local area networks.

Communications, of course, also includes getting on the World Wide Web, sending e-mail, and connecting to newsgroups. The Internet Explorer and associated Internet add-ons provide plenty of tools to help you do just that. We give you the skills you need to make full use of what Microsoft provides.

Part VI: Windows 95 Shareware

Shareware authors have been busy creating Windows 95-specific software to give you added features, more functionality, and more control. We provide you with the best Windows 95 shareware and freeware available.

Different Windows 95 Versions

Microsoft keeps putting out fixes and updates to Windows 95. First, there was Service Pack 1 in February 1996. Between February and October, Microsoft posted numerous other individual updates on their web site. In October, 1996, the OEM Service Release 2 went out to just hardware manufacturers. OEM SR2 included the previous individual updates, the Service Pack 1, and new updates available on Microsoft's web site, http:// www.microsoft.com/windows/software.htm.

In early 1997, Microsoft put the Internet Explorer version 4.0 into a public beta test (they called it the IE4.0 Platform Preview).

To see which version of Windows 95 you have, click the Start button, point to Settings, and then click Control Panel. Double-click the System icon. In the upper-right hand corner of the System Properties dialog box, read the System description. If it says 4.00.950, you have the original Windows 95 version. If it says 4.00.950 A, you have Service Pack 1. If it says 4.00.950 B, you have OEM Service Release 2.

If you install the Internet Explorer 4.0, you'll see an additional number under the one described in the previous paragraph. This number will be IE 4.0 4.71.xxxx, where xxxx is a four-digit number indicating the latest build of Internet Explorer 4.0.

The Internet Explorer version 4.0 can update and run with the original Windows 95 version. It can also update the Service Pack 1 and OEM Service Release 2 versions of Windows 95.

Microsoft has two development tracks for Windows 95: the user interface and the underlying computer management facilities. Internet Explorer 4.0 updates the user interface. Microsoft's service packs and releases add drivers and functionality to core elements. You'll want to get the latest updates of the core elements, but you don't have to have the latest service pack/release to be able to run the new interface.

You don't have to have OEM Service Release 2 with its 32-bit file system in order to use the latest user interface from Microsoft. You can still run Windows 95 with Internet Explorer 4.0 on hard disks formatted for the 16-bit FAT file system.

Service Pack 1

Released in February 1996, this pack of fixes cleans up a few nagging little problems. You have it installed if your System Properties dialog box lists 4.00.950 A in the System description. You'll find Service Pack 1 at http://www.microsoft.com/windows/common/aa2719.htm or http://www.microsoft.com/windows/software/servpak1/sphome.htm. Table 1-1 outlines the Windows 95 components that were updated and describes what fixes were made.

Table 1-1	Service Pack 1
Update	*Fixes*
OLE32 update	This update fixes the problem with deleted text. Before the fix, text you deleted was not actually erased, and you could see it if you were using Notepad to view documents with inserted ActiveX objects.
Windows 95 shell update	This update lets Windows 95 access fixes for NetWare Directory Services and fixes problems with copying files on NetWare servers that created zero-byte files.
Windows 95 common dialog update for Windows 3.1 Legacy printer drivers	This update fixes sporadic problems found with printers.
File and printer sharing for Microsoft Networks update	Before this fix became available, some network users could get unauthorized access to your hard disks.
File and printer sharing for NetWare Networks update	This update fixes the same problems regarding unauthorized access to your hard drives for NetWare Networks.
Windows 95 password list update	This update adds greater encryption to your password file. Unfortunately, the first version of this fix also corrupted your existing password file. Microsoft updated this fix with a patch and instructions on how to get rid of your previous password file.

(continued)

Table 1-1 *(continued)*

Update	Fixes
System Agent update	Microsoft found that the previous System Agent was off a little in its date/time calculation. This new System Agent fixes that problem.
Printer port (Lpt.vxd) update	When you installed Windows 95, the wrong Lpt.vxd was installed from the Windows 95 CD-ROM. This is the right one and it includes support for ECP ports.

Undocumented

If you have OEM Service Release 2, don't try to install Service Pack 1 over it. This causes all sorts of problems.

Stealth Updates

After the Service Pack 1 was released on the Microsoft web site, Microsoft continued to provide incremental updates to parts of Windows 95. You'll find them at http://www.microsoft.com/windows/common/aa2719.htm. Table 1-2 outlines what new Windows 95 components are available, where you can download them, and what they do for your computer.

Table 1-2	Stealth Updates	
Component	**Download Site**	**Fixes**
ISDN Accelerator Pack 1.1	http://www.microsoft.com/windows/software/isdn.htm	This pack includes ISDN drivers and an update to Dial-Up Networking. It also includes the DUN Server software, so you don't need Microsoft Plus! if you want to make your Windows 95 computer a Remote Access Server.
Internet Explorer	http://www.microsoft.com/ie	Internet Explorer is Microsoft's Internet browser. Depending on when you download it, you'll get either the standalone 3.01 version or the integrated 4.0 version.

Component	Download Site	Fixes
Kernel32 update	http://www.microsoft.com/ windows/software/krnlupd.htm	This is a replacement of the Windows 95 kernel DLL. It fixes a memory leak that drains system resources when you use TCP/IP applications over long periods.
32-bit DLC	http://www.microsoft.com/ windows/software/dlc32upd.htm	If you connect to mainframe computers using the DLC protocol, this fix gets rid of the stack overflow problem.
Fax cover page fix	http://www.microsoft.com/ windows/software/coverpg.htm	Before, setting the archive bit made the fax cover pages disappear. This fixes the problem.
Service Pack 1 password fix	http://www.microsoft.com/ windows/software/passwd.htm	The first version of Service Pack 1 corrupted your password file. This is a patch to fix Service Pack 1. You don't need this if you got Service Pack 1 after February, 1996.
PowerToys	http://www.microsoft.com/ windows/software/powertoy.htm	PowerToys contains TweakUI and lots of other user interface goodies.
KernelToys	http://www.microsoft.com/ windows/software/krnltoy.htm	KernelToys contains a number of separate utilities that track conventional memory, remap the keyboard, and more.
Internet Mail Service	http://www.microsoft.com/ windows/software/inetmail.htm	This is the Internet mail delivery driver that works with Windows Messaging and Microsoft Exchange. Formerly only available on Microsoft Plus!, you can now download it without having to buy Plus!.
Windows Messaging	http://www.microsoft.com/ windows/software/exupd.htm	This is the update of Microsoft Exchange. It is faster, smaller, and fixes bugs in the Internet mail delivery service.

(continued)

Table 1-2 *(continued)*		
Component	**Download Site**	**Fixes**
Wang Imaging for Windows 95	http://www.wang.com/ sbu/image95.htm	This replaces the fax imager in Windows Messaging and provides annotations to faxes and better TWAIN support to scanners.
IrDA 2.0 (Infrared Drivers)	http://www.microsoft.com/ windows/software/irda.htm	This enables wireless communication between infrared ports and external network or printer connections.
Large disk driver update	http://www.microsoft.com/ windows/software/dskts.htm	This fixes some EIDE drives with LBA and Int 13 problems.
Backup update	http://www.microsoft.com/ windows/software/backupd.htm	This provides performance improvements and bug fixes to the Windows 95 backup applet.

OEM Service Release 2

OEM Service Release 2 is not a retail product. That is, you can't go down to your local software store and pick up a copy. Microsoft only sold it to computer manufacturers. One of their reasons for doing this is that they didn't want to support old hard drive configurations with FAT 32 (their new file structure and format for hard disks).

If you have a copy (and a license to use) OEM Service Release 2, you can update your older version of Windows 95 (original or Service Pack 1) by booting your computer to the DOS prompt, renaming Win.com in your \Windows folder, and then running the OEM Service Release Setup.exe off the new CD-ROM.

One feature that Microsoft pulled from OEM Service Release 2 is the ability to dual boot. The discussion of dual booting in Chapter 6 doesn't apply to this version of Windows 95.

Table 1-3 is a version of a chart first published by Microsoft that describes OEM Service Release 2. We've edited out the Microsoft hyperbole. Some of the updates from OEM SR2 were already available as stealth updates.

The last two columns indicate whether a feature is available only when you order a new computer or whether you can download it from Microsoft's web site at http://www.microsoft.com/windows/common/aa2719.htm. You can find the latest version of this chart and links to download locations at http://www.microsoft.com/windows/pr/win95osr.htm.

Table 1-3	OEM Service Release 2		
Feature	*Description*	*New PC*	*Download*
FAT 32	Enhancements to the Windows 95 FAT file system designed to efficiently support large hard disks, up to 2 terabytes in size. Includes updates to Fdisk, Format, ScanDisk, and Defrag disk utilities to support FAT-32 partitions.	Yes	No
DriveSpace update	Windows 95 DriveSpace compression utility. Now supports compressed volumes up to 2GB in size. Note: DriveSpace compression is not supported on FAT-32 volumes.	Yes	No
Power management improvements	Support for Advanced Power Management (APM) 1.2 BIOS, wake-on-ring for modems, multi-battery PCs, drive spin down, and powering down of inactive PCMCIA modems.	Yes	No
Storage enhancements	Support for IDE Bus Mastering, 120MB Floptical disk drives, removable IDE media, Zip drives, and CD Changers. Also adds the SMART predictive disk failure APIs.	Yes	No
PCMCIA enhancements	Adds support for new PC Card 32 (Cardbus) bridges, PCMCIA cards that operate at 3.3 volts rather than 5 volts, multifunction PCMCIA network/modem cards, and PCMCIA Global Positioning Satellite (GPS) devices.	Yes	No
PCI Bridging/Docking	PCI Bridging/Docking	Yes	No
CDFS enhancements	Support for ISO 9660 disks up to 4GB in size and CD-I format CD-ROMs.	Yes	No
IRQ routing	Support for new PCI interrupt routers.	Yes	No
Internet Explorer 3.01	Microsoft's Internet browser.	Yes	Yes
Internet Connection Wizard	Makes it pretty easy to configure connections to worldwide Internet service providers through a centralized service, and assists in the sign-up process.	Yes	Yes
Internet Mail and News	Send and receive e-mail with this SMTP and POP3 mail client, and subscribe to newsgroups with a basic newsreader.	Yes	Yes

(continued)

Table 1-3 *(continued)*

Feature	Description	New PC	Download
NetMeeting	Make telephone calls over the Internet, including data calls with several people. You can remotely view and control any program, share a whiteboard, chat, and transfer files.	Yes	Yes
Personal Web Services	Allows publishing and hosting of HTML pages over the Internet/Intranet.	Yes	Yes
DirectX 2.0 (including Direct 3D)	Faster 2D and 3D graphics, sound, input, and communications for great games on virtually any PC. Will also ship with games that require it. Includes some sound and display driver updates.	Yes	Yes
ActiveMovie	Video architecture for Microsoft Windows. Playback of video, including QuickTime and MPEG-1 formats.	Yes	Yes
OpenGL	Support libraries for OpenGL graphics standard, plus some cool screen savers.	Yes	Available soon
Intel MMX support	Support for third parties to build software that exploits the Intel Pentium Multimedia Extensions (MMX) for fast audio and video support on the next generation of Intel Pentium processor.	Yes	No
Dial-Up Networking improvements	User interface enhancements, support for scripting, and hands-free dial-up.	Yes	Yes
Voice Modem support	Support for VoiceView and AT+V modems to allow switched voice and data transmission to occur, and to allow the modem to answer voice calls.	Yes	Yes
Service for NetWare Directory Services	Full client support for Novell NetWare 4.x, including NetWare Directory Services.	Yes	Yes
32-bit DLC	32-bit support for the Data Link Control protocol for SNA host connectivity.	Yes	Yes
Infrared support	Support for Infrared Data Association (IrDA) 2.0 compliant devices. Includes Infrared LAN connectivity.	Yes	Yes
Desktop Management	Support for Desktop Management Interface (DMI) 1.1. Allows a desktop management application to monitor devices on the PC.	Yes	Available soon

Feature	Description	New PC	Download
NDIS 4.0	Adds support for new NDIS 4.0 network interface card drivers.	Yes	No
Display enhancements	Support for dynamically changing screen resolution and color depth. Adapter refresh rate can also be set with most newer display driver chipsets.	Yes	Available soon
Wang Imaging for Windows 95	View image data from a variety of different file formats, including JPG, XIF, TIFF, BMP and FAX. Scan and annotate images with built-in TWAIN scanner support and imaging applet.	Yes	Yes
Fonts	Support for HP LaserJet 4 grayscale fonts.	Yes	Available soon
MSN 1.3	The latest version of the MSN client, which features performance improvements. (Note this has been outdated by updates to MSN.) Available from MSN.	Yes	Yes
Fixes/updates	Various Windows 95 updates, including: updated OLE components, enhanced Windows Messaging client with improved performance, and fixes to Microsoft Fax.	Yes	Yes
Automatic ScanDisk on boot	In situations where the PC was not shut down normally, ScanDisk will automatically run at the next reboot in order to check for damaged files.	Yes	No
Online services	FolderClient software for America Online 3.0, CompuServe 3.0, CompuServe WOW!, and AT&T Worldnet.	Yes	No

Internet Explorer 4.0

You can download Internet Explorer 4.0 from http://www.microsoft.com/ie. You can download additional Internet tools, including the latest versions of Outlook Express, NetMeeting, FrontPad, NetShow, Web Publishing Wizard, and Personal Web Server, from the same location.

Getting Commands Right the First Time

You'll be able to use the secrets in this book faster if you know exactly how to type the many Windows commands shown in the text.

Throughout this book, we've indicated many commands like this:

```
WORDPAD {/P} filename
```

or

```
Wordpad {/p} filename
```

In this command, *filename* is shown in *italics* to indicate that you should change *filename* to the actual name of the file you want to open in the WordPad text editor. The command /P is shown in curly braces {like this} to indicate that this *command line parameter* is optional. You should *not* type the curly braces if you decide to add /P to this command. Because Windows often uses square brackets [like this] to indicate the beginning of sections in initialization *(ini)* files and in the text version of the Registry, we do not use square brackets to indicate optional parameters. If you see a line that contains square brackets, you must type the square brackets along with the rest of the line.

If you want to print the Readme.txt file using WordPad, for example, you could click the Start button on the Taskbar, click Run, and then type this line followed by Enter:

```
Wordpad /p Readme.txt
```

or

```
WORDPAD /P README.TXT
```

When such a command is within the text of a paragraph, it usually appears in regular type, like the rest of the paragraph, because Windows itself is far more flexible than DOS in the formats it allows, and we want this book to reflect what you see when you use Windows. (At times, for clarity, the commands you should type are shown in **boldface**.) You can enter commands in any combination of upper- and lowercase — in all lowercase, ALL UPPERCASE, or A mixture Of both.

Whenever you see the term *filename* in italics, you can change it to any form of a valid filename that DOS or Windows will recognize, including drive letters and directory names. For example, if C:\Windows\Command is your current folder, any of the following names for the Readme.txt file are valid in this WordPad command:

```
WORDPAD README.TXT
Wordpad Readme.txt
WORDPAD C:\WINDOWS\COMMAND\README.TXT
WORDPAD \WINDOWS\COMMAND\README.TXT
```

We denote special keys on your keyboard with an initial capital letter, like this: Enter, Tab, Backspace, Shift, Alt (alternate), Ctrl (control), and Esc (escape). When you see a phrase such as *press Enter*, you know not to type the keys e, n, t, e, and r, but to press the Enter key.

If one of the shift keys (Shift, Alt, or Ctrl) should be *held down* at the same time that you also press another key, the two keys are written with a plus sign between them. For example, *press Ctrl+A* means *hold down the Ctrl key, then press the A key, then release both keys.*

If you are supposed to *let up* on a key *before* pressing another one, those keys are separated by commas. If we say, *press Alt, F, O,* this means *press and release Alt, then F, then O.* This sequence activates the menu bar of a Windows application, then pulls down the File menu, and then executes the Open command. This is the same as saying *click File, Open.*

In this book, we usually do not indicate a keyboard-only procedure every time we describe how to do something with your mouse. The phrase *click File, Open* always means *click the File menu and then click the Open command,* but it can also mean *press the keys on your keyboard to issue the File, Open command.*

Finding the Good Parts

Each chapter begins with an introduction that gives you a quick idea of the neat tricks in store in that chapter. The summary at the end of each chapter provides a more detailed look at what you can expect to learn in the chapter.

When we discuss a secret, an undocumented feature, a tip, or a set of steps to carry out a specific task, you'll see an icon in the margin of the page. If you want to just hit the high points of this book, you can go from icon to icon, reading the surrounding paragraphs for helpful supporting material.

Secret

The secret icon indicates some useful information that Microsoft would rather that the end user not be aware of. Microsoft feels that the rest of us need to be protected from ourselves, so it would prefer that you didn't mess with the Registry, for example.

Undocumented

An undocumented feature is an aspect of Windows 95 that really should be explained, but for some reason got left out of the manual. Windows 95 is filled with helpful features that the programmers put in but the documenters didn't have an opportunity to tell you about.

Tip

Tips are just that — little explanations about how to do a certain task in a particularly nifty manner. Windows 95 gives you lots of ways to do various things, and the documentation from Microsoft misses quite a few of them.

STEPS

We often give you step-by-step instructions on how to carry out a specific task. One of our goals in creating these steps is to make sure that nobody gets lost. So even if you're unfamiliar with the theory, we include enough details in the steps for you to complete specific tasks. You can breeze through some of the steps as you learn more about Windows 95.

Getting Technical Support for Windows 95

All Windows programs have bugs. This includes all retail Windows software and all shareware featured in *Windows 95 Secrets*. Every program, no matter how simple, has some unexpected behavior. This is the nature of software, and bugs are usually fixed with the release of a newer version.

It is not possible for the coauthors or IDG Books to provide technical support for Windows 95 or for the many DOS and Windows applications that may cause conflicts in your system. For technical support for the shareware on the *Windows 95 Secrets* CD-ROM, see the section *Technical Support for the Windows 95 Secrets CD-ROM* later in this chapter, and the discussion of this topic in Chapter 37.

For technical support for Windows 95, you will be better off contacting Microsoft directly — or using electronic support (which we describe in a moment).

Microsoft provides telephone technical support for its DOS and Windows products through these numbers:

Type of Support	Number to Call at Microsoft
Microsoft Windows 95 Support (90 days of free support starting with your first phone call)	206-637-7098
Microsoft Pay-Per-Call Support ($2 per minute to a maximum of $25)	900-555-2000 (U.S.) or 800-936-5700 (U.S.)
Microsoft Foreign Pay-Per-Call Support	206-635-3909
Microsoft International Support (for referral to a non-U.S. office)	206-882-8080
Microsoft General Support	206-454-2030
Microsoft Windows Environment	206-637-7098
Microsoft Windows Applications	206-637-7099
Microsoft Download Service (BBS)	206-936-6735
Microsoft Fast Tips — automated touch tone	800-936-4200 (U.S.)

Secret

The best technical support (in our humble opinion) has *never* been provided on phone lines — it has always been provided (this is the secret) on Microsoft's newsgroup server (see the *Accessing Microsoft Support Newsgroups* section below). This server replaces their technical support forums on CompuServe (although you can still get help on CompuServe in the same forums, which are now managed by Wugnet).

Online News about Windows 95

Here are some good places to seek technical support and read the latest news about Windows 95:

Where to Get Help	How to Get There
CompuServe	Type **GO WINNEWS**
AOL	Go to the keyword **Winnews**
Prodigy	Type **Jump Winnews**
WWW	**http://www.microsoft.com/support**
FTP	**ftp://ftp.microsoft.com/PerOpSys/Win_News**
MSN	Click the Microsoft icon, click Windows 95, and then click WinNews

Accessing Microsoft Support Newsgroups

The best place to get Microsoft support is from the Microsoft support newsgroups. These newsgroups combine peer support (for the most part), support from Microsoft volunteers (MVPs, ClubWin, and ClubIE members), and every now and then (depending on the newsgroup), actual support engineers from Microsoft.

Microsoft hosts the newsgroups on its server, and they aren't generally distributed to other servers at Internet service providers. To access the newsgroups, choose msnews.microsoft.com as your news server (or as one of a number of news servers) in your newsgroup reader. Microsoft Internet News is a good basic newsgroup reader that allows you to subscribe to multiple newsgroup servers. You can download it from http://www.microsoft.com/ie.

Log on to the Microsoft newsgroup server after logging on to your Internet service provider. Choose from the long list of product and interest area-specific newsgroups hosted by Microsoft and be prepared for a lot of reading. You can start here: http://www.microsoft.com/support/news/. Turn to Chapter 37 for a list of Microsoft Windows 95 support newsgroups.

If you want actual one-on-one contact with Microsoft support engineers, you are pretty much going to have to pay for it on a per-contact or contract basis. You get support for the first ninety days, but after that it's pay as you go.

Accessing Technical Support on CompuServe

The CompuServe Information Service (CIS) is a worldwide computer service (one of many) that, among other things, allows you to exchange messages with almost every other e-mail address in existence. Many vendors of Windows products maintain forums on CompuServe. A *forum* is a message area that technical support people monitor on a daily basis, answering questions and comments left by users of each vendor's products. Most companies are unwilling to provide telephone support, which they consider expensive and boring. But a company's top programmers often look in on the CompuServe forums devoted to the company's products. They like answering questions on the forums because they can post their responses anytime, day or night.

To get electronic technical support from Wugnet on CompuServe, for example, you call a CompuServe local number with your modem, then type **GO MICROSOFT** at any CompuServe prompt to get to the Microsoft Connection. You will see a list of services, including several Microsoft Connection forums. You can also go to the Microsoft Knowledge Base from this area.

If you need support from someone other than Wugnet, type **GO SOFTWARE** or **GO HARDWARE**. You will see a listing of scores of companies, each with its own forum or forums filled with technical messages posted by company technicians and users.

Once you're in the forum for your particular vendor, choose the menu option Announcements from Sysop. This displays a listing of system operators (sysops), along with the latest news about the forum, such as new program enhancement files you can copy (download) to your computer, for example. Write down the name and CompuServe number that corresponds to the sysop in your particular area of interest. Then switch to the Messages section of the forum, compose a detailed message about your problem, and address it to the number of the sysop you wrote down.

When you *post* a message in this way, it is seen not only by the sysop you addressed it to, but also by anyone else who reads the messages for that forum. Check the Messages section 24 to 48 hours later, and you'll probably find several responses. Some of them will likely be from people who are not employees of the vendor, but are more expert users of the company's products than many employees!

To gain access to CompuServe, call the Customer Service Dept. at 800-848-8990 in the U.S. or 614-457-8650 outside the U.S. Customer service is available 8 a.m. to 12 midnight, Eastern Time, Monday through Friday, and 12 noon to 10 p.m. Saturday and Sunday (except on U.S. holidays). CIS will send you a packet of information on how to find the closest local number in your area, and how to use the service.

Many Windows programs now include a coupon good for a free trial membership on CompuServe as well as information on how to reach that vendor's forum. You should look for these valuable free offers when you open the box of software.

If you don't already have a modem, we encourage you to buy the fastest modem available — 36 Kbps — and start taking advantage of online services such as CompuServe, as well as bulletin boards, newsgroups, and web sites for the excellent technical support they provide.

On CompuServe, you can type **GO WINNEWS** to go to the WinNews forum and get the latest information about Windows 95. The Microsoft Knowledge Base is available at **GO MSKB**. For Windows 95 shareware, type **GO WINSHARE** or **GO WUGNET**. To get to the Windows 95 help switchboard, type **GO WIN95**.

Microsoft Network Windows 95 Support

Microsoft now has its own online network. You can sign up for it as soon as you have installed Windows 95. The user interface for the Microsoft Network is the same as the Windows 95 user interface, so you will be able to use MSN as soon as you can use Windows 95.

On the Microsoft Network, forums are called *bulletin boards*. You can read messages posted to any of the bulletin boards and post your own. You can also enter chat areas and type messages to other MSN users while online.

There are support bulletin boards for Windows 95 on the Microsoft Network where you can get help from other Windows 95 users. To get to the Windows 95 support areas after you dial into MSN, double-click the Computers and Software icon in the Categories area, double-click the Software icon, the Operating Systems icon, and then the Windows 95 icon.

Windows 95 shareware is available on the Shareware bulletin board. If you want help regarding how to use the Microsoft Network, double-click the Microsoft Network icon on your Desktop (if you installed it during Windows 95 Setup).

You can also access the Microsoft Network through your own Internet service provider. Microsoft charges a monthly fee of $6.95 for unlimited access to the content and forums on MSN accessed over the Internet. Go to http://www.msn.com.

Technical Support for the *Windows 95 Secrets* CD-ROM

If the *Windows 95 Secrets* CD-ROM disc is damaged, you should of course contact IDG Books, which is committed to providing you with a CD-ROM disc in perfect condition.

However, the coauthors of this book and IDG Books are not familiar with the details of every program on the *Windows 95 Secrets* CD-ROM and do not provide any technical support for the programs on the CD-ROM. The programs are supplied as is. Most shareware authors, but not all, provide technical support to users after they register. Some shareware authors provide limited technical support to unregistered users if they have problems installing the software. In either case, the best way to get technical support is to look in the text file or help file that accompanies each program and send e-mail to the address listed there. Some shareware authors also provide technical support by fax or by U.S. mail.

Shareware authors do not usually have a technical support telephone line, although some do for registered users. If a program is freeware, it probably has no technical support. In this case, if a program does not work on your particular PC configuration, you probably will not be able to obtain technical support for it. See Chapter 37 for further information on the *Windows 95 Secrets* CD-ROM and its contents, and see the complete text of the IDG Books Worldwide License Agreement at the back of this book for a thorough discussion of the uses and limitations of the *Windows 95 Secrets* CD-ROM and its contents.

What Are Windows 95 Secrets?

Where do secrets come from? And what makes something a secret or an undocumented feature?

Windows 95 is the first operating system written with the reasonable expectation that it would sell more than 100 million copies. It is vastly more complex and feature-rich than its predecessor, Windows for Workgroups 3.11. All the people presently working at Microsoft who have worked on Windows 95 taken together do not know everything about Windows 95. Windows 95 is too complex to be completely understood.

Windows 95 is a very big piece of software. In fact, there is no way you can really call it a *piece* of software. A typical setup includes more than 1,000 files — and many more that are on the Windows 95 source diskettes or CD-ROM are not copied to your hard disk.

Many different programmers have worked to create Windows 95 — it's an evolving operating system. Much of its core functionality is found in Windows 386 version 2.0 and later versions of Windows. Because it has been created over time, because so many people have been involved in it, and because it is so multifaceted, no one person can document or even be aware of it all.

Windows 95 resembles an organism in its complexity. In the same manner that there isn't a book that completely describes a dog, there isn't a manual that completely describes Windows 95. We have to make do with books that help us understand dogs and operating systems. (No implication here that this operating system is a dog.)

We began participating in the Windows 95 (and previously Chicago) beta forums on CompuServe in December 1993, and we ran various versions of Chicago and then Windows 95 beginning with alpha version milestone 5. We collectively discovered and submitted over 570 bug reports to Microsoft, many of which resulted in improvements to the beta code. We started running the alpha version of Internet Explorer 4.0 in July, 1996, and began communicating with other alpha testers on the new Microsoft beta newsgroups.

Some of the secrets and undocumented features we discuss in this book were first discovered by other beta participants and shared freely on the beta forum. Other secrets were first discovered by participants in the newsgroups on the Microsoft news server.

By the time this book went to the printer, we had spent three years using Windows 95 every day, as our one and only operating system. We looked at and used almost every user-accessible aspect of it. It is this experience with the actual thing itself that has formed the basis of most of our secrets and undocumented features.

We had hoped that the Windows 95 beta forums on CompuServe would be a rich source of beta testers' "secrets." As the number of beta testers grew, the message traffic on the forum became a roaring river of more than 1,000 messages a day. We hoped to find little nuggets of wisdom in the flow.

We did find some gems, which we have included in this book, with the proper credit where applicable. We (and in turn, you) are indebted to the hardy adventurers who, without a map, braved the wilds of the Registry database to show us how to change the basic Windows 95 configuration. However, most of the messages on the forum were about problems that beta testers were having — problems that were often fixed by Microsoft. Some beta testers shared their discoveries, but most were looking for help from others who were more knowledgeable. We helped where we could and appreciated the help that others gave us.

We'd like to thank the staff of the Mt. BeautyBakery in Mt. Beauty, Victoria, Australia. Because they had an Internet connection and a helpful attitude, Dan was able to complete the last edits and the compilation of the electronic version of this book while attending the Bogong Cup hang gliding competition.

As we wrote this book, we had to rely on our own experience of Windows 95 as the rock bottom guide to what Windows 95 truly was. It didn't matter to us what was written about how it was supposed to work. What mattered was how it in fact did work. It is our experience that we have written about in this book.

The people responsible for the documentation of Windows 95 at Microsoft are under the impression that you don't read the documentation. Maybe you just don't read *their* documentation. We feel that Microsoft is justified in its cynicism, whatever the cause, and it really makes little sense for the company to write something that you won't read.

The documentation writers at Microsoft can't write a book about Windows 95 secrets, because they are obliged to maintain that there aren't any. They can't poke at the rough edges of the operating system and give you workarounds, because they need to put the operating system in the best light. Some areas just don't get mentioned.

We are not so constrained. So when we see something that definitely shows that an operating system is the handiwork of human beings, we point out how to get around its shortcomings.

The "secrets" and "undocumented features" were there waiting for us and others to find and document. The official documenters had their hands full with other issues. All of us taken together still haven't gotten it all down on paper.

Something is a "secret" or an "undocumented feature" if it is useful and isn't found in the documentation that you get when you purchase Windows.

This book is meant to be a reference work. It doesn't read like a novel. If you want to know more about an area, you should follow along on the computer as you read through the steps that we detail.

We feel that if you find just one really clever trick that helps you use Windows 95, then your purchase of this book will be worth it. We have striven to provide you many more than one really neat insight into how to effectively master this operating system.

Because the world of computers is increasingly online and wired together, this book is just one way of obtaining the information you need to better use Windows 95.

We hope you enjoy this book.

Internet Explorer 4.0 updates

This printing of Windows 95 SECRETS is based on information received before the public release of Internet Explorer 4.0. Because Microsoft reserves the right to change Internet Explorer, there may be some differences between the descriptions in this book and the public release of Internet Explorer 4.0. Please check www.idgbooks.com for updates.

Getting Updates on Internet Explorer 4

This printing of *Windows 95 SECRETS* is based on the beta release of Internet Explorer 4.0. Because Microsoft reserves the right to change Internet Explorer, there may be some differences between the descriptions in this book and the final release of the software. Please check the IDG Books Worldwide web site at www.idgbooks.com for updates.

To help you retrieve and print Internet Explorer 4.0 updates from the web easily, you can download an evaluation version of WebPrinter for Windows 3.x/95 v2.0 from the IDG Books Worldwide web site. WebPrinter enables you to print web pages as mini-booklets. This application automatically intercepts standard-size pages as they are sent to your laser/ink jet printer and then reduces, rotates, and paginates the pages to print as double-sided booklets.

Tip

You can print up to four documents before you have to purchase the full version of WebPrinter. For more information, visit the ForeFront Group's web site at www.ffg.com, or call (800) 475-5831.

Part I

Introduction and Installation

Chapter 2

Windows 95 Features Summary

In This Chapter

▶ A brief description of many of the features (both new and inherited from Windows 3.x) of Windows 95

Find a Feature and Get More Information

What's the point of writing a whole chapter summarizing the features of Windows 95? This chapter gives you another entry point into Windows 95. After skimming this list and finding features that you're interested in, you can turn to the associated chapter for details on how to implement or use those features.

Microsoft wants Windows 95 to be "discoverable." A novice user should be able to figure out how to do something useful by simply experimenting with Windows 95. This is a great feature (details later in this chapter), but it is also nice to have an overview that shows all the features in the territory. You could wander around "discovering" things for quite a while, but it sure is nice to have a map to help you through the jungle.

Here's a summary of the major features, and guidance about which chapters contain more information.

The User Interface

Simple user interface. What you see on your video monitor is the Windows 95 Desktop. The Desktop is simple and has an obvious entry point — the Start button on the Taskbar at the bottom, top, or one side of your screen. This Desktop is a radical departure from the Windows 3.x Desktop with its Program Manager and File Manager "shells." (See Chapter 7.)

When you start Windows 95, before you start changing things to suit you, there are only three or four things on the Desktop — the Taskbar with its Start button, plus icons for My Computer, Network Neighborhood, the Recycle Bin and, optionally, Windows Messaging, Microsoft Network, and the Internet. (See Chapter 7.)

Discoverability. This starts with the Start button. New Windows users can click the Start button — click, not double-click — and then follow the cascading menus to find out what is available. (See Chapter 11.)

The Start button. Clicking it once lets you find and start an installed application. One drawback is that the icons shown in the Start menus are only a quarter as large as they were in the Windows 3.x Program Manager. They are therefore significantly more difficult to identify. You exit Windows 95 (and prepare to turn off your computer) by clicking Shut Down at the bottom of the menu that pops up when you click the Start button. (See Chapter 7.)

Taskbar. The Taskbar contains the Start button and buttons for all the active programs — programs that you have already started. Only one click of a button in the Taskbar is required to bring a program to the top of the Desktop. Because all active applications (whether or not they have been minimized) show up on the Taskbar, it is easy to switch between active applications.

The icons in the Taskbar are a quarter as large as they were on the Windows 3.x Desktop — so they take up less room but are harder to recognize.

You can move the Taskbar from the bottom to the right, top, or left side of the Desktop and increase its size to half of the Desktop. You can also force it to always be on top, and/or hidden so that it only pops up when you move your mouse pointer to it. (See Chapter 7.)

Clock. You don't have to go searching for the time because the Taskbar contains a clock. Park your mouse pointer over the clock and the date pops up. Double-click the clock (or right-click it and choose Adjust Date/Time from the context menu) to display a dialog box where you can change the date and time. (See Chapter 7.)

My Computer. Double-click this icon on the Desktop to view the contents of the disk drives and folders (directories) stored on your computer. This feature is something of a combined Program Manager and File Manager. (See Chapter 8.)

Network Neighborhood. Same as My Computer, but for all the computers connected to yours. You see the shared resources — disk drives, printers, and other resources available to you on the network. (See Chapter 36.)

Windows Messaging. A unified e-mail and fax front end (user interface). You can route all your electronic mail communications through Windows Messaging, whether they be just across your local network, through information providers such as CompuServe or the Microsoft Network, or across the Internet. (See Chapter 32.)

The Desktop. You can put icons representing applications — and documents — right on the Desktop. Better still, put *shortcuts*, which are links to applications or documents, on the Desktop. This makes the Desktop look something like the Program Manager. (See Chapter 7.)

The Internet Explorer 4.0 Active Desktop. If you have installed Internet Explorer 4.0 you get an additional view of your computer, the Active Desktop. This view turns your Desktop into something like a web page with an active window of continuously updated information. (See Chapter 34.)

Folders. Directories are now called *folders*. When you double-click a folder icon in My Computer or Network Neighborhood, you get a *folder window* — a window displaying the contents of the folder. This is a very visual way of browsing to find the application or file you want. (See Chapter 8.)

Big icons in folder windows. You can browse through your local disks or those on the network, and you can display all your files with icons above their names. The icons are big, like they were in the Windows 3.x Program Manager. You can start an application by double-clicking its icon in the folder window. (See Chapter 8.)

New. You can create a new document in any folder — even on the Desktop — by right-clicking the folder window client area (or Desktop) and choosing the New command from the context menu. Windows 95 knows about all the software you have installed and prompts you for what type of document (bitmap or word processor, for example) to create. You can then double-click the new document and launch the application associated with it. (See Chapter 13.)

The Explorer. Right-click the My Computer icon and choose Explore. Up pops an Explorer window with a two-pane window. The left pane contains an outline, or *hierarchical,* view of the contents of your computer and the network connected to it. The right pane displays all the disk drives, folders, and/or files contained within the folder or drive highlighted in the left pane. The Explorer is especially useful for copying and moving files and folders. Although the File Manager in Windows 3.x often required that you open two separate windows in order to copy or move files, this is not necessary with the Explorer. (See Chapter 9.)

Help. Help is well organized, with a hypertext table of contents and index. Topic are thoroughly explained and frequently contain shortcut buttons that take you to the area you are searching for. There was no overall unified help in Windows 3.x. (See Chapter 11.)

Program Manager and File Manager. These applications are still there and provide for a transition to the new user interface for people familiar with Windows 3.x. You no longer exit Windows by exiting the Program Manager, as you did in Windows 3.x. (See Chapter 12.)

Right-click. Both buttons on two-button mice — and two out of three on three-button mice — do something useful now. When the mouse pointer is over a file or folder icon, clicking the right button — or left button for left-handed mousers — pops up a context menu. Right-clicking gives you many shortcuts to useful file or folder operations. It also lets you investigate and change the properties of the object you clicked. (See Chapter 24.)

Properties. There are *properties* associated with just about everything in Windows 95. This includes all the applications and files on your disk drives. For example, right-clicking the Desktop and choosing Properties from the context menu displays properties sheets that let you change display resolution or choose a different wallpaper or screen saver. (See Chapter 16.)

Find. You want to find a file and you don't know where you put it. Or you want to find a file that contains some known text. Find can do both of these tasks and much more. For example, it can find all the files that contain the word *seed* in their filename, have the words *cantaloupe* and *pineapple* in their contents, and were modified in the last three days. You can save and modify searches — oh, thank you, Microsoft (the Windows 3.*x* version of this was lame, at best). (See Chapter 11.)

Shortcuts. You can place a *shortcut*, or a link, on the Desktop or in a folder — somewhat in the manner of the Program Manager. You can gather all references to your applications in one or a few places, and launch them from there. This works without actually having to move the applications around. All the application icons shown on the Start menus are shortcuts. You can also place shortcuts in documents created by WordPad or Word for Windows — any OLE 2-compliant application client. (See Chapter 10.)

QuickView. Microsoft supplies more than 20 file viewers and expects application developers to provide more with their applications. A viewer lets you look at the contents of a file, most likely a document of some kind, without having to open the application that created it — presumably a quicker operation. Viewers exist for Quattro Pro, Excel, Word for Windows, WordPerfect 5 and 6, Word Pro, executable files (files with *exe* extensions), ASCII text files, and GIF and BMP graphics files.

These viewers are scaled-down versions of viewers found in the Windows utility Outside In, developed by Inso Corporation. QuickView Plus, which contains many more viewers and additional features, is available at http://www.inso.com. (See Chapter 13.)

Control Panel folder. Configuration information is consolidated in the Control Panel folder. Click the Start button, point to Settings, and then click Control Panel. If you want to configure anything about a network, double-click the Network icon in the Control Panel folder. We know this seems obvious, but previously it wasn't. (See Chapter 16.)

Themes. Microsoft Plus!, a Windows 95 add-on from Microsoft, comes with 16 themes that integrate Desktop icons, screen savers, wallpaper, sounds, mouse pointers, colors, and fonts. (See Chapter 22.)

Alt+Tab+Tab. Task switching is accessible from the keyboard. Instead of going to the Taskbar, you can quickly choose between active applications with this key combination. Hold down the Alt key and continue to press the Tab key to cycle through active applications. (See Chapter 21.)

Ctrl+Esc. Pressing Ctrl+Esc is just like clicking the Start button. (See Chapter 21.)

Communications

Windows Messaging, a universal mail client for all e-mail and fax communications. Windows Messaging provides a single user interface to connect with a myriad of electronic-mail providers. You can send and receive e-mail across your local network; over the phone lines from your mobile computer to your office network; through information service providers such as CompuServe, the Microsoft Network, and others; or through an Internet service provider (ISP) using a SLIP (Serial Line Internet Protocol) or PPP (Point-to-Point Protocol) account — all integrated through the Windows Messaging front-end and back-end message store. You can send and receive faxes using the same user interface. (See Chapter 32.)

Dial-Up Networking. Connect to your office computer or office network from home or your hotel room as though it were a local resource. Get your e-mail, copy files, and run programs on the distant computer as though you were directly networked to it. Dial into your Windows 95 desktop computer, a Windows NT server, a NetWare server, or a Unix-based server through Microsoft's 32-bit TCP/IP stack. Create a *connectoid* to connect to your Internet service provider. (See Chapter 28.)

Wizard helps set up Dial-Up Networking. Using a Wizard is like having someone lead you by the hand during the setup process. (See Chapter 28.)

Maintain the latest version of all your files on both your portable and desktop computers. Use the Windows 95 Briefcase to update the files that you are working on so both of your computers have the latest versions. (See Chapter 31.)

Access all Internet services. Connect to the Internet either through your local network or a dial-in Internet service provider with a SLIP or PPP account. Because Windows 95 comes with a high speed 32-bit TCP/IP networking stack, you are ready to connect to the net of nets. (See Chapter 33.)

World Wide Web browser. The Internet Explorer is integrated with the Windows 95 shell, Dial-Up Networking, and the Microsoft TCP/IP stack. You can dial out to the Internet and surf the web by double-clicking the Internet icon on your Desktop. (See Chapter 34.)

Internet News and Mail. Small, fast clients that work with the Internet Explorer. Internet Mail lets you connect to SMTP and POP3 mail servers. Internet News connects your to NNTP news servers. These programs offer basic functionality, but they have very well designed user interfaces. (See Chapter 35.)

High-speed communications, both foreground and background. Previous versions of Windows did not provide reliable background communications at high speeds. Certain tasks — such as formatting a diskette — would cause communications programs running in the background to drop transmitted characters. Windows 95 has been rewritten to significantly improve this situation, essentially through the use of 32-bit protected-mode code in file management and network system software, and hand optimization of time-critical code. (See Chapter 25.)

HyperTerminal. A 32-bit protected-mode terminal emulator, HyperTerminal provides easy access to bulletin boards and includes numerous file transfer protocols. It gives you a feel for how the new capabilities underlying the Windows 95 communications architecture can ease communications and improve reliability and speed. Of course, HyperTerminal still represents the old communications model in which, like a carriage turned into a pumpkin, your smart, fast computer becomes a semi-smart terminal connected to some "big" computer elsewhere. (See Chapter 29.)

TAPI. TAPI stands for Telephony Application Programming Interface. End users don't get to see this, but TAPI provides the basis for software developers to create new communications applications. TAPI shields end users from the arcana of modem AT commands. Developers of communications software can count on Windows 95 to recognize the installed modem. (See Chapter 26.)

Applications share the modem. No longer do you have to quit one communications application to use another — if these applications are TAPI-aware. Right now you can have Microsoft Fax at work monitoring the phone line for incoming faxes while you are using HyperTerminal to call an information service. You still have only one phone line, and your line is busy while you are using HyperTerminal, but fax monitoring restarts automatically when you finish communicating with the information service. (See Chapter 26.)

Single address book. Windows 95 maintains an address book that all TAPI-aware communication applications can use. You no longer need one book for faxes, another for e-mail, and a third for snail mail and voice communications. (See Chapter 32.)

File Management

Long filenames. You can give your files names up to 255 characters — assuming your application software supports these long names. The applications that come with Windows 95 do (except Program Manager and File Manager). (See Chapter 27.)

VFAT. The Virtual File Allocation Table is an extension of the existing file format for the DOS and Windows 3.*x* File Allocation Table (FAT). This means that you don't need to reformat your hard disk when you install Windows 95. You get access to long filenames without changing how files are stored. (See Chapter 27.)

Fast hard disk access with protected-mode disk drivers. Windows 95 doesn't have to switch your processor to real mode just to access your hard disks. This dramatically speeds up reading and writing to the disk. Windows 95 doesn't go through DOS or through your computer's BIOS to get to the hard disk, thereby saving lots of time. (See Chapter 27.)

A faster 32-bit CD-ROM file system. A major limitation in presenting video images on a computer display is the speed of reading the video frames off the CD-ROM. The new 32-bit protected-mode CD-ROM driver replaces the real mode Mscdex.exe driver and implements protected-mode caching for the CD-ROM drive. With your CD-ROM cached in RAM, you will be able to access its files and images much more quickly. (See Chapter 27.)

Dynamic caching in protected memory. Windows 95 provides faster caching. There's no need to allocate a fixed amount of hard disk space for swapping; it's all handled without any end user input. You don't need to use the SmartDrive disk cache, and you don't need to set a swap file size in the Control Panel. Setting up Windows to use virtual memory (swapping code and data out of RAM to the hard disk as necessary) no longer requires a permanent swap file. The swap file is automatically sized and resized as you run Windows 95. (See Chapter 27.)

Universal naming convention (UNC). You can now access files and folders on network servers without resorting to mapping the server name to a drive letter. The pathname for the file is now prefaced with the server name and two back slashes: \\server-name\folder-name\filename. This makes it as easy to access files and folders on servers as on your computer. (See Chapter 36.)

Ability to handle multiple file systems. Network servers don't necessarily use the FAT file system used by DOS and previous versions of Windows. With the Installable File System Manager, Windows 95 can speak to different types of network servers simultaneously, including Novell NetWare and Windows NT servers. (See Chapter 36.)

DOS

Virtual machines for each DOS application. Each DOS application thinks that it has all the hardware to itself. Windows virtualizes the hardware, so while the DOS application thinks it's talking to the hardware, it's really talking to software. DOS virtual machines are preemptively multitasked to prevent one application from hogging all the resources. If things get out of hand, you can kill a DOS virtual machine without having to end the DOS application first. (See Chapter 17.)

More memory for DOS applications. Because Windows 95 uses protected-mode components and drivers, conventional memory — the memory below the 640K boundary that DOS applications need — is not used up. Your computer may have hardware that requires a real-mode driver because Microsoft or the hardware manufacturer didn't write a 32-bit protected-mode driver to replace it. The Windows Setup program checks for this, and if the hardware doesn't have a protected-mode driver, Windows Setup puts the real-mode drivers in Config.sys. (See Chapter 18.)

Greater compatibility between DOS and Windows. DOS programs often take over hardware resources, causing conflicts. Because Windows 95 lets the DOS program think it has control of the hardware while continuing to control it itself, it is much easier for Windows and DOS programs to work together. (See Chapter 17.)

Run any DOS program "under" Windows. Almost all DOS applications can run in the DOS virtual machine provided by Windows 95. This was not true of previous Windows versions. For those few DOS programs that have a difficult time getting along with Windows 95, a special MS-DOS mode unloads Windows 95 and gives the finicky application access to 100 percent of the system resources. (See Chapter 17.)

DOS programs that run in VGA graphics mode can run in a window. Windows 3.*x* required that DOS VGA graphics applications switch to full-screen mode. Now you can more easily multitask DOS programs with Windows. (See Chapter 17.)

Toolbar for a DOS window. Just like a real Windows 95 window, the DOS window has a toolbar, which makes it easier to carry out such tasks as copying and pasting, switching to full-screen mode, changing the properties of the DOS virtual machine, and changing the font and size of the DOS window. (See Chapter 17.)

TrueType for DOS applications. You are not stuck with one font to display DOS text. Bitmapped and TrueType fonts are available, and you can change them quickly. You can also let the font size automatically change to match DOS window size. (See Chapter 20.)

25-, 43-, or 50-line DOS screens. You can set the number of lines in your DOS window or full screen, and make that setting specific to each of your DOS applications. (See Chapter 17.)

Separate Autoexec.bat for each DOS virtual machine. Each of your DOS applications can have a separate batch file that runs before the application begins. This is just like using an Autoexec.bat file to set up the DOS virtual machine environment to suit the application. (See Chapter 17.)

Clean killing of errant DOS applications. You can kill any DOS virtual machine, either with a simple close command or with Ctrl+Alt+Delete, without bringing down the Windows 95 operating system. This was not always the case with Windows 3.*x*. When you do this, all memory allocated to the DOS session is freed. (See Chapter 17.)

Start command. An extension to the existing DOS commands, Start lets you launch a DOS application in a new DOS virtual machine, start an application by naming its associated document, or start a Windows application. (See Chapter 17.)

Printing

Quick return to your application after initiating a print job. Windows 95 quickly puts the printing of your document into the background, releasing the application that initiated the printing to go on to other things. Windows 95 sends your documents to the print spooler using the compact Enhanced

Metafile Format (EMF). EMF is a new version of the Windows Metafile Format (WMF), an application-independent file type that includes graphical and formatted text information. The print spooler translates the EMF files — in the background and without stopping you from carrying out other work — into printer commands that are sent directly to your printer. (See Chapter 23.)

DOS file print spooling. Files you send to the printer from DOS and Windows applications now go to the same print spooler — there is no conflict about which application has control of the printer. (See Chapter 23.)

Print later. If you are not currently connected to a printer, you can queue up a batch of print jobs to print the next time you reconnect to your printer. This is very handy if you are on the road with your portable computer. (See Chapter 23.)

Printers folder. All print-related tasks are handled through one place — the Printers folder. You can install new printers, change a printer's configuration, and manage the print spooler here. You can place printer icons on your Desktop, and then drop documents on the icons to print to any of the printers connected to your computer, either directly or through the network. (See Chapter 23.)

A Wizard to help install your printers. A Wizard can guide you through printer installation. If your printer supports bi-directional communication, Windows 95 will query the printer for configuration information. (See Chapter 23.)

Bi-directional communication. Windows 95 supports bi-directional communication, which allows the printer to report on its current state, such as out of paper. This enables an application to take some appropriate measure — such as notifying you to get more paper, perhaps through a message on the sound board. (See Chapter 23.)

Support for plug and play printers. These printers support bi-directional communications and help in the installation process. If you change printers, you can force Windows 95 to query the new printer and switch to the other printer driver or install a new printer driver. (See Chapter 23.)

Print to a networked printer without the drivers for that printer having been installed on your computer. Using Windows 3.x, you had to install drivers for each kind of printer before you could use them. With all kinds of printers spread throughout the network, this was a hassle. With Windows 95, the drivers are automatically downloaded to your computer when you print to a shared printer if you don't have that printer configured on your computer. (See Chapter 23.)

No need for LPT port redirection. You can print to a printer with a UNC name (such as \\server\laser) without having to associate it with a logical port. (See Chapter 23.)

Hardware

Plug and Play. Installing a new piece of hardware will no longer be such a painful process. If you install plug and play-enabled hardware, configuration and conflict avoidance is automatic. Windows 95 knows what resources (one of 16 hardware interrupts, various DMA channels, and memory I/O addresses) are available and can assign them to the new device without user input. (See Chapter 19.)

Support for existing, pre-plug and play hardware. During setup, Windows 95 automatically detects much of the hardware currently in your computer, and it highlights any conflicts — say, between interrupts, ports, or addresses — to help you resolve them. Windows 95 Setup has a database of non-plug and play hardware and does a reasonable job of detecting such hardware. (See Chapter 19.)

Hot docking and hot swapping. You can connect portable computers — while running — to a network through a docking station. You can also pull PC cards from their sockets (or insert them into their sockets) without crashing the computer. Windows 95 tracks these events and notifies all applications regarding the new hardware configuration. Plug and play-aware applications can use this notification to take appropriate actions. How can this help? Windows Messaging can check for your e-mail when you come into the office in the morning, so when you plug your portable into its docking station, the messages will be waiting for you. (See Chapter 19.)

New device Wizards. Wizards provide a helping hand when you install new hardware. (See Chapter 19.)

Mice

One protected-mode mouse driver for DOS and Windows. You don't have to reduce the amount of memory available for DOS programs by loading a 16-bit mouse driver. If a DOS program is started in a DOS window, Windows 95 automatically activates the DOS mouse pointer. (See Chapter 24.)

Set multiple mouse features. The Mouse Control Panel gives you the power to change the mouse pointer size and color (great for LCD screens on portables), add mouse trails (again good for LCD screens), switch to a left-handed mouse, and change the mouse tracking speed. You can change the mouse pointer to an animated pointer. One thing that Microsoft still doesn't offer is support for the middle mouse button. Logitech provides software that lets you program the middle mouse button. Making it send a double-click is often very handy. (See Chapter 24.)

Support for serial ports 1 through 4. Windows 3.*x* didn't support COM3 and COM4. For example, serial mice could not use either. Windows 95 supports all four serial ports equally. This reduces the potential for conflict between other devices that want the first two serial ports. (See Chapter 25.)

Keyboard

Multi-language keyboard support. Easily switch between languages in one document with multiple-language keyboard layouts. If you have specified multiple-language and keyboard-layout options in the Keyboard Control Panel or in Windows 95 Setup, you can switch between keyboard layouts by pressing Alt+Shift. (See Chapter 21.)

Change the keyboard character repeat speed. The keyboard can never be fast enough for us. We want the arrow keys to move that cursor right along. Use the Keyboard Control Panel to set a fast (or slow) repeat rate and delay period for repeating the pressed key. (See Chapter 21.)

Use the navigation keys or the number pad to control the mouse pointer. If you don't like the mouse or can't use it, you can use your keyboard to control the mouse pointer instead. Use the Accessibility Options Control Panel to configure the speed and acceleration of the mouse keys. (See Chapter 21.)

Hard disks and floppy drives

Enhanced IDE support. With new IDE hard disks becoming available at sizes greater than 3GB, Microsoft has added protected-mode support for these bigger drives. (See Chapter 27.)

Protected-mode drivers for IDE based CD-ROM drives. You can hook these to the IDE hard disk controller in many computers. It's likely that you'll find one on your new computer. (See Chapter 27.)

SCSI support. No SCSI device drivers shipped with Windows 3.1, so SCSI hardware manufacturers had to write their own drivers. Windows 95 support is built-in. (See Chapter 27.)

Fast 32-bit floppy disk driver. No longer will formatting a floppy disk stop all other tasks under Windows. The routine responsible for formatting diskettes is now a protected-mode application. When a diskette is being formatted, Windows 95 creates a preemptively multitasked thread that can run in the background and won't hog your computer. The new driver also brings increased reliability and speed. (See Chapter 27.)

Display

Protected-mode display drivers. Microsoft is providing a broad range of video drivers for many popular display cards on the market. Video card manufacturers can use Microsoft's new display software technology to create additional protected-mode drivers that feature greater reliability and speed. (See Chapter 22.)

Safe mode to fix bad display drivers. If a display driver fails to work correctly, you can always bring Windows 95 up in Safe mode with the standard VGA display driver. This allows you to make the changes necessary to get Windows running properly. (See Chapter 22.)

The Display Properties Control Panel. Right-click the Desktop and choose Properties from the context menu to change any of the characteristics of the display. This includes wallpaper, screen savers, fonts used to display text on the display, Desktop and window colors, the magnification factor for your display, and so on. You can also access the Display Properties dialog box from the Control Panel folder. (See Chapter 22.)

Smooth fonts. Microsoft Plus! enables font smoothing to anti-alias TrueType fonts. This adds one of four shades around some of the edges of each letter to make them appear smoother. (See Chapter 22.)

Energy Star support. If your display adapter and monitor meet the Energy Star and VESA specifications, Windows 95 lets you control how long after keyboard inactivity the low-power standby mode of the monitor occurs. The display driver must support this feature. (See Chapter 22.)

Changing screen resolutions. You no longer have to restart Windows when you change video resolutions. (See Chapter 22.)

Modems

Unimodem. Centralized modem configuration is available to all Windows communications applications that are designed to take advantage of it. Windows 95 detects which modem you have and properly sets the modem initialization string. No longer do you have to configure each communications application for your modem — if you use only TAPI-aware or 32-bit communications applications. (See Chapter 25.)

16550A UART support. The 16550A is an advanced chip that handles serial communications in your modem or serial port. Windows 3.x didn't make use of all its advanced features. Windows 95 support for the 16550A makes communications more reliable as well as faster. (Not all computers have this chip.) (See Chapter 25.)

128 serial ports and 128 parallel ports. You probably won't need this many ports on your personal computer, but they are supported for people who pack their computers with special serial port boards. Modems that operate off the parallel port are now available. (See Chapter 25.)

Installation

Hardware detection. You might have some existing hardware conflicts that have gone unnoticed but will cause problems in the future. Windows 95 Setup thoroughly searches your computer and creates a database of hardware to identify all your components as well as conflicts. (See Chapter 3.)

Recovery of setup failures. If Windows 95 Setup fails — due to incorrect hardware detection, for example — you can start Setup again without having to worry about knowing where the failure occurred. Setup keeps track of the failure and skips over the area where it happened. (See Chapter 3.)

Multi-boot (allows you to boot older versions of DOS, Windows NT, OS/2, and Windows 3.x). You can keep your previous version of Windows — and Windows NT — and set up a new Windows 95 directory when you load Windows 95 for the first time. That way you can go back to the old version — or run Windows NT. Windows 95 has a multi-boot capability that lets you choose between a number of operating systems previously stored on your hard disk. (See Chapters 3 and 6.)

Support for batch file control of Setup. The Windows 95 Setup program requires that you answer a series of configuration questions. With a batch file working with Windows 95 Setup, the answers can be automatically provided without user input. (See Chapter 3.)

Installation from a network administrator's workstation. You can install Windows 95 on a local computer (or on a network server) from the workstation of a network administrator. You can configure Windows 95 to be used by a local computer with a hard disk, a local computer with just a floppy disk, or a diskless computer with a RIPL boot PROM (programmable read-only memory) chip and disk storage on a network server. (See Chapter 3.)

Verification of Windows 95 installation. What if you accidentally delete a file that is vital to the operation of Windows 95 or a file gets corrupted by some means? Rerunning Windows 95 Setup lets you verify your existing Windows 95 software. If there are problems, Windows 95 will reinstall the bad or missing files from the original diskettes or CD-ROM. (See Chapter 3.)

Fonts

New font installer/viewer. Click the Start button, point to Settings, click Control Panel, and then double-click the Fonts icon to invoke the new Font installer/viewer. You can copy fonts from fonts diskettes to the \Windows\Fonts folder, or leave them in separate folders on your hard disk. You can use the Fonts folder to uninstall fonts and/or delete font files from your hard disk. (See Chapter 20.)

32-bit TrueType rasterization. The TrueType rasterizer takes the TrueType font descriptions and turns them into the dots that are displayed on the computer screen. The new rasterizer does a better job of being faithful to the outline and hints of the TrueType fonts. (See Chapter 20.)

Font smoothing. Anti-aliasing improves the appearance of fonts on your display. To take advantage of this feature, your video driver has to be in at least 256-color mode, and you have to have Microsoft Plus! and a 486 processor. (See Chapter 22.)

Error Handling and Reliability

Local reboot. You can close DOS and Windows applications that have "hung" — quit responding —without also hanging Windows 95.

Safe mode. If Windows 95 can't start normally for any reason, it starts in Safe mode. This allows you to make changes to the configuration if necessary to solve the problem.

Better cleanup of resources. Windows 3.x applications often forgot to return memory resources that they borrowed from the operating system while running. This eventually caused Windows to run out of resources and stop running. Windows 95 cleans up after Windows 3.x applications.

Basic Structure

DOS and Windows combined. DOS functionality is now provided by 32-bit components. A portion of real-mode DOS is started when Windows boots in order to read and process real-mode drivers in Autoexec.bat and Config.sys. Windows is then automatically loaded and some of real-mode DOS unloaded from memory. (See Chapter 17.)

32-bit preemptive multitasking and multithreading. Much of the benefit of this new underlying structure for Windows 95 won't become apparent until you use 32-bit protected-mode Windows applications. The Windows 95 printing subsystem, HyperTerminal, and other applets are 32-bit applications that provide some of the benefits now. For example, the printing subsystem provides faster printing and releases the computer to other tasks by doing most of its work in the background.

32-bit protected-mode software drivers everywhere. Windows interacts with hardware devices through software components commonly called *drivers*. These drivers have been rewritten to place themselves above the 1MB memory boundary. Therefore, they take up no conventional memory — freeing up more for DOS applications — and they reduce many memory conflicts. Protected-mode drivers mean that Windows doesn't have to take time to switch the processor to real-mode whenever it interacts with hardware other than the processor and memory. (See Chapter 19.)

Rapid performance increases as you add more memory. Windows 95 runs at about the same speed as Windows 3.1 with 4MB of memory — very slowly. Add more memory and Windows 95 starts to run faster than its predecessor.

Compatibility with existing hardware and software. Microsoft would have been foolish not to make Windows 95 compatible with Windows 3.x. Upgrading everything would have been a major hassle. While some software utilities created for Windows 3.1 are not needed under Windows 95, all utility vendors have Windows 95 versions of their products.

More resources. Windows 3.*x* would run out of system resources long before it ran out of memory. This is due to the structure of the lists — the various memory heaps — of resources available to Windows 3.*x* applications. Microsoft has redesigned the resource allocation scheme in Windows 95 to reduce the chance it will run out of resources before you actually run out of memory. (See Chapter 18.)

Networking

Built for networking. While Microsoft updated virtually every area of the Windows operating system, it paid particular attention to networking. Microsoft worked hard to make networking easier, more reliable, faster, more security conscious, and more compatible with the leading networking operating systems, including Novell NetWare, Windows NT, and Banyan Vines. (See Chapter 36.)

Protected-mode networks. No more do you have to use up all that precious memory below 640K (or in the upper memory blocks) with network drivers. Windows 95 network components (drivers, clients, and so on) have no conventional memory footprints — they get loaded above the 1MB boundary. Accessing networked hard disks is much faster, and your DOS applications have memory enough to breathe. The drawback is that some third-party networks don't provide protected-mode network components. Microsoft provides 32-bit protected-mode network components for Microsoft Networks, Novell NetWare, and TCP/IP. (See Chapter 36.)

Reduced conflict between applications and networking components. Real-mode networking drivers compete with Windows 3.*x* for the same resources. They conflict in memory and attempt to exclusively control response to hardware and software interrupts. Windows 95 eliminates these conflicts. Again, this is true only with networks that provide protected-mode support such as Microsoft Networks, Novell NetWare, Windows NT, and TCP/IP. (See Chapter 36.)

Multiple simultaneous network support. You can use the same network card to hook your computer up to completely different kinds of networks at the same time. You get the protocol associated with Internet and Unix — TCP/IP, NetWare's IPX/SPX, and Microsoft's NetBEUI (pronounced *net buoy*). Windows 95 also works with protocols provided by other vendors. From your workstation you can "see" Unix servers, Windows NT servers, and Novell NetWare servers simultaneously. (See Chapter 36.)

One password for all logins. You can use one network logon password as the master logon password for resources you have previously logged onto. Enter your logon password once. When you access other password-protected resources (for example, a hard disk on a network server), Windows 95 sends the correct password from your encrypted store of passwords. (See Chapter 36.)

Protected-mode client for NetWare. This 32-bit protected-mode network component replaces the real-mode network drivers provided by Novell. You can still connect to NetWare servers, browse their file systems, and use NetWare command line utilities and logon scripts — as long as they don't have calls to TSRs. If you want to use Novell's real-mode components, you are still free to do so — but beware of conflicts. (See Chapter 36.)

File and printer services for NetWare. Disk drives, files and folders, and printers on local computers — not just NetWare servers — can be shared on the network. (See Chapter 23.)

Support for workstations with no local hard disks. You can install Windows 95 on a network server, allowing computers with no local storage (or floppy drives only) to run Windows from the server. (See Chapter 36.)

Network Administration and Security

Standard network system management protocols are supported. Windows 95 provides a Simple Network Management Protocol (SNMP) agent, allowing a network administrator to monitor and manage a local computer. Third-party network management tools can use SNMP to provide the network administrator with system information and management functions. (See Chapter 36.)

Registry-base systems management. The Windows 95 Registry replaces Win.ini, System.ini, and other *ini* files with a unified approach to storing system configuration information. This Registry information is available to the network system administrator. Microsoft provides the Registry editor. (See Chapter 36.)

System Policy Editor. The system administrator can set a number of configuration parameters with the administration-configuration application — the System Policy Editor. These policies — rules — determine if local workstations can share their files or printers, whether users can change their Desktop configurations, and so on. The editor provides network administrators with a point-and-click check box approach to network security. (See Chapter 12.)

Unified logon. A single logon dialog box can connect you to your workgroup or to multiple network servers. Password-protected resources — such as files and printers — are available to you after you have entered their passwords once. These passwords are stored with your master logon password. (See Chapter 36.)

Performance monitoring. From a single workstation, a network administrator can monitor the I/O performance of any or all local computers on the network. (See Chapter 36.)

Net Watcher. The network administrator can see who is currently logged onto various servers on the network and what resources they are accessing. Administrators can also add shared folders and files, and disconnect users from a server or from specific files. (See Chapter 36.)

Different users with different settings on the same local computer. Different users can use the same computer — at different times — and have it configured just for them. User data is stored in a Registry file separate from the computer configuration data. Users can have different Desktops and different privileges on the same computer. (See Chapter 12.)

User settings follow them around to different computers. Users can "roam" around the corporate network, logging on to different computers, and have their settings/configurations/permissions follow them around. You store the user portion of the Registry on a network server to allow this "roaming." (See Chapter 12.)

Summary

▶ Windows 95 is a vast and complex software system. We review the main elements of the territory without overwhelming you with details.

Chapter 3

Installing and Setting Up Windows 95

Take a Moment to Reflect

In this chapter we discuss how to install and set up Windows 95 on a single standalone computer. By *standalone* we mean the computer can (and will) boot Windows 95 from its local hard disk without requiring any connection to a network. The standalone computer can be attached to a network and operate as a server on a peer-to-peer network. A standalone computer can stand alone but is not necessarily unconnected.

Windows 95 can be installed on a network server, allowing network client computers to use and share this single copy of Windows 95. While we don't discuss this type of installation here, you can turn to Chapter 36 for a discussion of networking.

Requirements

Before you install Windows 95, you'll want to take stock of your situation. If you have just bought a new computer, Windows 95 is probably already installed on it. If you have an older computer, you'll want to be sure that it meets the requirements for Windows 95 shown in Table 3-1.

Table 3-1 Hardware Requirements for Installing and Running Windows 95

Component	Requirements
Processor	386 or greater. Windows 95, because of its 32-bit code, runs slower (when compared with Windows 3.x) on a 386SX processor, which has a 16-bit external data path. 386DX or 386 processors with 32-bit external data paths will run Windows 95 as fast as they did Windows 3.1 (which is relatively slow) — the faster the processor, the happier the user. If you have a B-step 386 processor (one marked ID 0303), you can't install Windows 95. We recommend at least a 486-33 MHz processor.
Memory	4MB of RAM is required for Windows 95 to work as well as Windows 3.x did with 4MB of RAM (marginally). Some Windows programs won't run in 4MB of RAM even with virtual memory (swapping to hard disk) turned on. And 8MB is recommended by Microsoft. More is better if you want to cut down on the virtual memory manager's swapping to the hard disk as you open multiple applications or use OLE objects in compound documents. We recommend at least 16MB. If you keep a lot of applications open at once, 32MB and beyond is even nicer.
Video	VGA is the minimum, with SVGA recommended by Microsoft. Larger monitors and higher resolution give you more real estate for multiple applications or larger areas for more text, numbers, and so on. Accelerated display cards make a real difference. We recommend at least 800 x 600.
Disks	Windows 95 comes on high-density diskettes or a CD-ROM. Getting Windows 95 in the CD-ROM format is vastly superior, just from the standpoint of ease of installation. You need between 24MB and 70MB of free hard disk space just for the Windows 95 files. You'll need the hard disk space for your Windows 95 files as well as for dynamically sized swap space. For your Windows 95 installation, you'll want to free up as much hard disk space as possible to prevent conflicts during installation. If you are installing Windows 95 into a directory containing Windows 3.x, you can subtract the size of the Windows 3.x files from this requirement. See *Hard disk space requirements* later in this chapter.

Component	Requirements
	Depending on choices that you make during installation, the amount can increase significantly. During the installation process, the required amount will be indicated on screen.
	If you are installing on a computer with compressed drives, you'll need at least 3MB of free uncompressed hard disk space during installation. This uncompressed disk space must be on your host drive (the physical drive or partition that "hosts" the compressed logical drive), such as C:.
	You must have a File Allocation Table (FAT) disk partition (required if you are running DOS and/or Windows 3.x). Computers that run Windows NT or OS/2 do not necessarily have FAT partitions on their hard disks.
	Just a note: If you have a new computer with Windows 95 already installed, it might have a FAT-32 partition, although most computer manufacturers continue to format their computers with FAT-16. FAT-32 is not compatible with earlier versions of Windows 95.
Others	Windows 95 takes advantage of modems, CD-ROM drives, sound cards, midi add-on cards, accelerated video, network cards, joy sticks, and so on.

Secret

The Windows 95 setup routines can determine how much memory you have installed in your computer. If you have less than 6MB of RAM, the setup routines install different system files than they would otherwise. If you initially installed Windows 95 with 6MB or less and later installed more memory, you should reinstall Windows 95 over itself to update these system files to take better advantage of the increased memory.

Unsupported hardware

The Windows 95 CD-ROM and diskettes come with a long list of hardware drivers, but they don't come with drivers for everything. There may not be any specific drivers for your add-on card, Windows 3.1 drivers may work, or you may need to get new Windows 95-specific drivers from your hardware manufacturer.

To find out what hardware is not supported, you can check the list at the Windows 95 Annoyances web site, http://www.creativelement.com/win95ann/devices.html.

Lots of older CD-ROM drives aren't supported by newer 32-bit drivers and require that you keep their existing drivers in your Autoexec.bat and Config.sys files that work with Windows 95. If you remove these drivers, you will not be able to access your CD-ROM after you install Windows 95. To see which CD-ROM drives are not supported, check out the Microsoft Knowledge Base article at http://www.microsoft.com/kb/articles/Q131/4/99.htm.

If your CD-ROM drive doesn't have a 32-bit driver, then Windows 95 won't cache the drive. You'll want to load SmartDrive (which you'll find in the root directory of the Windows 95 CD-ROM) to speed up access to data on your CD-ROM if it requires a 16-bit driver.

Starting with DOS

You may have heard that Windows 95 does away with DOS. It turns out that Microsoft got carried away with this claim, and many people actually wondered if they could install Windows 95 on their DOS and Windows 3.*x* computers.

You need to have at least DOS (version 3.2 or later) running on your computer in order to install the upgrade (retail) version of Windows 95. You must also have a copy of Windows 3.*x* installed, although not necessarily running, on your hard disk, or a handy Windows 3.*x* setup diskette. Your hard disk must contain a DOS FAT partition of at least 32MB, or Windows 95 won't install.

Undocumented

There is a way to fool the upgrade Windows 95 installation routines into installing Windows 95 if you don't have Windows 3.*x* installed and you don't have your Windows 3.*x* setup diskette handy. We assume that you have a license for Windows 3.*x*. Create a text file in the root directory of your hard disk. Rename it Ntldr with no file extension. Type one line in the file: **Rem** and save the file. Now when you install Windows 95 you won't be asked to insert a Windows 3.1 diskette.

The non-upgrade version of Windows 95 comes with a bootable DOS diskette that allows you to partition your hard disk, format the hard disk partitions for DOS, and install the necessary files to boot the computer from the hard disk into DOS 7.0. Windows 95 stores its files on a DOS-formatted hard disk just like DOS and Windows 3.*x* do. Windows 95 isn't some foreign invader that requires that you wipe out everything first and restructure it to work with Windows 95. You start with what you've got and make a few changes to get to Windows 95.

Making room for Windows 95

Before you install Windows 95, carefully consider its hard disk space requirements. If you have a 386 computer with a 40MB hard drive, Windows 95 is going to eat up a big chunk of your hard disk space. You might want to consider using disk compression software (built into Windows 95), a new hard disk, or a new computer.

No matter what computer you have, make sure there is plenty of room for Windows 95. The trend over the last few years with respect to the hard disk requirements of Windows programs should have prepared you for the demands that Windows 95 will make on your equipment and wallet. Windows 95 is no shrinking violet when it comes to using hard disk resources.

Windows 95 is not just one program, but a whole series of programs that provide a vastly greater amount of functionality than Windows 3.*x*. Unfortunately, you need a considerable amount of hard disk space to store these programs, and it gets worse as you install other Windows applications.

Hard disk space requirements

You can install Windows 95 into a new folder or over your existing Windows directory. Table 3-2 provides a rough approximation of the free additional disk space required to install and run Windows 95. These are rough estimates; they don't include additional requirements for fonts, application programs, DLLs, and so on.

Table 3-2	Free Disk Space Requirements	
	Installation Type	
New or Upgrade	*Typical*	*Compact*
New	56MB	49MB
Over Windows 3.1	41MB	34MB
Over Windows for Workgroups	41MB	34MB

Make sure you have plenty of room to install Windows 95. If you can move some directories to other hard disk volumes or off onto diskettes, you should consider doing so. After the installation is complete, you may be able to move some of these back.

The actual amount of hard disk space you need will depend on which options you choose when installing Windows 95. If you choose the Custom Setup option when you install Windows 95, you will have the opportunity to tailor your hard disk space usage. This is the option we recommend, unless you have a reason to use a different one.

If you are installing Windows 95 on a compressed volume, you will need at least double the hard disk space shown in Table 3-2, because the executable files that come with Windows 95 aren't very compressible.

After you install Windows 95, you can expect the size of the Windows 95 folder to increase. Not only do the programs that come with Windows 95 store themselves in the Windows 95 folder (and subfolders), but other programs store pieces of themselves there as well. Your C:\Windows or C:\Win95 folder will grow and grow and grow. This is actually a disaster.

The DLL mistake

Microsoft made a huge mistake that it has never fessed up to. It encouraged application software developers (including developers at Microsoft) to put parts of their programs into the \Windows or \Windows\System directories. This causes these folders to grow to an unmanageable size.

Most of these portions of programs are in the form of dynamic link libraries (DLLs). DLLs are both a curse and a blessing. Actually, they'd be just a blessing if they stayed in each application's folder or subfolders.

DLLs are loaded into memory by an application when you run it. They allow a programmer to create a file (a library) of functions that can be called by the program's executable file. DLLs are a neat way to package usable functions without having to put them all together in one huge executable file. They also can be called and shared by different programs while stored in memory.

Microsoft ships some DLLs that can (and are) used by application developers. These include the common dialog boxes (both 16-bit and 32-bit) that allow users to open and save files in applications. Microsoft put these DLLs in the \Windows\System folder. Because many programs use these DLLs, it is appropriate to store them in a commonly accessible folder.

However, most DLLs are used by only one program, so they do not need to be in a common location. These DLLs should be stored in their application's folder. Because application setup procedures store them in the \Windows or \Windows\System folders instead, these folders can grow to an unwieldy size.

While uninstall utilities allow you to track down these DLLs, they do nothing to solve the problem of bloated Windows folders if you want to keep programs that store DLLs in these folders installed. In addition, programs such as Microsoft Office and LapLink for Windows add more folders that are by default attached to the Windows folder, increasing the space requirements of the Windows folder and subfolders.

This problem is not solved by Windows 95. Programs can still put their DLLs in the Windows folder and subfolders. In addition, all the fonts that you add to Windows are stored in the \Windows\Fonts folder. Windows just gets bigger and bigger.

Because of this problem, you must be sure that you have enough space for Windows 95 and for all the files that get attached to it. If you have divided your hard disk(s) up into a number of smaller volumes, you may not have enough space on a given volume to store the ever-expanding Windows folders.

New or used?

All this adds up to a number of considerations:

1. Should you install Windows 95 over (and in) your existing Windows 3.1 directory? There is so much stuff in this directory and its subdirectories, stuff that you might not be using any more, that you might want to start fresh.

2. How much room do you need to set aside for the Windows folder and its subfolders as they continue to grow? If you install Windows in its own volume (say an uncompressed drive) and everything else on other volumes, how big should the Windows volume be?

3. How can you maintain some semblance of order and manage the growth of these folders?

If you are using a permanent swap file with Windows 3.*x*, you might want to get rid of that file, at least during Windows 95 installation. This will give the Windows 95 Setup program more free hard disk space. Some Windows 3.*x* programs, such as PhotoShop, however, require that you have a permanent swap file.

To get rid of the Windows 3.*x* permanent swap file, at least temporarily, take the following steps:

STEPS

Getting Rid of the Windows 3.*x* Permanent Swap File

Step 1. Run Windows 3.*x*.

Step 2. Double-click the Control Panel icon in your Program Manager. Double-click the Enhanced icon in the Control Panel.

Step 3. Click the Virtual Memory button and then Change.

Step 4. From the drop-down list in the Type field, choose Temporary. Click the OK buttons to exit from the Control Panel.

Step 5. Exit Windows 3.x to DOS.

Step 6. At the DOS command prompt, change directories to the root directory of the boot drive (**cd **).

Step 7. Type **attrib 386spart.par** and press Enter.

Step 8. If the result of step 7 is a listing for this file, type **del 386spart.par** and press Enter.

You have now freed up the hard disk space that was taken up by this file. You do not need a permanent swap file to run Windows 95. (It automatically creates a *dynamic* swap file, as described in the *Managing Your Swap Space* section of Chapter 27.) If you need a permanent swap file to continue running programs under Windows 3.*x*, you can re-create it using the Windows 3.*x* Control Panel.

Where to put the Windows folder

You can install the Windows 95 folder (and its subfolders) on any hard drives (or drive partitions or volumes) as long as the disk partition is a FAT partition. Some Windows 95 files will be installed on your boot drive (most likely C:).

The boot drive must have at least 3MB of uncompressed hard disk space. If your boot drive is completely compressed, you must uncompress enough of it to get 3MB of uncompressed space on the host drive. This may require you to move some files off your hard disk.

Windows 95 installs files on the boot drive. One of those files, Io.sys, will reside in the boot tracks. It takes over the startup process for your computer. In addition, Windows 95 has its own Command.com file and can have Autoexec.bat and Config.sys files that reside in the root directory of the boot drive. Windows 95 keeps other files on the boot drive as well. These are detailed in Chapter 6.

The total size of the files on the boot drive attributable to Windows 95 is less than 1MB. You can place the rest of Windows 95 in another volume. If your hard disk is partitioned into multiple volumes (each with a letter name), you can place Windows 95 into a non-bootable volume. If you have multiple physical hard drives, you can place Windows 95 on a non-bootable hard drive.

Compressed drives

Compressed drives are actually large files, called *compressed volume files* (CVFs), on a physical drive (the host drive) that are treated as (and named as) separate drives. You can install Windows 95 on a compressed drive.

Secret

Estimates of how much space you need on a compressed drive to store Windows 95 files are wildly inaccurate. This is because the Windows files can't be compressed as much as the estimated compression ratio used to report the amount of free space on compressed drives assumes they can be. If you are going to install Windows 95 on a compressed drive, you will need a lot more space than the amounts shown in Table 3-2.

Windows 95 manages a dynamically sized swap file. This swap file can be on the compressed drive that stores the bulk of the Windows 95 files or it can be on an uncompressed drive. To prevent file compression from slowing the swap file, Windows 95 places the swap file at the end of the CVF and doesn't compress it. The issues of file compression and the swap file are discussed in detail in Chapter 27.

Upgrade Windows 3.x or start anew

If you install Windows 95 in your existing Windows directory, you carry the past forward with you — all of the past. The up side is that you don't have to reconfigure or reinstall any of your applications. During the setup process, Windows 95 reads your Windows 3.x Win.ini, System.ini, and Protocol.ini files to find out what applications you have installed, and then it updates your Registry accordingly. (The *Registry* is a database that stores information about Windows and your Windows applications.)

In short, here are the advantages of installing Windows 95 in your existing Windows 3.x directory:

- The values stored in System.ini, Win.ini, and Protocol.ini are now stored in your Windows 95 Registry.

- The values stored in these files that refer to other applications are stored in the Registry, maintaining existing file/application associations and fonts.

- Existing network client software is automatically updated for a number of networks, including those from Microsoft, Novell, Digital Equipment Corporation, Sun, and Banyan.

- Existing Windows 3.x Program Manager groups are converted to menus on your Start button.

If you install to a new folder or delete your old Windows 3.1 directory and install to an empty Windows folder, you will need to reinstall some to most of your Windows applications. You have to do this because many Windows applications:

- Install portions of themselves in the Windows folder, and that folder is either wiped out or no longer on the path (the DLLs won't be found when the executable is called).

- Need to be registered in the Registry if they use OLE or create file associations.

- Install configuration files (*ini* files) in the Windows directory that need to be moved to the new Windows folders and, perhaps, re-edited.

Installing Windows 95 in a new folder makes a clean break with the past. You have to deliberately reinstall the applications that you use. You have to configure all the settings in your applications to match your preferences. You have to remember (or relearn) where all those settings were hidden. You have to go find all the diskettes for the applications you have to reinstall. All this because Windows 3.x got out of control.

If you install over Windows 3.x, you might first want to use an uninstall program and get rid of unused files. You can manually edit Win.ini and System.ini (using Sysedit.exe in the \Windows\System directory) to clean up references to the unused past. If you have a lot of fonts that you don't use, you can uninstall and delete them from your hard disk.

Another route you could take is to install Windows 95 over a *copy* of your Windows 3.*x* directory. With this method, the Windows 95 Registry is updated with all the information about your installed Windows applications, your program groups, and so on. But you would also have an intact installation of Windows 3.*x* to go back to if need be.

We give a complete step-by-step method of installing over a copy of your existing Windows directory, while keeping your Windows 3.*x* directory intact so that you can dual-boot back to Windows 3.*x* during the transition period. See the section later in this chapter entitled *Installing Windows 95 Safely Over Windows 3.x*.

If you choose to install over Windows 3.1, you do have the option of saving enough information to uninstall Windows 95 and to get back to Windows 3.1. We'll show you when to do that in the section entitled *The Setup Process* section later in this chapter.

Alternatively, you can keep your Windows 3.*x* directory intact and install Windows 95 in its own folder. This will allow you to dual-boot between these two operating systems. You just want to make sure you have enough disk space for both. Of course, you'll still have to reinstall some of your applications after you boot up Windows 95. Their DLLs will then be installed in both the Windows 3.*x* directory and the Windows 95 folder.

Secret

If you install Windows 95 in its own folder, a temporary way to get around reinstalling all these Windows 3.*x* programs is to include references in your path statement to the old Windows directory and System directory at the *end* of your Path *after* all other directories. This may let your old Windows applications find their DLLs. It doesn't update their file associations or register them for OLE.

Protecting your DOS files

Windows 95 installs its own DOS files in its Command folder (\Windows\Command). These files are updated versions of some of the DOS files that are installed in your DOS (version 5.*x* or 6.*x*) directory. Not all files that come with DOS 6.2*x* come with Windows 95.

Some of the utilities that came with earlier versions of DOS will cause problems if you run them after you install Windows 95. DOS 6.*x* versions of the disk utilities Scandisk.exe and Defrag.exe break the link between short filenames and long filenames maintained by Windows 95. You should not run these versions of these programs after you install Windows 95.

Some newer DOS programs that come with Windows 95 are really no different than the older DOS versions; they are just given a new file creation date and placed in the new Command folder when you install Windows 95.

When you install Windows 95, the setup procedures rename the older DOS programs that cause problems with long filenames. For example, Scandisk.exe becomes Scandisk.ex~. In addition, a batch file is created, Scandisk.bat, which is invoked when you type Scandisk at the DOS prompt (if you boot to the old operating system). This batch file essentially tells you to use the ScanDisk program in Windows 95. (You can do this by double-clicking Scandisk.exe in the Command folder or by right-clicking a hard disk icon, clicking Properties, Tools, and then clicking the Check Now button.)

Secret

If you install Windows 95 in an existing Windows 3.1 directory, about 2MB worth of DOS files will be deleted from your existing DOS directory, including the DOS 6.x version of Scandisk.exe. These files are not needed (as far as Microsoft is concerned), replaced by files installed in the Command folder, or too dangerous to use with Windows 95.

If you install Windows 95 to a new folder, the DOS files are not deleted. This allows you to have full DOS functionality when you dual-boot to the previous DOS version instead of into Windows 95. Even if you boot to the previous DOS version, you don't want to use the previous version's disk tools that cause problems with long filenames. That is why these previous disk utilities are renamed, no matter where you put Windows 95.

Microsoft decided to delete these older DOS programs because it replaced them in the new Command folder and saw a way to reclaim 2MB of disk space for you automatically. As long as you are overwriting Windows 3.x and changing your path to include the Command folder, Microsoft feels that the right thing to do is to get rid of replicated DOS programs.

Tip

If you want to make sure that the Windows 95 installation procedures don't change or delete any existing DOS programs, copy them to another directory that is not on your path, or compress a copy of all of them. Changing their attribute to read-only won't do any good. Check the section entitled *BootMulti* in Chapter 6 for more details.

After you have installed Windows 95, you can copy the files back from the other folder, or unzip the zipped files. Just be sure not to use the older disk utilities such as ScanDisk and Defrag.

Saving some Windows 3.x applets

Some applets that Microsoft included with Windows 3.x have not been upgraded or even made available with Windows 95. If you like using these applets, you'll need to make them available under Windows 95. If you installed Windows 95 in a new folder, you can create shortcut icons on the Desktop or add items to the Start menu that refer to these applets in the Windows 3.x directory.

Windows Write

Windows Write is not saved. If you install Windows 95 in your Windows 3.x directory, then the Write executable file (Write.exe) is written over by an executable stub (Write.exe) that merely calls Wordpad.exe. If you install Windows 95 to a new folder, this same stub executable is installed. All your Windows Write files will now be opened by WordPad.

Secret

To keep this from happening, make sure you save a copy of the original Write.exe and Write.hlp files. If you are going to install Windows 95 in the Windows 3.x directory, copy these files to a temporary directory before you install Windows 95. After installing Windows 95, you can copy these files back into the Windows 95 folder.

Secret

It does no good to write-protect Write.exe because Windows 95 Setup ignores the read-only attribute and writes right over it.

Microsoft wants you to use WordPad, its new 32-bit less-than-word-processor. Windows Write is now an out-of-date, 16-bit, half-text-editor, half-word-processor. But Write has the benefit of being smaller, faster, and more powerful than the newly updated Notepad.

Even after you restore Windows Write, you won't be able to engage it by double-clicking on files with the *wri* extension. You'll need to change the file extension association in the File Types tab of the View, Options dialog box. For step-by-step instructions on how to do this, turn to Chapter 13.

Tip

It's a good idea to create a folder that contains all your own system files, such as Write.exe and Write.hlp. That way they will be protected when you update Windows 95 in the future. You might want to name the new system folder My System.

The Recorder

The least-appreciated of Windows tools, the macro recorder, is not included with Windows 95 and doesn't work well with the new 32-bit applets. If you install Windows 95 over Windows 3.1, however, Windows 95 doesn't overwrite Recorder as it does Write.

While many sophisticated Windows applications have their own macro recorders, it is still great to have a general-purpose version that can help automate repetitive tasks. If you purchased Windows 95 without ever installing Windows 3.x, your system doesn't have a copy of Recorder.exe. We have featured some shareware on the CD-ROM that gives you some general macro capabilities with Windows 95.

Clipbook

Clipbook (which comes with Windows for Workgroups 3.11) doesn't come with Windows 95. Clipboard, however, does. If you installed over Windows for Workgroups 3.11, you still have Clipbook. Both Clipbook and Clipboard work the same way in Windows 95 as they did in Windows 3.x.

Secret

If you have any problems using the sharing facilities of Clipbook, put NetDDE.exe in your Startup folder (and start it up). Windows for Workgroups 3.11 automatically starts NetDDE; Windows 95 doesn't.

Other applets

Cardfile is also gone. During the beta cycle, Cardfile was replaced by WinPad, Microsoft's Personal Digital Assistant software. Microsoft subsequently dropped WinPad, but didn't replace it with anything.

Schedule+ 1.0 is gone, but the Windows 95 version of Schedule+ is integrated into Microsoft Office.

Dual-booting

Before you install Windows 95, you'll need to decide whether to keep the capability to start your computer using your old version of DOS and/or Windows. Windows 95 is no mere upgrade, and it is with some trepidation that you install it without a safety net.

If you are unsure whether some of your Windows applications will work with Windows 95 and you have the hard disk space, you should install Windows 95 in a separate folder. You can then migrate your Windows applications over one at a time to make sure everything is working.

If Windows 95 doesn't work out, you can then uninstall it and go back to your previous version of Windows. To have this option, however, you have to protect your DOS files, as described in *Protecting your DOS files* earlier in this chapter.

In order to easily reinstall Windows 3.1*x* later, you must also answer Yes to the question "Save system files?" when you install Windows 95.

Even though Windows 95 is not a run-of-the-mill upgrade, it is an upgrade nonetheless, and the purpose of installing it is to move from your previous version of Windows into the future.

A new face

Windows 95 has a completely new user interface, and this is going to take a little getting used to. It is possible to run slightly revised Windows 95 versions of the Windows 3.*x* Program Manager and File Manager. If you choose the Custom setup, you are presented (if you dig a little) with the option of starting the Program Manager when you boot Windows 95.

The Program Manager is not up to the task of handling the new capabilities of Windows 95. If you have to have it to provide a reassuring look to your users (perhaps including yourself), you can install it during setup, but it is not a long-term solution.

We recommend you make a clean break with the past and take the time to learn the new user interface. Throughout this book, we provide plenty of guidance for dealing with the many user interface issues.

Internet Explorer 4.0 adds yet another new user interface to Windows 95. Plenty of people have taken to the hypertext document interface displayed in web browsers. Microsoft has integrated a browser-like interface into the Desktop. The Program Manager begins to look like ancient history.

Clean up your Startup folder

If you install Windows 95 over your existing Windows directory, the applications in your Startup group will migrate to your new Startup folder. When you start Windows 95, these programs will also be started.

Some of these programs may not be applicable to Windows 95. For example, the Windows 3.1 version of Plug-In, a wonderful add-on to the Program Manager, will not work with Windows 95. Windows 95 Setup should find Plug-In and take references to it out of Win.ini.

You should remove all programs from your Startup group before you install Windows 95.

CD-ROM or diskette version?

If there is any way that you can swing it, get the CD-ROM version of Windows 95. It saves a tremendous amount of diskette-swapping aggravation. Windows 95 is just too big to fit on a convenient number of diskettes.

Microsoft ships Windows 95 on special extra high density (1.7MB) diskettes that can be read but not written to (without special formatting and diskette-writing software, which you will find on the *Windows 95 Secrets* CD-ROM). Microsoft chose these diskettes to cut down on the materials cost and to give you the benefit of fewer diskettes to swap. These diskettes are referred to as DMF diskettes.

Even if you are installing Windows 95 on a computer without a CD-ROM, you should still think about getting the CD-ROM version. Do this if you can copy the Windows 95 source files off the CD-ROM onto your computer's hard disk by connecting to a computer with a CD-ROM over a network, or through a serial or parallel cable to a PC with a CD-ROM.

The CD-ROM version has extra stuff on it. If you have the diskette version, you can download this extra stuff from http://www.microsoft.com/windows/software/cdextras.htm.

Loading the source files

Installing Windows 95 from diskettes or a dual-speed CD-ROM can be quite slow. Loading from diskettes is the worst. If you have a 6X or 12X CD-ROM, things are quite a bit brighter.

Tip

If you have the spare hard disk space, consider copying the CD-ROM or the diskettes to a temporary hard disk directory, and then installing Windows 95 from your hard disk. Copying diskettes can take a while, but the Windows 95 installation goes much faster. Furthermore, the original source files will always be available locally off a high-speed device (your hard disk). If you make changes to your Windows setup, the reconfiguration routines point back to the source files on your hard disk and quickly allow you to update Windows 95. You don't have to go searching for your Windows 95 diskettes or CD-ROM.

The problem is, of course, that you just used up 33MB of hard disk space ($4.95 worth at 15 cents a megabyte) that you might actually need. You can erase these source files after you have successfully installed Windows 95, but another problem arises. Any subsequent updates will point back to the now-erased source files, expecting to find them on your hard disk, so you will need to point the update routines toward your CD-ROM or diskettes when prompted to do so.

Most of the source files are in a compressed format and have the extension *cab*, which stands for *cabinet*. The setup routines extracts the files from the file cabinets.

You can use the regular DOS Copy command to copy the cabinet files from a CD-ROM. However, you can't use Copy to copy the files from the DMF formatted diskettes, nor can you copy these diskettes by using drag and drop in the File Manager. (The first Windows 95 setup diskette is not a DMF diskette, however, so you can use Copy to copy the files from that diskette to your hard disk.)To copy the files from the diskettes, you use the Extract command, which is on the first Windows 95 setup diskette.

To copy the DMF diskettes to your hard disk, first copy the Extract command (and all the files on the first, regular-density diskette) to your destination directory (say, C:\Win95src). Then copy the cabinet files from the second and further Windows 95 diskettes using the Extract /c command. You have to copy the cabinet files one at a time from the diskettes because wild cards don't work with the Extract /c command.

Use the Extract command (in DOS or a DOS window at the C:\Win95scr prompt) as follows:

```
extract /c a:\precopy2.cab c:\win95src
```

Replace *precopy2.cab* with the name of each cabinet file. Use the DOS DIR command to display the names of the files on the DMF diskettes. You can type **extract /?** to view the online documentation for the Extract command.

Tip

You can get a listing of all the files in the Windows 95 source cabinets (starting with Win95_02.cab) by using a variation of the Extract command and piping the results to a file. At the DOS prompt (while in the Windows 95 source directory) issue the command:

```
extract /d /a win95_02.cab > List95.txt
```

More details about the Extract command can be found in the Microsoft Knowledge Base. Turn your Internet Explorer (after you get this all set up) to http://www.microsoft.com/kb/articles/q129/6/05.htm.

Installing over a network or from a CD-ROM

If your computer is connected to a network and the source files are stored on a server, either on a hard disk or a CD-ROM, you can install Windows 95 from the server. Unless your system administrator has custom-designed the installation procedures, it is no different than installing Windows 95 from a local diskette drive, CD-ROM, or hard disk — with one exception.

Secret

Near the end of the Windows 95 installation, Windows 95 reboots your computer and grabs further files from the source cabinets. It reboots your computer under Windows 95. If, using the Windows 95 network or CD-ROM drivers, it is unable to make the connection to your network server or to your local CD-ROM drive, Windows 95 can't continue configuring itself.

If you're upgrading over a previous Windows directory, it may be difficult to get back to your previous connections to the server or the CD-ROM. There is obviously a bug if Windows 95 can't access your network or CD-ROM. But the bug shows up at an inopportune time.

While you won't be able to completely install Windows 95 because you don't have access to some files, in particular the printer files, you will have a semi-working version of Windows 95 at the end of your setup process. You will need to make some changes in your configuration to regain access to the network or your CD-ROM, perhaps using your previously working 16-bit drivers.

Windows 95 keeps track of the location of its source installation files. In most cases this location will be the \Win95 folder in your CD-ROM drive. It also tracks whether the files are stored in cabinet files, as they originally are, or have been expanded into separate files. Network administrators have the option of pulling all the Windows 95 files out of the cabinet files for easier management (see *Installing Copies of Windows 95 on Multiple Computers* section later in this chapter).

When you make certain changes to your Windows 95 configuration, Windows 95 will search for the files that it needs in the original location. If it doesn't find these files there it will ask you where it can find them. If you've installed from the Windows 95 CD-ROM, you'll just put it in your CD-ROM drive and continue. If the source files are stored somewhere other than their original location you can type in this new location when asked.

Windows 95 stores the source file location and the source file type (cabinet files or expanded files) in the Registry. You can edit your Registry, once you've installed Windows 95, to specify a new file location and to change the source file type. (Refer to Chapter 15 to learn more about the Registry editor.)

STEPS

Changing the Source File Location and Type

Step 1.   After you install Windows 95, double-click Regedit.exe in your \Windows folder.

Step 2.   Navigate in your Registry to HKEY_LOCAL_MACHINE\ SOFTWARE\Microsoft\Windows\CurrentVersion\SETUP. Highlight SETUP.

Changing the Source File Location and Type

Step 3.   Double-click SourcePath in the right pane of your Registry editor. Type a new path for the location of your source files. Click OK.

Step 4.   Double-click SourcePathType. To change it from the expanded, NETSETUP value to the cabinet value, type in **05 00 00 00.** Click OK.

Step 5.   If you are changing SourcePathType to the cabinet value, you'll also need to extract the Layout.inf file from the cabinet folders and place it in your \Windows\Inf folder. Follow the instructions in the *Loading the source files* section to do this. Backup your current Layout.inf file first.

Getting Ready to Start Windows 95 Setup

Your installation of Windows 95 may choke if you have loaded DOS TSRs into memory or are running Windows utilities or add-ons. Microsoft provides a list of TSRs known to cause problems in the file Setup.txt, which you will find on the Windows 95 CD-ROM or diskettes. Setup also searches through one of its files, Setupc.inf, to see if there are conflicts.

So many combinations of TSRs and Windows utilities could cause problems that Microsoft would prefer you eliminate as many variables as possible. Most support calls Microsoft receives concern setup issues.

Just before you install Windows 95, you should remark out as many of the calls to TSRs in Config.sys and Autoexec.bat as you can live without during the installation. You should also close any programs that are started by your Windows Startup group and eliminate unnecessary programs from the Startup group before installing Windows 95.

If your computer BIOS includes a virus-checking option, you'll need to turn off this function. Otherwise the Windows 95 Setup will freeze. The most common way to access this function is to press the Del key when booting your computer to bring up the built-in BIOS screen.

Back up some files

Changes are going to be made to a number of your existing files. If you want to play it safe, you can back them up and edit the newer versions later.

If you are updating your Windows 3.*x* directory, you'll want to back up all configuration *(ini)* files, Registry *(dat)* files, and password *(pwl)* files. No matter how you install Windows 95, you'll want to back up Autoexec.bat and Config.sys and any network configuration files and logon scripts.

Changes will be made

You don't want to remark out the real-mode drivers in Autoexec.bat and Config.sys before you start installation. Hardware detection procedures in Windows 95 Setup use these calls to help configure Windows 95.

Changes will be made to your Autoexec.bat and Config.sys files. Lines will be remarked out that are no longer needed. You will undoubtedly want to edit Autoexec.bat and Config.sys further or even remove these files.

If you have a Config.sys file with different sections for multi-configuration, only the currently active portion of the Config.sys file is used by Windows 95 Setup when configuring Windows 95. All other sections of Config.sys (and Autoexec.bat) are remarked out. If you want to use a multi-configuration version of Config.sys and Autoexec.bat with Windows 95, you will need to edit these files after the Windows 95 installation is complete.

Setup creates a new file called Dosstart.bat, which it places in the Windows 95 folder. Lines remarked out of your Autoexec.bat file are placed in this file. Dosstart is run when you start an MS-DOS mode session under Windows 95 (under some circumstances). Check out Chapter 17 for more details.

Running Setup from DOS or Windows 3.1*x*

Windows 95 Setup can be run from either your previous version of DOS (version 3.2 or higher) or from Windows 3.1*x* (not Windows 3.0). If you have only DOS on your computer, you can run Setup from DOS.

When you start Windows 95 Setup from DOS, it loads a mini version of Windows 3.1 from your Windows 95 source files and then runs Setup from this version of Windows. It will run a DOS 7.0 version of ScanDisk before it loads this mini version of Windows. If you start from Windows 3.1*x*, the DOS 7.0 version of ScanDisk will be run behind the scenes.

If a previous version of Windows 3.1*x* is loaded on your computer when you run Windows 95 Setup from DOS, Setup will find it and ask you if you want use this version of Windows to run Setup. There's no reason not to.

Setup switches

The easiest way to run the Windows 95 Setup is to start your Windows 3.1*x* File Manager and then double-click on the Setup.exe file in the Windows 95 source directory. However, if you run Setup from the DOS prompt, or if you choose File, Run in the Windows 3.1*x* File Manager, you can add some command line parameters. They are shown in Table 3-3.

Table 3-3	Command Line Parameters for Setup
Switch	*Resulting Action*
Setup /?	Lists some of the Setup switches.
Setup /d	Doesn't use the existing version of Windows to run Windows 95 Setup.
Setup /id	Doesn't check for minimum hard disk space requirements.
Setup /ih	Runs ScanDisk in the foreground. You get to see the results. Use this switch if the system hangs during the ScanDisk check or if you get error messages.
Setup /iL	Loads the Logitech mouse driver. Use this option if you have a Logitech Series C mouse.
Setup /in	Doesn't ask about or install network software. If you want to install Direct Cable Connection, don't use this switch.
Setup /ip	Doesn't run the hardware scan (plug and play).
Setup /is	Run Setup without first running ScanDisk. We recommend that you run ScanDisk first. If you get a message that there is not enough free conventional memory to run ScanDisk, and you have freed up as much conventional memory as possible, you can run Setup with this switch. This setting is also required if the Windows 95 Setup persists in believing there are errors on your hard drive, when this is not the case.
Setup /iq	This is the same as Setup/is except that you use it if you are running Setup from DOS. Use this switch or /is if you are using compression software other than DriveSpace or DoubleSpace.
Setup/IW	Bypasses the licensing screen (use uppercase letters).
Setup /nostart	Copies from the Windows 95 source files the minimum Windows 3.x DLLs required to run the Windows 95 Setup and then exit to DOS.
Setup *script-file*	If you have a script file that automates the setup process, this is how you run it. Often the script file will be on a network server, which you will need to log into before you begin setting up.

Undocumented (margin icon, beside Setup /is row)

Undocumented (margin icon, beside Setup /nostart row)

The Setup Process

You might be getting the idea that setting up Windows 95 is no simple matter. The setup procedures have to check for thousands of different hardware and software combinations. Developing the setup software was almost as complicated for Microsoft as creating the core of Windows 95 itself.

Running Windows 95 Setup is not that difficult because Microsoft has done so much to make it do the work for you. While we can't cover every step, we do point out some key areas and give you extra guidance about how to proceed.

Most of the dialog boxes that you'll see while Setup runs have Next and Back buttons. You get to choose when you go forward. If you want to go back and make a choice over again, you often have that option.

Starting Setup

You can start Windows 95 Setup using any one of the three methods described earlier in the section entitled *Setup switches*. If you are running Setup from Windows, you will see the dialog box shown in Figure 3-1. Click OK to continue.

Figure 3-1: The Windows 95 Setup opening dialog box. If you decide that you really aren't ready to start, you can exit Setup now. There will be other opportunities to quit or go back without consequences later during Setup.

If you are running Setup from the DOS prompt, you won't see this screen, but rather, you see the DOS 7.0 version of ScanDisk (found with the Windows 95 source files) running first.

Running ScanDisk

As soon as Setup starts, the ScanDisk program from the Windows 95 source files is called to check your hard disk.

If you start Windows 95 Setup from the DOS prompt, the DOS 7.0 version of ScanDisk will run in the foreground. If you start Setup from Windows, the DOS 7.0 version of ScanDisk runs in background while Setup tells you in a Windows message box that it is performing a routine check of your system, as shown in Figure 3-2.

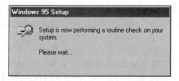

Figure 3-2: If you start Windows 95 Setup from Windows 3.1*x*, this message box appears while the DOS 7.0 version of ScanDisk (not the Windows 95 version) is running in the background.

If, while running Windows 95 Setup, ScanDisk reports a lack of conventional memory, quit Setup. You can then edit your existing Autoexec.bat and Config.sys files and restart your computer to get more conventional memory. This may allow the DOS 7.0 ScanDisk program to work correctly.

Undocumented

If Windows 95 Setup has trouble running the DOS 7.0 version of ScanDisk, you can run an earlier version of ScanDisk before you run Setup again. You'll need to be running DOS 6.2 or later to have ScanDisk. You can also run Defrag if you have DOS 6.0 or later. *Don't run the old versions of ScanDisk or Defrag after you have installed Windows 95.*

You can, alternately, run the DOS 7.0 version of ScanDisk that comes on the Windows 95 diskettes or CD-ROM (even though you are running an earlier version of DOS). You can run this version of ScanDisk from the DOS prompt before you start Windows 95 Setup again.

If you get an error message that says you must run ScanDisk to fix some problems encountered on your hard disk, you'll want to run the DOS 7.0 version of ScanDisk. To do so, take the following steps:

STEPS

Running DOS 7.0 ScanDisk to Correct Hard Disk Problems

Step 1.   Quit Windows 95 Setup (and Windows 3.1*x*).

Step 2.   Make sure that the first diskette in the Windows 95 set of diskettes is in your diskette drive, that your Windows 95 CD-ROM is in its drive, or that the Windows 95 source files are on your hard disk (they should already be there).

Step 3.   At the DOS command prompt type:

```
a:Scandisk.exe /all
```

Where *a* is the drive (and directory) designator for the location of the Windows 95 source files.

Step 4.   Follow the directions on the screen.

Step 5.   Start your earlier version of Windows again and run Windows 95 Setup again.

If you were originally running Windows 95 Setup from DOS, the DOS 7.0 ScanDisk will run and you'll be able to fix most disk problems without having to get out of Setup.

After ScanDisk runs under Setup, you are asked if you wish to continue running Setup. You can exit without any consequences at this point.

Warning about open programs

If Setup detects that some Windows 3.x programs are running, you will get the error message shown in Figure 3-3. Press Alt+Tab to switch to those programs, close them, and then continue Setup by clicking OK.

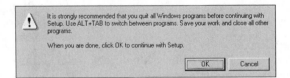

It is strongly recommended that you quit all Windows programs before continuing with Setup. Use ALT+TAB to switch between programs. Save your work and close all other programs.

When you are done, click OK to continue with Setup.

OK   Cancel

Figure 3-3: Windows 95 Setup detects running Windows programs. Click OK to continue Setup, press Alt+Tab to close the programs, or click Cancel to stop Setup.

Windows 95 Setup detects all running Windows programs, the vast majority of which will cause no problems. Microsoft just doesn't want any problems here, so it asks you to close all Windows programs. We have never had a problem with just proceeding, but for safety's sake, you might want to take the time to close your apps at this point.

Collecting information

You'll know that the next phase of setting up Windows 95 has begun when you see the dialog box shown in Figure 3-4. Setup is ready to get some information from you and from your computer. You can quit Setup by clicking Cancel or continue by clicking Next. Because this is the start of a new phase, you can't go back. You can, however, cancel and run the startup phase again.

The Windows 95 directory

Windows 95 Setup will, by default, attempt to install Windows 95 in your existing Windows 3.x directory. You have to tell it *twice* if you want to install Windows 95 in a new directory. You are presented with the dialog box shown in Figure 3-5. You can choose between the current Windows 3.x directory or another directory.

Figure 3-4: The Windows 95 Setup Wizard dialog box. You can quit Setup by clicking Cancel, or proceed to the fact-finding portion of Setup. The Back button is grayed out because the first phase has been completed and you can go back only by clicking Cancel and starting again.

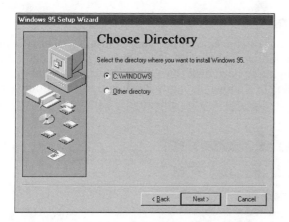

Figure 3-5: The Choose Directory dialog box. Windows 95 calls directories *folders*. Windows 95 Setup is the transition phase to Windows 95. Therefore the Windows 95 folder is called a *directory* in this dialog box. The default choice is to upgrade your existing Windows 3.*x* directory with Windows 95. Choose Other directory to put Windows 95 in a new directory.

If you choose to install Windows 95 into your existing Windows 3.*x* directory, you do have the option of saving crucial parts of your Windows 3.*x* directory so that you can uninstall Windows 95 and go back to Windows 3.*x*.

If you choose Other directory and click Next, you get the dialog box shown in Figure 3-6. Again, Setup wants to put Windows 95 into your current Windows 3.*x* directory. You have to type the volume, path, and directory name of your new Windows 95 directory if you want to install it in a directory other than your existing Windows 3.*x* directory.

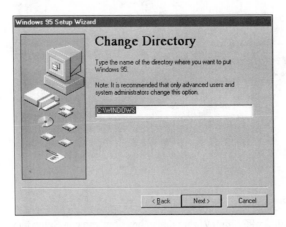

Figure 3-6: The Change Directory dialog box. The default is the current Windows 3.*x* directory — not much of a change. Type the name of a new directory if you want to install Windows 95 in a new separate directory.

Checking for free hard disk space

Windows 95 Setup now checks whether your computer meets the minimum requirements, including sufficient available disk space. If it determines that there is not enough free hard disk space for a Typical installation, it warns you with the dialog box shown in Figure 3-7. If you use the Compact or Custom install options, you may be able to get in under the limit.

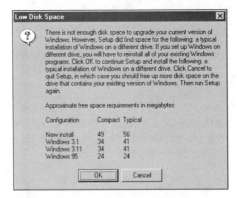

Figure 3-7: The Low Disk Space warning. If you feel that there is in fact enough free hard disk space to install Windows 95, click OK. If you are unsure, quit Setup by clicking Cancel and free up as much hard disk space as you can.

This dialog box can be quite confusing. You have already told Setup where Windows 95 should be installed, so you would think it should know if it's updating an existing Windows 3.*x* directory or being installed in a new one.

In addition, if you are updating Windows 3.*x*, Setup presented you with a Preparing Directory screen (in between the Choose/Change Directory dialog boxes and this Low Disk Space dialog box) to inform you that it was searching the current Windows 3.*x* directory for installed Windows components. Again, you would think that Setup would be smart enough to know which setup you're performing.

Instead, this dialog box presents you with a chart containing four rows, each representing a different upgrade or setup option. Since Setup doesn't appear to know whether it is upgrading or installing to a new Windows 95 directory, you have to know which one you want and which one Setup should have found to read this chart correctly.

Finally, since Windows 95 Setup doesn't yet know just what parts of Windows 95 you are going to install, it can't be sure that you *don't* have enough room to install Windows 95. It assumes you are going to choose the Typical option later on. You haven't made that choice yet, and you might not have even thought about it. You also don't know just what Typical means.

Did you check your hard disk space before you started? If not, click Cancel and do so before you begin Setup again.

Read the chart in this dialog box using the row that corresponds to the kind of upgrade or new setup that you want to perform. Combine that row with the column for the type of setup you will choose in a minute. We recommend that you do a Custom installation for the greatest flexibility, but make your best guess now.

If you feel you have enough free hard disk space, click OK and go to the next dialog box, which lets you choose from among four Setup options. If you are unsure about how much hard disk space you have, click Cancel and check things out before you begin Setup again.

If it turns out that you do not have enough free hard disk space, Setup will quit prematurely. You can recover from this and run Setup again from DOS if you have overwritten crucial parts of Windows 3.1*x* so that it doesn't run anymore.

Get connected

Microsoft wants to highlight the fact that Windows 95 is a very communicative operating system. Microsoft Exchange or Windows Messaging, its universal e-mail and fax client, gets installed if you install any of the options in the dialog box shown in Figure 3-8.

Don't install Microsoft Mail unless your computer is connected to a local area network and your co-workers are using Microsoft Mail. Though you can install the Microsoft Network now, that doesn't mean you've signed up for it. You do that later. Microsoft Fax is integrated with Microsoft Exchange or Windows Messaging so you can keep your e-mail and faxes in one unified message store, with one user interface.

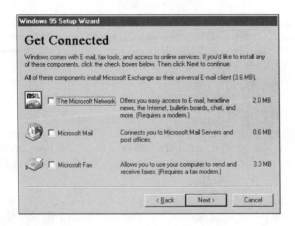

Figure 3-8: The Get Connected dialog box.

Early versions of Windows 95 came with the Microsoft Exchange client 4.0. More recent versions come with Windows Messaging.

Setup Options

After you choose a directory for Windows 95, you are given four options: Typical, Portable, Compact, and Custom. The dialog box that presents these choices is shown in Figure 3-9. You are not given enough information to intelligently decide what these choices mean — that is, what features of Windows 95 will be installed with each choice.

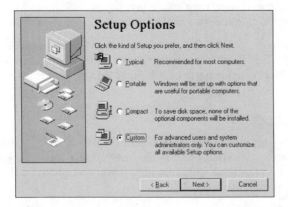

Figure 3-9: The Setup Options dialog box. We suggest choosing Custom so you that can make a more refined choice of specific Windows 95 features.

We suggest you take the Custom option. Later during the setup process, you'll get to define just what features you want to install.

Click Next to continue. If you want to go back, click Back at any time.

User Information

After you choose a type of setup, you are asked to supply user information. This information will show up in About boxes (See Figure 3-10), and in your Fax user properties sheet in Windows Messaging. If this is your personal copy of Windows 95 and your don't want to put in a company name, leave it blank.

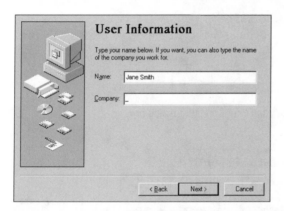

Figure 3-10: The User Information dialog box. The user name and company name shows up in the Help About dialog box and as the default when you set up Microsoft Fax.

Hardware detection

Setup next probes your computer for information about the hardware installed in it. It has previously checked to make sure your computer meets the minimum hardware requirements for a Windows 95 computer and that it has enough free hard disk space to install Windows 95. Now Setup looks at each piece of hardware and builds a list in your Registry of what it finds.

You will see the Analyzing Your Computer dialog box shown in Figure 3-11. Let Setup automatically detect your hardware unless you have a very good reason to specify it yourself. Knowing that you have some hardware that crashes Setup would qualify as a "very good reason."

Hardware detection may need some extra encouragement to look for certain pieces of hardware if it doesn't find references to them in Config.sys or Autoexec.bat and wonders if they are really there. After you click the Next button in the Analyzing Your Computer dialog box, you may get another Analyzing Your Computer dialog box like the one shown in Figure 3-12. You can tell Setup to look for these additional pieces of hardware.

After you click Next on this second Analyzing Your Computer dialog box, Setup performs hardware detection. This takes a while and you'll hear a lot of accesses to the hard disk.

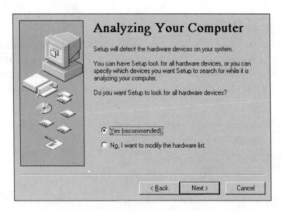

Figure 3-11: The Analyzing Your Computer dialog box.

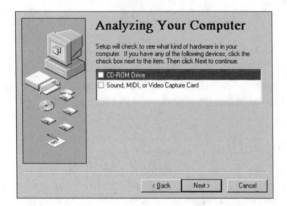

Figure 3-12: The second Analyzing Your Computer dialog box. Click the check boxes for the pieces of hardware you know you have installed in your computer.

Hardware detection may fail. If so, all is not lost. You can run Setup again and it will pass over the area where hardware detection failed. If hardware detection fails, you most likely will have to press Ctrl+Alt+Del or even the reset button on your computer.

Unless you have a computer that has a plug and play BIOS and is populated with plug and play cards, much of hardware detection will consist of the hardware detection routines probing hardware and testing what it finds against a database of known hardware. On older hardware it won't find ROM chips that contain properly formatted identifiers. The Setup hardware detection routines have to perform a lot of different little tricks to detect what is there.

The great thing about this is that you don't have to have plug and play hardware to be up to date with Windows 95. Microsoft has made the effort to bring along existing hardware and let it use the new operating system — a wise choice.

The hardware detection process also determines which resources (interrupts, memory addresses, memory ranges, and DMA channels) are used by the hardware. If conflicts over the use of these resources exist, hardware detection will note them for your later resolution.

Safe Recovery

If hardware detection crashes, you can start again. Setup will notice the fact that it had a problem because it left a trail behind it. The trail consists of four log files: Bootlog.txt, Detlog.txt, Setuplog.txt, and Detcrash.log.

- If Setup fails *before* hardware detection begins, Setup uses Setuplog.txt when you restart it to determine where it went wrong.

- If Setup fails *during* hardware detection, it creates Detcrash.log. When you rerun Setup, it finds this file and uses it to determine which detection module was running. Setup goes into Safe Recovery mode, reading the Registry to determine what hardware has been found and not using any failed detection modules.

- If Setup fails *after* hardware detection, Safe Recovery skips the hardware detection process.

- Bootlog.txt provides a record of each step in the bootup process and tells you where failures occur. If you call Microsoft support, they will ask you about the contents of this file.

- Detlog.txt is a list of the hardware detected during bootup. The Windows 95 startup routines always check for new hardware.

The Safe Recovery dialog box shown in Figure 3-13 will appear when you restart Setup. Choose Use Safe Recovery if there was a problem with your last attempt to run Setup and you want to skip over that problem.

Figure 3-13: The Safe Recovery dialog box. The Use Safe Recovery option is the default. Click Next to use this option if there was a problem with your last attempt to run Setup.

Select Components

If you chose the Custom setup option, you will get to choose just what add-on Windows 95 features you want installed using the Select Components dialog box, shown in Figure 3-14. *Read the text in this dialog box carefully.*

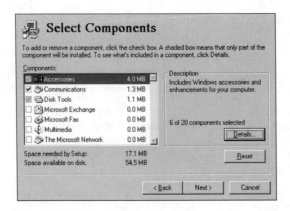

Figure 3-14: The Select Components dialog box. Use it to determine what features you want installed with Windows 95. Double-clicking items in the list box opens another dialog box with more choices.

The Select Components dialog box is the top of a hierarchy. Each element displayed in the list in the center of the dialog box leads to a further list of individual components that you can install. Double-clicking any item in the list (or highlighting an item and clicking Details) brings up an additional dialog box listing these individual components.

The Select Components dialog box also displays the amount of free hard disk space and the amount that will be consumed by installing Windows 95 and whatever components you choose. As you select each component for installation, the increased amount of hard disk space required to install Windows 95 is displayed under the Components list box. Notice that a certain amount of hard disk space is required to install basic Windows 95 and the default components.

In order to make wise choices about what components to install, you need to know:

■ What benefits/features the component offers

■ How much hard disk space it costs

If you are not familiar with the features offered, you may want to skim Chapter 2 or other chapters in this book that relate to these components as you install Windows 95.

The Custom setup option provides you with the greatest flexibility (after all, you get this Select Components dialog box), but it also asks you to make decisions that you may not be ready to make. You can easily add or delete any of these components anytime after you have installed Windows 95, so you can wait to make choices later if you so desire. See *Adding and Removing Parts of Windows 95* later in this chapter or turn to Chapter 16 for more details.

Accessories

Highlight Accessories in the Select Components dialog box and click the Details button. You will see a dialog box that lists the individual accessories you can install with Windows 95, as shown in Figure 3-15.

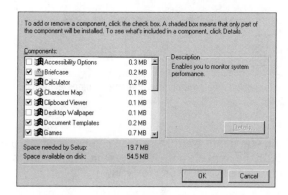

Figure 3-15: Accessories dialog box. Scroll through this list to see all the possible accessory choices.

When you highlight an individual accessory in this list, details about that accessory are shown in the Description area. The hard disk size requirements are shown to the right of each accessory named in the list box. To add an accessory to the list of components to be installed, click the check box to the left of the accessory name. When you are finished choosing accessories, click OK.

The Online Users Guide and the Windows 95 Tour (found in the Accessories list, but scrolled out of view in the dialog box displayed in Figure 3-15) include only the most basic of help files aimed at the neophyte Windows 95 user. The regular Windows 95 help files are installed automatically. The tour and the guide include some rather large video files, hence the 8.2MB size of the Online Users Guide. If you need very basic help and have the space, install them. You can always remove the video files (those with *avi* extensions) later.

Communications

If you want to connect two computers together using a parallel or serial cable to easily transfer files, select Dial-Up Networking and Direct Cable Connection from the Communications dialog box shown in Figure 3-16. If you want to dial into an Internet service provider or call your computer at work from your computer at home, you should also install Dial-Up Networking.

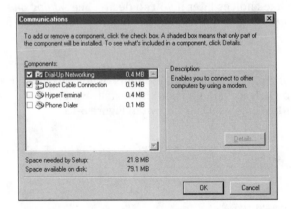

Figure 3-16: The Communications dialog box. The first two choices allow you to connect two computers.

If you have a modem, you might want to choose HyperTerminal to dial into bulletin boards and/or the applet Phone Dialer, which remembers a few phone numbers and can dial your phone for you.

Disk Tools

The Disk Tools component includes hard disk backup, defragmentation, and compression. Backup is not chosen by default. You might want it if you have a device that works with it (some tape drives). You need compression only if you have compressed hard drives and/or want to add compressed volumes later.

Microsoft Exchange (Windows Messaging)

Microsoft Exchange (the latest version is called Windows Messaging to clearly differentiate this messaging client from Microsoft Exchange Server) is a complete electronic mail and fax management system. It allows you to send and receive mail through the Internet (if you also purchase Windows 95 Plus!), over local and wide area networks, through CompuServe, or via the Microsoft Network. You'll need a network connection (either through a network card, or through a Direct Cable Connection over a serial or parallel cable) or a modem using Dial-Up Networking.

Microsoft Fax

Install Microsoft Exchange (Windows Messaging) if you want to install Microsoft Fax. Microsoft Fax lets you manage your faxes in Windows Messaging like e-mail. You'll need access to a fax/modem, either locally or over a LAN.

Multimedia

You need a sound card if you want to take advantage of any of the accessories offered in the Multimedia components list.

The Microsoft Network

To access the Microsoft Network (MSN), you need a modem or a network connection to a server that accesses the Microsoft Network. The Microsoft Network is an Internet service provider as well as a content provider and a web site. Some content is restricted to MSN members. You can use Windows Messaging to send e-mail through MSN.

Network connection

Windows 95 Setup configures a network connection for you if you have a network card installed, or if you chose to install Dial-Up Networking. You get complete access to all the network configuration dialog boxes. The top-level network configuration dialog box is shown in Figure 3-17.

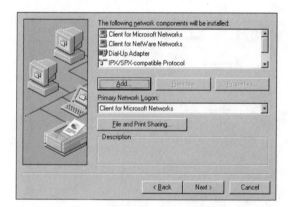

Figure 3-17: The network configuration dialog box. Components that will be installed are shown in the components list box in the upper right.

You can determine numerous network configurations and settings with this dialog box. You can set up your network now or you can wait and do it after Windows 95 is installed. We discuss the intricacies of network setup in Chapter 36.

If your computer will be connected to a Windows NT computer, you need to change the properties of Client for Microsoft Networks. Double-click Client for Microsoft Networks in the network configuration dialog box and mark the Log on to Windows NT domain check box, as shown in Figure 3-18.

Identification

In order to keep track of who is who on a network, Windows 95 needs a unique identifier for your computer. You enter this information, plus the name of your workgroup if you are on a Microsoft Windows network, in the dialog box shown in Figure 3-19.

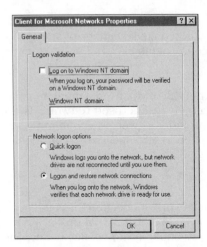

Figure 3-18: The Client for Microsoft Networks properties sheet.

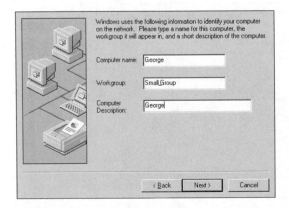

Figure 3-19: The identification dialog box. Enter a unique computer name, the name of the workgroup to which you wish to be attached, and, if you like, a description to help others identify your computer.

The computer must be unique on your network. The name cannot be longer than 15 characters and cannot contain spaces. The name should contain alphanumeric characters, and it can include the following special characters:

>   ! @ # $ % ^ & ( ) - _ ' { } . ~

Your workgroup name uses these same naming conventions (remember, no spaces). A workgroup name is shared among members of the workgroup. If you are connecting to an existing one, get the name from a network administrator or your fellow networkees.

Windows 95 displays the content of the Computer Description field as a comment to the right of your computer name when other users on the Microsoft Windows network search for your computer.

This computer name is used only if you are using NetBIOS. If you are using TCP/IP or IPX/SPX without NetBIOS, you don't need to worry about it.

Network Information Required

Unless your network card is plug and play compatible, Setup may not be able to correctly configure its driver to match the card's setup. If this is the case, you will see the dialog box shown in Figure 3-20. If you know the network card's settings, you can enter them. If you want to wait until later to correctly configure this card, choose the first option in this dialog box.

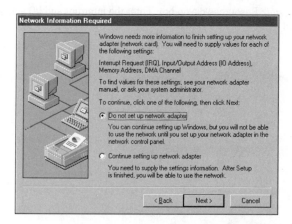

Figure 3-20: The Network Information Required dialog box. You'll need to know how your network card is configured to use it with Windows 95. With non-plug and play cards, you have to set hardware jumpers on the board or use a DOS or Windows 3.x program. You may have to take your computer apart to find the values, or run the program that came with the card.

If you are able to remember or find the values for your network card, click the second option button in the Network Information Required dialog box and click Next. You can set these values in the Network Resources dialog box shown in Figure 3-21.

Computer Settings

Remember early in this setup process when Setup went out and detected your hardware? Some of the results of that search are displayed in the Computer Settings dialog box, as shown in Figure 3-22. You get to change these settings if they don't actually match what you know your hardware configuration to be.

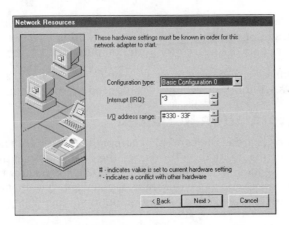

Figure 3-21: The Network Resources dialog box. Enter the interrupt and I/O address range for your network card.

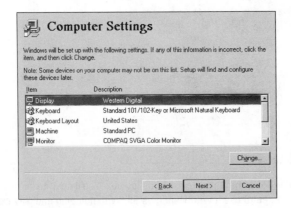

Figure 3-22: The Computer Settings dialog box. Scroll through this description of your hardware. If anything needs to be changed, double-click it.

Scroll down the list of Computer Settings. If you find an item you want to change, highlight it and click the Change button.

Tip

Windows 95 Setup may not have been able to correctly identify your video card. If so, it may show your display as VGA. You can change this later. You should wait to do this because Setup sometimes has difficulties if you make that change now.

Keyboard Layout is used by Windows to correctly identify the layout of keys on your keyboard. Setup will also modify Autoexec.bat and Config.sys to match that layout when you are in a Windows DOS session. If you change keyboard layout later using the Keyboard icon in the Control Panel, you will need to edit Autoexec.bat and Config.sys.

Setup looks for some odd computers that Windows 95 treats a little differently. If you double-click the Machine item in the list, you can see this list of computers. If you have one of these computers and it has not been correctly identified by Setup, choose it now.

Most likely, Setup will not correctly identify your monitor unless you have a plug and play version. You can double-click Monitor and choose from the list.

You can change almost all of these settings later using icons in the Control Panel (with the exception of Machine, User Interface, and Power Manager, if you don't have any power-management features in your computer). You can change User Interface settings using other methods.

Tip

The last item in the Computer Settings list box is User Interface (use the scrollbar to get down to it), which defaults to Windows 95. The other option is Windows 3.1. If you choose Windows 3.1, you actually get both interfaces. Setup places a shortcut to the Windows 95 version of the Windows 3.*x* Program Manager in the Startup folder, so that when you start Windows 95, it automatically launches the Program Manager.

Startup Disk

If there is a problem with booting your computer under Windows 95 from the hard disk, you have to be able to boot from a diskette. Setup displays the Startup Disk dialog box (see Figure 3-23) to give you the opportunity to create such a diskette.

You can always create a bootable Startup diskette later using the Add/Remove Programs icon in your Control Panel. The Startup diskette will not be able to connect you to your network. It will contain the files listed in Table 3-4.

Table 3-4	Files on Startup Diskette
Files	*Function*
Io.sys	Boot DOS
Msdos.sys	Startup configuration
Command.com	DOS prompt
Attrib.exe	Change file attributes
Chkdsk.exe	Disk status
Debug.exe	Low-level debugger
Ebd.sys	Emergency boot disk marker
Regedit.exe	Registry editor

(continued)

Table 3-4 *(continued)*

Files	Function
Uninstal.exe	Windows 95 uninstaller
Edit.com	DOS-based editor
Fdisk.exe	Low-level disk partition utility
Format.com	Disk format utility
Scandisk.exe	Utility to check and repair disk drives
Scandisk.ini	Configuration file for ScanDisk
Sys.com	Utility to allow creation of bootable drive

You might want to add the following files after setup is complete (You'll find them all in the \Windows\Command folder):

Files	Function
Autoexec.bat	
Config.sys	
Edit.hlp	Help file for Edit.com
Fc.exe	File compare utility
Mem.exe	Display memory status
More.com	Display one page at a time
Mscdex.exe	CD-ROM driver
Msd.exe	System diagnostics
Setver.exe	Utility to set DOS versions for some programs
Xcopy.exe	Extended copy utility

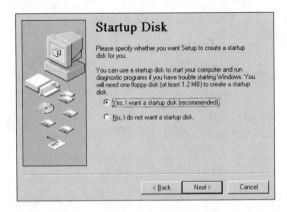

Figure 3-23: The Startup Disk dialog box. Choose whether you want to create a Startup diskette or not. If you have a bad floppy drive and might have trouble creating such a diskette, wait until later.

If you subsequently install Microsoft Plus!, you need to update your Windows 95 Startup diskette. You can do this when you install Plus! or when (and if) you install DriveSpace 3.

If you don't have an updated Startup diskette and you do use DriveSpace 3, you won't be able to access your compressed volumes when you boot off your Startup diskette. If you can start Windows 95 normally (booting off the hard disk) you can update the Startup diskette by going to the Control Panel, double-clicking the Add/Remove Programs icon, and clicking the Create Disk button on the Startup Disk tab.

If you can't start Windows 95 normally, follow these steps if you have the Plus! CD-ROM:

STEPS

Updating the Startup Diskette with the Microsoft Plus! CD-ROM

Step 1.   Boot your computer with the Startup diskette in drive A.

Step 2.   Using Edit.com, examine Autoexec.bat and Config.sys on the Startup diskette to make sure they have lines that call your CD-ROM 16-bit driver and the Mscdex.exe file. If not, you are going to have to use the drivers on the diskettes and the manufacturer's instructions that came with your CD-ROM to create these lines in your Startup diskettes' Autoexec.bat and Config.sys files.

Step 3.   If you can access your CD-ROM, continue to step 4. If not, boot with your Startup diskette in drive A after updating your Startup diskette's Autoexec.bat and Config.sys files to include the CD-ROM driver and Mscdex.exe file.

Step 4.   Put your Microsoft Plus! CD-ROM in the CD-ROM drive. At the command prompt, type **Copy d:\Win95*.* a:**. (We assume that D is your CD-ROM drive volume letter.)

Step 5.   Type the following commands, pressing Enter after each command:

```
ren scandisk.exe scandisk.w95
ren drvspace.bin drvspace.w95
ren scanplus.exe scandisk.exe
ren drvplus.bin drvspace.bin
```

Step 6.   Restart your computer with the Startup diskette in drive A.

You should now be able to see the compressed volume drives. For more information, visit the Microsoft Knowledge Base at http://www.microsoft.com/kb. Search for articles Q136900 and Q135174.

Copy files

Once Setup has gathered the information it needs from you and your computer to successfully configure and install Windows 95, it copies the files that it needs from the Windows 95 cabinet source files. You initiate this process by clicking Next in the Start Copying Files dialog box, shown in Figure 3-24.

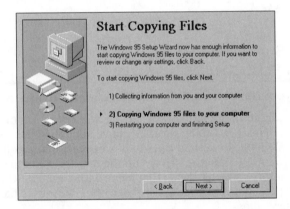

Figure 3-24: The Start Copying Files dialog box. You can go back, cancel Setup, or go forward with Setup by clicking Next.

Setup takes a while to copy the files that it needs to install Windows 95. If you are installing over an existing Windows 3.x directory, most of the files will be copied to that directory over previous versions of these files. The previous versions will no longer exist unless you have stored copies of them in some other directory.

If you have the hard disk space, you can make a complete copy of your Windows 3.x directory and store it on another volume. You can then install Windows 95 over Windows 3.x, secure in the knowledge that you have the option of restoring your Windows 3.x directory if things go very wrong.

You can also back up your hard disk or just your Windows 3.x directory and restore it later if there is a problem. Of course, you'll want to do this before you start Setup, or at least before you take this somewhat irreversible step.

Finishing Setup

Copying files proceeds automatically and at the end (if you didn't run out of hard disk space), Setup takes you to the Finishing Setup dialog box shown in

Figure 3-25. You're not really finished with Setup, but Setup is now going to force your computer to reboot and start up in Windows 95. It configures a number of files before it starts Windows 95.

Finishing Setup

The Setup Wizard is ready to start Windows 95 and begin the last part of Setup.

Remove any disks from their drives, and then click Finish to restart your computer and finish Setup.

1) Collecting information from you and your computer

2) Copying Windows 95 files to your computer

▶ 3) Restarting your computer and finishing Setup

Back   Finish

Figure 3-25: The Finishing Setup dialog box. If you get this far, click Finish.

After you click Finish, Setup reboots your computer. It takes a while for the Windows 95 files to be configured and Windows 95 to start. If you didn't correctly configure your network card, you will receive a message to that effect, and you'll be told that you can make the required changes later.

Next, Windows 95 will set up your Control Panel, configure your Start menus, and set up your help files. It will also ask you to choose your time zone setting. In addition, Windows 95 will prompt you to set up your printer, your modem if you have one, and Microsoft Exchange (or Windows Messaging) if you installed it.

If you like, you can ignore these Setup dialog boxes and simply click the Cancel button. Later, you can use the Control Panel to set up your time zone and other devices.

If VGA was chosen for your display during Setup, you can change it after Windows 95 starts by right-clicking the Desktop, clicking Properties, and clicking the Settings tab. Click the Change Display Type button (or the Advanced Properties button) and choose a new video adapter. See Chapter 22 for more details.

Installing Copies of Windows 95 on Multiple Computers

You can automate the process of installing Windows 95, both over a network and on standalone computers. Microsoft provides four utilities to help system administrators manage this process. You can find three of the utilities in the \Admin\Nettools\Netsetup folder on your Windows 95 CD-ROM. The other utility is available for download from the Microsoft web site, and it's included in Windows 95 Service Pack 1.

The first utility, Netsetup.exe, expands the Windows 95 cabinet files to place all the source code for Windows 95 in separate expanded files on your hard disk. Most likely, you'll want to place these files on a network server. Be prepared for 130MB of code.

As Windows 95 files are updated and as you get new drivers, you can copy the new files over the existing files in your Windows 95 source code directory.

The remaining three utilities help you create and edit the Windows 95 install files, as well as modify the overall Windows 95 install file, Msbatch.inf. Batch.exe helps you predetermine various variables that the user would normally be prompted for during a typical Windows 95 install. You can download the latest version of Batch.exe from http://www.microsoft.com/windows/download/batch20.exe.

Infinst.exe is stored in \Admin\Nettools\Netsetup. You use it to merge existing install files into your Msbatch.inf file. You can download Infinst.exe from http://www.microsoft.com/windows/software/servpak1/infinst.htm. This applet gives you further control over install variables, including whether or not various online services are installed.

You can find instructions on how to use these files to create and modify Msbatch.inf at http://www.halcyon.com/cerelli/install.htm. Microsoft documents this process in its *Windows 95 Resource Kit*.

Installing Windows 95 Safely Over Windows 3.x

The Windows 95 Setup offers two options: install Windows 95 in its own directory or install it in the same directory as your Windows 3.x files. If you install Windows 95 into your Windows 3.x directory, it will be impossible to dual-boot between the two versions of Windows (although you can manually configure your computer to dual-boot between your older version of DOS and Windows 95). Installing Windows 95 in its own directory also has drawbacks: Windows 95 won't inherit your Windows 3.x preferences. Nor will it inherit your application settings in Win.ini and System.ini. (To re-establish these settings, you'll have to painstakingly reinstall your applications.)

Windows 95 also offers you the option during Setup to "save your System files" (save Windows 3.1 in compressed form). This helps if you need to uninstall Windows 95, but doesn't help you preserve both Windows 3.x and Windows 95 so you can dual-boot between them.

Secret

For the best of both worlds, we recommend *copying* your Windows 3.x directory and installing Windows 95 over the copy of Windows 3.x. This not only saves your Windows 3.x settings, but it also lets you dual-boot. Here's how to do it.

STEPS

Installing Windows 95 in a Copy of the Windows 3.x Directory

Step 1.   Exit Windows 3.x and return to the C:\prompt.

Step 2.   At the C:\ prompt, type **Xcopy C:\Windows*.* C:\Win95*.* /s /e /v.**

This command duplicates your Windows 3.x files. Substitute the name of the directory in which your Windows 3.x files reside (*.*). Then name the directory where you want to place your Win95 files (*.*). The /e switch copies all subdirectories, including empty ones (handy when programs create directories that aren't used initially, such as Tmp directories). When you install Windows 95 in its new directory, it replaces most of the files there but still needs an extra 20MB to fully install. If the Setup routine issues a message that there's not enough disk space, it may not be considering the space it recovers by overwriting files. So if Setup complains you don't have the space available when in fact you do, you can ignore the message.

Step 3.   You should still be at the C:\ prompt. Type **Xcopy C:\DOS*.* C:\DOSSave*.*. /e /v.**

This command saves your DOS files. When you install Windows 95 into a directory containing Windows 3.x, Windows 95 deletes older DOS files that aren't compatible with such Windows 95 features as long filenames. But you'll need these files later to dual-boot.

Step 4.   At the C:\ prompt, type **Edit C:\Autoexec.bat**. In your Autoexec.bat file, replace references to C:\Windows with C:\Win95. Save the file and exit. Also change Config.sys in the same way.

Next, type **Edit C:\Win95\Progman.ini** and change references to C:\Windows to C:\Win95. Unfortunately, some Windows applications (including Word) reference C:\Windows in their *ini* files. To ensure that these apps work in Windows 95, you'll have to edit every single *ini* file in the C:\Win95 directory. The best command to do this is:

```
For %f in (C:\Win95\*.ini) Do Edit %f
```

This loads, in turn, each *ini* file. Save each file and exit. Now reboot. Windows 3.x should start normally in the renamed directory (C:\Win95).

If you have Tessler's Nifty Tools batch file creator (Dir2Bat), you can make this process easier using the following command:

```
Dir2Bat /F /X C:\Windows C:\Win95\*.ini "edit !"
```

(continued)

STEPS *(continued)*

Installing Windows 95 in a Copy of the Windows 3.*x* Directory

This creates a batch file that edits only the *ini* files that contain the string "C:\Windows."

You can download this utility from http://ourworld.compuserve.com:/homepages/NIFTY_TOOLS/tnt.htm.

Edit any Program Manager icons that mention C:\Windows by right-clicking each icon in each Program Manager group and changing any references to C:\Windows to C:\Win95.

Again, this process will be easier if you use two Tessler Nifty Tools applets. We refer you to his site at http://ourworld.compuserve.com:/homepages/NIFTY_TOOLS/tnt.htm for further instructions.

Step 5.   Now you're in Windows 3.*x*. Choose File, Run and then type **regedit/v.** In the Registry editor, search for all instances of C:\Windows and change them to C:\Win95. Exit the Registry editor. Now run Windows 95 Setup from inside your altered copy of Windows 3.1.

Setup will see a copy of Windows 3.*x* in C:\Win95, and it will install there by default. (You've not preserved your Windows 3.*x* preferences under Windows 95, and you still have a stored copy of your Windows 3.*x* configuration.)

Step 6.   Delete your old C:\DOS directory using the Windows 95 Explorer.

Then rename C:\DOSSave to C:\DOS. (You've just restored your old DOS utilities.)

Remember: When running Windows 95, your new DOS 7.0 utilities will be in C:\Win95\Command. But when you dual-boot to Windows 3.*x*, your DOS 5 or 6 files are in C:\DOS. Either way, Windows 95 automatically switches between two sets of Autoexec.bat files to set the correct path statement.

Step 7.   When you boot to Windows 95, your edited Config.sys and Autoexec.bat files for Windows 3.*x* are renamed Config.dos and Autoexec.dos. Open these files with a text editor and change the references to C:\Win95 back to C:\Windows (or whatever folder holds your original Windows 3.*x* installation). The Window 95 setup created new Autoexec.bat and Config.sys files from the old ones. You may wish to delete these old files, or edit them. See *Cleaning Up Config.sys and Autoexec.bat* in Chapter 18 for guidance.

Step 8.   Exit to DOS and change the properties of Msdos.sys (a hidden file in the root directory) so it is not read-only, hidden, or system. Do

Installing Windows 95 in a Copy of the Windows 3.*x* Directory

this by changing to the C:\Windows\Command directory, then typing **Attrib -r -h -s C: \Msdos.sys.** Now, open Msdos.sys with a text editor.

In the [options] section, add this line, and then save the file:

```
BootMulti=1
```

You can also use the batch file EditMSDOSSys.bat to help edit this file — see *Editing Msdos.sys* in Chapter 6.

Step 9. Reboot your PC. When you see the message that Windows 95 is starting, press F8 to intercept the boot process. You'll be presented with a series of options, the last one of which is Previous version of MS-DOS. Choose this option and your system will boot to Windows 3.*x*. If you don't press F8, you boot to Windows 95. You can also just press F4 to boot directly to Windows 3.*x*.

Tip

After you install Windows 95 over your Windows 3.*x* directory, you can delete your old Win32s directory or back it up to removable media. You'll find it under the \Windows\System directory. This directory contains the 32-bit code needed to run 32-bit apps under Windows 3.*x*. If you're not going back to Windows 3.*x*, you won't need it anymore. Be sure to edit your System.ini file to remove any references to it.

Is Your Windows 95 Sick?

What happens if you accidentally delete a file that is needed to run Windows 95? What if a spot on your hard disk goes bad? Have you ever copied over a system file with a file of the same name but an earlier date?

You can rerun Windows 95 Setup in file-verification mode to fix problems that might be due to corrupted or missing Windows 95 files. When you double-click Setup.exe, Setup knows (by looking at Setuplog.txt) that you have already installed Windows 95 and asks you if you want to verify your copy of Windows 95.

Using Setuplog.txt, Setup checks your files. If it finds one that fails its integrity check, it copies a new copy from the source files onto your hard disk.

Adding and Removing Parts of Windows 95

You can revisit the list of Windows 95 components you saw in the Select Components dialog box during Setup, and then add or remove parts of Windows 95. Here's how to make changes:

STEPS

Adding or Removing Parts of Windows 95

Step 1. Click the Start button. Point to Settings, and then click Control Panel.

Step 2. Double-click the Add/Remove Programs icon.

Step 3. Click the Windows Setup tab. Highlight a category of components and click Details.

Step 4. You can uncheck installed components that you want removed, and check uninstalled components that you want installed.

This can get quite confusing because you can quickly forget which components you are installing and uninstalling, and there is no way to see which is which. You'll have to click Cancel and start again if you get confused. Too bad the check marks don't have different colors.

Secret

A subfolder of Windows 95, named Inf, contains the setup-information files that guide the installation and removal of Windows 95 components (as well as Windows 95 Setup). These files have an *inf* extension.

You can view and edit these files by double-clicking them. They are all short enough to be edited by Notepad. The *Windows 95 Resource Kit* from Microsoft provides some documentation on the structure of these files, but they are somewhat self-explanatory if you open them in Notepad.

If you want to do away with your (or someone else's) ability to easily add or remove Windows 95 components, and save about $1.50 worth of hard disk space, you can delete this folder.

Upgrading Earlier Versions of Windows 95

You may have an earlier version of Windows 95. The original file date used for Windows 95 was 7/11/95. The original Microsoft Plus! files were dated 7/14/95. Plus! was updated first on 10/24/95.

Service Pack 1 for Windows 95 was released in early 1996. The OEM Service Release 2 went to computer manufacturers in October 1996. Internet Explorer 4.0 became available as a public beta in early 1997.

If you have an earlier version of Windows 95, you can download updates from Microsoft's web site at http://www.microsoft.com/windows/software.htm. For more information about Service Pack 1, visit http://www.microsoft.com/windows/software/servpak1/moreinfo.htm. Information about OEM Service Release 2 is available at http://www.microsoft.com/windows/pr/win95osr.html.

A Complete Bootable Copy of Your Windows 95 Setup

You can make a copy of your Windows 95 hard disk setup, including all the applications that you have installed, on a new hard disk. This makes the transition to a bigger hard disk a lot easier. Errol Nielson provided the original methods.

STEPS

Copying Windows 95

Step 1. If you are moving to a hard disk that is bigger than your BIOS can handle, you are going to have to use the manufacturer's setup instructions before you follow these steps. You'll either have to upgrade your BIOS, or use a program in the boot tracks of the new hard disk that supersedes your BIOS settings.

Step 2. Physically install your new hard disk as a slave (setting the correct jumper position) and using your BIOS settings to tell the computer to see it as the secondary drive. We'll refer to the first drive as C and the new one as D.

Step 3. Make sure you have a Windows 95 Startup diskette. If you haven't already created one, click the Start button, Settings, Control Panel, and double-click the Add/Remove Programs Icon. Click the Startup Disk tab, and follow the instructions.

Step 4. Start Windows 95 and click the Start button, Programs, Windows Explorer. Right-click on each of the two hard disk icons, and click Properties. Label the C drive *Old Disk* and the D drive *New Disk*.

Step 5. Click the Start button, Programs, MS-DOS Prompt. Type **fdisk** and select Change current fixed disk drive. Select the number that stands for your new drive, usually 2.

Step 6. In Fdisk, select Create DOS partition or logical DOS drive, and then select and create a primary DOS partition. Exit Fdisk and restart the computer.

Step 7. Click the Start button, Programs, Windows Explorer. Right-click the D drive (the New Disk drive). Select Format, Full, and Copy System Files.

Step 8. In the Windows Explorer, choose View, Options, click the View tab, and select Show all files.

Step 9. You are now going to copy everything from C to D. The one file you don't want to copy is WIN386.swp (located in your \Windows folder on drive C). You can right-drag all the files and folders from C to D, but don't drag the Windows folder because that will copy this file also.

(continued)

Copying Windows 95

You can also get rid of WIN386.swp by turning off virtual memory and rebooting your computer. If you do this, you can just copy everything from C to D without worrying about working around this file. Click the Start button, Settings, Control Panel, double-click the System icon, click the Performance tab, click the Virtual Memory button, and mark "Let me set my own virtual memory settings," and "Disable virtual memory." Click OK and OK. Reboot.

If you don't disable virtual memory, you'll need to create a new \Windows folder on drive D and right-drag all the files (except WIN386.swp) and folders in the \Windows folder on C to the \Windows folder on D. Turn to Chapters 8 and 9 to see how to copy files using the Explorer.

Be sure to use the right mouse button to drag and drop because if you drag with the left mouse button, Windows 95 won't actually copy the executable files. Rather, it will create shortcuts to them on the destination drive. When you right-drag and choose Copy Here from the context menu, Windows 95 copies the files themselves.

Step 9a. There is an alternative to right drag and drop copying. You can click the Start button, click Run, and then type:

```
XCOPY C:\ D:\ /c /e /f /h /r /s
```

Do not use XCopy in DOS or from a DOS prompt because it will destroy long filenames.

Step 10. Right-click your D drive hard disk icon. Choose Properties, and then click the Tools tab. Click the Check Now button and click the Thorough option button in the ScanDisk dialog box. Click the Start button.

Step 11. When error checking is complete, exit Windows 95 and turn off your computer. Unplug or remove the old drive (the C drive). Reset the jumpers on the slave to turn it into the master.

Step 12. Place your Windows 95 Startup diskette in the A drive. Restart your computer, press the key that gets you into your BIOS editor, change the drive table settings to reflect the changes in the hard disk configuration. Continue the boot process, saving your new BIOS settings to boot off your floppy drive.

Step 13. Type **fdisk**. Select Set active partition. Exit FDisk, remove the Windows 95 Startup diskette from the floppy drive. Restart your computer. You should be running Windows 95 off your new hard disk.

Copying Windows 95

Step 14. If everything is working, you can reinstall your original hard disk as your D drive. Set the jumpers on it to be the slave, exit Windows 95 and turn off the computer. Re-plug in your old drive. Restart your computer and go to your BIOS settings. Edit the BIOS table to match your current hard disk configuration.

Some computers won't boot with a bootable drive set up as a slave drive. If you find this to be the case, place your Windows 95 Startup diskette in your floppy drive, boot to it and use FDisk to "Delete partition of logical disk drive" on drive D. Don't do this until you are sure that your new disk drive is working.

There are more automated ways of accomplishing this task. You can find a program designed for system administrators at http://www.ghostsoft.com (it costs $250). Another option is the wonderful program Partition Magic 3.0. This programs lets you resize your hard disk partitions without losing all your files and data. It also lets you move all of Windows 95 to a new disk. Check it out at http://www.powerquest.com/partitionmagic.

Installing Windows 95 with Other Operating Systems

If your computer has OS/2, Windows NT, or DR DOS installed as its operating system, you can still install Windows 95 on it and have both operating systems living in harmony. There are a few basic requirements.

DR DOS

Installing Windows 95 on a computer with DR DOS version 3.x through 7.x is similar to installing it on a computer with MS-DOS. None of the DR DOS files are erased. Certain DR DOS programs will cause a conflict with Setup. Setup checks to see if these programs are running. Remark them out of Autoexec.bat and Config.sys if there is a problem with Setup.

When Setup creates new Autoexec.bat and Config.sys files at the end of Setup, it comments out the command lines that start DR DOS utilities that cause problems for Io.sys.

Remove password protection for your volumes before you start Windows 95 Setup.

Windows NT

Windows NT has its own multi-boot capability, the Windows NT Boot Loader. This is not true of MS-DOS, DR DOS, or Windows 3.*x*.

On a computer that will have both Windows NT and Windows 95 installed, you want the Windows NT Boot Loader to be in charge. The Windows NT Boot Loader will be in the boot tracks of the boot device, your bootable hard disk.

When you boot your computer, the Windows NT Boot Loader will appear first and let you choose between NT and DOS. Windows 95 Setup doesn't change this arrangement. To run Setup, you need to choose MS-DOS.

Once Setup has run and rebooted your computer, you must choose MS-DOS again to let Windows 95 Setup configure all the files that it needs to continue successfully. Choosing MS-DOS from the Windows NT Boot Loader will allow your computer to load Windows 95.

It is possible that the copy of Windows NT on your computer was installed in your Windows 3.*x* directory. Both Windows NT and Windows 3.*x* can successfully run from the same directory. This is not true of Windows NT and Windows 95. You will need to install Windows 95 in a different directory than your Windows NT directory.

After installing Windows 95 on a Windows NT computer, you can boot to Windows 95 by booting to MS-DOS at the Windows NT Boot Loader. The Windows 95 file Io.sys will actually be started if you make this choice at boot time. Io.sys reads Msdos.sys to determine whether it should boot into Windows 95, DOS 7.0, your previous version of DOS, or Windows 3.*x*, if Windows 3.*x* is installed on your computer.

You can edit Msdos.sys to specify which way your Windows NT computer will boot if you choose MS-DOS. See Chapter 6 for guidelines on editing this file. The same guidelines apply whether you have a Windows NT or a Windows 95 computer.

Secret

You can only set up Windows 95 on a disk partition that is formatted for the FAT file system. This is the file system that works with DOS. Windows NT can manage this kind of disk partition as well as NTFS driver partitions. Windows 95 won't even see these NTFS partitions.

You can install Windows NT on a Windows 95 computer. Io.sys will be moved out of the boot tracks by the Windows NT setup, just as though it were the DOS version of Io.sys. The Windows NT Boot Loader will be placed there instead.

You should install Windows NT from the DOS 7.0 prompt.

OS/2

Like Windows NT, you let the OS/2 Boot Manager have the first crack at deciding which operating system is going to be loaded. Like Windows NT,

OS/2 has its own file system (HPFS) that it manages along with any FAT drive partitions on your computer. Windows 95 must be installed in a FAT partition. It cannot see the HPFS partitions.

You have to run Windows 95 Setup from MS-DOS. Be sure that your OS/2 system is configured to dual-boot to MS-DOS. You may need to reconfigure OS/2 before you run Windows 95 Setup.

The OS/2 Boot Manager is disabled by Windows 95 Setup. You'll want to re-enable it by running the OS/2 Fdisk utility from your OS/2 boot diskette after Windows 95 is completely installed.

An OS/2 computer will most likely have Windows 3.*x* installed also. You need to install Windows 95 in a new directory. This will give you the option of booting to OS/2, DOS, Windows 3.*x*, or Windows 95.

Secret

You can install OS/2 after you have installed Windows 95. Like Windows NT, the OS/2 installation thinks that the Windows 95 Io.sys file in the boot tracks is the DOS version.

Uninstalling Windows 95

You can uninstall Windows 95, and there are various levels of uninstall. If you chose to save your existing Windows 3.*x* installation when you installed Windows 95, you can uninstall Windows 95 by just going to the Add/Remove Programs icon in the Control Panel and choosing to uninstall Windows 95. If you didn't do this, you can use the following procedures.

You can uninstall just the Windows portion of Windows 95 and keep the DOS 7.0 portions. You can remove the DOS 7.0 portions and go back to booting your computer to an earlier version of DOS. It helps if you have protected your previous DOS files, although you can also restore them from your DOS diskettes.

If you installed Windows 95 to a directory other than your Windows 3.*x* directory, you can go back to your earlier version of Windows. If you installed Windows 95 in your Windows 3.*x* directory and didn't save the information necessary to uninstall Windows 95, you'll need to reinstall Windows 3.*x* (as well as nearly all of your Windows programs).

Most of Windows 95 is installed in the Windows 95 folder. This folder may be named Windows, Win95, or whatever other name you chose when you installed Windows 95.

Back to DOS 7.0

Secret

You can remove Windows 95 and still boot to its DOS 7.0 portions. You can run Windows 3.*x* from DOS 7.0 (although you may have to reinstall Windows 3.*x* if you installed Windows 95 over it). You can use the DOS 7.0 that comes with Windows 95 just like an upgraded version of DOS, which it is (although not completely).

STEPS

Deleting Windows 95 Back to DOS 7.0

Step 1.   Turn on your computer. When you see the message that Windows 95 is starting, press F8. Choose Command prompt only.

Step 2.   Create a DOS 7.0 folder and copy the DOS 7.0 files into this folder. At the DOS 7.0 command prompt, type:

```
c:
cd\
md\DOS70
cd\DOS70
xcopy \Win95\Command\*.*
xcopy \Win95\Emm386.exe
xcopy \Win95\Smartdrv.exe
xcopy \Win95\Command.com
xcopy \Win95\Msd.exe
xcopy \Win95\Setver.exe
```

\Win95 is your Windows 95 folder.

Step 3.   Delete most of the Windows 95 files. At the DOS 7.0 command prompt type:

```
path c:\DOS70
deltree c:\WIN95
```

Step 4.   Edit your Autoexec.bat and Config.sys files to refer to the \DOS70 directory instead of the \Win95 or \Win95\Command directory. You may want to put Smartdrv back into your Autoexec.bat file to get disk caching. You can add Emm386.exe to Config.sys to get memory management. Turn to Chapter 17 for more details on DOS.

Step 5.   Edit Msdos.sys to start at the DOS 7.0 command prompt. At the DOS 7.0 command prompt type:

```
attrib -r -h -s Msdos.sys
edit Msdos.sys
```

Add the following lines to the [options] section of Msdos.sys:

```
BootGUI=0
BootWin=1
```

When you are finished editing Msdos.sys, save it and type the following at the command prompt:

```
attrib +r +h +s Msdos.sys
```

Step 6.   You can delete some extraneous files. At the DOS 7.0 command prompt, type:

```
del Setuplog.*
del Bootlog.*
```

Deleting Windows 95 Back to DOS 7.0

```
del Setlog.*
del Sudhlog.*
del Netlog.*
del System.1st
```

Back to an earlier version of MS-DOS

You can remove Windows 95 completely and revert to your earlier DOS and perhaps Windows 3.*x* operating system.

You remove Windows 95 from the command line prompt (as only seems fitting). You can do this from either the DOS 7.0 command line prompt or the command prompt of your earlier version of DOS (if you have dual-boot capability).

STEPS

Removing Windows 95 Completely

Step 1. Make sure you have a DOS diskette that will boot your computer to your previous version of DOS. This diskette must contain the file Sys.com. If you have deleted your earlier version of DOS from your hard disk, you also need diskettes containing all your earlier DOS files. The number 1 diskette in the DOS 6.*x* set is bootable. This is not true of earlier versions of MS-DOS, and you may need to create such a bootable diskette, perhaps using another DOS computer.

Step 2. Turn on your computer. When you see the message "Starting Windows 95," press F8. Choose Command prompt only or Previous version of MS-DOS. Choosing Command prompt only boots your computer to DOS 7.0. Choosing Previous version of MS-DOS boots it to your older DOS (if you have dual-boot capability).

Step 3. Copy the Windows 95 versions of Deltree.exe and Scandisk.exe to the root directory. At the command prompt type:

```
c:
cd\
copy \Win95\Command\Deltree.exe
copy \Win95\Scandisk.*
```

(We assume that \Win95 is your Windows 95 folder.)

(continued)

STEPS *(continued)*

Removing Windows 95 Completely

Step 4. Edit your Scandisk.ini file so ScanDisk can clean up your long filenames. At the command prompt type:

```
edit scandisk.ini
```

Set labelcheck=on and spacecheck=on so ScanDisk will check for invalid characters and spaces in volume labels and filenames.

Step 5. Run ScanDisk to remove these bad filenames (long names that are proper under Windows 95). At the command prompt type:

```
Scandisk c:
```

You can scan all your volumes from inside ScanDisk.

Step 6. Delete most of your Windows 95 files. At the command prompt type:

```
deltree c:\Win95
```

Step 7. You can now delete files in the root directory that are associated with Windows 95. If you chose menu item 6 in step 2, at the command prompt type:

```
del Autoexec.bat
del Config.sys
ren Autoexec.w40 Autoexec.bat
ren Config.w40 Config.sys
```

If you chose menu item 8 in step 2, at the command prompt type:

```
del Autoexec.w40
del Config.w40
del Winboot.sys
```

Step 8. Delete additional files in the root directory associated with Windows 95. At the command prompt type:

```
del Setlog.*
del Detlog.*
del Bootlog.*
del Sudhlog.*
del netlog.*
del System.1st
del *.---
```

Step 9. Delete the real-mode DOS files associated with Windows 95. If you chose menu item 6 in step 2, at the command prompt type:

```
del Io.sys
del Msdos.sys
del Command.com
```

Removing Windows 95 Completely

If you chose menu item 8 in step 2, at the command prompt type:

```
del Winboot.sys
del Msdos.w40
del Command.w40
```

If your boot drive is compressed, you need to erase these files from the root directory of your host drive.

Step 10. If you were using DoubleSpace or DriveSpace compression under Windows 95, you can also delete the compression drivers. Don't do this if you are using Stacker version 3.1. At the command prompt type:

```
del D??space.*
```

If your boot drive is compressed, you need to erase these files from the root directory of your host drive.

Step 11. Put your bootable DOS diskette into drive A and reboot your computer.

Step 12. Place the boot portion of your earlier version of DOS in the boot tracks of your bootable hard disk by typing at the command prompt (after your computer starts):

```
sys c:
```

Step 13. You may need to copy Command.com from your boot diskette to the root directory of your hard disk. Also, you may need to edit Autoexec.bat and Config.sys.

Step 14. If you have MS-DOS version 6.*x* and you are using disk compression, you'll want to place the real-mode DOS 6.*x* version of the DoubleSpace or DriveSpace compression driver in the root directory.

Step 15. Remove the bootable floppy from drive A and restart your computer.

Back to Windows NT

If you have installed Windows 95 on a computer that has Windows NT with its Boot Loader managing the bootup process, you can erase Windows 95 and restore your computer to its previous configuration.

STEPS

Removing Windows 95 from a Computer with Windows NT

Step 1.   Follow all the steps used in the previous section to get back to your previous version of MS-DOS.

Step 2.   Reboot your computer with the first Windows NT Setup diskette in drive A.

Step 3.   Choose the Repair option after you boot off this diskette.

Step 4.   When you are prompted to do so, put your Windows NT emergency repair diskette in drive A and choose the option to repair the boot files.

Step 5.   You may need to edit your MS-DOS Autoexec.bat and Config.sys files and reinstall Windows 3.x if it is in a separate directory from Windows NT and you installed Windows 95 in that directory.

Summary

▶ Lots of little wrinkles come with installing and setting up Windows 95.

▶ Follow our guidelines to determine if your computer can run Windows 95.

▶ We show you how to free hard disk space so that you can have enough room to install Windows 95.

▶ Microsoft made a big mistake when it encouraged developers to put parts of their applications in the Windows directory, which is now growing out of control.

▶ If you want to maintain your old DOS setup, we show you how to protect your existing DOS files.

▶ Did you like Windows Write? We get it back for you.

▶ The Windows 95 Setup is slow. We show you how to speed it up.

▶ You can run into problems setting up Windows 95 from a CD-ROM or a network server. We show you now to avoid these problems.

▶ Windows 95 Setup goes on and on. We help you each step of the way.

▶ If your Windows 95 has gone bad, we give you a method to get it straightened out.

▶ Want to inhabit a multioperating system environment? We show you how Windows 95 can co-exist with OS/2 and Windows NT.

▶ If you want to revert to an earlier operating system, you can uninstall Windows 95.

Chapter 4

A Quick Look at Windows 95

In This Chapter

This chapter is an introduction to the workings of Windows 95. Follow along and in a few minutes you will have a good grasp of the basic notions that underlie Windows 95.

▶ What are those icons doing on my Desktop?

▶ Where do I start?

▶ How do I run a program?

▶ Where do I find help?

▶ What is the My Computer icon?

▶ What happens when I double-click the My Computer icon, a drive icon, a folder icon?

▶ How do I see what is on My Computer?

▶ How do I quit Windows 95?

The Desktop

We assume that you have been able to install and set up Windows 95 correctly (or that it was already installed on your computer), and that the Windows 95 Desktop is now displayed on your screen. Your screen should look something like Figure 4-1. If this is not the case, first check Figure 4-2 in the next section to see if you are in Web view. If your screen doesn't resemble that figure either, then you should go back to Chapter 3 to get Windows 95 installed properly.

On the left side of the Desktop you'll find three or more icons, depending on the options you chose during installation. You use these icons to find and view the files and folders that are stored on your computer (and, if you are connected to other computers, on the network of computers).

At the bottom of the Desktop is the Taskbar with its Start button and clock. The Taskbar is a switcher — it lets you easily move between open documents and active applications. If it's on the Taskbar, you need to click it only once.

Figure 4-1: The Windows 95 Desktop. Single-click the Start button, but double-click the icons on the Desktop.

Tip

If you don't see your Taskbar at all: Slide your mouse pointer to the bottom of your screen. The Taskbar should jump into view. Right-click a part of the Taskbar without buttons or icons, and choose Properties. In the Taskbar Options tab, clear the Auto hide check box and click OK.

For a little fun, try moving the Taskbar around the edges of the Desktop. Take the following steps:

STEPS

Moving the Taskbar

Step 1. Position your mouse pointer over the Taskbar, but not over the clock or the Start button (or any other buttons representing applications that are currently open).

Step 2. Press and hold the left mouse button.

Step 3. Holding the left mouse button down, move the mouse pointer to a side or the top of the Desktop.

Step 4. When an outline of the Taskbar appears on a side or the top of the Desktop, release the mouse button.

Moving the Taskbar

Step 5.   Repeat steps 1 through 4 to move the Taskbar around the Desktop.

Active Desktop

So you say that your screen didn't look anything like the one in Figure 4-1. The integrated shell version of Internet Explorer 4.0 incorporates the interface of the Microsoft web browser into the Windows 95 user interface. This combined interface mixes two metaphors: the Desktop, with its files and folders, and Web view, with its hyperlinks between documents. Microsoft calls this interface *Active Desktop*.

If you have installed Internet Explorer 4.0, your screen may look like the one shown in Figure 4-2.

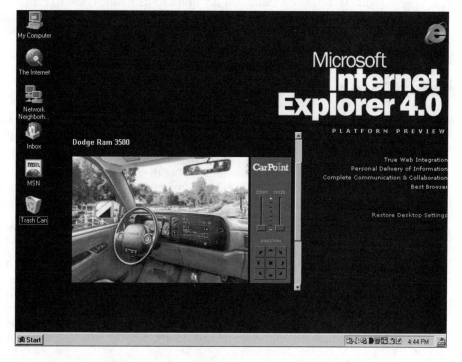

Figure 4-2: The Windows 95 Active Desktop. Single-click the Start button, and (by default) single-click the icons on the Desktop.

By default, when you're using Active Desktop, you can just single-click Desktop icons — instead of double-clicking them as you normally do — to open the associated program or window. Throughout this book, whenever you see instructions to double-click Desktop icons, you can simply single-click if you are using the Active Desktop (and have selected the option button labeled "Single-click to open any item" in the View tab of the Options dialog box [displayed by right-clicking the Desktop and choosing Properties]). If you want to change this behavior, see the *Single-click or double-click* section of Chapter 9.

The Start Button

Click the Start button. Among the commands on the menu is Help. Click (once) on Help to launch general help for Windows 95 (you can learn a lot here). If a command is on a menu, you need to click it only once.

The Start menu also contains several menu names (Programs, Documents, and so on). Note that menu names all have small black triangles to their right. To display a menu, simply point to its name. Point to Programs, then to Accessories, then to Games (if you installed Games during the setup process), and then click on FreeCell. This is an example of how you run programs from the Start button in Windows 95.

What's on the Desktop?

There are at least three icons on the Windows 95 Desktop. Unlike the icons on the Windows 3.*x* Desktop, these icons do not represent active programs or "tasks," which is why we are emphasizing this point.

The icons represent *capabilities* sitting there waiting for you to do something. Nothing happens or is happening until you double-click one of the icons. When you double-click one of these icons, you open a *window*.

The My Computer icon looks like a computer and it represents your computer. Double-click this icon and see what you get. (See Figure 4-3.)

If you have installed Internet Explorer 4.0, you have the option of using Web view in your My Computer window. Web view divides your My Computer Window into two panes with an active window on the right. To change views, right-click the My Computer window, point to View, and choose Web View. Then right-click the My Computer window again, point to View, and choose one of the following: Large Icons, Small Icons, List, or Details.

Figure 4-3: The My Computer window. Your computer is displayed in the My Computer window. This computer has two drive volumes, two floppy diskette drives, a CD-ROM drive, a host physical drive for a compressed drive volume, and three folders — Control Panel, Printers, and Dial-Up Networking. You can double-click any of them.

What's in the My Computer Window?

In the My Computer window, you'll find icons that look like disk drives and, in fact, represent the disk drives connected to your computer. (The drives may be connected directly to your computer or to other computers on your network.) These drive icons act just like icons on the Desktop. That is, you can double-click them (or single-click them if you're in Web view).

You also see three folder icons labeled Control Panel, Printers, and Dial-Up Networking. You can double-click these icons as well.

Double-click the C: drive icon in the My Computer window. (In Figure 4-3, the C: volume is named Belinda.) The C: drive window appears on your Desktop, as shown in Figure 4-4.

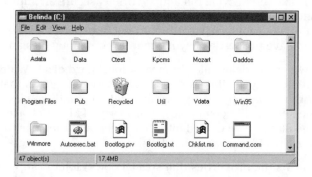

Figure 4-4: The C: drive window contains icons representing folders and files.

The My Computer icon on the Desktop and the drive icons in the My Computer window respond in the same manner. Double-click them to open a window.

Disk Drives, Folders, and Files

The C: drive window contains icons that look like manila folders with tabs on the left side. These folder icons represent folders. Folders can contain files and other folders.

The other icons in the C: drive window represent different kinds of files. One icon that's present in drive windows for local hard disks is the Recycled icon, which vaguely looks like a recycle receptacle. This icon is equivalent to the Recycle Bin icon on the Desktop. (You'll learn about the Recycle Bin in Chapter 14.)

You started with the My Computer icon, which looks like a computer. When you opened My Computer, you found that it contained drive icons and some folder icons. When you opened a drive icon, you saw that it contained icons representing folders and files, including one that displays the Recycle Bin. Double-clicking on a folder icon in turn displays the folders and/or files it contains.

All the icons that are on your Desktop the first time you start Windows 95 represent containers. They can contain disk drives, folders, and/or files.

Special Folder Windows

Everything on your computer is stored within a window. You open a window by double-clicking an icon that represents a computer, a network, a drive, or a folder. Some icons, such as the Recycle Bin and the My Briefcase icons (if you installed the Briefcase) represent special kinds of folders.

Special folders, like the Recycle Bin and My Briefcase, are an improvement on the old concept of *directories* in DOS. Like a directory, a folder can contain files and other folders (subdirectories). But special folders are *objects* that can have properties beyond merely containing files and folders.

For example, when you delete files from your local hard disks, Windows 95 stores them in the Recycle Bin. A property of the Recycle Bin is that you can *restore* files within it back to their previous locations (until you issue the File, Empty the Recycle Bin command). A property of My Briefcase is that you can change files you've copied into this folder, and then use them to "update" the original files on your hard disk.

Windows 95 knows the properties that special object folders support, and it automatically takes advantage of them when acting on files within these folders.

Finding Stuff the Web Way

Desktop, folders, files, documents — the Windows 95 Desktop view is based on these office-related metaphors.

In contrast, the Active Desktop and Web view are based on the metaphor of linked objects. When you point to an icon on the Active Desktop, the mouse pointer becomes a pointing hand, and clicking once takes you to the object represented by the icon, be it on your local hard disk, your network, or the Internet. Screens in Web view are often *active*, meaning that they incorporate multimedia effects such as movies, sound, and 3D images.

The standard Desktop view emphasizes where things are stored. The Active Desktop concentrates on showing you what content is available (regardless of where it is stored) and how you can interact with it.

Quitting

If this is enough and you want to quit now — after all, this is just a first look — click the Start button at the left end of the Taskbar, and then click Shut Down. In the Shut Down Windows dialog box, choose Shut down the computer, and click the Yes button. After a moment, Windows 95 displays a message stating "It's now safe to turn off your computer." At this point, you can safely turn off your machine.

You will find a great deal of discussion about the Desktop, the Start button, folders, and windows in *Part II: The Windows 95 User Interface*.

Summary

We provide a quick look at the Windows 95 user interface. If you followed the steps in this chapter, you should now have a good grasp of the most basic structure of Windows 95.

▶ Explore what's on the Desktop.

▶ Move the Taskbar around the Desktop.

▶ Switch between Desktop view and the Active Desktop.

▶ Use the Start button to start a program and find help.

▶ See what is in the My Computer window.

▶ Open a drive or folder window.

▶ Quit Windows 95.

Chapter 5

A Tutorial for Windows 95

In This Chapter

We provide a step-by step tutorial that introduces the basic features of the Windows 95 user interface. You will learn about:

▶ Switching between the standard and the Active Desktop

▶ Creating files and folders

▶ Moving a file between folders

▶ Creating a shortcut to the file and putting it on the Desktop

▶ Deleting the shortcut and the file

▶ Restoring the file and shortcut

Starting

Complete this tutorial and within a few minutes you'll be familiar with the main concepts underlying Windows 95. Grasp these concepts and the logic of Windows 95 is revealed. Using this logic, you can explore on your own.

Before continuing, be sure to go over the steps in Chapter 4 so you are familiar with the concepts we use in this chapter.

Windows 95 comes with its own guided tour (if you installed it). Before you start this tutorial, you should take the guided tour. Follow these steps to start the tour:

STEPS

Starting the Windows 95 Guided Tour

Step 1. Click the Start button.

Step 2. Click Help on the Start menu.

Step 3. Highlight "Tour: Ten minutes to using Windows" in the Contents tab of the Help Topics window.

(continued)

STEPS *(continued)*

Starting the Windows 95 Guided Tour

Step 4.   If you get an error message stating that Windows 95 can't run the tour because you are using large fonts, right-click the Desktop, click Properties in the context menu, click the Settings tab, choose Small Fonts from the Font size drop-down list, click OK, and then click OK again to restart Windows. Finally, follow steps 1 through 3 again.

Step 5.   Click the Display button.

After you finish with the guided tour, you're ready for the following tutorial. If you were using large fonts before taking the tour, you can switch back to this setting if you like.

Switching Views

All versions of Windows 95 let you choose among four different views in the My Computer window and your drive and folder windows. In addition, if you have Internet Explorer 4.0, you can switch to Web view. If you have Internet Explorer 4.0, follow all three of the steps below. If you have Windows 95 without Internet Explorer 4.0, follow step 1 only:

STEPS

Switching Views

Step 1.   Double-click the My Computer icon on your Desktop (or single-click if you've set Web view to single-click). Right-click an empty part of the My Computer window to display a context menu. Point to View, and choose Large Icons, Small Icons, List, or Details from the cascading menu that appears. Try all four views to see which one you prefer. The view you choose only affects the current window, so you can use different views for different drive and folder windows.

Step 2.   Right-click the Desktop, steering clear of your icons. Check Active Desktop at the top of the context menu and see your Desktop transformed. Right-click the Desktop again, and this time clear the check mark next to Active Desktop to switch views again. Do this a few times until you are comfortable with it.

Step 3.   Double-click the My Computer icon on your desktop. Right-click an empty part of the My Computer window. Point to View, and then mark or clear Web View.

Creating a Folder or Two

The first thing you need to do is create some folders to store files. You can easily delete these folders later if you choose.

STEPS
Creating a Folder

Step 1. Double-click My Computer (the My Computer icon on the Desktop).

Step 2. Double-click the C: drive icon in the My Computer window.

Step 3. Right-click in an empty area of the C: drive window, away from any icons.

Step 4. Point to New in the context menu.

Step 5. Click Folder in the cascading menu that appears. A new folder icon appears in the client area of the C: drive window, and the name of the folder (New Folder) is highlighted.

Step 6. Type **Temporary** as the name of the folder and press Enter. (The text you type replaces the original folder name.)

Step 7. Right-click the client area of the C: drive window (away from any icons) to display the context menu, and this time point to Arrange Icons, and then click Auto Arrange. (This command is not available if you are using List or Details view. See step 1 under Switching Views in the previous section.)

Step 8. Repeat steps 3 through 6, but this time type **Temporary 2** as the folder name.

You have just created two folders in the root directory of the C drive. They are named *Temporary* and *Temporary 2* so you'll know you can delete them later with no negative consequences.

Creating a File

Now, you are going to create a file and edit it a bit. Windows 95 lets you create a document first before opening an application. It also associates the appropriate application with that document.

STEPS

Creating a File

Step 1. Double-click the Temporary folder in the C: drive window. Click View, Options, View, and uncheck "Hide MS-DOS file extensions for file types that are registered" (or "Hide file extensions of known file types" if you're using Internet Explorer 4.0). Click OK. You want to be able to see the file extension of the file you are about to create.

Step 2. Right-click the client area of the Temporary folder window.

Step 3. Point to New in the context menu.

Step 4. Click Text Document in the cascading menu. A file icon with the name New Text Document.txt appears in the Temporary folder. The name is highlighted.

Step 5. Type **Temporary File.txt** as the new name for the document and press Enter.

Step 6. Double-click the Temporary File.txt icon. The Notepad application will start and give you a blank client area in which to type some text. When you have a bit of text in the file, click File and then Save on the Notepad menu.

Step 7. Click the Close box (the X) in the upper-right corner of the Notepad window to quit the application.

You have created a new file, added some text to it, and saved the edited file in the Temporary folder.

Moving a File

Next, you will move the Temporary File.txt from the Temporary folder to the Temporary 2 folder. You'll find that the Windows 95 user interface makes it easy to move, copy, and delete files and documents.

STEPS

Moving a File

Step 1. Right-click the Temporary File.txt icon in the Temporary window.

Step 2. Click Cut in the context menu. The icon for the Temporary File.txt is now grayed out to show that the file will be moved from this location.

Moving a File

Step 3. On the Taskbar, click the button with the drive icon, which should represent your C drive.

Step 4. Right-click the Temporary 2 folder icon in the C: drive window. You may have to scroll the client area of the window by clicking the scrollbars (if any) on the right and bottom edges of the window.

Step 5. Click Paste in the context menu. The Temporary File.txt document disappears from the Temporary folder window. If you can't see the Temporary folder window, click its button in the Taskbar.

Step 6. Double-click the Temporary 2 folder icon in the C: drive window. If this folder icon is obscured by the Temporary folder window, click the title bar of the C: drive window to bring it to the top.

Step 7. Notice that Temporary File.txt is now in the Temporary 2 folder.

You have just moved a file from one folder to another using the Cut and Paste commands. You could have also used *drag and drop* to drag Temporary File.txt from the Temporary folder and drop it in the Temporary 2 folder. You'll learn more about this technique in Chapter 8.

If you want to copy a file instead of moving it, you can use the steps above, but click Copy instead of Cut in step 2.

Creating a Shortcut

Temporary File.txt is now in the Temporary 2 folder. If you are going to work on this file a bit, it is not a bad idea to put a shortcut icon for it on your Desktop. A *shortcut icon* is simply a pointer to an object (such as a document, folder, or application). When you double-click a shortcut icon, Windows 95 opens the associated object for you. Here are the steps to create a shortcut for Temporary File.txt:

STEPS

Creating a Shortcut to a File

Step 1. Double-click the Temporary 2 folder icon in the C: drive window.

Step 2. Point to the Temporary File.txt icon and press and hold down the right mouse button.

Step 3. Drag the icon over to a clear space on your Desktop.

Step 4. Release the right mouse button.

Step 5. Click Create Shortcut(s) Here in the context menu.

(continued)

STEPS *(continued)*

Creating a Shortcut to a File

Step 6.   Press F2, and then type a new name for the shortcut, something like **Temporary File.**

Step 7.   Notice the little curved arrow in the lower-left corner of the file icon. This indicates that this icon is a shortcut (and not the file itself).

Step 8.   Click the button for the Temporary 2 folder on the Taskbar and notice that the Temporary File.txt icon is still there. Putting a shortcut to a file onto the Desktop (or anywhere else) doesn't move the file.

Step 9.   Double-click the Temporary File shortcut icon on the Desktop. Windows 95 launches Notepad and opens Temporary File.txt for you.

Step 10.   Click the Close box in the upper-right corner of the Notepad application to close it.

Deleting a Shortcut

You can delete a shortcut to a file, folder, or application without affecting the object itself. Here's how:

STEPS

Deleting a Shortcut

Step 1.   Right-click the Temporary File shortcut icon on the Desktop.

Step 2.   Click Delete in the context menu.

Step 3.   A message box appears asking if you are sure you want to delete the shortcut to Temporary File.txt.

Step 4.   Click Yes.

Step 5.   Click the Temporary 2 folder button on the Taskbar. Notice that Temporary File.txt is still there.

Deleting a File

Deleting a shortcut doesn't affect the associated file. Now you will delete (and restore) the actual file.

STEPS

Deleting a File

Step 1. Right-click the Temporary File.txt icon in the Temporary 2 folder.

Step 2. Press the Delete key on your keyboard. You will be asked if you want to delete the Temporary File.txt file.

Step 3. Click Yes.

Step 4. Notice that the Temporary File.txt icon has disappeared from the Temporary 2 folder window.

Step 5. Double-click the Recycle Bin icon on the Desktop. Notice that both Temporary File.txt and the Temporary File shortcut are stored in the Recycle Bin.

Step 6. To restore Temporary File.txt to the Temporary 2 folder, right-click the Temporary File.txt icon in the Recycle Bin window and click Restore.

Step 7. Notice that Temporary File.txt is back in the Temporary 2 folder window.

Step 8. Click the Close box in the upper-right corner of the Recycle Bin window.

You can also restore the Temporary File shortcut to the Desktop. Note that it doesn't do much good to restore a shortcut if you've deleted (or moved) the object it points to. If you like, delete Temporary File.txt again, and then restore only the Temporary File shortcut from the Recycle Bin. Try double-clicking the shortcut (which now points to a file that you've deleted) and see what happens.

So What Was the Point?

My Computer contains icons representing each of your drives, which in turn contain folders. In this tutorial, you opened your C drive and created two new folders in it.

A folder can contain other folders, files, and shortcuts to folders and/or files stored elsewhere.

The Desktop is actually a folder. You will learn more about this in Chapter 10.

You can start an application by double-clicking a file icon. When you do this, Windows 95 starts the application used to create the file, and then opens the file in the application for you.

Shortcuts don't move the associated object (a document, folder, or application), they just give you quick access to it.

Deleting a shortcut doesn't delete the associated document, folder, or application. Deleted shortcuts and files reside in the Recycle Bin until you either restore them or empty the Recycle Bin.

Summary

In this chapter we provide a hands-on, step-by-step tutorial to familiarize you with some of the basic concepts of working with the Windows 95 user interface.

▶ You create folders and create and store files in those folders.

▶ You move a file between folders.

▶ You create a shortcut to a file on the Desktop.

▶ You delete a shortcut and a file.

Chapter 6

Customizing Your Windows 95 Startup

In This Chapter

Your computer can start up in all sorts of different configurations. We show you how to set the options for how Windows 95 starts. We discuss:

▶ Getting rid of the Windows 95 startup logo

▶ Booting your computer to a DOS 7.0 prompt instead of to the Windows 95 graphical user interface

▶ Using a hot key to start Windows in Safe mode if there is a problem with your hardware

▶ Booting to your previous version of DOS or Windows

▶ Choosing a startup hardware profile depending on your computer's hardware configuration

▶ Using multiconfiguration Config.sys and Autoexec.bat files to control startup

Do I Need to Do This?

Do you need to customize your Windows 95 startup? No. Not if all the defaults are just right for you. The Windows 95 Setup program creates all the necessary files and sets up everything invisibly and automatically, so you may not need to worry about anything.

But if you installed Windows 95 in a separate directory from your Windows 3.*x* directory and you want to be able to switch between operating systems, you'll find the tricks provided here useful. If you want to know the sequence of commands and actions that occur when your computer starts up, you'll find them here.

This chapter also explains what basic changes you might want to make to your Autoexec.bat and Config.sys files for Windows 95, and it outlines the function of the files in your root directory.

How Windows 95 Starts Up

A lot happens between the time you turn on your computer and when the Windows 95 Desktop appears on your screen.

First, the BIOS

First, the commands stored in your computer's BIOS (and your video card's ROM) chips are carried out. These commands provide low-level drivers for some of your basic hardware (disk drives, ports, video cards, and so on). The last command of the BIOS is to execute the program that resides in the boot tracks of the boot device (most likely your hard disk).

The BIOS will find Io.sys in the boot tracks unless you have Windows NT or OS/2 installed. In those cases, their boot program will be found in the boot tracks. These operating systems allow you to start Io.sys, if you desire, instead of their boot programs.

Often the BIOS settings are displayed on your screen as your computer goes through the startup process. Right under the BIOS settings you may see on the left side of your screen a message that Windows 95 is starting. This is your clue that you can now press one of the startup keys to alter the startup process. For more information, see the section later in this chapter entitled *Startup Keys*.

Then, DOS

Io.sys is DOS. Just as in DOS 4, 5, and so on, Io.sys is a hidden file in the root directory of your boot drive. Io.sys starts your processor in real mode, sets up the DOS data structures in conventional memory, and initializes the low-level DOS functions. DOS starts before Windows 95 starts. DOS starts Windows 95. Your processor is set to real mode and runs DOS before Windows 95 gets going.

Io.sys also calls some DOS real-mode programs, carries out the commands in Config.sys, and loads the command interpreter for Autoexec.bat, if these files exist. Depending on what it finds in Config.sys and Autoexec.bat, it may carry out a number of DOS real-mode commands.

Before Io.sys reads Config.sys and Autoexec.bat (if they exist), it reads Msdos.sys, which is a text file that determines the startup configuration for Windows 95. Msdos.sys may tell Io.sys to ignore your Config.sys and Autoexec.bat files.

Finally, Windows 95

Io.sys reads Config.sys and Autoexec.bat next, in that order, unless you have asked (perhaps through pressing a startup key or through the parameters of

Msdos.sys) that they be ignored. (If you hold down the Shift key during
startup, Io.sys ignores Config.sys and Autoexec.bat.) If Msdos.sys is configured so Windows is set to start, Io.sys loads Windows 95. If Winstart.bat
exists, Io.sys reads it and carries out the commands in it. After all this, your
computer is finally under the control of the Windows 95 operating system.

Msdos.sys

Undocumented

Msdos.sys is a very important configuration file. Io.sys reads this file early
on. You can use it to determine whether you will start in DOS 7.0 or
Windows 95, whether you will boot to a previous version of DOS or not,
whether you see the Windows 95 startup logo or not, and whether you can
use the startup function keys.

You will find Msdos.sys in the root directory (folder) of your boot hard disk,
most likely the C drive. In spite of its *sys* extension, it is a text file like
Config.sys. You can edit it with Notepad or Microsoft Edit (Edit.com in the
\Windows\Command folder).

Msdos.sys is a hidden, read-only system file. To find and check out the
attributes of this file, take the following steps:

STEPS

Viewing the Attributes of Msdos.sys

Step 1.   Right-click My Computer on your Desktop and then click Explore.

Step 2.   Click View, Options. Mark the Show all files option button.
Click OK.

Step 3.   Click the hard disk icon in the left pane of the Explorer that represents your boot drive, most likely C:. Scroll the right pane until
you see Msdos.sys.

Step 4.   Right-click Msdos.sys, and then choose Properties.

You can change the attributes of Msdos.sys by marking or
clearing the boxes on its General properties sheet. You can't,
however, change the System property. To be able to edit
Msdos.sys, clear the Read-only check box.

Editing Msdos.sys

We have created a batch file that you can use to help edit Msdos.sys. The
batch file changes the attributes of Msdos.sys, opens Microsoft Edit, allows
you to make changes to the files, and then resets the attributes of the file
back to their original values.

To use this batch file to edit your Msdos.sys file, take the following steps:

STEPS

Using a Batch File to Edit Msdos.sys

Step 1. Using the Explorer, copy the file Edit Msdossys.bat from the DOS folder of the *Windows 95 Secrets* CD-ROM to an appropriate folder on your hard disk. You might have a folder where you store batch files, but you can use any folder.

Step 2. Right-drag Edit Msdossys.bat from this folder to the Desktop. Click Create Shortcut(s) Here in the context menu. Press F2 and edit the shortcut's name to **Edit Msdos.sys**.

Step 3. Right-click the Edit Msdos.sys icon on your Desktop and choose Properties. Click the Program tab. Click Change Icon.

Step 4. You will be presented with icons from the Pifmgr.dll file. Pick one that reminds you that you are editing the Msdos.sys file.

Step 5. Click OK in the Change Icon dialog box, and OK in the Properties dialog box.

Step 6. Double-click the Edit Msdos.sys icon on your Desktop to begin editing Msdos.sys.

Msdos.sys file contents

Your Msdos.sys file may look something like this:

```
[Paths]
WinDir=C:\WINDOWS
WinBootDir=C:\WINDOWS
HostWinBootDrv=C
[Options]
BootGUI=1
Network=1
;
;The following lines are required for compatibility with other
programs.
;Do not remove them (MSDOS.SYS needs to be >1024 bytes).
;xxxxxxxxxxxxxxxxxxxxxxxxxxxxxxxxxxxxxxxxxxxxxxxxxxxxxxxxxxxxxxxxa
;xxxxxxxxxxxxxxxxxxxxxxxxxxxxxxxxxxxxxxxxxxxxxxxxxxxxxxxxxxxxxxxxb
;xxxxxxxxxxxxxxxxxxxxxxxxxxxxxxxxxxxxxxxxxxxxxxxxxxxxxxxxxxxxxxxxc
;xxxxxxxxxxxxxxxxxxxxxxxxxxxxxxxxxxxxxxxxxxxxxxxxxxxxxxxxxxxxxxxxd
;xxxxxxxxxxxxxxxxxxxxxxxxxxxxxxxxxxxxxxxxxxxxxxxxxxxxxxxxxxxxxxxxe
;xxxxxxxxxxxxxxxxxxxxxxxxxxxxxxxxxxxxxxxxxxxxxxxxxxxxxxxxxxxxxxxxf
;xxxxxxxxxxxxxxxxxxxxxxxxxxxxxxxxxxxxxxxxxxxxxxxxxxxxxxxxxxxxxxxxg
;xxxxxxxxxxxxxxxxxxxxxxxxxxxxxxxxxxxxxxxxxxxxxxxxxxxxxxxxxxxxxxxxh
```

```
;XXXXXXXXXXXXXXXXXXXXXXXXXXXXXXXXXXXXXXXXXXXXXXXXXXXXXXXXXXXXXXXi
;XXXXXXXXXXXXXXXXXXXXXXXXXXXXXXXXXXXXXXXXXXXXXXXXXXXXXXXXXXXXXXXj
;XXXXXXXXXXXXXXXXXXXXXXXXXXXXXXXXXXXXXXXXXXXXXXXXXXXXXXXXXXXXXXXk
;XXXXXXXXXXXXXXXXXXXXXXXXXXXXXXXXXXXXXXXXXXXXXXXXXXXXXXXXXXXXXXXl
;XXXXXXXXXXXXXXXXXXXXXXXXXXXXXXXXXXXXXXXXXXXXXXXXXXXXXXXXXXXXXXXm
;XXXXXXXXXXXXXXXXXXXXXXXXXXXXXXXXXXXXXXXXXXXXXXXXXXXXXXXXXXXXXXXn
;XXXXXXXXXXXXXXXXXXXXXXXXXXXXXXXXXXXXXXXXXXXXXXXXXXXXXXXXXXXXXXXo
;XXXXXXXXXXXXXXXXXXXXXXXXXXXXXXXXXXXXXXXXXXXXXXXXXXXXXXXXXXXXXXXp
;XXXXXXXXXXXXXXXXXXXXXXXXXXXXXXXXXXXXXXXXXXXXXXXXXXXXXXXXXXXXXXXq
;XXXXXXXXXXXXXXXXXXXXXXXXXXXXXXXXXXXXXXXXXXXXXXXXXXXXXXXXXXXXXXXr
;XXXXXXXXXXXXXXXXXXXXXXXXXXXXXXXXXXXXXXXXXXXXXXXXXXXXXXXXXXXXXXXs
```

While only two options are listed in this sample file, you can add numerous options to change how your computer starts up. Note that if you have installed Windows 95 onto another hard drive volume or in a different directory, the WinDir folder in your copy of Msdos.sys may in fact be named something other than C:\Windows.

Msdos.sys options

The options you can specify in Msdos.sys are listed in Table 6-1. If an option is not listed in the Msdos.sys file, Io.sys uses its default value. The default value varies depending on the option. Most of the options' default values are 1. The default value for each option is the first value listed after the equal sign.

Table 6-1		Options for Msdos.sys
BootMulti	=	0 or 1
BootWin	=	1 or 0
BootGUI	=	1 or 0
BootMenu	=	0 or 1
BootMenuDefault	=	n (default is either 1 or 3)
BootMenuDelay	=	n (default is 30 seconds)
BootKeys	=	1 or 0
BootDelay	=	n (default is 2 seconds)
Logo	=	1 or 0
DrvSpace	=	1 or 0
DblSpace	=	1 or 0
DoubleBuffer	=	1 or 0
Network	=	1 or 0
BootFailSafe	=	0 or 1
BootWarn	=	1 or 0
LoadTop	=	1 or 0

BootMulti

If you recently purchased your computer, the manufacturer may have installed Windows 95 OEM Service Release 2 and configured your hard disk as a FAT-32 volume. While this is unlikely, if it is indeed the case, you won't be able to boot between a previous version of DOS or Windows 3.*x* and your version of Windows 95. DOS and earlier versions of Windows 95 don't work with the 32-bit file system, FAT 32. Microsoft turned off the capability to multi-boot when it released this service release.

OEM Service Release 2 can configure FAT-16 hard disk volumes, and you can use these volumes with previous versions of DOS and Windows. Microsoft has promised to release a utility that will let you multi-boot if you have OEM Service Release 2 and have configured your hard disks in this manner. You'll need to search for and download this utility from http://www.microsoft.com/windows95.

BootMulti=1: You can boot to a previous version of DOS and/or Windows using the F4 or F8 keys.

BootMulti=0: This is the default. You can start only Windows 95 (or DOS 7.0). If no reference to BootMulti is found in Msdos.sys, you will not be able to boot to your previous version of DOS or Windows.

If you do not have this option in Msdos.sys and if Io.sys is in the boot tracks of your hard disk, you will not be able to start previous versions of DOS or Windows. If either the Boot Manager for OS/2 or the Windows NT Boot Loader is in the boot tracks, then these programs control whether you are able to multi-boot or not.

DOS by itself doesn't have a multi-boot capability. You will not have a multi-boot capability if you set up Windows 95 over your existing Windows 3.*x* directory (you updated Windows 3.*x*). If you installed Windows 95 in a separate directory (folder), you will have the ability to start your previous version of DOS.

Undocumented

You must be careful when setting up Windows 95 because the setup routines automatically delete a number of DOS files without telling you. These DOS files have almost exact DOS 7.0 equivalents, but these new files will be stored in the C:\Win95\Command directory and not in your old DOS directory. If your path statements vary depending on which operating system you start up (very likely), you may not have access to your previous DOS functions.

If you want to save existing DOS programs that would otherwise be erased, you need to take some steps before you set up Windows 95.

Copy all your DOS files to a separate directory that is not found in your path statement. The Windows 95 Setup program looks for a set of files and uses the path statement to help it find them. Once it finds them it erases them. For an extra margin of comfort you might compress this backup copy of your DOS directory.

After Windows 95 is set up, you can copy all your DOS files back to your regular DOS directory and erase the temporary directory.

If Windows NT or OS/2 controls the boot tracks, and you indicate when prompted by one of their multi-boot dialog boxes that you want to boot to DOS and BootMulti=1, you will then have the option of booting to your previous version of DOS or Windows 95 (or DOS 7.0).

If BootMulti is not found in Msdos.sys, the F4 function key will not do anything at startup.

The program System Commander from V Communications lets you boot to any operating system set up on your computer and works great with Windows 95. You can also boot any other PC-compatible OS. Call V Communications for more information at 408-296-4224 or 800-648-8266.

BootWin

BootWin=1: The default value. Boot to Windows 95 (or DOS 7.0). BootWin means to boot to Windows 95, which includes DOS 7.0.

BootWin=0: Without any intervention by the user, boot automatically to the previous DOS version. BootWin=0 means to boot to DOS 5 or 6, or Windows 3.x, instead of Windows 95.

If the value is 1, then Windows 95 (or DOS 7.0) is started by default — without any action required by you.

If the value is 0, then your previous version of DOS is started by default. Autoexec.dos and Config.dos are renamed Autoexec.bat and Config.sys, and the commands in them are executed.

The BootWin setting determines the effect of the F4 startup key. After Msdos.sys is read, a startup message appears. If BootWin=1, then this message will say that Windows 95 is starting. If you press F4 at this point, a new message appears, saying that MS-DOS is starting.

If BootWin=0, then the initial message states that MSDOS is starting. You'll need to press F4 before this message appears to get the message that Windows 95 is starting.

If the boot programs for OS/2 or Windows NT are in the boot sectors of your boot device (your hard disk), they determine first if you can boot to another operating system. If you choose to boot to DOS from their boot programs, you then have the choice of booting to Windows 95 or to your previous version of DOS.

If BootWin=0, using MS-DOS mode automatically restarts your computer using your previous version of DOS. You must press F4 to avoid this. See Chapter 17 for details on MS-DOS mode.

BootGUI

BootGUI=1: The default value. If BootWin=1 (or BootWin is not in the Msdos.sys file), start Windows 95.

BootGUI=0: If BootWin=1, don't start Windows 95 after starting DOS 7.0.

If BootWin=0, and you do not press F4, the value of BootGUI is ignored.

If BootWin=1 and BootGUI=1, the WIN command is issued automatically after your Autoexec.bat file (if any) is processed. If BootWin=1 and BootGUI=0, no WIN command is given and you will be presented with the DOS 7.0 prompt after the Autoexec.bat file is processed.

Whether BootGUI=1 or BootGUI=0, all the commands in Config.sys and Autoexec.bat will be carried out. All the default commands, including the loading of Himem.sys, will also occur.

If BootGUI=0, your computer starts up DOS 7.0 and you are presented with the DOS prompt. Your computer is now running real-mode DOS. You can run Windows 95 by typing **win** at the command prompt and pressing Enter.

Tip

You can also create a Win.bat file in the root directory. If this file is empty, Windows 95 boots to the command prompt. This is the same as setting BootGUI=0 in the Msdos.sys file.

You can use TweakUI to set BootGUI to 0 and boot to the command prompt. Download TweakUI, a component of PowerToys, from http://www.microsoft.com/windows/software.htm.

Undocumented

If you boot to the command prompt instead of to the Windows 95 Desktop, you can get to the Desktop by typing **win** and pressing Enter. If you start Windows 95 in this manner, when you shut down Windows 95, you can get back to the DOS 7.0 command prompt when you see the message "It's now safe to turn off your computer." Simply type **mode co80** and press Enter. You won't see the keystrokes you're typing (because the graphical screen covers them up), but when you press Enter, you will be back at a C:\ prompt. There is an even better way to do this, which you can check out in the *DOS after Windows* section of Chapter 17.

BootMenu

BootMenu=1: Display the Startup menu.

BootMenu=0: The default value. Don't display the Startup menu.

The default is to require that you press F8 to display the Startup menu. Setting BootMenu=1 forces the menu to appear each time you start up or reboot your computer.

The Startup menu (shown in Figure 6-1) obviously provides you with a number of different ways to start up your computer. Some of these mirror the values that you can set in the Msdos.sys file.

```
Microsoft Windows 95 Startup menu
=================================
   1.    Normal
   2.    Logged (\BOOTLOG.TXT)
   3.    Safe mode
   4.    Safe mode with network support
   5.    Step-by-Step confirmation
   6.    Command prompt only
   7.    Safe mode command prompt only
   8.    Previous version of MS-DOS
Enter a Choice: 1       Time Remaining: 30

F5=Safe mode Shift+F5=Command Prompt Shift+F8=Step-by-Step Confirmation [N]
```

Figure 6-1: The Startup menu. Choose whether your computer starts in Windows 95 or your previous version of DOS, whether your computer starts in Safe mode, and whether Autoexec.bat and Config.sys are read.

You can use TweakUI to set BootMenu to 1. Download TweakUI, a component of PowerToys, from http://www.microsoft.com/windows/software.htm.

You should only include BootGUI in the Msdos.sys file if it is set to 1. If you include it set to 0, you won't be able to boot to the Windows 95 Desktop even if you choose 1 (Normal) from the Startup menu. The BootMenuDefault and BootMenuDelay values work with the BootMenu value. If you want to be able to boot to your previous DOS, BootMulti must be equal to 1.

BootMenuDefault

BootMenuDefault=*n*: The default value is 1 if the last time you ran Windows 95 you exited normally, 3 if you exited abnormally and don't have a network connection, and 4 if you exited abnormally and do have a network connection. Set the value you want the BootMenu to use without user input.

The Startup menu is not static. Whether certain values appear in this menu depends on the values you set in Msdos.sys and Config.sys. You may want to choose which value in your menu is the default choice.

BootMenuDelay

BootMenuDelay=*n*: The default value is 30 seconds. This option sets the number of seconds the Startup menu is displayed before the default menu item is acted upon. You can also use TweakUI to set the BootMenuDelay value.

BootKeys

BootKeys=1: This is the default. The function keys that work during the boot process (F4, F5, F6, F8, Shift+F5, Ctrl+F5, Shift+F8) are enabled.

BootKeys=0: These function keys don't work.

If you, as a system administrator, want to disallow certain actions, you can disable the actions taken by these function keys. These function keys are described in detail in the section later in this chapter entitled *Startup Keys*. This does nothing to make a PC "more secure," because anyone can change Msdos.sys from within Windows or DOS.

BootDelay

BootDelay=*n*: The default is 2 seconds. The time in seconds the bootup process will wait for you to press a startup key (BootKey) after the message that Windows 95 is starting is displayed.

If you want to have enough time to press a BootKey, you should put in a value greater than 2 seconds. If BootKeys=0, there is no delay.

Logo

Logo=1: The default value. Display the Windows 95 logo screen as Windows 95 boots up.

Logo=0: Leave the screen in text mode.

Some third-party memory managers have trouble when this logo is displayed. Also, it can be annoying in general, and it can prevent you from seeing important messages from real-mode drivers. You can replace Logo.sys with another *bmp* file. See the section later in this chapter entitled *Changing the Startup Graphic*.

Drvspace

Drvspace=1: The default value. Load Drvspace.bin if it is there.

Drvspace=0: Don't load Drvspace.bin even if it is there.

If you have a drive that is compressed with Drvspace, you most likely will want to have it mounted and available. If not, you can disable this action.

Dblspace

Same as Drvspace, except for the spelling. DoubleSpace and DriveSpace drives are now handled by one 32-bit driver, Drvspace.bin.

DoubleBuffer

DoubleBuffer=1: The default value. You only need this if you have a SCSI drive that requires double buffering.

DoubleBuffer=0: If you don't think that your SCSI driver requires this, then set it equal to 0.

Network

Network=1: The default value if network components are installed. Enables the Startup menu option *Safe mode with network support.*

Network=0: Either the network isn't installed or you don't want the option of booting in Safe mode with network support. If Network=0, then menu item 4 will not appear in the Startup menu, and the items below it will be renumbered.

BootFailSafe

BootFailSafe=0: The default value. Windows 95 doesn't boot into Safe mode automatically.

BootFailSafe=1: Forces your computer to start in Safe mode.

BootWarn

BootWarn=1: The default value. When BootWarn=1, you see a warning message box when you boot in Safe mode.

BootWarn=0: Don't show the Safe warning message box.

LoadTop

LoadTop=1: The default value. Command.com and Drvspace.bin or Dblspace.bin can be loaded at the top of conventional memory. This is standard.

LoadTop=0: If there is a problem with NetWare or other software, forces these programs not to load at the top of conventional memory.

The Windows 95 Startup Menu

The Windows 95 Startup menu (shown in Figure 6-1), gives you a set of choices regarding how your computer starts before Io.sys carries out its default commands and before it reads Autoexec.bat and Config.sys. Io.sys reads Msdos.sys before the Startup menu appears.

Normal

If BootGUI=1, start Windows 95; otherwise go to DOS 7.0 prompt. Carry out the commands in the Autoexec.bat and Config.sys files. Hangs if BootWin=0.

Logged

Same as Normal but writes out the file Bootlog.txt, which tracks the load and startup sequence. Hangs if BootWin=0.

Safe mode

If BootGUI=1 and BootWin=1, start Windows 95 in Safe mode. Safe mode is a generic Windows 95 startup with VGA graphics, but no networking. It doesn't read or carry out the commands in Config.sys or Autoexec.bat, and it boots to DOS 7.0 or Windows 95 (depending on BootGUI) even if BootWin=0.

Safe mode with network support

Same as Safe mode but also loads the network drivers. You would want to do this if you are loading Windows 95 off the network or need network resources when trying to change your incorrect drivers.

Step-by-step confirmation

Same as Shift+F8. Ask for confirmation before carrying out each command from Io.sys, Config.sys, and Autoexec.bat. Helps to isolate trouble. Boots to DOS 7.0 or Windows 95 (depending on BootGUI) even if BootWin=0.

Command prompt only

Carry out a normal boot sequence but don't start Windows 95. If BootWin=0, starts previous DOS version.

Safe mode command prompt only

Same as Safe mode but don't start Windows 95. Autoexec.bat and Config.sys are not read; nor are their commands carried out.

Previous version of MS-DOS

Same as F4. Load the previous version of DOS. If BootWin=0, restart Windows 95 Startup menu, and if chosen again load previous version of DOS.

Startup Keys

Table 6-2 shows which keys are read before the Windows 95 graphic appears on your screen, and right after the text message that Windows 95 is starting appears. You can use the keys to modify how Windows 95 starts. If BootKeys=0 in Msdos.sys, the keys won't work.

Table 6-2	**Keys That Modify How Windows 95 Starts**
Key	**Result**
F4	If BootWin=1, starts the previous version of DOS. If Windows 95 has been installed in its own directory on a computer that has MS-DOS 6.*x* or a previous DOS operating system, then this key will start that version of DOS instead of Windows 95. This also works if Windows 95 has been installed on a computer that already has OS/2 and Windows NT installed after you use their multi-boot menus.
	If BootWin=0, pressing F4 boots up Windows 95.
	Only works if BootMulti=1. Same as menu item 8 on the Windows 95 Startup menu.
F5	Safe startup of Windows 95. This allows Windows 95 to start with its most basic configuration, bypassing your Autoexec.bat and Config.sys files, using the VGA driver for video, and not loading any networking drivers. You can use Safe startup if there are any problems starting Windows 95.
	Same as menu item 3 on the Windows 95 Startup menu.
Shift+F5	Command line start. Boots to real-mode DOS 7.0. MS-DOS, Command.com, and Dblspace.bin (or Drvspace.bin) are loaded in low memory, taking up valuable conventional memory space. Bypasses Config.sys and Autoexec.bat.
	Same as menu item 7 on the Windows 95 Startup menu.
Ctrl+F5	Command line start without compressed drives. The Dblspace.bin and Drvspace.bin files are ignored and DoubleSpace and DriveSpace drives are not mounted.
F6	Safe startup (like F5) but with the addition of the network. Same as menu item 4 on the Windows 95 Startup menu.
F8	Starts the Windows 95 Startup menu.
Shift+F8	Interactive start that goes through Config.sys and Autoexec.bat one line at a time and lets you decide if you want that line read and acted upon. Also goes through each command that Io.sys initiates before it carries out the commands in Config.sys. (This is interesting to watch in itself.)
	Same as menu item 5 on the Windows 95 Startup menu.

What Gets Loaded When

Undocumented

Io.sys carries out a default sequence of commands. These commands can be overridden or modified by entries in Config.sys. You can easily see just what commands Io.sys carries out if you don't have a Config.sys or an Autoexec.bat file (rename your existing files) or if these files are empty. You can also just instruct your interactive startup (Shift+F8) to ignore these files.

When you see the message that Windows 95 is starting, press Shift+F8 to start interactive startup. You will be asked to confirm if you want various actions to be carried out. Here's how to interpret the questions:

```
Load DoubleSpace driver [Enter=Y, Esc=N]?
Process the system registry [Enter=Y, Esc=N]?
```

If you are actually going to start Windows 95, you want the Registry to be processed.

```
Create a startup log file (BOOTLOG.TXT) [Enter=Y, Esc=N]?
```

The file Bootlog.txt is created and a backup of the previous Bootlog.txt is written to Bootlog.prv.

```
Process your startup device drivers (CONFIG.SYS) [Enter=Y, Esc=N]?
```

If you have a Config.sys file, Io.sys will read and carry out the commands within it. Answer **N** to this question to see the bare commands that Io.sys carries out.

```
DEVICE=C:\WINDOWS\HIMEM.SYS [Enter=Y, Esc=N]?
```

Windows can't start unless Himem.sys is loaded first. Your Windows directory may be C:\Win95, or some other name and drive letter.

```
DEVICEHIGH=C:\WINDOWS\IFSHLP.SYS [Enter=Y, Esc=N]?
```

This is the helper file for the installable file system. This is needed for the Virtual File Allocation Table (VFAT) file system that Windows 95 uses to imitate the standard DOS and Windows FAT file system and still store long filenames.

```
DEVICEHIGH=C:\WINDOWS\SETVER.EXE [Enter=Y, Esc=N]?
```

This command reads in a table of program names and values that fools these named programs into thinking that an earlier version of DOS is running. Notice that the last two commands asked to be loaded high. They are in fact loaded in conventional memory as long as you haven't loaded Emm386.exe.

```
Process your startup command file (AUTOEXEC.BAT) [Enter=Y, Esc=N]?
```

Answer **N** to this request.

```
AUTOEXEC [Enter=Y, Esc=N]?
```

Answer **N** again.

```
WIN [Enter=Y, Esc=N]?
```

If you say no to the last question, you are left at a command line prompt with the Windows 95 version of DOS loaded. Windows hasn't been loaded because you answered no to that command. This is the same as choosing Shift+F5 or putting the line BootGUI=0 in Msdos.sys.

This default load sequence gives you an idea why Config.sys and Autoexec.bat are not needed. Many of the functions that would be carried out by Config.sys are carried out by Io.sys, if you let it. In the next sections, you will see that Io.sys sets values that are normally set in Config.sys. You also will see that Io.sys sets parameter values normally set in Autoexec.bat.

Undocumented

You can suppress the commands loaded by Io.sys by putting the following line in your Config.sys file:

```
DOS=NOAUTO
```

Config.sys

There is a great deal more, hardware-wise, to the standard personal computer than was the case when MS-DOS was designed. Your Config.sys file has undoubtedly reflected that growth. This file on most modern computers is filled with calls to software drivers that support additional hardware.

Mice, sound cards, CD-ROM drives, and network cards are among the hardware components that didn't have built-in support in the original MS-DOS operating system. Memory management, including the ability to load programs in high memory and provide expanded memory for DOS programs that required it, also necessitated software drivers that were called by references to them in Config.sys.

These software drivers are now (with the advent of a mostly 32-bit operating system, Windows 95) called *real-mode* or *16-bit* drivers. Under MS-DOS or Windows 3.*x* these drivers had to be loaded either in conventional memory (below the 640K line) or in upper memory between the 640K line and the 1MB line.

Windows 95 incorporates most of these drivers into the operating system. In other words, they are part of Windows 95. No longer are these drivers stored in conventional or upper memory blocks. This frees up a significant amount of conventional memory that can be used for DOS programs that require it.

The new drivers are called *32-bit* or *protected-mode* drivers. They are loaded above the 1MB boundary. Information about them is stored in the Registry. When Windows 95 starts, it reads the Registry files and loads the appropriate protected-mode drivers.

You do not need a Config.sys file unless you have to use real-mode drivers for a piece of hardware that is not supported by 32-bit drivers. Windows 95 includes 32-bit mouse drivers that provide full mouse functionality to DOS programs in a Windows DOS session, so you don't need a 16-bit mouse driver.

Config.sys variables

Various values that were previously set in Config.sys, such as Files= or Fcbs=, are now set at values higher than the previous defaults. You may or may not need to set higher values for some of these variables.

The new default values:

```
files=30
fcbs=4
buffers=22
stacks=9,256
lastdrive='
```

Memory Management

If you have real-mode drivers (say you have a CD-ROM drive that isn't supported with 32-bit drivers) and want to load them in upper memory, you need to use the expanded memory manager (with perhaps the expanded memory option turned off) to access the memory between 640K and 1MB. Loading these drivers into upper memory gives you more conventional memory for DOS programs. If you are not running DOS programs that require a lot of memory, then there is no point in doing this.

Put the following lines in Config.sys before any lines that load real-mode drivers:

```
DEVICE=C:\WINDOWS\HIMEM.SYS /TESTMEM:OFF
DEVICE=C:\WINDOWS\EMM386.EXE NOEMS
DOS=HIGH,UMB
```

You should put calls to the real-mode drivers after these lines, and start the lines that load the real-mode drivers with Devicehigh=.

For a more thorough discussion of memory management, see Chapter 18.

Autoexec.bat

Much of the functionality that was found in Autoexec.bat and Config.sys is now incorporated into the Registry or into Windows 95 defaults, so these files can be much shorter or even eliminated altogether.

Tip

For example, the default DOS prompt is now the equivalent to that created by the PROMPT pg line in Autoexec.bat. This prompt command creates a DOS command prompt that includes the volume and directory name and the greater-than symbol (C:\Windows>). If you want a different DOS prompt, you still need to create an Autoexec.bat file and put in your own prompt statement.

The Windows 95 default path is C:\Windows;C:\Windows\Command. If your programs require additional directories in the path, you need to create a path statement in your Autoexec.bat. There is no reason why a Windows program should require a path value, but a lot do. DOS programs use them extensively.

If you have a DOS program that requires a path, you can create a batch file that runs before the program starts and sets the path for the program in a Windows DOS session. You don't have to mangle the global path statement to accommodate these DOS programs. You can name the batch file by creating a specific shortcut (actually a *pif*) to the DOS program. See Chapter 17 for more details.

It is a good idea not to store the temporary files that are created by Windows 95 and various application programs in the extensive folder Windows. Windows 95 automatically sets the environment variables Tmp and Temp to C:\Windows\Temp. This makes it convenient to browse this folder and erase old temporary files.

You should have your Autoexec.bat file load any program whose capabilities you need when you open any DOS window on the Windows 95 Desktop. For example, if you want to keep a history of DOS commands in your DOS window so you can easily go back to previous ones and edit or run them again, you should put the statement Doskey in Autoexec.bat.

Multiple Configurations

In previous versions of DOS, you could create a menu of configuration choices to be displayed when you first started your computer. You used special commands in Config.sys and Autoexec.bat to create the menus and respond to your choices.

Windows 95 also accommodates multiple configurations. The menu of configuration choices is displayed after a normal startup (after Config.sys and Autoexec.bat files have been read) but before Windows 95 itself is started. (See Figure 6-2.)

```
Microsoft Windows 95 Startup menu
============================
    1.   Normal
    2.   Logged (\BOOTLOG.TXT)
    3.   Safe mode
    4.   Safe mode with network support
    5.   Step-by-Step confirmation
    6.   Command prompt only
    7.   Safe mode command prompt only
    8.   Previous version of MS-DOS
Enter a Choice: 1          Time Remaining: 30

F5=Safe mode Shift+F5=Command Prompt Shift+F8=Step-by-Step Confirmation [N]
```

Figure 6-2: If you have BootMenu=1 in your Msdos.sys file or press F8 during Windows 95 startup, this Startup menu is displayed.

Here are example Config.sys and Autoexec.bat files that illustrate how to create a multiple configuration menu.

Config.sys

```
;config.sys, Config.w40 when booted to DOS 6.2x
[menu]
Menuitem=windows,Load Windows for Workgroups 3.11
Menuitem=win95,Load Windows 95
Menudefault=win95,7
[global]
DEVICE=C:\WIN95\himem.sys /testmem:off /v
DEVICE=C:\WIN95\EMM386.EXE NOEMS /V
dos=UMB,High
[windows]
include=global
BUFFERS=20,0
FILES=99
LASTDRIVE=H
FCBS=16,0
BREAK=ON
STACKS=9,256
DEVICEHIGH=C:\WIN95\SETVER.EXE
DEVICEHIGH=C:\UTIL\SFXCD\DEV\MTMCDE.SYS /D:MSCD001 /P:310 /A:0 M:64
/T:S /I:5 /X
DEVICEHIGH=c:\windows\IFSHLP.SYS
DEVICEHIGH=C:\WIN95\COMMAND\DRVSPACE.SYS /MOVE
shell=C:\WIN95\COMMAND.COM c:\WIN95 /e:512 /p
[win95]
include=global
shell=C:\WIN95\COMMAND.COM c:\WIN95 /e:512 /p
```

Autoexec.bat

```
@rem autoexec.bat, autoexec.w40 when booted to DOS 6.2x
@echo off
goto %config%
:windows
PROMPT $P$G
PATH;
PATH C:\WINDOWS;C:\WIN95\COMMAND;C:\UTIL\BATCH
SET TEMP=C:\UTIL\TEMP
SET LMOUSE=C:\UTIL\LOGITECH
LH C:\UTIL\LOGITECH\MOUSE
LH C:\WINDOWS\SMARTDRV.EXE /X 2048 128
LH C:\WINDOWS\MSCDEX.EXE /S /D:MSCD001 /M:10
LH C:\WIN95\COMMAND\doskey
WIN
GOTO END
:win95
PATH;
PATH C:\WIN95;C:\WIN95\COMMAND;C:\UTIL\BATCH
LH C:\WIN95\COMMAND\doskey
:END
```

Both of these files assume you want to start in DOS 7.0. They allow you to choose between running Windows for Workgroups 3.11 or Windows 95. If you want to boot to Windows 95 and not to DOS 7.0, set BootGUI to 1 in Msdos.sys. If BootWin=0, these files will not be read and their associated configuration menu will not be displayed.

These files create the Startup menu shown in Figure 6-3.

```
Microsoft Windows 95 Startup menu
==============================
    1.   Load Windows for Workgroups 3.11
    2.   Load Windows 95

Enter a Choice: 2      Time Remaining: 07


F5=Safe mode Shift+F5=Command Prompt Shift+F8=Step-by-Step Confirmation [N]
```

Figure 6-3: The Multiple Configuration menu. In spite of the heading for this menu, it is not the same as the Windows 95 Startup menu. You can display that menu before this menu appears. Shift+F8 won't work. Shift+F5 will.

Multiple Hardware Configurations

You can create multiple hardware configurations for one computer. For example, if you have a non-plug and play portable computer that is sometimes connected to a docking station, you might want to create a hardware configuration that includes the cards in the docking station and the network connected to the docking station.

The startup sequence for a computer with multiple hardware configurations includes a menu that allows you to choose which hardware configuration you want to use. An example hardware configuration startup menu is shown in Figure 6-4.

```
Windows cannot determine what configuration your computer is in:
Select one of the following:

   1.    Docking Station with Network
   2.    Disconnected Portable
   3.    None of the Above

Enter your choice:
```

Figure 6-4: The multiple hardware configuration menu. This text menu appears after the Windows 95 logo is displayed.

To create multiple hardware configurations, take the following steps:

STEPS

Creating Multiple Hardware Configurations

Step 1.   Click the Start button, point to Settings, and then click Control Panel.

Step 2.   Double-click the System icon, and then click the Hardware Profiles tab to display the Hardware Profiles list, as shown in Figure 6-5.

Step 3.   Click the Rename button to rename your current profile to something that appropriately describes your current hardware configuration.

Step 4.   Click the Copy button, highlight the new hardware profile, and click Rename to rename the new hardware profile.

Step 5.   Click the Device Manager tab. Click the plus sign next to the device types that will vary between hardware profiles.

Step 6.   Click a device that will be found in one hardware profile but not in the other. Clear the check box next to the name of the hardware profile that will not use this device, as shown in Figure 6-6.

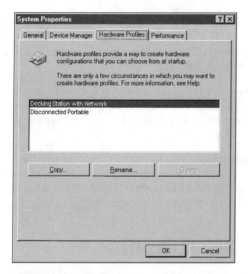

Figure 6-5: The Hardware Profiles list. You can copy, remove, and rename hardware profiles. You define hardware profiles in the Device Manager.

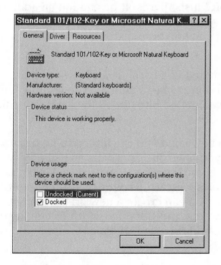

Figure 6-6: Choose which devices go with which hardware configuration.

Your Device Manager may not list all the devices that are available among your various hardware configurations. You have to install device drivers for these devices before you can assign them to your different hardware profiles.

To learn how to add hardware device drivers, turn to Chapter 19.

QEMM and F4

Tip

If you are using QEMM 7.*x* and it loads a file called Dosdata.sys in Config.sys, this file will reboot to optimize memory.

When you press the F4 key to boot your previous operating system, Dosdata.sys reboots the machine to re-optimize the memory, and then you see the message that Windows 95 is starting. Pressing F4 again should boot the previous operating system.

The only resolution to this problem is to remark out the QEMM lines in Config.sys and Autoexec.bat or to remember to press F4 two times. You need to be very careful about remarking the QEMM lines, since QEMM may be loading some important 16-bit device drivers in real mode.

Changing the Startup Graphic

Before your computer displays the Windows 95 Desktop, you're treated to an animated (640 x 400) Microsoft Windows 95 advertisement. This graphic is embedded in the Io.sys file in your root directory.

Undocumented

If you have installed Microsoft Plus!, Microsoft has added an additional file to your root directory, Logo.sys, which contains a slightly edited version of the original advertisement. In spite of its *sys* extension, it is a *bmp* file and can be edited by MS Paint.

You can create your own animated Logo.sys file and replace Microsoft's billboard with your own. You don't have to animate the graphic, but you can if you want to. Logo.sys is an animated bitmapped file, so if you edit it with MS Paint, you'll lose the animation.

If you decide that you want a new Logo.sys, the first step is to save the original Logo.sys (assuming you have one), perhaps as Oldlogo.sys. Next, if you view Logo.sys in MS Paint, you'll notice that it is sized 320 pixels wide by 400 pixels high. The Windows 95 startup routines stretch it out to 640 x 400 when it's displayed. You can create a new graphic at 640 x 400 (or at 533 x 400 if you want to maintain the 4:3 ratio (width to height) that is the standard for video monitors), and then use MS Paint or Paint Shop Pro to shrink the graphic to 320 x 400.

Your logo.sys file must have a color depth of 256 colors (8 bit), and its file size must be 127K. If it is 320 pixels x 400 pixels x 256 colors, it will be 127K in size. The Windows 95 startup routine will reject a Logo.sys file that doesn't meet these criteria.

There are lots of animated Logo.sys replacements available online. We suggest that you point your browser at http://www.nucleus.com/~kmcmurdo/win95logo.html. Karl McMurdo, who maintains this site, has collected more animated logos than you'll ever need. You will also find a tool called XrX Animated Logo Utility at the site. This program will help you animate your *bmp* files. The site has complete directions for creating more animated logos.

Secret

If you delete Logo.sys, the graphic embedded in Io.sys will be used instead. Getting rid of Logo.sys doesn't make the graphic go away. But if you set Logo=0 in your Msdos.sys file, no graphic will be displayed before the Windows 95 Desktop appears.

You can use TweakUI to set Logo=0 in Msdos.sys so that the startup graphic is not displayed.

Your \Windows folder contains two additional graphics files named Logos.sys and Logow.sys. These are the two screens you see when you exit Windows 95. Just as with Logo.sys, you can edit these two files or create replacements for them. If you delete, rename, or move them, you may be dumped to the DOS prompt when you exit Windows 95. To see under what conditions this occurs, turn to the *DOS after Windows* section in Chapter 17.

Dual-Boot Configuration

You can have multiple operating systems running on your computer. DOS 6.2x combined with Windows 3.1x, Windows 95, OS/2, and Windows NT can all coexist on the C drive (or on multiple drives) of your computer as long as you have the room for them (and you use the FAT file system).

You can put almost all of DOS 6.2x, Windows 3.1x, and Windows 95 on a non-bootable hard disk, even a compressed hard disk. The only files you need to leave on the boot drive are the bootup files (Io.sys, Msdos.sys, Config.sys, and Autoexec.bat) and the files that work with a compressed drive.

When you first install Windows 95 over an existing DOS/Windows system, you have the option of installing over an existing Windows 3.1x directory or in a new directory. Windows 95 uses the existing DOS file structure, so there is no need to start by reformatting your hard disk. If you install Windows 95 to a new directory, then you have the option of booting either DOS (which can get you to Windows 3.x) or Windows 95.

If you have a computer that dual-boots between DOS and Windows 95, the files in the root directory will be renamed depending on whether you have booted into DOS or booted into Windows 95. Assuming that you previously booted into Windows 95, the renaming shown in Table 6-3 will take place if you boot into DOS.

Table 6-3	Files Renamed in Dual Boots from Windows 95 to DOS
From	*To*
Io.sys	Winboot.sys
Msdos.sys	Msdos.w40
Command.com	Command.w40

(continued)

Table 6-3 *(continued)*

From	*To*
Autoexec.bat	Autoexec.w40
Config.sys	Config.w40
Io.dos	Io.sys
Msdos.dos	Msdos.sys
Command.dos	Command.com
Config.dos	Config.sys
Autoexec.dos	Autoexec.bat

The Startup Folder

When Windows 95 starts, it runs the programs in the Startup folder. Windows 95 knows which folder is the Startup folder because there is an entry in the Registry specifying a particular folder, usually \Windows\Start Menu\Programs\Startup. You can change which folder is used as the Startup folder, as well as which folders are used for other special functions, by editing the entries found in the Registry under the following branch:

HKEY_CURRENT_USER\Software\Microsoft\Windows\CurrentVersion\Explorer\shellfolders

Even better, use TweakUI to designate which folders are used for special functions. Click the General tab in TweakUI, choose the folder, and then choose the location.

You may want to load a file and execute it when Windows 95 starts up, but you don't want to place the file (or a shortcut to it) in the Startup folder. You could put it on the load or run line in Win.ini. But there is a special set of branches in the Registry where calls can be made to start programs without those programs showing up in the Startup folder.

If you want to know why you can't find the call to System Agent, or if you're curious about other programs that start up without you knowing about it, get out your Registry editor and check this out:

STEPS

Seeing and Creating Hidden Startup Programs

Step 1.   Double-click Regedit.exe in your \Windows folder.

Seeing and Creating Hidden Startup Programs

Step 2. Navigate to either
HKEY_LOCAL_MACHINE\SOFTWARE\Microsoft\Windows\CurrentVersion\
RunOnce
or
HKEY_LOCAL_MACHINE\SOFTWARE\Microsoft\Windows\CurrentVersion\Run.

You can also check the RunServices or RunServicesOnce keys.

Step 3. Highlight Run in the left pane. You'll see which programs are currently running when you start up.

Step 4. To enter a call to a new program to run at startup time (once or always) Right-click in the right pane with either Run or RunOnce highlighted. Click New, String Value.

Step 5. Type any name you want to identify the application that is going to be run at startup.

Step 6. Double-click this new name. Type the complete path and filename for the application. Click OK.

Step 7. Exit the Registry editor.

For more information about editing your Registry, turn to Chapter 15.

Windows 95 Troubleshooting

If you press F8 at startup and go to the command prompt, you can start Windows 95 with the debug switch. Here's the debug syntax:

WIN {/D:{F}{M}{N}{S}{V}{X}}

/D:	Used for troubleshooting when Windows does not start correctly.
F	Turns off 32-bit disk access. Equivalent to SYSTEM.INI file setting: 32BitDiskAccess=FALSE.
M	Enables Safe mode. This is automatically enabled during Safe start (function key F5).
N	Enables Safe mode with networking. This is automatically enabled during Safe start (function key F6).
S	Specifies that Windows should not use ROM address space between F000:0000 and 1MB for a break point. Equivalent to SYSTEM.INI file setting: SystemROMBreakPoint=FALSE.
V	Specifies that the ROM routine will handle interrupts from the hard disk controller. Equivalent to SYSTEM.INI file setting: VirtualHDIRQ=FALSE.

| X | Excludes all of the adapter area from the range of memory that Windows scans to find unused space. Equivalent to SYSTEM.INI file setting: EMMExclude=A000-FFFF |

Microsoft provides troubleshooting guidelines to help you determine what is causing a problem when you can't start Windows 95 in the normal fashion. To access those guidelines, connect to Microsoft's Knowledge Base on their web site at http://www.microsoft.com/kb/articles/q136/3/37.htm.

Summary

Windows 95 gives you a great deal of control over how your computer starts up. By editing a few files you can control the startup process.

▶ Boot your computer to a DOS 7.0 prompt either by creating an empty Win.bat file or by editing Msdos.sys.

▶ Start up in your previous version of DOS or Windows either by pressing a function key or by default.

▶ Edit Msdos.sys in order to get rid of the Windows 95 logo.

▶ Use function keys to go step-by-step through the startup process, start Windows 95 in Safe mode if there is a problem with your hardware, or bring up the Startup menu.

▶ Create different hardware profiles and choose between them at startup depending on your current hardware setup.

▶ Develop multiconfiguration Config.sys and Autoexec.bat files to design your own Windows 95 Startup menu.

Part II

The Windows 95 User Interface

Chapter 7

The Desktop and the Taskbar

In This Chapter

Windows 95 presents itself to you as a graphical user interface — pretty
pictures on your display. The Desktop is represented by a graphical background. The Taskbar sits on top of the Desktop and is attached to an edge.
Here, we discuss:

▶ Arranging the icons on your Desktop the way you want them

▶ Replacing existing icons with new ones and fixing corrupted icons

▶ Changing the invisible grid that determines icon spacing

▶ Changing the font and font sizes used for icon titles

▶ Placing new blank documents on your Desktop ready to be opened by an
  application with a double-click

▶ Putting the Taskbar where it will do you the most good

▶ Getting rid of "sliding" windows

▶ Task switching between applications and folders using the keyboard

▶ Using the Task Manager as a floating task switcher

What You See Is What You Get

The Windows 95 user interface is a Desktop with stuff on it. The background
graphic represents the Desktop. The icons on your Desktop represent all
kinds of different applications and documents, sort of like a regular desktop.
The Taskbar keeps track of whatever you are currently working on. The
Start button helps you start something new. The clock . . . well, you can
figure that out for yourself.

Internet Explorer 4.0 adds an Active Desktop that lets you single-click to
navigate on your Desktop as you would in web pages.

We discuss the Desktop and the Taskbar in this chapter. We discuss some
aspects of the Start button, but leave deeper details to Chapter 11. Each
of the icons on the Desktop has its own chapter — see *The Icons on the
Desktop* later in this chapter for more information.

First, Your Password

Before you can use Windows 95 for the very first time, it prompts you to enter your name and password as shown in Figure 7-1. Windows 95 uses this information to differentiate you from other people who may share your computer. If you set up Windows 95 for multiple users, it can remember different configurations for each person, and it uses each person's name and password to determine which configuration to display. If you are on a network, your name and password let you log on to other servers.

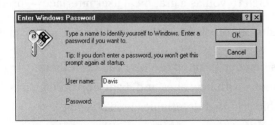

Figure 7-1: The user logon dialog box.

If you type a name and a nonblank password, this logon dialog box will appear every time you start up Windows 95. You can make this logon dialog box go away and not reappear the next time you start your computer by typing your name and then clicking the OK button without entering a password. You will be asked to confirm that you want a blank password.

While Windows 95 lets you use login names and passwords, it is not a secure system. Other users can get into your computer by simply pressing the Esc key when asked for their name and password. You can, however, use the System Policy Editor (see *Icons on the Desktop*) and third-party software (see *Securing the Windows 95 Desktop* in Chapter 12) to improve the security of Windows 95 computers. Passwords, multiple users, and multiple Windows 95 configurations are discussed in Chapter 12.

After you've closed the logon dialog box, the Windows 95 user interface appears, as shown in Figure 7-2. The background used for the Desktop can vary (based on how you set it up later) from one solid color to a photographic image. There are three (but maybe four, five, or six) icons — 32 x 32-pixel pictures — in the upper-left corner of the Desktop. On the bottom edge is the Taskbar, a rectangular bar with a Start button on the left-hand side and a digital clock on the right.

The Welcome screen announces the fact that you are new to Windows 95 and may need a few hints. You can have this reminder of your neophyte-hood come up every time you start Windows 95 or you can ask it to quiet down. Simply click the "Show this Welcome screen next time you start Windows" check box to clear it, and then click the Close button. It's easy to get the Welcome screen back any time you want — just double-click the Welcome.exe file in your Windows 95 folder.

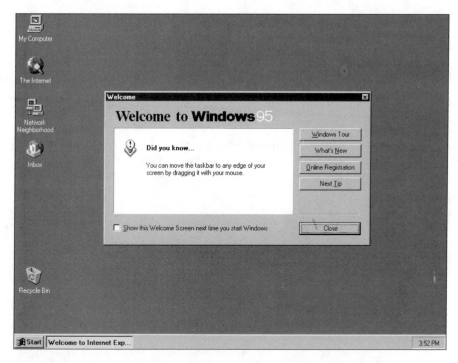

Figure 7-2: The Windows 95 user interface. It will soon look different as you change it to suit your preferences. Of course, if you are using the Internet Explorer 4.0 Active Desktop, the Desktop will be a bit more cluttered.

Want to create your own tips, or modify the existing ones? Turn to the *Your own tips* section in Chapter 15.

The Desktop

The Windows 95 user interface is based on the *desktop* metaphor, which originated at the Xerox Palo Alto Research Center in the 1970s. (You must have heard this story by now.) Your screen is turned into a graphical desktop with lots of little items on the desktop for you to work with.

In fact, the Windows 95 Desktop doesn't look much like a real desktop, although it doesn't really matter whether it looks like one or not. The primary purpose of the Desktop is to provide a background on which to display graphical objects such as icons and windows. In Windows 95, your open applications and documents appear in separate windows, and you can use the Desktop (and the Taskbar) to determine how these windows are displayed.

With the advent of the World Wide Web, the computing world quickly adopted a new *hyperlink* metaphor, which was popularized by the browser software you use to travel the web. This metaphor emphasizes the connections (hyperlinks) between documents, both locally and globally.

Microsoft saw that it was in its strategic interest to incorporate this approach into the part of the computer that it owns almost completely, the operating system. Starting with Internet Explorer 4.0, the Microsoft browser is completely integrated into Windows 95. When you use the Active Desktop, the Desktop expands and morphs a bit, taking on many browser-like characteristics. The same icons are there, but you can single-click them instead of double-clicking, and your mouse pointer becomes a pointing hand, a familiar shape to anyone who has used web browsers.

If you right-click an empty part of the Desktop (regardless of your version of Windows 95), a context menu appears that lets you control the Desktop. This basic menu — it does change — is shown in Figure 7-3.

Figure 7-3: The Desktop context menu. Right-click anywhere on the Desktop to bring up the menu.

Click Properties to change many aspects of the Desktop. Move the icons around with Arrange Icons and Line up Icons. If you have Internet Explorer 4.0, click Active Desktop to switch between the standard Desktop and the new Active Desktop.

Undocumented

When the context menu is showing, you can only carry out the actions listed on that menu until you left-click (a right-click won't work) on the Desktop or click (either left or right) in a window or someplace other than the Desktop. If you have a hidden Taskbar, it will not pop up as long as the Desktop context menu appears on the Desktop.

The invisible grid

There is an invisible grid on your Desktop. The icons on the Desktop are centered in the cells defined by this grid and placed on the left side of the Desktop, starting at the top of the screen. You can place the icons in other locations, although most are not as convenient as this default top/left positioning. You can also determine the size of the grid cells.

This grid exists in both standard and Active Desktop views.

Arranging the icons

To align your icons in the center of the grid cells, right-click the Desktop and then click Line up Icons. This lets you drag icons to different parts of the Desktop and still have them look orderly when you are finished.

To arrange the icons in one of four predefined orders, right-click the Desktop, point to Arrange Icons, and then choose by Name, by Type, by Size, or by Date. The icons will arrange themselves starting in the upper-left corner and proceeding down to the next cell in the sort order specified. Additional columns of icons will be added to the right if there are more icons than can fit in the first column.

If you want the icons to always place themselves in columns starting at the left-hand side of the Desktop, right-click the Desktop, point to Arrange Icons, and then click Auto Arrange. Auto Arrange is a toggle switch; when it's active, you see a check mark next to the command. If Auto Arrange is checked, the icons always move back into the columnar arrangement no matter where you move them or where you originally place them.

Undocumented

Auto Arrange does not sort the icons. When Auto Arrange is checked, you specify the order for the icons by simply dragging them to new positions in the columns. If you move an icon to the right of the column(s) of icons, it gets placed at the bottom of the right-most column.

If you turn Auto Arrange off (clear it), you can place icons wherever you like and in any order. If you don't want to be restricted to placing your icons in a particular order or location on the Desktop, don't use the Line up Icons, Arrange Icons, or Auto Arrange commands. If you don't use these commands, you can drag and drop your icons wherever you like and space them as close together or as far apart as you want.

Sometimes your icons get moved around for you. This can happen when Windows 95 crashes. The next time you start up your computer, your meticulously placed icons are now lined up on the left side of the Desktop in type order.

Tip

While you can't stop the occasional crash, you can save your icon arrangements and restore them after the crash. You may find the little Desktop utility EZDesk to be just the ticket. Download it from ftp://users.aol.com/EzDesk95/ezdesk17.zip.

The 1.7 version of EZDesk doesn't save the icon placements on the Active Desktop. Hopefully, it will be updated by the time you read this book to work with Active Desktop in Internet Explorer 4.0.

Changing the size of the grid

The grid starts in the upper-left corner of the Desktop. The vertical line that marks the right-hand edge of the first cell is so many pixels to the right of the left edge of the Desktop. The horizontal line that marks the bottom edge of the first cell is so many pixels below the top edge of the Desktop. The invisible grid is revealed in Figure 7-4.

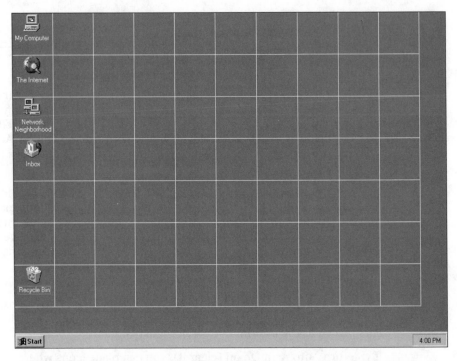

Figure 7-4: A faux icon spacing grid. The size of each cell in the default grid spacing in pixels (assuming a display magnification set at Small Fonts) is 75 pixels high and 75 pixels wide.

Secret

The size of the cells depends on the icon pixel size, icon spacing (both horizontal and vertical), and display magnification (Small Fonts, Large Fonts, or Custom), as discussed in Chapter 22. The default cell size (for Small Fonts) is 75 x 75 pixels with a default icon size of 32 pixels and default icon spacing of 43 pixels (32+43 = 75). The grid in Figure 7-4 is set at 75 pixels high by 75 pixels wide.

You can change the size of the icon spacing grid by editing the vertical and horizontal icon spacing values. To do this, take the following steps:

STEPS

Editing Icon Spacing

Step 1. Right-click the Desktop. Click Properties. Click the Appearance tab.

Step 2. Click the drop-down arrow in the Item field to open up the drop-down list of Desktop items.

Editing Icon Spacing

Step 3.   Click, one at a time, Vertical Icon Spacing and Horizontal Icon Spacing.

Step 4.   Adjust the size of each — in pixels — using the spin controls in the Size field to the right of the Item field. (Click the up and down arrows or enter a new number value to change the size.) The total vertical size of the cell will be the sum of the icon size plus the vertical spacing. Horizontal size is calculated similarly.

Step 5.   To see what the effect is on icon spacing, click the Apply button when both sizes are adjusted. Keep adjusting icon spacing until you are pleased with the results.

Step 6.   Click OK.

If an icon's title text doesn't fit within the boundaries of the cell, Windows 95 truncates the text and adds ellipses. If you make the vertical or horizontal spacing too small, the icons will overlap — not a good idea.

Undocumented

If you make the horizontal spacing of the cells too large, you may receive an "Explorer Caused a Divide error in Module Shell32.dll" error message. You'll know then that you've gone too far.

Changing the font and size of icon title text

By default, the icon titles use the MS Sans Serif 8-point font (at 800 x 600 display resolution — higher resolution displays default to a 10-point font). You have the option of changing the font used to display the icon titles. You can also change the font's point size and make it boldface and/or italic. You can't change the text color to something other than black unless you set your Desktop to a dark color, in which case Windows 95 automatically sets the text color to white.

Tip

MS Sans Serif is a *screen* font, which means that it has been designed to be readable at 96 or 120 pixels per logical inch. You can use any font that you want, including Arial, which looks a lot like MS Sans Serif but is a TrueType font. Check out the various fonts and choose one that you find easy to read.

If you increase the font point size, icon titles get bigger and may not fit in the grid cells.

To change the font used for the icon titles, take the following steps:

STEPS

Changing Icon Title Fonts

Step 1.   Right-click the Desktop. Click Properties. Click the Appearance tab.

Step 2.   Display the Item drop-down list.

Step 3.   Click Icon. You can change the Font and Size fields. You can also use the Bold and Italic buttons (see Figure 7-5).

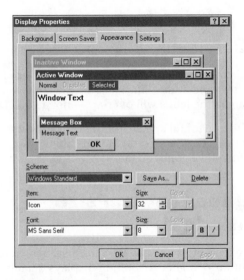

Figure 7-5: The Appearance tab of the Display Properties dialog box. Display the Item drop-down list and then choose Icon. Pick a font style from the Font drop-down list and a point size from the Size field. The B and / buttons stand for bold and italics.

Step 4.   Click the Apply button when you have chosen a font, point size, and so on, to see the effect of the choices. Keep adjusting these values until you are pleased with the results.

Step 5.   When you are done, click OK.

Changing other properties of the Desktop

You can change the background graphics, the colors used on the Desktop, the size of the icons, as well as many other properties of the Desktop. All of these changes are described in Chapter 22.

Putting new items on the Desktop

It is easy to put new items, represented by icons, on the Desktop. You can place new (empty) folders, new shortcuts, or new (blank) documents on the Desktop. By default, you can create new documents of the these types: Text, WordPad, Bitmap Image, Briefcase, or Wave Sound. And if you like, you can add more document types to the list, or remove document types from the list. (You learn how to do this in Chapter 13.)

When you create a new shortcut (right-click the Desktop, point to New on the context menu, click Shortcut), a Wizard starts that guides you through the process of linking your new shortcut to an application. When you install new applications, they often add their own document type to the New menu. You can edit the list of new types in the new menu using the steps detailed in the *Adding Items to the New Menu* section in Chapter 13.

Tip

Placing new blank documents on the Desktop is a pretty nifty feature and contributes to the document-centric character of Windows 95. When you double-click a new document icon on your Desktop, Windows 95 brings up the appropriate application and opens the blank document within it so that you can edit the document. To add new document icons to the Desktop, right-click the Desktop, point to New, and then click the document type that you want to add.

The new documents don't necessarily have to be empty or unformatted. You can create forms or certain subtypes of documents, such as "my standard format letter," and use them as a basis for creating new documents.

Pasting and undoing actions

The Paste command on the Desktop context menu lets you copy (or move) a file (or application, folder, or shortcut) to the Desktop. For example, if you want to copy a file to the Desktop, you first select a file in a folder window or in the Explorer. Then you right-click the file and choose Copy, which means "copy this file to someplace as soon as I tell you where." Finally, you right-click on the Desktop and choose Paste to tell Windows 95, "this is where I want you to copy the file." (We discuss folder windows, the Explorer, and shortcuts in Chapters 8, 9, and 10, respectively.)

Windows 95 includes the Paste command in context menus for a variety of other (yet to be investigated) Desktop icons. As you can see, the Cut, Copy and Paste commands (and functionality) have made their way out of the word processor and into the operating system.

Your Desktop context menu might include an Undo command below the Paste command. The specific Undo command that appears depends on what actions you have taken in folder windows. If you have just renamed a file, for example, you will see the Undo Rename command. If you have just deleted a file, you will see the Undo Delete command.

The Undo command shows up in the Desktop context menu (and in most context menus) whenever you have taken an action that can be undone. If you remember what it was that you did and you want to undo it (as long as you haven't quit and restarted Windows 95), here's your chance. For additional details, see the section entitled *The Undo Command* in Chapter 8.

The Icons on the Desktop

The icons that first appear on the Desktop stand for powerful Windows functions. They are discussed in later chapters. The My Computer icon is discussed in Chapter 8. The Recycle Bin is covered in Chapter 14. The My Briefcase icon is discussed in Chapter 31. The Internet icon is covered in Chapter 34, and the Inbox icon in Chapter 32.

The great thing about the Desktop is that there are icons on it. The Desktop takes over much of the function of the Windows 3.*x* Program Manager. Put up a digitized photograph as your background and the icons hang there in space on your Desktop. In contrast, the Windows 3.*x* Program Manager presented a rather boring background for your program groups (unless you had a specialized wallpaper application).

You can put any icon on the Desktop that you want. It is much more natural to put your stuff on the Desktop than it is to be constrained to the confines of the Program Manager. We discuss this in a lot more detail in Chapter 10.

You can use the System Policy Editor to get rid of all the icons on your Desktop or to just get rid of the Network Neighborhood icon. (Turn to Chapter 36 to see how to install the System Policy Editor.) To use the System Policy Editor, take the following steps:

STEPS
Getting Rid of Icons on the Desktop

Step 1.   Install the System Policy Editor from the Windows 95 CD-ROM. You'll find it in the Admin\Apptools\Poledit folder. You can also download it from the Microsoft web site at http://www.microsoft.com/windows/software.htm.

Step 2.   Click the Start button, point to Programs, Accessories, System Tools, and then click System Policy Editor.

Step 3.   Double-click the Local User icon in the System Policy Editor window. Choose File, Open Registry.

Step 4.   Click the plus sign next to the word *Shell*, and then click the plus sign next to the word *Restrictions*.

Step 5.   Click the check box next to "Hide all items on Desktop" or "Hide Network Neighborhood."

Getting Rid of Icons on the Desktop

Step 6. Click OK. Choose File, Save from the System Policy Editor's menu bar. Choose File, Exit.

Step 7. Restart Windows 95.

If you want to selectively choose which icons to display on the Desktop, use TweakUI instead of the System Policy Editor. You can download TweakUI as a part of the Microsoft PowerToys at the Microsoft web site, http://www.microsoft.com/windows/software.htm.

If you have installed Internet Explorer 4.0, you can quickly get the icons off your Active Desktop by right-clicking the Desktop and clearing the check mark next to Show Icons. (The Show Icons command only appears in the context menu when you are using the Active Desktop.)

New icons for Desktop items

You can choose new icons to replace the default ones that come with your Desktop. The Microsoft Plus! CD-ROM includes a dozen themes, each of which allows you to choose different icons for the Desktop items in keeping with the theme. For example, the Mystery theme uses a deer stalker cap to represent My Computer.

If you want to choose your own new icons instead of using the default Windows 95 icons or those in a Microsoft Plus! theme, you need to do manually what the themes application does automatically. You have to edit the Registry. You also have to find a source of new icons.

You can find icons in some executable files (files with *exe* extensions), in some dynamic link libraries (files with *dll* extensions), in icon files (files with *ico* extensions), and in icon libraries. The easiest way to find the icons that are already stored on your hard disk is to use one of the shareware icon search and library manager programs found on the *Windows 95 Secrets* CD-ROM.

You can use built-in Windows 95 functions to search an individual file for icons:

STEPS

Looking at Icons

Step 1. Double-click My Computer. Choose View, Options, and then click the File Types tab.

Step 2. Click any file type in the Registered file types list. Click the Edit button.

(continued)

STEPS *(continued)*

Looking at Icons

Step 3.   Click the Change Icon button. The icons you see under Current Icon are contained in the file listed under File Name. To see icons in other files, click the Browse button. You can now search for another file that contains icons. (For more on searching for a file, turn to Chapter 9.)

Step 4.   Be sure to click the Cancel buttons when you are done looking at icons.

Secret

To replace the Desktop icons, you need to edit your Registry as follows:

STEPS

New Icons for Old

Step 1.   Double-click My Computer. Double-click the drive icon for your hard disk. Double-click your Windows folder icon. Double-click Regedit.exe in the \Windows folder. (To find out more about the Registry, turn to Chapter 15.)

Step 2.   Using the Registry editor, click the plus signs in the left pane to navigate to HKEY_CLASSES_ROOT\CLSID. Click the plus sign next to CLSID.

Step 3.   To change the My Computer icon, scroll down the left pane of the Registry editor to {20D04FE0-3AEA-1069-A2D8-08002B30309D}. This is the Class ID for the My Computer object. Click the plus sign next to it and highlight DefaultIcon in the left pane.

Step 4.   Double-click Default in the right pane. Type the name of the file that contains the icon you want to use instead of the existing icon. Follow the complete path and filename with a comma and then a number representing the icon's position in the file. (You can determine an icon's position using the steps for Looking at Icons above. In step 3, the icons in the Current Icon box are numbered from left to right, beginning with 0 for the left-most icon.)

Step 5.   Click OK, and then exit the Registry editor.

You can change the icons of the other Desktop items by going to the following Class IDs in step 3 of New Icons for Old steps:

Inbox (Windows Messaging)   {00020D75-0000-0000-C000-000000000046}

Network Neighborhood   {208D2C60-3AEA-1069-A2D7-08002B30309D}

Dial-Up Networking   {992CFFA0-F557-101A-88EC-00DD010CCC48}

Printers	{2227A280-3AEA-1069-A2DE-08002B30309D}
Briefcase	{85BBD920-42A0-1069-A2E4-08002B30309D}
Control Panel	{21EC2020-3AEA-1069-A2DD-08002B30309D}
Internet Explorer	{FBF23B42-E3F0-101B-8488-00AA003E56F8)
Internet Mail	{89292102-4755-11cf-9DC2-00AA006C2B84}
Internet News	{89292103-4755-11cf-9DC2-00AA006C2B84}
Microsoft Network	{00028B00-0000-0000-C000-000000000046}
Recycle Bin	{645FF040-5081-101B-9F08-00AA002F954E}

The Recycle Bin has two icons, one for empty and one for full. Double-click *empty* and *full* in the right pane of the Registry editor to assign new icons to each of them.

Make your own icons

You can easily make your own icons, just by using MS Paint. Here's how:

STEPS

Make Your Own Icons

Step 1. Click the Start button, Program, Accessories, and then Paint.

Step 2. In the Paint window, choose Image, Attributes. Make the Height and Width 32 pels (pixels), and click OK.

Step 3. Click View, Zoom, and then Show Grid.

Step 4. Click View, Zoom, Custom. Choose 800% and click OK.

Step 5. Create your new icon. Save it as a *bmp* file.

Step 6. You can now treat this file as a regular icon file. Following the New Icons for Old steps in the previous section, you can point to it and use it on your Desktop.

When you replace a Desktop icon with one you made yourself, you don't need to refer to it by anything other than its filename (see step 4 under New Icons for Old). You don't need to use an index number (in this case 0) because there is only one icon in the file.

High Color icons

While icons were originally limited to 16 colors, you can now have 16-bit (High Color, or 64 thousand colors) or 24-bit (True Color, or 16 million colors) color icons. If you create your own icons with MS Paint, you can choose the color depth.

To display High Color or True Color icons, you need a video card with enough memory at a given resolution. Right-click the Desktop, click Properties, and then click the Settings tab. Check the Color palette field to find out what your color depth is. If you have enough memory, you'll see High Color (16 bit) or True Color (24 bit) in the list. If you don't see these values, reduce your screen resolution using the Desktop area slider bar. Turn to the *Changing Resolution, Color Depth, and Magnification* section of Chapter 22 for more details.

Secret

To display High Color or True Color icons, you also need to change a Registry setting using your Registry editor, as described here:

STEPS

Fixing the Registry to Allow the Display of High Color or True Color Icons

Step 1. Double-click My Computer. Double-click the drive icon for your hard disk. Double-click your Windows folder icon. Double-click Regedit.exe in the \Windows folder. (To find out more about the Registry, turn to Chapter 15.)

Step 2. In your Registry editor, click the plus signs in the left pane to navigate to HKEY_CURRENT_USER\Control Panel\desktop\WindowMetrics.

Step 3. Double-click Shell Icon BPP in the right pane. If your display supports High Color, type **16**. If it supports True Color, type **24**.

Step 4. Exit the Registry editor.

If you have installed Microsoft Plus!, you don't have to make changes in your Registry file. All you have to do is right-click the Desktop, click Properties, click the Plus! tab, mark the "Show icons using all possible colors" check box, and click OK.

You don't have to purchase Microsoft Plus! in order to get this capability. It also comes with the Microsoft font smoother, which you can download from http://www.microsoft.com/truetype.

Corrupted Desktop icons

If your Desktop icons get sick, you can refresh them. Windows 95 stores all the icons on the Desktop in a file named ShellIconCache, which is stored in the \Windows folder. It is a hidden file, so be sure to choose View, Options in your Explorer or My Computer window, click the View tab, and click Show all files if you want to see the file listing. Windows 95 caches the shell icons in this file so that it can access them quickly instead of having to search through all the files that hold these icons every time it starts up.

Secret

You can refresh the icon cache by deleting ShellIconCache from your \Windows folder. To do this, first restart your computer in MS-DOS mode or exit to MS-DOS mode. Then type **del ShellIconCache**. (If you type **dir sh*.*** at the DOS prompt while in the \Windows folder, ShellIconCache won't show up because it's still hidden. However, you can still delete the file.) Exit MS-DOS mode and restart Windows 95. The ShellIconCache file is automatically rebuilt from the original icons in their source files.

It's even easier to rebuild your icons using TweakUI. Just click the Repair tab, and then click the Rebuild Icons button. You still need to restart Windows 95 after following these steps.

Scraps

Some Windows 95-aware applications can place *scraps* on the Desktop (or in any folder window). You can try this out using WordPad. Open up a WordPad document. Select some text. Drag and drop it onto the Desktop.

An icon with the name Scrap appears on the Desktop. This is a document that can be read by WordPad. It is made up solely of the text that you dropped on the Desktop. Double-click its icon on the Desktop, and WordPad launches.

Scraps give you an easy way to pile up a bunch of notes or graphics on your Desktop (or in any other folder) and then make something of them later. Scraps give you an alternative to the Clipboard, and the advantage of using them is that you can keep multiple pieces available at one time. Put your company logo on the desktop and paste it into any document as you edit it.

It is possible to store a bit of boilerplate text in your Tray on the Taskbar. (See the section entitled *The Tray on the Taskbar* later in the chapter.) You'll need to download a small shareware application to be able to do this. You'll find TrayText at http://ourworld.compuserve.com/homepages/ MJM_Software/traytext.htm.

The Taskbar

The Taskbar starts off with just the Start button and a digital clock in the Tray. It is the home of the *active* applications — those applications that you started by double-clicking a file or an application icon, as well as Explorer and folder window buttons. There is a button on the Taskbar (or an icon in the Tray) for every major active application or window. Maybe this is a good time to step back and examine just what Windows 95 means by an *active* application.

When you first turn on your computer, only Windows 95 and whatever applications are in the Startup folder are read off the hard disk and loaded into your RAM. An application or a document needs to be read into memory from the hard disk before it can act or be acted upon.

We refer to an application that has been loaded into memory as an *active* application. Applications that are stored on your computer's hard disk but haven't been loaded into memory are *inactive*. A document is loaded into memory with its application. There aren't any stray documents out there in memory without their associated applications.

Some documents are *compound* documents — they were created using multiple applications. Not all applications that were used to create a compound document will be loaded into memory when the document is loaded.

Some applications don't put buttons on the Taskbar or icons in the Tray. These "hidden" applications run in the background and aren't looking for any user input. You can hide the Taskbar buttons of whatever applications you choose. You can also move Taskbar buttons over to the Tray, where they are displayed as small icons. To make these changes, you need to use shareware apps that are included on the *Windows 95 Secrets* CD-ROM. (See *The Tray on the Taskbar* later in this chapter for more information.)

Internet Explorer 4.0 lets you add additional toolbars to the Taskbar. These toolbars resemble the Taskbar and are connected to it. Right-click your Taskbar, point to Toolbars, and choose Address, Link, Desktop, or New Toolbar. New Toolbar lets you define your own toolbars.

The Taskbar buttons

Each Taskbar button includes the application's or window's icon and name. If there is an associated document or file with the application, its name is supposed to appear first on the button (according to the Windows 95 software design guidelines). The icons on the Taskbar button are smaller versions of the icons you see on the Desktop. They are 16 x 16 pixels instead of 32 x 32 pixels.

Windows 3.*x* or multidocument applications place the name of the application first on the Taskbar button. For example, if you open a copy of Microsoft Word, you'll see a button labeled Microsoft Word on the Taskbar, and you will be hard pressed to see the name of the open document. If you open the Windows 95 Notepad without a document, Untitled appears as the first name on the Taskbar button.

Tip

Every major active application or window is represented on the Taskbar, regardless of whether the application is currently minimized, restored, or maximized. (The only exceptions are applications that run behind the scenes, which don't need Taskbar buttons, and those that have icons in the Tray instead of Taskbar buttons.) *This means that the Taskbar is a task switcher.* No matter if the active application has been minimized or is now buried under other application windows on the Desktop, you can bring it to the top by clicking its button (a single click at that) on the Taskbar.

The Taskbar is one of Window 95's most fundamental "ease of use" improvements over Windows 3.*x*. It is also an advantage that Windows 95 has over the Apple Macintosh. This new feature makes it almost impossible to lose track of which documents and programs are open, even when they are stacked on top of each other.

The Taskbar takes the place of the minimized active application and window icons that by default were displayed at the bottom of your Windows 3.*x* Desktop. Because it has a button for every major active application, whether the application is minimized or not, the Taskbar has much of the task-switching functionality of the Windows 3.*x* Task Manager.

Tip

The single-click operation of the Taskbar makes it easy to switch between *tasks* — which are simply active applications or windows. Combine this with Windows 95's enhanced resource management, and it is easy to find yourself using multiple active applications and opening multiple instances of your Explorer or My Computer windows. Windows 95 makes multitasking (defined from the user's perspective as quickly jumping among active applications and windows) easy enough to be useful.

Drag and wait to a Taskbar button

You can drag a file to a Taskbar button and continue to hold down the mouse button after you reach the Taskbar button. As you hold the file over the Taskbar button, the application associated with that button will spring to life. If it was minimized, it will open into a window on the Desktop. If it was buried under other windows, it will come to the top.

Tip

Once the application window has appeared, you can drop the file icon on it. The application determines what happens next. If the application is a Windows editor or word processor, it will open or insert the dropped file, depending on where you drop it. Drop it on the title bar and the document opens. Drop it in the client window, and the document may be inserted into an existing document.

If the program is a DOS editor, dropping a file will put the name of the dropped file at the insertion point in a DOS file. This behavior isn't all that useful unless you want to build a text document full of file names.

Specialized Windows 3.*x* applications that are meant only to be displayed as icons and never expanded into windows do not work with Windows 95.

Undocumented

If you have Internet Explorer 4.0, you'll notice that you can minimize a window on the Desktop by clicking its Taskbar button. Of course, you just click it again to maximize the window.

Hiding the Taskbar

The Taskbar has two mode switches:

> Always on top or not
>
> Auto hide or not

Always on top means always on top of other windows on the Desktop (not exactly *always*, but often enough anyway). Turn on this feature and other windows do their best to stay out of the way of the Taskbar. Turn off this feature and other windows don't know that the Taskbar is there.

If you turn on Auto hide, the Taskbar disappears unless it is the last thing you clicked on. An Auto-hidden Taskbar doesn't take up Desktop real estate except when you want to do something with it — such as switch to another task.

When Auto hide is on, the Taskbar hides itself as soon as you click on another application. To get the Taskbar to display itself, move the mouse pointer to the edge of the screen on which you've docked the Taskbar. You'll see a 2-pixel-wide line along the edge that is a remnant of the Taskbar. When your mouse pointer hot spot gets within 2 pixels of the edge of the Desktop, the pointer becomes a resize arrow, and the Taskbar pops up. The mouse pointer then changes back to a normal selection arrow.

Undocumented

If you move your mouse pointer more than 10 pixels away from the Taskbar without clicking it (or one of the Taskbar buttons) first, the Taskbar disappears. It doesn't disappear instantly. Depending on what is beneath the Taskbar, the screen usually takes longer to repaint the Desktop to show what was obscured by the Taskbar than it took to pop up the Taskbar in the first place. This can be quite a bother.

If you click the Taskbar after it pops up, it gains the focus. You can then move the mouse pointer around the Desktop and the Taskbar doesn't disappear until you click another window or the Desktop. You have to click directly on the Taskbar and not on any of the buttons. Sometimes this is a little difficult, because much of the Taskbar itself might be covered by buttons.

If Auto hide is on and Always on top is off, when the Taskbar pops up, it will pop up behind any window that it might have otherwise obscured. You may still be able to have a partial view of the Taskbar and be able to switch tasks, and so on.

If Auto hide is off and Always on top is on, the Taskbar sits on top of your Desktop and other windows try to get out of its way. When you maximize a window, it does not cover up the Taskbar. The application calculates the maximum window size as the actual screen resolution minus the number of pixels in the Taskbar.

If Always on top is on, this doesn't mean necessarily that the Taskbar will always be on top. Other windows can have this same property. If two windows have this "always on top" property, whichever window has the focus will be on top.

To change the Auto hide and Always on top modes, take the following steps:

STEPS
Changing Taskbar Modes

Step 1. Right-click the Taskbar and click Properties to display the Taskbar Properties dialog box, as shown in Figure 7-6. (You can also get to this dialog box by selecting Start button, Settings, Taskbar.)

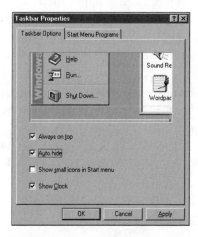

Figure 7-6: The Taskbar Options tab of the Taskbar Properties dialog box. Check the Auto hide and/or Always on top boxes to change these Taskbar modes.

Step 2. Click Auto hide and/or Always on top to change the Taskbar modes. Click the Apply button to see the effect of these modes.

Step 3. When you are done, click OK.

Sizing the Taskbar

The Taskbar starts out thin, but you can make it bigger. In fact, you can make it as large as one-half of the Desktop.

Move your mouse pointer to the top edge of the Taskbar so that the mouse pointer turns into a resize arrow. Hold down the left mouse button and drag the Taskbar's edge upward. The Taskbar increases in height in button-height increments.

Windows 95 sizes the buttons on the Taskbar automatically. All the buttons are the same size, no matter how long the names of the application and its associated document are. If the names are too long to fit in the button, Windows 95 truncates them and places an ellipsis after them, if there is room.

You can see the full name of the application and document associated with a given button by placing your mouse pointer over the button and waiting for less than a second. A ToolTip (a small pop-up box with text) appears next to your mouse pointer. This happens only if the full name of the application and its associated document can't fit on the button face.

Undocumented

As you open additional applications, the Taskbar buttons shrink, unless you increase the size of the Taskbar. When the buttons become so small that they are just big enough to contain the 16 x 16 pixel icons within them, they get no smaller. If you add more active applications at that point, all the icons will not be displayed at the same time on the Taskbar.

In this situation, a *spin control* appears on the Taskbar. You can spin the control to see icons that are not currently showing on the Taskbar.

The Taskbar is attached to an edge of the Desktop. If it is on the bottom, you can't narrow it by detaching it from the right or left edge. The resize arrow appears only when the mouse pointer is near the top of the Taskbar.

Tip

The icons on the Desktop move to avoid the Taskbar when you resize it (as long as it isn't in Auto hide mode, as explained in the *Which Desktop edge is best for the Taskbar?* section that follows). You have to have quite a few icons on the Desktop to see this effect.

Moving the Taskbar

The Taskbar doesn't have to be on the bottom of your Desktop. You can move it to any other edge (the top, bottom, left, or right side of the screen).

To move the Taskbar, position the mouse pointer over it, but not over any of the buttons on the Taskbar. Press down the left mouse button and drag the mouse pointer toward one of the other Desktop edges. As you begin moving the mouse, an outline of the Taskbar appears. Release the mouse button when the outline of the Taskbar is positioned on the desired edge.

Which Desktop edge is best for the Taskbar?

In application windows, the menu bar is at the top of the window, and a scroll bar is often at the right. No doubt you use menus and scroll bars quite often. You are probably used to moving your mouse to the right, top, and bottom of a Windows application client area, in that order of frequency. The left and bottom edges of the screen are the least "natural" areas to point to. You may find yourself doing a lot of extra mousing around if you place the Taskbar in these "unnatural" areas.

Tip

If you dock your Taskbar on the right side, you can get to the buttons on the Taskbar with an easy movement of the mouse. If the Taskbar is hidden, however, it may be too easy and quite a bother. If your document is anywhere near the right edge of your screen and you move the mouse quickly to the right to scroll, you are likely to overshoot the scroll bar and move to the Desktop edge. Up pops the Taskbar, which you didn't want. Now you have to move the mouse at least 10 pixels to the left of the Taskbar to get it to disappear — a waste of time.

The advantage of placing the Taskbar on the right is that it is easy and natural for you to get to it. And if Auto hide is off, the Taskbar stays in view so you don't have to worry about making it pop up accidentally. However, there are disadvantages to placing the Taskbar on the right as well. If Auto hide is turned on, you have to be accurate with your mouse to avoid inadvertently displaying the Taskbar. Furthermore, a vertical Taskbar with horizontal buttons is most likely fatter than a horizontal Taskbar with horizontal buttons, because the buttons have to be wide enough to display the names (although this is only an issue if Auto hide is off).

One advantage of leaving the Taskbar on the bottom or moving it to the left is that you can have Auto hide on and still not accidentally pop up the Taskbar so often that it becomes annoying. And if you are left-handed, it might feel natural to attach the Taskbar to the left edge of the Desktop. However, docking the Taskbar on the left side will probably be a difficult adjustment for most people, and if you place it on the bottom, the Start menu on the Taskbar pops up instead of dropping down.

Placing the Taskbar on the top edge of the Desktop will make it feel like a menu bar or a toolbar, and moving the mouse to the top of your screen is a "natural" movement for Windows users. The Start menu also drops down from the Start button in a familiar manner. If you have the real estate, put the Taskbar on the top edge and keep Always on top turned on and Auto hide turned off. This option will probably feel comfortable to you. (Just remember that if you turn on Auto hide, you'll have the problem of mouse overshoot when you choose menu items, although it won't be nearly as bad as if the Taskbar is at the right.)

Test out each location to figure out which one works the best for you. Be sure to give yourself a reasonable amount of time to try each one — a couple days is about right.

Secret

Windows applications may get partially covered by the Taskbar if they are at their restored size and the Taskbar is attached to the top edge of the Desktop with Always on top turned on and Auto hide turned off. When Windows applications are maximized, they do not get obscured by the Taskbar.

The fact that Windows applications can't seem to find the Taskbar when they are at their restored size can be quite annoying. If a window's title bar is covered by the Taskbar, you have to use the keyboard to lower the window enough to bring the title bar into view. (Press **Alt+Spacebar**, **M**, press the down arrow repeatedly to move the window down, and then click once.) You could also just maximize the application's window by pressing Alt+Spacebar, X.

Resizing and moving windows on the Desktop

Using the Taskbar, you can cascade, tile, or minimize all the sizable windows on the Desktop. Right-click the Taskbar and choose one of these sizing options.

Minimize All Windows is a very powerful function, because it is paired with Undo Minimize All. (When you right-click the Taskbar after choosing Minimize All Windows, the context menu contains an Undo Minimize All command.) You can clear your Desktop with one command, and then place everything back where it came from with the opposite command. This is a very handy feature if you want to get to some icons on your Desktop that are covered up by your application windows.

Internet Explorer 4.0 adds a new button to the Taskbar that lets you toggle between Minimize All Windows and Undo Minimize All. You'll see it on the right-hand side of the Tray.

The Start button

We discuss many of the Start button's interesting secrets in Chapter 11, but here are a few of the high points.

The Start button contains the Stop button, in the form of the Shut Down command. Click the Start button and then click Shut Down to get out of Windows 95.

Clicking the Start button displays the Start menu. This menu provides a series of cascading menu choices that give you access to much of the functionality of Windows 95. You can easily change all of the menus that are attached to the Programs menu item to display the menus, folders, files, and applications that you want displayed.

Right-clicking the Start button lets you open and explore your computer and easily change items in the Start menus.

You can add items to the Start menu by dragging them over and dropping them on the Start button.

Ctrl+Esc displays the Start menu.

The Tray on the Taskbar

The little indented area on the right edge of the Taskbar is called the *Tray*. Some applets that start up when Windows 95 starts up put their icons in here. The idea is that by putting small icons in the Tray, applets that are always running don't take up as much space on the Taskbar as bigger applications, which run only when you choose to start them.

G.L. Liadis Software, publisher of numerous shareware applications for Windows 95, has come out with WinTray. If you put this 249K application in your Startup folder, you gain the ability to store up to eight icons of your choice in the Tray.

Once you've used the WinTray dialog box to select the applications you want in the Tray, their icons automatically show up in the Tray every time you start Windows. You can configure the icons to launch your favorite apps with a double-click or a single-click (your choice). You can keep the WinTray dialog box open during your Windows session or instruct it to hide. Right-clicking any icon you placed in the Tray brings up the WinTray window again so you can reconfigure the program, adding or removing icons from the Tray.

The Tray is usually used for small system utilities, such as resource monitors and diagnostic tools that you want to frequently check on with a double-click. For example, the Windows 95 Resource Meter (C:\Windows\Rsrcmtr.exe) automatically places itself in the Tray when you run it. WinTray lets you store other utilities in the Tray as well.

There's no particular reason, however, that you should be limited to putting utilities in the Tray. Any major application that you use frequently could be a candidate — your word processor, say, or a favorite game. These applications are probably two or three levels down in your Start Menu, whereas icons in the Tray are a lot easier to find.

You can download an unregistered shareware version of WinTray from the Internet by setting Internet Explorer to http://www.vpm.com/glliadis. Click the Utilities keyword to download WinTray or see a listing of many other programs from this prolific shareware author.

Another shareware application, Icon Corral, not only lets you place application icons in the Tray, it allows you to remove the space-wasting buttons for these applications from the Taskbar itself while they're running. You can download a fully-functional version from http://cs.washington.edu/homes/erask/win95.html. (The full version costs only $5.)

Tray Shortcuts is a free program that doesn't remove apps from the Taskbar, but does place icons in the Tray like WinTray does. You can find Tscuts.zip at http://rsko.gel.ariadne-t.gr/ftp/win95/sysutil.

The clock

The Taskbar has a digital clock. If you rest your mouse pointer over the time, you'll see the date in a ToolTip. If you right-click the time, you can choose Adjust Date/Time in the context menu to display the Date/Time Properties dialog box, as shown in Figure 7-7.

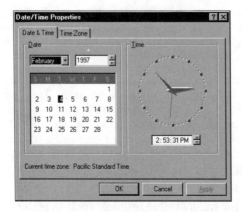

Figure 7-7: The Date/Time Properties dialog box. You can set the date and time by typing new values or clicking the spin controls in the date and time fields.

You can change the date by choosing the month from the drop-down list, spinning the year field, and clicking on a day. You can change the time by typing in a new time or by using the spin control. To change the clock to a 24-hour display (instead of AM and PM), take the following steps:

STEPS

Changing the Time Format Display

Step 1. Click the Start button, point to Settings, and then click Control Panel.

Step 2. Double-click the Regional Settings icon.

Step 3. Click the Time tab.

Step 4. Display the Time style drop-down list and choose a style with an uppercase H.

Step 5. Click the OK button in the Regional Settings Properties dialog box.

If you want to change the date format, click the Date tab in step 3 instead of the Time tab.

If you change the Short date style, the new style won't be used until you restart Windows 95.

You can also set your time zone by clicking the Time Zone tab, as shown in Figure 7.7. Check out the nifty world map with the highlighted time zone (shown in Figure 7-8). Even if this function didn't do anything useful, it would be worth it just to have this graphic.

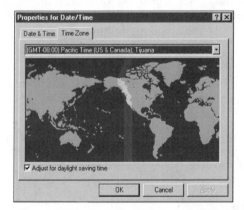

Figure 7-8: The Time Zone map. Display the drop-down list above the map to pick a time zone. Watch the map move from side to side as you pick out different ones. Or drag the "sun" until it's over your time zone — cooler still. You can also use your arrow keys to move the time zone around.

You can tell your computer what time zone it is in by dragging the "sun" in the map until it is over your time zone. You can also use the arrow keys to move the sun around. If you prefer using more conventional methods, just choose a time zone from the drop-down list.

There are 51 separate entries in the list of time zones (in the original version of Windows 95) even though you might assume that there are only 24 unique time zones. Windows 95 keeps track of the daylight savings time rules for various locations, so, for example, there is a unique entry for Arizona (USA) that doesn't honor daylight savings time. There are also separate entries for Darwin and Adelaide (Australia), both of which are plus $9^{1}/_{2}$ hours from Greenwich Mean Time.

Using your arrow keys (and not your mouse) you can move the time zone map to each of these different locations. Some odd time zones in the south-western Pacific are not accounted for.

When the first day of daylight savings time arrives, you get a message asking you if you want to have your computer's clock moved an hour ahead.

The time zone value does have something of a practical value. If you are on a network that crosses time zones, say, your own company's WAN, your computers will use this time zone value to get everyone's time synched to a universal standard such as Zulu, Greenwich Mean Time, or whatever arbitrary one you choose. Your computers can correctly compare files that are time-stamped on the West Coast with files that are time-stamped on the East Coast.

The Windows 95 Time Zone Editor is a customization tool for those with an abiding interest in the start and end dates of daylight savings time and other time-related policies. You can edit the start and end dates of daylight savings time, create new time zones, and so on. Download Microsoft's Kernel Toys from http://www.microsoft.com/windows/software/krnltoy.htm. Inside Kernel Toys, you'll find the Time Zone Editor.

Microsoft has added new time zones with additional daylight savings times and rules. OEM Service Release 2 incorporates these additions into the basic product. If you have an earlier version, download the latest updates from http://www.microsoft.con/windows/software.htm.

You can add a date display to the Tray. This lets you see the date without having to place your mouse pointer over the time display. You can download TrayDay from http://ourworld.compuserve.com/homepages/MJM_Software/trayday.htm.

Sliding windows

You'll notice as you click application buttons on the Taskbar that the title bar of the application is displayed first in a shrunken form and then expanded until the complete application is displayed in a window on the Desktop. This is called *sliding* or *zooming* windows, and it occurs only if the application has been minimized first.

If you minimize an application on the Desktop, the opposite effect occurs. The window's title shrinks, and then the application's window disappears. Windows 95 is trying to show you that your application has now gone to the Taskbar and to get it back you need to click its button there.

Secret

If you don't like this effect, you can turn it off. Here's how:

STEPS

Turning Off Sliding Windows

Step 1. Double-click Regedit.exe (the Registry editor) in the \Windows folder. See Chapters 8 and 9 for more on viewing the \Windows folder in the Explorer or a folder window.

Step 2. Click the plus sign to the left of HKEY_CURRENT_USER. (This will make the change for the current user only. Often the current user is the only user.)

Step 3. Click the plus sign to the left of Control Panel and then Desktop. Highlight WindowMetrics.

Turning Off Sliding Windows

Step 4. Click Edit, New, String Value in the Registry editor menu bar. Type **MinAnimate** as the new name for the string value.

Step 5. Double-click MinAnimate in the right pane. Type the value **0**. Click OK.

Step 6. Exit the Registry editor and restart Windows 95.

If you want the sliding windows effect to reappear, you can always change this value back to 1. If you find that someone has already created MinAnimate, you can change its value by double-clicking it.

TweakUI makes it easier to get rid of the zooming windows effect. Just click the General tab in TweakUI and clear the Window animation check box. (Download TweakUI from Microsoft's web site at http://www.microsoft.com/windows/software/powertoy.htm.)

Task Switching with the Keyboard

Three keyboard combinations let you switch between active applications and folders.

Hold down Alt and press the Tab key. A window that contains the icons of the active applications and folders appears on the Desktop. By pressing and releasing the Tab key, you can switch among the active applications and folder windows.

If you want to get back to the Start button, press Ctrl+Esc. This displays the Taskbar and the Start menu. You can get to the menu items on the Start menu by using the up and down arrow keys or the key corresponding to the letter underlined in the menu. Press the Enter key to choose the menu item. Menu items in the other menus (that cascade off the Start menu) don't have assigned letters. You can still use the up and down arrows to get to them and the Enter key to choose them.

Undocumented

You can get to the icons on the Taskbar or the icons on the Desktop with the keyboard. Press Ctrl+Esc to get to the Start menu. Press Esc to put the focus on the Start button and hide the Start menu. Press Tab to put the focus on the Taskbar. You can now use the arrows keys to move among the Taskbar icons.

Press a second Tab after the first to shift the focus to the icons on the Desktop. You can then use the arrow keys to highlight one icon after another. The Tab key (or the F6 key) toggles the focus between the Start button, the Taskbar, and the icons on the Desktop. (The focus must first be on one of these items for this to work.) The Start button doesn't open the Start menu until you focus on it and press the Enter key. If the Taskbar is in Auto hide mode, it appears when the focus shifts to the Start button or the Taskbar and disappears when the focus shifts to the Desktop.

You can switch to the Desktop by placing the Desktop (actually a folder that contains the icons on the Desktop) on the Taskbar. To see how to do this, check out the *Putting the Desktop on the Taskbar* section in Chapter 8. You can also place the Desktop on the Start button. For details, see Chapter 11.

Undocumented

If you are in a full-screen DOS Windows session, you can return to the Desktop by holding down Alt, pressing the Tab key, and clicking the pop-up window that is displayed when you press Alt+Tab.

You can also switch between tasks by holding down Alt and pressing the Esc key. If the task you switch to is minimized, the only action you will notice is that the task's button on the Taskbar is depressed and the title bar of the previously active application changes to its inactive color.

The Task Manager

The Windows Task Manager is still here, although in a new suit of clothes. Many of its functions have been taken over by the Taskbar, but that doesn't mean it isn't useful. It might be just the right tool for you.

The nice thing about the Windows 3.*x* Task Manager was that it was always right there, a double-click on the Desktop away. You always had the option of bringing up the Task Manager and using it to switch to another task, no matter how deeply it was buried in the pile on your Desktop. Short of minimizing all the covering windows, this was often the only way to switch to a non-minimized task.

Third-party vendors had a field day with the Windows 3.*x* Task Manager, finding lots of ways that they could improve upon it. They turned their Task Manager replacements into shells that replaced the Windows 3.*x* Program Manager.

The Task Manager in Windows 95 is a floating Taskbar without the Start button or the clock.

The Task Manager is Taskman.exe in the \Windows folder. You can always double-click it in a folder window or the Explorer. Bring it up and you get a button for every active task, as shown in Figure 7-9.

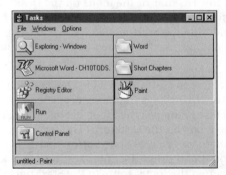

Figure 7-9: The Task Manager. Click a button to switch to that task.

You can change the size of the buttons and choose whether or not you want text in them by clicking Options in the menu bar. One nice thing about the Task Manager is that it has buttons that display the big icons.

Unfortunately, the Windows 95 Task Manager does not appear when you double-click the Desktop, like the Windows 3.*x* Task Manager did. If you'd like to use the Task Manager, you should create a shortcut for it and assign a hot key to it so that you can get to it when you need it. To do this, follow the steps detailed in Chapter 10. You can put a shortcut to the Task Manager in your Startup folder so that it is available to you when you start Windows.

The Windows 95 Task Manager does get activated when there is a problem with the normal Windows 95 shell program, Explorer.exe — suddenly there it is on your Desktop. You can switch tasks or shut down Windows.

Summary

The Desktop and the Taskbar form the core of the Windows 95 user interface. In this chapter (and Chapter 22) we show you how to set them up your way.

▶ We show you how to arrange the icons on your Desktop and change the underlying invisible grid that determines their placement.

▶ It is easy to place empty documents on the Desktop and then double-click them to bring up applications to edit these documents.

▶ The Taskbar can be transformed into a useful tool if you take the time to move and size it for your needs. We show you what kind of problems you will run into using it in certain configurations and how to find the right edge of the Desktop to use.

▶ Use shareware applets to put Taskbar buttons in the Tray.

▶ If you don't like the sliding windows effect when you minimize and restore application windows, we show you how to get rid of it.

▶ You can use Alt+Tab, Alt+Esc, and Ctrl+Esc to choose among active applications and folders.

▶ The Task Manager is still with us. You can use it as a floating task switcher.

Chapter 8

My Computer — Folders and Windows

Viewing Your Computer

You need a window, or several windows, on your computer in order to see what is there. This chapter focuses on how to use folder windows (or *single-pane* windows) for file management. In Chapter 9, we discuss the Windows Explorer, a *dual-pane* window. Much of what you learn in this chapter can be applied to both folder windows and to the Windows Explorer.

If you have installed Internet Explorer 4.0, you'll see that it integrates the Internet Explorer — Microsoft's web browser — into the Windows 95 user interface. With this new interface, specifically its Web view and Active Desktop, you can open a window with a single click (although you can change this setting to require a double-click if you prefer). The earlier version of the Windows 95 user interface requires a double-click.

In this chapter, we use double-click — the previous default — as a stand-in for both methods. Whenever we refer to a double-click in this book, keep in mind that you can use a single-click instead, if you've downloaded and installed the Internet Explorer 4.0 and are using the Web view in the default configuration. You learn how to change this setting in *Other View options* later in this chapter, and in Chapter 9.

My Computer, Your Computer

There it is in the upper-left corner of your display — My Computer. Wait a minute, it's *your* computer. *My* computer is here. As far as you are concerned it's *your* computer, but then you would tell us that "It's *My* Computer."

Microsoft was well aware of this "Who's on first, What's on second, and I don't know who's on third" problem but went ahead and called it My Computer anyway. You can imagine some computer instructor saying to his or her students, "Double-click My Computer," and then having to say, "No, I mean double-click the My Computer icon on the screen of *your* computer."

Not only that, My Computer is just an icon on your computer's screen. It's not your computer. It's a computer within a computer. Microsoft hopes that this doesn't confuse you.

As you shall see, this is not just a semantic issue. When something has a representation of itself within itself, the representation has to be distorted so as not to go on endlessly. After all, My Computer is on the Desktop, but the Desktop is both in My Computer and is displayed on your computer. For an example, see the section later in this chapter entitled *Putting the Desktop on the Taskbar*.

Changing My Computer to Fred

Tip

Fortunately, you can change the My Computer icon to something else, like Your Computer. Highlight the My Computer icon, press F2, and type a new name.

You can also change the Network Neighborhood to something like Network Neighbourhood if you are in England. And if you use the Registry editor, you can change the name of the Recycle Bin (see Chapter 14).

The My Computer Window

When you first set up Windows 95, you will see three to six icons on the left side of your Desktop. The number depends on which options you chose during the Windows 95 setup process.

The My Computer icon (and a rather generic-looking computer icon it is) is the first icon on the Desktop — an indication of its importance in the hierarchy of items on the Desktop. You can place it somewhere else, if you want, but if you arrange the Desktop icons in any of the predetermined sort orders (by right-clicking the Desktop, pointing to Arrange Icons, and choosing from the submenu), it will again appear in the upper-left corner.

When you double-click My Computer, a single-pane window much like the one shown in Figure 8-1 appears on your Desktop. Don't worry if your My Computer window looks slightly different. This is the version of the My Computer window that comes with Internet Explorer 4.0. In the figure, it's displayed with the Large Icons view selected and the regular toolbar showing.

Figure 8-1: The My Computer window. Double-click the My Computer icon on the Desktop to open it.

Tip

You don't have to double-click the My Computer icon to open it. You can just right-click it and then click Open from the context menu. The Open command is at the top of this menu. You can left- or right-click the menu item — it doesn't care which mouse button you use.

Double-clicking My Computer opens a window that displays the contents of My Computer. *Open* means to display in a window. If you open an application, it will be displayed in a window. If you open a document, it will also be displayed in a window. Opening an icon such as the My Computer icon means to display its contents within a window.

You don't find windows on real-world desktops — so much for metaphors. You might think of a window as the thing itself plus its edges. A window displays a document on the Desktop, and the edges of the document contain commands that determine how the document is displayed.

The contents that are displayed are not the physical contents of the computer — what you would normally expect to see when you "opened" up your computer — but its logical contents. The My Computer window contains icons that look like physical items: your floppy drive(s) and your hard disk drive(s). The window also has some manila folder icons with graphics on them.

The diskette and hard disk drive icons represent the logical contents — the files, folders, documents, and applications — that are stored on these devices. The folder icons stand for directories (or *folders*) that are stored on the hard disk(s). While most folders can contain any type of file, the folders in the My Computer window contain specific types of files. For example, the Printers folder contains the printer driver files. We discuss these particular folders in much more detail in other chapters. To open and display the contents of any drive or folder icon, double-click it.

If you have installed Internet Explorer 4.0, you can display the contents of My Computer in Web view (right-click the My Computer window and choose View, Web View). In Web view, you see something like the My Computer window shown in Figure 8-2. To open a drive or folder icon when you are in Web view, single-click it.

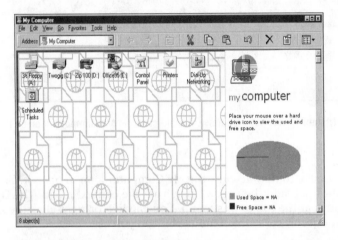

Figure 8-2: My Computer window in web view. Single-click a drive or folder icon in this view of My Computer to display its contents.

Internet Explorer 4.0 also lets you view web sites in your computer window. Just click Favorites, and then choose a Favorites web site. You can also click Go and choose a site. We discuss in this further in the *What Is This Explorer Thing?* section of the next chapter.

Folders

The My Computer window looks something like a single-pane version of the Windows 3.*x* File Manager. In the File Manager, each directory on your disk drive has a little manila folder icon to the left of its name. The File Manager icon is a file cabinet. The idea is that all the folders are stored in the file cabinet.

Windows 95 has replaced the term *directory* with *folder* — a more office-oriented name. Also, folders can do much more than directories. Some specialized folders, such as the folders in the My Computer window, have additional capabilities. You can place folders on the Desktop and they can have windows of their own (folder windows).

A folder icon can be on the Desktop or contained within a window. Folders can contain other folders, just as directories can contain subdirectories. Because they are not stuck in the File Manager, the Windows 95 folders are more accessible. Instead of using the File Manager to organize and locate your files, you double-click a folder icon to bring up its window.

In the Windows 3.*x* File Manager, the hard disk and floppy disk drive icons used to sit on a special bar above the client area of the window. With Windows 95, they have come down to join the folders and files in the client area.

If you use Web view to display the My Computer window as a web page, you will still see folders in the window. Although web pages out on the World Wide Web could conceivably have folder icons in them, they rarely do. Microsoft is clearly stretching it a bit in its efforts to get the two metaphors (Desktop and World Wide Web) to work together.

The special folders in the My Computer window

The four folders (three folders if you haven't installed Internet Explorer 4.0) in the My Computer window are unlike most other folders on your hard disk. They have special functions, and their contents are not stored within the folder. For example, the contents of the Control Panel folder are stored in the \Windows\System folder in files with the *cpl* extension.

Microsoft made an arbitrary design decision to put these special folder icons in the My Computer window and to put little graphics on them. They were placed in the My Computer window because this provides an easy way for you to get to folders that contain useful Windows 95 functions. We have devoted a chapter each to three of these folders.

The Printers folder is covered in Chapter 23, the Control Panel folder in Chapter 16, and the Dial-Up Networking folder in Chapter 28.

You can use the Scheduled Tasks folder (available if you have installed Internet Explorer 4.0) to create a list of actions that Windows 95 will perform at a certain time without further input from you. Examples include running ScanDisk, running Defrag, and so on.

My Computer window properties

If you right-click on an empty part of the My Computer window, a context menu like the one shown in Figure 8-3 appears. This menu is similar to the one you get when you right-click the Desktop. It has an additional View command, which lets you change how the icons in the window are displayed: Web View, Large Icons, Small Icons, List, and Details. (Web View is only available if you have installed Internet Explorer 4.0.)

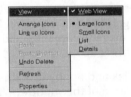

Figure 8-3: The context menu for the My Computer window with the view options showing.

The Properties command displays the System Properties dialog box, which functions as the Windows 95 hardware interface. Turn to Chapter 19 for details on setting system-wide properties using one of the components of this dialog box, the Device Manager.

Drive properties

When you click a drive icon in the My Computer window, a report of its free space and disk capacity appears in the status bar. To view or change the properties of a drive, right-click the drive icon and click Properties. You can change the drive's volume label, as shown in Figure 8-4. You can also check the drive for errors, back it up, or defragment it by clicking the Tools tab. Check out Chapter 27 for details.

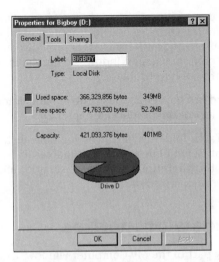

Figure 8-4: The General tab of the Properties dialog box for a disk drive. Type a new volume label for your drive. If you want to check for errors, click the Tools tab. You can share your drive with others on your network by setting your share configuration in the Sharing tab. To compress your drive or change its compression ratio, click the Compression tab (not shown).

Opening a new window

Double-click a drive icon in the My Computer window to open a new window that displays the contents of the drive. The contents will consist of folder and file icons.

Each icon has an associated window. And if you double-click an icon in one of these windows, you will open yet another window. My Computer has its own window, and all your disk drives have their own windows.

You can continue to double-click folder icons to move hierarchically through the folders stored on your drive. Folders can contain subfolders, which can in turn contain more subfolders. You can move sideways by returning to a parent folder and then moving to a different subfolder.

If you have installed Internet Explorer 4.0, you can also go backward and forward along the path that you have traveled. Notice the Back and Forward arrow buttons on the toolbar. (If you don't see a toolbar, choose View, Toolbar.) Click the Back button to go back to the previous folder or view that you chose. If you've gone back, you can click the Forward button to move forward to where you were before you went back. These two buttons only work if you view your computer's contents through one window (see the next section, *One window or many?*).

One window or many?

Choose View, Options in the My Computer window (or in any drive or folder window) to display the Options dialog box, as shown in Figure 8-5. The Folders tab gives you two options for browsing folders. If you choose Browse folders using a separate window for each folder, Windows 95 opens a separate window each time you double-click an icon within the My Computer window, a drive window, or a folder window. If you choose Browse folders by using a single window that changes as you open each folder, Windows 95 reuses and renames the My Computer window each time you double-click an icon within the window.

Your Desktop can fill up pretty quickly if you choose to open a new window every time you double-click a drive or folder icon. (See *Closing a folder window* later in the chapter to learn how to close folder windows.) However, opening multiple windows does let you see the contents of several windows at one time. It also makes it easier to move items from one folder to another. When you open a window, a button for it appears on the Taskbar, so you can simply click Taskbar buttons to switch among multiple open windows.

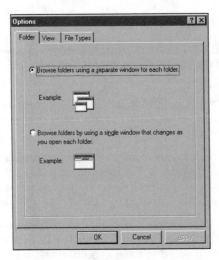

Figure 8-5: The Folder tab of the Options dialog box. You can choose to browse folders in separate windows or in a single window.

Switch to a single window view on the fly

Secret

If you are opening separate windows as you go from folder to folder, you can still choose to open the next folder in the current window instead of opening a new window. Instead of double-clicking a folder icon, which would display the new folder in its own window, hold down the Ctrl key as you double-click the icon. The existing window will now display the contents of the double-clicked folder.

By the way, this trick doesn't work with the middle mouse button if you have defined the button to be a double-click. You actually have to double-click with the left mouse button. See Chapter 24 for details on how to define the middle mouse button as a double-click.

If you want to use this trick in Web view, hold down the Ctrl key as you single-click a folder icon.

Open a window in the Explorer view

Secret

If you hold down the Shift key as you double-click a folder icon, the new window opens as an Explorer window (see Chapter 9). You need to make sure the focus is on the folder icon you want to open before you hold down the Shift key and double-click. Otherwise, you could easily open a few more Explorer windows than you had planned. The reason for this is that you also use the Shift key with the mouse to select multiple items (see *Selecting a group of files and/or folders* later in this chapter).

This option, unlike the one described in *Switch to a single window view on the fly*, does work with the middle mouse button defined as a double-click.

Two copies of the My Computer window

You get only one copy of the My Computer window no matter how many times you double-click the My Computer icon. This is not true of the Explorer, which we discuss in Chapter 9.

Secret

If you have set the View, Options, Folder property to browse folders using a single window, you'll find it difficult to get two copies of any window. There is a tricky way you can get an extra copy (or as many copies as you want) of a window, even if you have chosen the single window option. If you want to copy files from one folder to another it is awfully handy to be able to create a second window on the fly.

STEPS

Getting Two Windows of the Same Folder

Step 1. Double-click the My Computer icon. Click View, Options, Folder, and choose Browse folders using a separate window for each folder.

Step 2. Double-click a drive icon in the My Computer window.

Step 3. In the drive window, choose View, Options, Folder, and choose Browse folders by using a single window that changes as you open each folder.

Step 4. Click the Up One Level button in the drive window's toolbar. (Choose View, Toolbar if the toolbar is hidden.)

You now have two My Computer windows. You can use this same trick to get an extra copy of any drive or folder window. Change your View, Options, Folder setting to browse in separate windows, and then double-click any icon in the window to open a second window. Change back to browsing in a single window, and click the Up One Level button in the second window. Of course, if you use separate windows as your default View, Options, Folder setting, you can use a variation on this theme to create multiple copies of any window.

Change Your Window View

You can use options on the View menu to choose whether the My Computer window (or a drive or folder window) displays a toolbar and/or a status bar. If you've installed Internet Explorer 4.0, the toolbar changes if you view HTML documents or web sites. If you're using the previous version of Windows 95, you only have one toolbar available.

You can choose how the drive icons, folder icons, and other icons are displayed in a window by choosing among four views: Large Icons, Small Icons (rows), List (columns), and Details. (If you've installed Internet Explorer 4.0, you can also choose Web view.) To switch views, click one of the four view buttons on the right end of the toolbar (or, if you've installed Internet Explorer 4.0, click the Views toolbar button and then click the desired view in the drop-down menu). To see how to order your icons, refer to *Order the icons* later in this chapter.

Undocumented

You can globally set some of these display preferences so that they will apply to folder windows you haven't ever opened. When you open a window for the first time, it establishes its own settings for these variables. To change the settings for windows you've already opened, you must change them individually for each window.

In the pre-Internet Expoloer 4.0 version of Windows 95, the global settings for all folder windows are: Use large icon view, don't show the toolbar, show the status bar, and order icons by name. When you open a folder window for the first time, Windows 95 uses these global settings. If you change the settings within a window, however, Windows 95 uses the new settings the next time you open the window. Windows 95 only applies the global settings to windows you haven't yet opened.

If you have installed Internet Explorer 4.0, you'll find that Microsoft has changed the global settings. The defaults are now: Display background graphics and custom HTML, display the toolbar and the status bar, and order icons by name. If you like, you can change the default settings from Web view to the standard Windows 95 ones. If you like, you can change the default settings from Web view to the standard Windows 95 ones. To do this, choose View, Options, click the View tab, and select the option button labeled "Display standard Wndows appearance." We discuss this dialog box in more detail in Chapter 9.

You can't globally change the settings for all folder windows (including those you have already opened). There is also no way for you to change all the global display settings (including icon sort order) for as yet unopened folders. You can't choose a subset of folders and set the view properties of only those folders.

Secret

You can set some view parameters for as yet unopened folder windows. To do this, open a window and arrange it using the View menu. Choose to show or hide the toolbar and status bar. Choose from the four (or five) views.

When you are finished, hold down the Ctrl key and click the Close box. Windows 95 will use your changed settings as the new defaults when you open folder windows for the first time. Note that you can't use this method to set the Auto Arrange option or the icon sort order (in the View, Arrange Icons submenu) for new folder windows.

One problem you may notice is that when you start Windows 95, your folder windows might be slightly shorter than they were when you last shut down. If a window is too short to display the last row of icons, you will see a vertical scroll bar on the right side of the window, which you can use to scroll the last row into view. (If you want to fix the size, point to one of the window's edges, and when the mouse pointer becomes a black double-headed arrow, drag until the window is the desired size and release the mouse. If you drag one of the window's corners, you can change both the height and width of the window at the same time.)

The whole issue of window view properties is dealt with poorly by Windows 95. Many users want to be able to make their windows look "just so," and they don't appreciate it when the appearance of their windows changes (even a little bit). Users would greatly appreciate a global or semi-global way to change window view properties. Unfortunately, Microsoft hasn't been able to program a decent way to do it.

Other View options

When you choose View, Options in the My Computer window or any drive or folder window, Windows 95 displays the Options dialog box, which contains three tabs. The Folder tab is discussed in *One window or many?* earlier in this chapter. The two remaining tabs, View and File Types, are discussed in Chapter 9 and Chapter 13, respectively.

Order the icons

You can specify the order in which your icons are displayed in a window. Choose View, Arrange Icons, and then choose Name, Type, Size, or Date from the submenu that appears. If you are using details view, you can also choose which variable to sort on by clicking the heading buttons (Name, Size, Type, and Modified) located at the top of the client area. If you have installed Internet Explorer 4.0, the My Computer window has an additional Attributes heading button, as shown in Figure 8-6.

If you want to toggle between ascending and descending order, click the desired heading button a second time.

Line up your icons

Secret

If you use the large or small icon view of a window, you can place the icons where you like. They will stay where you put them, even if you switch views, resize the window, close the window, and go back to it. The large icon view will mirror the small icon view, and vice versa.

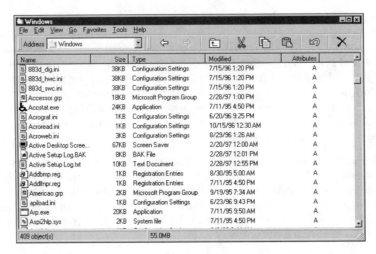

Figure 8-6: A folder window in details view. Click one of the heading buttons (Name, Size, Type, Modified, and Attributes) at the top of the client area to order the icons by that variable.

As with the Desktop, every folder window contains an invisible grid, although Windows 95 only uses the grid in the large and small icon views. The size of the grid depends on the size of the icons, the font size (magnification), and the display resolution. You can snap your icons to the center of the cells in the grid by choosing View, Line up Icons.

Changing the column widths in details view

When you choose the details view of a folder window (View, Details), heading buttons appear above each column. At the edge of each of these buttons is a black vertical spacer line. When you rest your mouse over the vertical line, the mouse pointer becomes a vertical line with two horizontal arrows.

You can change a column's width by dragging the spacer line on the right edge of the column's heading button to the left or right. If you drag the spacer line for the Name button to the right, for example, the Name column widens, and the remaining columns shift over to the right.

Tip

If you want to temporarily hide a column in details view for a given folder window, drag the spacer line on the right edge of the heading button all the way to the left edge of the column. You can redisplay the column — even though you can't see it — by dragging the now-invisible heading button's edge to the right.

Each folder window has its own properties. Before you adjust the width of the columns in a window, they have the default properties. After you change the column widths, Windows 95 retains the new settings and uses them the next time you open that particular folder. This is true even if you open the folder window through My Computer and make changes to it, and then open the same folder in Explorer view (see the next chapter).

Secret

Do you want to adjust a column's width in details view so that none of the entries in the column are truncated? Rest your mouse pointer over the spacer line, and double-click. Windows 95 widens (or narrows) the column just enough to fit the widest entry. This is the same method you use to "AutoFit" columns in Excel and Access.

Freshening up the folder window

Tip

A folder window may not always accurately display the actual contents of the folder. You might have copied files in and out of the folder without the window noticing and updating itself. Files may also have changed in size, content, or name. You can update the display of a window by pressing the F5 key, by choosing View, Refresh, or by right-clicking the client area of the My Computer window and clicking Refresh.

Checking the status bar

The status bar at the bottom of your My Computer, drive, and folder windows can provide some useful information, as you may have seen earlier if you opened a drive window. Open a window full of files; the status bar shows you how much disk space the files use, how many files there are, and how much free disk space you have.

Closing a folder window

The three buttons in the upper-right corner of a window allow you to minimize, maximize or restore, and close a folder window, respectively from left to right. The Close button (aso called the *Close box*), is new to Windows 95.

Undocumented

Hold down the Shift key as you click the Close box to close not only the window with the focus but all its parent windows as well. If you opened a number of windows to get to the current one, this method gives you an easy way to get rid of all the preceding windows.

Creating a New File, Folder, or Shortcut

You can create a new file, folder, or shortcut in a window, just as you can on the Desktop. Right-click the window and point to New in the context menu (or choose File, New) to display a submenu containing options that let you create a new folder, a new shortcut, or a new document of a particular type.

Once you have created a folder or file, you can open it by double-clicking it. We discuss creating new folders in more detail later in this chapter.

Folder Window Properties

Previously in this chapter, we mentioned the properties sheets of My Computer and of a drive icon. An ordinary folder also has properties. To see them, right-click the folder window (or right-click a folder icon) and choose Properties from the context menu.

Undocumented

The first tab in the Properties dialog box is General, as shown in Figure 8-7. You can set the folder attributes (Read-only, Archive, Hidden) by clicking the check boxes. This properties sheet also displays the total size and number of the files stored in the folder. In addition, it tells you the number of subfolders and includes the files in these subfolders (and further sub-subfolders) in its total file size and number count. This information is not shown on the status bar of the folder window.

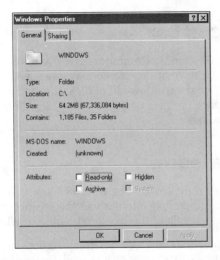

Figure 8-7: The General properties sheet for a folder. While not too exciting, this properties sheet does give you some very useful information about the size and number of files (and subfolders) within the folder and its subfolders.

You can share your folder with others on the network by changing settings on the Sharing tab. You can give other network users the ability to read-only or read-write to this folder, and you can optionally require a password to access the folder. If the Sharing tab is not visible, you have to go to the Network icon in the Control Panel and activate file and printer sharing.

There is no properties sheet that displays the view properties of a folder window. This is unfortunate. While you can change these properties by using the window's menu bar, it would be convenient if you could modify them in a properties sheet as well.

Moving Forward and Back Using a Folder Window

Double-click the My Computer icon on the Desktop and, if you've installed Internet Explorer 4.0, make sure the toolbar is displayed. Click the down arrow next to the drop-down list on the left side of the toolbar, or press the F4 key. (If you don't see the toolbar, choose View, Toolbar.) The drop-down list contains an indented list of icons.

Click the Up One Level button to the right of the drop-down list. The Desktop icon is now displayed in the list along with the other icons, as shown in Figure 8-8.

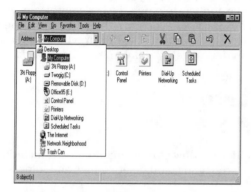

Figure 8-8: The My Computer window with its drop-down list displayed. You can display any of the items in the list by clicking once on it. The My Computer window changes to the window associated with the item you pick.

Notice that the items in the drop-down list are indented. The indents indicate which icons belong to which other icons. The icons that are two indents to the right of My Computer are displayed in the My Computer window. The icons that are one indent (and one indent only) to the right of the Desktop icon are displayed on the Desktop.

If you click the Desktop icon, the My Computer window becomes the Desktop window, and the icons on the Desktop itself are also displayed in the Desktop window.

When you click various icons in this drop-down list, the contents of the item you click — the folder, disk drive, Desktop, or whatever — is displayed in the transformed My Computer window.

Only certain items appear in the drop-down list: Desktop, My Computer, Network Neighborhood, Recycle Bin, special folders, and the first level of items contained in My Computer. If, starting in the My Computer window, you double-click on a drive icon, double-click on several more folders, and then display the drop-down list, the list will contain the current folder and all of its parents. The current folder's siblings will not be displayed in the list.

You can use the current folder to display the contents of the parent folder, or of any other icon in the drop-down list just by clicking that icon. As you saw earlier in this chapter in the section entitled *Opening a new window*, you open child windows by double-clicking folder icons within the window.

Secret

You can move up through a thread of parent folders by pressing the Backspace key. This works even if you are browsing folders in a single window. If your current window is displaying the contents of a folder or a subfolder, you can backspace all the way back to My Computer if you like.

If you are browsing folders in separate windows, you can use Alt+Tab+Tab to go either direction. Hold down Alt and press the Tab key until you get to the folder window you want.

If you have installed Internet Explorer 4.0, you can use the Back and Forward buttons on the regular toolbar to move "historically" from window to window. While the drop-down list lets you move hierarchically, the arrow buttons let you move back to the contents of your previous folder or web site, forward to the next folder or web site if you have gone back.

New, Copy, Cut, Paste, Rename, and Delete

You can use drive and folder windows for file maintenance, including creating, copying, moving, renaming, and deleting files and folders.

Creating a folder

It's easy to create a new folder. All you have to do is right-click in the folder window within which you want to place your new folder. Follow these steps:

STEPS

Creating a New Folder

Step 1. Double-click the My Computer icon on the Desktop.

Step 2. Decide which drive you want to store your folder in, and double-click the appropriate drive icon to open the drive window.

Step 3. If you want to store your folder in the root — in other words, at the top of the hierarchy of folders on that disk drive — go to step 5. If you want to store your folder within another folder on the drive, then double-click that folder icon in the drive window.

Step 4. Continue double-clicking folder icons until you get to the folder window that you want to contain your new folder.

Step 5. Right-click the client area of the window (or choose File, New, Folder). In the context menu, point to New, and then click Folder from the submenu. A new folder icon appears in the window.

Creating a New Folder

Step 6. To replace the temporary name *New Folder* with a name of your choosing, simply type over it with the new name.

Moving a file or folder

There are numerous ways to move a file or folder from one folder to another. As a general suggestion, you'll have an easier time accomplishing this task and learning how it's done if you have both the source folder window and the destination folder window open on your Desktop and fully visible.

Move with Cut and Paste

Follow these steps to move a file or folder with the Cut and Paste commands.

STEPS

Moving a File or Folder with Cut and Paste

Step 1. Double-click the My Computer icon. Choose View, Options, Folder, and if you haven't already done so, choose the option to browse folders using separate windows. Click OK.

Step 2. Double-click the drive icon that contains the file or folder you want to move. If the file or folder is in a subfolder, continue double-clicking folder icons until you open the folder window that contains the item you want to move. (This is the source folder.)

Step 3. If the destination folder window — the folder to which you want to move the item — is already open, click its title bar (or its Taskbar button) to bring it to the front, and go on to the next step. If it isn't open yet, first open the window of its parent folder (or an ancestor folder), and then continue double-clicking folder icons until you open the destination folder window.

Step 4. Make sure that you can see both the source and the destination folder windows. They don't have to be fully visible.

Step 5. Right-click the folder or file you want to move, and click Cut in the context menu. (Or click the folder or file to select it, and then choose Edit, Cut.)

Step 6. Right-click an empty part of the destination folder window, and click Paste (or choose Edit, Paste).

Yes, a move is, in this case, referred to as a *cut and paste*. It makes you think you are in a word processor.

Move with right drag and drop

You can also drag and drop the file or folder to the destination folder window. As you drag the file or folder icon, it looks semi-transparent.

STEPS

Moving a File or Folder with Right Drag and Drop

Step 1.   Carry out the first four steps in the *Move with Cut and Paste* section earlier in this chapter.

Step 2.   Position the mouse pointer over the file or folder to be moved. Press the right mouse button and, while holding it, pull the file or folder over to the destination folder window.

Step 3.   Release the right mouse button when the mouse pointer is over the destination folder window. You can drop the file or folder when you're pointing to the title bar, the menu bar, the toolbar, or the client area. Just make sure you don't point to an icon.

Step 4.   Choose Move Here from the context menu.

Move with left drag and drop

If you use the left mouse button to drag and drop, you don't have to deal with a context menu. But it helps to know what kind of file you are moving and where you are moving it to.

STEPS

Moving a File or Folder with Left Drag and Drop

Step 1.   Carry out the first four steps in the *Move with Cut and Paste* section earlier in this chapter.

Step 2.   Position the mouse pointer over the file or folder to be moved. Press the left mouse button and, while holding it, drag the file or folder over to the destination folder window.

Step 3.   Release the left mouse button when the mouse pointer is over the destination folder window. You can drop the file or folder on the title bar, the menu bar, the toolbar, or the client area, but not on any icons in the folder.

Secret

If you have followed the steps in this section, you've taken the steps required to open two windows. You therefore know which drives the destination and source folders are stored on. When you drag and drop a file or folder, Windows 95 only *moves* the item out of the source folder and into the destination folder *if both folders are on the same drive*.

If you drag and drop a file or folder from a folder on one drive to a folder on another drive, then Window 95 *copies* the file instead of moving it.

In both cases, this is *not* true if you are dragging a file that isn't a document or a data file, but rather an application. When you drag and drop an application, Windows 95 creates a *shortcut* to the application in the destination folder. What is an *application file*? You can identify application files by their extensions if you have cleared the box labeled "Hide MS-DOS file extensions for file types that are registered." (Choose View, Options in the My Computer window and click the View tab; see Chapter 9 for more information.) Application files have extensions such as *exe* or *com*. There is an even easier way to tell, as you'll see if you keep reading.

You can force a *move* by holding down the Shift key after you have selected the file or folder to move. Don't press Shift until you have selected the file or folder. If you do, you may instead change which icons are selected because the Shift key is also used to select.

Tip

If you drag an executable file (an application file), Windows 95 creates a shortcut to the application when you release the mouse. You can tell before you actually release the mouse if Windows 95 intends to create a shortcut. As you drag the file over the destination folder window, you'll see a black curved arrow in a white box in the lower-right corner of the semi-transparent file icon. Press and hold the Shift key and the arrow disappears, indicating that Windows 95 will *move* the file or folder instead. This is one way to tell that Windows 95 thinks you are dragging an application file.

Windows 95 treats the Desktop just like a folder. Like all folders, it is located on a disk drive, most likely your C drive. If you try to *move* something to the Desktop (most often you will want to create shortcuts on the Desktop), and the Desktop is on a drive other than the one that contains the file or folder you are dragging, Windows 95 will, by default, *copy* the file or folder instead (unless you hold down the Shift key).

Tip

You can tell if a file or folder is going to be copied because a plus sign appears in the lower-right corner of the semi-transparent icon representing the file or folder icon as you drag it over the destination folder window (or Desktop). If you see this black plus sign in a white box, you know a *copy* will occur if you release the left mouse button. Press and hold the Shift key to force a *move*.

If you decide not to move the icon, just put it back where you got it — in the same window. If you were using a left drag and drop, then nothing will happen. If you were using a right drag and drop, a context menu will appear. Click Cancel.

Secret

If you don't want to continue with your drag and drop, press Esc while holding down the mouse button. We love this secret because it makes Windows 95 just that much more user friendly. You don't have to worry that you will do something wrong. If it looks wrong, just press Esc. Later, you will see how you can undo by releasing the mouse button.

There is an even trickier way to cancel a drag and drop. Click the other mouse button before you release the primary mouse button.

Tip

You can drop your file or folder on a folder icon to move it into that folder. You don't have to open the destination folder window. If the destination folder icon is visible in its parent folder window, you can drop the file or folder icon on it to move it to that folder.

You can't move a drive icon. The disk drive is fixed in place. You can't move the total contents of the disk by dragging the drive icon. If you try to move the disk drive, you will be given the option of creating a shortcut to the drive. You have to select the contents of the disk if you want to move them.

You can't move any of the icons in the My Computer window. You can only create shortcuts to them.

Secret

If you point to a file or folder icon in a window that has the focus (its title bar is highlighted) and press and hold down either mouse button, the name of the icon becomes highlighted. This makes it obvious that the icon is selected and ready to be moved. If you do the same thing to an icon in a window that does not have the focus, the icon will not become highlighted (nor will the window gain the focus). However, the icon is still selected and ready to be moved.

What this means is that if the destination folder window happens to have the focus and be partially obscuring the source folder window, as shown in Figure 8-9, you can still left or right drag a file or folder icon from the source folder window and drop it into the destination folder window. The source folder window won't gain the focus when you select the icon and drag, so it won't cover up the destination folder window.

If you download the Microsoft PowerToys (http://www.microsoft.com/windows/software/powertoy.htm), you can completely change this mouse behavior using X Mouse. The focus will stay with the mouse pointer and shift from window to window as you move the pointer. X Mouse does cause some incompatibilities with some programs, so you'll need to test it if you want your mouse to behave this way.

Move with Send To Any Folder

You'll need to download the PowerToys utilities from the Microsoft web site (http://www.microsoft.com/windows/software/powertoy.htm) before you can use Send To Any Folder.

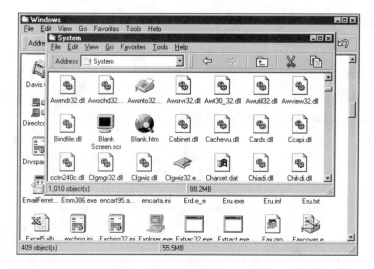

Figure 8-9: The destination folder window is on top of, and partially obscuring, the source folder window. When you drag a file or folder icon from the source window into the destination window, the source window doesn't gain the focus and cover the destination window.

Once you install SendToX (part of PowerToys), you'll be able to move or copy files or folder to other folders by right-clicking a file or folder name, clicking Sent To in the context menu, and then clicking Any Folder. SendToX maintains a history of previous destination folders so you can easily send files to a common folder.

You can also add a common destination folder or two to the Send To folder to allow you to move files or folders to a common folder just using the Send To option on the context menu. Turn to the *Right-Click to a Powerhouse* section of Chapter 10 for instructions on how to set this up.

Copying a file or folder

You copy a file or folder to a new folder or disk drive using pretty much the same methods that you use to move a file or folder, but with a slight variation — just enough of a variation to perform a copy rather than a move. Therefore, much of the information in *Moving a file or folder* applies to the copy command. This is your clue to look there for further help with the copy methods, and pay special attention to the tips and secrets.

Copy with Copy and Paste

Follow these steps to copy a file or folder with Copy and Paste:

STEPS

Copying a File or Folder with Copy and Paste

Step 1.   Double-click the My Computer icon. Click View, Options, Folder, and if you haven't already done so, choose the option to browse folders using separate windows. Click OK.

Step 2.   Double-click the drive icon that contains the file or folder you want to copy. If the file or folder is in a subfolder, continue double-clicking folder icons until you open the folder window that contains the item you want to copy. (This is the source folder.)

Step 3.   If the destination folder window — the folder to which you want to copy the item — is already open, click its title bar (or its Taskbar button) to bring it to the front, and go on to the next step. If it isn't open yet, first open the window of its parent folder (or an ancestor folder), and then continue double-clicking folder icons until you open the destination folder window.

Step 4.   Make sure you can see both the source and the destination folder's windows. They don't have to be fully visible.

Step 5.   Right-click the source folder or file you want to copy, and click Copy in the context menu. (Or click the file or folder to select it, and then choose Edit, Copy.)

Step 6.   Right-click an empty part of the destination folder window, and click Paste (or choose Edit, Paste).

Yes, a copy is, in this case, referred to as a *copy and paste*. It makes you think you are in a word processor. Yes, we know that we just copied and pasted the *Move with Cut and Paste* section and edited it slightly to create this section. Pretty cheap of us.

Copy with right drag and drop

Follow the instructions in the *Move with right drag and drop* steps, but with the following exception: Choose Copy Here instead of Move Here from the context menu. Is that better?

You can also use this method to create a copy of a file in the same folder as the original file. After you drop the file in the same folder and choose Copy Here, Windows 95 creates a duplicate file with the prefix "Copy of."

Copy with left drag and drop

Follow these steps to copy with left drag and drop:

STEPS

Copying a File or Folder with Left Drag and Drop

Step 1. Carry out the first four steps in the *Copy with Copy and Paste* section.

Step 2. Position the mouse pointer over the file or folder to be copied. Press the left mouse button and, keeping it held down, drag the file or folder over to the destination folder window.

Step 3. Press and hold the Ctrl key.

Step 4. Release the left mouse button when the mouse pointer is over the destination folder window, and then release the Ctrl key. You can drop the file or folder on the title bar, the menu bar, the toolbar, or the client area, but not on any icons in the folder.

Notice that step 3 says to press the Ctrl key, which forces a copy operation. If you are copying from a folder on one drive to a folder on another drive, you don't have to use the Ctrl key. When you drag and drop between volumes (between local disk drives or over a network) Windows 95 assumes you want to copy instead of move.

Remember that if you are *copying* a file or folder, a small black plus sign in a white box will appear on the icon when you drag it over the destination folder window. If you don't see the plus sign, press and hold the Ctrl key.

Tip

You can't copy a drive icon. Instead, double-click on the drive icon to display its contents in a drive window, and then copy the contents of the drive. You can't copy any of the icons in the My Computer window.

Secret

You can make a copy of a file in the same folder as the original by holding down the Ctrl key while you left drag and drop the file in the same folder window. Windows creates a new file with the prefix "Copy of." This doesn't work in Explorer view. To do this using the Explorer, see Chapter 9.

If you drag and drop a file onto an icon that represents an executable file, Windows 95 will start the application. If the application can read and use the file you dropped, it will do so. For example, if you drop a file icon with the extension *doc, rtf,* or *txt* onto the WordPad icon, WordPad will start and open the file.

Cut or Copy now, Paste later

While it's easy to see what you're doing if you have both the source and the destination folder windows on the Desktop, you don't have to do it this way. You can first cut or copy a file or folder, and then paste it to its new location when you get to it later. As long as you don't do another cut or copy, the files or folders remain on the Clipboard waiting to be pasted.

Renaming files and folders

You can rename a file or folder (but not a disk drive) in a window by clicking the name once, and then clicking it again to select it. Once the name is selected, you can type the new name right over it. The clicks have to be far enough apart that they qualify as separate clicks and not a double-click. You might find it easier to select the file or folder with a single click, and then press the F2 key (or right-click the filename and choose Rename from the context menu).

If you have installed Internet Explorer 4.0 and are in Web view and have chosen "Single-click to open any item" in the View tab of the Options dialog box (displayed by right-clicking the Desktop and clicking properties), it won't work to click once and then click again to select the name of a file, because clicking once actually opens the item you click on. Instead, right-click on the icon, and then choose Rename from the context menu.

Another way to rename a file or folder is to select the item, choose File, Rename, and then edit the name as usual.

Tip

After you click twice on a file or folder name (or issue the Rename command), a dotted line appears around the name, and the name becomes highlighted, ready to be wiped out as soon as you type a letter. If you want to edit the existing name instead of typing a new one, press an arrow key or click on the name. The highlighting goes away and you get an insertion point. You can now edit the name using the arrow keys to move the insertion point, and Backspace and Delete to delete individual characters. Press the Home or End key instead of the arrow keys to move quickly to the beginning or end of the name.

If you are displaying file extensions (check out Chapter 9) and you change an extension, Windows 95 displays a message box when you finish editing the name asking if you are sure you want to change the extension. In the few hundred times we have done this, neither of us has ever said no.

Change File Type, a freeware application, lets you change a file extension without having to reassure Windows 95 that it's really what you mean to do. It's available at http://www.windows95.com.

This renaming process can get quite tedious if you are renaming a lot of files, for example, all your *.w4w files to *.doc files. If you want to do group renames, you must use the File Manager (which doesn't support long file names) or the DOS command line. The standard commands you can use in folder windows aren't quite strong enough. Turn to Chapter 9 to learn more about the File Manager or to Chapter 17 to learn more about DOS.

Microsoft would rather that we not discuss file extensions. They want file extensions to go away and for Windows users to quit seeing them in their windows. For now, we feel it is a much better idea to display file extensions because Windows (and DOS) use them so heavily. In fact, it is easier and more reliable to change file extensions when they are displayed than when they are not. Check out Chapter 13 for more details.

Valid file and folder names are discussed in the *Valid filenames* section of Chapter 27.

Deleting files and folders

To get rid of a file or folder, highlight its icon and press the Delete key. You can also right-click an icon and choose Delete in the context menu or choose File, Delete. If the file or folder is on a local nonremovable drive, it gets sent to the Recycle Bin.

Dragging and dropping an icon from a folder window to the Recycle Bin on the Desktop also works. The benefit of this method is that Windows 95 does not ask you to confirm the delete. (You can configure the Recycle Bin to not require a confirmation for a file delete.) Note that your files and folders aren't necessarily deleted just yet. The Recycle Bin provides a safety net for us careless users. We tell you more about deleting in Chapter 14.

Tip

To delete a file or folder without sending it to the Recycle Bin, hold down the Shift key while you press the Delete key. Windows 95 will delete the highlighted file or folder, and won't put it in the Recycle Bin.

The Undo Command

Undocumented

Every time you perform an action such as renaming, copying, moving, or deleting, you have a chance to undo it (in the same Windows 95 session). Not just now, but later as well. Windows 95 builds an undo stack as you do things, adding new actions to the top of the stack. You can only undo multiple actions in the reverse order that you did them.

The Undo command and an associated action verb — Rename, Copy, Move, or Delete — appears in the context menu that appears when you right-click a window or the Desktop (but only if you have performed an undoable action). For example, if you just renamed a file, Undo Rename will appear on the context menu when you right-click the client area of a window.

This undo business is global. It doesn't matter if you renamed a file in one window and deleted a file in another, they both show up (actually you see only the last action) on the context menu in any window. After you issue the Undo command once to undo the most recent action, choosing Undo a second time undoes the previous action, and so forth.

This can get kind of confusing. You may not remember in which window you renamed or deleted or copied a file or folder. But when you right-click any window, the reference to that previous action shows up.

It's best to undo something within the window that you did it in. This way, you can see the action get undone — for example, the file takes back its old name. If the action you're undoing is a few actions down the stack, it might be hard to remember which window you did what in. Unless you are working in just one or two windows, it's all too complicated.

Undo is a great confidence builder. You just can't mess up too badly because you can undo the damage that you did. This gives you a little leeway to experiment with Windows 95.

Tip

The keyboard shortcut to undo your most recent action is Ctrl+Z.

Selecting Items in a Window

You click an icon to select it, and then choose an action — such as Move, Copy, Delete, or Rename — to do something to the icon. This is an illustration of the Windows syntax: first a noun (the object), then a verb. You can also right-click on an icon in a window to select it. When you right-click, a convenient context menu appears with a series of verbs — actions — you can take.

Undocumented

If you click an icon in a window, the window is automatically highlighted and given the focus. If you simply drag an icon from a window, the window doesn't get the focus. The icon isn't highlighted either. This comes in handy when you're copying or moving files or folders between windows. See the *Move with left drag and drop* section earlier in chapter.

Selecting multiple files and folders

If you want to move, copy, or delete (but not rename) more than one file or folder, you can select all of the items first, before issuing the command. That way, you only have to issue the command once instead of numerous times. To select multiple files and/or folders, click on the first icon, and then Ctrl-click on the additional icons. The Ctrl key is just a continue-selection key.

Tip

You can't rename more than one file or folder at a time. It just won't work. If you have multiple files and/or folders selected when you choose Rename, Windows 95 automatically deselects all the icons but the one you most recently selected.

Selecting a group of files and/or folders

You can select a group of adjacent icons with the Shift key. Click (or right-click if you like) the first icon in the group. Then hold down the Shift key as you click the last icon in the group. Windows 95 will select all the icons in between the two you clicked (and Shift-clicked).

When you display your icons in details view, it is pretty clear what *in between* means. You click one file or folder and then you Shift+click a second one located either above or below the first. All the icons in between these two icons get selected.

Undocumented

In other views, *in between* means different things. For example, in large icon or small icon view, *in between* means all the icons that fit in a rectangle formed when you take the diagonal corners of the rectangle as the two selected icons. To select the group of large icons shown in Figure 8-10 using the Shift key method, you would select the icon in the second row, fourth column, and then hold down the Shift key as you select the icon in the sixth column, fourth row.

Figure 8-10: The large icon view of a window. The icons were selected by clicking an icon in one corner of a rectangle and then Shift+clicking the icon in the opposite corner.

In the large icon or small icon view, if both the icons you select with the "click, Shift-click" method are in the same row or column, all the icons between the two selected icons in the same row or column will get selected.

Undocumented

The list view orders icons by columns — sort of like wrapping columns of text in a word processor. You can't select rectangular groups of icons in this view as you can in large or small icon view. If you click an icon in the first column, and then Shift+click another icon in the second column, all the icons below the selected icon in the first column get selected, along with all the icons above the Shift-selected icon in the second column, as shown in Figure 8-11.

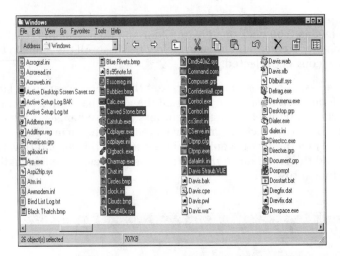

Figure 8-11: Selecting icons in list view. List view arranges icons by column. Click an icon in the second column and then Shift+click an icon in the third column. All the icons below the selected icon in the second column and above the Shift+clicked icon in the third column are selected.

Lasso those icons, cowboys and cowgirls

You can draw your own rectangle (or *lasso*) around or through the icons that you want to select. You don't have to completely enclose an icon to get it lassoed.

Undocumented

To drag a rectangle around the icons that you want to select, move the mouse pointer to an area near the icons. Press and hold down the left mouse button. Drag the mouse pointer over the additional icons that you want to select. The icons are highlighted as you lasso them. Release the mouse button when you have highlighted all the icons. A group of icons selected with a lasso is shown in Figure 8-12.

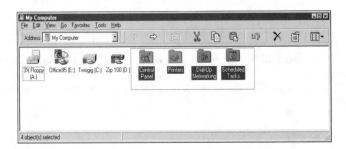

Figure 8-12: Lassoing the icons. Drag a rectangle around a group of icons to select them. Use either the left or right mouse button.

Secret

You can lasso with the right mouse button. When you release the right button, a context menu appears. You can select an action from the context menu to perform on all the icons you have rounded up. Exactly which context menu appears depends on what kind of icons you have rounded up. Windows 95 displays a menu containing actions that can be used on almost all the selected files and/or folders. Some of the actions may not be applicable to some of the icons.

You can use the lasso on the Desktop just like you use it in a folder window.

Select everything

If you want to select everything in a folder window, choose Edit, Select All, just as you would to select all the text in a document. See, you already knew how to do this.

Tip

To select all the icons in a folder window with the keyboard, highlight the window (make sure the window's title bar shows that it has the focus) and press Ctrl+A.

Select everything but

Select, by whatever means you want (except, of course, Select All) everything that you *don't* want to select. Then choose Edit, Invert Selection. This selects everything in the folder window that you didn't select the first time. This is a great way to select everything but a few things.

Deselect with Ctrl+click

After you've selected everything in a window or selected a bunch of icons with the lasso or Shift+click, you might want to remove a few icons from the selection. To do this, Ctrl+click each icon you want to deselect. This is an easy way to select a bunch of icons, and then pull out a few that you don't want selected. You can then right-click one of the selected icons if you want to display a context menu.

Select a few bunches of icons

Combine click and Ctrl+click with Shift+click and Ctrl+Shift+click to select bunches of icons. Ctrl+Shift+click (that is, holding down Ctrl and Shift while clicking) works the same as Shift+click, but it doesn't wipe out previous selections. The Ctrl key continues to be the continue-selection key.

Choose some icons with click, Ctrl+click, and/or Shift+click. Choose another bunch of icons with a Ctrl+click and then a Ctrl+Shift+click. By mixing and matching these selection methods, you can grab little grouplets of icons in the folder window. There are many variations on how this works (we'll let you experiment rather than go through them all) but the behavior of the Shift and Ctrl keys is consistent — trust us on that.

Grabbing the icon group

If you have selected a group of icons and want to move or copy them with drag and drop, you need to drag all of them together. To left or right drag the group, point to one of the selected items and start dragging — you'll bring the whole group with you. If you start dragging when the mouse pointer is between the selected icons, you end up deselecting the icons.

Dragging multiple icons

Here is where it gets ugly, literally. When you drag a single icon (and its name), you get an aesthetically-pleasing transparent version of the icon with its name in black. You can tell right away what you're dragging around. When you drag a group of icons, you get a group of box outlines that stand for the icons and lines that stand for the icon names, as shown in Figure 8-13.

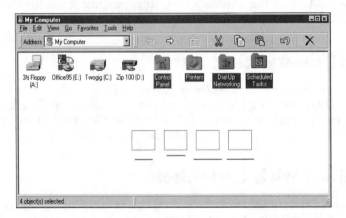

Figure 8-13: Dragging multiple files and folders in a folder window. The icons in this large icon view are portrayed as box outlines and the icon names are portrayed as lines.

We find these icon ghosts quite displeasing; Microsoft can't be too happy about them either. The Windows 3.x File Manager didn't use such ugly icon stand-ins. We assume that users just didn't understand the stacked-documents icon that the File Manager uses to represent multiple icons.

Why didn't Microsoft just make all the icons in the group transparent like when you choose one icon? Because on slower computers with unaccelerated video cards, the repaint time is too slow.

Not only are the ghosted icons ugly, they are hard to manage because they are so spread out. Your mouse pointer still tells you where the hot spot is, but you can easily get confused as to where the icons are if you drag them to another folder window or onto the Desktop. It feels like you're dragging around this big blob of stuff, which is no fun at all.

Undocumented

Normally, when you select and then drag an executable file, Windows 95 creates a shortcut to the executable in the destination folder and leaves the executable itself in its original folder. If you select a group of files that includes executable files (but includes other file types as well), Windows 95 moves (or copies) *all* the files instead. This is dangerous, because it can make some programs cease to work.

Press Esc to cancel

We mentioned this earlier in the *Moving a file or folder* section, but we want to emphasize it again here. If there is a problem while you're dragging an icon or a group of icons around, just press Esc. This aborts the drag operation, but leaves the icons selected.

You can also just click the other mouse button.

Put the Desktop on the Taskbar

It is easy to cover your Desktop with windows so you can't get to the icons on your Desktop. In Chapter 7, we showed you how to use the Minimize All Windows and Undo Minimize All commands to solve this problem. There is another way to deal with this problem that is even more powerful.

Secret

Put a copy of your Desktop on your Taskbar. That way, you can always get to your Desktop because you can always get to your Taskbar (if you have it set for Always on top).

Unfortunately, you can't put the Desktop in the Startup folder, but then it doesn't really matter. Just leave it minimized on the Taskbar when you shut down Windows 95, and it will be there the next time you start up. Here's how you do it:

STEPS

Putting Your Desktop on Your Taskbar

Step 1.   Double-click the My Computer icon. Make sure the toolbar is displayed.

Step 2.   Click the down arrow to the right of the drop-down list, and then use the scroll bar to move up to the top of the list.

Step 3.   Click the Desktop icon. Size and format the Desktop window the way you want it.

Step 4.   Minimize the Desktop window.

The Desktop window is now on your Taskbar. You can use Alt+Tab to task switch to the Desktop. You can do this even if you are running a DOS program in a full-screen DOS box. Hold down the Alt key and press and release the Tab key until you highlight the Desktop icon.

If your computer crashes or does not close down in a normal fashion, you may have to open this Desktop window again.

In the section entitled *The Desktop on the Start menu* in Chapter 11, we show you how to put the Desktop on the Start menu. The Microsoft PowerToys add-on comes with an applet called Deskmenu, which lets you put the Desktop in the Tray of the Taskbar. Just download Powertoy.exe from http://www.microsoft.com/windows/software/powertoy.htm. The Deskmenu icon is small because it is a Tray icon, so it is a bit harder to get at. Also, because it is a Tray icon, you can't use your arrow keys to navigate to it from the Start button (see the *Keyboard Control of the Start Menus* section in Chapter 11). The *Windows 95 Secrets* CD-ROM also contains a small applet, Tab2desk, that lets you get to your Desktop using Alt+Tab.

If you have installed Internet Explorer 4.0, you can add the Desktop toolbar to your Taskbar. Just right-click the Taskbar, point to Toolbars, and then click Desktop.

Folder Windows Are Like the Program Manager

Putting the Desktop on the Taskbar is sort of like turning the Desktop window into the Program Manager. All the icons on the Desktop are now in a window. If a folder window is in the large icon view, it looks like the Windows 3.*x* Program Manager. If you have folders (or shortcuts to folders) on your Desktop, they can act like program groups in the Program Manager. We discuss these issues further in Chapter 7.

Folder windows are a great deal more useful and powerful than the Program Manager, and unlike the Program Manager, you can have multiple folder windows, but some of that old look and feel is still there.

The Explorer is the complement of the File Manager; it gives you a hierarchical view of your computer. We discuss the Explorer in the next chapter. We discuss the Program Manager and the File Manager, which Microsoft included in Windows 95 to provide a transition to the new user interface, in Chapter 12. But you don't really need a transition, do you, if you're reading this book?

Summary

If you want to know how to manage your computer most efficiently, this chapter and the next chapter are the places to look.

▶ We show you how to change the name of My Computer.

▶ We provide you with a score of secrets and tips on how to speed your way through the maze of files and folders on your computer. Get these tips down and your computer is a delight.

▶ We show you how to get multiple copies of any folder window.

▶ The folder window views let you look at your computer in many different ways, and we show you how to change these views to suit your needs.

▶ We provide a number of methods you can use to quickly select files and folders in a folder window.

▶ Afraid of drag and drop? Don't be. We show you how to use this powerful technique with all the safety built in.

▶ Want to have a copy of the Desktop on the Taskbar so you can hot key to it from a full-screen DOS session? We show you how.

Chapter 9

The Explorer — Displaying the Hierarchy

In This Chapter

We show you how to use the Explorer to really grab hold of your computer and wrestle it into shape. We discuss:

▶ Modifying the Explorer on the Start button to act the way you want it to

▶ Putting the Explorer on the Desktop

▶ Using the Explorer to quickly copy and move files and folders

▶ Using keyboard shortcuts to reduce mouse clicking in the Explorer and My Computer windows

▶ Controlling multiple Explorer windows on your Desktop

▶ Making sure that you can see all the files on your computer

▶ Learning to use the Explorer for just about everything you did with the File Manager, and much more

What Is This Explorer Thing?

The Windows 95 Explorer is the hierarchical file cabinet or outline view of My Computer — actually *your* computer. It lets you easily understand the file and folder structure of your computer. It is a replacement for the Windows 3.*x* File Manager. You can use the Explorer to move, copy, rename, compress, view, and delete files and folders on your computer and on the network. It gives you a two-paned view of a folder window.

Internet Explorer 4.0 updates the Explorer to provide a tree view of web sites. Webmasters will have to implement the specific HTML tags that allow the Explorer to display a hierarchical view of their sites. When you visit a site that has used the proper tags, you see the structure of the web site in the left pane of the Explorer, just as you see the structure of your own computer's filing system.

Files and folders get stored on your disk drives in a hierarchical structure before you ever get a chance to get in there and muck it up. You'll find folders dividing up a hard drive, subfolders dividing up folders, and sub-subfolders dividing up subfolders. This natural organization of your drives is shown in Figure 9-1. The Explorer makes this structure evident to you.

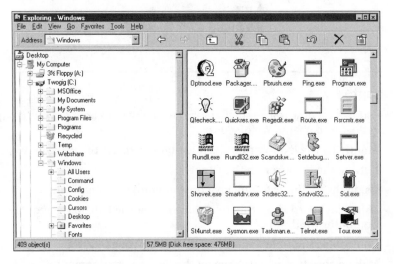

Figure 9-1: An Explorer view of the organization of My Computer. Notice that the hard disk (C:) is connected to and to the right of My Computer. This indicates that it is a part of My Computer. The folder labeled Windows is a part of C:, and Command is a subfolder of the Windows folder.

Like the Windows 3.*x* File Manager, the Explorer shows both a tree view and a folder (directory) view. The left pane gives you a hierarchical view of your computer, disk drives, and folders. The right pane displays the contents of the folder, disk drive, computer, or networked server computer currently selected in the left pane.

The right pane of the Explorer can display either a web page-like view of your file and folder icons or an HTML document. When you visit a web page, its address (or URL) is shown in the left pane of the Explorer window attached to the Internet icon, as shown in Figure 9-2. To display a web site, click Go or Favorites in the menu bar.

Unlike the Windows 3.*x* File Manager, you can view each branch of the tree in the Explorer by single-clicking the small plus signs to the left of the folder and drive icons. Gone is the need to double-click the icon to expand the branch. A click on the plus sign does not highlight the folder or display its contents in the right pane. This ability to navigate the tree without display-ing the contents of folders makes the Explorer easier to use and more versatile than the File Manager.

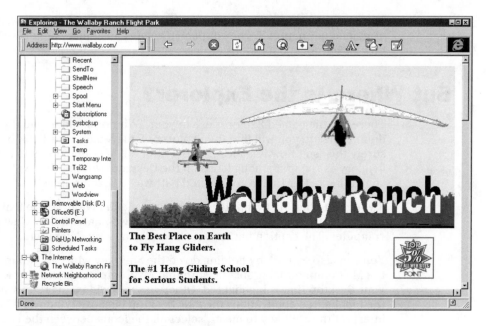

Figure 9-2: An Explorer view of a web page.

Tip

You can quickly navigate through your folders and subfolders by clicking the plus signs next to folder names. The Explorer won't try to read the filenames in a folder until you actually select a folder name; therefore, it is much faster than the File Manager.

Web designers can structure web documents hierarchically, with topics/ documents divided into subtopics/subdocuments. Some folks (apparently a minority in the wider world, but a majority among computer nerds) like hierarchical structure. Most people who browse the web, however, prefer the topical connectedness afforded by hyperlinks, which tie ideas and documents together through their not-necessarily hierarchical association with one another.

If you've installed Internet Explorer 4.0, you can use the Explorer to browse web sites either hierarchically (if the web designer as implemented the proper tags), or through hyperlinks. Use the left pane (the left brain?) to see the overall structure of the web site, and use the right pane to follow the hyperlinks embedded in the text.

Almost everything that we said in Chapter 8 regarding My Computer is applicable to the Explorer. All the various ways of copying, moving, renaming, and deleting files and folders are exactly the same for the Explorer.

The Explorer is just a dual-pane version of the single-pane windows we examined in Chapter 8. The left pane provides an additional navigation tool that makes some operations easier.

But Where Is the Explorer?

There is a file named Explorer.exe in your \Windows folder, and if you double-click it, you will find the Explorer displayed on your Desktop. But surely this isn't how it is meant to be. After all, My Computer sits there in all its glory as the first among icons on the Desktop. Doesn't the Explorer rate something better than a convoluted pathway to Explorer.exe?

If you right-click My Computer, the context menu invites you to Explore. Click Explore and My Computer turns into a two-pane window view of your computer. The caption bar says it all: Exploring - My Computer.

Tip

You can also explore by holding down the Shift key while you double-click the My Computer icon. Just be sure that My Computer is the only icon on your Desktop that is highlighted. Otherwise you will inadvertently open all the highlighted applications on your Desktop because Windows 95 will interpret the Shift key to mean "select all the icons between the last one highlighted and the My Computer icon."

The Explore menu option is available when you right-click the Network Neighborhood icon, the Recycle Bin, the Microsoft Network icon, the Start button, or any folder or disk drive icon. You can view the contents of any of these items in the Explorer view.

You can change My Computer into My Explorer. We discuss ways to do this in the *Turning My Computer into the Explorer* section later in this chapter.

The Windows Explorer and the Start button

The Explorer (actually a shortcut to Explorer.exe) has its own icon on the Start menu.

Click the Start button, point to Programs, and click on Windows Explorer in the Programs menu. You can determine just how the Explorer starts up (when you start it from the Programs menu) by editing the properties of this menu item. See the section later in this chapter entitled *Explorer Command Line Parameters*.

Putting the Explorer on the Desktop

My Computer is on the Desktop. You can put the Explorer on the Desktop, too. By doing this you are saying that the Explorer view is just as important as the My Computer view of your computer. The easiest way to do this is to put a shortcut to the Explorer on the Desktop. To do this, take the following steps:

STEPS

Putting the Explorer on the Desktop

Step 1. Click Start, point to Programs, and click Windows Explorer.

Step 2. Click the Windows folder icon in the left pane of the Explorer. Scroll down the right pane until Explorer.exe is showing.

Step 3. Drag Explorer.exe to the Desktop and drop it. There's no need to choose Create Shortcut(s) Here from a context menu since dragging the icon from Explorer to the Desktop creates a shortcut to the program automatically. (Dragging an executable file to the Desktop always creates a shortcut rather than moving the file itself. Dragging other file types, however, actually moves them into the \Windows\Desktop folder.)

Step 4. Press F2, and change the Explorer shortcut icon's name to **Explorer** or whatever else you want.

Turning My Computer into the Explorer

There are two ways to turn My Computer into My Explorer. The first requires editing your Registry, but it only affects My Computer. The second changes the default action that takes place when you double-click My Computer from Open to Explore, but it also makes the same change for other Desktop objects (such as Network Neighborhood, the Recycle Bin, Internet Mail, Internet News, and the Internet icon).

Thanks to Dan Norton for pointing out this first method:

Secret

STEPS

Changing My Computer to My Explorer

Step 1. Double-click Regedit.exe in your \Windows folder.

Step 2. Click the plus sign next to HKEY_CLASSES_ROOT. Scroll down the left pane of the Registry editor to CLSID. Click the plus sign next to CLSID.

Step 3. Scroll down the left pane of the Registry editor to {20D04FE0-3AEA-1069-A2D8-080022B30309D}. Click the plus sign next to this identifier.

Step 4. Highlight *shell* in the left pane. Right-click the right pane, and then choose New, Key. Type **Open** as the name for the new key.

(continued)

Changing My Computer to My Explorer

Step 5.   Highlight the Open key in the left pane, right-click the right pane, choose New, Key, and create a key called Command.

Step 6.   Highlight the new Command key, right-click the Default key, choose Modify, and set the Default value of Command to Explorer.exe. You can use any of the parameters detailed in *Explorer Command Line Parameters* later in this chapter to modify this command.

Step 7.   Exit the Registry editor. These changes take effect immediately.

Step 8.   Highlight the My Computer icon on your Desktop, press the F2 key, and change the name from My Computer to My Explorer, or whatever you like. Press Return.

If you right-click My Explorer, you'll notice that the context menu now contains two different Open commands. The second Open command is the one you just created. It's displayed in boldface to indicate that it's the default action Windows 95 takes when you double-click My Explorer. The first Open command is an action associated with the general class of objects of which My Explorer is a member. Clicking it opens a My Computer window. Both Open commands work without interfering with each other.

Secret

If you would rather not edit your Registry, you can simply change the default action associated with a file type. In this case, you'll change the default action of My Computer from Open to Explore:

Opening My Computer with Explore

Step 1.   In the Explorer, choose View, Options, and then click the File Types tab.

Step 2.   Select the Folder entry in the Registered file types list. Click the Edit button to display the Edit File Type dialog box.

Step 3.   Click Explore in the Actions box, click the Set Default button, and then click OK.

Step 4.   Click the OK button to exit the Options dialog box.

Step 5.   If you wish, you can also change the name of My Computer to My Explorer.

This change not only affects My Computer, it also affects every other object on the Desktop that normally opens in a folder window. For example, if you double-click the Recycle Bin icon, it now opens in Explorer view. If you ever want to see My Computer, the Recycle Bin, and so on, in the old folder windows, simply right-click the icon and select Open. To reverse the whole change, follow the steps above and make Open instead of Explore the default action.

Getting an Overview of Your Computer

The Explorer displays icons arranged hierarchically in its left pane, as shown in Figure 9-3. The topmost icon is the Desktop. At the second level you'll find My Computer, the Internet (if you have installed Internet Explorer), the Network Neighborhood, and some additional icons. Floppy-disk drive icons, hard-disk drive icons, folder icons (some with little graphics on them), are attached to My Computer.

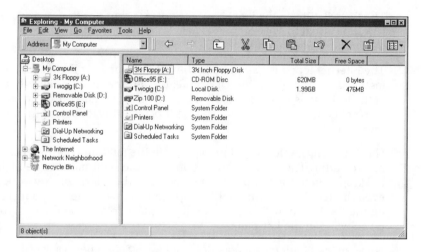

Figure 9-3: The Explorer view. The left pane shows the Desktop and the items that are attached to it.

The view of your computer in the left pane of the Explorer is somewhat strange. It states that everything is part of and contained within the Desktop. But it is clear if we view the contents of the \Windows folder (after marking "Show all files" as described in the *Seeing All the Files on Your Computer* section later in this chapter) that the Desktop is a subfolder of your \Windows folder. The \Windows folder is contained within a disk drive that is contained within My Computer. In addition, the Explorer (remember it is Explorer.exe) is contained within \Windows.

The Desktop appears at the top and the Desktop appears as a sub-sub-sub-folder of itself. The Explorer appears as a window on top of the Desktop, and at the same time it displays the Desktop (in two forms) within the Explorer, which is itself a member of the Desktop.

So making a conceptual leap, you see that My Computer is connected to the Desktop, and that the disk drives, hard and floppy, are connected to My Computer.

The dotted lines are your guides. If a vertical dotted line comes out of the bottom of an icon, the icons connected to that line by horizontal dotted lines are contained within the top icon. My Computer, Network Neighborhood, and Recycle Bin are all contained within the Desktop. The disk drives are contained within My Computer.

The Network Neighborhood icon represents all the computers connected to yours over a LAN. You won't have a Network Neighborhood icon on your Desktop unless you have installed a network or set up Dial-Up Networking or Direct Cable Connection.

Network Neighborhood and Recycle Bin are displayed on the same level as My Computer. Microsoft wants you to think of the network in the same way as you think of your computer.

The Recycle Bin spans local hard disk drives (but not floppy drives). In this way, it is equal to My Computer. Also, Microsoft wanted the Recycle Bin on the Desktop permanently.

The Internet icon also appears in the left pane of your Explorer if you have installed Internet Explorer. Of course, the Internet icon is right there on your Desktop as well. Microsoft wants to be sure that you know how easy it is to get connected to the Internet so it placed this icon near the top of the hierarchy.

Shortcuts on the Desktop don't appear in the left pane of the Explorer — too much clutter. They do, however, appear in the right pane if you highlight the Desktop icon in the left pane. The Inbox and the Microsoft Network icons, even though they are on the Desktop, don't show in the left pane. File icons on the Desktop don't show either. If you place folders on the Desktop, they do show up in the left pane.

Some special folders, such as Control Panel, Scheduled Tasks (if you have Internet Explorer 4.0), and Printers, are displayed on the same level as the disk drives. Microsoft doesn't want you to have to go searching for them through the hierarchy of folders. Like cream, they have risen to the top.

Ordinary folders are stored in the disk drives, and the folder icons are connected to the drive icons. Figure 9-3 doesn't show any folder icons attached to the drive icons because the view in the left pane hasn't been expanded to include them. You can see them in Figure 9-2. File icons never show up in the left pane of the Explorer window.

Special folders

When you install Windows 95, it sets up a number of preconfigured folders that have special characteristics. These include \Recycled, \Program Files, \Windows\Recent, \Windows\SendTo, and \Windows\Fonts. Internet Explorer also creates a \Windows\Favorites folder for Internet web pages, and a \Windows\History folder to keep track of the URLs for previously visited web sites.

Some of these folders contain a hidden file, Desktop.ini, which contains a reference to a dynamic link library file that defines a particular set of behaviors for the folder. Others are just regular folders that Windows 95 uses as default storage locations for certain kinds of files. For example, the default storage location for new applications is \Program Files.

Windows 95 keeps track of some of these folders in the Registry. You can edit their entries to point to other locations. This can be useful if you want to move one of these folders to another drive. This doesn't appear to work for the Fonts folder, however.

You can use your Registry editor (see Chapter 15) to review the settings in HKEY_CURRENT_USER\Software\Microsoft\Windows\CurrentVersion\Explorer\shellfolders. You can also use TweakUI to make the necessary Registry changes.

When you install Microsoft Office, it creates the \My Documents folder. This folder is especially handy as a top-level branch for storing all your work files (and folders). Putting everything under this branch makes it easy to backup your work and copy it to other computers.

We suggest that you create another branch under the root directory, \My System. You can use this folder to store files and applications that modify the behavior of your computer, but are specific to your computer alone. We have included a number of batch files and *reg* files on the *Windows 95 Secrets* CD-ROM that you might want to place in this folder. Then, no matter how often you update your \Windows or \Windows\System folders, your still have your original files in \My System.

Two panes — connected and yet independent

The two panes of the Explorer window are connected. You click on an icon in the left pane, and the contents of that drive or folder are shown in the right pane. If you have the Explorer description bar turned on (choose View, Options in the Explorer, and mark the box labeled "Include description bar for right and left panes"), the right pane is labeled Contents of '*xxx*,' where *xxx* is the name of the selected icon in the left pane.

Much of the power of the Explorer comes from the fact that the two panes, although connected, are also independent of each other. You can view the contents of one folder in the right pane and, without disturbing that view, expand the tree in the left pane to find another folder. This makes it easy to copy or move files and folders from one folder to another.

Think of the right pane of the Explorer window as a folder window. It acts just like a folder window, except that the default action when you double-click a folder icon in the right pane is to open the folder in the existing Explorer window, rather to open another folder window.

If you have Internet Explorer 4.0 and are viewing the Explorer in Web view, you only have to single-click a folder icon in the right pane to display its contents. If a document is displayed in the right pane, you can single-click on any hyperlinks it contains to go to their targets.

Navigating with the Explorer

The Explorer is your navigator. It guides you to the files and folders on your computer's disk drives or, if you are connected to a network, on other computers. The Explorer displays, in an expandable tree, your computer's drives and the drives of other computers to which you are networked. You search through the drives by clicking the Explorer tree to expand it. The Explorer also gives you an easy way to copy, move, and link files or folders across disk drives, folders, or the network.

Because the Explorer gives you an overview and a road map of your computer and the server computers you are connected to, you can use it to find your way around computer space. The key to navigating is using the little plus signs to the left of the icons in the folder tree. Clicking on a plus sign expands that branch of the tree. For example, clicking the plus sign next to your C drive icon expands the tree to allow you to see all the folders attached to the root directory of the C drive.

Click the plus sign next to any of the folders on the C drive, and you'll see the folders contained within that folder. Each branch of the folder tree gets expanded as you climb out the branches.

To collapse a branch, click the minus sign to the left of an icon. The minus sign appears as soon as you expand a branch.

If you have Internet Explorer 4.0, you can also navigate by clicking the Back and Forward arrow buttons on the toolbar. They allow you to move back to a previously viewed document or folder, and then move forward again to the document or folder you viewed most recently.

Highlighting a folder icon

If you click a folder icon in the left pane, you see the contents of that folder in the right pane. If the contents of the right pane include folder icons, you can expand a branch by double-clicking one of them. The folder tree in the left pane of the Explorer also expands when you do this.

The default action of clicking a folder icon in the left pane is to display the contents of the folder in the right pane. If you instead right-click a folder icon and choose Open in the context menu, Windows 95 opens a new folder window on the Desktop with the contents of the folder.

Tip

If you double-click a folder icon in the tree, you both expand the branch at that node and display the contents of the folder in the right pane.

Secret

If you double-click a folder icon in the right pane of the Explorer, the Explorer view expands to display the contents of that folder in the right pane. By making a change to the Folder definition in your Registry, you can have this action display the contents of the folder in a new window instead of in the Explorer.

STEPS

Making Single-Pane Views from the Explorer

Step 1. Double-click Regedit.exe in the \Windows folder. Click the plus sign next to the HKEY_CLASSES_ROOT key. Scroll down to the Folder key.

Step 2. Click the plus sign next to the Folder key, and highlight the *shell* key.

Step 3. Double-click Default in the right pane to display the Edit String dialog box. Type **Open** in the Value Data field and click OK.

Step 4. Double-click a folder icon in the right pane of the Explorer and notice this action now opens a new window. If you double-click a folder icon in the left pane in the Explorer, the right pane still displays the contents of that folder.

Folder icons in the Explorer

Double-click a folder icon in the left pane of the Explorer. If this folder has subfolders, double-clicking it will display them in the folder tree. The double-click is a toggle. If you double-click the folder icon again, the folder tree collapses to hide the subfolders.

Undocumented

If you have Internet Explorer 4.0, try this: Drag and hold a file or folder icon from the right pane over a folder icon in the left pane. If the folder in the left pane has subfolders that were previously not displayed (the folder had a plus sign next to it), they are now displayed. This allows you to navigate down the folder tree and find the target subfolder as you are dragging.

Toolbar or Internet toolbar

As we saw in the Chapter 8, Internet Explorer 4.0 provides two toolbars, the standard toolbar, which looks something like the toolbar in the earlier version of Windows 95, and the Internet toolbar. The Explorer automatically switches between toolbars depending on whether you are viewing a web document or a folder or disk drive on your computer (or network).

The Internet toolbar should be familiar to those of you who have used the Internet Explorer in its previous incarnations. Now this toolbar finds itself attached to other windows, including the Explorer and My Computer. We discuss this aspect of the Windows 95 user interface in more detail in Chapter 34. You can increase the height of either toolbar by pulling down on its bottom edge. If you do this, the toolbar will include text names as well as icons.

Making the left pane bigger

The two panes of the Explorer window are divided by a vertical bar. You can increase the width of the left pane so that you can see more of its contents as you expand branches of the folder tree. To do this, rest your mouse pointer over the vertical bar. When the mouse pointer turns into a vertical line with two arrows, drag the bar to the right.

The Network Neighborhood

The Network Neighborhood icon contains the shared resources of the computers to which your computer is connected. Double-click this icon to see the disk drives, folders, and printers that are available (shared) to you.

You can expand branches of the folder trees found on other computers just as easily as you can on your computer. Windows 95 treats the networked computers just like My Computer to encourage you to do likewise. You can use the Explorer window to browse networked computers just as you do your own computer.

If you like, you can map a shared folder or disk drive to a drive letter, thereby making it appear as though it is part of My Computer. If you have an earlier version of Windows 95, click the Map Network Drive icon in the Explorer toolbar and choose which shared disk to map to which drive letter. If you have Internet Explorer 4.0, choose Tools, Map Network Drive.

If you want to connect to a shared printer, use the Printers folder (located in the My Computer window).

Using the keyboard with the folder tree

Secret

You can, if you like, expand all the branches of the folder tree at once. To do this, hold down the Alt key and press the asterisk above the number pad. We don't really recommend expanding all branches at once because it can take a long time.

To expand or collapse branches with your mouse, you click the plus and minus signs next to the branches. If you want to use the keyboard instead, press Tab if necessary to bring the focus to the left pane of the Explorer window, use the arrow keys to highlight the branch you want to expand or collapse (or type the first few letters of the folder or drive name), and then press the plus key to expand the branch or the minus key to collapse it.

Normally, if you collapse a high-level branch when branches underneath it are displayed, the next time you expand the branch, all the branches within it are redisplayed as well. If you want to only see the first level of folders under the branch the next time you expand it, press F5 after you collapse it. Windows 95 "invisibly" collapses the branches under the high-level branch so that they won't show the next time you expand it.

Creating New Folders

Windows 95 and your applications create the folders they need during installation. If you want additional folders for your own work, you need to create them yourself. To create folders using the Explorer, take the following steps:

STEPS

Creating a Folder

Step 1. Right-click the My Computer icon on the Desktop. Choose Explore in the context menu.

Step 2. Expand the folder tree in the left pane of the Explorer window until you see the folder in which you want to place your new folder. Click this folder icon to select it. Make sure that the folder name is highlighted and that its name is in the Explorer window title bar.

Step 3. Right-click a blank part of the right pane to display a context menu. Point to New, and then click Folder.

Step 4. A new folder icon appears in the right pane, and its name is highlighted. Type an appropriate name for the folder and press Enter.

It would seem natural to right-click a folder or drive icon in the left pane of the Explorer and choose New from a context menu to create a new folder, shortcut, or whatever within the selected folder (or root directory if you right-click on a drive icon). Unfortunately, there is no New option on the context menu that appears when you right-click on items in the folder tree.

Copying and Moving Files and Folders

You can move and copy files a lot more easily with the Explorer dual-pane window than with a single-pane folder window. You just have to be willing to put up with this hierarchical view of your computer, the attached network, and the Internet (if you're using Internet Explorer 4.0).

You can view the contents of the source folder in the right pane and independently find the destination folder in the left pane. Once you see both source and destination in your Explorer window, you can copy or move the files and/or folders from the right pane to the left.

Almost all the copying and moving techniques detailed in Chapter 8 work the same with the Explorer. Instead of dragging and dropping between folder windows, you select icons in the Explorer window's right pane and drop them on folder icons in the left pane.

Secret

You can't copy a file into the same folder that contains the original file by pressing the Ctrl key as you drag and drop the file in the right pane of the Explorer. Instead, Ctrl-drag the file from the right pane and drop it on the folder icon of the same folder in the left pane of the Explorer. A copy of the file will then appear in the folder with the prefix "Copy of."

If you want to move or copy files or folders in the Explorer, first select the icons in the right pane with any of the techniques detailed in the previous chapter. Issue the Cut or Copy command, display the contents of another folder in the right pane, and issue the Paste command to move or copy the selected files and/or folders to the new folder.

If you have downloaded Microsoft's PowerToys utility (http://www.microsoft.com/windows/software/powertoy.htm), you can use Send To Any Folder to move or copy a file or folder to another folder (see the *Right-click to a Powerhouse* section in Chapter 10).

Creating Two Explorer Windows

In the Windows 3.*x* File Manager, it was much easier to manage files if you had two child windows open at the same time. Each window had two panes (the directory tree on the left and the directory contents on the right), so when two child windows were open, the File Manager contained a total of four panes.

You could use one child window to display the source directory and the other window to display the destination directory. This made it much easier to copy and move files, or to simply compare the contents of two directories.

In the File Manager, you couldn't expand the directory tree while maintaining the same contents in the right pane. In contrast, the tree and folder panes in the Explorer are more independent, which allows you to manage files with just two panes.

The File Manager does have an advantage over the Explorer. The File Manager has a multidocument interface. It can contain two child windows within its window border. Microsoft has decided to drop this interface and have the operating system, not the applications, control the window borders.

As a result of this decision, the Explorer does not have a multidocument interface. So if you want to reduce the amount of scrolling you have to do to find the source and then go to the destination folder when you're moving and copying files, you might find it easier to open two Explorer windows at the same time on the Desktop. This is quite easy to do, because Windows 95 opens a new copy of the Explorer each time that you right-click My Computer and click Explore, or each time you double-click an Explorer shortcut on the Desktop (see *Putting the Explorer on the Desktop* earlier in this chapter).

Undocumented

You can open another copy of the Explorer that's already focused on a particular folder by following these steps:

STEPS

Opening a Second Copy of the Explorer

Step 1. In the left pane of an Explorer window, right-click the folder icon you want to Explore. This could be either the source or destination folder.

Step 2. Click Open in the context menu.

Step 3. Right-click the system menu icon (at the left end of the title bar) of the newly opened folder window.

Step 4. Select Explore from the context menu.

Step 5. Click the Close box in the upper-right corner of the folder window you created in step 2.

This will open a new copy of the Explorer with the focus on the selected folder. Once you have two Explorer windows, you can display the contents of the destination folder in one and the source folder in the other.

Tip

You can arrange the Explorer windows like the child windows in the File Manager by right-clicking the Taskbar and choosing Cascade, Tile Horizontally, or Tile Vertically. (Before you issue one of these commands, make sure all your other open windows are minimized.) When tiled, the two Explorer windows cover your Desktop completely and look like the two child windows in the Windows 3.x File Manager when it was maximized.

Undocumented

If you leave two tiled Explorer windows open when you shut down your computer, they will be ready to go when you start it again. Unfortunately, the two windows won't stay tiled, but will instead be stacked on top of each other. (This is because Window 95 erroneously saves the position of only one Explorer window.) You'll need to right-click the Taskbar and choose Tile Horizontally or Tile Vertically to separate the windows again.

Explorer (And My Computer) Keyboard Shortcuts

The Explorer and the My Computer folder windows share a common set of keyboard shortcuts. They are listed in Table 9-1.

Table 9-1	Explorer and Folder Window Keyboard Shortcuts
Key	*Action*
F1	Help
F2	Rename the highlighted file or folder.
F3	Bring up the Find dialog box.
F4	Display down the drop-down list in the toolbar. This is a toggle switch.
F5	Refresh the windows. You saw one use for this command in *Using the keyboard with the folder tree* earlier in this chapter. If the files or folders in a window have changed and have not yet been updated, this will update the display.
F6	Move the focus from left pane, to the drop-down box in the toolbar, to the right pane, and back to the left pane again. In a folder window there is only one pane.
F10	Put the focus on the File menu.
ALT+*	Expand all the branches in the folder tree.

Key	*Action*
*	Expand all branches below the focused node (folder or drive icon).
Backspace	Move up one level in the folder hierarchy.
Tab	Same as F6; shift the focus between the two panes and the toolbar. This is very useful for navigating the folder tree or picking out files and folders in the right pane.
Arrow keys	Move up and down the folder tree in the left pane or the list of files and folders in the right pane. If you move quickly enough in the left pane, the highlighted folder's contents do not show in the right pane. If you leave the focus on one icon for more than a second, its contents are displayed in the right pane.
Right arrow	Expand the highlighted folder if it isn't expanded already. If it is, go to the subfolder.
Left arrow	Collapse the highlighted folder if is it expanded. If not, go to the parent folder.
Ctrl+Arrow keys	Scroll the left or right pane, depending on which pane has the focus. You can use PgUp and PgDn keys also. The focus isn't changed.
Enter	Does nothing in the folder tree. In the right pane, pressing Enter runs the selected file or opens the selected folder, just as double-clicking would.
Shift+F10	Display the context menu. Same as right-click. Throughout the Windows interface, pressing Shift+F10 is equivalent to clicking the right mouse button.
+	The keypad plus sign. When a folder name is highlighted and the branch below it is collapsed, expand the branch.
−	The keypad minus sign. When a folder name is highlighted and the branch below it is expanded, collapse the branch. When combined with F5, collapse all the branches below.
Alt+Spacebar	Open the system menu. This menu allows you to move, minimize, maximize, size, or close the folder or Explorer window.
Alt+Enter	Display the folder's properties sheets.
Ctrl+G	Open the Go To Folder dialog box. This allows you to enter the name of a folder or computer to go to.
Ctrl+X	Cut highlighted item.
Ctrl+C	Copy highlighted item.

(continued)

Table 9-1 *(continued)*

Key	*Action*
Ctrl+V	Paste copied or cut item.
Ctrl+Z	Undo a previous action.
Letter(s)	Jump to the first folder whose name starts with that letter(s). If you type the same letter(s) again, jump to the next folder whose name starts with those letters. You need to type multiple letters quickly or Windows 95 will interpret the second letter as a new first letter.
Alt+F4	Close the application window. Throughout the Windows interface, Alt+F4 closes all applications.

Seeing All the Files on Your Computer

Microsoft is somewhat ashamed of the three-letter file extensions it uses to define file types. It is also a bit embarrassed by its 8- followed by 3-character filenames. It has created a way of doing long filenames (255 characters long) without upsetting its existing file structure (FAT, for file allocation table), and now it wants Windows 95 users to forget about file extensions.

When you first install Windows 95, it doesn't show files with certain extensions in folder windows or in Explorer windows. And it doesn't show the three-letter extensions for files of registered file types. You can tell Windows 95 to display these missing files and extensions. Here's how:

STEPS

Viewing All Files and File Extensions

Step 1.   Open a folder or Explorer window. One way to do this is by right-clicking My Computer and choosing either Open or Explore.

Step 2.   Click View, Options to display the Options dialog box, and click the View tab if necessary, as shown in Figure 9-4. (This figure shows the version of the Options dialog box that you will see if you have installed Internet Explorer 4.0.)

Step 3.   Mark the Show all files option button and clear the check box labeled "Hide MS-DOS file extensions for file types that are registered." (If you're using Internet Explorer 4.0, this check box is labeled "Hide file extensions for known file types.")

Step 4.   Click OK.

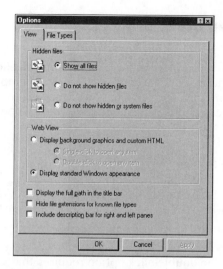

Figure 9-4: The Options dialog box that comes with Internet Explorer 4.0.

Notice that you can make these changes in either a folder window or an Explorer window. We chose to write about this capability in this chapter only because Microsoft views the Explorer as an advanced interface and sees the capability to view file extensions as an advanced feature. Of course, the whole point of this book is to make every advanced feature visible to anyone who wants to take advantage of it.

Seeing hidden folders

Secret

If you mark the Show all files option button, you also get to see more folders contained in the Windows folder. Microsoft appears to think that less "advanced" users will have a problem with these folders showing up in their folder windows, so it hides them from the view of users who choose to hide files of certain types.

You can see which folders get hidden by opening an Explorer window and expanding the branch connected to your \Windows folder icon in the folder tree. Watch the list of folders change as you switch back and forth between Show all files and Hide files of these types (or Do not show hidden files/Do not show hidden or system files if you have installed Internet Explorer 4.0).

Single-click or double-click

If you have installed Internet Explorer 4.0, the View, Options dialog box also lets you choose between two options for the Web view. You can choose to have Explorer and My Computer windows display background graphics and custom HTML or use the standard Window appearance (see Figure 9-4). If you choose the former, you can choose between Single-click to open any item and Double-click to open any item.

When the single-click option is turned on, you can select an icon by hovering your mouse pointer over it. Once you've selected an icon this way, you can perform some action on it by issuing commands (such as Cut, Copy, Rename, Delete, and so on) via the keyboard, menus, or toolbar. (The icon stays selected as long as you don't move your mouse pointer over another icon.)

The single-click option lets you open a window by single-clicking a folder icon or an application icon. The double-click option requires that you double-click an icon to open its window.

Explorer Command Line Parameters

Take a moment to look at how the Explorer command line parameters work:

STEPS

Viewing the Windows Explorer Command Line Parameters

Step 1.   Right-click the Start button and then click Explore.

Step 2.   Click Programs in the left pane of the Explorer.

Step 3.   Right-click Windows Explorer in the right pane and then click Properties.

Step 4.   Click the Shortcut tab and then look at the Target field.

The target for the Windows Explorer shortcut is:

```
C:\WINDOWS\EXPLORER.EXE /n,/e,C:\
```

With the command line parameters /n,/e,C:\, an Explorer window you open by clicking Windows Explorer in the Start menu looks like Figure 9-5.

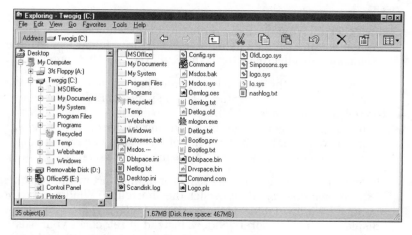

Figure 9-5: An Explorer window focused on the C drive.

The syntax for the Explorer command line is:

```
C:\Windows\Explorer.exe {/n,}{/e,}{options,}{folder}
```

The parameters have the following meanings:

/n,   Opens a *new* Explorer window — by itself, this commands
          opens a window in folder view

/e,   Opens an *expanded* folder with its contents displayed in
          Explorer view

options   may be either one of the following:

/root,   Selects a folder as the *root* of a folder tree

or

/select, Highlights a folder and displays the folder's parent

folder   may be any folder name or path, such as:

    C:\

or

    C:\Windows

Note that you have to use commas between switches on the Explorer
command line.

Undocumented

If there were no command line parameters after Explorer.exe, clicking
Windows Explorer in the Start menu would bring up an Explorer window
focused on the C drive.

If you add C:\Windows or any other folder name to the Explorer command line, clicking Windows Explorer in the Start menu displays a folder window containing the contents of that folder. Adding a folder name to the Explorer command line effectively turns the Explorer into My Computer.

Undocumented

If you insert /e, (the comma is required) in front of the folder name, clicking Windows Explorer in the Start menu displays an Explorer window focused on the specified folder with the folder expanded and the contents of the folder displayed in the right pane. Putting a folder name in the Target field (command line) takes Explorer out of its default behavior. Using /e, restores some of that default behavior; /e, means *Explorer view*.

If instead of clicking Windows Explorer in the Start menu, you open an Explorer window and double-click the shortcut to Windows Explorer found in the C:\Windows\Start Menu\Program folder, Windows 95 does not display another Explorer window. Instead, it refocuses your existing Explorer window on the folder in the Target field. To force Windows 95 to create a new Explorer window, you need to add the /n, command line parameter. Adding /n, restores the rest of the Explorer's default behavior (except for its focus); /n, means *new*.

Undocumented

When you click Windows Explorer in the Start menu, you get another Explorer window even if you don't use the /n, command parameter. The only situation in which you need the /n, parameter to get another Explorer window is if you launch the Explorer by double-clicking the Windows Explorer shortcut within an Explorer window.

You can't replace C:\Windows with My Computer or Network Neighborhood. Desktop will work, but it doesn't get you to the top of the hierarchical view of your computer. You might try it to see what we mean.

Undocumented

The normal topmost icon in the Explorer is the Desktop. This is referred to as the *root* of the folder tree. You can specify a different root if you want. Add /root, to the command line and follow it with your new root. The new root could be My Computer, or C:\Windows, or whatever you like. Here's an example:

```
C:\WINDOWS\EXPLORER.EXE /n,/e,/root,C:\
```

This example produces an Explorer window that looks like Figure 9-6.

You can use the /select, parameter to highlight a given folder and open the folder's parent. Here's an example (see Figure 9-7):

```
C:\WINDOWS\EXPLORER.EXE /n,/e,/select,C:\
```

Figure 9-6: An Explorer window with the C drive as its root (`/root,`).

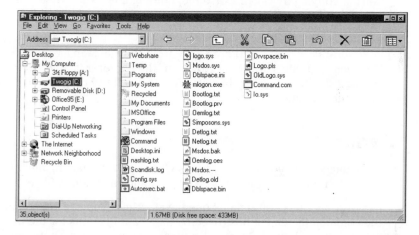

Figure 9-7: An Explorer window focused on the C drive with its parent, My Computer, open (`/select,`).

Notice the differences that these command line parameters produce by comparing Figures 9-6 and 9-7 with Figure 9-5.

Going from the File Manager to the Explorer

How do you go from using the File Manager to using the Explorer? In this section, we review almost all the things you can do with the File Manager and show you how to do them better with the Explorer or another part of the Windows 95 interface. Much of what we say here about the Explorer is the Windows 95 interface. Much of what we say here about the Explorer is also true of the My Computer folder windows. Where it isn't true, and isn't obviously *not* true, we point it out.

Open, Copy, Move, Delete

The File Manager's File menu offers these choices: Open, Copy, Move, and Delete.

The Explorer accomplishes those same tasks with the context menu, substituting the Cut and Paste commands for Move, and the Copy and Paste commands for Copy. Because the Explorer can use the right mouse button, it can use right drag and drop, which allows for easier-to-understand copy and move operations. The Explorer also supports the Windows 3.*x* conventions of copying by clicking on a file, holding down the Ctrl key and dragging it to a new folder and moving a file by clicking on the file, holding down the Alt key and dragging it to a new folder.

In Windows 3.*x,* you could drag a file from the File Manager to the Program Manager to create a shortcut. However, the Explorer is much better at creating shortcuts, mainly because it makes full use of drag and drop and the context menu.

Rename

File Manager lets you use wild cards when you're renaming files. This makes it easy to rename a group of files, or to change a bunch of file extensions.

Explorer only lets you rename one file at a time. You can also rename files in the common file dialog box (used by many applications for the Open and Save As dialog boxes). Just click a filename twice slowly (but don't double-click it), type a new name or edit the existing name, and press Enter. You can also click a file to highlight it, and then press F2 to rename it. Finally, you can right-click an icon and choose Rename from the context menu.

The File Manager doesn't work with long filenames. It is possible to upgrade the File Manager to handle long filenames using a shareware application, File Manager Long File Name Support for Windows 95. You can download this application from http://ourworld.compuserve.com/homepages/sweckman/winfilee.htm.

Run

File Manager lets you run an executable file by choosing File, Run to display the Run dialog box, typing the filename, and adding command line parameters. If you are focused in the File Manager on a particular directory, it puts the directory's pathname in the command line.

In Windows 95, Run is on the Start menu in the Taskbar. It doesn't know which folder you have highlighted, so it doesn't put your current path in the Run dialog box's command line. Run keeps a history from session to session of past command lines.

File association

File Manager can create an *association* with an application to open and print associated documents.

The Explorer has a similar easy-to-use file association feature, but one that is much more powerful. You can create many more commands than opening and printing. Just double-click an unregistered file type, enter an optional name for the file type, and pick an application to open it.

In the Explorer, the Print command only appears in the context menu for files of registered types. The File Manager doesn't dim the File, Print command even when you highlight a file that it doesn't know how to print.

With the Explorer, you can add other commands or change an existing association by choosing View, Options, and changing settings in the File Types tab. Check out Chapter 13 for details.

Open an unassociated file

With the File Manager, you can drag a file to an open application or a minimized icon on the Desktop to view or open it.

With the Explorer, you can put a shortcut in the Send To folder that points to a default file opener (or two). Then you can right-click a file in the Explorer, and use the Send To command to send the file to the default file opener. (See Chapter 13 for details.) You can drag a file to a minimized application button on the Taskbar, or to an application window that is open on the Desktop.

You can also right-click a file, choose Open, and pick which application you want to open the file with.

Create directory

One of the main reasons you use the File Manager or the Explorer is to create new directories (or, in Windows 95 terminology, new folders). You can use both the File Manager and the Explorer to build hierarchical folder structures.

To create a folder in the Explorer, highlight the folder icon in the left pane that will contain the new folder. Right-click the right pane, point to New in the context menu, and click Folder. Rename the folder from New Folder to whatever you like.

Create file

You can't create a new, empty file in the File Manager.

You can in the Explorer. Right-click in the right pane and choose New. Then click on the desired document type in the New menu.

Search or File Find

You can use the File Manager to find a file using wild cards, and you can tell it what directory (and subdirectories) to search.

The Explorer has a much more powerful Find capability. It remembers your past searches, so you can edit them and use them again. The Find feature allows you to use a greater number of search criteria, and you can search for files by looking for text within them. There is no comparison. Check out Chapter 11 for details.

You initiate a Find with the Explorer by choosing Tools, Find, Files or Folders or by pressing F3 if your focus is on the Desktop, a folder window, or an Explorer window. You can also search for computers on your local network, or for documents on the Microsoft Network or on the Internet.

File view filters

If you choose View, By File Type and type an extension or filename, the File Manager restricts the files it displays to ones that have the extension or filename you specify.

The Explorer lets you do this with Find. You can display in the Find window only files that have a given name or extension. This is slower than the File Manager's way of doing it, but less prone to error.

Copy, Label, Format, make a system disk

The File Manager lets you do a disk copy. You can also change the label of a disk drive, including a hard disk drive. And you can format a diskette (or a hard drive) and create a system diskette.

To disk-copy a diskette in the Explorer, right-click the floppy icon and select Copy Disk from the context menu.

To label a hard disk drive or a diskette, right-click the drive icon, click Properties, and then type the new label.

To format a drive, right-click the drive icon, and click Format.

To make a system disk or diskette, right-click the drive icon and choose Format. If you want to format the diskette and make it bootable, select the Full option button, and mark the Copy system files check box under Other options (see Figure 9-8). If the disk is already formatted, select the Copy system files only option button, and click Start.

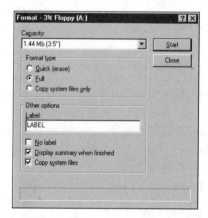

Figure 9-8: The Format dialog box. Mark the Copy system files only check box to make a system diskette of a formatted diskette. Select Full and Copy system files to format a bootable diskette.

To create an emergency boot diskette, click the Control Panel icon in the left pane of the Explorer window, double-click the Add/Remove Programs icon, click the Startup Disk tab, and then click the Create Disk button.

Change the font used

In the File Manager, you can choose what font you want to use to display files, and so on.

The font that the Explorer uses is determined by the Icon font setting in the Appearance tab of the Display Properties dialog box. Right-click the Desktop and click Properties. Click the Appearance tab, and then select Icon in the Item drop-down list. Choose the desired font and size, and click OK.

Print a directory listing

Tip

You can't print a directory listing in either the File Manager or the Explorer. In the File Manager, choose File, Run (or in the Explorer, click the Start button and click Run) and then type:

```
COMMAND/c DIR *.* >LPT1
```

This command prints a directory listing. You need to manually eject the last page on a laser printer. See Chapter 17 for more details on how to do this.

Put two directory listings side-by-side

The File Manager has a multidocument interface, which lets you compare two directories side-by-side, or show a source and destination directory within one window controlled by the File Manager.

The Explorer has a single-document interface. To get two copies of a folder or two different folders on the Desktop, you need to open two Explorers. If you want to arrange them next to each other, you need to minimize all other applications, and then right-click the Taskbar and choose Tile Vertically or Tile Horizontally from the context menu.

The Explorer has a stronger mechanism for expanding the folder tree, which allows you to copy and move files and folders between folders without needing two separate windows, as you do with the File Manager.

Click the plus and minus signs next to folder names in the Explorer to expand and collapse branches of the folder tree. This doesn't affect the contents of the right pane.

The Explorer shows all your disk drives in one folder tree; you don't need two windows to see more than one disk drive's folders.

Sort files by name, date, file type, size

The File Manager lets you click a toolbar icon or choose a menu item to sort your files. The order is fixed for each variable: ascending for name, descending for date, and so on.

The Explorer lets you sort on name, date, file type, or size in all four icon views (the File Manager has only two icon views). It also lets you order your files and folders by ascending or descending order. If you sort by type, the Explorer sorts on the file type name, while the File Manager sorts alphabetically by extension.

Tip

If you're using details view in the Explorer (View, Details), you can sort files or folders by clicking any of the gray header buttons at the top of the right pane. Click twice to reverse the sort order.

View file contents

The File Manager doesn't have a set of file viewers that let you see the file without launching the program that created the file.

The Explorer comes with a raft of file viewers that Microsoft calls *Quick Viewers*. You can access them by right-clicking a file. You can put the Quick View manager in the SendTo folder. (Quick View is actually a stripped-down version of the popular Outside In program for Windows from Inso Corp., which also markets additional Quick Viewers.)

Undo and Delete

Undo is not available in the File Manager. The Explorer has an Undo command on the context menu that lets you undo rename, copy, move, and delete operations. You can also recover a previously deleted file from the Recycle Bin.

When you delete a file using the File Manager, you have to confirm that you want to delete the file. If you do, it's gone (unless you use the DOS program Unerase). If you delete a file using the Explorer, it goes to the Recycle Bin, and you can recover the file later if you realize you acted in haste (unless you turned off this capability or you deleted the file from a removable or network drive).

Share a disk drive or folder

In the Explorer, right-click on the folder or drive icon and choose Sharing. This option isn't available in the File Manager.

Customize the toolbar

The File Manager lets you customize the toolbar. Just double-click it.

You can't do this with the Explorer. You can customize the context menu, although it is more difficult.

See hidden files

In the File Manager, you can see a file with the hidden or system attribute turned on if you choose View, By File Type, Show Hidden/System Files.

The Explorer automatically hides files with certain extensions unless you choose View, Options, View and turn off this option.

If you have installed Internet Explorer 4.0, it ghosts the hidden file icons so you can quickly see that these hidden files are actually half hidden. It's kind of cute.

See free disk space

Both the Explorer and the File Manager show the available disk space in the status bar.

File attributes

The File Manager displays the file attribute for all the files at once in its All File Details view.

If you installed Internet Explorer 4.0, the Explorer displays file attributes in its detail view. In earlier versions of Windows 95, you have to right-click a file and choose Properties to see the file attributes for that one file. If you select multiple files and then right-click any of the selected files and choose Properties, Windows 95 shows you the common file attributes for the selected files.

File size

The File Manager displays a greater degree of precision than the Explorer when giving the file size. The Explorer only shows the number of bytes to the nearest 1K.

Additional File Manager strengths

The File Manager is very fast. You can ask the File Manager to minimize itself after you start a file by double-clicking it in the File Manager.

Additional Explorer strengths

The Explorer gives you immediate access to the Control Panel, Network Neighborhood, the Printers folder, Dial-Up Networking, Scheduled Tasks (if you have installed Internet Explorer 4.0), and so on.

You can use the universal naming convention (UNC) to access a networked drive without having to map it to a drive letter.

Summary

The Explorer is the most powerful tool that Windows 95 provides to manage your computer. Unfortunately, much of its power is hidden.

▶ Use the Explorer to navigate throughout your computer and the network connected to your computer.

▶ We show how to make sure that file types aren't hidden from your view.

▶ We reveal the hidden command line parameters that determine how the Explorer behaves.

▶ We show you how to put the Explorer on the Desktop, or just about anywhere that makes sense to you.

▶ If you know how to use the Explorer, you can quickly copy and move files and folders around on your computer.

▶ The Explorer and My Computer come with keyboard shortcuts, and we show you what they are.

▶ We show you how to size and display the Explorer or multiple Explorers on your Desktop.

▶ We compare what the Windows 3.*x* File Manager does with how the Explorer handles the same tasks.

Chapter 10

Using Shortcuts to Open Up Your Computer

In This Chapter

Shortcuts make your Windows 95 computer a lot easier to use. We discuss:

▶ Putting shortcuts to anything in your computer on your Desktop

▶ Viewing any document with a shortcut to the Quick View file viewers built into Windows 95

▶ Starting any program when Windows 95 starts

▶ Copying, moving, opening, compressing, and viewing files easily with Send To

▶ Starting DOS programs and DOS/Windows batch files from icons

▶ Starting different versions of your applications with different icons

▶ Printing files by dragging and dropping them to an icon on the Desktop

▶ Making the full power of your computer visible

▶ Making sure your applications can find all their accessory files without having to add folder names to your Path statement in your Autoexec.bat file

What's a Shortcut?

We want to clear up something right away. We use the word *shortcut* to mean two very different things in this book. When we say something like *keyboard shortcut*, we mean a keystroke that does something that otherwise would have taken a bunch of keystrokes or a lot of mousing around. The *shortcuts* we talk about in this chapter refer to icons that represent, and are linked to, applications and documents.

This kind of shortcut is a shortcut in the sense that you don't have to use the Explorer or My Computer windows to find your document or application. You can just put a shortcut (a link) to it in a convenient place. Double-clicking the shortcut is the same as — and sometimes even better than — double-clicking the original file.

Didn't Windows 3.1 have something like shortcuts? Yes, the Program Manager was full of them. You could drag a file from the File Manager and drop it on the Program Manager to create a new program item within a program group. Double-clicking the program item started the application or opened a file with its associated application (if its file type was registered).

Shortcuts have escaped the confines of the Program Manager. They are no longer limited just to files and applications. No longer babies crawling on their hands and knees, they are on their way to high school.

Shortcuts are easily recognizable because the lower-left corner of a shortcut icon has a curved black arrow in a little white box. This icon on an icon shows up automatically when you create a shortcut. Take a look at the example in Figure 10-1.

Figure 10-1: A shortcut icon. All shortcut icons have a black arrow in a little white box in the lower-left corner.

An important fact to remember is that if you delete a shortcut icon from the Desktop (or anywhere else, for that matter) you have deleted only the shortcut, not the item to which the shortcut points. But if you move an actual file to the Desktop and then delete that file's icon, you have deleted the file.

If you attempt to delete the icon of a program on your computer, you receive this warning from Windows 95: "The file *appname.exe* is a program. If you remove it, you will no longer be able to run this program or edit some documents. Are you sure you want to delete it?" If you answer yes, Windows 95 sends the program file to the Recycle Bin, unless you held down the Shift key when you pressed Delete or you have configured the Recycle Bin to purge deleted files. In all these cases, the program will no longer be available. So be careful out there.

Shortcuts Are Great (Here's Why)

Just because a folder is a good place to store something doesn't mean that it's a convenient place to go when you want to get the item you stored. You probably have really good reasons for putting some files or applications in a particular folder, but it also makes perfect sense to give yourself a way to get at them quickly.

Disk drives are getting big. The amount of information that can be stored on one can quickly overwhelm the most meticulous person. If you stack a lot of boxes in a room, you're going to have a hard time getting around in it.

Our computers are getting hooked up ever more tightly to other people's computers. We're looking for stuff on their machines and they are doing the same on ours. A gigabyte here, a gigabyte there, and pretty soon it adds up to real chaos.

Shortcuts make your information much more accessible. Microsoft has made shortcuts flexible and powerful. It isn't obvious at first, but you will soon discover that Windows 95 shortcuts are a huge improvement in the Windows interface. They will help you be more productive.

You can even make shortcuts to web pages. Double-click a shortcut to a web page, and the Internet Explorer will start, dial up your Internet service provider (if that is how you are connected to the Internet) and take you to the target web page.

The same thing is true if you are on a local area network and want to get to a page on your Intranet web server. You can use shortcuts in the Favorites list to quickly get to your favorite web sites. Shortcuts not only open up your computer and your network, they open up the Internet.

Put your favorite files and programs on the Desktop

Your Desktop is an icon container, and the perfect spot for shortcuts. It may remind you of the Windows 3.*x* Program Manager. You don't really want to put your documents or applications on your Desktop. Keep them in the folders that they share with other similar applications and files. For example, keep all your game applications in subfolders of the Games folder, but put shortcuts to your favorite games on the Desktop.

Put shortcuts to documents on the Desktop — just the ones that you are currently working on. Working on a set of similar documents? Create a shortcut to the folder that holds them.

If you want a bunch of similar applications on the Desktop, but not covering the Desktop, put a folder (or, even better, a shortcut to a folder) on the Desktop and put shortcuts to the applications in the folder. This is sort of like a Windows 3.*x* Program Manager program group.

Want the Explorer on the Desktop? Put a shortcut to Explorer.exe on the Desktop, but leave the file Explorer.exe where it belongs, in the \Windows folder.

Tip

Wouldn't it be convenient to drag and drop files to the Quick Viewer so you could take a peek at their content? Put a shortcut to \Windows\System \Viewers\Quickview.exe on the Desktop and rename it Quick Viewer.

If you put a shortcut to your printer on your Desktop, you can drag and drop a document to your printer.

Remember — the Desktop is itself a subfolder of the \Windows folder. Its full pathname is C:\Windows\Desktop. You usually don't want to *move* files to the Desktop folder. Instead, you want to create *shortcuts* in the Desktop folder, and these shortcuts will appear on your Desktop.

Automatically start programs when Windows starts

You no doubt have some programs that you want to start when you start Windows.

You can put shortcuts to these programs into the Startup folder, and leave the programs where they are. The Startup folder is very similar to the Startup program group in the Windows 3.*x* Program Manager.

Undocumented

Want to make sure that the programs start in the order that you want them to? It's easy.

Create a DOS batch file that is nothing but a series of calls to the programs you want to start, in the order that you want, preceded by the Start command. For example:

```
start Winapp1.exe
start Winapp2.exe
start Winapp3.exe
```

Create a shortcut to this batch file in the Startup folder.

The Start button is full of shortcuts — add more

Like a hierarchical version of the Windows 3.*x* Program Manager, the Start menus cascading across the Desktop are filled with shortcuts. When you install a Windows 3.*x* application under Windows 95, it thinks it is creating a program group. In fact, it is creating a folder full of shortcuts to the application and its companion files.

Shortcuts in the Start menu make it easy to get to applications. Click the Start button and follow the menus out to the shortcut to the application you want.

Tip

You can put a shortcut on the Desktop (or in any folder) to a folder that holds the shortcuts to a set of documents or applications — shortcuts within a shortcut to a folder. Right-drag a folder from the Start Menu folder (in the Explorer, not from the Start menu itself) to the Desktop and drop it. Here are the steps:

STEPS

Putting a Shortcut to a Start Menu Folder on the Desktop

Step 1. Right-click the Start button. Click either Open or Explore.

Step 2. Double-click the Programs icon if you want a folder further down the hierarchy of Start menus, for example, the Accessories folder.

Step 3. Right-drag a Start menu folder to the Desktop and click Create Shortcut(s) Here after you drop it.

You now have part of your Start menu on your Desktop. You can add or remove shortcuts from this folder with ease just by dragging and dropping. Adding and removing shortcuts from this folder adds and removes the same shortcuts in the target Start menu.

Move, copy, compress, print, and view files and folders easily

Put shortcuts to your Briefcase software, default file opener, Quick Viewer, printer, file compression program, or whatever into your SendTo folder. Then, whenever you right-click a file or folder, you have the option of sending it to one of these destinations.

Send a file to the shortcut for your default file opener, and the application opens it. Send a file of an unregistered type to the shortcut for Quick Viewer, and the viewer does its best to display the file.

We use the ability to send a file to WinZip (featured on the *Windows 95 Secrets* CD-ROM) all the time. Right-click a file, click Send To, click WinZip, enter the name of the compressed file to be created, and it's done.

Start DOS programs by double-clicking icons

Put a shortcut to DOS on your Desktop. There's already one in your Start menu, but it's that much closer if it is on the Desktop (at least when the Desktop isn't covered up).

You can create shortcuts to all your DOS programs. You can use icons from any icon library or from the files that come with Windows 95. You can treat your DOS programs just like Windows programs. Why not? Most DOS programs run fine in a window.

Use a shortcut to do more than one thing at a time

Create a shortcut to a DOS batch file that calls a Windows program in addition to calling some DOS functions. This is a neat way to do programming, given that Microsoft does provide a Windows batch language. You can combine DOS and Windows programs in the batch file, and they can all do more together. Here's an example that uses a couple of proprietary DOS utilities:

```
echo off
:: The next line switches COM2 from modem to port
c:\util\ams\encom
:: The next line runs the Direct Cable Connection
:: Start /w is used to suspend the batch file processing
start /w c:\Windows\Directcc.exe
:: This utility switches COM2 back to the internal modem
c:\util\ams\modem
```

The Start command is described in Chapter 17.

Modify how a Windows program operates

A shortcut allows you to combine the call to your Windows application with some of its command line parameters. The Windows Explorer shortcut on the Start, Programs menu is a good example of this (see Chapter 9).

If your program has the ability to take command line parameters, you can create different versions of the command line in different shortcuts to the same program. Who cares if it is just one program behind the scenes (behind the shortcut)? If it acts differently when you call it with one shortcut than with another shortcut, it might as well be a different program.

Use a different program to open a document

If you have a shortcut to a document, you can change the application that opens or acts on that document. The default shortcut just names the document and its path. Insert the name of the application that you want to act on the document into the definition of this shortcut (in the Target field) to override the file/application association found in the Registry.

The properties sheet for such a shortcut is displayed in Figure 10-2. The name of the application (and any command line parameters) precedes the name of the file. If the pathname to the application includes a space, surround the pathname and filename with double quotes.

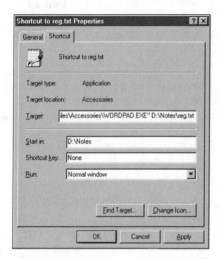

Figure 10-2: The properties sheet for a shortcut to a file ending in the *txt* extension. By default, Windows associates *txt* files with Notepad. To override this file association, we have specified that the WordPad application open this file. The file is too big for Notepad.

Put shortcuts to parts of documents on the Desktop

You can copy a paragraph from a document and paste a shortcut to it on the Desktop. Just highlight the paragraph, issue the Copy command, right-click the Desktop, and click Paste Shortcut.

The "scrap" on the Desktop is now a piece of data or text you can insert into another document. If you double-click it, Windows 95 invokes the application that created it, and the scrap is displayed in the application's window. The application that opens the document must be OLE-enabled.

Send shortcuts through (some of) the mail

You can paste a shortcut to a document into an e-mail message, and send the message over Microsoft Mail on your local area network. The recipient can open the document by clicking the shortcut icon if the document is stored in a shared folder or disk drive. All you have to send by mail is the shortcut, not the document itself. One advantage of e-mailing shortcuts is that you don't overburden the e-mail post office with numerous documents.

You can e-mail shortcuts to other Microsoft Network users by sending shortcuts to Microsoft Network bulletin boards, chat areas, documents, and so on. Users can double-click the shortcut and go to the targeted area or document.

You can e-mail shortcuts to people over the Internet as long as their mail clients can handle attachments in MIME or UUENCODE format. You can put shortcuts to various Internet sites in an e-mail attachment. When the recipient double-clicks a shortcut in the attachment, it launches his or her browser, which then jumps to the targeted site or document.

(If you have Office 97, you'll notice that e-mail and Internet addresses in documents are automatically live. You can click on them and immediately call up your e-mail client or web browser to send e-mail or go to the web site.)

Creating Shortcuts

The whole point of shortcuts is to put them in convenient places, which include the Desktop, the Start menu, the SendTo folder, folders on the Desktop, and whatever windows you regularly have open on the Desktop. You can put shortcuts wherever you want, but then, what's the point of some of the possible locations?

Drag and drop to create a shortcut

Undocumented

If you drag and drop a binary executable file to a folder or to the Desktop, Windows 95 automatically creates a shortcut to the file. Executable files have *exe*, *com*, or *bat* extensions. However, *bat* files are a major exception to this rule. If you drag a *bat* file to the Desktop, it gets *moved* — a shortcut is *not* created. (Files that end with the *pif* extension used to be executable files. They are now shortcuts.)

If you left-drag a binary executable file icon from a folder or Explorer window into another window or onto the Desktop, you will see a black curved arrow in the lower-left corner of the transparent file icon. This tells you that Windows 95 will create a shortcut if you release the left mouse button.

Undocumented

You can choose to create a shortcut when you drag and drop an icon by holding down the Ctrl and Shift keys. You can also do this by right-dragging the icon. In both cases, you will get a context menu asking if you want to Move Here, Copy Here, Create Shortcut(s) Here, or Cancel the operation. To explicitly create a shortcut with drag and drop, click Create Shortcut(s) Here from the context menu.

Name that shortcut

Tip

You can change the name of a shortcut. It is a good idea to change the name to something meaningful, rather than a short filename. Don't hold back; make the names work for you.

If a shortcut icon is already highlighted, press F2 to invoke the rename function. If it isn't highlighted, right-click the icon and then click Rename on the context menu. When you see a black box around the name, type the new name, and then press Enter.

Give your shortcuts names that are long enough to be meaningful, but not so long that they fill up the Desktop. Windows 95 wraps names to fit in the icon grid on the Desktop. It shortens single words with ellipses.

You can't use the following symbols in a shortcut name:

/ * ? .< > |

Get rid of "Shortcut to"

Do you get tired of seeing "Shortcut to" as the first part of your shortcut's name? You can teach Windows 95 to quit putting it on every shortcut that you create. To give Windows 95 the idea of how you want to do things, place one shortcut after another on your desktop. After you create each one, edit the name of the shortcut to remove "Shortcut to." After seven or eight shortcuts, Windows 95 wises up and quits putting "Shortcut to" in the name of the newly created shortcut. However, this workaround is far from ideal, as explained in the next few paragraphs.

The "Shortcut to" workaround is an experiment by Microsoft to add adaptive behavior to Windows 95. In other words, the operating system "notices" what the user is doing and adjusts its behavior to fit the user's preferences.

The implementation of such adjustments is maintained in the Registry. When you start Windows 95 for the first time, a value named *link* is set to a default value of 20. Every time you create a shortcut, this value is increased by 1 and written to the Registry. If you have created any shortcuts, you should be able to fire up Regedit.exe and see the value of *link* by selecting HKEY_CURRENT_USER\Software\Microsoft\Windows\Current Version\ Explorer. The value of *link* is stored in hexadecimal math, so the number 21 will look like 15, and so on.

Each time you rename a shortcut to remove the "Shortcut to" prefix, the value of *link* is reduced by 5. When *link* equals zero, Windows 95 stops adding the prefix to your shortcuts.

So far, so good. But a bug in the adaptive behavior prevents this from being a permanent fix. If *link* equals zero and you restart Windows, the value is set back to 20 — as if you'd just installed Windows 95.

Fortunately, there's an easier way to defeat this behavior than manually renaming shortcuts every time you start Windows. Download PowerToys from the Microsoft web site. It includes a Control Panel applet called TweakUI that turns off the behavior from a dialog box. To download PowerToys, just set your Web browser to http://www.microsoft.com/windows/software/powertoy.htm.

Cut and paste a shortcut

You can create a shortcut whose first location is the same folder as the application or document itself and then move it to the folder that you want. Right-click an icon in a folder window or the Explorer and click Create Shortcut. A shortcut to the file that you right-clicked will appear.

You can then move the shortcut out of this folder to your desired destination by using the Cut and Paste commands (see Chapter 8). This combined method avoids dragging and dropping.

Create a new "unattached" shortcut, then create the link

You can create a new shortcut first, and link it to an application or document second. (You can't use this method to create a shortcut to a folder.) To do this, take the following steps:

STEPS

Creating a New Shortcut

Step 1. Right-click the Desktop or a folder or Explorer window. Point to New, and click Shortcut. This launches the Create Shortcut Wizard, as shown in Figure 10-3.

Step 2. Type the complete path and filename of the program, document, or file that you want to create the shortcut to. Click the Browse button if you would rather find the file instead of typing in the name.

Step 3. Click the Next button. You can type a new name for the shortcut or leave the default name (the name of the file you linked to).

Step 4. Click the Finish button.

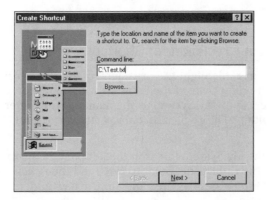

Figure 10-3: The Create Shortcut Wizard. You can type the path and filename of the application, document, or file that you want to create a shortcut to, or you can click the Browse button to look for the file.

Shortcuts on the Desktop

The Desktop is like any other folder, except that it is always open on the Desktop, so to speak. Drag an application icon from a folder or Explorer window and drop it on the Desktop and you automatically create a shortcut. Right-click the Desktop, point to New, and click Shortcut to create a new shortcut on the Desktop.

Tip

You can create folders on the Desktop and put shortcuts in them. This a handy way to put a lot of stuff on the Desktop without cluttering it up. To do this, right-click the Desktop, point to New, and click Folder. You can change the folder name at any time.

The new folder is now a subfolder of the C:\Windows\Desktop folder. You can use the Explorer to find the Desktop folder. Click the plus sign next to the Windows folder icon in the folder tree and you will see it (if you have configured the Explorer to show all files with View, Options, View).

Tip

You can drag and drop shortcuts to the new folder on your Desktop. Double-click the new folder to open its folder window. Right-drag icons from other folder windows and drop them onto the new folder window. Click Create Shortcut(s) Here.

Creating a Shortcut to a Folder of Shortcuts

Tip

You don't have to put a folder of shortcuts on the Desktop. Instead, you can put a shortcut to a the folder on the Desktop. To do this, use the Explorer to find an appropriate location for a folder that will contain shortcuts. You might, for example, create an AllGames subfolder under your Games folder.

STEPS

Creating a Shortcut to a Folder of Shortcuts

Step 1. In the Explorer, highlight the drive icon of your boot drive. Right-click the the right pane of the Explorer window. Point to New and click Folder. Type **My System** as the name for the folder. You can use this folder to store files that are particular to your Windows 95 setup.

Step 2. Highlight the My System folder in the left pane of the Explorer, right-click the right pane, point to New, and then click Folder. Type **Desktop Folders** as the name for the new folder.

Step 3. Highlight Desktop Folders in the left pane of the Explorer, right-click the right pane of the Explorer window, point to New, and then click Folder. Type the name of a folder that will hold shortcuts to documents or applications of a certain type. For example, **Graphics**.

Step 4. Right drag the Graphics folder icon to the Desktop and click Create Shortcut(s) Here.

Step 5. You can now drag and drop shortcuts to graphics files and/or graphics applications to this Graphics folder shortcut on the Desktop. These shortcuts will actually be stored in the \My System\Desktop Folders\Graphics folder, but they will be visible and available via the shortcut to the Graphics folder sitting on your Desktop.

You now have a shortcut to a Graphics folder on your Desktop. You can double-click the shortcut to display the contents of the Graphics folder. You can drag and drop icons to it to create shortcuts that will be stored within the folder.

Shortcuts to Folders, Disks, Computers, Printers, and On and On

You can have shortcuts to items other than files, documents, or applications. The following sections describe some suggested shortcut opportunities.

Folders

Let's say that you are working on documents you have placed in the C:\JonesAccount\BillsIssues folder. You can right-drag this folder from a folder window or Explorer onto the Desktop, and then choose Create

Shortcut(s) Here in the context menu. Double-clicking the shortcut to the BillsIssues folder quickly displays the contents of the folder in a folder window.

Disk drives

Tip

Right-drag a drive icon from the Explorer and drop it on the Desktop. The context menu will let you choose only between Create Shortcut(s) Here and Cancel. You'll find it particularly useful to create shortcuts to mapped drives representing shared resources (folders or drives) located on other peer computers or server computers.

Do you want to know the properties of a hard disk whose shortcut icon you have on your Desktop? Right-click the shortcut, click Properties, click the Shortcut tab, click the Find Target button, right-click the target drive icon in the folder window, and click Properties.

Computers

You can put a shortcut to an entire computer on the Desktop (or anywhere you like). Right-click the My Computer icon on the Desktop and click Create Shortcut. You've got yourself a shortcut on the Desktop to something already on the Desktop.

Undocumented

You can also do this with networked computers, even computers that you remotely dial into. Just right-drag them out of Network Neighborhood and onto the Desktop (or another folder window), and choose Create Shortcut(s) Here. If you are dialing into the computer through remote access, you can put a shortcut to the computer on your Desktop and initiate the call by double-clicking the computer's shortcut icon.

Printers

Right-drag a printer icon out of your Printers folder and drop it on the Desktop. Click Create Shortcut(s) Here. Now you can drag and drop files to the printer.

Control Panel icons

Open the Control Panel (Start, Settings, Control Panel). Right-drag one of the icons from the Control Panel to the Desktop, to a folder on the Desktop, or to a shortcut to a folder on the Desktop. Click Create Shortcut(s) Here. Now you have immediate access to whatever that icon does. Want to keep changing your mouse properties? You got it.

We would like to thank Matthias Koenig for his great investigative work in finding the following undocumented features.

Undocumented

To display the Device Manager the "long way," you right-click My Computer, click Properties, and then click the Device Manager tab of the System Properties dialog box. Want to put a shortcut to the Device Manager on your Desktop? Take the following steps:

STEPS

Creating a Shortcut to the Device Manager

Step 1. Right-click the Desktop, point to New, and then click Shortcut.

Step 2. In the Command line field type

C:\Windows\Control.exe Sysdm.cpl, System,1

Click Next.

Step 3. Type **Device Manager** in the Name field. Click Finish.

Undocumented

You normally display the Settings tab of the Display Properties dialog box by right-clicking the Desktop and choosing Properties (or double-clicking the Display icon in the Control Panel), and then clicking the Settings tab. How about a shortcut to this properties sheet?

STEPS

Creating a Shortcut to the Display Control Panel

Step 1. Right-click the Desktop, point to New, and then click Shortcut.

Step 2. In the Command line field type

C:\Windows\Control.exe Desk.cpl, Display,3

Click Next.

Step 3. Type **Display Settings** in the Name field. Click Finish.

The format of the above examples is

```
Control.exe {cpl filename} {,applet name} {,tab#}
```

You can find the *cpl filename* of any of the Control Panel icons by searching (using Find as detailed in Chapter 11) for files with the *cpl* extension in the \Windows\System folder. The *applet name* you can find by looking in the

Control Panel. Double-click any of the Control Panel icons to figure out the applet's tab number (if any). In the dialog box that appears, count the tabs, starting with 0 for the first tab on the left.

HyperTerminal connections

Right-drag the desired connection icon out of the HyperTerminal folder (open it from Start, Programs, Accessories, HyperTerminal). Drop it on the Desktop and click Create Shortcut(s) Here. Now when you want to call, double-click the connection's shortcut icon on the Desktop.

Shortcuts to files far, far away

You can create a shortcut to a document that resides on a computer that you have to dial into with Dial-Up Networking. If you double-click the shortcut for the file, your modem dials the phone number and makes the connection to the other computer. Once it gets into the other computer, the linked document is displayed on your Desktop.

Mail out shortcuts

You can mail a shortcut by dragging and dropping it into an e-mail message. When the recipient receives the message, he or she can access the file or folder that is linked to the shortcut by double-clicking the shortcut in the mail message. This works with Microsoft Mail and with the Microsoft Network. You can also mail shortcuts to web sites, ftp sites, and so on.

Paste shortcuts into documents

Microsoft has attempted to blur the line between the shell (the Desktop or user interface) and the Windows applications that you use while in Windows 95. The fact that Cut and Paste are now part of the Windows user interface is one example of this.

Another is the fact that you can place shortcuts — which you place in folders for the most part — in documents and e-mail messages. To paste a shortcut into your document, right-click a shortcut in a folder, click Copy, right-click the client window area in your word processor, and then click Paste.

As an example of when this would be useful, you can give someone a document that contains shortcuts to other documents on the Internet. The recipient can then double-click the shortcuts to access to the latest versions of all the targeted documents. When you double-click a shortcut in a document, Windows 95 takes the appropriate actions to retrieve that document from wherever it is.

And on and on

Do the same for Direct Cable Connection, Dial-Up Networking, Phone Dialer — whatever you want or need on the Desktop. The idea is to not hold back. Make your computer convenient for you. Put the shortcuts where they do the most good for you.

Don't hide your computer under a bush or in the Explorer. The Explorer is obviously well named: You use it when you have to go exploring for the functionality that you want. Shortcuts can help you reduce this work to a minimum.

Right-Click to a Powerhouse

Secret

Placing shortcuts in the SendTo folder can turn your context menu into a powerhouse. The Send To command is on almost all context menus. And it doesn't really mean *send to*. It means *drop this file on this application or folder*.

However the recipient application or folder deals with drag and drop is how the application reacts when something is sent to it. You can modify the application's behavior using command line parameters. (See the section later entitled *The Target field*.)

Applications in the Send To menu are like commands on the context menu. You can do such things as send files to be compressed in the background, print files, view files, or open files with a particular editor. The difference is that with the Send To menu items, you don't have to associate a file type with an action as you would to create a context menu item. You can just send any file to an application in the Send To menu and let it take the action.

Tip

Use the Explorer to expand your folder tree so you can see the \Windows\SendTo folder. To see how Send To works, right drag and drop a printer icon from your Printers folder to the SendTo folder to create a shortcut to the printer. Now when you want to send a file to the printer, you can right-click the file, point to Send To in the context menu, and click on the shortcut to your printer in the Send To submenu.

If you haven't turned off (using TweakUI) the "Shortcut to" text that gets added when you create shortcuts, you'll probably want to edit the names of these shortcuts to get rid of this extraneous text.

You can place other items in the SendTo folder: a shortcut to a folder on a server computer perhaps; a shortcut to an application that you want to use to open files of unregistered types (see Chapter 13); or a shortcut to the Quick Viewer (Quickview.exe in the \Windows\System\Viewers folder).

Undocumented

When you use Send To, Windows 95 acts as though you used your left mouse button and dragged the file or folder you right-clicked to the application, folder, or object in the Send To menu. For example, say you are using the Send To command to send a file to a folder. If the file is on the same disk drive (or volume) as the folder, it gets moved. If it is on another disk drive, it gets copied.

PowerToys, Microsoft's little user interface fixer-upper, contains a pair of SendtoX files that add four new destinations to your Send To menu: Send To Any Folder, Send To Clipboard As Contents, Send To Clipboard As Name, and Send To Command Line. If you don't like any of these destinations, you can delete them from the SendTo folder. You can download Powertoys.exe from http://www.microsoft.com/windows/software/powertoy.htm.

Send To Any Folder allows you to copy or move a file from one folder to any other folder. Using the Send to Any Folder's dialog box, you can browse to find the target folder, or find it in the Send to Any Folder's drop-down history list if it's a previous target.

Send To a Printer

If you have access to two or more printers — whether they are attached to your PC or to your network — you can Send To any of your printers. This is a lot faster than manually changing your current printer every time you want to print a document to one or the other.

One way to get a printer onto your Send To menu is to right-drag its icon from the Printers folder (in the Control Panel) to the C:\Windows\SendTo folder.

You can even have the same printer show up twice on the Send To menu with different settings — for instance, draft versus presentation quality. To do this, double-click the Add New Printer icon in the Printers window, then select a printer model you already have installed. When Windows asks if you want to "replace" or "keep" the existing driver, reply "keep" (unless you really do possess an updated driver).

After you finish installing this "new" printer driver, you should have a "Copy 2" icon in your Printers folder. Right-click this icon, click Properties, and configure this copy of your printer driver any way you like. Then right-drag it into the SendTo folder to create a shortcut to it. Your new alternate printer settings will appear on your Send To menu the next time you right-click a file icon.

Other things you may want to add to your Send To menu are the Desktop, the Start menu, and the Startup folder. To get these in the menu, right-drag the subfolders named Desktop, Start Menu, and Start Menu\Programs\ Startup from your \Windows folder to the \Windows\SendTo folder. When you find a file that you want on your Desktop, in your Start menu, or in your Startup folder, right-click the file, then point to Send To, and click on the desired option.

There are some caveats. Remember that when you drag a file to a folder in the Explorer, the file is *moved* if the folder is on the same drive, but *copied* if the folder is on a different drive. It works the same way if you send a file to a folder in the Send To menu. Also, if you send an executable file to the Desktop or to any part of the Start menu via the Send To command, the file doesn't get moved. Instead, Windows 95 creates a shortcut to the file (which is actually what you want).

Send To Send To

You can put a shortcut to the SendTo folder in the SendTo folder.

If you want to browse for executables that you want to put in the SendTo folder as targets, you can send them there easily by right-clicking them, pointing to Sent To, and then clicking Shortcut to Send To. A message box appears telling you that you cannot move or copy the executable to this location, and it asks if you want to create a shortcut instead, which you do.

Attempting to right-drag the SendTo folder from the left pane of the Explorer into the SendTo folder in the right pane doesn't work. All you get is Open and Cancel items on the context menu that appears — not Create Shortcut(s) Here.

What you need to do instead is right drag the SendTo folder from the right pane of the Explorer to the SendTo folder in the left pane.

Now browse through your whole system, looking for executable files that would be great targets for sending documents to. When you find one, right-click it and select Send To, Shortcut to Send To.

Send To the Desktop

You can create a shortcut to the Desktop folder, which is a subfolder of your \Windows folder. You can even create the shortcut on your Desktop. Then drag this shortcut to the SendTo folder, which is also a subfolder of your \Windows folder. This makes for an easy way to send stuff to the Desktop when it's not visible.

Create Shortcuts to DOS Programs

You can drag and drop a DOS application file to the Desktop or to a folder window just as easily as you can a Windows executable file. You automatically create a shortcut when you drop the file.

You'll probably want to make some changes to a DOS program's shortcut. You might want a different icon than the default MS-DOS icon that you get, and you may need to change some other properties as well. (All shortcuts have properties, which we'll get to in the next section.)

You can create a folder to store the shortcuts to your DOS programs, or you can mix these DOS program shortcuts with your Windows shortcuts. It's up to you.

If you have DOS files, such as files that you edit with the DOS Edit program, you can create shortcuts to these and store them on the Desktop or in a folder. The DOS programs and files can fit right in with the Windows programs and files, as long as they can run in a Windows DOS session.

Tip

You can run a mixture of DOS and Windows programs from a DOS batch file. Windows programs will run from the DOS prompt of a DOS virtual machine, so you can combine commands to run these programs with DOS programs.

You can call a DOS batch file with a shortcut, and the batch file can contain lines that start Windows programs. If you include the following command in a batch file, you can have a DOS batch file run a Windows program and wait for you to quit the Windows program to continue processing the commands in the batch file:

```
Start /w {Windows program}
```

We discuss many aspects of running DOS programs in Chapter 17.

What's Behind the Shortcut?

Right-click a shortcut and click Properties. A properties sheet similar to the one shown in Figure 10-4 will be displayed on your Desktop.

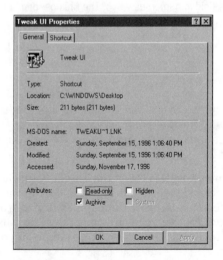

Figure 10-4: A shortcut's General properties sheet. You can change the file attributes if you like.

A shortcut has two properties sheets: General and Shortcut. The filename of the shortcut (after all, it is a file) has a *lnk* extension. A shortcut is a link (or *lnk*) to another file. The only things you can change on the General properties sheet are the file attributes of the shortcut file.

Click the Shortcut tab to display the Shortcut properties sheet, as shown in Figure 10-5.

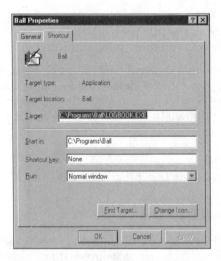

Figure 10-5: A shortcut's Shortcut properties sheet. The Target field contains the name of the target file. You can change this field in numerous ways. The Change Icon button lets you change the shortcut's icon.

The Target field

The Target field in the Shortcut properties sheet lists the file that is linked to the shortcut. You can modify this field in many ways. If the target file is an application that accepts command line parameters, you can include them after the application name.

Tip   If you want to view the document or data file in the Target field with an application other than the one assigned to this file's file type in the Registry, you can type the path and filename of the desired application in front of the file's path and filename. In addition, you can add command line parameters after the application's name to alter its behavior. For example, if you type this entry in the Target field:

```
"C:\Program Files\Accessories\Wordpad.exe" /p D:\Myfolder\Thisfile.txt.
```

The shortcut will print the file Thisfile.txt using WordPad.

Secret

The command line parameters in the Target field won't work if you drag a file to a shortcut. This is also true if you place a shortcut like this in the SendTo folder and then right-click a file and send it to the shortcut. Windows 95 acts as if the command line is as follows:

```
"C:\Program Files\Accessories\Wordpad.exe" %1
```

In this command line, %1 is the name of the dragged or sent file. The /p parameter is ignored.

The Start in field

The field now labeled *Start in* used to be called the Working Directory in Windows 3.*x*. This field is blank unless you put something in it. You may need to do this if the application in the Target field needs to find some application helper files in another folder and can't do so without help from you.

If the application doesn't require assistance in finding any helper files, you can make the Start in folder the folder that you want to contain the documents that use the application.

Hot keys

A *hot key*, which we also refer to as a *shortcut key* or an *accelerator key,* is a key combination that runs a shortcut. For example, press Ctrl+Alt+F and up pops FreeCell. Well, not actually, but it could if you defined the hot key for FreeCell. (If you're in Word for Windows, it opens the footnote pane.) Hot keys give you a keyboard method of quickly getting to the applications and files you use most often.

Secret

The problem with hot keys is that you have to remember which keyboard combination does what. (You also have to make sure you are not in a program that uses that hot key for another function.) When you use the mouse, the visual user interface gives you feedback that you are headed in the right direction. In contrast, you have to rely exclusively on your finger memory if you want to use hot keys. But then, to each his or her own.

To define a hot key, type the letter in the Shortcut key field. Crtl+Alt will automatically be added to and precede the letter, making the hot key Ctrl+Alt+{*letter*}. If you want Ctrl+Shift+{*letter*}, then hold down the Ctrl key and the Shift key as you press the letter.

You can also define hot keys for shortcuts to DOS programs. The Shortcut key field in a *pif* (the shortcut file to a DOS program) operates somewhat differently than it does in a shortcut to a Windows file. See Chapter 17 for more details.

If you have just created a shortcut, you have to restart Windows to have the hot key take effect.

Want to create a hot key to call the Task Manager? Why not create one that resembles the Windows 3.1 keystrokes that called it? How about Ctrl+Alt+~ (Ctrl+Alt+*tilde*)?

Just define a shortcut to the Task Manager, which you'll find in the \Windows folder, and put the shortcut in one of the Start menus or on the Desktop. Define the hot key for this shortcut and you're in business.

Run in which size window?

Most of the time you want a shortcut to display the application or document in its normal (restored) window, in other words, a window that is bigger than the button on the Taskbar, but smaller than the whole Desktop (minus the Taskbar). The Run field lets you choose among these three alternatives.

If the shortcut just prints a document, for example, you might as well leave it minimized. If you want the application or document to fill the whole Desktop, then choose Maximized.

Change the shortcut's icon

When you create a shortcut to an application, Windows 95 uses the first icon referenced in the application's executable file. Often this is adequate. If you have different shortcuts to the same application, though, you might want to distinguish them with different icons. You can choose among the icons that may be stored in the application's executable file (not all executable files have icons).

If your shortcut is to a document, Windows 95 chooses the first icon in the associated application's executable file. If a document doesn't have an associated application, then Windows 95 chooses the blank document icon. Just how documents get associated with applications is discussed in Chapter 13.

To browse for icons, click the Change Icon button. In addition to looking for icons in the application's executable file, you can look in many other executable files as well. Three files that contain icons are \Windows\Explorer.exe, \Windows\Moricons.dll, and \Windows\System\Shell32.dll.

Lots of icons are available to use with your shortcuts. You can pick icons from icon libraries distributed as shareware, or from other executable files. The shareware on the *Windows 95 Secrets* CD-ROM features numerous icon editors and managers. These applications search through your files and automatically create icon libraries. This cuts down on the time it takes to choose new icons.

Find that target

Tip

If you have a shortcut, you can get back to the file linked to the shortcut by clicking the Find Target button. This is helpful if you want to run the application without any of the command line switches you may have put in the Target field.

When you click the Find Target button, Windows 95 opens a folder window that contains the target. If the Target field contains an application, Windows 95 opens the folder that contains the application, even if the field also contains a document. If the Target field only contains a document, the folder window containing the document opens.

DOS shortcut sheets

If the shortcut targets a DOS application or a DOS file (a file whose file type is associated with a DOS application), you'll get a different set of shortcut properties sheets than the ones you get with Windows shortcuts. These sheets are so extensive and so interwoven with the workings of DOS programs under Windows 95 that we devote an entire chapter to them. Turn to Chapter 17 for further details.

Undocumented

The DOS shortcut sheets are stored in files that used to be called Program Information Files, or *pif*s. The shortcuts that link to Windows files use the *lnk* extension. The shortcuts that link to DOS files use the *pif* extension. You can see these extensions if you use the File Manager or a DOS window. The *pif* extension isn't visible in the Explorer or in a folder window.

There is a folder named \Windows\Pif. This folder can contain the *pif*s that are associated with DOS programs. Anytime you double-click a DOS program name in the Explorer, you create a default *pif* for it in the same folder as the DOS program, unless it can't be created there, in which case Windows 95 places it in the \Windows\Pif folder. For example, if the DOS program is in a folder on a CD-ROM, Windows 95 won't be able to place the *pif* file on the CD-ROM (when you double-click the DOS program) so it will put the *pif* in the \Windows\Pif folder. If you drag a shortcut to a DOS file or DOS application onto your Desktop, the *pif* is stored in \Windows\Desktop.

All *pif*s are shortcuts. You can open an Explorer window and focus on a folder that contains a *pif* to see that it has the little black arrow in the white box in the lower-left corner of the MS-DOS icon.

Secret

Let's say that you create a shortcut to a Windows file or application. Later you decide to change this shortcut and have it link to a DOS batch file that calls your Windows application after running some other functions. What happens to your shortcut?

Windows 95 automatically changes the *lnk* file to a *pif*. Easy as can be.

This doesn't work the other way. If you edit the Target field in a *pif* so that it refer to a Windows file, the *pif* does not automatically change to a *lnk* file.

Shortcuts on the Start Button

We discuss how to put shortcuts on the Start button and in the Start menus in Chapter 11.

A Shortcut to a Shortcut

In *Creating a Shortcut to a Folder of Shortcuts* earlier in this chapter, we showed you how to make a shortcut to a folder that contains shortcuts. Can you create a shortcut to a shortcut? After all, a shortcut is a file, and if we can have shortcuts to files, why not a shortcut to a shortcut file?

Right-drag one of the shortcut icons that you have created from its source folder and drop it on the Desktop. Click Create Shortcut(s) Here. Now, right-click the shortcut on the Desktop and click Properties. If this is a DOS link, or *pif,* you need to click the Program tab and look at the Cmd line field to see the equivalent of the Target field used for shortcuts to Windows files. If it is a Windows file shortcut, click the Shortcut tab, and look at the Target field.

Notice that the name in the Cmd line or Target field is not the name of the shortcut in the source folder, but rather the name of the file that the original shortcut is linked to. A shortcut to a shortcut isn't really a shortcut to a shortcut; it is a shortcut to the original file.

What Happens If I Move or Delete the Linked File?

Shortcuts are linked to a specific item — a file, a folder, and so on. If you move or delete that item, what happens when you double-click the shortcut?

If you have moved the item, Windows 95 tries to find it the next time you open its shortcut. While Windows 95 is searching, it displays the Missing Shortcut dialog box, as shown in Figure 10-6.

Figure 10-6: The Missing Shortcut dialog box. If you know where you moved the target, you can help out by clicking the Browse button.

When Windows 95 creates a shortcut, it records the creation time and date of the linked file or folder down to a fraction of a second and stores this information in the shortcut file. It is extremely unlikely that any two files or folders would be created at the same time and date to this level of precision.

Using a built-in function, Windows 95 begins searching for the lost file, folder, or object starting at its original location. You may have edited the file or changed its name — Windows 95 doesn't care, because it is searching on the file or folder's creation time/date.

The search method is not foolproof. If you move the target object (say a linked file) from one volume (say the D drive) to another volume (say the C drive), it won't find it. If your shortcut is to a file on a mapped networked drive, and the mapping of that drive changes (say from D to F), the link to the target is lost.

If you delete the file or folder, then of course Windows 95 won't find it. As it's looking, Windows 95 does keep track of the file or folder that is nearest in time/date to the actual linked item. If it can't find what it is looking for, it gives you the option of choosing the item closest in time, which can provide some weird "matches." You don't have to accept the file that Windows 95 suggests.

Shortcuts in the Help Files

The Windows 95 help files are filled with shortcuts that take you to the item that you have a question about. Of course, you may already be there.

The shortcut icon in the help file is a little like the black arrow used to indicate shortcut icons. It is a purple arrow curving to the upper-left corner instead of a black arrow curving to the upper-right corner.

Click the shortcut arrows in the help files to take the action that is explained in the sentence surrounding the arrow icon.

Creating Application-Specific Paths

If you start an application from a shortcut, you may find that it won't work because you haven't correctly identified the location of necessary accessory files in the Start in or Working directory (see Chapter 17). You might also want to be able to run an application from the Run dialog box (Start, Run) without specifying the path to the executable file.

Secret

By editing the Registry, you can associate a set of folders that house the accessory files an application needs to work correctly. In addition, you can specify the complete pathname to the application. Michael Giroux gave us the basis for these steps:

STEPS:

Specifying Paths to Applications in the Registry

Step 1.   Double-click Regedit.exe in your \Windows folder.

Step 2.   Click the plus signs in the left pane of the Registry to drill down to the following branch:

```
HKEY_LOCAL_MACHINE\SOFTWARE\Microsoft\Windows\
CurrentVersion\App Paths
```

Step 3.   Right-click the App Paths icon in the left pane, point to New, and then click Key. A new key folder appears in the left pane of the Registry editor. Type the name of the executable file, including the *exe* extension.

Step 4.   Double-click Default in the right pane while the new folder is highlighted in the left pane. Type the full path to the executable file in the Edit String dialog box. Click OK.

Step 5.   You will now be able to type the name of the executable file in the Run dialog box without the pathname and have the application actually run.

Step 6.   Define the path to the executable file's associated files by right-clicking the right pane of the Registry editor while the focus is on the new folder.

Step 7.   Point to New, then click String Value. Enter the name **Path** in the highlighted name field in the right pane of the Registry Editor.

Step 8.   Double-click Path in the right pane. In the Edit String dialog box, enter the complete path to the folders that contain the associated files. If there is more than one folder, separate the pathnames with semicolons. Click OK.

Step 9.   If you have any trouble with these steps, look at the other examples under the App Paths folder. When you are done, exit the Registry.

The paths that you entered in step 8 will be added temporarily to your path statement when you invoke the executable file, whether by double-clicking a shortcut to it, by entering its name in the Run dialog box, or by double-clicking it in the Explorer or a folder window.

Summary

Windows lets you put links to your applications and files on your Desktop and anywhere you find useful. Shortcuts are an incredibly powerful and convenient means of accessing resources on your computer.

▶ We show you how to use the power of shortcuts to put your most important applications and documents within easy reach.

▶ We guide you through the many ways of creating shortcuts.

▶ We show you how you can drag and drop files to a Desktop file viewer, a Desktop printer, or a default file opener.

▶ DOS and Windows applications can get along much better under Windows 95, and you can even make them appear to like each other.

▶ If you add application-specific paths to your Registry, you can run applications from the Run dialog box without specifying their paths.

Chapter 11

The Start Button and Finding

In This Chapter

You can mold the Start button to help you get at your applications more easily. We discuss:

▶ Shutting down Windows 95

▶ Optimizing your Start and Programs menus

▶ Deleting unwanted shortcuts to recent documents from your Documents menu

▶ Adding and removing items from your Start menus

▶ Putting the Desktop on the Start button

▶ Running the Start menus from the keyboard

▶ Creating and saving complex file searches

▶ Using Find to build Start menus and get rid of unwanted files

Starting

In Chapter 7, we looked at the Desktop and the Taskbar. The Start button is attached to the Taskbar, but there is so much going on with it that it gets its own chapter. It is the primary entry point into Windows 95. As you change your Desktop to match your needs, the Start button continues to provide many useful services.

The Start button is the Windows 95 replacement for the Windows 3.x Program Manager. And like the Program Manager, the Start button gives you a way to quit Windows.

You can also think of the Desktop as the Program Manager. You can fill it up with shortcuts. And if you put shortcuts to folders on the Desktop and fill the folders with shortcuts, these folders then look like program groups. But it is the Start button that inherits all the program groups and program items when you convert your existing Windows 3.x to Windows 95.

Secret

If you want, you can change the name on the Start button to something like Panic. The new name has to be five letters to exactly replace Start. You use a hex editor (see the *Windows 95 Secrets* CD-ROM) or WinHacker to edit the Explorer.exe file. This is truly a hack. Different versions of Windows 95 have different Explorer.exe files, so WinHacker may not work for you. WinHacker saves a good copy of Explorer.exe as Explorer.old in your \Windows folder before it makes the change, so you can recover by booting to the DOS prompt and copying the "old" Explorer over the hacked version. To change the name, replace all instances of *Start* in Explorer.exe with your new five letters (after you save a copy of original Explorer.exe).

Stopping

We start our discussion of the Start button by talking about the Stop button. The most important function you can find on a computer is how to stop it, how to get it ultimately under your control so that if you have any problems you can just stop the whole thing.

Click the Start button. Click Shut Down and select the first option button, Shut down the computer. We're outta here. We know it seems funny that the Start button is also the Stop button, but there it is.

Clicking Shut Down presents you with the dialog box shown in Figure 11-1. This dialog box gives you four choices. The default is Shut down the computer. You can also choose to Restart the computer, Restart the computer in MS-DOS mode, or Close all programs and log on as a different user. Depending on your configuration, you may not have the last option.

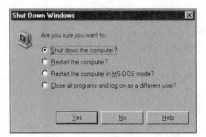

Figure 11-1: The Shut Down Windows dialog box. Make one of four choices.

Windows 95 always defaults to the Shut down the computer option unless you have installed Internet Explorer 4.0, in which case the default option is the one you chose the last time you made a selection in this dialog box.

Shut down the computer

Shut down the computer actually means to shut down Windows 95. Unless you have implemented the Windows 95 Advanced Power Management functions, you'll have to turn off your computer yourself.

Click the Yes button in the Shut Down Windows dialog box to shut down the computer. It is best to wait until you see the message "It's now safe to turn off your computer" before you actually flip the switch to power down your computer. If you turn off the power before this, the Registry files may not have been updated with the latest configuration information.

If you want to restart Windows, wait until you see the "It's now safe to turn off your computer" screen and then press Ctrl+Alt+Delete.

Undocumented

The Windows 95 shut down screens are Windows bitmap (*bmp*) files. Microsoft gave them *sys* extensions just to keep your prying eyes out of them. If you want to change them, you can edit them with MS Paint. Their names are Logos.sys and Logow.sys. You'll find them in the \Windows folder.

Undocumented

After you quit Windows 95, you are back under the control of Io.sys. If you had pressed the F8 key when the "Starting Windows 95" message appeared on your screen, and then started Windows 95 by typing **Win** and pressing the Enter key at the DOS command prompt, you would now be able to get back to real-mode DOS (to the DOS command prompt) by typing **mode co80** and pressing Enter when you see "It's now safe to turn off your computer."

There is a better way to do this, which you can check out in the *DOS after Windows* section of Chapter 17. But this method does illustrate that DOS is still there after you quit Windows 95. We don't suggest that you start Windows 95 in this manner, because it won't manage conventional memory as effectively as it normally does. One reason for this is that if you start Windows 95 this way, the real-mode compression driver Dblspace.bin is not unloaded and replaced by the protected-mode double-space driver.

Undocumented

Using Microsoft Plus! or other Windows 95-aware clock-tracking software and a shareware utility called Shutdown95, you can automatically close down Windows 95 at a pre-arranged time. You'll find Shutdown95 and ClockMan95 on the *Windows 95 Secrets* CD-ROM.

Troubleshooting Windows 95 shut down problems

If your computer hangs when you shut it down, you may have an incompatible device driver, incorrectly configured hardware, or other problems. Microsoft provides a detailed troubleshooting guide. You can find it in the Knowledge Base at http://www.microsoft.com/kb/articles/q145/9/26.htm.

Restart the computer

If you have had a problem with Windows 95 and just want to start over again, you can choose Restart the computer in the Shut Down Windows dialog box. This option works the same way as Shut down the computer, but it doesn't require that you press Ctrl+Alt+Delete to restart Windows 95. It also doesn't tell you when you can safely turn off your computer.

Windows 95 saves its Desktop configuration (open folders, for example) and then quits. As soon as it quits, it restarts with a warm reboot.

Undocumented

To restart Windows 95 quickly without going through the complete warm reboot process, hold down your Shift key while clicking the Yes button in the Shut Down Windows dialog box.

Restart the computer in MS-DOS mode

Choosing Restart the computer in MS-DOS mode means closing down Windows 95 and going to the DOS command prompt. Your computer isn't rebooted (not even a warm boot), so when DOS starts, it doesn't read a special Config.sys or Autoexec.bat file. Instead, it reads the file DOSstart.bat, which is located in your \Windows folder. You can get out of MS-DOS mode and back to Windows 95 by typing **Exit** or **Win** at the DOS prompt.

To get the full details on how to use this option to run recalcitrant DOS programs, turn to the *DOS in MS-DOS mode without a reboot* section of Chapter 17.

Log on as a different user

The option to Close all programs and log on as a different user doesn't even appear if you don't have a network, have never installed or used Direct Cable Connection, or haven't enabled user profiles. If you have done any of these things, you will see it.

"Close all programs and log on as a different user" is the same as "Restart the computer," but it lets you log on as a different user. Windows 95 keeps track of different users, so you can have different Desktop and network setups for each. This shut down option allows you to get out of the current user's setup and into a new user's configuration. Turn to Chapter 12 for more details.

Click Here to Begin, Boing . . .

Secret

When you first start Windows 95, you get a bouncing message in the Taskbar: "Click here to begin." We haven't seen this message in a while on our computers. The message goes away if you have applications in your Startup folder (or referenced in the run or load line in your Win.ini), if you left folders open when you last shut down, or if there are applications (such as the System Agent) in the Tray on your Taskbar.

Secret

You can get rid of this message manually by editing the Registry. Using the Registry editor, navigate to HKEY_CURRENT_USER\Software\Microsoft\ Windows\CurrentVersion\Policies\Explorer. Double-click NoStartBanner in the right pane. Enter the value **01 00 00 00**. You can make this same change at HKEY_USERS\.Default\Software\Microsoft\Windows\CurrentVersion\ Policies\Explorer.

If you would like to see this little pest come back, you need to be sure that none of the conditions described in the first paragraph in this section are true. In addition, Windows 95 beta tester John Bode tells us to take the following steps:

STEPS

Bring Back "Click here to begin"

Step 1. With no active tasks minimized or running (that is, you want an empty Taskbar with no Tray icons), press Ctrl+Alt+Delete. Highlight Explorer and click End Task.

Step 2. Answer No when asked if you want to shut down Windows 95.

Step 3. In about 15 – 20 seconds, a dialog box appears that says the Explorer is not responding. Click End Task.

Step 4. The Taskbar will now run the "Click here to begin" animation. There is no need to restart Windows 95.

TweakUI, which you can download from the Microsoft web site, http:// www.microsoft.com/windows/software/powertoy.htm, also lets you turn this annoying behavior on or off.

The Start Menu

Click the Start button and up pops the Start menu, as shown in Figure 11-2. This is the first of the cascading menus. The nice thing about the Start button is that it is a starting point. There never was much of a starting focus with the Windows 3.*x* Program Manager.

What is not so great about the Start button is that it takes a lot of mousing to get to where you want to be. Following the cascading menus to get to the application or document that you want can get pretty tedious. Turn to the *Change Menu Display Speed* section later in this chapter for details on how to make menus appear more quickly.

Figure 11-2: The Start menu — your window into the world of Windows 95. If you have Advanced Power Management enabled on your computer, you will see the Suspend command. If you haven't installed Internet Explorer 4.0, you won't see the Favorites command.

One way to cut down on extra mousing is to drag an icon for an application, folder, or document and drop it on the Start button to create a shortcut to the item in the main Start menu. We discuss Start menu shortcuts in more detail later in this chapter.

The Start menu has eight or nine items. The Programs menu at the top gets you to most of your applications. Favorites opens Internet Explorer 4.0 (if you have installed it) at a specific address that you choose. Documents is a list of the last 15 files that you double-clicked in an Explorer or a folder window. Settings gets you right to the Control Panel, Printers folder, or Taskbar — areas where you can update many Windows 95 properties. Find lets you search your computer, your LAN, the Internet, your e-mail and fax message store, or the Microsoft Network (MSN) for files, people, or services that meet criteria you define. Help is a combined help file for all of Windows 95. Run lets you type the name of an application that you want to run or a document that you want to work on (its associated application will load along with it). Suspend (if you have it) let's you put your computer in low power mode.

Programs

Notice the Programs icon in the Start menu. It looks like a folder window to remind you that the Programs menu is like a folder window that contains applications. Windows 95 comes with a collection of shortcuts to applications and accessory programs, which it stores in the \Windows\Start Menu\Programs folder. If you installed Windows 95 in your existing Windows 3.x directory, all your previous program groups are converted to folders and placed in the Programs folder as well. What you see in the Programs menu is the contents of the Programs folder.

You aren't restricted to putting applications in the Programs folder. You can organize it any way you want. You can put documents in the Programs folder just as you could with the program groups in the Windows 3.x Program Manager.

Unlike the Program Manager, which had only one level, you can have as many subfolders in the Programs folder as is practical, and they can each have subfolders. Each subfolder displays as a separate cascading menu (or submenu) in the Programs menu. Of course, the cascading menus can get pretty complicated after a while.

Using tools built into the Start button, you can easily organize everything in the Programs folder to suit your preferences. You can create a flat or hierarchical structure of subfolders. You can name the icons anything you want.

If you set up Windows 95 in a new folder, the Programs menu has three submenus and between two and five applications. If you set up Windows 95 over your existing Windows 3.x directory, you will have additional submenus.

To get to an application, click the Start button, move the mouse pointer over the Programs icon, and follow the cascading menus until you get to the application that you want to run. Click the application once to run it.

Can't find your application? We'll show you how in the *What you can do with Find* section later in this chapter.

Accessories menu

The Accessories submenu under the Programs menu contains a few of the new applications that come with Windows 95. You'll find games, faxing, WordPad, and other applications here.

Startup menu

If you have applications that you want to start when Windows 95 starts, you need to put shortcuts to them in this menu (which corresponds to the \Windows\Start Menu\Programs\Startup folder). You can close a program that started when Windows started any time you choose. If you then decide you want to start the program again, click the application in the Startup menu.

We show you how to put shortcuts in the Startup folder/menu later in this chapter.

Favorites

You won't find this Start menu item unless you have installed Internet Explorer 4.0. This is another way of starting the Internet Explorer and choosing a destination.

Documents

The last 15 documents that you started by double-clicking an icon in an Explorer or My Computer window are displayed in this menu. You can restart a document and its associated application by clicking it once in the Documents menu.

For Windows 95 to add a document to this list, you have to have started it from an Explorer or folder window. That way, Windows 95 can grab the document name. If you open a document from inside your application, Windows 95 doesn't know how to put it on the list. However, applications written specifically for Windows 95 can also place their newly opened documents on the menu.

The list contains shortcuts to the documents. You can delete all the shortcuts at once (without affecting the documents themselves). Right-click the Taskbar. Click Properties in the context menu. Click the Start Menu Programs tab, and click the Clear button. All the shortcuts in the Documents menu are gone.

Undocumented

You can also remove shortcuts individually. Windows 95 puts the shortcuts to your recently opened documents in the \Windows\Recent folder. You can edit these shortcuts or delete them as you like. You need to be sure that the Show all files option button is marked in the View tab of the Options dialog box (choose View, Options in any folder or Explorer window). Otherwise, the Recent folder will be hidden from view.

STEPS

Cleaning Up the Documents Menu

Step 1.   Open an Explorer window.

Step 2.   Click the plus sign next to the \Windows folder. Highlight the Recent subfolder under the \Windows folder.

Step 3.   The shortcuts to the documents are displayed in the right pane. You can delete them in any manner you choose.

You can use TweakUI to clear the Documents menu every time you restart Windows. Just click the Paranoia tab, and then click Clear Document history at logon. You can also use EZDesk or WinHacker. Check out the *Windows 95 Secrets* CD-ROM.

Put a shortcut to your recent documents folder on the Desktop

Tip

If you want to be able to quickly edit the contents of your recent documents folder, put a shortcut to it on the Desktop. Open the Explorer and focus on the \Windows\Recent folder. Right-drag the Recent folder to the Desktop and drop it there. Click Create Shortcut(s) Here. Edit the name of the shortcut folder icon to **Recent Docs** or whatever.

Now you can quickly get to the folder of recent documents and remove the documents that you don't care to have there.

Settings

Settings gets you down deep into Windows 95 if you follow it very far. It contains the Control Panel, the Printers folder, and the Taskbar properties sheets.

The Control Panel

Click the Control Panel menu item to bring up the Control Panel. You'll find lots of applications for configuring your computer and Windows 95.

Tip

The Control Panel is a special folder. It is hidden, so if you use the Explorer to look for a subfolder called Control Panel under your hard disk drive, you won't find one. You will see it in the Explorer in the left pane, on the same level as the local hard drives and the Printers folder, Fonts folder, and Dial-Up Networking folder. We discuss the Control Panel in Chapter 16.

You can use the System Policy Editor, as discussed in the section entitled *The Icons on the Desktop* in Chapter 7, to keep users out of the Control Panel.

The Printers folder

All your currently installed printers are stored in the Printers folder. This folder also contains the Add Printer icon, which lets you add new printers. You can reach the Printers folder through the Control Panel and the My Computer window as well as the Settings menu. The Printers folder is a special folder, so it only shows up in the left pane of the Explorer window. There are no files associated with the Printers folder (other than printer driver files) — just Registry settings. As you create new printers, their properties are stored in the Registry.

We cover the Printers folder in Chapter 23.

The Taskbar properties sheets

Clicking the Taskbar item (or Taskbar & Start Menu if you've installed Internet Explorer 4.0) in the Settings menu brings up the Taskbar Properties dialog box. You can display the same dialog box by right-clicking the Taskbar and choosing Properties. The first tab in the dialog box is Taskbar Options.

We describe the first two check boxes in the Taskbar Options tab in Chapter 7. The Show small icons in Start menu check box lets you change how the Start menu looks. Mark and clear this box to see which look you prefer. The Show Clock check box lets you choose whether or not to display the clock at the right end of the Taskbar.

The Start Menu Programs tab is where you will find much of the power to add, remove, clean up, and move menu items (which are just shortcuts) in the various Start menus. This properties sheet is shown in Figure 11-3.

Figure 11-3: The Start Menu Programs properties sheet. If you have an earlier version of Windows 95, you will have Add and Remove buttons instead of the Wizard button. The Wizard button adds additional Start menu cleanup capabilities.

If you have installed Internet Explorer 4.0, you can easily move items (those that can be moved) from one part of the Start button to another without invoking the Start Menu Wizard. Just drag a Start menu item from its present location to a new location on the start menu. This trick also works on the Favorites menu, both the one displayed on the Start menu and the one in My Computer and Explorer windows.

The Start Menu Organizer Wizard

If you have installed Internet Explorer 4.0, you can click the Wizard button in the Start Menu Programs tab of the Taskbar Properties dialog box to start the Start Menu Organizer Wizard, shown in Figure 11-4. This Wizard will help you semi-automatically clean up little problems often found in Start menus. You can add shortcuts to existing menus, create new menus, and remove menus and shortcuts you no longer want.

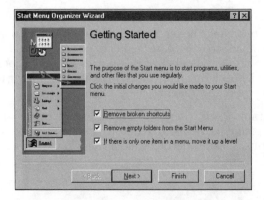

Figure 11-4: The Start Menu Organizer Wizard. The Wizard will help you clean up and customize your Start menu.

Add Start menu items

You can use the Start Menu Programs tab of the Taskbar Properties dialog box to add items to the Start menu, to the Programs menu, or to submenus of the Programs menu. If you have an earlier version of Windows 95, you click the Add button as shown in Figure 11-5 to launch the Create Shortcut Wizard. This Wizard lets you browse for the application you want to create a shortcut to, asks which Start menu you want to place it in, and asks what you want to call the item.

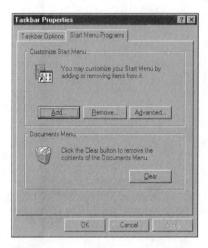

Figure 11-5: The Add button on the earlier Windows 95 version of the Taskbar Properties dialog box.

If you've installed Internet Explorer 4.0, you click the Wizard button in the Taskbar Properties dialog box to run the Start Menu Organizer Wizard. After you work through the first few Start Menu Organizer Wizard dialog boxes, you'll see a dialog box that contains an Add button to let you add items to the Start menu. You can browse to find the application file whose shortcut you want to add. In the next dialog box, you can choose an existing menu to place the item in, or you can create a new menu for the item. Following that is a dialog box that lets you choose a name for the item.

The menu items, which are after all shortcuts, don't display the little black arrow in the lower-left corner of their icons. We normally expect to see this black arrow on shortcut icons. Because all menu items are shortcuts, the Microsoft designers felt that there was no need to add the arrow to the icons displayed in the menus. Keep in mind that the menus themselves are not shortcuts, but rather subfolders of the \Windows\Start Menu folder.

Remove Start menu items

To remove menu items or entire menus, use the Remove button in the Start Menu Programs tab of the Taskbar Properties dialog box (if you have an earlier version of Windows 95) or the Wizard button (if you have installed

Internet Explorer 4.0). Be careful — these removals aren't stored in the Recycle Bin for you to put back in place. The Remove Shortcuts/Folders dialog box, which is displayed when you click the Remove button (see Figure 11-6), lets you navigate among the menus/folders to find the items (or folders) that you wish to remove. (The Start Menu Organizer Wizard provides a similar dialog box.)

Figure 11-6: The Remove Shortcuts/Folders dialog box. You can highlight the menu item or menu/folder that you want to remove. If you remove a menu/folder you also remove (delete) all the shortcuts in that menu.

Edit, move, add, delete Start menu items — the Advanced button

Click the Advanced button from the Start Menu Programs properties sheet to open an Explorer view of your Start Menu. This clipped Explorer works like any other Explorer window. (The Start Menu folder is set as the root — see Chapter 9 to learn how this is accomplished.)

You get all the capability you need to move menus from node to node. You can right-drag menu items (shortcuts) from another Explorer window and drop them in any menu folder that you like. You can create new menu folders in the Start menu or in any submenu folder.

The Start Menu Explorer, as shown in Figure 11-7, demonstrates very clearly that the Start menu is really just a series of folders — special folders, but folders nonetheless. You can manipulate them as you would any other folders.

The menu folders are meant to hold shortcuts. If you want to add a shortcut to a menu folder, the best way to do it is to right-drag an application icon from another Explorer window to the Start Menu Explorer, drop it in the menu folder that you want, and choose Create Shortcut(s) Here. Once you create the shortcut, you will probably want to edit out the "Shortcut to" text. (If you use the Start Menu Organizer Wizard or TweakUI to add menu items, the shortcuts you place in the Start menus won't have the "Shortcut to" prefix, so you won't have worry about removing it.)

You can copy or move application icons (and document or folder icons) to the menu folders in the Start menu if you wish, but the menu folders are really intended to hold shortcuts to applications.

The Start Menu Explorer is especially useful for moving menus about. You can't move menus using the Add and Remove buttons (in either version of Windows 95).

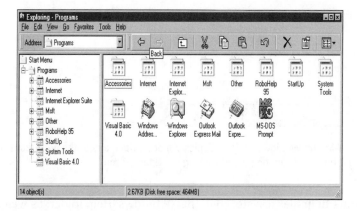

Figure 11-7: The Start Menu Explorer. If you highlight a menu folder icon name in the left pane, the contents of that menu folder appears in the right pane.

Find

The Find command is on the Start menu, it's located in the Tools menu in the Explorer window menu, and it's available by pressing the F3 key. We discuss the Find capability later in this chapter.

You can eliminate Find (although not the F3 key version) using the System Policy Editor.

Help

The Start menu Help command gets you to the unified help for all of Windows 95. Click Help and you get the Windows 95 Help Topics window, as shown in Figure 11-8.

Since Windows 95 help is a unified help system, you don't have to search a lot of separate help files to learn about Windows 95. Click the Find tab to build a complete word index to the help system.

Figure 11-8: The Windows 95 Help Topics window. Open any of the book icons by double-clicking it (or by highlighting it and clicking the Open button).

Windows help files are stored in the \Windows\Help folder, as well as the \Windows, \Windows\System, and \Windows\Command folders.

Adding to Help

You can add the contents of a help file to the Help menu item in the Start menu. You can then make Windows automatically index the contents of the additional help file, so that its contents (as well as the normal Windows help contents) show up when you perform a search in the Windows 95 Help Topics dialog box.

You can use this technique with any help (*hlp*) file that provides its own contents (*cnt*) file. Microsoft Plus!, for example, blends its own help files into Windows 95's help in exactly this way.

Windows 95 Secrets is available as a help file in *Windows 95 Secrets Gold* and *Windows 95 Secrets Bonus Pack*. You can add this help file to your Windows 95 help file in the manner detailed in these steps.

STEPS

Adding Help to Help

Step 1.   In the Windows Explorer, click View, then Options. In the View tab, click the Show all files option button if it isn't already selected.

Adding Help to Help

Step 2. You can copy any set of help and contents (*hlp* and *cnt*) files into your C:\Windows\Help folder.

For example, on the *Windows 95 Secrets Gold* or *Bonus Pack* CD-ROM, find and select the Secrets.hlp and Secrets.cnt files. Copy these two files into your C:\Windows\Help folder.

Step 3. Make your C:\Windows\Help folder the current folder in Explorer. Make a copy of the Windows.cnt file, and name the copy Win95cnt.bak as a backup.

Step 4. Open Windows.cnt in Notepad or any plain-text editor. Near the top of the file, you should see several lines that begin with :Index. Immediately after the last :Index line, add the following new line:

```
:Index Yourhelpfile title=yourhelpfilename.hlp
```

Step 5. Press Ctrl+End to move to the end of the file. After the last line, add the following new line:

```
:include yourhelpfilename.cnt
```

Press Enter at the end this line, and move your insertion point below your new :include line to make sure you have created a blank line.

Step 6. Save and close the file.

There's no need to restart Windows. You can immediately click the Start button and click Help to see the addition. You should find new "books" (help chapters) at the end of your help list.

To add the new help files topics to the ones you can search, click the Find tab in the Help Topics dialog box. The first time you do this, you will be asked whether you want to maximize or minimize the database used in the search process. If you've got the disk space, we recommend you choose the maximize option because it offers more powerful searches.

Run

This is a command line interface. If you want to run a program by typing its path and name and perhaps some command line parameters, then this is the place for you. This is like calling a program from the DOS command line, especially now that you can run Windows programs from the DOS command line.

The Run dialog box (shown in Figure 11-9) keeps a little history. You can bring up previous commands, edit them, and run them again.

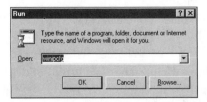

Figure 11-9: The Run dialog box. Type the path and filename of your DOS or Windows application, document, or Internet URL. Put in some command line parameters, if you like.

You can type the name of a document that has an associated application (as defined in the Registry) and run it. For example, you can type the name and path of an *ini* file. When you click the OK button, Notepad is invoked, and it displays the *ini* file in its client window area.

Undocumented

Want to quickly open a window that displays the files and folders in the root directory of your boot drive? Click the Start button, and then click Run. Type a backslash (\) in the Run dialog box, and then click the OK button.

You can use TweakUI to clear the Run history every time that you start Windows 95. Click the Paranoia tab, then check Clear Run history at logon. You can also use the System Policy Editor to hide the Run command.

Suspend

Although we don't show it in Figure 11-2, your Start menu may contain a Suspend command. It will be there if you have a computer that you can implement Advanced Power Management on, such as a portable Pentium or a Pentium Pro computer.

The Suspend command puts the computer into suspend mode immediately. Normally, your computer goes into suspend mode if you haven't typed or used the mouse for a specified interval of time. You can set the suspend parameters by double-clicking the Advanced Power Management icon in the Control Panel. You might choose to put your computer into Suspend mode to reduce its power usage while you are not using it.

Right-Click the Start Button

You can right-click the Start button and choose Open, Explore, or Find. Choose Open to display a folder window focused on the Start Menu folder, which is a subfolder of the \Windows folder.

The Start Menu folder contains an icon for the Programs folder. Notice that the icon is the same as the one displayed next to Programs in the Start menu. Double-clicking the Programs folder icon opens a folder window containing the Accessories folder, the Startup folder, and other folders and applications. The hierarchy of folders and subfolders in the Start Menu folder corresponds to the cascading menus and submenus within the Start menu.

The Start Menu folder gives you a way of traversing the menus using folders, a different style for those who wish to use it. Because the Start menu is also a folder, you can drag shortcuts into it and its subfolders. You can double-click icons in the Start Menu folder window to open up other folder windows, and then navigate back up to the parent folders.

When you right-click the Start button and click Explore, Windows 95 displays an Explorer window focused on the Start Menu folder. Unlike the Explorer window that's displayed when you click the Advanced button in the Start Menu Programs tab of the Taskbar Properties dialog box, this is a full Explorer. The folder tree in the left pane will take you anywhere you want to go; it's not restricted to the Start Menu folder and its subfolders.

The Find command opens the Find dialog box. We describe this dialog box in the *Find* section later in this chapter.

The Programs Menu/Folder

Secret

You can use the Explorer to move the \Windows\Start Menu\Programs folder onto the Desktop. To do this, right-click the Start button and click Explore, and then drag the Programs folder out of the Start Menu folder and onto the Desktop. All sorts of havoc ensues.

After you move the Programs folder to the Desktop, it still contains all the subfolders/menus that it had when it was a subfolder of the Start Menu folder. The cascading menus are still attached to the Programs menu item on the Start menu, the menu items/shortcuts in the Programs folder are still in their proper subfolders, and the items within them are still functional. The icon for the Programs folder (and for all its subfolders), however, changes to an ordinary folder icon, instead of the icon used for subfolders of the Start Menu folder (a manila folder with a little window on top).

When the Programs folder is stored within the Start Menu folder, the Programs folder and the Programs menu are separate but connected items. However, now that the Programs folder is on the Desktop, if you try to add a menu item using the Add button (or Wizard button if you've installed Internet Explorer 4.0) in the Start Menu Programs tab of the Taskbar Properties dialog box, the shortcut is added to the Programs folder on the Desktop, but not to the Programs menu. To avoid this type of problem, we suggest that you leave the Programs folder and its subfolders in the Start Menu folder. It is a much better idea to just place a *shortcut* to the Programs folder on the Desktop.

The Start Menu Folder

Secret

Unlike the Programs folder, if you move the Start Menu folder, \Windows\Start Menu, it maintains its relationship with the Start menu. You can use the Add button (or the Wizard button if you've installed Internet Explorer 4.0) to add a menu item to the Start Menu folder in its new location, and you will find the menu item in the correct subfolder of the Start Menu folder and in the correct cascading menu in the Start menu.

If you try to delete the Start Menu folder, Windows 95 will ask you to designate another folder as the Start Menu folder. If you don't, you won't be allowed to delete it. Deleting the original Start Menu folder and designating a new one is one way to create a new Start Menu folder that contains only the shortcuts and menus you want.

You can rename the Start Menu folder, but it continues to function in the same way.

Secret

The name of the Start Menu folder is stored in the Registry. If you want to designate another folder as the Start Menu folder, you can change the name of the Start Menu in the following branch of the registry using the Registry editor:

```
HKEY_CURRENT_USER\Software\Microsoft\Windows\CurrentVersion\Explorer\Shell
Folders
```

Turn to Chapter 15 to see how to use the Registry editor. You'll need to restart Windows 95 to have this change take effect.

You can also use TweakUI to name another folder as the Start Menu folder, another as the Programs folder, and another as the Startup folder. You should do all three if you want to completely move the Start Menu. You might want to copy the Start Menu to its new location first, edit it, and then use TweakUI to designate this new folder as the Start Menu folder. Once all that is working, you can delete the original Start Menu folder.

Drop It on the Start Button

There is an easy way to add menu items to the Start menu. Drag and drop icons from the Desktop or from a folder or Explorer window to the Start button. This works only if Auto hide is turned off in the Taskbar Options tab of the Taskbar Properties dialog box.

When you drag an icon to the Start button, Windows 95 automatically adds a shortcut to it in the Start menu. When you click the Start button to display the main Start menu, any icon's you've added in this way appear in their own little section above the Programs command, as shown in Figure 11-10.

These menu items are shortcuts just like the other menu items. The nice thing about them is that the icons are full size so you can see them more easily. These shortcuts are stored in the Start Menu folder.

Figure 11-10: The Start menu with additional shortcuts. Notice that, as with other menu items, these shortcuts don't have the little black arrow in the lower-left corner.

Tip

Shortcuts you drop on the Start button order themselves alphabetically. However, you can change their order by changing their names. Start the name of the shortcut you want to be first with A or 1, the second with B or 2, and so on. You can also start a shortcut name with the nonprinting space character (Alt+0160) to place it first. If you have installed Internet Explorer 4.0, you can place the movable Start menu items in any order that you like. Just drag and drop them to the appropriate location.

The Desktop on the Start menu

Undocumented

A neat trick is to put the Desktop itself on your Start button. Since the Desktop is also a folder, you can drag it from the Explorer onto the Start button. The Desktop folder is located under the \Windows folder.

When you click on the Desktop icon on the Start menu, you open a window to your Desktop. You now have a Desktop window on your Desktop. This is very handy if the icons on your Desktop are covered with other windows. You just place a window to your Desktop over them.

This trick also comes in handy when you use the keyboard to get to the Start menu. Press Ctrl+Esc to get to the Start menu from anywhere — even full-screen DOS sessions. After the menu pops up, you can use your arrow keys to get to the Desktop icon. This gives you a quick way to switch to an inactive application that has a shortcut on the Desktop.

In Chapter 8, we show you how to put the Desktop on the Taskbar. That way, you can get to it with Alt+Tab. Putting your Desktop on the Start menu gives you another way to get to it with a different set of keystrokes. The Desktop folder on the Start menu does not contain My Computer, Network Neighborhood, or Recycle Bin — but the Desktop on the Taskbar does.

You can use the Deskmenu item that comes with Microsoft's PowerToys to easily get to your Desktop. It creates a Tray icon called Deskmenu. When you click the icon, a menu of Desktop items is displayed on top of all the windows on your Desktop.

You can also use a little shareware application called Tab2Desk that allows you to use Alt+Tab to get to the Desktop. Tab2Desk works the same as Minimize All Windows (available when you right-click on an uncovered part of the Taskbar). When you press Alt+Tab, you can choose the Tab2Desk icon to minimize all open windows on the Desktop.

Folders in the Start menu folder

If you create a folder in the Start Menu folder, its folder icon includes a little window graphic. The Start Menu folder is a special folder; it automatically adds this window graphic to the icon of any folder stored within it. You can see this by navigating in your Explorer to your \Windows\Start Menu folder. You'll notice that all the subfolders of the Start Menu folder have icons that include this graphic.

If you move the Programs folder from the Start Menu folder, it and all its subfolders revert to displaying their folder icons sans window graphic. And if you then add more shortcuts to this relocated Programs folder or its subfolders, they won't appear in the Start menu.

At times, it may be more convenient for you to create a new folder in the Start Menu folder than to add a shortcut to a folder. When you click an item in the Start menu for a *shortcut* to a folder, Windows 95 just opens the folder window for you. In contrast, if you add an *actual* folder to the Start Menu folder and then put shortcuts inside the folder (to documents, executables, or other folders), then when you point to the menu item for the folder in the Start Menu, a cascading menu appears with all the shortcuts you placed in the folder.

To do this while in the Explorer view of the Start Menu folder, right-click a blank area of the right pane. Then point to New, and click Folder. Type a name for your folder, press Enter, and it's ready to go. You can now right-drag executables, documents, and so on into this new folder in the Start Menu to create shortcuts. Once you've done this, you can easily pick them from the Start Menu.

One difference between creating a folder in the Start Menu versus creating a shortcut to a folder is that a folder containing shortcuts does not change when you add or subtract items in the actual folder. A shortcut to a folder, by contrast, is dynamic and always remains up-to-date with the contents of that folder.

Control Panel on a Start menu

Secret

You normally get to the Control Panel by clicking the Start button, pointing to Settings, and finally clicking Control Panel. The Control Panel is usually displayed in a folder window. However, you can make the Control Panel a menu item in any of the Start menus, and you can display it as a menu and not as a window. To do so, take the following steps:

STEPS

The Control Panel As a Menu

Step 1. Right-click the Start button, and click Open. If you want to place the Control Panel on the main Start menu, stop here. Otherwise, continue to open up windows of menu items until you open the menu item/folder that you want to contain the Control Panel.

Step 2. Right-click an open area of the window. Point to New in the context menu, and then click Folder.

Step 3. The temporary name New Folder is highlighted so that you can type over it with a new name. Type the following text exactly as we have printed it here:

Control Panel.{21EC2020-3AEA-1069-A2DD-08002B30309D}

Step 4. Press Enter, and the New Folder icon is replaced with the Control Panel icon.

Step 5. Click the Start button. The Control Panel icon appears as a menu item, and all the Control Panel icons are listed in a cascading menu attached to it.

The long identifier given in step 3 is unique to the Control Panel. You can find it by using your Registry editor and searching for Control Panel. We discuss some additional ways that you can put Control Panel applets on your Start menu in the *Shortcuts to the Control Panel* section of Chapter 16.

You can use the same trick for the Printers and/or the Dial-Up Networking folder, as well as for many other Desktop objects. The unique identifiers for these folders are as follows:

Dial-Up Networking	Dial Up Net.{992CFFA0-F557-101A-88EC-00DD010CCC48}
Printers	Printers.{2227A280-3AEA-1069-A2DE-08002B30309D}
Inbox	Inbox.{00020D75-0000-0000-C000-000000000046}
My Computer	My Computer.{20D04FE0-3AEA-1069-A2D8-08002B30309D}
Recycle Bin	Recycle Bin.{645FF040-5081-101B-9F08-00AA002F954E}
Network Neighborhood	Network Neighborhood.{208D2C60-3AEA-1069-A2D7-08002B30309D}

Desktop	Desktop.{00021400-0000-0000-C000-000000000046}
My Briefcase	Briefcase.{85BBD920-42A0-1069-A2E4-08002B30309D}
Fonts	Fonts.{BD84B380-8CA2-1069-AB1D-08000948F534}

Use these identifiers in step 3 of The Control Panel As a Menu steps to put these folders on the Start menu.

Keyboard Control of the Start Menus

You can run the Start menus with your keyboard. The most important keyboard combination is Ctrl+Esc, which displays the main Start menu.

You can choose menu items on the Start menu by pressing the letter key that corresponds to the underlined letter in the name. If you have added items to the Start menu that begin with the same letter, the letter key will take you to these items first. The letter keys operate in round-robin fashion, going to the first item that starts with that letter, and then the next, until it starts over at the top again.

The letter keys work in all the submenus also. There is no underlined letter in the shortcut names under the Programs menu, so you type the first letter of the item.

The arrow keys can also move you through the menus. The up and down arrow keys move you within a menu. When you get to the bottom of a menu, pressing the down arrow again takes you up to the top. (By the same token, pressing the up arrow when you're at the top of a menu takes you to the bottom.) The right and left arrow keys move you forward and back between the cascading menus. When you reach a menu item that you want to run, press Enter.

Undocumented

If you press Ctrl+Esc and then Esc, the Start menu disappears, but the focus stays on the Start button. When the Start button has the focus, you'll see the focus rectangle on it. You can confirm the Start button still has the focus by pressing Enter after you've pressed Ctrl+Esc, Esc. The Start menu will reappear.

Once the Start button has the focus, you can press Tab repeatedly to change the focus from the Start button to the Taskbar, from the Taskbar to the Desktop, and then from the Desktop back to the Start button.

If the focus is on the Taskbar, you can use the arrow keys to move the focus from button to button. To restore an application or bring it to the top of the windows on the Desktop, move the focus to the Taskbar button for that application, and press Enter.

If the focus is on an icon on the Desktop, you can use your arrow keys to move among the Desktop icons to focus on the application, folder, or file you want to open. Press Enter when the focus is on the desired icon.

It's hard to see whether the focus is on the Start button, the Taskbar, or the Desktop, and using the Windows 95 default color scheme (called the Windows Standard scheme) makes this even more difficult. If the Start button has the focus, you'll see the typical dotted rectangle around the word *Start*. If the Taskbar or the Start button has the focus, and if your color scheme has an Active Window Border color that differs from the 3D Object color (something that is not true of the default Windows color scheme), you will see a border line around the Taskbar. If the Desktop has the focus, the Taskbar border will display the Inactive Window Border color, and an icon on the Desktop will be highlighted. See Chapter 22 for details on how to change these colors.

If you have defined hot keys for the shortcuts on the Start menus, you can start the application immediately without going through the Start button, just by pressing its hot key combination. We describe how to create hot keys in Chapters 10 and 17 .

Change Menu Display Speed

If you position your mouse pointer over one of the menu items on the Start menu, you'll notice that after a short delay the menu appears. If instead you click the menu item, the associated menu appears immediately.

Secret

You can set the length of time that elapses before the menu appears. You can make the menu appear instantaneously or make the time interval so long that the menu doesn't pop up until you click the menu item. The current default value for the time delay is $1/4$ of a second (or 250 milliseconds). To change this value, take the following steps:

STEPS

Change the Menu Display Speed

Step 1. Double-click Regedit.exe in an Explorer window focused on your \Windows folder.

Step 2. Click the plus sign next to HKEY_CURRENT_USER, and then click Control Panel. Highlight Desktop under Control Panel.

Step 3. Right-click in a clear area in the right pane of the Registry editor window; click New and then String Value.

Step 4. Type **MenuShowDelay**.

(continued)

STEPS *(continued)*

Change the Menu Display Speed

Step 5.   Double-click MenuShowDelay. Type the length of the time delay that you want to wait until the menus pop up in milliseconds (thousandths of a second). Type **0** for no delay, and **100000** for almost never.

Step 6.   Click OK.

Step 7.   Exit the Registry, and restart Windows 95 to have these values take effect.

You can also set the value of MenuShowDelay using our old favorite TweakUI, which you can download from the Microsoft web site, http://www.microsoft.com/windows/software/powertoy.htm.

Find

Windows 95 includes a search capability. The Windows 3.*x* File Manager had a very rudimentary one, but it has been much improved for Windows 95.

You can get to this Find function in a number of ways. If you want to search for files or folders, right-click the Start button, the My Computer icon, or any folder icon, and then click Find in the context menu.

If you want the option of searching for computers (available only if you have installed networking) as well as files or folders, you can click the Start button, and then choose Find from the Start menu, or choose Tools, Find in an Explorer window. If you just want to search for a computer, you can right-click the Network Neighborhood icon and click Find Computer in the context menu.

The easiest way to find a file or folder? Press the F3 key when the focus is on the Desktop, a folder window, an Explorer window, or the Taskbar.

Just because the command is called *Find* doesn't necessarily mean the usefulness of this function is limited to finding things. For example, you can use Find as a filter to list all the executables in a folder or in a set of folders in one window.

Finding files or folders

You can find files and/or folders that match the criteria you set in a Find dialog box. Windows 95 gives you a significant number of options to define your search strategy.

File or folder name

Undocumented

If you are looking for a specific file or folder and you know its name, type the name in the Named field, as shown in Figure 11-11. You can search for multiple folders, files, or file types. Just separate their names by a comma, as in:

```
*.bat, *.sys, *.txt, bill?.*
```

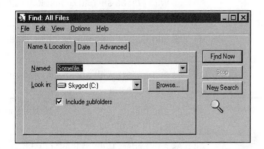

Figure 11-11: The Name & Location tab of the Find dialog box. Type a file or folder name or partial name. If you know the general area (folder or drive) where the file or folder is located, choose a drive from the Look in drop-down list, and/or type the pathname to a folder in the Named field.

Secret

You can type a partial name with wild cards. The wild cards are ? and *. The question mark stands for one letter and the asterisk for one or more letters. Table 11-1 shows these and other options.

Table 11-1	Find Options
Entered in Named Field	*Search Location*
*	All files and folders.
.	All files and folders.
*.	All files.
.	No files or folders.
.exe	No files or folders (because a filename cannot start with a period).
abc	All files and folders with *abc* in name (including extensions).
exe	All files and folders with exe in name or extension. Most likely executable files.
*.exe	All files with exe in extension only.

(continued)

Table 11-1 *(continued)*

Entered in Named Field	*Search Location*
abc	All files and folders with *abc* in name.
*abc	All files with *abc* as last letters in name (not including extension).
*abc?	All files with *abc* as second to last letters in name (not including extension).
?abc	All files and folders with *abc* as at least second letters in name if not later.
?abc*	All files and folders with *abc* as the second through fourth letters in name.
??abc	All files and folders with *abc* as at least the third letters in name if not later.
?abc?	All files and folders with at least one letter in front of *abc* and at least one behind in name.
?a?.*	Three-letter file name with middle letter of name given and extension unknown.

Notice that unlike searching in DOS for filenames, you can have the asterisk or question marks in front and still get meaningful results. In fact, the search algorithm is much more flexible and powerful than what was available with DOS or Windows 3.*x*.

In the Look in field, enter the general location for the file or folder. If you know a file or folder is on a certain disk drive, choose that drive letter. If you can narrow it down further, use the Browse button to choose a folder, or include a pathname in the Named field.

By default, Windows 95 includes subfolders in the search. You probably want to do a top-down search, so leave the Include subfolders check box marked unless you know what folder the file is in.

Secret

Find will search for your files in hidden subfolders if you have marked the Show all files option button in the View tab of the Options dialog box (click View, Options in an Explorer or folder window). Find will not find your fonts in the Fonts folder (which has the system attribute set, but is not hidden) if the Look in field in your Find dialog box is set to \Windows and not to Windows\Fonts. The hidden subfolders under the \Windows folder are NetHood, Recent, Pif, Sysbckup, ShellNew, Spool, and Inf.

Date

Windows 95 lets you limit your searches based on dates. You can restrict a search to a particular time frame, and you can further restrict the search by specifying whether you're looking for files/folders that were modified during that period. If you have installed Internet Explorer 4.0 you can also restrict the search to a time period during which the files or folders were created or last accessed.

To set search criteria based on the date, click the Date Modified tab if you're using an earlier version of Windows 95, or the Date tab if you've installed Internet Explorer 4.0 (shown in Figure 11-12).

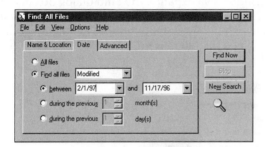

Figure 11-12: The Date tab of the Find dialog box. You can limit the search for files and folders based on the time/date they were modified, created, or last accessed. If you're looking for a recently changed file, search for files that have been modified in the last few days.

File type, specific text, file size

You can search for files that contain certain pieces of text, are of a certain file type, or are at least as big as or greater than a certain size. Click the Advanced tab in the Find dialog box, as shown in Figure 11-13.

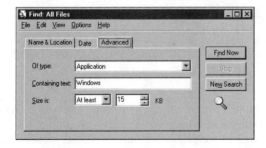

Figure 11-13: The Advanced tab of the Find dialog box. If all you know about a file is that it contains a particular block of text, you can search for files containing that text.

This is a good method to use if you've completely forgotten the name of the file you're trying to track down, but you still remember something about its content. For example, you could search for all the files that contain the words *Sincerely Yours*.

You can also use the Advanced tab to limit the search to files of a certain type — for example, all text files, all Word for Windows files, or all Quattro Pro files. And if you have some idea of how large the files you're looking for are, you can use size as a search criteria.

Starting the search

After you have entered all the criteria in the various tabs of the Find dialog box, click Find Now. Windows 95 expands the Find dialog box and displays the search results in the pane below the search criteria, as shown in Figure 11-14. You can use the View menu to choose among the four standard views (large icon, small icon, list, details).

Figure 11-14: The results pane of the Find dialog box displayed in large icon view. If you use details view (the default), you can sort the results in ascending or descending order by filename, folder name, date, size, or file type.

The results pane looks like a folder window with one exception: When you view the results in details view, Windows 95 adds a column named In Folder that lists the folder in which each item was found. You can sort the found files and folders by filename, folder name, date, size, or file type, in either ascending or descending order.

If you want to go to the folder that contains a file or folder listed in the results pane, select the file or folder and choose File, Open Containing Folder.

Saving the search

Windows 95 retains your search criteria after you've performed the search. If you don't like the results of a search, you can modify the criteria and do another one. In Windows 3.*x* the search criteria disappeared after each search. This caused extreme frustration, and it gave rise to many third-party products for finding files.

If you want to use a particular set of search criteria as the basis of future searches, you can save it as an icon on your Desktop. To do this, make sure the criteria you want to save is specified in the Find dialog box, and choose File, Save Search.

Tip

The saved search will end up as an icon on your Desktop, which is not the best of locations. You might want to create a folder under the \Windows folder called Find. You can then drag these icons off the Desktop and into this folder, and then create shortcuts to them on the Desktop or another convenient location.

When you want to perform a search you've saved as an icon, double-click the icon (or a shortcut to it). Windows 95 displays the Find dialog box with all the search criteria specified. Optionally modify the criteria, and then click Find Now to perform the search.

What you can do with Find

Tip

You can use Find to locate all the executable files in your games folder and then drag shortcuts to all these games to a newly created games submenu on your Start menu. It is great to be able to see all the executables within the subfolders of a folder that defines a general class of applications. This is especially true if you use the large icon view in the results pane.

This is a good way to create menus under the Start menu. You can search for all executables on your hard disk and then drag them in groups to new menu folders. You can also create folders or shortcuts to folders on the Desktop, and then drag documents or executables over to these folders.

The Find command really opens up your computer and lets you see what is hiding under the covers. You'll be surprised at what you have ignored.

Tip

Use Find for file management. You can use it to find all the files on your entire hard disk so that you can order them by size or age or file type. You can get rid of all the *tmp* (temporary) files, or all the really old text files.

If you want additional capabilities (such as search and replace) check out http://home.sprynet.com/sprynet/funduc/ for a complete search-and-replace program that supports regular expressions.

Finding a computer on your network

You can use a completely different Find function to find a server or computer on your local network, as long as you know its unique name. Click the Start button, point to Find, and then click Computer. This option won't appear unless you have installed the network options on your computer.

You can also right-click the Network Neighborhood icon on your Desktop and then click Find Computer. Or, in your Explorer, choose Tools, Find, Computer.

You have to know the exact name of the computer; you can't use wild cards. Needless to say, a find utility isn't worth much if you have to know exactly what it is you are looking for.

If you do use this feature, you need to preface the name of the computer you are looking for with two back slashes (\\). This is the universal naming convention for a server — and therefore a computer — name.

Searching The Microsoft Network

If you like, you can search The MSN for services related to a topic. In an Explorer window, choose Tools, Find, On the Microsoft Network. You can also click the Start button, point to Find, and click On the Microsoft Network.

The search engine will look for your search text in the names and descriptions of bulletin boards and chat rooms.

Searching the Internet

If you have installed Internet Explorer 4.0, you can click the Start button, point to Find, and then click On the Internet. This starts the Dial-Up Networking connectoid that connects to your Internet service provider (if this is how you connect to the Internet). After you connect, the Internet Explorer starts up and displays your default search page.

You can configure which search service you want to use to find things on the Internet. The default service is Microsoft's search page. If you are using the Internet Explorer, you can change the default search page (or search engine) by choosing View, Options, Navigation, and then selecting Search Page in the Page drop-down list. Type the URL for the search page in the Address field. You can also search for people's e-mail addresses (found by web crawlers) if you have installed Internet Explorer 4.0. Just choose Find, People. You can find your local store of e-mail addresses by choosing Find, E-mail Addresses. This command takes you to your Windows address book.

Summary

You can use the Start button and the Find function to make your work easier and increase your efficiency.

▶ We show you how to create and modify Start menus to match the way that you work.

▶ We provide a means to trim the unnecessary files from the recently used files list.

▶ If you find that Desktop icons are often covered up, you'll appreciate being able to put the Desktop on the Start menu.

▶ Windows 95 has a very powerful search engine. You can define intricate searches that are quite useful in file management, and you can use searches to build Start menus and create Desktop folders.

Chapter 12

Desktop Strategies — Making Windows 95 Your Own

In This Chapter

Windows 95 is a set of tools waiting for an artist. This is a chance to let your creativity shine. We discuss:

▶ Cleaning up the clutter in your Start menus

▶ Putting the Start button to work with your heavily used applications

▶ Letting loose and just piling it on the Desktop

▶ Putting folders on the Desktop to hold your shortcuts

▶ Turning a folder window into your Program Manager and using the Explorer as your File Manager

▶ Using the real Program Manager and File Manager as your user interface without giving up of the power of the *new* interface

---

It Comes with a Start Button

"But, I don't know where to start."

Microsoft went for the uncluttered look in Windows 95. Many of its customers thought the Windows 3.*x* Program Manager was ugly. In a reaction to this criticism, Microsoft reduced the Desktop to a Taskbar, a Start button, and a few icons.

If you have installed Internet Explorer 4.0, your Desktop is now a bit more cluttered. Microsoft apparently saw all that unused space and decided to fill some of it up. As a result, the Desktop now sports an *active window*, which you can set up to download specific information off the Internet as it is updated.

The addition of the active window, however, does nothing to change a basic reality: You have to build your own virtual computer — which, after all, is the real computer — for yourself. Windows 95 provides the tools, but leaves the design up to you.

Your documents and applications are well hidden on your hard disk or across the network. To create a usable computer, you need to bring them forth. You may have expected that it would all be there for you. If that's the case, it's time to leave home and make your own way in the world.

Windows 95 gives you shortcuts, cascading menus off the Start button, a Desktop that can contain icons, folders with properties, a powerful browser in the Explorer, a configurable context menu, a SendTo folder, a configurable connection to the Internet, and a moveable/hideable Taskbar. We provide you with a collection of add-on utilities to increase your computer's functionality still further.

A Desktop Strategy

Every single one of you will set up the Windows Desktop in a different manner to match your own preferences. Only if a network administrator or system information manager has set up your computer over the network — and enforced a mandatory style (stored on a secure server) — will you be prevented from making the changes that make your computer your own.

Windows 95 provides a great deal of flexibility — although, of course, there will never be enough to completely please any of us. In this chapter, we present five major strategies for designing a Windows Desktop. You can ignore all our hard work here and go off on your own, or you can start with one of our approaches that closely matches your own style, and then build on it.

The major considerations in developing a Desktop strategy are getting the tools and putting them close at hand. Windows 95 doesn't include everything that you need in the user interface, so you are going to have to add a number of utilities to make it work for you. We have some, and we point out areas where you'll need to get more.

Don't hide the power of Windows 95 under a bush. Bring it out, make it accessible, make it easy. Take advantage of additional utilities and make them accessible, too.

Whose Desktop Is This Anyway?

When you start Windows 95 for the very first time, you get a logon dialog box similar to the one shown in Figure 12-1. (Depending on your version of Windows 95, your dialog box may differ slightly from the one in the figure.) The point of the logon box is to let the computer know who you are and whether you really are who you say you are. Windows 95, in turn, will let you configure your own Desktop, so even if other people use the computer they won't mess with your Desktop settings.

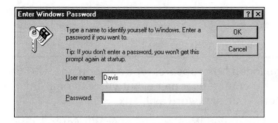

Figure 12-1: The Windows 95 logon dialog box. Type your user name and password to protect your Desktop.

You can configure Windows 95 to make the logon dialog box go away and not come back. If you do this, you are telling Windows 95 that either you are the only user of this computer or that everyone should be treated the same and should get the same Desktop with this computer. You are also saying that you do not want to log on to a local area network at Windows 95 startup.

You must satisfy these three conditions to make the logon box go away.

1. You must have a blank password.

2. You must disable user profiles.

3. You must have Windows configured so that it won't log you on to a local area network.

If you meet these conditions (described later in this section), Windows 95 won't display the logon box the next time it loads because it won't have any need for your user name and password.

You could also make the logon dialog box go away by simply clicking the Cancel button or pressing the Escape key. However, if you use this method, you only cancel the logon process this one time. The next time Windows 95 starts, it will display the logon box again. Furthermore, if you cancel the logon process and then try to use Windows 95 features that require your account name and password, such as Dial-Up Networking, you'll find that Windows 95 won't remember this information, and you won't be able to save any passwords.

If you want your computer to be able to change Desktop settings depending on who is using it, you need to enable user profiles:

STEPS

Configuring User Profiles

Step 1.   Start your computer after installing Windows 95.

(continued)

STEPS *(continued)*

Configuring User Profiles

Step 2.   When the logon box appears, type a user name, and click OK. You have to enter a user name, but you can omit the password. This enters your password as blank.

If you have installed Windows 95 over Windows 3.1, you won't necessarily have a logon box. If not, go to step 3 and finish the rest of the steps. This will configure Windows 95 to call up a logon box the next time you start.

Step 3.   Click the Start button, point to Settings, and then click Control Panel.

Step 4.   Double-click the Passwords icon in the Control Panel to display the Passwords Properties dialog box, and click the User Profiles tab, as shown in Figure 12-2.

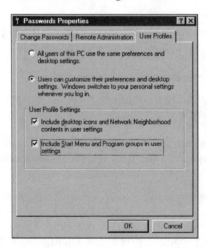

Figure 12-2: The User Profiles tab of the Passwords Properties dialog box. Use one Desktop for all users, or let each user set up his or her own Desktop.

Step 5.   Choose between "All users of this PC use the same preferences and desktop settings" and "Users can customize their preferences and desktop settings. Windows switches to your personal settings whenever you log in."

Step 6.   Click OK. You'll be given the option of restarting your computer. To have your changes take effect now, do so, or wait until after you take the next steps.

If you choose to use the same Desktop for all users, any changes you make to the current user in the Registry and any changes you make on the Desktop or in the Start menus will apply to all users. If you let different users customize their own Desktops and Start menus, their changes will apply only to their configuration.

You can use the Passwords icon in the Control Panel to change your password. In the Password Properties dialog box, click the Change Passwords tab, and make the desired changes. You can even change your password to blank if you have previously put in another password.

Different users can log on to different servers on the network. To log on to the network when you first start Windows 95, you have to enter your user name in the logon box. If you want to just get into Windows 95 locally, you don't need to log on to a network, and you can forego the logon box at startup time. To set up your logon options, follow these steps:

STEPS

Configuring Logon Options

Step 1. Click the Start button, point to Settings, and then click Control Panel.

Step 2. Double-click the Network icon in the Control Panel. Display the Primary Network Logon drop-down list (see Figure 12-3).

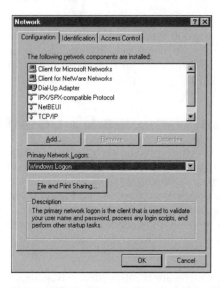

Figure 12-3: The Network dialog box. If you click the Primary Network Logon field, the Description field tells you about the field. To get more detailed information, right-click the field and choose What's This?.

(continued)

STEPS *(continued)*

Configuring Logon Options

Step 3.   Choose Windows Logon, Client for Microsoft Networks, Client for
NetWare Networks, or other possible choices.

Step 4.   Click OK. Restart Windows to have your changes take effect.

If you choose Windows Logon in step 3, you are saying you don't want to log
on to the network, whatever network that might be. If you choose Windows
Logon and you've met the first two conditions described earlier in this
section, the logon box won't appear the next time you start Windows 95.

You can choose Client for Microsoft Networks in step 3, and as long as you
aren't logging on when you start up Windows 95, you can still make the
logon box disappear. If your network connection is through Dial-Up Networking, for example, and not through a local area network, you won't have
to see the logon box nor actively log on to your Windows 95 computer. You
will have to log on to the computer that you dial into.

Even though you can set up Windows 95 so that you don't see the logon box,
this doesn't mean that you haven't logged on to your computer. If you have
a user name and a blank password, you are logged on as your user name
when you start Windows 95, and all your other passwords (for example,
your DUN passwords) are stored in your password file.

Secret

You can selectively get rid of user profiles by booting into DOS, changing to
the \Windows\Profiles directory and deleting the directory named for the
specific user. Be sure you aren't logged on as that user when you do this.
This gets rid of the User.dat file for that particular user, so that it will no
longer be merged with the System.dat file to create the Registry.

Securing the Windows 95 Desktop

Windows 95 is designed to be user-friendly, not secure. Your Windows 95
computer is not protected from unauthorized use, even if you set up a name
and password to protect (sort of) your Desktop configuration. Anyone with
physical access to your computer can just log on under a new name and
password or press Escape when the logon dialog box appears. You need
add-on utilities to provide higher levels of access restriction. Passwords and
security features are not "friendly," but neither is the experience of discovering that someone has tampered with your computer.

We have included shareware utilities on the *Windows 95 Secrets* CD-ROM or
at http://www.windows95.com that provide an additional measure of safety.
If you don't control physical access to your computer, you might consider

using them. Also, if you have enabled user profiles, you can modify Windows 95 to be more secure. Details are available at http:// www.conitech.com/windows/secure.html.

You can also download Clasp97 from http://www.cyberenet.net/~ryan/, StormWindows from http://www.hotfiles.com/swbrowse/000/A/X/ swlib-000AXR.html, or the killer security application StopLight 95 ELS at http://www.safety.net/stoplite.htm.

Dealing with a corrupted password file

If you have logged on to Windows 95, Windows 95 creates a password file and saves all your other passwords in this file. You gain access to the additional passwords in this password file by logging on to your computer with your user name and password (which may be blank). Windows 95 will not create and save a password file for you if you have not logged on under your user name (at least once) and it will not let you access that password file unless you are logged in under that user name. If you canceled the logon dialog box, then you aren't logged on, so you won't have access to any passwords and you won't be able to save any passwords.

If you have never seen the Windows 95 logon box, check to see if you have any password (*pwl*) files stored in your \Windows folder. If not, you can either configure user profiles for multiple users as described in the *Whose Desktop Is This Anyway?* section earlier in this chapter or install Dial-Up Networking. Either of these actions will let you log on anew.

If you find that other applications are unable to remember their passwords, but their Save Password check boxes are not grayed out and are checkable, your password file might be corrupted. You will need to either delete or rename it.

If you find that your DUN connectoids no longer have attached passwords, your password file might be corrupted. See the *Saving your DUN connectoid passwords* section in Chapter 33.

If you get the error message "MPREXE Caused an Invalid Page Fault in Kernel32.dll" while you're trying to access your Internet service provider or when you're using Dial-Up Networking, you most likely have a corrupted password file.

The initial release of Service Pack 1 included a security update that damaged existing password files. Microsoft subsequently released an update to this update at http://www.microsoft.com/windows/software/passwd.htm, but it may have been too late for you. You'll have to delete or rename your corrupt password file.

If you suspect that your password file is corrupted, delete or rename your *pwl* files found in your \Windows folder. Restart Windows and let Windows rebuild them. You'll have to enter all new passwords, but now they can at least be saved.

You can look at a number of Microsoft Knowledge Base articles that deal with password issues. Go to http://www.microsoft.com/kb/articles/Q135/1/97.htm or http://www.microsoft.com/kb/articles/Q137/3/61.htm or http://www.microsoft.com/kb/articles/Q148/9/25.htm.

Dealing with the Start Button

If you installed Windows 95 over your existing Windows 3.*x* directory, you will likely find a large number of submenus attached to the Programs menu on your Start button. Windows 95 transforms all your program groups into menus (and their corresponding subfolders in the \Windows\Start Menu\ Programs folder), and it turns your program items into shortcuts. All these menus add up to a big mess.

Windows 95 has its own collection of menus and shortcuts on the Programs menu as well, and these only add to the clutter. You'll probably want to reorganize things soon after you set up Windows 95. You may wonder if you can get rid of some of the menus. You also may not remember the functions of the applications that now have shortcuts in your various new menus.

Tip

One way to deal with all this clutter and still have a manageable set of Start menus is to drag the menu folders out of the \Windows\Start Menu\Programs folder into a temporary holding folder. Take the following steps to clean up your Start menus:

STEPS

Uncluttering Your Start Menus

Step 1.   Right-click the My Computer icon on your Desktop. Click Explore to display the Explorer window.

Step 2.   Make sure that Show all files is turned on (choose View, Options, and click the View tab).

Step 3.   In the left pane of the Explorer window, highlight the drive or folder in which you want to put a folder that will temporarily store some Start menu items.

Step 4.   In the right pane, right-click, point to New, click Folder, and then type a name for the folder such as **TempStart**.

Step 5.   Navigate to the \Windows\Start Menu folder in the left pane.

Step 6.   Highlight the Programs folder, find the menu folders in Programs that you want to temporarily move out of the Start menus, and drag (move, not copy) them from the Programs folder over to the TempStart folder.

You can also temporarily move shortcuts out of the menus; you might want to drag them to a subfolder of the TempStart folder.

You can use the Explorer to rearrange the menu folders under the \Start Menu\Programs folder so that they make more sense to you. Unlike the Windows 3.*x* Program Manager, the Start menus are hierarchical. The hierarchy of folders and subfolders under the Programs menu corresponds directly to the hierarchy of menus and submenus in the Start menu.

You can continue to move folders and subfolders back and forth between TempStart and your \Windows\Start Menu\Programs folder, rearranging their order, pulling shortcuts from one folder to another, and so on. TempStart gives you a place to store all the extra folders from your Windows 3.1 configuration until you decide what to do with your new configuration.

The Start button itself

You can place shortcuts right on the main Start menu by dragging folder, application, or document icons over to the Start button and dropping them on it. You should only put your most heavily used applications (or folders or documents) on the main Start menu. To start an application you've dropped on the Start button, all you have to do is click the Start button and then click the application icon (or press Ctrl+Esc, use the down arrow key to highlight the application icon, and press Enter). This level of convenience demands that you list just the applications (or folders) that deserve it.

There is a cost to this strategy. As the main Start menu gets bigger, it takes longer to draw, and the shortcuts you add make it hard to get to the other items on the Start menus. The icons on the main Start menu are full-size (unless you right-clicked the Taskbar, clicked Properties, and then checked Show small icons in Start menu), which means they take up a considerable amount of room. You should restrict the number of icons you place on the main Start menu so that they don't bog you down.

The menus on the Programs menu

The Programs menu is the replacement for the Program Manager. It can contain submenus as well as icons for applications or documents. You can choose how to mix these different elements. If you like, you can create a Programs menu that duplicates the program groups you had in your Program Manager. You just configure it to have only submenus, and you configure the submenus to correspond to your program groups.

Tip

If you have just one level of submenus in your Programs menu, these submenus will contain the shortcuts to your applications. If you prefer, you can create a hierarchy of two or more levels of submenus. With this type of setup, you could group similar submenus together (for example, all editing and word processing submenus), and then put them under a more general submenu (say, editors), which would be located directly under Programs.

You can use the Programs menus as often or as infrequently as you like. It can take a fair amount of mousing to get to applications in your Programs menu because you may have to navigate through several cascading menus. You might want to use the Programs menu for applications that you use only once in a while. Another idea is to place the applications you use the least out in the most far-flung submenus, and put the programs you use all the time in the main Programs menu.

Pile It on the Desktop

Your computer Desktop can take it, so why not pile it on? You can throw just about anything that you want on the Desktop, but the best idea is to put shortcuts to applications, folders, and documents there. There is little need to hold back; if you have something that you are dealing with right now, put a shortcut to it on the Desktop.

The Desktop is often easy to get to (especially if you have a large high-resolution monitor) so you may want to put shortcuts to your most heavily used applications on the Desktop. But just because shortcuts to your most important applications (in terms of use) end up on the Desktop doesn't mean you should reserve the Desktop for only these high-priority items. You can put just about anything there.

The Desktop is a very convenient temporary storage area. You can right-drag files out of a folder window or the Explorer and drop them there (creating shortcuts when the context menu appears) without having to open another folder window. You can go back later and drag these shortcuts to new locations. Alternatively, you can drop the actual files on the Desktop, and move them later.

You can even drag text selections out onto the Desktop from documents created in WordPad or other Windows 95-aware word processors. When you use the Desktop this way, it functions like a permanent Clipboard.

It's easy to get things off your Desktop. Just select the icon and press the Delete key, or drag the icon to the Recycle Bin. If the icon is just a shortcut, then no harm is done. You've just removed a link to your application or document. If the icon represents a file, however, you've deleted the whole file. That's why it's a good idea to not put important files and applications on the Desktop, but only shortcuts to them. You reduce the risk of deleting something that you wanted.

Tip

You can use the Explorer or My Computer to create folders on the Desktop, and then put shortcuts in them. You could just as well put folders containing shortcuts somewhere else in your filing system, and then put shortcuts to the folders on the Desktop. If you do this, the Desktop becomes, in effect, the Program Manager. The shortcuts on the Desktop that point to folders are like program groups. It's as though your Program Manager had wallpaper.

Tip

Putting shortcuts to folders on the Desktop is particularly convenient when you're working on a project with many different files in many different folders. You can create a folder to store shortcuts to the files in the project. Put a shortcut to this folder on the Desktop (or on the main Start menu). Now you have a quick way to access all the files in the project.

If the project is divided into recognizable subsets, put the shortcuts to files in each subset into a folder identifying that subset. Put shortcuts to the subset folders into an overall project folder. Put a shortcut to the project folder on the Desktop.

If you have a document that you are working on, drag a shortcut to it onto the Desktop. Double-click the shortcut, and the document opens in the application you used to create it.

Sometimes you might find it inconvenient to reach the Desktop, especially if you don't have much real estate. For example, you might be running at 640 x 480 on a 14-inch monitor, or maybe you're running your applications in maximized windows. In these situations, you can still use your Desktop. In Chapters 8 and 11, we show you ways to put the Desktop (the\Windows\Desktop folder) on the main Start menu or on the Taskbar so that you can always access it, even if it is covered up.

Undocumented

If you put the Desktop folder on the Taskbar or on the main Start menu, the folder will function as a variant of the Program Manager. If you open the Desktop folder window on the Desktop and display its contents in large icon view (View, Large Icons), it looks a lot like the Program Manager. Windows 95 gives you many Program Managers: the Start menus, the Desktop, folder windows with large icons, and a variation on the Windows 3.*x* Program Manager itself. If you have Internet Explorer 4.0 installed, you can add a Desktop toolbar to your Taskbar. Just right-click the Taskbar, click Tools, and then click Desktop.

Massage the Context Menu

Both the Explorer and My Computer provide navigational windows that give you a view of your computer. Because the Explorer has a folder tree view in the left pane, it has greater navigational abilities, but both display all your folders, applications, and documents.

If you right-click any of the icons displayed in these views, you get a context menu. You can modify the context menu to make it significantly easier to use. In Chapters 10 and 13, we discuss how to modify the context menu and add destinations — such as a default file opener for all files of unregistered types, Quick View, a file compression program, and your printer — to the Send To menu item. Some of these changes are very easy to make, while others require that you edit the Registry a bit.

The Active Desktop

In *Turn a Folder Window into the Program Manager...* and *Use the Real Program and File Managers* later in this chapter, we show you how to connect the Windows 95 Desktop to the rapidly fading Windows 3.*x* past. Here, we talk about the present and future incarnations of the Desktop.

By default, Internet Explorer 4.0 displays the Windows 95 Active Desktop, but it also makes it easy to switch back to the standard Windows 95 Desktop. Microsoft did this on purpose, because it is moving toward fully integrating the Internet/Intranet into your computer, and it wants to make this transition as painless as possible.

Microsoft came out with the Windows 95 Desktop just as the World Wide Web was getting hot. They didn't have time to prepare an integrated browser for shipment by August 24, 1995, when they shipped Windows 95. If they could've, they would've. Bill Gates showed an early demo of the integrated interface on December 7, 1995.

If you have installed Internet Explorer 4.0, you have two Desktops: the standard Windows 95 Desktop and the Active Desktop (see Chapter 34). Right-click the Desktop and click Active Desktop in the context menu to switch back and forth.

Turn a Folder Window into the Program Manager . . .

. . . and turn the Explorer into the File Manager.

Windows 95 integrates the File Manager and Program Manager functions into the Explorer window and My Computer folder windows. The Explorer is just a window with two panes. My Computer gives you access to single-pane folder windows. Shortcuts, which are similar to program icons in Windows 3.*x*, are now stored in folders. You can view shortcuts in both the Explorer and My Computer windows. If you use large icon view (View, Large Icons in the Explorer or any folder window), your shortcuts will look something like your program icons did in the Program Manager.

The Program Manager window

Undocumented

You can set up your Desktop so it resembles the Windows 3.*x* interface. You can use a Windows 95 folder window to function as the Program Manager.

STEPS

Creating a Program Manager-Like Folder

Step 1.   Right-click My Computer on your Desktop. Click Explore. Navigate until you find a convenient place (any folder or root of a disk drive that's easy to find) to store a hierarchy of folders that will be your Program Manager folders.

You'll be able to move your Program Manager folders later, so it doesn't matter if you don't choose the best spot at first.

Step 2.   Create a folder called PMShortcuts. Do this by right-clicking in the right pane of the Explorer when it is focused on the folder or disk drive root that you chose in step 1. Point to New in the context menu, and then click Folder. Type the name **PMShortcuts**.

Step 3.   Highlight the new PMShortcuts folder in the left pane of the Explorer. Right-click the right pane, Point to New and click Folder. Type the name **Program Manager**.

Step 4.   Continue to right-click the client area of the PMShortcuts folder, adding new folders that are the equivalent of program groups. You will place shortcuts to them in the Program Manager folder.

Give each program group-like folder a name that represents all the shortcuts to applications that you will store in them. For example, you could create a folder named Microsoft Office that will store all of your shortcuts to Microsoft Office applications.

Step 5.   After you have created all the program group-like folders, right-drag the Program Manager folder icon to the Desktop. Click Create Shortcut(s) Here after you drop it there, and change the name of the new shortcut to **Program Manager**.

Step 6.   Double-click the Program Manager icon and it opens up a Program Manager window. Right-drag the other folders you created from the PMShortcuts folder, drop them on the Program Manager folder window, and choose Create Shortcut(s) Here to create shortcuts to them. Change the shortcut names to get rid of the "Shortcut to" prefix.

Step 7.   Now you can right-drag shortcuts or application icons from the Explorer, or maybe from a Find window, to any of the shortcuts to folders within the Program Manager folder window. To make it easier to drop the icons on the folders, you can double-click the shortcuts to folders to open the folder windows first.

You now have a Program Manager folder window that resembles the Program Manager in Windows 3.x. You also have a shortcut to it on the Desktop; any time you want to open the Program Manager window, just double-click this icon. You can also drag this shortcut icon to the Start button to place it on the main Start menu. This is very similar to placing a shortcut to the Desktop folder on the main Start menu.

Because you put a shortcut to the Program Manager folder on the Desktop instead of the folder itself, you won't accidentally delete the folder. The same is true of all the folders displayed within the Program Manager window. All the icons within these folders are also just shortcuts.

You can leave this Program Manager window open on your Desktop, just as you could with the Windows 3.x Program Manager.

The Explorer as File Manager

If you use details view (View, Details), the Explorer looks a lot like the Windows 3.x File Manager. It can accomplish many, but not all, of the functions that the File Manager can and quite a few that the File Manager can't. You can certainly use it as a replacement for the File Manager. For a comparison of the two, see Chapter 9.

Secret

You can't place a shortcut to Explorer.exe in the Startup folder without making any modifications to the shortcut. Explorer.exe contains the complete user interface (Desktop, Taskbar, and so on), so it causes a problem to have the Explorer (the user interface) call itself when it starts up. You can, however, put a shortcut to Explorer.exe in the Startup folder if you modify the Target field of the shortcut (right-click the shortcut, click Properties, and click the Shortcut tab) to C:\WINDOWS\EXPLORER.EXE /n,/e, {*pathname* and *filename*}. (Yes, the commas are necessary in that command line.) The command line parameters that follow Explorer.exe modify this command to start the Explorer and not the complete user interface.

You don't have to put a call to the Explorer in the Startup folder to keep the Explorer close at hand. When you quit Windows 95, just be sure that the Explorer icon is on a Taskbar button; that is, that the Explorer is active. The next time you start Windows 95, the Explorer is one click away.

You can also place a shortcut to the Explorer on the Desktop so you can double-click it to start the Explorer. Right-drag Explorer.exe from the \Windows folder. Drop Explorer.exe on the Desktop and click Create Shortcut(s) Here. Shorten the name of the shortcut to Explorer. Alternatively, you could drag Explorer.exe to the Start button to put a shortcut to the Explorer in the main Start menu. By default, the Programs menu contains a shortcut to the Explorer, called Windows Explorer.

The Explorer isn't the File Manager. It doesn't have a multidocument interface, so you can't display two folder trees next to each other within the Explorer window. Microsoft wants to get away from the multidocument interface and let the operating system manage multiple documents and applications. You can, however, run more than one copy of the Explorer by double-clicking its shortcut on the Desktop twice.

Want to put up two Explorer windows side by side? Here's how.

Tip

Minimize all active windows. If you have created a shortcut to the Explorer on your Desktop, double-click it twice, and then right-click the Taskbar and click Tile Vertically. You now have two Explorer windows side-by-side.

Use the Real Program and File Managers

Program Manager and File Manager are still there (\Windows\Progman.exe and \Windows\Winfile.exe) and you can use them. No shame in that. You can place shortcuts to the Program Manager and File Manager in the Startup folder, so that they come up every time you start Windows 95. You can choose (by right-clicking the shortcut, choosing Properties, and clicking the Shortcut tab) whether they will start up restored, maximized, or minimized on the Taskbar.

Program Manager and File Manager act the same as they did in Windows for Workgroups 3.11. That is their charm. You don't have to learn something new, and you get all the advantages of these applications.

The File Manager is quicker than the Explorer. For one thing, it doesn't have to display all the file icons. For another, it doesn't have to go looking for long filenames. Of course, you can't use the File Manager to display long filenames, because it knows nothing about them.

You can use the File Manager to rename groups of files (as long as the filenames are less than nine characters), which is something you can't do with the Explorer or My Computer. You can configure the Program Manager to minimize itself after you launch an application, and you can't do this with the Explorer or My Computer either.

Even if you don't use File Manager or Program Manager as your primary interface, you can place shortcuts to them in your other interface areas and call them when you want to use their power.

If you leave the Program and File Manager active (on the Taskbar) when you quit Windows 95, you won't have to worry about putting them in the Startup folder. They will return to their positions the next time you start up Windows. You might also want to put shortcuts to them on the Desktop, the main Start menu, or the Programs menu, so that you can start them quickly if you need to.

You can think about ways to combine the use of the Desktop, Start menus, and the Program Manager and File Manager. Some applications, perhaps less-used ones, could go on the Start menus. Applications you use the most frequently could go in the Program Manager.

Some of you may have used the File Manager as your primary shell or user interface. The Start menu mimics the File Manager with its hierarchical structure. You might mix and match these two means of getting to your files.

You can change the shell setting in System.ini. For example, you can set shell=Winfile.exe to make the File Manager your shell (or user interface) in Windows 95. You can then quit Windows 95 by quitting the File Manager. (The default shell is, of course, the standard Windows 95 Explorer shell, which includes the Desktop, the Start button, and the Taskbar.)

There are some problems with using the Program Manager and the File Manager as the Windows 95 user interface. Right-clicking doesn't work in the Program Manager or the File Manager. You can't drag things out of the File Manager and put them on the Desktop, although you can drag applications from the File Manager and drop them into a program group in the Program Manager.

In addition, Ctrl+Esc gets you to the Start button, not to the Task Manager as it did in Windows 3.1. Also, you won't find program group icons in your Program Manager. Instead you see the rather ugly minimized application icons common to multidocument interfaces under Windows 95.

Making Windows 95 a Complete Operating System

Microsoft's strategy, because it owns the operating system, is to include within the operating system increasing levels of basic functionality that appeal to a broad market. That's why it built the Internet Explorer 4.0 into the user interface.

No matter how good Windows 95 is, however, it is never going to be good enough. There will always be something that could improve it dramatically. With time, it will age and your needs will change as you see other possibilities.

Microsoft can't provide everything (neither can we), and Windows 95 needs some improvements. That's why we provide shareware on the *Windows 95 Secrets* CD-ROM. Programs on the *Windows 95 Secrets* CD-ROM can add to the basic Windows 95 software set to make a system that you can use every day.

The *Windows 95 Secrets* CD-ROM includes lots of shareware and freeware applications, many of which have been designed to extend the Windows 95 operating system. We suggest that you look through the categories of shareware on the CD-ROM and see for yourself how you might want to enhance the power of the basic system.

Summary

Windows 95 is still in the box and waiting for you to assemble it. You might want to add some batteries.

▶ We show you how to dredge up the good stuff and put it where the sun does shine.

▶ We give you a way to clean up the clutter Windows 95 created on your Start menus when you set it up over your Windows 3.*x* directory.

▶ We encourage you to use the Desktop as you would any horizontal surface in your office — pile it on. We also show you how you can keep it neat with shortcuts to folders.

▶ Want the Windows 3.*x* retro look? Turn a folder window into the Program Manager.

▶ We show you that you can still use the real Program Manager and File Manager as your user interface.

Chapter 13

Documents First

Document-Centric?

Microsoft has touted the "document-centric" nature of Windows 95. What are they getting at? To get perspective, you have to shift your focus to a non-computer-mediated way of dealing with a document.

If you were going to write a personal letter, perhaps to your mother, you might decide to take out a nice piece of stationery, retrieve a serviceable pen from your desk drawer, and begin the letter. Your attention was on the letter first, the paper second, and the writing implement third.

If you were to write the letter on a computer, you would have to start a letter-writing application before you started writing the letter. The letter-writing software package is the container for the letter. It's as though the pen contains the paper and the letter.

Windows 95 lets the letter-writing application take its more "natural" place as the means (perhaps one of many) of getting the words (and numbers, pictures, and sounds) into the document. The document has gained a measure of independence from the application.

This document-centric approach is reflected in a number of Windows 95 features. Windows 95 has eliminated the Program Manager and File Manager as two separate and distinct ways of viewing the contents of your computer. Their functions are now integrated into My Computer and the Explorer windows. You can place new blank documents on the Desktop or in any folder window. You can access documents via the Documents menu on the Start menu. You can double-click a file icon and have its associated application open it, and you can define actions to be taken on a file and display those actions as options in the context menu.

If you have installed Internet Explorer 4.0, this document-centric orientation is expanded to include documents on the Internet as well as on your own computer or network. You experience the World Wide Web as a web of interconnected documents. Your browser (or the Explorer) is just a window you use to view documents. The documents can be active — for example, they may be forms that let you purchase something — but they still look like documents and not like applications.

Internet Explorer 4.0 modifies the Windows 95 user interface so that it can display HTML documents, including their GIF and JPEG files, ActiveX Objects, Java applets, and anything that can be viewed in a web browser.

You can access HTML documents from the Windows 95 Desktop with a single click, if you stay with the default single-click Web view. If you click an HTML document icon when you're using the Explorer, it appears in the right pane of the window. To traverse from one HTML document to another, you click hyperlinks embedded in the text.

Associating Actions with File Extensions

Like Windows 3.1, Windows 95 uses file extensions to designate file type. A file with the extension *txt* can be, and is by default, designated as having the file type of *text*. Your computer can take certain *actions* on files depending on their file type. For example, sound cards can play music files.

Usually, applications perform the actions. For example, a file with the extension *ht* contains information necessary to successfully call a bulletin board, but it needs HyperTerminal (or any other application that can read *ht* files) to perform the action — to actually make the call.

You can choose (and modify) the actions that will be taken on a file from among all the possible actions that are open to you. The available actions depend on what Windows 95 provides and which other applications you have installed on your computer.

File types and their associated actions are defined (registered) in the Registry files. Windows 95 defines more than 50 file types (and their associated actions) before you get a chance to define your own.

Where Are These Actions?

If you right-click a file of a registered (defined) file type, a context menu appears on the Desktop. In the top section of the context menu are the actions defined for this file type, including any actions you have added. The action listed in boldface (usually the first choice) is the default action. If you double-click the file, this action occurs.

It is quite possible for an application to be able to take literally thousands of different actions on a file. Just think of the many different ways that a word processor (with your help) acts on a document. Not all the actions that an application can undertake need to or should be defined in the Registry.

It only makes sense to define certain kinds of actions in the Registry. Actions that can be taken without significant additional user input come to mind, such as opening, printing, translating the file from one format to another, playing (musically speaking), and updating.

Creating and Editing File Types and Actions

The file type/action association is fundamental to the document-centric character of Windows 95. Without it, you could not double-click a file name or file icon on the Desktop or in a window and have it and its application open in a window. You would always have to start an application first, and then search for the document in the application's File Open dialog box.

One of the main purposes of the Windows 95 Desktop metaphor is to make applications subservient to the data or document. This metaphor falls down when you can't get to your data without going through an application. If you can right-click a file and choose among associated actions in the context menu, it feels like the file is in charge.

You can change which file extensions are associated with which actions. You can add (or register) new extensions. When you install Windows 95 over your existing Windows 3.x directory, the setup program reads your existing Windows 3.x Win.ini and Registry files and places all your existing file types and their associated actions in the Windows 95 Registry files.

When you install a new application under Windows 95, the application stores all its defined file types and their associated action(s) in the Registry. The associated action may simply be opening a file.

You can edit or add new file type/action associations in either a My Computer window or an Explorer window. To do so, take the following steps:

STEPS

Viewing File Types

Step 1.   Open a folder or Explorer window. One way to do this is by right-clicking My Computer and choosing either Open or Explore.

Step 2.   Choose View, Options to display the Options dialog box, and click the File Types tab (see Figure 13-1).

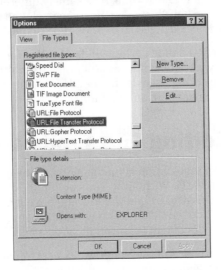

Figure 13-1: The File Types tab of the Options dialog box. Scroll the Registered file types list to view all registered file types.

Step 3.   You can use the New Type, Remove, and Edit buttons to create a new registration for an extension, remove an existing registered extension, or edit the description and associated actions for an existing file type.

Creating a new file type

New file types are usually created when you install a new application. The application developers designate a set of file extensions that are associated with their application, and they include code in the application setup routine that edits your Registry to register their file types and associated application actions.

You can edit the Registry directly to create your own file types and application actions. You can also create new file types quickly using the Open With dialog box (see *Multiple extensions — one application* later in the chapter). However, you can't use the Open With dialog box if you have to add actions to the new file type you're creating. In these situations, you'll need to use the Add New File Type dialog box. If you haven't already done so, follow the Viewing File Types steps in the previous section to display the File Types tab of the Options dialog box, and then continue with the steps below.

STEPS

Creating a New File Type

Step 1. Click the New Type button to display the Add New File Type dialog box (see Figure 13-2).

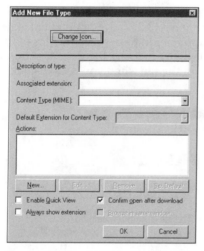

Figure 13-2: The Add New File Type dialog box.

Step 2. Press Tab once. Enter a description of the file type in the Description of type field. The new file type will be listed in the File Types tab of the Options dialog box in alphabetical order by the first letter of this description. Any name that is relevant to you is okay.

Tip

Windows 95 also uses this field to sort files in folder and Explorer windows when you use details view and order by type. When you order by type, Windows 95 doesn't sort files by their extension, as was true under Windows 3.*x*. Rather, it sorts them in alphabetical order by the contents of the Description of type field.

(continued)

Creating a New File Type

Step 3.   Enter the file extension in the Associated extension field. The extension should be no longer than three letters if the application can't handle long filenames — that is, a Win-16 application or one written for Windows 3.*x*. You don't have to type the period.

You won't be allowed to enter an extension that is already registered. This prevents Windows 95 from having to choose between applications when you double-click a file.

Step 4.   If your file type has a defined content type (such as HTML, GIF, JPF, AVI, or MPEG), select it from the Content Type (MIME) drop-down list. The Default Extension for Content Type field will display the default extension as soon as you choose the content type.

Step 5.   Click the New button. The New Action dialog box is displayed, as shown in Figure 13-3. In the Action field, enter an action that you want an application to perform on files of this file type. You might want to begin by defining the default action that an application performs on the file when you double-click it.

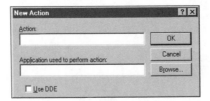

Figure 13-3: The New Action dialog box.

You can use any action name you like. You will associate your action name with an action that you define. You can define a number of different actions, and name each one.

For example, Open and Print are possible action names. Windows 95 will use the action names you choose to describe the associated actions, so you should make them understandable.

Put an ampersand (&) in front of the letter that you want to use to select the action from a context menu with the keyboard. For example, &Open underlines the letter O, so you can press the O key and then Enter to execute this action from the keyboard. Capitalize the first letter of the action.

Creating a New File Type

Step 6. In the Application used to perform action field, enter the name of an application that will perform the named action and that is associated with the file type. Type the complete pathname and the application filename. Add to the application name the command line parameters that will instruct the application to perform the action.

For example, if you want a text file to be printed, you might define the action named Print as **C:\Windows\Notepad.exe /p.** If the application is in a folder with a space in its name, you need to surround the application and its pathname with double quote marks:

```
"C:\Programs Files\Accessories\MSPaint.exe" "%1"
```

This action will open a file (referenced by the parameter %1) using Microsoft Paint.

The possible actions that an application can take on files of this type and the macro language of the application program determine which action names make sense. The default action for most applications is Open. If you put the filename of the application in the Application used to perform action field without any command line parameters, the action it will most likely carry out is to open the file that you right-clicked.

If you put in command line parameters, don't put double quote marks around them. For example:

```
"C:\Program Files\Accessories\MSPaint.exe" /p "%1"
```

Undocumented

Step 7. You can also use Dynamic Data Exchange (DDE) to modify the behavior of the application by passing it a message. If the application has a macro language, you can use that macro language to make the application behave in all sorts of different ways when you choose some action on the context menu. If you want to use DDE to define an action, mark the Use DDE check box. Windows 95 expands the dialog box to display additional fields that let you specify how you want to use DDE.

Figure 13-4 shows a way to modify how files with extensions other than *doc* can be opened by Word for Windows without opening a new copy of Word when it is already active. If you don't use DDE to send a message to Word, another copy of Word is opened when you double-click a file with an extension other than *doc*.

(continued)

STEPS *(continued)*

Creating a New File Type

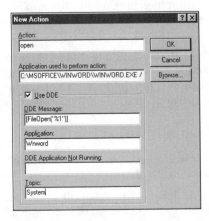

Figure 13-4: Using DDE to modify how a file is opened by Word for Windows.

Step 8.   Click OK when you have finished defining the application's action to return to the Add New File Type dialog box. You can continue defining new actions to take on a given file type by clicking the New button and repeating steps 5 and 6. The actions you define will be listed in the Actions box in the middle of the Add New File Type dialog box. When you've finished defining actions, select one of the actions in the Actions box, and click the Set Default button. This will define the selected action as the action that occurs when you double-click the file.

Step 9.   If you want to change the icon that will represent the new file type, you can do so by clicking the Change Icon button in the Add New File Type dialog box. Optionally mark one or more of the check boxes at the bottom of the dialog box (see the next three sections for descriptions of these options), and then click OK, and click OK again to close the Options dialog box.

You now have a new file type — a new file extension that is associated with a given set of actions, which most likely originate in one or more applications. All of the actions appear on the context menu that is displayed when you right-click a file of this type.

Confirm Open after Download

If the Confirm Open after Download check box at the bottom of the Add New File Type (or Edit File Type) dialog box is marked — the default choice — Windows 95 will ask whether you want to open files of this type after you download them from an Internet site. This is a safety measure to guard against viruses that could be hiding in executable or document files. The Confirm Open after Download check box is only available if you've installed Internet Explorer 4.0.

Enabling Quick View

If you mark the Enable Quick View check box at the bottom of the Add New File Type (or Edit File Type) dialog box, you can use Quick Viewers to see a file on the Desktop without having to open (or even own) an application that is normally used to open it. Windows 95 ships with more than 20 viewers for some common file types. Application developers can ship their own Quick Viewers with their applications. In addition, Inso Corporation, the maker of Outside In and the Quick View technology, ships Quick View Plus, which contains many more viewers.

Quick View is not installed during the typical Windows 95 setup. If you used our guidelines in Chapter 3 and did a custom setup, you had the opportunity to install Quick View then. If you want to install it now, click the Start button, point to Settings, and click Control Panel. Double-click the Add/Remove Programs icon, click the Windows Setup tab, click Accessories, and then click the Details button. Scroll down to the Quick View check box. Check it and then click OK twice. You may be asked for your Windows 95 CD-ROM or diskettes.

You can implement this feature for a file type that has an associated Quick Viewer by clicking this box. If you installed the application, it should have checked this box during setup.

Always show extension

If you mark the Always show extension check box in the Add New File Type (or Edit File Type) dialog box, Windows 95 will show the extension for this file type even if the option to "Hide MS-DOS file extensions for file types that are registered" is checked in the View tab of the Options dialog box (choose View, Options in any Explorer or folder window).

Editing an existing file type

To edit an existing file type, choose View, Options (in any Explorer or folder window) and click on the File Types tab. Select the file type whose actions, or icons, or associated application(s) you want to change, and click the Edit button. You will be presented with the Edit File Type dialog box, which, with the exception of the name, looks just like the Add New File Type dialog box.

You can use the Edit File Type dialog box to add new actions, edit or remove existing ones, or declare a different action as the default. You can also change the icon associated with the file type if you like. The steps for editing a file type are very similar to the ones detailed in the Creating a New File Type steps earlier in the chapter.

One application associated with two file extensions

Secret

If you scroll carefully through the list of registered file types in the File Types tab of the Options dialog box, you will find some file types that show two file extensions. If you use the File Types tab of the Options dialog box, you can't create a file type with two extensions and only one entry in the list. You can, however, do this using the Registry editor or the Open With dialog box. (See the section entitled *Multiple extensions — one application* later in this chapter.)

File associations via the Registry

Undocumented

The File Types tab of the Options dialog box is a front end to the Registry — but then so are most of the properties sheets and dialog boxes that you deal with in Windows 95. You can edit the Registry entries for your file types directly, if you like, using the Registry editor.

STEPS

Editing File Types in the Registry

Step 1. Go to Chapter 15 if you need to learn more about the Registry. If you have put a shortcut to the Registry editor on your Desktop, double-click it. Otherwise, find Regedit.exe in the \Windows folder using the Explorer or My Computer, and double-click it.

Step 2. Click the plus sign next to HKEY_CLASSES_ROOT. This branch of the Registry will expand. The first keys shown are the file extensions. They all start with a period. There should be at least 50 keys, all marked with folder icons.

Step 3. Click any of the keys that are file extensions. A file type name will be associated with each one (listed in the right pane). Look at a few of these names to get an idea of how they are associated with the extension.

Step 4. Scroll down the HKEY_CLASS_ROOT branch until you pass the extension keys and get to the file type names. Click the plus sign next to a file type name that corresponds to a file type or extension that you previously viewed in step 3.

Step 5. Click the plus sign next to *shell* under the file type name. Notice that the action names associated with that file type are displayed. Click the plus signs by those action names and then click the *command* key.

Step 6. Notice that the action defined in the New Action (or Editing Action) dialog box is defined here. If DDE is used, you will find references to it under whichever action is was defined for.

Editing File Types in the Registry

Step 7. Use the Registry editor's New, Delete, and Rename commands (in the Edit menu) to create new file types or edit existing ones, using the models you explored in steps 1 through 6. You may need to turn to Chapter 15 for more information on how to edit these values. When you are done, exit the Registry.

You may find old file types and file type names that no longer apply. You can prune them out of the Registry if you like.

Change the edit application for batch files

Tip

If you right-click an MS-DOS batch file (a file with the *bat* extension) while it is displayed in a folder window, and then click Open, you will notice that Notepad is used to edit the file. To use WordPad instead of Notepad as the editor for *bat* files, take the following steps:

STEPS

Editing the Action Associated with *bat* Files

Step 1. Open a folder or Explorer window. One way to do this is by right-clicking My Computer and choosing either Open or Explore.

Step 2. Choose View, Options, and click the File Types tab.

Step 3. Select MS-DOS Batch File in the Registered file types box. Click the Edit button.

Step 4. Highlight Edit in the Actions field and notice that the Edit button is grayed out. You can't change the application associated with editing a batch file this way. This is why you need access to the Registry.

Step 5. If you have a shortcut to the Registry editor on your Desktop, double-click it. Otherwise, find Regedit.exe in the \Windows folder using the Explorer or My Computer, and double-click it.

Step 6. Click the plus sign next to HKEY_CLASS_ROOT. Scroll down to *batfile*. Click the plus sign next to *batfile*. Click the plus signs next to *shell*, and then *edit*.

Step 7. Select *command*. Double-click Default in the right pane of the Registry editor.

Step 8. Type **"C:\Program Files\Accessories\Wordpad.exe"** %1.

Multiple extensions — one application

Secret

Using the Registry editor you can create multiple extensions, and associate them with one application. If you have Microsoft Word installed, you will notice that the extensions *.dot* and *.doc* in the Registry (under HKEY_CLASSES_ROOT) both refer to Word Document. This is how multiple extensions are associated with one application.

Using the Registry editor, you can edit an entry for an extension to change the application that the extension is associated with. Highlight an extension entry in the Registry editor, double-click Default in the right pane of the Registry editor, and type a new file type name or the name of an existing file type.

If you created a new file type name, you will then need to create a new key value in HKEY_CLASSES_ROOT by that name. In addition, you will need to define some actions that are associated with that file type. Use the existing keys in this section of the Registry as examples.

You can also use the Open With dialog box to associate a new file type with the Open action for an existing application. Unfortunately, when using Open With, the only action you can associate with this new file type and extension is the Open action. Other actions may be associated with the file types that were created when the application was first installed, and you can't use the Open With dialog box to associate these actions with the new file type and extension. However, once you've used Open With to associate a file type with an application, you can edit the file type to associate it with other actions.

To see how the Registry is changed when you use the Open With dialog box, take the following steps:

STEPS
New File Types with Open With

Step 1. Right-click the Desktop, point to New, and click Text Document.

Step 2. Rename the document Test.tst. Click OK when warned about changing the extension.

Step 3. Right-click Test.tst. Choose Open With on the context menu. Choose some existing registered application, or click Other to specify any other application. Exit the application after Test.tst has been opened.

Step 4. Now open up your Registry editor, scroll down HKEY_CLASSES_ROOT to *.tst* and find the application name associated with this extension. Scroll further down and find this application name. Notice the associated command for opening a file in the application. Close the Registry editor.

Editing (not merging) exported Registry files

Tip

Exporting your Registry or a branch of your Registry creates a file with a *reg* extension. The default action for this file type is Merge, as in merge this file back into the Registry. We find this a bit dangerous. Fortunately, you can easily change the default action for this file type.

STEPS

Changing the Default Action for an Exported Registry File

Step 1. Open a folder or Explorer window. Choose View, Options, and click the File Types tab.

Step 2. Scroll through the Registered file types list and select Registration Entries.

Step 3. Click the Edit button.

Step 4. Select Edit in the list of actions. Click the Set Default button.

Step 5. Click the Close button twice to close the Edit File Type and Options dialog boxes.

Re-associating RTF files with WordPad

Tip

If you install Word for Windows after you install Windows 95, the Open action for Rich Text Format (RTF) files is associated with Word and not WordPad. If you want to open this type of file with WordPad, edit the Open action associated with rtf files so it points to \Program Files \Accessories\Wordpad.exe instead.

Secret

If you find that your new associations are reverting to their previous association (for example, if after changing the *rtf* association to WordPad, it goes back to Word), you are the victim of Microsoft's not-too-smart Registry association update routines. These go in after you install a new program and update the Registry based on what is in the [Extensions] section of the Win.ini file.

If you have an old association of *rtf* with Word in the Win.ini file, Windows 95 might use it to "update" your Registry and wipe out your new change. A way to get around this is to erase this association in the [Extensions] section of Win.ini. Unless you are using cc:Mail, you can erase this whole section. You might want to make a copy first, just in case.

Associating more than one program with a given file type

You can define many actions for a given file type. And you can associate each of these actions with a different application. Each action has to have a unique name. The following example describes one situation in which you might want to associate multiple programs with a single file type.

Tip

Files of the file type screen saver have an *scr* extension. Script files used by many different programs (although not by the Windows 95 DUN scripting application) also use the *scr* extension. You can create an action, which we call Edit Scripts, that is associated with script files. To do so, take the following steps:

STEPS

Adding an Edit Scripts Option to the File Type Screen Saver

Step 1.   Open a folder or Explorer window. Choose View, Options, and click the File Types tab.

Step 2.   Scroll through the Registered file types list and select Screen Saver.

Step 3.   Click the Edit button, and then click the New button.

Step 4.   Type **Edit Scripts** in the Action field. Browse to \Windows\Notepad.exe in the Application used to perform action field.

Step 5.   Click OK, then Close, and then Close again.

Opening Unregistered File Types

If you double-click a file that has an extension that is not registered, Windows 95 will not try to open the file. Instead, it will display the Open With dialog box, as shown in Figure 13-5. This dialog box lists all the programs associated through actions to registered file types.

The "Always use this program to open this file" check box is marked by default. If, in general, you want files with this extension to be opened by the application that you are about to choose, then leave this box checked. You can also type a description of the file type in the Description of '*.xxx*' files field. Choose a program to open this file by double-clicking the program name in the list box or by clicking the Other button to find the program that you want.

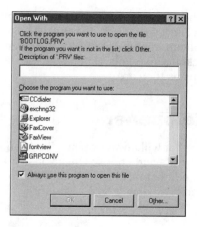

Figure 13-5: The Open With dialog box.

If you just want to open this file now and not worry about establishing an association between its file type and an application, clear the "Always use this program to open this file" check box and double-click an appropriate program to open the file.

This method of opening files of an unregistered type gives you a great deal of flexibility, at a cost of having to scroll to find an appropriate application. It also lets you create new file types and associate them with applications without using the File Types tab of the Options dialog box.

Opening a registered file type with another application

Sometimes, you might want to open a file whose file type is already registered and whose Open action is already associated with an application that you would rather not use this time. If you double-click the file in the Explorer or a folder window (or right-click the file and choose Open from the context menu), the associated application will open it.

Tip

Hold down the Shift key and right-click the file in an Explorer or folder window. The Open command in the context menu becomes Open With to allow you to choose an application other than the one already associated with this file type.

When you choose Open With, the Open With dialog box (refer to Figure 13-5) appears, but the "Always use this program to open this file" check box is not marked. If you want to change the associated Open action for this file type to the new application, you'll need to mark this box.

This is a quick way of changing the associated Open action for a given file type. You don't have to go to the File Types tab in the Options dialog box and edit the reference to the application associated with the Open action. When you use the Shift+right-click method, you just change the default Open action, and leave the other actions as they are.

Create a default file opener

Secret

You can define a default program that will always open a file of an unregistered type when you right-click the file and choose OpenNote (or a different name of your choosing) from the context menu. This lets you avoid going through the rigmarole of the Open With dialog box. A variation on this method lets you open the file with a double-click.

STEPS

Defining a Default File Opener

Step 1.   If you have a shortcut to the Registry editor on your Desktop, double-click it. Otherwise, find Regedit.exe in the \Windows folder using the Explorer or My Computer, and double-click it.

Step 2.   Click the plus sign next to HKEY_CLASS_ROOT. Scroll down the left pane until you find Unknown. Click the Unknown folder icon. Click *shell*.

Step 3.   Choose Edit, New, Key. Type **OpenNote**, and then select OpenNote.

You don't have to name the command OpenNote. You can type any name that will make sense to you as a menu item in the context menu, and that corresponds with the action or command that you are about to define.

Step 4.   Choose Edit, New, Key. Type **command**. Highlight the *command* folder icon.

Step 5.   Double-click Default in the right pane of the Registry editor. Enter the filename and path to the application that you want to use as the default file opener. For example, type **C:\Windows\Notepad.exe %1**.

Step 6.   Click OK, and exit the Registry editor.

A variation on the above steps lets you double-click to open a file of an unregistered file type with the default file-open application. You need to first examine the *openas* key under the Unknown key because you are going to delete it (and the *command* key under it) and then put it back in.

The steps required to do this are the same as the ones given above — but before you take step 3, examine *openas*, write down the command data, and then delete the *openas* key. After step 5, use Edit, New, Key to put the *openas* key and its *command* key back in as before, but now under OpenNote (or whatever name you chose).

Now when you double-click a file of an unregistered type in Explorer, it will open the file in the specified program. Both OpenNote and Open With will now be in the context menu when you right-click an unregistered file. You can still use Open With if you want to choose a different program to open the file.

You can substitute other applications instead of Notepad for your default file opener. You might try WordPad. Unlike Notepad, which chokes on non-text files, WordPad can open files of almost any format except executables. If you have a hex editor, use that in this example instead.

General actions on any file type

Secret

You can define a set of actions that will apply to any file type or to any unregistered file type. These actions will then appear in the context menu when you right-click any file or when you right-click any file of an unregistered file type. Matthias Koenig showed us this little gem.

In the earlier section entitled *Create a default file opener*, we showed you how to use the Registry editor to create OpenNote, an action that would open unknown file types with Notepad.exe. You had to use the Registry editor to create this action because the "file types" Unknown and All are not displayed in the File Types tab of the Options dialog box.

You can, if you like, display these two "file types" in the File Types tab of the Options dialog box. Once they are there, you can define any actions you care to for them.

STEPS

Defining Actions for Any File Type

Step 1. Right-click the Desktop, point to New, and then click Text Document.

Step 2. Rename the text document **All.reg**. Click OK when asked about the extension change. (Be sure that you are showing your MS-DOS extensions. To do this in the Explorer, choose View, Options, View, clear the check box labeled Hide MS-DOS file extensions for file types that are registered, and click OK.)

(continued)

Defining Actions for Any File Type

Step 3.   Right-click the new document icon that you have just created, and choose Edit. Type the following text into the document, save, and close it when you are done:

```
REGEDIT4
[HKEY_CLASSES_ROOT\Unknown]
"EditFlags"=hex:02,00,00,00
[HKEY_CLASSES_ROOT\*]
"EditFlags"=hex:02,00,00,00
```

Step 4.   Right-click the All.reg document icon, and then click Merge.

Step 5.   Open an Explorer or folder window. Choose View, Options, and then click the File Types tab.

Step 6.   The first entry should now be an asterisk (*), which stands for All file types. Scroll down the file types list to find the Unknown file type. You can use the methods described in this chapter to add new actions to these "file types."

Printing files using other applications

One of the biggest limitations of the Send To menu item is that you cannot configure a Send To command line with parameters. Say you have *txt* files associated with Notepad, but you frequently want to print *txt* files with WordPad because you like the fact that WordPad doesn't automatically add headers and footers to the output, as Notepad does. You could try adding /P as a parameter to WordPad.exe's command line in a Send To shortcut, but it doesn't work. Windows ignores any parameters that follow the executable name in the shortcut. (To see the command line underlying a Send To shortcut, right-click the shortcut in the C:\Windows\SendTo folder, click Properties, and then click the Shortcut tab.)

The best way to get around this limitation is to define a shortcut that will appear on your context menus and do anything you desire. This will let you use your right mouse button to select a file and launch almost any action you can think of.

It's easy to define a new action for all files with a particular extension. Here's how to create a new context menu item that appears when you right-click a *txt* file in the Explorer or a folder window, and automatically prints text files through WordPad instead of Notepad:

STEPS

Print a Text File Using WordPad

Step 1. In the Explorer, choose View, Options, and click the File Types tab.

Step 2. In the list of Registered file types, scroll down and select Text Document, click the Edit button, and then click the New button.

Step 3. In the New Action dialog box that appears, type **Print Using WordPad** as the Action. In the Application used to perform action box, type the following:

```
"C:\Program Files\Accessories\WordPad.exe" /P
```

In this example, the quotes are necessary because one of the folder names contains a space. The parameter /P causes WordPad.exe to print the *txt* file.

Step 4. Click OK, and then click Close twice to exit the dialog boxes.

Back in the Explorer window, find a *txt* file and right-click it. You should see a new Print Using WordPad command on the context menu. Click this choice. You should see WordPad flash for a moment as it reads the file and automatically sends it to the printer.

You can create all kinds of commands for all types of files. Many applications support a variety of command line parameters that launch different kinds of behaviors on files you open. Word for Windows, for example, supports the parameter /m followed by a Word command. For example, if you use /mFilePrintPreview with *doc* files, you can open documents in Print Preview mode, rather than in Normal view. (In Word, choose Tools, Customize, Menus to see other possible commands you can use.)

Changing BMP Icons to Show Thumbnail

Secret

Each file type displays its associated icon in the Explorer, on the Desktop, or in folder windows. Instead of using a single uniform icon for all your *bmp* files, you can display a crude thumbnail sketch of each file. Thanks for this secret go to Firas El-Hassan, who sent a message to the Windows 95 beta forum on CompuServe about how to create a unique icon for each graphic. If you use this trick, you will know in advance what you're going to see when you double-click a *bmp* file icon:

STEPS

Thumbnails for *bmp* Files

Step 1. Double-click Regedit.exe in your \Windows folder.

Step 2. Click the plus sign next to HKEY_CLASSES_ROOT. Scroll down the left pane of the Registry editor to Paint.Picture.

If you have installed another bitmap editor that has supplanted the default action for *bmp* files, which is to open them with MS Paint, you have to scroll down to that application name instead. To find out the action name, highlight *.bmp* under HKEY_CLASSES_ROOT in the left pane of your Registry editor.

Step 3. Click the plus sign next to Paint.Picture, and select DefaultIcon in the left pane of the Registry editor.

Step 4. Double-click Default in the right pane.

Step 5. In the Edit String dialog box, delete the existing value in the Value data field, and type **%1** instead. Click OK.

Go to an Explorer or folder window and focus on a folder that contains *bmp* files. Choose View, Large Icons, and check out the new thumbnails. They should each display a tiny thumbnail of each bitmap, not the generic paint icon.

Viewing a File without Starting an Application

If you right-click a file icon in the Explorer, a folder window, or on the Desktop, you may see Quick View in the context menu (if you don't, see the *Enabling Quick View* section earlier in this chapter). You have this option if the file that you right-click is of a registered file type and Windows 95 has a file viewer for that type.

Windows 95 ships with more than 20 file viewers. These viewers know about the file format of the documents of a given file type. They can load quickly, read the document, and display it on your Desktop.

Microsoft encourages application developers to ship file viewers with their applications, so you may have additional viewers stored in the \Windows\System\Viewers folder. Windows 95 ships with Quick Viewers for the file types shown in Table 13-1. Many of the applications that Quick View can display are either rarely used or not the latest versions.

Table 13-1	Files Windows 95 Recognizes
File Extension	*File Type*
asc	ASCII
bmp	Windows bitmapped graphics
cdr	CorelDRAW versions 4 and 5
dib	Windows bitmapped graphics
dll	Dynamic link libraries (application extensions)
doc	Microsoft Word 2.0 and 6.0, WordPad, others
drw	Micrographic draw
exe	Executable format
inf	Windows setup files (text)
ini	Windows configuration files (text)
mod	Multiplan versions 3, 4, 4.1
ppt	PowerPoint version 4
pre	Freelance Graphics for Windows
rle	Bitmapped graphics (Run Length Encoded)
rtf	Rich Text Format
sam	Ami, Ami Pro
wb1	Quattro Pro for Windows
wdb	MS Works Database
wk1	Lotus 1-2-3 versions 1 and 2
wk3	Lotus 1-2-3 version 3
wk4	Lotus 1-2-3 version 4
wks	Lotus 1-2-3 or MS Works version 3
wmf	Windows Meta File
wp5	WordPerfect 5
wp6	WordPerfect 6
wpd	WordPerfect demo
wps	MS Works word processing
wq1	Quattro Pro for MS-DOS
wq2	Quattro Pro for MS-DOS version 5
wri	Windows Write
xlc	MS Excel Chart
xls	MS Excel versions 4 and 5

All you have to do is right-click a file of one of the above file types (or with one of the above file extensions) and choose Quick View in the context menu. Quick View will display the file in a view window. If you want to edit the file and you have the associated application, click the Edit button in the view window, and Quick View will load that application for you.

Undocumented

You can create a shortcut on the Desktop for the Quick Viewer, and then drag and drop files to the Quick Viewer from the Explorer or a folder window. If you drag a file to the Quick Viewer that is not associated with any viewer, Quick View will ask if you want to view it with the default viewer.

STEPS
Putting the Quick Viewer on Your Desktop

Step 1.   Use My Computer or the Explorer to view the \Windows\System\Viewers folder.

Step 2.   Right-drag Qvstub.exe to the Desktop and drop it there.

Step 3.   Change Qvstub's icon name to **Quick Viewer**.

For an even easier and quicker way to view files without a specific viewer, see the next section.

Inso, the manufacturer of Quick View, also offers Quick View Plus, which has a much more extensive list of file viewers. Inso's latest version works with Internet Explorer and Netscape Navigator (as an ActiveX component or as a Netscape Plug-In) to allow you to view other types of documents while online. You can find Inso at http://www.inso.com.

Easiest Way to View/Open an Unregistered File

If you right-click a file in the Explorer or in a folder window, you will see the Send To command in the context menu. When you point to it, a submenu appears, as shown in Figure 13-6. When you first set up Windows 95, this submenu should contain such items as $3^1/_2$ Floppy and Fax Recipient.

The Send To list contains your common destinations.

Undocumented

You can add shortcuts to the Quick Viewer and your text file opener. To view or open a file of an unregistered type, right-click it, click Send To, and then click either the Quick Viewer or an application icon. Here's how to set up Notepad as a text file-open application:

Figure 13-6: The Send To menu.

STEPS

Send File to Notepad

Step 1.   Open an Explorer window. Make sure you can see all file extensions. If you can't, choose View, Options, View to set this.

Step 2.   Navigate to the \Windows folder in the left pane, and click the plus sign next to it. Then select the Windows folder icon.

Step 3.   Scroll down the right pane until Notepad.exe is visible. Right-drag Notepad.exe to the SendTo folder icon in the left pane and drop it there. Click Create Shortcut(s) Here.

Step 4.   Select the SendTo folder icon in the left pane of the Explorer. Select the Shortcut to Notepad.exe icon in the right pane, and then click it again. Rename this icon **Notepad**.

Step 5.   Notepad will now be a choice in your Send To menu. You can place a shortcut to Qvstub.exe in the SendTo folder in a similar manner. (See *Viewing a File Without Starting an Application* earlier in this chapter for more information about Quick View.)

Of course, you don't have to choose Notepad as your text file opener. You can also put numerous other shortcuts in the SendTo folder.

Documents on the Start Menu

If you open a file by double-clicking it (or by right-clicking it and then choosing Open) in a folder window or an Explorer window, a reference to it will show up on a list under the Documents submenu of the Start menu. The last 15 documents you open this way appear on this list. If you want to work with one of these documents, simply click on its name in the Documents menu. Windows 95 will start the application you used to create the document, and then open the document inside it.

If you open a document within a Windows 3.*x* application — using the File, Open command, for example — it does not show up on the Documents list.

Undocumented

To clear the Documents list, right-click the Taskbar, click Properties, click the Start Menu Programs tab, and then click Clear. To clear just the documents that you want cleared, open the \Windows\Recent folder in the Explorer or a folder window and delete the undesired documents. (Make sure you have Windows 95 set to show all files; otherwise, you won't see the Recent folder. To check, choose View, Options, View in any Explorer or folder window.)

You can put a shortcut to \Windows\Recent on your Desktop. This is another way to get to these recently opened documents, and it also lets you easily edit the list.

You can clean out the contents of the Recent folder every time that you start up Windows 95 using a setting found in TweakUI. Just click the Paranoia tab and then select Clear Document history at logon.

New Blank Documents

Creating new blank documents on the Desktop, in a folder window, or in the Explorer is discussed in Chapter 8. You can create blank documents by right-clicking the Desktop (or an empty part of a folder or Explorer window), pointing to New, and then clicking the desired document type.

Tip

If your desired file type isn't on the New menu, don't worry. Click any file type. When the new blank document icon appears, its name is selected. Type a new name with an extension of the registered file type you want. You will get a dialog box asking you if you are sure you want to change the extension. You do.

The new file will contain the data associated with the file type you just chose (but not the file type associated with the new extension). If you chose to create a new document of the Text Document file type, but later change the file extension to *doc,* the file will still contain plain text until you save it in Word for Windows or another word-processing document format.

Adding Items to the New Menu

You can use TweakUI to add items to the New menu (or remove them from the menu). It's a simple matter of dragging and dropping a blank document or file of the correct file type onto TweakUI's New tab. The document you drag needs to be associated with an application.

You might have installed an application, but an association with the file extension you want to use for the new blank document has not been created. You can easily create an association by first creating a new blank document in your application. Rename the document with the new extension that you want to associate with this application. Then Shift+right-click the new document in an the Explorer or folder window, and choose Open With. Make sure the Always use this program to open this file check box is marked. Click the Other button in the Open With dialog box, and browse to your application.

Once you have created an association between the document and an application, you can create a New menu item by dragging the blank document onto TweakUI's New tab.

Secret

You can also edit your Registry to manually create the New menu item. This gives you complete control over the process.

If you are going to manually create a New menu item, the first step is to make sure you have registered the document type in the Registry. Do this by following the steps in the section entitled *Creating a new file type* earlier in this chapter.

Next you need to edit the new file type's entry in the Registry. The following steps show you how to do that:

STEPS

Creating an Item on the New Menu

Step 1.   Go to Chapter 15 if you need to learn more about the Registry. If you have put a shortcut to the Registry editor on your Desktop, double-click it. Otherwise, find Regedit.exe in the \Windows folder using the Explorer or My Computer, and double-click it.

Step 2.   Click the plus sign next to HKEY_CLASSES_ROOT. This branch of the Registry will expand. The first keys shown are the file extensions. They all start with a period. There should be at least 50 keys, all marked with folder icons.

Step 3.   Click the file extension key that matches the file type you just created.

Step 4.   Right-click the right pane of the Registry editor. Choose New, Key. Change the name of the key to **ShellNew**.

Step 5.   Click the new ShellNew key in the left panel of the Registry. Right-click the right panel. Choose New, String Value. Type the name **NullFile**.

Step 6.   Exit the Registry editor when you are done.

The file type description for a file with this extension is now added to the New menu. When you select this file type from the New menu, Windows 95 will create a text file, but it will have the extension you just picked in the Registry.

Immediately invoke an application with a new file

If you want to have an application called immediately when you create a new blank file using the New menu, you can add a command string value to the ShellNew key. To do so, take the following steps:

STEPS

Invoking an Application when You Create a New File

Step 1. Follow the first five steps in the previous section.

Step 2. If it is not highlighted, click the ShellNew key in the left panel of the Registry. Right-click the right panel. Click New, String Value. Type the name **command**.

Step 3. Double-click *command*. Type the path and filename of the application that will be invoked. Include a space and then a **%1** after the filename to allow the new file to be opened by the application. If the application is stored in a folder with a pathname that includes a space, put double quote marks around the combined path and filename of the application, and put double quote marks around the %1.

Step 4. Exit the Registry editor.

Make the new file of the correct file type

If you want the new file you created in the previous section to be the correct file type, you need to create an empty file with your application, store it in the \Windows\ShellNew folder, and tie this empty file to the ShellNew command that is associated with the application.

For example, you can create an empty Windows Write file and store it in the \Windows\ShellNew folder. You can then edit the Registry so that the ShellNew command associated with the *wri* extension points to this new empty file.

In Chapter 15 we show you the hard way to do this in order to illustrate some of the lower-level functions found in the Registry. What follows is an easier way. The easiest way? Use TweakUI and drag a blank document created by an application into the New tab.

In the following steps we use Windows Write as an example of how to create a new file of the correct file type. You can do this with any file type.

STEPS

Creating a New File of the Correct File Type

Step 1. Double-click your Windows Write icon and create a new file. Save it in a temporary folder with the name Write.wri. Using the Explorer, move the file to the \Windows\ShellNew folder. This folder is hidden, so you will need to have your Show all files option marked in order to see it. (Choose View, Options in the Explorer, and click the View tab.)

Step 2. Go to Chapter 15 if you need to learn more about the Registry. If you have put a shortcut to the Registry editor on your Desktop, double-click it. Otherwise, find Regedit.exe in the \Windows folder using the Explorer or My Computer, and double-click it.

Step 3. Click the plus sign next to HKEY_CLASSES_ROOT. This branch of the Registry will expand. The first keys shown are the file extensions. They all start with a period. There should be at least 50 keys, all marked with folder icons.

Step 4. Click a file extension key that matches the file type you just created (let's say the *wri* extension). Click the ShellNew key that you created using the Creating an Item on the New Menu steps earlier in this chapter.

Step 5. If you created a NullFile entry, delete it by highlighting it in the right panel of the Registry editor and pressing the Delete key.

Step 6. Right-click the right panel. Choose New, String Value. Type the name **FileName**.

Step 7. Double-click FileName. Type the name of the empty file, which in this case is Write.wri.

Step 8. Exit the Registry editor when you are finished.

Now when you use the New menu to create a new blank document associated with Windows Write, it will create a properly formatted document.

We wish to thank Matthias Koenig for providing much of this information.

Taking items off the New menu

Install a bunch of applications and pretty soon your New menu gets unwieldy. You can take document types off the menu and put them back on when you need to. Again, TweakUI to the rescue. Just click the New tab and choose which items to keep on the menu.

TweakUI accomplishes its New menu management task by placing a minus sign as the last character in the ShellNew key name associated with the file type extension in the HKEY_CLASSES_ROOT section of the Registry. You can use your Registry editor to examine some of the file extensions listed and see how this works.

Summary

We describe how to make it easy to get to your documents without having to go through your applications first.

▶ The Desktop and folder windows can give you a view of your documents. It is such a bother to have to open an application first to see these documents and work on them. We show you how to get right to the document and let the application take care of itself.

▶ We show you how to create new file types and define actions that can be taken on files of those types — actions that can automate your work.

▶ We show you how to use DDE and the macro languages built into your applications to automate your work even further.

▶ We use the Registry editor to change the assigned edit application for MS-DOS batch files from WordPad to Notepad.

▶ We show you how to create new menu choices for the right mouse button so that you can right-click (or double-click) your files and have something useful happen.

▶ We give you a couple of ways to create shortcuts to opening and viewing files of unknown file types.

▶ Finally, we describe how to clear the Documents list on the Start menu and open new blank documents on your Desktop.

Chapter 14

The Recycle Bin — Going Through the Trash

In This Chapter

We reveal the secrets and subtleties of deleting files, folders, and shortcuts, including:

▶ Using the Recycle Bin to store your deleted files and shortcuts until you are sure that you want to get rid of them

▶ Seeing how files are stored in these hidden folders

▶ Deleting (and copying, moving, and renaming) files in the common file dialog boxes

▶ Restoring deleted files and folders or moving the files to new locations out of the Recycle Bin

▶ Deleting files over a network

What's Recyclable about the Recycle Bin?

The Recycle Bin doesn't recycle anything but your disk space. If you want to stretch the analogy a bit, you could say that if you delete unused files, you won't have to go out and buy new hard disks, but that is stretching it.

Our take on the use of this symbol for the trash can is Microsoft's realization that people would rather have a Recycle basket on their Desktop than a trash can. It is cooler. Right?

So why the Bin part of Recycle Bin? During the early stages of the Windows 95 (then code-named Chicago) beta testing, its name was Recycle.bin. This is a pun. In a Unix file system, *bin* is a standard subdirectory where the *binary* files (executable programs) are stored. Combine the trash-receptacle meaning of the word *bin* with its Unix-world meaning, and the nerds at Microsoft got .*bin* on the Chicago Desktop. An art designer or somebody in marketing made them get rid of the period and capitalize the *b*.

Secret

Want to change the name of the Recycle Bin to Trash Can? All you need to do is search your Registry for all occurrences of the name *Recycle Bin* and change each one to *Trash Can*. You can also open the Registry editor and navigate to HKEY_CLASSES_ROOT\CLSID\{645FF040-5081-101B-9F08-00AA002F954E}, double-click Default in the right pane, and type the new name. Searching and editing the Registry is discussed in Chapter 15.

The Recycled Folders

The Recycle Bin is an alias (a stand-in) for the special folders labeled Recycled. You can use the Explorer to see these folders — you'll find one on every hard disk and every logical drive on the hard disk. (If you have divided the hard disk into multiple drives, such as C, D, and so on, you will see a Recycled folder on each logical drive.) The Recycle Bin icon is displayed on the Desktop, and it's attached to the Desktop icon in the Explorer, on the same level as the My Computer and Network Neighborhood icons. The Recycled folder icons are attached to the hard disk drive icons along with your other folders. (The Recycled folders are indeed folders, even though they don't have the standard folder icons.) They are designated as file type Recycle Bin.

If you double-click the Recycle Bin icon or any of the Recycled folder icons, you will find that they all display the same contents. Opening the Recycled folder icon attached to one hard disk will show the files deleted from your other local hard disks as well.

Microsoft made it a point to put the Recycle Bin on the Desktop and made it hard to remove. The Recycle Bin stores all the files that have been deleted from your hard disks. You have to go to only one place to find all your deleted files.

Want to get the Recycle Bin icon off the Desktop? Use TweakUI to clear it. Don't worry, you can still get to the Recycle Bin by going to the Recycled folders.

Secret

You can change the name of the Recycled folders; it just doesn't do any good. If you change the name *Recycled* to *Wasted*, the next time you start Windows 95, it creates a new Recycled folder. You end up with two recycle receptacle icons, both of which display the same list of deleted files when you double-click them.

If you were following along and really created a Wasted folder, now we have to bail you out. You have a Recycled folder and a Wasted folder. How do you erase or get rid of the Wasted folder? It's not so easy.

STEPS

Getting Rid of the Wasted Folder

Step 1. Click the Start button, point to Programs, and click MS-DOS Prompt to open a DOS window.

Step 2. Change directories to the \Wasted directory. (You'll find it in the root directory.)

Step 3. Type **dir /a** to see if any files are stored in the Wasted directory. You are going to purge these files, so be sure to restore any that you might want to keep before you take the next step. To restore any of these files, right-click the Wasted folder, click Open, right-click any file that you want to restore and click Restore.

Step 4. Type **Attrib -r -s -h Desktop.ini**.

Step 5. Type **del *.*** and press the Enter key.

Step 6. Change directories to the root directory of the hard disk partition that contains the Wasted directory (**cd **).

Step 7. Remove the Wasted directory by typing **rd Wasted** at the DOS prompt.

The Recycled folders are system resources. Windows 95 regenerates them if you change the name of a Recycled folder. It doesn't want you to mess with these resources because it needs them to manage deleted files.

Secret

The Recycled folders are indeed folders, but they are special ones. When you display the contents of a Recycled folder in details view, you'll see an additional column named Original Location. Recycled folders don't use the folder icon. And the Recycled folders are hidden so that you can't see them if you go to DOS and type **dir** (although you can see them if you type **dir /a**).

Windows 95 puts the deleted files in these folders, but it stores them under new names (although you don't see this). Each Recycled folder contains an additional file named Info. Again, you don't see this file (unless you type **dir /a** at the DOS prompt). Windows 95 combines the deleted files and the Info file to create entries that look like the original deleted filenames with the addition of a column that lists their original location.

What is really unusual about these Recycled folders is that their folder windows display the names and icons of all the deleted files, not just the ones stored in that particular folder or deleted from that particular logical disk drive. The files deleted from a particular drive, however, are actually stored in the Recycled folder on that drive. You can see this for yourself by going to the DOS prompt, changing directories to the Recycled folder on a particular drive, and typing **dir /a**.

The code that makes the Recycled folders special is stored in a dynamic link library named Shell32.dll. This file is referenced in the Desktop.ini file.

Figure 14-2: The Windows 95 common file dialog box. You can highlight a file listed in this box and delete it by pressing the Delete key. You can also drag and drop files to and from this dialog box.

You can't delete files in the older common file dialog boxes, such as those used by Windows 3.*x* Write. Microsoft now refers to these as *Win-16* common dialog boxes.

Deleted, what does that mean?

To *delete* a file means to move it to the Recycle Bin.

The fact that deleted files are stored in the Recycle Bin means that they aren't "really" deleted. They are still taking up space on your hard disk. If you don't get around to emptying the Recycle Bin until your disk is full, you will experience performance slowdowns or problems with other applications as your free disk space shrinks.

What is great about the Recycle Bin is that it allows you to organize and clean up your file system without having to make a decision that you may regret a few minutes later. If you delete something and then realize it's more important than you had thought, you can restore it easily.

The Recycle Bin provides a trade-off between the safety and convenience of not deleting the file until later and the valuable disk space taken up by these deleted items. It is up to you to decide when to empty it.

Secret

Files that you delete in a DOS session are not sent to the Recycle Bin. Likewise, if an application deletes files without using an Explorer window, folder window, or the new common file dialogs, these files are not sent to the Recycle Bin. As far as the Windows 95 or DOS file-management system is concerned, the files are deleted.

Do you want the files you delete in a DOS window to go to the Recycle Bin? You can if you use a little freeware application called Delete.exe. You'll find it at http://ourworld.compuserve.com/homepages/vrangan/.

When you empty the Recycle Bin or delete files in a DOS session, the names of the deleted files are altered so that they don't show up in the file listings in the Explorer, folder windows, or DOS directory lists. The disk space taken up by the files is now available to be written over by new files. If they haven't been written over yet, you can recover these files by using low-level tools. For additional information, see the section entitled *Undelete and Unerase* later in this chapter.

To summarize, there are three levels of delete. If you delete a file in a folder or Explorer window, it is stored in the Recycle Bin. If you delete it from the Recycle Bin or delete it in a DOS window, it is deleted from the file management system. If you use low-level tools to wipe the space on the hard disk that it occupied, it can't be recovered. Still, a slightly earlier version of the file may be intact on the hard disk in some other location — in which case it would be recoverable.

Deleting shortcuts

If you delete a shortcut, only the shortcut goes to the Recycle Bin, not the target (whether it be a file, application, or folder). The original item stays right where it was and continues to work fine. You are only deleting the shortcut file itself — which has an extension of *lnk, pif* or *url* — not the target of the shortcut.

Right- or left-drag to the Recycle Bin

There are many ways to delete a file. You can drag the file to the Recycle Bin icon, to a Recycled folder icon, or to an open Recycle Bin or Recycled folder window. If you left-drag the file icon, it is moved to the Recycle Bin. If you right-drag it, you are given the choice to move the file or cancel the move.

You can drag files back out of the Recycle Bin and place them in any folder, not just in their original location. If you right-drag a file out of the Recycle Bin to a folder window, you will be given the chance to move the file or cancel the move.

If you right-click a file icon and click Delete in the context menu, or if you highlight a file icon and press the Delete key, you will be asked to confirm your deletion. It doesn't matter if the Recycle Bin has been set to remove files immediately on delete or not; you will still be asked for confirmation of the deletion.

If you drag a file (either left- or right-drag) to the Recycle Bin, you will not be asked for confirmation unless you've set the "Remove files immediately on delete" option. The Windows 95 designers assumed that if you were willing to go to all the trouble of dragging a file to the Recycle Bin, you meant it.

You can turn off the delete confirmation message by following these steps:

STEPS

Turning Off Delete Confirmation

Step 1.   Right-click the Recycle Bin icon on your Desktop.

Step 2.   Click Properties in the context menu.

Step 3.   Click the Global tab (if necessary).

Step 4.   Clear the check box labeled "Display delete confirmation dialog."

Shift+Delete

You can delete files without sending them to the Recycle Bin — in other words, purge them — by highlighting their filenames, holding down the Shift key, and pressing the Delete key. (You can also hold down Shift while clicking Delete in a context menu.) The files won't be sent to the Recycle Bin because by deliberately holding down the Shift key, you are telling Windows 95 that you want these files purged. Don't confuse this use of Shift+Delete with the use of Shift+Delete in word processors to send selected text to the Clipboard. Most newer word processors now also support Ctrl+X to cut to the Clipboard, so if you use this key combination, you won't mix up the meaning of Shift+Delete.

Don't Delete Your Hard Disk

If you right-click a hard disk drive icon in the Explorer or in a folder window, you won't find Delete on the context menu. It's not a good idea to delete a hard disk. You can't. But you can delete — or move to the Recycle Bin — all the files on the hard disk by dragging the drive icon to the Recycle Bin.

We don't suggest you do this, especially if the space taken up by the current files on the hard disk is greater than the space set aside for deleted files in the Recycle Bin. If you delete a hard disk, you are moving all the files on the hard disk to the Recycle Bin. This is not possible if there isn't room for them there.

All this can get quite confusing. The Recycled folders are attached to a hard disk, but they show all the files that have been deleted or moved to the Recycle Bin, no matter which hard disk (or disk partition) they were deleted from. If you drag a hard disk drive icon to the Recycle Bin, are you also deleting the files stored in the Recycled folder? The next section addresses this question.

You Can't Delete My Computer or Other Key Components

You can drag My Computer, Network Neighborhood, and the Recycle Bin and drop them on the Recycle Bin folder window. But when you do, you will just get a beep. Windows 95 won't let you delete these things, thankfully.

The same is true of the Printers folder, the Control Panel, the Fonts folder, and the Dial-Up Networking folder. You just get a beep. You can try deleting one of these folders with a right-drag, which feels safer because right-dragging normally gives you a context menu confirming the move.

You *Can* Delete a Floppy Disk

Files on a floppy disk are not moved to the Recycle Bin when you delete them. (In fact, files you delete from any removable media are not sent to the Recycle Bin.) You can drag the floppy drive icon to the Recycle Bin (icon or folder window), and all the files will be purged after you are first advised of that fact and allowed to change your mind. The message box that appears displays an icon of a file being shredded as a way of indicating that your files will be very difficult to recover if you continue.

If you highlight a file that is stored on a floppy disk and press the Delete key, you will get the same notification. Windows 95 just doesn't provide as much safety for files on floppy disks as it does for files on your local hard disks, although it does ask every time for confirmation of the deletion (purge).

Going Through the Trash — Retrieving Deleted Files

It is easy to get files back from the Recycle Bin. Just double-click the Recycle Bin icon on the Desktop to open the Recycle Bin folder window, as shown in Figure 14-3. Right-click the item that you want to restore, and then click Restore. The file is restored to its original location. If the folder that it was stored in has been deleted, it is restored also.

You can also just drag the files out of the Recycle Bin and move them to wherever you want. Dragging only moves files in and out of the Recycle Bin, no matter whether you right-drag or left-drag. If you right-drag, you won't see options for Copy, Create Shortcut(s) Here, or any other command you usually see in a context menu when you right drag and drop.

 Tip
You can use any of the selection techniques discussed in Chapter 8 to choose which files you want to move or restore to their original location. If deleting a file was the last file management action you carried out, you can choose Edit, Undo Delete in the Recycle Bin window, or right-click the window, and choose Undo Delete from the context menu.

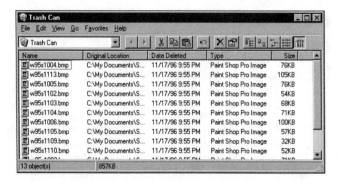

Figure 14-3: The Recycle Bin window (note that we've renamed it Trash Can). The second column lists the original location (folder) of the deleted file. Right-click the file you want back and then click Restore from the context menu.

Undocumented

Do you want to check out a graphic or text file that you have already put in the Recycle Bin? Maybe you want to edit it after you deleted it. As long as you haven't emptied your Recycle Bin, you can drag and drop the file from the Recycle Bin onto your application icon. After you're done viewing the file you don't have to worry about deleting it, because it wasn't undeleted in the first place.

If you edited a file that's currently in the Recycle Bin and want to save its new version, save it to another folder. The name of the file in the Save As dialog box will default to its Recycle Bin name, which is not its original name (even though the original name is shown in the Recycle Bin window). This name is used internally by the Recycle Bin to track the deleted files. You may want to change it if you save the edited file to a new folder.

Tip

Unlike moving, copying, or deleting a file, emptying the Recycle Bin is not a recoverable action. You won't find Unempty the Recycle Bin on the context menu. (If the emptied files haven't yet been overwritten by other files, however, you may still be able to get them back with an Undelete utility, as we discuss later in this chapter.)

Emptying the Recycle Bin

As you have seen, dropping a file into the Recycle Bin or pressing the Delete key after selecting an icon does nothing more than move the files to the Recycle Bin. It certainly doesn't delete them — unless you chose the Remove files immediately on delete option in the Recycle Bin properties sheet (right-click the Recycle Bin icon and choose Properties). If you want to delete the items in the Recycle Bin, you need to choose Empty Recycle Bin.

STEPS

Emptying the Recycle Bin

Step 1. Double-click the Recycle Bin icon on the Desktop.

Step 2. Choose File, Empty Recycle Bin in the Recycle Bin window.

Step 3. All the files in the Recycle Bin are purged.

If you want to purge only some of the items in the Recycle Bin, select those items first and then choose File, Delete. Or, you can right-click the items that you want purged and click Delete in the context menu.

Remove Files Immediately on Delete

You can set a Recycle Bin property to remove files immediately on delete. When you delete a file, it is not moved to the Recycle Bin but is immediately purged from the file system.

When this option is set, if you drag files to the Recycle Bin or highlight them and press the Delete key, Windows 95 confirms the file deletion because now they will be purged. This is also true if you right-click a file and choose Delete.

To set the properties of the Recycle Bin, right-click the Recycle Bin icon or the Recycle Bin folder window and choose Properties. The Recycle Bin Properties dialog box, as shown in Figure 14-4, appears on the Desktop.

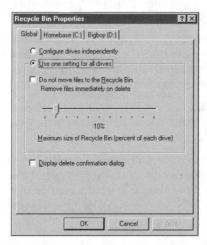

Figure 14-4: The Recycle Bin Properties dialog box. You can choose whether to remove files immediately on delete or not. You can choose the maximum size of the Recycled folders on each hard disk, and you can choose whether to configure the hard disks separately.

In the Recycle Bin Properties dialog box, check whether you want the files to be removed immediately on delete or not. You can set the maximum size of the Recycled folder on all or any of the hard disks.

The Recycle Bin and Networks

If the Recycle Bin shows you all the deleted files, what if you are connected to a local or wide area network? Are you going to see all the deleted files on all the servers in your Recycle Bin? Nope.

Undocumented

You see only the files that you deleted from your local hard disks. It doesn't matter if the server resources (a hard disk or folder) are mapped to a local drive letter or not. You can double-click a Recycled folder on the host or server computer and you still will see only the files that you deleted from your local hard disks.

If you delete a file on the host, it is the same as if you deleted a file from a floppy disk — it is purged. The deleted file is not saved to the Recycle Bin.

Undelete and Unerase

If a file is purged, it is no longer recognized by the Windows 95 file management system. Files are purged when you choose Empty Recycle Bin, when you hold down the Shift key and press the Delete key to delete a selected file, or when you delete a file and the Recycle Bin properties sheet has been set to remove files immediately on delete.

When a file is purged, all that happens is that the first letter of its filename is changed so that it is no longer recognized as a legitimate filename by the file management system. The space taken up by that file is now available for use when other files are written to the hard disk.

DOS 6.x came with an Undelete utility. This utility is not available with Windows 95. But you can use the old DOS 6.x Undelete utility to unpurge files. You just need to be sure to keep this utility around after you upgrade to Windows 95. You'll find Undelete.exe in your old DOS directory.

You can also find it on your Windows 95 CD-ROM. Just check in the Other\Oldmsdos folder. And you can download it from http://www.microsoft.com/kb/softlib/mslfiles/pd0646.exe.

Undelete works to recover files that haven't been overwritten by new files. It doesn't do much good if more than a short time has elapsed between the time that you purged the file and the time you want to undelete it. The probability that it has been overwritten increases as time passes.

Undocumented

To use Undelete, you need to run it in MS-DOS mode with the file system locked. One way to do this is to choose Start, Shut Down, and choose Restart the computer in MS-DOS mode in the Shut Down Windows dialog box. At the DOS prompt, type **Lock**, and then **Undelete**. When you are done, type **Unlock** and then **Exit** to relaunch Windows 95. Be sure to copy Undelete.exe to your \Windows\Command directory before you do this, so that you can find it when you type Undelete at the DOS prompt.

If you want to be even safer, you can run Undelete's deletion sentry to store deleted files for seven days before really deleting them. This works whether you delete files at the DOS command prompt or by emptying the Recycle Bin. After you copy Undelete to your \Windows\Command folder, type **Undelete /?** at a DOS prompt to see how to use this feature.

Symantec provides Norton Utilities for Windows 95. These utilities are integrated with the Windows 95 Desktop and user interface, and they include an unerase capability. If you have installed Norton Utilities for Windows 95, when you right-click the Recycle Bin icon, you'll see some new commands in the context menu. Norton Utilities provides additional backup for deleted files by taking over the functions of the Recycle Bin.

Norton Utilities let you unerase files that have been purged without having to use the Undelete utility in MS-DOS mode. Unerase has to deal with the same issues as Undelete: the deleted file's name has been altered, so although the hard disk space may still contain the purged file's contents, the space has been marked available. Use Norton Utilities' Unerase as soon as you can after you inadvertently purge a file to increase your chances of recovering it.

Summary

There are three layers of delete. We show you how the Recycle Bin helps you delete files without undue worry.

▶ You can access and manage the Recycle Bin with minimal effort. It is right there on the Desktop.

▶ We show you how deleted files are stored in a special hidden system folder that displays their properties in the Recycle Bin manner.

▶ The common file dialog boxes are like mini folder windows. We show you how to use them to delete files listed in them. You can also copy, move, and rename files listed in these common dialog boxes.

▶ You can move files into and out of the Recycle Bin to or from any location that you please. You can drag with either the right or left mouse button.

▶ If you delete files on a floppy or over a network, they really do go away without going to the Recycle Bin first.

Chapter 15

The Registry — The Real User Interface

ini Files, RIP

Microsoft intends to stop using configuration files, otherwise known as *ini* files, and it hopes other developers will do the same. Windows directories throughout the world are filling up with these files. Win.ini and System.ini, Microsoft's main contribution to this blight, have grown as some developers took the easy route and put their applications' vital parameters in these files.

This has led to a number of difficulties as users and system administrators try to access the computer's and user's configurations. There are so many different files that no one can keep track of what is where. In addition, there is no systematic distinction between values that are user-specific and those that are machine/software-specific.

Windows 3.1 introduced the Registry (Reg.dat), which stored file association and OLE information. The Registry was greatly expanded in Windows NT, and in Windows 95 it is (for the most part) the central repository of user and system configuration data.

The fact that Microsoft programmers still use *ini* files, such as Telephon.ini, in Windows 95 means that Microsoft hasn't yet gotten it together to completely make the transition. Telephony (TAPI) was developed before the Windows 95 Registry was ready.

Win.ini and System.ini (and other *ini* files) are provided with Windows 95. These files are still necessary for Windows to operate properly. That is, not all the information they contain has been transferred to the Registry. For example, a list of font substitutes is still kept in Win.ini.

Microsoft also retained the Win.ini and System.ini files to maintain compatibility with Windows 3.*x* applications and other previous methods of storing system and user configuration information.

The Registry Keys and Structure

The Registry is a storehouse for configuration values and settings that are used to determine how Windows 95 operates. It is supposed to, over time, assume all the functions of the configuration files found in the Windows folder.

The Registry also keeps track of a list of hardware and hardware configurations that the Windows 95 setup and hardware detection routines discovered. If you change your hardware configuration, the Registry is updated.

The *keys* in the Registry are similar to the bracketed headings in the Win.ini or System.ini files. Registry keys, unlike *ini* file headings, can and do contain subkeys. While only text strings were allowed in *ini* files, values in the Registry can consist of executable code.

The Registry is a database divided into six main branches, as can be seen in Figure 15-1. Each branch is a *handle* to a different set of key values, hence the names HKEY_CLASSES_ROOT, and so on, shown in Figure 15-1. The branches are described in the following sections.

[HKEY_CLASSES_ROOT]

This branch contains the file extensions and file/application associations as well as OLE data. This branch is an *alias* (simultaneously updated copy) of HKEY_LOCAL_MACHINE\Software\Classes. Changes in this area of the Registry are discussed in Chapter 13.

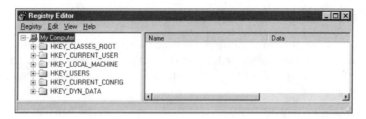

Figure 15-1: The Registry editor. Click a plus sign to open a branch of the Registry.

[HKEY_USERS]

The information displayed under this key is stored in the User.dat file. This includes the user-specific Desktop configurations, network connections, and the Start menu. If your computer is configured using user profiles, a separate User.dat file is created for each user. When a user logs on to the computer, Windows 95 reads that person's User.dat file and integrates it into the Registry.

[HKEY_CURRENT_USER]

This is the portion of HKEY_USERS that is applicable to the current user. If there is only one user, the default user, then both branches are the same.

Many of the examples of editing the Registry used in this book make the assumption that you are editing the values only for the current user or for the default user. Therefore, many of those changes take place along this branch of the Registry.

If you want to make the indicated changes for other users with different login names, you need to track down the appropriate locations in the HKEY_USERS branch.

There are similar values in this branch and in the next one, HKEY_LOCAL_ MACHINE. The values in this branch take precedence over the values in the next one.

Software developers can store user-specific information here. If they do, their programs will be customized for each individual user. It doesn't matter that one user changes his or her settings. As long as those values are stored here, other users keep their settings. It's up to the software developers to put all their user-specific values in this branch. You'll find this information by looking at

HKEY_CURRENT_USER\Software*CompanyName**App Name**Version*

Check out the values under HKEY_CURRENT_USER\Software\id\Doom95 (if you've installed Doom95).

[HKEY_LOCAL_MACHINE]

This is the branch for computer hardware and its installed software. If the computer can have multiple hardware configurations — such as hooked up to the network or not, or docked or not — the information on each configuration is stored here.

Look down the HKEY_LOCAL_MACHINE branch under SOFTWARE, and you'll find the names of the companies that make the software that you have installed. This branch is meant to be a convenient location for machine-specific information about each company's products. Programmers don't have to use this area to store various settings, but it sure makes it easy if they do.

This is where you'll find application names, version numbers, application pathnames, and hardware settings — settings that apply to all users. Of course, Microsoft uses this branch to register its software.

Programmers are also encouraged to store their Windows 95-compatible uninstall information under this key. You'll find it in

HKEY_LOCAL_MACHINE\SOFTWARE\Microsoft\Windows\CurrentVersion\Uninstall.

[HKEY_CURRENT_CONFIGURATION]

The display settings and the available printers are here.

[HKEY_DYN_DATA]

The Registry keeps data on Windows performance parameters, and these values are stored here. This information is kept in RAM after Windows 95 loads, and it is updated on an ongoing basis. You can view these statistics using the System Monitor. Plug and play devices and the software that monitors these devices make use of the information stored here.

Each of the six main branches is divided into further branches. Each node is a key. You can follow any of the branches out until you run out of keys and have only data.

Secret

To expand all branches below a node, highlight the node and press Alt+*. (that is, press Alt plus the numeric keyboard asterisk). To collapse all the branches below a node, click its minus sign, highlight the node, and press F5.

Much of the Registry is not that useful to a user or system administrator. It is maintained by the operating system, configured when you install new software, and often better edited through user interface elements in the Control Panel and elsewhere.

We have, however, found wide applicability for editing the HKEY_CLASSES_ROOT branch and the HKEY_CURRENT_USER branch. You may find that the other branches also provide useful areas for individual customization.

The Registry Files

System.dat and User.dat are the two hidden, system, read-only files that make up the Registry. Unlike the *ini* files, they are binary files that can't be read easily with an ASCII file editor. You need the Registry editor to examine the variables and values stored in the Registry.

Actually, you can use WordPad to read the Registry, but you need to export it to a text file first. This is an option found in the Registry editor. The resulting file (if you export the whole thing instead of just a branch) is too big to be read by Notepad. You can make changes to the exported Registry file and import the altered file back into the Registry database, updating the previous Registry entries. We discuss this more in the later section entitled *The Registry Editor*.

There is only one Registry on your computer, but it is made up of the two files — System.dat and User.dat. If there is a policy file (a file with the *pol* extension), it is also part of the Registry. We discuss policy files and their implications for the Registry in the *System Policy Editor* section of Chapter 36. The Registry editor displays the two files as one Registry when you invoke it.

The Registry files and their backups (System.da0 and User.da0) have the DOS file attributes of hidden, read-only, and system. This doesn't prevent you from displaying them in the Explorer or a folder window, as long as you have the Show all files option turned on. (In any Explorer or folder window, choose View, Options, click the View tab, and mark the Show all files option button.)

System.dat and User.dat are by default stored in the \Windows folder, or the main Windows folder created during installation. (Remember that while we call our folder Windows, you may have named yours something else, such as Win95 or Win.) If your \Windows folder is on a compressed drive, these files (and their backups) are stored on the boot drive. Other variations are possible with networked computers.

System.dat stores information specific to a computer and to the software on that computer. System.dat tracks the detected hardware and its configuration as well as Windows and other installed programs (that put their information in the Registry).

User.dat stores user-specific information, including mouse speed, color scheme, cursor scheme, wallpaper, accessibility settings, icon spacing, fonts, keyboard layout, keyboard delay and speed, regional settings, Explorer settings, attributes of standard Windows software, and network passwords.

A user's Desktop icons and network connections are stored in User.dat. If you make the appropriate choice in the User Profiles tab of the Passwords Properties dialog box (double-click the Passwords icon in the Control Panel), each individual user can have his or her own Start menu and Desktop settings.

Registry recovery

Every time you successfully start (or restart) your computer, Windows 95 backs up System.dat and User.dat to System.da0 and User.da0, respectively. If Windows 95 fails to start, you can use the backup files from the last successful start to recover.

When Windows 95 fails to start successfully, it reverts to Safe mode. You can tell if you're in Safe mode because the word *Safe* appears in each corner of your screen. If you find yourself in Safe mode, you know that you have had an unsuccessful start and that the Registry files were not written to their backups. The backup files are the ones that worked the last time there was a successful start.

Secret

You can recover the last good Registry files from their backup files by double-clicking on the Registry Recovery icon (follow the steps below to set this up), shutting down Windows, and restarting.

STEPS

Installing the Registry Recovery Batch File

Step 1.   Using the Explorer, copy Regrecov.bat from the Registry folder on the *Windows 95 Secrets* CD-ROM to your \Windows folder.

Step 2.   Right-click the Desktop. Point to New, and then click Shortcut.

Step 3.   Click the Browse button. Find Regrecov.bat in your \Windows folder. Double-click it, and then click Next.

Step 4.   Type the name **Registry Recovery**. Click Next.

Step 5.   Click the cloud and lightning icon, and click Finish.

Step 6.   Right-click the Registry Recovery icon on your Desktop. Click Properties.

Step 7.   Click the Program tab, choose Minimized in the Run drop-down list. Mark the Close on exit check box, and then click OK.

You now have an icon on your desktop that will copy the last successful version of your Registry files over the files that didn't work. Double-click it to use it. When it has completed its work, shut down Windows and restart with the recovered files.

The cloud with lightning icon is quite appropriate for this function. It combines the saving-for-a-rainy-day aspect with the lightning-is-now-striking aspect.

You have one additional System.dat backup file, System.1st. This file is stored in the root directory of your boot drive (or its host). System.1st was created when you first installed Windows 95, and it contains your hardware and software configuration as the Windows 95 setup program understood it.

If your Registry becomes so corrupted that you can't recover it, you can always copy this file over System.dat in your Windows 95 folder. Unfortunately, you will lose all the Registry entries for programs that you have installed since you first installed Windows 95.

Registry backup

Tip

Even though the Registry files are backed up after every successful start, it is a very good idea to make a backup of these files periodically. You also might want to do it just before you edit the Registry. You can do this by using a DOS batch file, which is included on the *Windows 95 Secrets* CD-ROM. (Isn't it amazing how useful DOS can be?)

STEPS

Installing the Registry Backup Batch File

Step 1. Using the Explorer, find Regback.bat in the Registry folder on the *Windows 95 Secrets* CD-ROM. Copy it to your \Windows folder (or any folder that you find convenient).

Step 2. Right-click the Desktop. Point to New, and then click Shortcut.

Step 3. Click the Browse button. Find Regback.bat in your \Windows folder. Double-click it, and then click Next.

Step 4. Type the name **Registry Backup**. Click Next.

Step 5. Click the umbrella icon, and click Finish.

Step 6. Right-click the Registry Backup icon on your Desktop. Click Properties.

Step 7. Click the Program tab, choose Minimized in the Run drop-down list. Mark the Close on exit check box, and then click OK.

Make sure that you have room on your hard disk for the backup copy of the Registry files (approximately 500–600K). By default, the Registry Backup batch file places the backup in your \Windows folder. You can copy these files to a floppy disk if you like, or edit the batch file to save these files directly to a floppy.

Tip

In the *Registry recovery* section, we describe the Registry Recovery batch file (Regrecov.bat), which uses the Registry backup files automatically created each time Windows 95 starts successfully. You may want to use the backup files that you create yourself (with the help of the Registry Backup batch file) instead of these automatically generated batch files. If so, you need to copy the files created by the Registry Backup batch file over System.dat and User.dat.

The Registry Backup batch file (Regback.bat) creates two files — System.dak and User.dak. You can use the batch file Regman.bat, stored in the Registry folder on the *Windows 95 Secrets* CD-ROM, to copy these two backup files over System.dat and User.dat. Copy Regman.bat to your \Windows folder (or any folder that you find convenient). You can place a shortcut to it on the Desktop or in any location that you like. Follow a variation of steps 2 through 7 in the Installing the Registry Backup Batch File steps, choosing an appropriate name and icon for the shortcut.

Microsoft's Registry backup applets

The CD-ROM version of Windows 95 contains an applet called CfgBack that backs up your current Registry and allows you to restore it later (as long as you can at least boot into Safe mode). You'll find the applet in the \Other\Misc\Cfgback folder. Copy it into your \Windows folder, and copy its help file (Cfgback.hlp) into your \Windows\Help folder. Create a shortcut to Cfgback.exe on your Desktop or in a utilities folder.

You can save up to nine different named versions of the Registry. We recommend that you run CfgBack any time you are about to make any manual change to the Registry. If you make a mistake, running CfgBack and restoring the latest named backup gets you up and running as you were before.

There are one or two minor drawbacks, so to speak, with CfgBack. If your system is set up for multiple users, CfgBack won't save the User.dat portion of your Registry. You have to copy User.dat from your System folder manually. In addition, you have to save the *rbk* files created by CfgBack in your \Windows folder for CfgBack to be able to restore them later.

Windows itself does save one copy of your Registry for you, as the hidden files System.da0 and User.da0 in your \Windows folder. These files contain a copy of the Registry as it existed the last time Windows started successfully. In case of an emergency, you can copy System.da0 over System.dat and User.da0 over User.dat to restore your Registry to its most recent working condition. However, CfgBack still gives you more protection because it lets you save numerous, successive copies of the Registry, and it is quick and easy to use.

While CfgBack (and another utility called ERU, which is described in the next section) are by no means a complete backup program, they are so easy to use that you may want to place shortcuts to them in your Startup folder to remind you to run them once a day (or whenever you boot up).

CfgBack, ERU, and all the other utilities found on the Windows 95 CD-ROM, are available for download at no cost from the Microsoft web site (http://www.microsoft.com/windows/software/otherutils.htm).

Microsoft provides further Registry recovery and backup guidance in its Knowledge Base. You can find the relevant articles at http://www.microsoft.com/kb/articles/q131/4/31.htm.

Secret

Neither CfgBack or ERU will work unless you have Autoexec.bat, Config.sys, and Command.com in your root directory. If you want to use these utilities and you do not have an Autoexec.bat or Config.sys file, you can use a text editor to create "dummy" files with just the word *rem* in them.

Emergency Recover Utility

Microsoft provides another backup and disaster-recovery utility called ERU (Emergency Recovery Utility), which adds the major user-configuration files to a boot diskette, including a compressed version of User.dat. This utility is on the Windows 95 CD-ROM in the \Other\Misc\Eru folder.

While CfgBack only backs up the Registry, ERU saves additional configuration files. If you can't start Windows, reboot your PC with a bootable floppy disk that includes files placed there by ERU, and ERU will automatically restore these important files for you.

STEPS

Creating a Bootable Diskette and Adding the
Emergency Recovery Utility

Step 1. You need to create a bootable diskette in order to use ERU. You can do this by right-clicking your A drive in Explorer, clicking Format, and then selecting Copy System Files Only. (This performs the same function as typing FORMAT A: /S at your command prompt.) The resulting bootable diskette contains only four files: the two "hidden" files, Io.sys and Msdos.sys, along with Command.com (to process commands) and Drvspace.bin (to access your hard drive if it is compressed).

A Startup diskette is also bootable, but you create it through the Control Panel, and it contains many more files. To create a Startup diskette, click Start, Settings, Control Panel, Add/Remove Programs, Startup Disk, Create Disk. This results in a diskette that contains 16 files. In addition to the four files that comprise a vanilla bootable diskette, it also contains tools such as ScanDisk (to repair hard drive sectors), RegEdit (to update the Registry),

(continued)

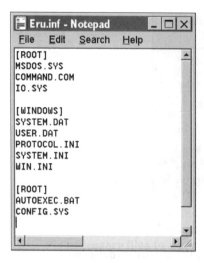

Figure 15-3: The sample Eru.inf file.

Eru.inf controls which files are copied from your hard disk to your emergency disk, and in which order. Files are copied in the order they are listed in the Eru.inf file, until ERU runs out of diskette space.

This text file is a place for you to add any drivers or other files that may be necessary for your system to boot up. For example, if you have real-mode drivers listed in a Config.sys file, you should add those to the list in Eru.inf.

You'll notice in the Eru.inf file that the section entitled [ROOT] is listed twice. This is deliberate. If ERU runs out of diskette space, it will skip the files at the end of the Eru.inf listing — in this case, Autoexec.bat and Config.sys. Listing the [ROOT] folder twice lets you put the less-critical files last.

The Registry Editor

In a number of chapters in this book, we reveal how to use the Registry editor to change a value or add a key. Microsoft has created numerous user interface elements — the Control Panel, dialog boxes, and properties sheets — that are designed to let you change the values stored in the Registry without having to edit it directly. Microsoft hopes that these elements are enough. They aren't.

If you can make the changes you need without using the Registry editor, by all means do so. Changes you make in properties sheets and dialog boxes are reflected immediately in changes in the behavior of that portion of the operating system affected by the values stored in the Registry.

Changes you make using the Registry editor are often not used until the next time you start Windows (and the Registry values are read and stored in memory). We have indicated throughout the text when the changes you make take effect immediately versus when you need to restart Windows.

Secret

There is a way to make the changes that you've made to the Registry take effect quickly, if not immediately. Click the Start button, click Shut Down, choose Restart the computer, hold down the Shift key and click Yes. Your computer will restart Windows 95 without rebooting.

Making changes to Registry values using the Windows 95 user interface elements is the safest means of changing these values. It is quite possible, using the Registry editor, to delete or alter vital elements of the Registry. Some changes may prevent Windows 95 from operating correctly.

One precaution that you can take to recover from such an unfortunate editing session is to make a backup of the Registry files before you edit them. If you have copied our Registry Backup batch file (Regback.bat) to your hard disk and made a shortcut to it, you can run it every time before you edit the Registry. You can even edit the shortcut that you use to start the Registry editor to call Regback.bat first.

If you engage in a course of action that damages the Registry, you still have your automatic backups. If you restart Windows after an editing session that has gotten out of hand, and Windows can't start successfully, you can always go to the backups.

On the other hand, you may have done some damage during your editing session — perhaps made some inadvertent changes that you don't remember and certainly didn't want to make — but the damage is not great enough to prevent Windows 95 from starting the next time. If you have started Windows after one of these rash editing sessions, an intentional backup you did right before your last editing session would be very handy, because at this point, your backup and your master are identical — and both contain settings that you don't want.

If you backup intentionally before you make editing changes, you can always recover to your intentional backups. Otherwise, you will have to manually undo your egregious labors.

We have included numerous additional Registry editors and Registry editor extensions on the *Windows 95 Secrets* CD-ROM. One extension saves the paths within the Registry that you have visited, allowing you to get back to them quickly. You can download the latest version at http://www.dcsoft.com/ftp/regeditx.zip.

Starting the Registry editor

You'll find the Registry editor in the \Windows folder. Windows 95 Setup does not place it on any of the Start menus. Microsoft is not that eager for the uninitiated to use this tool. The application file name is Regedit.exe. Your system administrator may have removed it from your computer.

If you are going to use the editor, it is a good idea to create a shortcut to access it. Place the shortcut on the Desktop or in the Start menus. If you don't know how to create shortcuts, you shouldn't be messing around with the Registry editor (unless you are following our explicit step-by-step instructions).

Editing with the Registry editor

Chapters throughout this book contain discussions that point to areas of the Registry to be edited. Let's take a minute to see what the editing commands are and how to use them.

To learn how to edit the Registry, it helps to get to a location that has some useful keys, constants, and values. We'll use the current Desktop in the following steps as an example of a very fruitful location.

STEPS

Editing the Registry

Step 1.   Click the plus sign to the left of HKEY_CURRENT_USER. Click the plus sign to the left of Control Panel, and then the one next to Desktop. (The name HKEY refers to the fact that this is a handle to a key. The Registry is filled with keys that eventually have data attached to them.)

Step 2.   Highlight the WindowMetrics name next to its folder icon. Notice that the right pane is now filled with constant names (Name) and values (Data).

Step 3.   In Chapter 7, we showed you how to create a new constant (MinAnimate) to turn off the sliding windows effect. If you haven't created this constant, you can do so now (you can easily get rid of it or change its value so that your current configuration remains the same).

Step 4.   Right-click in the right pane of the Registry editor (but not on a constant name or value). A New button, as shown in Figure 15-4, appears. Point to the New button, and a menu appears. You can choose to create a Key, a String Value, a Binary Value, or a DWORD Value. The key and/or any of the constants will be attached to the WindowMetrics key.

Step 5.   Right-click the Desktop key in the left pane of the Registry editor. As shown in Figure 15-5, the context menu will give you the choice of collapsing this expanded branch of the Registry; creating a new key, string value, or binary value; finding a text or numerical string in the local branch; or deleting or renaming the key.

Editing the Registry

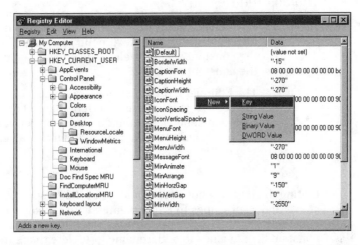

Figure 15-4: Inserting new keys or values in the Registry. Right-click the right pane of the Registry editor to insert new keys or constants.

It is not a good idea to delete or rename a key unless you know exactly what you are doing. Adding a new key or value (actually a constant that has a value, which the Registry editor refers to as *Data*) may change the way the Windows 95 operates, but it won't do any damage.

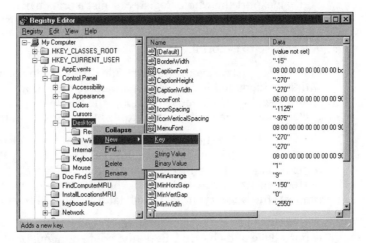

Figure 15-5: Right-click next to a key in the left pane of the Registry editor to access a context menu.

(continued)

Step 6.   Right-click a constant in the Name column in the right pane of the Registry editor. A context menu appears, allowing you to modify the constant's value, delete the constant and its value, or rename the constant.

Step 7.   The Edit menu provides similar choices to those that appear on the context menu when you right-click a key or a constant. The Edit menu changes depending on whether you have highlighted a key or a constant. You can't highlight a value (or Data).

Editing the Registry consists of adding or deleting keys, adding new constants and their values to be associated with the keys, and modifying those constants and their values — pretty straightforward. It's knowing what keys, constants, and values to add, rename, or delete that's the trick.

Exporting and importing the Registry

You can export the Registry to an ASCII file with the *reg* extension. If you do this, Windows 95 writes the keys, constants, and values stored in System.dat and User.dat to an ASCII text file that can be read by WordPad. The size of the file for the whole Registry is about 500K (before additional applications are registered).

You can export the whole Registry or just a branch of the Registry. To export either, choose Registry, Export Registry File in the Registry editor. To export a branch, highlight the branch in the left pane of the Registry before you choose to export it.

Choosing Registry, Export Registry File displays the common file dialog box with an added modifier extension attached at the bottom, as shown in Figure 15-6. You can choose to export the whole Registry or just a branch by clicking one of the two option buttons at the bottom of the dialog box.

You should export the Registry or a branch of the Registry into a file with a *reg* extension (the default choice in the Export Registry File dialog box). The *reg* extension will be added automatically if you type a filename. The exported Registry is a text file. Using the *reg* extension makes it easy to merge (import) the Registry or its branch later if you edit the exported file.

The exported Registry file can be read easily by WordPad. Right-click the exported file and choose Edit on the context menu. Don't double-click the file, because the default action for a file of this file type is to merge it back into the Registry. Figure 15-7 shows how part of an exported Registry file looks in WordPad.

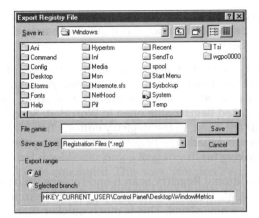

Figure 15-6: The Export Registry File dialog box. You can determine how much of the Registry is exported (the highlighted branch or all of the Registry) by clicking one of the two option buttons at the bottom of this dialog box.

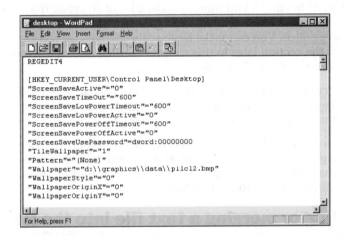

Figure 15-7: The Control Panel\Desktop key area in the Registry exported to a text file. The key values are surrounded by square brackets. The constants and their string values are surrounded by double quotes.

Tip

The exported text file encloses the key name, including all preceding key names, in square brackets. The constant names are enclosed in double quote marks. String values associated with the constant names are also enclosed in double quotes. DWORD values (double word in either decimal or hexadecimal format) begin with *dword:*. Binary values begin with *hex:*.

Searching an exported Registry file

One reason to export a Registry file is to be able to search it quickly. The Registry editor has a find facility, but it is slow. You can bring the exported then put it (or a shortcut to it) in your \Windows\StartMenu\Programs\Startup folder. This file would contain the following text:

```
REGEDIT4
[HKEY_CURRENT_USER\Software\Microsoft\Windows\CurrentVersion\Explorer]
"link"=hex:00,00,00,00
```

This will only work if Merge is the default action for *reg* files. If Edit is the default action, but you actually want to merge the file, edit the Target field of the shortcut file to include *regedit.exe* followed by the *reg* file's name and extension.

Of course, it is easier to use TweakUI to turn off this particularly obnoxious Windows 95 behavior, but you may think of other reasons why you want to write into the Registry at startup.

After Windows 95 runs a *reg* file, it displays a dialog box saying the merge was successful. You can get rid of this dialog box with the RtvReco utility (http://www.windows95.com). Actually, there's a free and easy way around this. The trick is an undocumented switch to RegEdit that J.T. Anderson of Los Angeles was kind enough to point out to us.

RegEdit supports an /s switch, which stands for *silent*. When you add this to a RegEdit command line, the switch suppresses the usual "merge was successful" dialog box that you would otherwise have to click OK in to get rid of.

Therefore, if you have a reason to create a shortcut to a *reg* file that you commonly want to merge into the Registry, use the /s switch on the command line. Instead of creating a shortcut to Filename.reg, for example, you would use the following command line in the Target field of the shortcut:

```
Regedit.exe /s filename.reg
```

If you like the way this eliminates the annoying "merge is successful" dialog box, you don't have to limit yourself to eradicating it for a single shortcut. You can suppress this dialog box every time you run RegEdit by editing the default action for RegEdit.

STEPS

Silencing RegEdit

Step 1.   In the Explorer, click View, Options, File Types.

Step 2.   In the Registered file types listing, select Registration Entries, and then click the Edit button.

Step 3.   In the Actions box, select Merge, and then click the Edit button.

Step 4.   In the Application used to perform action box, change regedit.exe to regedit.exe /s. Click OK, and then click Close twice to exit.

This changes the default command line for RegEdit. Of course, changing the command line globally in this way does mean you see no confirmation box when you merge a *reg* file. For this reason, you might want to stick with editing only those shortcuts where you really need the silent treatment.

Adding a Windows Write file type definition to the New menu

Secret

Windows Write is a small editor — sort of a word processor — that comes with Windows 3.*x*. Microsoft did not include Windows Write with Windows 95. It has not been revamped to take advantage of the new common file dialog boxes, the print preview facility, long filenames, and other Windows 95 features. That doesn't mean it is not useful. It is awfully fast, and if you have saved your copy from Windows 3.*x,* you can still use it.

You'll find the easy way put Windows Write documents on your New menu in *Adding Items to the New Menu* section of Chapter 13. You can just use TweakUI.

In this section, we discuss how to edit the Registry to accomplish the same result as an exercise in seeing how the Registry editor works.

You have to be sure that you save Write.exe to another name before you set up Windows 95 over your existing Windows 3.*x* folder. You can then copy it back over the phony Write.exe that Windows 95 constructs in your \Windows folder. This phony Write.exe just calls WordPad.

You can create a file type definition for Windows Write by editing the Windows 95 *wri* extension file type to associate it with Windows Write instead of WordPad. You make this change using View, Options, File Types in an Explorer window. Review the section entitled *Creating a new file type* in Chapter 13 to understand how to do this, or follow the steps below.

Secret

After you have changed the association of *wri* files from WordPad to Windows Write, use the instructions in the *Adding Items to the New Menu* section of Chapter 13 to create a new menu item for Windows Write files. Chapter 13 shows you the easy way to create a new empty Windows Write file and associate it with the ShellNew command in the Registry under the .*wri* extension. In this section, we'll create the file header for an empty Windows Write file and place it in the Registry as data.

Even if you know what the Windows Write file header is, it will take a long time to type it using the Registry editor. This is where the ability to export a branch of the Registry, edit it, and merge it back in comes in handy.

Changing the Registered Owner

Windows 95 tracks your name and the name of your company. To see this information, choose Help, About in almost any application.

Secret

You can change your name and company settings, which are stored in your Registry, using the Registry editor:

STEPS

A New User

Step 1.   Double-click Regedit.exe in your \Windows folder.

Step 2.   Navigate to HKEY_LOCAL_MACHINE\SOFTWARE\Microsoft\ Windows\CurrentVersion.

Step 3.   Double-click RegisteredOwner and/or RegisteredOrganization in the right pane to change the names.

Step 4.   Exit the Registry editor.

Your own tips

As we show in the *First, Your Password* section of Chapter 7, Windows 95 provides a few tips to the first-time user. You can use TweakUI to turn the display of tips on and off. You can also edit the tips that come from Microsoft and create your own new tips for another user. Here's how:

STEPS

Creating New Tips

Step 1.   In your Registry editor, navigate to HKEY_LOCAL_MACHINE\ SOFTWARE\Microsoft\Windows\CurrentVersion\explorer\Tips

Step 2.   Right-click the right pane of the Registry editor. Choose New and then String Value.

Step 3.   Type a number one greater than the highest number of the existing tip number. For example, the last tip from Microsoft is number 47, so type **48**. Press Enter.

Step 4.   Double-click the number you just typed. Type a new tip. Click OK.

Creating New Tips

Step 5.   You can also edit an existing tip by double-clicking its associated number. When you are done, exit the Registry editor.

Editing other people's Registries

The Registry editor gives you the option of editing Registries on other computers that you are networked to over a dial-up line, Direct Cable Connection, or LAN. This feature requires a Windows NT server on your network to provide user-level (as opposed to share-level) network security.

In addition, if you are going to let your Registry be edited by someone else on your network, you must configure your networking options on your computer to add the Remote Registry Service. Only other users who have user-level access to your computer will be able to edit (or use their Registry editor to view) your Registry.

Setting user-level security

If you have a Windows NT server on your network, set your computer to use user-level security by taking the following steps:

STEPS

Setting User-Level Security

Step 1.   Click the Start button, point to Settings, and then click Control Panel.

Step 2.   Double-click the Network icon.

Step 3.   Click the Access Control tab. Mark the User-level access control check box. Type the name of the Windows NT server that keeps the list of users.

Setting up a computer to allow its Registry to be edited

You can set up your computer to be a Registry server. That is, you allow people at other computers to edit or view your Registry. To do this, take the following steps:

> **STEPS**
>
> Configuring Your Computer as a Registry Server
>
> **Step 1.** Click the Start button, point to Settings, and then click Control Panel.
>
> **Step 2.** Double-click the Network icon.
>
> **Step 3.** Click the Add button. Double-click the Service icon in the Select Network Component Type dialog box.
>
> **Step 4.** Click Microsoft in the Manufacturers box of the Select Network Service dialog box, and Microsoft Remote Registry in the Network Services box.
>
> **Step 5.** Click OK and then OK again. You will have to restart your computer for this change to take effect. You may need to obtain the source floppy disks or the Windows 95 CD-ROM to get the files for this service.

Using the Registry editor to edit someone else's Registry

If another computer user on your network has set up his or her computer as a Registry server and you have user-level access to that user's computer through a list kept on a Windows NT server, you can edit that user's Registry. Double-click your Registry editor icon. Choose Registry, Connect Network Registry in the Registry editor. Type the name of the computer containing the Registry you are going to edit. When you are done, choose Registry, Disconnect Network Registry.

You'll need to add the software that enables you to do this. It doesn't come on the Windows 95 diskettes, but it's there on the Windows 95 CD-ROM. You'll find it in the \Admin\Nettools\Remotreg folder. Double-click the Add/Remove Programs icon in the Control Panel, and add this software using the Windows Setup tab. Be sure to click the Have Disk button and then browse to the correct folder.

You can find further details on editing other people's Registries at http://www.microsoft.com/kb/articles/q141/4/60.htm.

The DOS Version of the Registry Editor

You can edit the Registry from the DOS command prompt. This is useful if you are having difficulties starting Windows 95. To go to the DOS prompt without starting Windows, press F8 at the Starting Windows 95 notification.

If you type **Regedit /?** at the DOS command prompt, you will get a little help on how to import and export the Registry. You need to use the program Edit to edit the exported Registry. Use Regedit to import the edited Registry file back into the Registry.

The DOS Regedit syntax is as follows:

```
REGEDIT    {/L:system}    {/R:user}    filename1
REGEDIT    {/L:system}    {/R:user}    /C filename2
REGEDIT    {/L:system}    {/R:user}    /E filename3 {regpath}
/L:system           Specifies the location of the System.dat file
/R:user             Specifies the location of the User.dat file
filename1           Specifies the file(s) to import into the Registry
/C filename2        Specifies the file to create the Registry from
/E filename3        Specifies the file to export the Registry to
regpath             Specifies the starting Registry key to export from
                    (Defaults to exporting the entire Registry)
```

You can export and edit the whole Registry or just a branch of it. Don't import a branch back into the Registry with the /C (create) option. This will create a Registry with only one branch.

Numerous problems have been reported when using the DOS version of RegEdit with large Registry files. Make sure to backup your Registry before you use RegEdit. It can't edit files much larger than 600K.

Cleaning Up the Registry

As you load on new software, many file associations get disconnected in the Registry. A few of these missing connections and other bits of displaced pointers get removed or straightened out when you run RegClean, a utility that you can download from Microsoft's web site at http://www.microsoft.com/softlib/RegCln.exe. You can read more about it at http:/www.microsoft.com/kb/articles/q147/7/69.htm.

Unfortunately, RegClean disassociates Internet Explorer from HTML files. You can easily make Internet Explorer the default browser again, but you've got to wonder about just how clever that programmer at Microsoft was. We experienced no problems with RegClean, but others have stated that it didn't remove old associations from their Registry.

Check out the *Windows 95 Secrets* CD-ROM for other tools that clean up your Registry much more thoroughly. You can also download the latest crippled version of Lifesaver at http://members.aol.com/aeroblade/index.html.

Summary

If you can edit the Registry, you have complete control of Windows 95.

▶ We provide you with a means of recovering from fatal conditions in the Registry.

▶ We show you how to get that extra margin of safety by manually backing up your Registry using our batch files and Desktop shortcuts.

▶ We describe a number of keystroke shortcuts to help you edit and display the Registry more quickly.

▶ As an example of how to use the ability to export the contents of your Registry to edit the Registry, we bring Windows Write back to life and show you how to create Windows Write files of the proper type from the New menu.

▶ We introduce you to editing Registries across a LAN.

▶ If there is a real problem starting Windows 95, we tell you how to edit the Registry in DOS.

Chapter 16

The Control Panel and Properties Sheets

In This Chapter

We cover the Control Panel and general features of properties sheets.

▶ Getting to the Control Panel settings quickly

▶ Installing and removing Windows applications

▶ Creating a bootable Startup disk

▶ Controlling your multimedia hardware and drivers

▶ Configuring Windows 95 for your local currency, time, and dates

▶ Associating sounds with Windows 95 events

▶ Locating those missing parameters in properties sheets

What Will You Find Where?

Windows 95 has to keep track of itself and the computer it is running on. You need a way to see (and change) your Windows 95 configurations. Thousands of little pieces of information running around in your computer need to be right for everything to work.

In the Control Panel, you'll get a handle on most of your computer's hardware and the software drivers that work with it. You'll also find the Fonts folder (it's also in your Explorer under \Windows\Fonts) and the settings for currency, dates, time, and other location-specific information.

Properties sheets, an innovation with Windows 95, provide another means to get at the parameters that define your files, and in some cases, your hardware.

Many of the specific Control Panel settings are described in the chapters in "Part IV: Plug and Play". In this chapter, we discuss the Control Panel settings that aren't described there.

Getting to the Control Panel

It's easy to get to the Control Panel (see Figure 16-1). Just click the Start button, point to Settings, and then click Control Panel. But this isn't the only way to get to the Control Panel, nor is it necessarily the most convenient.

Figure 16-1: The Control Panel. Double-click any icon to change the settings associated with that icon.

Here are some other ways to get to the Control Panel:

- If you want to use the Display Control Panel (the Display icon in the Control Panel), right-click the Desktop and click Properties.

- You can get to the Date/Time Control Panel by double-clicking the clock on the Taskbar.

- The Fonts and Printers folders are accessible through the Explorer. (The Fonts folder is under your C:\Windows folder, and the Printers folder is under My Computer.)

- You can get to the System Control Panel by right-clicking My Computer and clicking Properties.

- Access the Modem Control Panel by clicking HyperTerminal in your Start menu (if you installed it), and then double-clicking the HyperTerminal application icon in the HyperTerminal folder. Choose Files, Properties in the HyperTerminal window, and then click the Configure button in the New Connection Properties dialog box.

- You can also get to the modem through the System Control Panel, by choosing the Device Manager tab, selecting Modem, and then double-clicking the desired modem.

- Another way to the modem is through a Dial-Up Networking connectoid. Right-click a DUN connectoid (not a shortcut to one), click Properties, and then click Configure.

- To get the Network Control Panel, right-click the Network Neighborhood icon on the Desktop and choose Properties.

Shortcuts to the Control Panel

If you want a shortcut to an icon in the Control Panel, open the Control Panel, right-click an icon, and click Create Shortcut. You'll see a dialog box saying you can't create a shortcut in the Control Panel and asking whether you want to place the shortcut on the Desktop instead. You can certainly make that choice.

Shortcuts to Control Panel icons make it easy to get at the specific settings that you want changed. While the Control Panel is a reasonable organizing folder for these items, you may have one or two that you change a lot. Bring them out to the Desktop.

Tip

You can place shortcuts to Control Panel applets on your main Start menu. Even better, create a folder, perhaps under your My System folder (which we suggested you create in Chapter 7), and then drag the folder icon and drop it on the Start button. You can then put all your shortcuts to the Control Panel applets in the new folder. That way, you can determine just which applets you want on the main Start menu, and you can put all the shortcuts in one place. You can name the shortcuts anything you like, and they can point to a certain tab within an applet, such as the Device Manager tab in the System Control Panel (as described in the next section, *Fine-tuning your Control Panel shortcuts*).

Microsoft made the Control Panel much slower in Windows 95 and Windows 3.1 than it was in the bad old days of Windows 3.0. Starting with Windows 3.1, opening the Control Panel causes Windows to read through every file in your System folder, looking for files with a *cpl* extension. These *cpl* files are, of course, Control Panel applets.

Making the Control Panel read through all these files enables third-party vendors to add their own applets to the Windows interface, so this delay does have some merit. Independent developers can now install Control Panel applets for multimedia devices, tape drives, and other peripherals.

But sometimes you *don't* want to wait for the Control Panel to assemble its little list of applets. You want fast access to the *one* applet that you use all the time. Perhaps you frequently need to change a setting for your mouse or your keyboard. Or you like to change your Desktop colors or fonts every day. Or you need quick access to the handy Device Manager buried within the System applet. The next two sections teach you how to customize your Control Panel shortcuts to display the exact components you want to access.

Fine-tuning your Control Panel shortcuts

The Control Panel occupies a special place in the Desktop hierarchy. If you look for Control Panel in the Explorer, it doesn't appear as an icon under the Windows\Start Menu folder, as you might expect. Instead, it appears in the left pane of the Explorer *after* all your floppy drives and hard drives. This implies that Control Panel isn't on any of your disks at all.

This isn't the case, of course. Control Panel is, in reality, a normal executable file stored in your \Windows folder. You can see this by clicking the Start button, clicking Run, and then typing the following command:

```
C:\Windows\Control.exe
```

When you click OK, you see the same Control Panel window appear as you do when you run Control Panel directly from the Start menu (Start, Settings, Control Panel).

If you've visited the Control Panel before, you know it includes icons for changing your keyboard, mouse, and modem settings, and for many other functions of your system. The exact complement of Control Panel applets in your Control Panel window depends on the hardware and software you've installed. But the Control Panel holds a lot of secrets beneath its humble exterior. Control.exe supports a number of parameters that can dramatically speed up your access to the settings in its applets.

For example, let's say you want to change your dialing properties frequently, perhaps because you travel a lot. You could click Start, Run and type the following:

```
C:\Windows\Control.exe Modem.cpl
```

Even better, you can create a command that displays an individual tab of an applet, rather than having to start out at the first one and click your way across to the tab you really want.

For example, you can create a command that takes you directly to the Device Manager, a tab in the System applet. That command should look as follows:

```
C:\Windows\Control.exe Sysdm.cpl, System, 1
```

This command causes Control Panel to open Sysdm.cpl, the System applet, and jump to the second available tab. (In programmer-speak, the first tab is numbered 0, the second is 1, and so forth.) You need to specify the applet name in this command line because some applets contain more than one function within them.

What the three examples above have in common is the Control Panel's built-in command syntax. Stripped down to skeletal form, the syntax goes like this:

```
Control.exe {filename.cpl} {,applet-name} {,tab#}
```

If you run Control.exe with no parameters, only the Control Panel dialog box is displayed. If you add the correct *filename.cpl*, the first tab of that applet's dialog box is displayed. And if you tack on the correct applet name and tab number, then *that* tab is displayed.

In actual practice (as opposed to theory), there seem to be some quirks in the way Windows processes the tab number for an applet. Some Control Panel applets, particularly Display, dutifully jump to the correct tab when you specify a number in the command line, such as 1, 2, or 3. Other applets refuse to display any tab but the first (tab 0) even if you've used the "correct" syntax. Apparently, some of the programmers at Microsoft didn't know they were supposed to build in this feature, so they didn't. If a particular tab doesn't seem to want to let you "jump to it," the tab simply may not be programmed to do so.

You can place commands like these on the Start menu, on your Desktop, or elsewhere, and access them with a mouse click or a hot key.

Table 16-1 shows some of the *cpl* files available in most Windows systems, and the applet name you'll need in order to jump to a particular tab. (The applet Main.cpl contains several different functions, which are listed separately below.)

Table 16-1	Control Panel File and Applet Names
Filename	*Applet Name*
Main.cpl	Fonts
Main.cpl	Keyboard
Main.cpl	Mouse
Main.cpl	Printers
Access.cpl	Accessibility Options
Appwiz.cpl	Add/Remove Programs
Desk.cpl	Display
Intl.cpl	Regional Settings
Joy.cpl	Joystick
Mmsys.cpl	Multimedia
Modem.cpl	Modems
Netcpl.cpl	Network
Password.cpl	Passwords
Sysdm.cpl	System
Timedate.cpl	Date/Time

Now that you know the filenames and applet names to use, let's make sure you never have to type these lines more than once. It's easy to create a shortcut icon on your Desktop that takes you directly to the tab of your choice in a Control Panel applet's dialog box. Here's how:

STEPS

Control Panel Shortcut Icons on the Desktop

Step 1.   Right-click an unoccupied spot on your Desktop.

Step 2.   On the context menu that appears, point to New, and then click Shortcut.

Step 3.   In the Create Shortcut Wizard, type a command line such as the following:

```
C:\Windows\Control.exe Desk.cpl, Display, 2
```

Step 4.   Click the Next button. Type a name for your new shortcut, such as Display Appearance, and then click the Finish button. You're done!

You should see a new icon on your Desktop. Double-click it, and you will be almost instantly transported to (in this case) the Appearance tab of the Display Properties dialog box.

You'll probably want to change the icon for the shortcut, because this method produces one that looks pretty boring. Check out how to do this in the *Change the shortcut's icon* section of Chapter 10. You might also want to edit the shortcut's Target field to change the command line parameters. To do so, right-click the shortcut, click Properties, and then click the Shortcut tab.

Assign hot keys to Control Panel shortcuts

Once you've put a command for a Control Panel applet in a shortcut and placed the shortcut icon where you want it on the Desktop or your Start menu, you can assign it a hot key combination. This lets you to open the dialog box at almost any time by pressing Ctrl+Alt+A or a similar key combo.

To assign a shortcut icon a hot key, right-click the icon, and then click Properties. Click the Shortcut tab, click in the Shortcut key field, and then press a letter key on your keyboard. Windows automatically adds Ctrl+Alt to the key you press. For example, pressing the letter *a* assigns the hot key Ctrl+Alt+A to that shortcut. To assign a Ctrl+Shift or Shift+Alt combination, hold down those keys while you press the letter key.

To assign a hot key to an item in your Start menu, right-click the Start button, and then click Explore. Change to the subfolder of \Windows\Start Menu that contains your Start menu item. In the right pane of the Explorer, right-click the shortcut icon that corresponds to your menu item, and then click Properties. Once you see the Properties dialog box, you can assign a hot key in the same manner as we described in the previous paragraph.

We provide some additional examples of how to make shortcuts to the Control Panel icons in the *Control Panel icons* section of Chapter 10. You can find further details on how to put the Control Panel on the Start menu in the *Control Panel on a Start menu* section of Chapter 11.

Control Panel Settings

Most of the Control Panel settings are discussed in other chapters, as outlined in Table 16-2. In this chapter, we discuss those that aren't covered elsewhere.

Table 16-2	Settings Covered in Other Chapters
Control Panel Icon	*Chapter*
Add New Hardware	19
Date and Time	7
Display	22
Fonts	20
Internet	34
Keyboard	21
Mail (or Mail and Fax)	32
Microsoft Mail Postoffice	32
Modems	25
Mouse	24
Network	36
Passwords	32 and 36
PC Cards	19
Printers	23
System	19
Desktop Themes	22

Add/Remove Programs

The Add/Remove Programs Control Panel gives you three functions:

- Installing and removing programs that utilize the Windows 95 version of Install Shield

- Installing or removing programs that are covered by the Windows 95 setup routines or that have *inf* files consistent with the Microsoft standard for install files

- Creating a bootable Startup diskette, as described in Chapter 3

Install/Uninstall

Microsoft has attempted to provide a standard Windows application installation-and-setup procedure so you don't have to fathom a new set of steps every time you install a new piece of software. By licensing portions of the Install Shield software and integrating it into Windows 95, Microsoft provides application developers with a tool that will help you install and uninstall their programs.

To install a piece of compatible software, click the Install button, as shown in Figure 16-2.

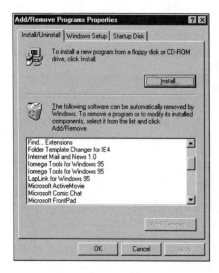

Figure 16-2: The Install/Uninstall tab of the Add/Remove Programs Properties dialog box. Use this tab to install software that uses the built-in Install Shield procedures. Developers of small shareware applications may opt not to use these.

If you install software using the Install/Uninstall tab, the Registry gets updated correctly and Windows retains enough information about the setup so that you can uninstall the software if you choose to later.

If you want to uninstall a program, it is best to use the Install/Uninstall tab so that you can remove most (if not all) of the bits and pieces of an application that are stored in various parts of your computer. If the application's programmers have written a proper uninstall routine, it will also remove references to the program in the Registry.

Secret

If you delete an application manually or find that you can't remove an uninstalled program's name from the list in the Install/Uninstall tab, you can remove these entries manually using the Registry editor.

STEPS

Removing Program Names from the Install/Uninstall List

Step 1. Double-click Regedit.exe in your \Windows folder.

Step 2. Click the plus sign next to HKEY_LOCAL_MACHINE in the left pane of the Registry editor. Navigate down through the branch to SOFTWARE, Microsoft, Windows, and finally Uninstall.

Step 3. In the left pane, highlight the name of the application whose name you wish to erase from the Install/Uninstall list. Choose Edit, Delete.

Step 4. Close the Registry editor.

You can also use TweakUI — a Microsoft "use at your own risk" Desktop applet — to remove these superfluous names. Download it from http://www.microsoft.com/windows/software/powertoy.htm.

Network Install

If you commonly install software to several PCs in your company, save yourself some shoe leather. You can add a Network Install tab to the Add/Remove Programs Properties dialog box that lets you or individual users easily install new applications across a network at the click of a mouse.

Let's assume you have a site license to distribute software within your company to all users, or a license to distribute it to a certain number of users. The Network Install tab allows you to install an entire application from another PC — without diskettes or a CD-ROM. (The other PC is usually a network server, but it could be any other PC in a peer-to-peer network.)

To make the Network Install tab appear, you must create the two short text files shown here:

```
Example Contents of Netinst.reg:
REGEDIT4
Hkey_Local_Machine/SOFTWARE/Microsoft/Windows/CurrentVersion
AppInstallPath=\\\\Server1\\Win95\\Apps.ini

Example Contents of Apps.ini:
[AppInstallList]
Microsoft Internet Explorer=\\Server1\Apps\Msie30.exe
Mapped Application=*\\Server1\Dummy\Dumsetup.exe
```

Sounds

The Sounds Control Panel lets you associate a given sound with a given Windows event. Windows 95 stores the sounds it uses in files with the *wav* extension. Windows 95 understands *wav* files and can "play" them through your sound card.

Windows 95 comes with lots of sounds that you can associate with Windows events (if you installed the sound files). You can also purchase CD-ROMs full of *wav* files, download sound files from online services or bulletin boards, or get them over the Internet.

The sounds that come with Windows 95 are arranged as "sound schemes," so you can apply them all at once to the designated Windows events. This makes it a lot easier to apply sounds. You can even create your own sound schemes by choosing from among the *wav* files that are installed on your computer.

You can test the sounds by selecting an event, choosing a sound from the Name drop-down list, and clicking the triangular play button to the right of the Preview window, as shown in Figure 16-4.

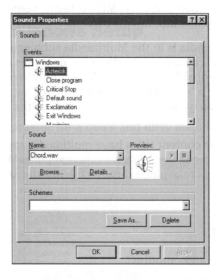

Figure 16-4: The Sounds Control Panel. Highlight a Windows 95 event, select or browse for a sound, and then click the triangular play button next to the Preview box.

If you didn't install the sound schemes when you installed Windows 95, there won't be any listed in the Schemes drop-down list. To install the sound schemes that come with Windows 95, double-click the Add/Remove Programs icon in your Control Panel, click the Windows Setup tab, highlight Multimedia, and then click the Details button. Mark the sound schemes you want to install, click OK twice, and insert your Windows 95 CD-ROM when prompted.

Undocumented

Microsoft Plus! contains *Desktop themes*, which include unnamed sound schemes, as well many other Desktop elements. The sounds within the themes are associated with Windows events, but no name appears in the Schemes field. If you like, you can name and save a theme's sound scheme. First double-click the Desktop Themes icon in the Control Panel, choose a theme, and click OK or Apply. Second, open the Sounds applet, click the Save As button, type a name for the new scheme, and click OK.

You've now associated the sounds that came from the Desktop theme that you chose with a sound scheme name. Later, if you choose a new Desktop theme, or no theme, you can still use the sounds associated with the previous theme by using the sound scheme that you just named.

Applying sounds to application events

Windows comes with sounds and sound schemes that you can apply to various Windows events. Application programmers can also add sounds to events that are specific to their application. If an application doesn't have a sound associated with a particular event, Windows uses the Windows sound that is associated with that event. For example, Windows uses the sound associated with its own Open program event when you open an application, unless the application has a different sound (or no sound) associated with that event.

Events are organized by application. The first application is Windows. Scroll down the Events window in the Sounds dialog box to see other applications and events.

Secret

Windows users can add sounds to specific applications and specific application events, even if the application programmers neglected to do so. This means that each application can have its own unique sounds for similar types of (or different) events. This requires editing the Registry. Here's how:

STEPS

Adding Sounds to Application Events

Step 1. Double-click Regedit.exe in your \Windows folder.

Step 2. Navigate to

HKEY_CURRENT_USER\AppEvents\Schemes\Apps

Step 3. Highlight Apps in the left pane. Right-click the right pane, and choose New, Key. Type the name of the application's executable file. For example, type **Write** for Windows Write. Press Enter. (If your application already is listed under the Apps key, you can skip this step.)

Step 4. Highlight the key that you just created (or the existing key if your application was already listed) in the left pane of the Registry editor, right-click the right pane, and choose New, Key. Type one of the following event names:

(continued)

STEPS *(continued)*

Adding Sounds to Application Events

> AppGPFault
>
> Close
>
> MailBeep
>
> Maximize
>
> MenuCommand
>
> MenuPopup
>
> Minimize
>
> Open
>
> RestoreDown
>
> RestoreUp
>
> SystemAsterisk
>
> SystemExclamation
>
> SystemQuestion
>
> SystemHand
>
> You can see more about what these event names mean by navigating to
>
> HKEY_CURRENT_USER\AppEvents\EventLabels
>
> and then clicking any one of the event names.

Step 5. Highlight the new key that you just created in the left pane of the Registry editor, right-click the right pane, and choose New, Key. Type **.current**.

Step 6. Repeat steps 4 and 5 to name events associated with your application until you have named all the events that you care to. Exit the Registry.

Step 7. Double-click the Sounds applet in the Control Panel. Scroll down the Events list until you find the name of the application that you just named sound events for in the Registry. Click on a sound event, and select a *wav* file to associate with that event by selecting it from the Name list, or by browsing for it with the Browse button.

You can make this all a little easier by exporting the HKEY_CURRENT_USER\AppEvents\Schemes\Apps key from the Registry using the Registry editor. You can use this text file as a basis for creating a *reg* file that you can merge into the Registry. Edit this *reg* file to duplicate the steps above for each application whose events you want to add sounds to.

To learn more about *reg* files, turn to the *Exporting and importing the Registry* section of Chapter 15.

TweakUI

Of course, we've mentioned TweakUI throughout this book. It won't be in your Control Panel unless you download it first from Microsoft's web site (http://www.microsoft.com/windows/software/powertoy.htm).

You can use TweakUI to "tweak" all sorts of user interface settings. Double-click it and play with it for a while. (See Figure 16-5.)

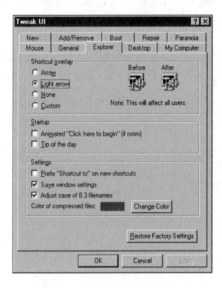

Figure 16-5: TweakUI. Click a tab to find a whole new set of "tweaks."

Properties Sheets

Right-click an object and click Properties. The object's properties sheet(s) are displayed.

Tip

An even quicker way of displaying an object's properties sheet(s) is to hold down the Alt key and double-click the object's icon. You can also highlight an object, hold down the Alt key and press the Enter key.

Pretty much anything you see on your Desktop has a properties sheet, except, interestingly enough, the Control Panel icons, which are often properties sheets themselves. For example, the Display icon contains the Desktop's properties sheets.

Every file has a properties sheet. Every shortcut to a Windows program has a properties sheet, as does every shortcut to a DOS program.

Like the settings in the Control Panel, most properties sheets are discussed in the relevant chapter. We mention properties sheets here because we want to point out that they are a general phenomenon. While they aren't universal — you may run lots of Windows 3.x applications that don't use them — they will become more common as developers integrate them into applications.

Summary

The Control Panel settings let you configure hardware and software drivers.

▶ We show you how to quickly get to the different Control Panel settings.

▶ You can install and remove Windows applications through a consistent interface.

▶ You can choose your settings for displaying currency, time, and date.

▶ The Control Panel has a setting for associating sounds with Windows 95 events.

Part III

DOS Secrets

We'll give you a little bit of the flavor of Schulman's book here, because it applies to how DOS and Windows 95 actually work on your computer. You can turn to Chapter 18 for further discussion of conventional and expanded memory.

DOS and Windows, Together at Last, at Least

Microsoft says that Windows 95 is an integrated operating system. Does that mean that DOS 7.0 and Windows 95 come in the same box? Or does it mean something more radical, that Windows 95 is a whole new operating system that leaves DOS with but a small role to play?

Andrew Schulman argues in his book that Windows has been a real operating system since 1988 with the advent of Windows/386 2.*x*. What he means is that Windows code has been handling the requests that programs make of the computer, and, when necessary, it has been handing those requests to DOS to let it do some of the work. With the advent of Windows for Workgroups 3.11, and especially the 32-bit file access that came with it, DOS has had even less of the grunt work to do.

According to Achulman, 32-bit file access (which was introduced with Windows for Workgroups 3.11), is "pre-beta" code for the disk/file access subsystem of Windows 95. In Windows for Workgroups, 32-bit file access really did not work well, failing under some conditions. For example, certain legitimate DOS-read functions cause Windows for Workgroups with 32-bit file access to halt with a "system integrity" error. In Windows 95, it is hard to turn off 32-bit file access, and we have not seen any reports of difficulties with it.

It is the fact that Windows is first in line to deal with disk-access requests that makes it an operating system. Windows makes the decision about how to handle these requests and uses some of the DOS code routines if they are useful. Windows 95 treats DOS as a real-mode driver.

Schulman states early in his book:

> "If I had to explain how Windows 95 relates to DOS in 25 words or less, I'd say this: *Windows 95 relates to DOS in the same way that WfW 3.11 does.* Windows provides 32BFA [32-bit file access]. For non-file calls, it calls (in V86 mode) the real-mode DOS code in WINBOOT.SYS *[now called Io.sys in the released version of Windows 95]*. Windows 95 is a genuine operating system; so were WfW 3.11, Windows 3.1 Enhanced mode, and Windows 3.0 Enhanced mode."

It Sure Looks Like DOS

Of course, as a user, it sure looks like DOS when you start your computer. Right there is a text screen with familiar messages. The first text messages are probably output from your BIOS.

The Basic Input/Output System (BIOS) chip(s) used to play a much more important role. In the days before 386 systems, the BIOS chips contained the only code that told DOS enough about the hardware to allow DOS to talk to said hardware. Some DOS programs bypassed the BIOS to get directly at the hardware and speed their screen display. Later versions of DOS bypassed the BIOS to use their own descriptions of the hard disk to provide quicker access. Now, Windows — and especially Windows 95 — keeps its own account of the hardware and provides all the hardware drivers it needs.

This doesn't mean the BIOS is ignored by Windows 95. Instead, once the hardware description is read from the BIOS, Windows uses its own routines to interact with the hardware.

Soon after the BIOS display (if any), your screen gives you the reassuring message "Starting Windows 95." But where did this message come from? Well, from DOS, of course. The file Io.sys sits in the boot tracks of your hard disk and starts after the BIOS completes its work. Io.sys *is* DOS.

Many of you may think of Command.com as DOS. But Command.com is only the user interface (the *shell*) for DOS. It can easily be replaced by another user interface, such as 4DOS.

Io.sys does the work of reading Config.sys. If you have an Autoexec.bat file, Io.sys loads Command.com to execute the statements in Autoexec.bat. Even if these files don't exist, Io.sys does much of the work that they would have done, such as loading Ifshlp.sys and Setver.exe. The last thing Io.sys does is start Windows by sending out the instruction Win.com as though it were a line in Autoexec.bat.

This Windows startup process is discussed in much more detail in Chapter 6.

The data structures and routines created by Io.sys are still there after Windows 95 starts up, and Windows 95 calls upon them (in V86 mode) as it needs them. As developers rewrite more Windows components using 32-bit equivalents, Windows needs less and less of Io.sys.

A Thing on a Thing

The fact that you first boot into real-mode DOS, that you have DOS-looking text on your screen, and that DOS is necessary for Windows to run, creates the perception that Windows is "a thing on a thing." IBM, in its marketing of OS/2, does as much as it can to foster this perception.

Microsoft wants us to see Windows 95 as a "real" operating system, which it is. In order to enhance that perception, Microsoft constructed Io.sys so that it calls Windows 95 automatically without your having to put a line in your Autoexec.bat file to call Win.com. Microsoft also made it somewhat difficult to get to DOS outside of a Windows DOS box.

Internal DOS commands (DIR, Copy, CD, and so on) are resident in Command.com. External DOS commands (XCopy, Find, Mem) are DOS files — separate executable programs.

All the internal DOS commands found in DOS 6.*x* are still there in the DOS that comes with Windows 95. But only some of the DOS external commands (executable files) that came with DOS 6.*x* come with Windows 95.

Secret

When you write DOS commands, you need to put double quote marks around long folder and filenames than contain spaces (for example, CD \"Another folder").

Windows 95 doesn't come with a virus checker, an undelete program, or DOS-based backup. These were big new functions that came with DOS 6.2*x*. Microsoft decided to drop virus checking in Windows 95 and let others provide that functionality.

Windows 95 comes with a Recycle Bin, but files deleted from the DOS prompt (or over the network or on diskettes) don't go to the Recycle Bin. If you want to undelete files deleted at the DOS prompt, you have to use the DOS 6.2*x* Undelete command or a package from another developer such as Norton Utilities for Windows 95.

Windows 95 does come with a Windows-based backup program that works with floppy-based tape backup hardware. More extensive backup software (for example, for SCSI tape drives) is provided by other developers.

To find out how to undelete files at the lower DOS levels by using the DOS 6.2*x* Undelete command, turn to Chapter 14.

The remaining DOS commands

Microsoft claims that DOS commands are now native Windows 95 commands. They certainly are in the sense that they have been changed to work with long filenames and the VFAT (Virtual Fat Allocation Table, the DOS file system). All of the previous internal DOS commands are available and have been updated.

Table 17-1 lists the DOS external commands that come with Windows 95.

Table 17-1	DOS External Commands in Windows 95
Filename	**Definition**
Attrib.exe	Show or change file attributes
Chkdsk.exe	Check disk and provide status report (use ScanDisk instead)
Choice.com	Accept user input in a batch file
Debug.exe	Debug hexadecimal editor and viewer
Deltree.exe	Delete tree (directory and subdirectories)

Filename	Definition
Diskcopy.com	Full copy of diskettes
Doskey.com	Edit command lines, recall them, create macros
Edit.com	File editing application
Extract.exe	Extract files from a cabinet file
Fc.exe	Compare two files
Fdisk.exe	Low-level disk partitioning and configuration
Find.exe	Find text in a file
Format.com	Format a disk
Label.exe	Label a disk
Mem.exe	Display memory use
Mode.com	Mode of port or display, or code page (character set)
More.com	Pause for output one screen at a time
Move.exe	Move files (copy and delete original)
Scandisk.exe	Fix disks
Share.exe	File locking
Sort.exe	Sort the contents of a file
Start.exe	Run a Windows program
Subst.exe	Substitute a drive letter for a directory
Sys.com	Create a system disk
Xcopy.exe	Extended file and directories copy
Xcopy32.exe	Improved version of Xcopy.exe, called by Xcopy.exe

You can't copy long file or folder names with Xcopy.exe (or Xcopy32.exe) in MS-DOS mode (even when you use double quote marks around the file names), but you can in a Windows DOS session.

Secret

Xcopy /k copies the file attributes correctly but not the directory attributes. This is an acknowledged bug in Windows 95.

You can learn how to use all of these commands, and the internal ones as well, by consulting the online DOS help. Type the command and add /? before pressing Enter.

DOS 6.2*x* came with a DOS help program. You could get extensive information about DOS commands by just typing **help** at the DOS prompt. This help program (Help.hlp) wasn't updated for the Windows 95 version of DOS commands. You'll find it on Microsoft's Windows 95 CD-ROM in the \Other\ Oldmsdos folder. You can run it in a DOS window.

You can copy Help.hlp into the \Windows\Command folder, and because this folder is on the path, you will then be able to get to the help program by typing **help** *command* at any DOS prompt. The help information will be somewhat out of date, but still useful.

You can use any of the DOS programs that you find in the \Other\Oldmsdos folder. If you don't have newer versions in your \Windows\Command folder, you can copy any of these DOS programs to the Command folder from your Windows 95 CD-ROM.

DOS Edit

Windows 95 ships with a new version of DOS Edit. Written by a contractor to Microsoft, Emory Horvath, it is a nifty little editor, and it's quite useful for dealing with text and batch files. You can easily create a shortcut to it and put it on your Start menu or your Desktop (see Chapter 10). You'll find Edit.com in your \Windows\Command folder.

Undocumented

Edit can load up to nine files and can have two windows open at any one time. It can use up to 5.5MB of virtual memory to load and manage files, handling files up to 64,000 lines. The maximum line length is 1024 characters. It doesn't require Windows 95 to run, and it should run on any processor equal to or greater than a 286. It requires only 160K of conventional memory.

Edit is great for looking for text in binary files, and it has a switch in its File Open dialog box to give you that option. The Edit command's File Open dialog box defaults to opening files with any extension — a big improvement over the early version if you use it to edit batch files.

Secret

The Edit command doesn't recognize a mouse double-click setting in the Registry. If you have set your middle mouse button on a Logitech mouse to double-click (as described in Chapter 24), it won't work with Edit. You'll have to remember to double-click with the left mouse button.

Config.sys commands

A number of commands are used only in your Config.sys file. They include:

break	files	rem
buffers	include	set
country	install	shell
device	lastdrive	stacks
devicehigh	menucolor	submenu
dos	menuitem	switches
drivparm	numlock	verify
fcbs		

DOS commands that are no longer around

The following DOS commands did not come with Windows 95:

append	interlnk	recover
assign	intersvr	replace
backup	join	restore
comp	memcard	ramdrive.sys
dosshell	memmaker	romdrive.sys
edlin	mirror	share
ega.sys	msav	smartmon
fasthelp	msbackup	tree
fastopen	power	undelete
graftabl	print	unformat
graphics	print.sys	vsafe
help	qbasic	

Some of these external DOS command files are stored in the \Other\Oldmsdos folder on the Windows 95 source CD-ROM. They are the MS-DOS 6.22 versions, and they haven't been updated.

Cautions about some DOS commands

Chkdsk has been superseded in functionality by Mem.exe and Scandisk.exe. ScanDisk is now both a Windows program and a DOS program that checks for problems with your disk (hard or floppy). Mem gives you a great deal more information than Chkdsk about your available conventional memory. Chkdsk /f is rejected both in a Windows DOS session and in MS-DOS mode. You can type it, but you just get a message that you "Cannot obtain exclusive access to drive *X*:."

Share.exe is not needed in Windows DOS sessions. A virtual device driver takes care of file locking. You can still use it in MS-DOS mode.

Subst.exe hasn't fully worked for quite a while. It doesn't work with networked drives, and it fails with Fdisk, Format, and Sys. It will work just fine in a Windows DOS session or in MS-DOS mode to substitute a drive letter for a path or folder name. This makes it easier to use really old DOS programs that weren't designed to use pathnames.

Do not use the earlier DOS Append utility. It prevents Windows 95 and Windows-based applications from creating valid pathnames for the files they are using.

Wonderful DOS commands

If you want to rename a set of files, you have to use either the File Manager or the DOS Ren command. To compare files, you need to use either Fc.exe or the file-matching shareware that we feature on the *Windows 95 Secrets* CD-ROM.

DOS 7.0 adds the ability to navigate up the folder tree just using dots as names for grandparent and great grandparent folders. The dots are stand-ins for the various folders as follows:

.   The current folder

..   The parent folder

...   The grandparent folder

....   The great grandparent folder

You can use these stand-in dot names in place of the actual names in DOS commands. For example:

Copy *thisfile.ext* ...   Copies *thisfile.ext* to the grandparent folder

CD ....   Changes the current folder to the great grandparent folder

Modifying DOS commands

You can modify the default behavior of some DOS commands so that they do just what you want them to. You do this by setting the value of certain environmental variables. For example, if you want to change the default behavior of the DIR command, you can add the following line to your Autoexec.bat file (or to a batch file that runs when you start a Windows DOS session):

```
set dircmd=/p /l /o:-d
```

This line modifies the DIR command to pause after each screen-full of listed files, display the filenames in lower case, and order the filenames in descending date order.

You can modify the Copy command by setting the value of *copycmd*.

How do you know which modifiers to use when changing these commands? They are the same ones you could type in manually when you enter the command. Type **copy /?** or **dir /?** at the command prompt and press Enter to see the available modifiers.

Doskey lets you define macros, so you can redefine any of the DOS internal or external commands, as long as you run them after you load Doskey and the macro definitions (most likely in your Autoexec.bat file or in a batch file that is run when you start a Windows DOS session). For example, if you want to redefine the Mem command to pause after each page of information, add the following to your batch file:

```
c:\Windows\Command\Doskey
Doskey mem=mem.exe $* /p
```

The Mem command is now changed to mean "Mem with the page pause modifier." The symbol $* means "include whatever is typed after Mem on the command line." For more information on Doskey, type **doskey/?** at the command prompt.

Shortcuts to DOS commands

You can make further modifications to DOS commands by using shortcuts to MS-DOS programs (also known as *pif*s) to call the commands. Some of these are carried out automatically. To see what we mean, take the following steps:

STEPS

Creating a Shortcut to Mem.exe

Step 1.   Using your Explorer, navigate to the C:\Windows\Command folder. Right-click Mem.exe. Click Properties.

Step 2.   Click the Program tab. Notice that the Cmd line field has the following entry:

C:\WINDOWS\COMMAND\MEM.EXE /c /p

This entry modifies the Mem command to display greater details about memory allocation, and to pause after displaying one page of information. These commands were automatically added to the command line.

Step 3.   Click OK.

Step 4.   Press the F5 key to refresh the Explorer window. Scroll through the Command folder until you find the MS-DOS icon labeled Mem. It will be right below the Mem.exe file (if you are using details view and name order) and its type is listed as Shortcut to MS-DOS Program.

Step 5.   Double-click the shortcut to Mem icon.

Double-clicking the shortcut to Mem icon opens a Windows DOS session, displays the memory details, and then pauses, waiting for you to press another key. You will want to edit this shortcut so that it doesn't close on exit (right-click the shortcut icon, click Properties, click the Programs tab, and clear the Close on exit check box).

You can create a Windows shortcut for any of the DOS commands. You can put these shortcuts anywhere that makes sense to you — on your Desktop, in the Start menus, in a DOS folder that has a shortcut on your Desktop. In this way, the DOS commands become Windows programs.

If you create a shortcut that can't be added to the same folder, Windows will put it in the \Windows\Pif folder. You'll notice this if you create a shortcut to a DOS command in the \Other\Oldmsdos folder on your Windows 95 CD-ROM.

If you have DOS parameters or filenames that change, add a space and a question mark after the DOS command name in the command line, as in **Edit ?**.

DOS commands you shouldn't run

We want to be sure to cover a few DOS commands and applications that you must *never* run while in a Windows DOS session or in MS-DOS mode.

Don't ever run any disk utilities that haven't been updated to work with long filenames, unless you have saved your long filenames. This includes Norton Utilities version 8 and previous versions, as well as any earlier versions of Central Point disk utilities. You can run earlier versions of Norton Disk Editor, but do so after pressing F8 at the Windows 95 startup message and getting to a command prompt.

Don't ever run backup programs that are unaware of long filenames unless you have saved your long filenames with Lfnbk.exe (Long filename backup). This program saves the long filenames and restores them after you run an older DOS-based backup program.

You won't be able to run Chkdsk /f. Don't run Fdisk, Format C: (but Format A: and Format B: are fine), or Sys C: while in a Windows DOS session.

Don't ever run any disk optimization packages other than Defrag (which comes with Windows 95) if they haven't been updated for long filenames. Don't run programs that change your hard disk interleave from a Windows DOS session.

Windows has a built-in disk cache. Don't run third-party disk cache programs that aren't specifically designed for Windows 95.

Don't ever run utilities that undelete files unless they have been specifically designed for Windows 95. You can use the DOS 6.*x* version of Undelete using the steps provided in Chapter 14.

The path and Windows 95 applications

The default path that is set if you don't have an Autoexec.bat file is

```
C:\Windows;C:\Windows\Command
```

This assumes, of course, that your Windows 95 folder is called Windows and that it is on the C drive.

You can add more folders to the path if you have an Autoexec.bat file. You can also change the path in a batch file that you run when you open a DOS window.

Undocumented

Windows 95 applications can set a pointer to the folder that contains their executable files. The reference is stored in the Registry at HKEY_LOCAL_MACHINE\Software\Microsoft\Windows\CurrentVersion\ AppPaths.

When a Windows 95 application starts, the shell looks at the entry at this location and appends the referenced folder(s) to the path.

You can set up references at this location in the Registry so you don't have to type the full pathname in front of an executable file's name when you use the Run menu item to run a program. This also works with the Start command in DOS batch files.

Use the Registry editor to add folder references, patterned after the ones already in the Registry at the above location, for your own Windows applications that don't know about this new Windows 95 feature. You can then reference the applications in Start commands without using their full pathname.

Running DOS Programs

Our major concern in this chapter is providing you with the tools to make it easier to run DOS programs, both in Windows DOS sessions and in MS-DOS mode. You'll find significant improvements relative to Windows 3.*x* in Windows 95's ability to run DOS programs, and we want you to be able to take advantage of these improvements.

You can run DOS programs:

- Before Windows 95 starts by booting to a command prompt
- After Windows 95 starts in a Windows DOS session
- By quitting Windows to get to MS-DOS mode without a reboot
- By warm booting to MS-DOS mode with a call to send you back to Windows with an exit command
- By exiting Windows 95 after starting it with an Autoexec.bat file and switching to the DOS prompt

DOS before Windows

To get to the DOS prompt before Windows 95 starts, press F8 when you see the message that Windows 95 is starting. Choose menu item 6, Command prompt only. You can edit your Msdos.sys file to have your computer automatically start at the DOS prompt or give you a menu of choices before Windows 95 starts. (For more information, see Chapter 6.)

Windows 95 hasn't loaded yet, but the commands in your Config.sys and Autoexec.bat files (if you have such files) are executed. You won't have access to any hardware devices such as your mouse, CD-ROM, or sound card unless you have loaded their 16-bit drivers. Windows 95 loads the 32-bit drivers for these devices only when Windows 95 is loaded.

Unless you have configured your Autoexec.bat and Config.sys files to work with DOS programs that you would normally start before you start Windows 95, it is unlikely you will have these 16-bit drivers loaded. Windows 95 doesn't need them and can, by itself, provide these services to DOS programs that run in Windows DOS sessions.

To increase conventional memory, you may want to load your 16-bit drivers and DOS TSRs in the upper memory blocks. If your DOS program requires expanded memory, you should put a line in your Config.sys file to load an expanded memory manager. Turn to Chapter 18 for more details.

At this point, because Windows 95 hasn't loaded, you are in DOS 7.0. You have real-mode direct disk access, not 32-bit file/disk access. If you want disk caching, you are going to need to run SmartDrive (Smartdrv.exe). Chkdsk /f works just fine (whereas it will not work in MS-DOS mode).

While you certainly can run your DOS programs by booting up DOS instead of Windows 95, this may not be the best method. You will probably want to optimize Autoexec.bat and Config.sys to run Windows 95, not DOS programs. You can run DOS programs in MS-DOS mode with their own individually optimized Autoexec.bat and Config.sys files, so this is a better place for them. You can also run DOS programs in Windows DOS sessions, which provide 32-bit drivers, thereby reducing demands for conventional memory.

DOS in Windows

If your DOS programs run in Windows DOS sessions, by all means run them there. Windows 95 creates a "virtual machine" for each Windows DOS session. As far as your DOS program is concerned, it is running in its own computer.

Each Windows DOS session is its own virtual machine. Each virtual machine can be different. You can run a number of them at once. Each is preemptively multitasked. This means no one session can hog all of your computer's resources.

You can set a number of virtual machine operational parameters. You determine what the computer looks like to the DOS program by editing Windows DOS session properties sheets. These sheets are found in Program Information Files, or *pif*s.

The easiest way to run a DOS program in Windows 95 is to double-click its icon in a folder window or the Explorer. In many cases, the DOS program will just run and that's all there is to it. You can create shortcuts to DOS programs and documents and treat them just like you would shortcuts to Windows programs and documents. *Pif*s have been enhanced to take on the function of shortcuts to DOS programs.

You can also run a DOS program from the Run command in the Start menu. Click the Start button, and then click Run. Type the full name of the program, including its path. Type any command line parameters after the program's name.

Undocumented

If you want to run the DOS internal commands such as Copy from the Run command, you need to use something like the following syntax:

```
command /c copy filename lpt1
```

The /C switch allows you to run internal commands.

If you have an application that writes a PostScript file to disk, and later you want to send that PostScript file to the printer, there is no "Windows" way to do this. You have to copy the file to the printer port, as shown in the example above — one good reason to keep DOS around. (Note that the previous example will not eject the last page of text files from laser printers; you must do this manually.)

Windows 95 provides Windows DOS sessions with 32-bit file access to the hard drive as well as disk caching. This significantly speeds hard disk access by DOS programs. DOS programs have full mouse functionality (if they are designed to use a mouse) without having to load a 16-bit mouse driver. You don't need 16-bit sound card drivers, CD-ROM drivers, or network drivers, because these services are provided by Windows 95 32-bit drivers.

You can run DOS programs in a window or full screen. To switch a DOS session between windowed and full-screen modes, press Alt+Enter. To switch between DOS sessions, press Alt+Tab. You can copy data in a DOS window and paste it into a Windows 95 window.

Your Start menu contains an MS-DOS Prompt menu item. Click the Start button, point to Programs, and click MS-DOS Prompt. This is a generic Windows DOS Session. You can run a DOS program in the Windows DOS session from the DOS prompt. You can open multiple Windows DOS sessions by choosing this Start menu item.

Given all the features you get when you run your DOS programs in a Windows DOS session, you might conclude that Windows 95 provides a better DOS than DOS. If all DOS programs were able to take advantage of the DOS box, this would surely be the case.

DOS in MS-DOS mode without a reboot

If your DOS program won't run in a Windows DOS session, no matter how you set the properties of its virtual machine, you'll need to run it in MS-DOS mode. You don't have to quit Windows to use this version of MS-DOS mode, but you are given that option when you do quit Windows.

To quit Windows to MS-DOS mode without rebooting, take the following steps:

STEPS

Quitting Windows to MS-DOS Mode

Step 1.   Click the Start button.

Step 2.   Click Shut Down.

Step 3.   Click Restart the computer in MS-DOS mode.

Step 4.   Click Yes.

Undocumented

All but a 4K stub of Windows is unloaded from memory, and the file Dosstart.bat is run. This file is in your \Windows folder. It was created when you first installed Windows 95, and it consists of the calls to DOS TSRs that were remarked out of your previous DOS/Windows 3.x Autoexec.bat file.

You can edit the Dosstart.bat file so it calls the TSRs that are appropriate for when you start MS-DOS mode (such as Smartdrv.exe and/or a 16-bit mouse driver). Because you are not doing a warm boot when you start non-rebooted MS-DOS mode, you will be unable to start any 16-bit drivers you would have normally called from a Config.sys file that you configured for DOS. If you need to load these drivers to run DOS programs in MS-DOS mode, either load them in the Windows 95 Config.sys file or use the warm-boot version of MS-DOS mode.

Secret

If you want to access your CD-ROM while in MS-DOS mode, you'll need to load your real-mode CD-ROM driver in your Config.sys file or load it in a private Config.sys if you use the reboot version of MS-DOS mode. In addition, Mscdex.exe, which is normally loaded by your Autoexec.bat, must be loaded. When Windows 95 is installed, Mscdex.exe is remarked out (because Windows 95 has its own 32-bit protected-mode version of Mscdex.exe) and the unremarked call from your previous Autoexec.bat file is moved to Dosstart.bat. The real-mode CD-ROM driver in your Config.sys file is not remarked out.

When you go to MS-DOS mode, Mscdex.exe is called by Dosstart.bat, and because the real-mode CD-ROM driver has been previously loaded, you will now be able to access your CD-ROM drive in MS-DOS mode. If you remove the real-mode CD-ROM driver from your Config.sys (perhaps to reclaim the conventional memory it uses), you won't be able to access your CD-ROM in MS-DOS mode without a reboot. In addition, you will get a series of error messages about Mscdex.exe unless you also remove it from Dosstart.bat.

If you have plenty of conventional memory even when you load the real-mode CD-ROM driver, you will be able to play your CD-ROM-based DOS games without having to go to rebooted MS-DOS mode. If this is not the case, you should load your real-mode CD-ROM drivers in private Config.sys files, and load Mscdex.exe in private Autoexec.bat files.

Undocumented

A shortcut to a DOS program, Exit to dos.pif. is automatically created when you exit to MS-DOS mode in this manner. You'll find it in the Windows 95 folder.

You can edit Exit to dos.pif. If you right-click this file in your Explorer and click Properties in the context menu, you can set whatever properties you like, including creating your own private Autoexec.bat and Config.sys. Of course, if you go that far, you are rebooting into DOS when you restart the computer in MS-DOS mode, which we discuss next.

Undocumented

You can also get to the non-reboot version of MS-DOS mode by creating a shortcut to MS-DOS (a *pif*) that doesn't create its own Autoexec.bat and Config.sys files. This is an option in the Advanced Program Settings properties sheet, which we discuss later in this chapter in the section entitled *Advanced button.*

When you exit this non-reboot version MS-DOS mode, your computer restarts Windows 95.

DOS in MS-DOS mode with a reboot

Windows 95 restarts (warm boots) your computer when it goes into rebooted MS-DOS mode. You exit this mode back into Windows 95 by typing **exit** at the command prompt and pressing Enter. Your computer is again restarted (warm booted) and Windows 95 reloads.

Undocumented

A restart is a warm boot. Io.sys runs again and reads Msdos.sys, Config.sys, and Autoexec.bat. Be careful: If you have edited your Msdos.sys file so that BootMulti=1 and the default boot is to DOS 6.2 (BootWin=0), you will restart to your previous version of DOS instead of MS-DOS mode. A way around this is to press F4 at reboot time to boot to Windows 95. You'll also need to do this when you exit MS-DOS mode.

To get to rebooted MS-DOS mode, you first need to create an icon with the proper properties. We show you how to do this in the *MS-DOS Mode* section of this chapter. Each DOS program that uses MS-DOS mode can have its own icon with these properties.

DOS after Windows

Secret

Just as it's possible to run DOS before Windows 95, it is also possible to shut down Windows 95 and go to the DOS prompt and real-mode DOS. This is just like it was with Windows 3.*x*, and you can run your DOS programs after you leave Windows 95.

Microsoft has made it somewhat difficult to get back to the DOS prompt after running Windows 95, but you can do it automatically by taking a few easy steps. First, you need to create an Autoexec.bat if you haven't already done so. If Io.sys finds an Autoexec.bat file, it loads Command.com, the DOS user interface, to read and execute the commands in Autoexec.bat.

Your Autoexec.bat and Config.sys files should contain the commands that will load the 16-bit drivers for your mouse, CD-ROM, and any other devices that you'll want accessible when running real-mode DOS. Because Io.sys loads Command.com, the DOS user interface will be available to you when you shut down Windows 95. And because Command.com is already loaded, Windows 95 doesn't have to load it again whenever you open a DOS window, thereby speeding up that process.

Second, you need to edit your Autoexec.bat file. The last line should contain the statement *win*. This statement will start Windows 95 after the previous commands in the Autoexec.bat file are executed.

Third, you need to edit your Msdos.sys file to boot your computer to the DOS command prompt, by setting BootGUI=0. Read the BootGUI section of Chapter 6 for more details about how to do this. This setting tells your computer not to automatically load Windows 95, because that's what your edited Autoexec.bat already does.

Fourth, rename the file Logos.sys in your \Windows folder to Logos.sav. This *bmp* graphics file is the one that displays the message "It's now safe to turn off your computer." When Windows 95 shuts down and doesn't find this file, your computer displays the DOS prompt instead, if you have carried out the other steps.

If you have a portable computer and have implemented the Advanced Power Management feature, you need to go to the Advanced Power Management icon in the Control Panel and disable this feature, which would turn off your computer when you shut down Windows 95.

Starting Windows 95 in this manner makes it less effective in managing conventional memory. For example, the real-mode compression driver Dblspace.bin is not unloaded and replaced by the protected-mode double-space driver if you start Windows 95 this way. Therefore, less conventional memory will be available for DOS windows sessions.

Gary Tessler worked out many of these details and makes them available at his site. For more Windows 95 tricks check out his site at: http://ourworld.compuserve.com/homepages/NIFTY_TOOLS.

DOS in a Box

You can either display a DOS program that's running in a Windows DOS session in a window on the Windows 95 Desktop, or full screen. A DOS window can have a toolbar just like any respectable Windows program (see Figure 17-1). If your DOS window doesn't have a toolbar, click the system menu icon on the left end of the DOS window's title bar, and choose Toolbar.

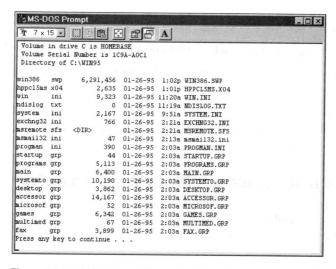

Figure 17-1: A Windows DOS session. Notice the toolbar. The title bar is at the top of the window. The system menu icon is on the left end of the title bar.

You can use the DOS window toolbar to:

■ Change the DOS font size and thereby the DOS window size

■ Mark, copy, and paste text to and from the DOS window and the Clipboard

■ Expand the DOS window to full screen

■ Change the properties of the shortcut to the DOS application

■ Choose to not suspend the DOS program when it is in the background (doesn't have the focus)

DOS window versus DOS screen

There is a difference between a DOS *screen* and a DOS *window*. In full-screen mode, there is no DOS window, and the DOS screen is the same as your computer's screen. A DOS screen on the Desktop is contained in a DOS window. In Figure 17-1, the DOS screen is the area underneath the toolbar and inside the edges of the DOS window.

You will frequently want to see the whole DOS screen inside the DOS window, because DOS programs are designed with the assumption that you can see the entire screen. If you can't see the complete DOS screen in the DOS window, it may be more difficult to run the program effectively.

The DOS window is smaller than the DOS screen if you can see a horizontal and/or vertical scroll bar in the DOS window. In this case, the DOS window only shows you a part of the DOS screen at any one time.

STEPS

Choosing a DOS Font, First Method

Step 1.   If your DOS application is displayed at full-screen size, press Alt+Enter to get DOS into a window.

Step 2.   If the DOS window does not have a toolbar, click the system menu icon in the upper-left corner of the DOS window, and select Toolbar.

Step 3.   Click the arrow on the font size combo box at the left end of the toolbar.

Step 4.   Use the scroll bar on the font list box to review the choices.

Step 5.   Choose a font size and type.

The second method is as follows:

STEPS

Choosing a DOS Font, Second Method

Step 1.   Click the Font button (the button with an *A* on its face) at the right end of the DOS window toolbar.

Step 2.   Choose a font from the Font size list, as shown in Figure 17-2. A preview of the DOS window size appears along with a preview of the font itself.

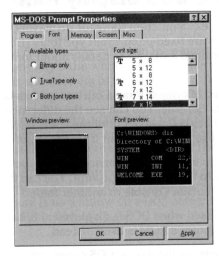

Figure 17-2: The Font tab of the MS-DOS Prompt Properties dialog box. When you choose a font from the list in the upper-right corner, the result is displayed in the two preview boxes.

Choosing a DOS Font, Second Method

Step 3.   Click OK.

Secret

If the Both font types option is marked in the Available types area, only 23 fonts are shown, in addition to Auto. This is in spite of the fact that 25 fonts are available (sixteen TrueType and nine bitmapped). There is an overlap of the 4 x 6 and 7 x 12 TrueType and bitmapped fonts. Only the bitmapped fonts for these sizes are shown when this box is checked.

To choose the TrueType font for these two font sizes, mark the TrueType only option button. These fonts of the same size look quite a bit different.

Auto font

If you want the font to change based on the size of the DOS window, set the font size to Auto. As you drag the window, Auto will choose the font size that best fits your DOS window size from among 23, 18, 16, or 9 fonts (depending on your choice of available fonts).

Mark, copy, and paste text or graphics to and from the DOS window and the Clipboard

The toolbar in a DOS window makes it easy to mark and copy data and text to and from the Clipboard. You can copy data and text into DOS documents from Windows documents and vice versa.

STEPS

Copying DOS Data to the Clipboard

Step 1.   To start marking data (graphics or text), click the Mark button (it shows a dotted square) on the left side of the toolbar.

Step 2.   Move your mouse pointer to anywhere just outside the area that contains the data or text that you want to copy to the Clipboard.

Step 3.   Press and hold the left mouse button.

Step 4.   Drag until the rectangle that you are dragging with your mouse pointer completely covers the desired data or text.

Step 5.   Release the mouse button.

Step 6.   Click the Copy toolbar button (it shows two pieces of paper), or press Enter.

To paste text or graphics from the Clipboard to your DOS application, position your cursor in the DOS document, and click the Paste toolbar button (it shows a clipboard), located to the right of the Copy button.

Changing directories in a DOS window

Undocumented

Here's a cool trick from Kaleb Axon, a Windows 95 beta tester. It is an interesting way to change directories in a DOS window.

STEPS

Changing Directories in DOS

Step 1. Open a DOS window by clicking the Start button, Programs, MS-DOS Prompt.

Step 2. Open an Explorer window by right-clicking My Computer, and then clicking Explore. Navigate in the Explorer to any folder or subfolder.

Step 3. Type **cd** at the DOS prompt in the DOS window. Press the spacebar.

Step 4. Drag and drop a folder icon from the Explorer window to the DOS window.

Step 5. The folder name now appears on the DOS command line.

This is an example of a general class of behaviors. Drag and drop works with DOS, sort of. While you can't drag and drop text from a Windows 95 application into a DOS application, you can drag and drop filenames to the command line of a DOS application. (If you do need to drag and drop text from a Windows application, you can copy it to the Clipboard, and then paste it into a DOS text-editing application.)

Connecting a DOS window to the Explorer

Undocumented

Want to quickly open a DOS window into the current directory while you are navigating about your hard disk in the Explorer? This makes it easy to use DIR to look more closely at the files in that folder.

STEPS

DOS Windows and Folder Together

Step 1. Open an Explorer window.

Step 2. Choose View, Options, and click the File Types tab.

DOS Windows and Folder Together

Step 3.   Click File Folder in the Registered file types list, and then click the Edit button.

Step 4.   Click New.

Step 5.   In the Action field, type **MS-DOS Prompt**.

Step 6.   In the Application used to perform action field, type **C:\Command.com /k cd**.

Step 7.   Click OK, click Close, and then click Close again.

Step 8.   Right-click any folder icon in the Explorer window, and click MS-DOS Prompt in the context menu.

You now have a new context menu command, MS-DOS Prompt, associated with any folder. This always works, regardless of whether you right-click a folder icon in the right or left pane of the Explorer, a folder icon in a folder window, or a shortcut to a folder on the Desktop (or in any other folder). The DOS window opens up with its current directory equal to the folder that you right-clicked. This gives you a quick way to open a DOS window on any current folder in the Explorer.

You can use Doshere.inf, a file in the Microsoft PowerToys, to do this automatically. Doshere.inf edits your Registry to insert the command shown in step 6 above. It puts the words *DOS Prompt Here* in your context menu. If you'd rather have Doshere.inf add the words *MS-DOS Prompt*, you can edit it by opening it in Notepad. Download PowerToys from http://www.microsoft.com/windows/software/powertoy.htm.

Expand the DOS window to full screen

You can run DOS in a DOS window or you can run it at the full-screen size. It's easy to switch back and forth. Press Alt+Enter to switch between the two modes. If you have the toolbar displayed, you can switch to full screen by clicking the Full Screen toolbar button (the button with four arrow heads).

Change the properties of the shortcut to the DOS application

Click the Properties button in the DOS window toolbar. It is the fourth button from the right, and it shows a hand holding a sheet of paper. We discuss the effect of changing these properties in the *Editing Shortcut Properties Sheets* section later in this chapter.

Background button

Click the Background button on the DOS window toolbar to *not* suspend the DOS application while it is in the background; that is, when the DOS application doesn't have the focus. (This button is turned on by default.) See the *Background* section later in this chapter.

Closing a DOS application

Under normal circumstances, you exit your DOS application by whatever means the developer of your DOS program provided. If you mark the Close on exit check box in your DOS application's *pif,* the DOS window will also close when you exit your application.

If you are unable to exit normally, you can exit by clicking the Close box (the X) at the right end of the DOS window's title bar. You will get a warning message if the Warn if still active check box is marked in the DOS application's *pif.*

Using Windows 3.*x,* you exited from the DOS command prompt in a Windows DOS session by typing **exit** and pressing Enter. You can now just click the Close box. Placing an X.bat file on your path that contains the single line *exit* also gives you an easy way to end a DOS session. If you do this, you can simply press the letter *X,* and then press Enter to exit.

Creating a Virtual Machine for DOS Programs

Windows creates a "virtual machine" for every DOS program you start from Windows (every Windows DOS session). You have the option of designing this "virtual machine." Instead of interacting with your computer hardware (the real machine), the DOS program interacts with something that it "sees" as a real machine: the virtual machine.

Undocumented

If you start your DOS programs from MS-DOS Prompt in the Start menu, they will run in the virtual computer associated with that MS-DOS prompt. This virtual machine is defined by properties sheets stored in the MS-DOS Prompt shortcut in the \Windows\Start Menu folder. You can edit these properties sheets to redefine the virtual machine associated with the Start menu's MS-DOS Prompt.

Undocumented

When you double-click an icon that represents a DOS program in a folder window, the Explorer, or File Manager, you automatically create a shortcut. This is also true if you choose Run from the Start menu. This shortcut to a DOS program is stored in the same folder the DOS program is stored in. If a shortcut is already there, a new one isn't created.

Undocumented

If you delete or move the shortcut, double-clicking the DOS application's icon in the Explorer creates a new shortcut in the folder that contains the DOS application, unless you moved the shortcut to the \Windows\Pif folder. If the DOS program doesn't execute, the shortcut won't be created.

These shortcuts to DOS programs are like shortcuts to Windows programs. However, the properties of a shortcut to a DOS program, a *pif,* are different from those of a shortcut to a Windows program because the properties sheets of a shortcut to a DOS program define a virtual machine.

Double-click a shortcut to a DOS program and the program starts. You can move and copy these shortcuts. You can place them on your Desktop or on your Start menus. You can have multiple shortcuts for one DOS program, just as you can have multiple, and different, shortcuts for Windows programs or documents.

Shortcuts to DOS can be associated with documents instead of programs, just like Windows shortcuts. You can associate the DOS applications that open these documents with the documents' extension. See Chapter 13 for details on how to associate applications with document extensions.

Undocumented

While the task of identifying the needs of each and every DOS program is too daunting for Microsoft to attempt, Windows 95 comes with Apps.inf, which is stored in the \Windows\Inf folder. Apps.inf provides the basic virtual machine configuration for over 300 DOS applications. You don't have to do anything to access this file; Windows 95 automatically uses it to help create shortcuts for the DOS programs referenced in it.

In many cases, the default shortcut that is created when you double-click a DOS application icon works just fine.

Undocumented

Many DOS software developers include *pif*s with their DOS applications. *Pif*s created for Windows 3.*x* are compatible with shortcuts to DOS programs for Windows 95. You can place them wherever they are appropriate for your work.

Secret

When a shortcut is created automatically, it has the same name as the DOS program, but a different extension: *pif.* You won't see this extension even if you have chosen View, Options, View in the Explorer and cleared the check box labeled "Hide all MS-DOS file extensions for file types that are registered." Likewise, you won't see the *lnk* extension used for shortcuts to Windows programs. You will see the file type Shortcut to MS-DOS Program.

Secret

There is a difference between starting a DOS program at the MS-DOS prompt within a Windows DOS session and double-clicking the DOS program icon in a folder window.

- If you start the DOS program from the MS-DOS prompt in a Windows DOS session, no shortcut is created.

- If you double-click the DOS program icon (or run the DOS program by choosing Run from the Start menu), a shortcut is created.

You can also create a shortcut by right-clicking a DOS program icon and clicking Create Shortcut.

Program properties sheet

The Program properties sheet is the meat of the matter. Take a look at Figure 17-3 to see what we mean. A Program properties sheet contains the command line for the DOS program, its working directory, an optional startup batch file that runs before the DOS application, a hot key definition, a window configuration, and buttons to change the associated shortcut's icon and define MS-DOS mode. You'll find a big chunk of DOS program functionality here.

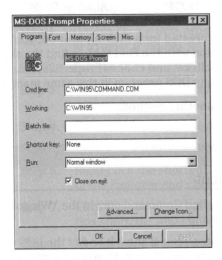

Figure 17-3: The Program properties sheet. Define the title of the application, its command line, working directory, startup batch file, shortcut key combination, state of the DOS window, and icon. Also specify whether the application needs to run in MS-DOS mode or not.

The Program properties sheet for a shortcut to a DOS program is a lot like the Shortcut properties sheet associated with Windows programs. Figure 17-4 shows the similarities. Where there are differences, we point them out.

Notice that the Program and Shortcut properties sheets have titles, command lines (Cmd line and Target), working directories (Working and Start in), Shortcut key and Run fields, and Change Icon buttons. For more on shortcuts, see Chapter 10.

Title

The title is displayed on the left side of a DOS application's title bar, which appears when the application is running in a window (not in full-screen mode). The title is also displayed on the Taskbar button for the window. By default, Windows uses the name of the shortcut for the title, but you can change it by typing a new title in the field at the top of the Program properties sheet.

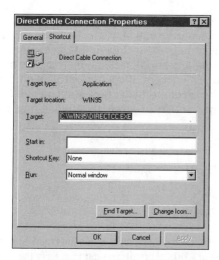

Figure 17-4: The Shortcut properties sheet for a Windows shortcut. The Target field is like the Cmd line field in Program properties. The Start in field is similar to the Working field. Both properties sheets have Run and Shortcut Key fields, and both have Change Icon buttons.

Command line

When you start a DOS program for the first time by double-clicking its icon in a folder window, you automatically create a shortcut that contains the complete pathname of the DOS application in the command line field. The command line can contain the driver letter, folder name, filename, extension, and any command line parameters.

You can set the values for what are referred to as *environmental variables* in your Autoexec.bat file and other DOS batch files. You do this with a Set command. You can use these variables in the command line in a properties sheet to insert their associated values into the command line. You use the following form:

```
%variablename%
```

For example, if you entered the command Set location = ABC in your Autoexec.bat, you could then enter the command line c:\%ABC%\Myprog.exe in a properties sheet to run the program Myprog in the ABC directory.

Secret

If you move the DOS program, or if you want the shortcut to refer to another program, you can edit this command line. Unlike shortcuts to Windows applications or documents, a shortcut to a DOS program or document will not go looking for the associated DOS program or document if you move it. You have to edit the command line to give it a new location.

The Shortcut properties sheet has a Find Target button. There is no such button in a shortcut to a DOS program. You have to navigate to the DOS application's folder by yourself, using the Explorer or a folder window.

If your DOS program can accept different command line parameters and you want to be able to type them whenever you start the DOS program, you need to add a space and a question mark at the end of the command line string. You only need to type one question mark, no matter how many parameters your DOS program can accept. If you make this modification to your command line, the MS-DOS Prompt dialog box, shown in Figure 17-5, will appear each time you start the DOS program to let you enter your parameters.

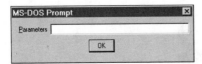

Figure 17-5: The MS-DOS Prompt dialog box. If you enter a question mark after the program name in the command line of a DOS shortcut, you get to specify the command line parameters every time you start this DOS application.

If you use the same command line parameters every time you start a DOS application, just type them in the Cmd line field after the program's pathname. You can create multiple shortcuts associated with one DOS program, each with different command line parameters, and perhaps one with a question mark.

Undocumented

When you run a shortcut from the Run command on the Start menu, any parameters you type after the shortcut name *override* the parameters that you specified in the Cmd line field of the shortcut's Program properties sheet. For example, doing a command such as Run Myapp.lnk /abc forces your app to use the parameter /abc instead of whatever command line you defined in the shortcut. This is one way to use one set of switches to start the application most of the time, and use a different set occasionally.

Undocumented

The command line can contain a DOS application name and a filename, something like C:\Windows\Command\Edit.com C:\Windows\Temp \New.txt, for example. The shortcut will be a shortcut to the document, just like a Windows shortcut to a document.

Undocumented

If the DOS application is associated with a file extension, you can easily create a *lnk* shortcut to a DOS document. Right-click a document with that extension and click Create Shortcut. This creates a Windows shortcut, a file with the *lnk* extension, not a *pif*. You have to create the association between the file extension and the DOS program first. Turn to Chapter 13 for details.

Undocumented

You can change a *lnk* file to a *pif* just by adding the DOS application name in front of the document filename in the Target field of the Shortcut properties sheet. For example, assume you have a shortcut to a text file that is normally associated with Notepad. You can edit the command line in the Shortcut properties sheet for this document to use Edit.com instead. When you do, the *lnk* file turns into a *pif*.

You can't create a *lnk* shortcut from a *pif*. If you right-click a *pif* and choose Create Shortcut, you'll create another *pif*.

Working directory

The working directory is the folder that is meant to contain files that work in conjunction with your DOS application or the data or text files you edit with the DOS application. The DOS program will search the directory you enter in the Working field for any files it needs. Whether an entry is needed here or not depends on the DOS program.

Tip

For example, one of the authors runs the DOS program Doom (don't so many misguided souls?). The Doom shortcut is stored in \Windows \Desktop. The command line for Doom is d:\games\doom\doom.exe. The working directory for Doom is d:\games\doom. If the Working field is blank, Doom 1.2 won't run when you double-click the Doom shortcut icon. Heretic, another product from id Software, the developers of Doom, doesn't require an entry in the Working field.

Batch file

You can run a DOS batch file before your application starts up.

This is one way to set certain environmental variables for a DOS application before you run it. For example, put the following line in this batch file:

```
Set Mydir=C:\thisone
```

Alternatively, you can load TSR programs in the batch file before your primary DOS application starts. You then can access the TSR from within that DOS application — without using memory in every DOS session by loading that TSR prior to starting Windows.

Hot key(s)

You can type an entry in the hot key field (it's labeled Shortcut key) to define a set of keys that you press at the same time to start a DOS application. Hot keys work for shortcuts that are in the Start menus or on the Desktop.

Hot keys let you start an application from the keyboard without mousing around. People who use DOS applications in full-screen mode and want to quickly start and switch between applications are particularly fond of them.

While the name of the field, Shortcut key, is singular, it is best to assign a *set* of keys to be pressed together as one hot key. That way, you can define three keys that probably won't be used for something in another application that might be open at the time you press these three keys. For example, you could define Ctrl+Alt+D to start the MS-DOS Prompt window.

If you use the Ctrl, Alt, and/or Shift key, it is easy to press and hold down one or two of these keys while you press the last key, most likely a letter key. These keys are modifier keys, and usually your applications won't react to them until you press another key. This makes it easier to press three keys at once.

Even if another application has the focus and you are in full-screen DOS mode, the hot key will work. The hot key takes precedence. If you define a hot key combination that was originally used in another application, that application loses the ability to use that combination, even if it has the focus. The keyboard combination opens the application for which you defined the hot key instead.

Tip

For example, if you define a hot key as Shift+D without Ctrl or Alt, you would be unable to type a *D* (uppercase *d*) in your word processor. Or if you define a hot key as Ctrl+Shift+D and that combination is used in your spreadsheet for some function, the spreadsheet will not be able to see that combination, because Windows will grab it before the spreadsheet can get a hold of it — even if the spreadsheet has the focus.

Undocumented

Your hot key should (by convention) include either an Alt or Ctrl key, plus a function key or printable key. The Windows 95 help files say it has to, but it doesn't. You can include the Shift key in the combination, but not the keys Backspace, Enter, Esc, Print Screen, Spacebar, or Tab. Ctrl+Shift or Ctrl+Alt plus a letter key is often a good combination. Windows applications often leave combinations with these keys undefined so you can define macros with them.

Something else to try is Ctrl or Alt in combination with the punctuation keys (period, comma, and so on). Windows applications rarely use these combinations.

If you just want to switch to running applications, an easier way to do this is to press Alt+Tab. This allows you to switch to any running application, DOS *or* Windows. You can also use Ctrl+Esc to get to the Start menu.

Tip

If you set a hot key for a shortcut and later want to get rid of it, you can't just delete the key combination from the Shortcut key field, and then save the shortcut. The previous key assignment isn't actually deleted unless you succeed in entering None in the box. And you can't just type the word *none* — you must place your insertion point in the field and press Backspace to specify None.

Undocumented

The Shortcut properties sheet of a *lnk* file also has a hot key definition field. While hot keys work the same way with both types of shortcuts (*pif* and *lnk*), entering keystrokes into the hot key field works differently. If you type the *d* key in the Shortcut key field of the Program properties sheet for a *pif* file, it gets entered as a *d*. In contrast, if you type a *d* in the same field of the Shortcut properties sheet for a *lnk* file, Windows automatically adds Ctrl+Alt+ before the *d*.

It is not a good idea to redefine function keys, such as F1 (help), as hot keys. This reduces the functionality of Windows 95. Many applications also use the combinations Ctrl+F1, Ctrl+Shift+F1, and so on.

Run — normal, minimized, maximized

What size window do you want to start your DOS application in?

If your font size is set to Auto, you can maximize the DOS window so that it fills up the Desktop as much as possible. DOS windows are sized based on the height-to-width ratio of the DOS font you're using, and their size is limited by the size of the Desktop. If you choose Maximized with Auto font sizing, you'll get a large DOS window.

If you have a fixed DOS font size, the Maximized setting will display a DOS *window* that encompasses a whole DOS *screen* at the set DOS font.

If you choose Normal, you will get a DOS window that is the restored size. If the maximized and restored size are the same because you are using a fixed DOS font size, and the DOS window is big enough to display the whole DOS screen, the only difference between Normal and Maximized may be the location of the window.

If you choose Minimized, the DOS application opens as a button on the Taskbar. This is great for running DOS programs that don't require any interaction with the user (as is true of many batch files).

Close on exit

The Close on exit check box is a very nice feature. If you want to run a quick DOS batch file, you can have it show up only as a button on your Taskbar and make it go away as soon as it carries out its work.

In many cases, you will want the DOS window to close after you have completed working with the DOS application or document. This is the way all Windows programs work; nothing is left open after you quit them. The only reason you would want to leave the DOS window open is if you wanted to run another DOS program after you finished working on the one that you are currently running.

You can open a DOS window with just the DOS prompt, as you do when you click the MS-DOS Prompt item in the Start menu. Even with Close on exit checked, the DOS prompt is there ready for you to run the next DOS pro-gram. You don't exit the command prompt DOS window until you type **exit** at the prompt or click the Close box (the X) in the upper-right corner of the DOS window.

Tip

If your DOS program does some work, writes some output to the DOS screen, and then quits, you won't be able to see what the output was if you mark Close on exit. Lots of DOS programs do this, so clear this check box if you want to see their output.

If you quit a DOS application and the DOS window is still on the Desktop, the title bar of the DOS window states that the application is inactive. To get rid of the DOS window, click its Close box.

Memory properties sheet

The amount of memory available to a DOS program running in a Windows DOS session depends on the configuration of the Autoexec.bat and Config.sys files (if you have them), and whether DOS TSRs and 16-bit drivers are loaded in conventional memory or in the upper memory blocks (UMBs). You can find further details in Chapter 18.

Windows 95 can provide DOS programs with expanded, extended, and/or DOS protected-mode memory (DPMI). The DOS programs must comply with Windows expanded, extended, and/or DPMI memory specifications in order to be able to use this memory.

Because Windows 95 makes extensive use of 32-bit protected-mode drivers that do not use conventional memory or UMBs, it can provide up to 612K of conventional memory for DOS programs that run in Windows DOS sessions.

The Memory properties sheet in the Properties dialog box, as shown in Figure 17-8, is divided into four sections, one for each type of memory available to DOS programs. You can use these sections to set the amount of each type of memory that's available to your DOS program.

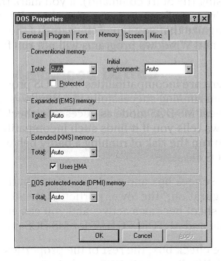

Figure 17-8: The Memory properties sheet. You can set the amount of available conventional, expanded, extended, and/or DPMI memory.

The default setting is Auto, which means "let the DOS programs determine how much they need or want." Some DOS programs don't do a good job of restraining themselves and need to be limited in their memory acquisition.

Conventional memory

The maximum amount of conventional memory available is about 612K under the best of circumstances. DOS games and other large programs will likely take all they can get. The only reason to limit the amount of conventional memory available to a DOS program is to let it load slightly faster. This may help on slower computers, but won't be noticeable on faster ones.

Tip

You could create a separate shortcut, for example, for "small" DOS sessions in which you plan to run only DOS commands such as DIR, Del, and so on. Setting conventional memory at 160K would be adequate for these tasks. This would conserve physical memory for other applications while a "small" DOS session is running.

Protected

Does your DOS program contain a bug? Does it write to memory in areas that it shouldn't? If so, click the Protected check box to help protect Windows from crashing because of bugs caused by your DOS application.

When the Protected check box is marked, the MS-DOS system memory area is write-protected so your DOS application can't write into this area and corrupt it.

Environment

If you are running a batch file to set environment variables before your DOS application runs, you might want to expand the size of the environment that stores these variables. You may have a smaller environment size in your common Config.sys file. Use the Initial environment drop-down list to set aside a larger environment for environment variables that are particular to your DOS application.

Expanded (EMS) memory

If a DOS program makes use of expanded memory that meets the LIM 4.0 specification, Windows itself can provide it with expanded memory. Windows includes its own expanded memory manager separate from Emm386.exe. DOS games such as Xwing use expanded memory for handling sound effects and music. Some DOS spreadsheets also use expanded memory.

You can set the value for expanded memory to Auto if you want the DOS program to determine how much it needs, or you can limit its appetite. Some DOS programs don't know when they have had enough, so you'll have to tell them.

If you have a Config.sys file with a line calling the MS-DOS expanded memory manager (Emm386.exe), and if the parameter *noems* is on that line, expanded memory will not be available to DOS programs running in Windows DOS sessions. The Memory properties sheet will be altered to show this state of affairs, as shown in Figure 17-9.

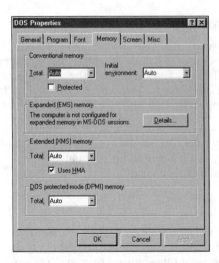

Figure 17-9: The Memory properties sheet with no expanded memory available. If you have a line such as Device=Emm386.exe noems in your Config.sys file, there will be no expanded memory available to your DOS programs.

For most DOS programs, you can set expanded memory equal to zero. If you have any DOS programs that use expanded or extended memory, you should give these programs their own shortcuts.

Extended (XMS) memory

If your DOS application makes use of extended memory in a way that is compatible with running under Windows, the XMS memory settings allow you to specify the amount of available extended memory.

Applications that use DPMI (DOS Protected Mode Interface) — which Microsoft prescribes as the correct way to access extended memory under a multitasking environment — can use this extended memory. (DPMI applications obtain extended memory through Himem.sys or other "XMS managers.")

HMA

If DOS or other 16-bit drivers are loaded high in your Config.sys file, marking the Uses HMA check box doesn't do anything. Otherwise, you can use this memory like extended memory.

The High Memory Area (HMA) is the first 64K of extended memory. It is the only part of extended memory that an application running under DOS can access while still in real mode. Very few DOS applications currently use this memory area. This is unfortunate, because if they did, they would be able to add almost 64K to the amount of conventional memory available to them (unless the line DOS=High is in your Config.sys file). The Windows memory manager, Himem.sys, and all other compatible memory managers make this 64K area available to Windows or any program that requests it.

The rule for the Uses HMA check box is: If you start two shortcuts under Windows — both using the HMA — Windows will switch this memory between them in turn, so they can both benefit from using it.

If you turn *off* this Uses HMA check box, an application started from that shortcut cannot access any HMA from within Windows, even if it would otherwise be capable of doing so.

If, however, DOS or a DOS application claims the HMA *before* you start Windows, then no Windows application or shortcut to a DOS program can ever use it.

DOS applications that can use the HMA generally make this fact very well known in their publicity and documentation. You can leave this check box *on,* unless you know that two particular applications using it at once would conflict. In that case, turn it off for the application that requires less memory.

DOS protected-mode memory

Some DOS programs use this specification for turning extended memory into something that DOS programs can use.

Screen properties sheet

The default setting for a new shortcut is to run your DOS application windowed on the Windows 95 Desktop. This makes DOS programs look and feel more like Windows programs, which is a nice touch.

Tip

MS-DOS programs that run in VGA graphics mode can run in a window on the Desktop. This wasn't the case in Windows 3.*x*. DOS games that rely on hand-eye coordination will probably run too slowly in a window. You'll want to run them at full-screen size.

You can always switch between full-screen and windowed views with Alt+Enter.

Starting a Windows DOS session in a small window takes slightly more memory than starting it full-screen. So if your application won't start in a window, mark the Full-screen option button in the Screen properties sheet of the Properties dialog box (see Figure 17-10).

Initial size — number of lines displayed

If your video display driver can provide support for more than 25 lines of DOS text in a DOS window or full-screen display (and most VGA or higher-resolution systems can) the Initial size drop-down list will be active. You can change the number of lines displayed in the first box.

This works great for a windowed DOS session, even one that merely displays the good old DOS C:\> prompt. When you configure Windows for a number of screen lines greater than 25 — let's say 50 — DOS commands *know* that the screen now contains that many lines. For example, the command dir /p, which halts a directory listing at the end of each screen page, now stops scrolling the display after showing 50 lines instead of 25.

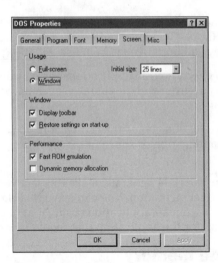

Figure 17-10: The Screen properties sheet. Choose how your DOS program will be windowed.

DOS applications themselves vary in their support for higher-than-25-line screens. Some applications automatically adjust to the number of lines in effect when they start up. Other applications, presuming that no one would ever have a display with more than 25 lines, are hard-coded to force themselves into that mode every time.

No matter how many DOS screen lines you configure Windows for, Windows won't open a windowed DOS session any taller than your screen will allow. If you specify a number of lines that would make a windowed DOS session extend beyond the top and bottom of your screen (with the DOS screen font you're using), Windows creates a window only the height of your physical screen — with scroll bars so you can see the rest.

Most VGA adapters support 25-, 43-, and 50-line modes, although if yours doesn't, this setting won't change anything. A 43-line display takes up less room on your display than a 50-line display, while still giving you a lot more information than the bad old 25-line display.

Restore settings on start-up

You can change your font, window size, and position while running your DOS application. If your want your original values to be used the next time you start the application, mark the Restore settings on start-up check box.

If this check box is cleared, Windows retains the values you used in your last session. For example, if you exit your DOS application and close the DOS window while you are in full-screen mode, the next time you start this application, it will come up in full-screen mode.

Fast ROM emulation

Applications that display text run faster if you mark the Fast ROM emulation check box. This allows Windows to use faster routines in RAM if the application normally uses standard ROM BIOS calls to write text to the screen. You must turn off this setting if garbage appears on the application's screen or if you lose control of its mouse when you run it under Windows.

Dynamic memory allocation

If your DOS application switches back and forth between text and graphics modes or starts in text mode and switches later to graphics mode, you need to be sure to always have enough memory for the graphics mode. In these cases, you'll want to clear the Dynamic memory allocation check box. Otherwise you can release this memory for other programs if they start in graphics mode and then switch to text mode. This switch appears to be written in the most part for Microsoft Word for MS-DOS.

Check this box if you want to let other programs use the small amount of extra available memory when the DOS application goes into text mode.

Misc properties sheet

Microsoft had no other place to put these properties of the DOS virtual machine, so it created a Misc properties sheet, as shown in Figure 17-11. Not too original, but what the heck.

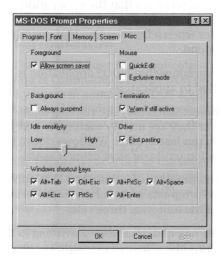

Figure 17-11: The Misc properties sheet. This is the grab bag of the DOS properties sheets. Whatever didn't fit elsewhere is here.

Windows shortcut keys

Windows has a defined set of what we call *hot keys,* which it refers to as *shortcut keys.* It grabs them first whenever you press them. If your DOS program wants these keys for its own uses, you have to configure a shortcut for that application that tells Windows to back off and let the keystrokes go to the DOS application.

Table 17-2 lists these hot keys and their definitions.

Table 17-2	Windows Hot Keys
Hot Key	*Definition*
Alt+Tab	Tab from one active application to another. Switch to graphics mode if DOS is in full-screen text mode. This is the "cool switch." Windows 3.*x* has a text-mode version of the cool switch that doesn't switch to graphics mode when you switch between full-screen DOS applications.
Alt+Tab+Click	If your DOS application is in full-screen mode and you press and hold the Alt+Tab key combination, clicking any mouse button brings up the Desktop.
Ctrl+Esc	Switch to graphics mode, if necessary, from full-screen DOS, display the Desktop and the Taskbar, and click the Start button.
Alt+Print Screen	Copy the active window to the Clipboard. If the DOS application is in a DOS window, copy it as a graphic; if the DOS application is in full-screen text mode, copy it as text.
Alt+Spacebar	Click the system menu icon.
Alt+Esc	Switch to the next active application.
Print Screen	Copy the complete Desktop, including all windows, to the Clipboard. In full-screen DOS text mode, copy all the text to the Clipboard.
Alt+Enter	Switch between full-screen and DOS window.

To let the DOS application use any of these keystrokes while it has the focus or is in full-screen mode, clear the check box associated with the appropriate keystrokes.

If you clear the PrtSc check box and the Windows DOS session is in full-screen mode, the Print Screen key sends the current DOS screen to the printer in the same way it would under the DOS operating system.

Undocumented

Pressing Alt+Enter toggles between the Window and Full-screen option buttons in the shortcut's Screen properties sheet. You may want your DOS application to come up the same way you set it the first time and not the way you left it the last time. To preserve the settings in a shortcut's properties sheets, you can set the shortcut's file attribute to read-only. Right-click the shortcut icon, click Properties, and then mark the Read-only check box in the General properties sheet.

MS-DOS Mode

If your DOS program doesn't work in a Windows DOS session, you can run it in MS-DOS mode (real-mode DOS). Rebooted MS-DOS mode works by shutting down Windows 95, performing a warm reboot, and booting into MS-DOS after calling a second copy of Command.com. When you exit MS-DOS mode, Windows 95 restarts.

Non-rebooted MS-DOS mode doesn't require a reboot before DOS starts. It runs the Dosstart.bat file right after it switches to DOS mode. You can exit back to Windows 95 by typing **exit** at the DOS prompt.

To get to a command prompt (the DOS prompt) in rebooted MS-DOS mode, you need to create a shortcut for Command.com with the proper properties (see the next section). You can put the icon associated with this shortcut on your Desktop, in one of your Start menus, or wherever is convenient. You can create properly configured shortcuts for every DOS application that requires MS-DOS mode.

Creating an MS-DOS mode shortcut

To create an MS-DOS mode shortcut for your Desktop, carry out the following steps:

STEPS
Creating a Shortcut for MS-DOS Mode

Step 1. Open the Explorer and navigate to your Windows 95 folder. Find Command.com.

Step 2. Right-click Command.com, and click Properties.

Step 3. Click the Program tab and then the Advanced button.

Step 4. Mark the MS-DOS mode check box. If you don't want a warning before you switch to MS-DOS mode, clear the Warn before entering MS-DOS mode check box.

(continued)

STEPS *(continued)*

Creating a Shortcut for MS-DOS Mode

Step 5. The default is to use the current MS-DOS configuration. This means that you won't need to reboot to get to MS-DOS mode. If you want private Autoexec.bat and Config.sys files for this DOS application, you should mark the Specify a new MS-DOS configuration option button. See the next section.

Step 6. Click OK in the Advanced Program Settings dialog box, and click OK again in the Properties dialog box.

Step 7. Click F5 to refresh your Explorer. If you order your Explorer window in details view by name, a new MS-DOS shortcut icon labeled Command will be right below Command.com. If not, check in the \Windows\Pif folder. Right-drag the shortcut to the Desktop. Click Move Here in the context menu.

Step 8. The name of your new shortcut icon, Command, will be highlighted. Press F2 and type **MS-DOS mode.**

You now have an icon on the Desktop that will get you to the non-rebooted MS-DOS mode (real-mode DOS) and give you a DOS prompt. The MS-DOS mode created in this fashion will use versions of the same Autoexec.bat and Config.sys files (if you have them), that are read when Windows 95 starts, as well as the Dosstart.bat file.

Private Autoexec.bat and Config.sys files

Each MS-DOS mode shortcut can have its own private Autoexec.bat and Config.sys files. The information used to create these files is stored in the shortcut. The files will be created when you switch from Windows 95 to rebooted MS-DOS mode; that is, when you double-click the icon associated with the shortcut.

Having private Autoexec.bat and Config.sys files is a great idea. Each DOS program that runs in rebooted MS-DOS mode can have its own special configuration or drivers and DOS TSRs that work just right for it. You can also create a MS-DOS mode shortcut just for the command prompt, but with Autoexec.bat and Config.sys files that are completely independent of those used to start Windows 95.

Previously, the only way to have different startup configurations was to create a multiconfiguration Config.sys file by creating different sections of your Config.sys file as documented in your MS-DOS manual.

At startup, you then chose which set of drivers and DOS TSRs you wanted to load from a menu. You often had to create a multiconfiguration Config.sys file to have enough conventional memory for some DOS programs, or to allow for expanded or extended memory for other DOS programs.

Allowing completely different Autoexec.bat and Config.sys files is a much cleaner and easier-to-understand solution to the problem of multiple configurations. (Of course, the best solution is to have one configuration that works for all programs.) You create and save in the shortcut the information necessary to create the Autoexec.bat and Config.sys files that work with your DOS application.

Creating private Autoexec.bat and Config.sys data

To see how to create private Autoexec.bat and Config.sys files, you will use the shortcut that you just created for Command.com. You already configured it to start in MS-DOS mode.

STEPS

Creating Private Autoexec.bat and Config.sys Files

Step 1. Right-click the MS-DOS mode icon on the Desktop (assuming you created it using the steps for Creating a Shortcut for MS-DOS Mode in the *Creating an MS-DOS mode shortcut* section earlier in the chapter).

Step 2. Click Properties, click the Program tab, and then click the Advanced button. The Advanced Program Settings dialog box will appear, as shown in Figure 17-12.

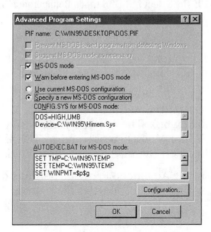

Figure 17-12: The Advanced Program Settings dialog box. You can create your own private Autoexec.bat and Config.sys files by typing what you want in these files in the two fields at the bottom of this dialog box, or by clicking the Configuration button.

(continued)

STEPS *(continued)*

Creating Private Autoexec.bat and Config.sys Files

Step 3. Mark the MS-DOS mode check box.

Step 4. Mark the Specify a new MS-DOS configuration option button. The bottom half of this properties sheet becomes active.

Step 5. Type what you want in the CONFIG.SYS for MS-DOS mode and AUTOEXEC.BAT for MS-DOS mode fields. You can get a head start by clicking the Configuration button to display the Select MS-DOS Mode Configuration Options dialog box, shown in Figure 17-13.

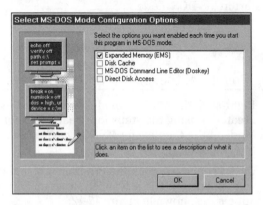

Figure 17-13: The Select MS-DOS Mode Configuration Options dialog box. As you highlight each option, its description appears at the bottom of the dialog box.

Step 6. Choose the options you want in this dialog box. If you highlight an option, its description appears at the bottom of the dialog box. You can highlight it before you click its check box.

Step 7. Click the OK button in the Select MS-DOS Mode Configuration Options dialog box. The options you chose will be used to fill the CONFIG.SYS for MS-DOS mode and AUTOEXEC.BAT for MS-DOS mode fields. You can further edit these fields now.

Step 8. Click OK in the Advanced Program Settings dialog box, and then click OK again in the Properties dialog box.

Editing private Autoexec.bat and Config.sys data

Secret

You should carefully edit the CONFIG.SYS for MS-DOS mode and AUTOEXEC.BAT for MS-DOS mode fields. They will include lines from your Autoexec.bat and Config.sys files that are read before Windows 95 starts. You may not want some of these lines in the private Autoexec.bat and Config.sys files for MS-DOS mode.

These fields may also include some instructions that are (by default) carried out by Io.sys. For example:

```
SET TMP=C:\Windows\Temp
SET TEMP=C:\Windows\Temp
```

You may want to delete these lines or edit them.

Tip

If you choose to install the expanded memory manager (Emm386.exe), you can load 16-bit drivers and DOS TSRs in UMBs, and they will be loaded in UMBs by default, if you choose them from the Select MS-DOS Mode Configuration Options dialog box. You need to add the *noems* or *ram* parameter to the line with the Emm386.exe driver (after Emm386.exe).

Disk caching in MS-DOS mode is handled by the 16-bit driver Smartdrv.exe. It will be loaded high if you use Emm386.exe.

If you want to have an easily accessible history of your previous DOS commands while in MS-DOS mode, load Doskey. It is also loaded high if you load Emm386.exe with the *noems* or *ram* parameter.

If your DOS program requires direct disk access, choose this option from the Select MS-DOS Mode Configuration Options dialog box. This option adds the Lock command as the last line in your private Autoexec.bat file.

Tip

You'll need to add a 16-bit mouse driver to your private Autoexec.bat or Config.sys file if you want to have a mouse in rebooted MS-DOS mode.

Where are the private files?

Secret

The lines that you add to the CONFIG.SYS for MS-DOS mode and AUTOEXEC.BAT for MS-DOS mode fields are stored in the MS-DOS mode shortcut you created for your DOS application or for Command.com. You can use Edit.com to see this for yourself. To do so, take the following steps:

STEPS

Seeing the Internals of the MS-DOS Mode Shortcut

Step 1. Click the Start button, point to Programs, and then click MS-DOS Prompt.

Step 2. Type **Edit** and press Enter.

Step 3. Choose File, Open. In the Directories field navigate to C:\Windows\Desktop.

Step 4. In the Files field, scroll to MS-DOS mode.pif and double-click it.

You'll see the lines from your CONFIG.SYS for MS-DOS mode and AUTOEXEC.BAT for MS-DOS mode fields at the bottom of the file. Be sure *not* to save this file when you are finished looking at it.

The private files exposed

Secret

When you switch to rebooted MS-DOS mode, new private Autoexec.bat and Config.sys files are created just for that session. The lines in the shortcut used to start this MS-DOS session are used to create these files. The existing Autoexec.bat and Config.sys files used to start Windows 95 are stored in temporary files with the extension *wos* (Windows Operating System?).

When you exit MS-DOS mode (by typing **exit** at the DOS prompt, or by quitting your DOS application if the Close on exit check box is checked), the private Autoexec.bat and Config.sys files are deleted, and the temporary Autoexec.wos and Config.wos files are renamed to their original names.

This is an example of what a temporary private Autoexec.bat looks like:

```
@ECHO OFF
SET TMP=C:\Windows\Temp
SET TEMP=C:\Windows\Temp
SET WINPMT=$p$g
SET Path=C:\Windows;C:\Windows\Command
LoadHigh C:\WINDOWS\SmartDrv
LoadHigh C:\WINDOWS\Command\DOSKey
Lock
REM
REM The following lines have been created by Windows. Do not modify them.
REM
CALL C:\WINDOWS\COMMAND.COM
C:\WINDOWS\WIN.COM /WX
```

Notice that Command.com is called to create the DOS prompt in the MS-DOS mode session. Command.com was already loaded before this Autoexec.bat was read, so this is a second copy of Command.com. You exit from MS-DOS mode by typing **exit** at the DOS prompt and pressing Enter.

Exiting from this call allows the next line of the Autoexec.bat file to be carried out. The next line is the call to restart Windows with the /WX switch. This switch starts Windows 95 with a text-mode message that Windows is restarting.

When MS-DOS mode starts, it displays a text-mode message that Windows 95 is starting the MS-DOS based program.

This is an example of what a temporary private Config.sys file looks like:

```
DOS=SINGLE
Device=C:\Windows\Himem.sys
DeviceHigh=C:\Windows\Emm386.exe noems
DOS=HIGH,UMB
```

You don't need to load the memory manager, Himem.sys, unless you want to load Emm386.exe and thereby provide access to the UMBs and expanded memory.

Tip

You must add the *noems* parameter manually. This parameter allows upper memory to be used as UMBs. There is no reason for DeviceHigh= in the third line. This line is automatically written when you choose to load the ex-panded memory manager option from the Select MS-DOS Mode Configuration Options dialog box. Emm386.exe is loaded in conventional memory, so it might as well read Device=.

MS-DOS Wizard, part of Microsoft's Kernel Toys, gives you a new level of control over drivers and commands in your system. You load separate Config.sys and Autoexec.bat files for the various 16-bit programs that need them. Download Kernel Toys from http://www.microsoft.com/windows/software/krnltoy.htm.

Creating a Distinct Prompt for DOS

You can create a prompt for Windows DOS sessions that is different than the DOS prompt you see in MS-DOS mode (or before Windows 95 starts up). You can also create a different prompt for each MS-DOS mode shortcut.

Windows 95 prevents you from starting another instance of itself if you type **win** at a DOS prompt while in a Windows DOS session or in MS-DOS mode. (If you try, it just displays a warning message.) But you still might find it desirable to remind yourself — in full-screen DOS sessions — whether you are running a Windows DOS session or an MS-DOS mode session.

There is a good reason to have a reminder that you are in a DOS session under Windows 95. While it is safe to turn off your PC while in DOS before Windows starts (or MS-DOS mode), it is not such a good idea when you're at a DOS prompt in a full-screen Windows DOS session. Even in rebooted MS-DOS mode, you should return to Windows so your Autoexec.bat and Config.sys files get renamed correctly.

DOS prompt for Windows DOS sessions

Tip

You can alert yourself to the fact that you are in a Windows DOS session by adding a line to your Autoexec.bat file. This line might look like the following:

```
SET WINPMT=Press ALT+ENTER or type EXIT to return to Windows 95.$_$_$P$G
```

The $_ symbols insert blank lines between your message and the normal path and greater-than signs used in the default prompt. (PG means path and greater-than sign). Be sure to make this all one line in Autoexec.bat.

After you shut down and restart Windows 95 so this Autoexec.bat file is executed, you should see your new prompt inside a Windows DOS session.

If you type **set** by itself in a Windows DOS session, you can see what's happening. The set command displays the contents of the DOS environment. In Windows DOS sessions, Windows reverses the meaning of Set Prompt and Set Winpmt. Set Winpmt is either equal to PG (which is the default) or to whatever your normal prompt setting is in your Autoexec.bat file. Set Prompt is equal to your longer message.

DOS prompt for MS-DOS mode sessions

Just as you can create a distinctive DOS prompt for your Windows DOS sessions, you can also create unique DOS prompts for every different MS-DOS session type. Each shortcut you use to start a DOS program in MS-DOS mode can have its own Autoexec.bat file. Edit the Winpmt settings in these Autoexec.bat files, and you can have unique prompts.

You can create and edit the CONFIG.SYS for MS-DOS mode and AUTOEXEC.BAT for MS-DOS mode fields for a given MS-DOS mode shortcut using the Select MS-DOS Mode Configuration Options dialog box. If you do, the Winpmt setting from your Windows 95 Autoexec.bat is placed by default in your AUTOEXEC.BAT for MS-DOS mode field. You can edit it or replace it with a more appropriate choice.

You can create a distinct DOS prompt for your shortcut that just opens with Command.com. You might want to set a prompt by adding the following line to your AUTOEXEC.BAT for MS-DOS mode field:

```
Set Winpmt=Type EXIT and press Enter to return to Windows 95.$_$_$P$G
```

A Way Cool DOS Banner Instead

A distinctive DOS prompt is nice, but a DOS banner is way cool. It sits at the top of your DOS window (as well as in full screen) and quietly informs you that you are indeed in DOS.

The wording, "Press Alt+Enter or type Exit to return to Windows 95," certainly reminds you that you are in a Windows DOS session, but this black-and-white prompt is tiresome, especially as you watch it repeated over and over again, every time you type a command.

You can replace boring DOS prompts with a colorful prompt. To create a prompt like this, you need to have the DOS screen and keyboard driver Ansi.sys loaded in your Config.sys file. Add this line anywhere in Config.sys:

```
Device=C:\Windows\Command\Ansi.sys
```

If you want to load this driver in the UMBs, make it Devicehigh= (but be sure to include a call to the real-mode expanded memory manager, Emm386.exe, first, as well as the line DOS=High,UMB).

If you have a third-party replacement for Ansi.sys with a slightly different name (such as Fansi.sys), change the Device= line to reflect the name and location of your version of this driver. If you've just added this line to Config.sys, you must shut down Windows and restart to make the change take effect (but don't do that just yet).

Next, you have to add a new line to your Autoexec.bat file. Put this line (and only this line) in the file Winpmt.txt. You'll find this file on the *Windows 95 Secrets* CD-ROM. You can copy and paste this line from this file into your Autoexec.bat or you can type it out as shown below.

The Windows prompt is one long line in Ansi.sys's terse jargon, which we explain in the *Making your own prompt using Ansi.sys* section later in this chapter:

```
SET WINPMT=$e[s$e[f$e[0;30;46m$e[K DOS Session In Windows 95
$e[16CAlt+Tab to switch; type Exit to
close$_$e[0;40;37;1m$e[K$e[u$P$G
```

(Again, this should be one long line in your Autoexec.bat file; it should not be split over multiple lines, as it is shown here.)

Now that you have edited both your Autoexec.bat and Config.sys files, you can shut down Windows and restart so these changes take effect.

Open a Windows DOS session (click the Start button, point to Programs, and click MS-DOS Prompt). You should see something like Figure 17-14.

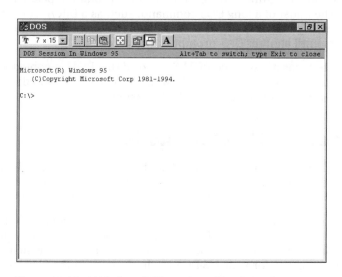

Figure 17-14: A Windows DOS session with our new banner prompt. Notice that the banner hangs out at the top of the window and doesn't bother the C:\> prompt.

This prompt is an improvement over the plain C:\> prompt in many ways. First of all, it's all on the top line, so it isn't repeated on every line down the side of the screen as you type commands. And instead of listing Exit as the

Table 17-4	Commands for Designing Your Own Prompt
Command	*Action*
$e[B	Move cursor 1 line down (for a new C:\> prompt).
$e[*n*A	Move the cursor up *n* rows.
$e[*n*B	Move the cursor down *n* rows.
$e[*n*C	Move the cursor right *n* columns.
$e[*n*D	Move the cursor left *n* columns.
$e[2J	Clear the screen with current colors and move the cursor to the Home position: row 1, column 1.

And if you want to design your own colors, you need to refer to Table 17-5, which lists the numbers that stand for each available color:

Table 17-5	Commands for Choosing Colors
Command	*Action*
0	Reset all attributes to light gray on black
1	Intensify the foreground (text) color
4	Underline text (on monochrome systems)
5	Make the foreground text blink
7	Turn on reverse video
8	Make canceled (invisible) text; black on black
30	Black foreground
31	Red foreground
32	Green foreground
33	Yellow foreground
34	Blue foreground (underlined on mono)
35	Magenta foreground
36	Cyan foreground
37	White foreground
40	Black background
41	Red background
42	Green background
43	Yellow background
44	Blue background

Command	Action
45	Magenta background
46	Cyan background
47	White background

You set the colors in the table by using the command

`$e[color1;color2;...;colorNm`

where *color1* is one of the numbers in the list of color attributes. You can have as many of these attributes in the same command as you need. They must be separated by semicolons (;) and the command must end with a lowercase *m*.

You usually begin a color command with a zero (0) to reset everything — turn blinking off, for example — and then continue with the numbers for foreground color (the text color) and background color. If you use the number 1 as one of the attributes, the text color is made brighter (intensified). Intensified colors are not always what you would expect. Intensified yellow is yellow, but "unintensified" yellow is actually brown.

You could set all of your DOS sessions to black text on a light gray background (similar to Windows' own black-on-white color scheme) by using the following in your Winpmt= statement:

`$e[0;30;47m`

If you set your Winpmt to this color, don't forget to then clear the entire screen to this color scheme. This requires the DOS command CLS in batch files you start from Windows. Using white on black in DOS sessions is easier.

Windows/DOS Batch Files

In Chapter 15, we describe three DOS batch files for backing up and restoring your Registry files. These batch files all have accompanying shortcuts and icons that make them look like Windows programs. They run in minimized windows, so their buttons only display on the Taskbar for a few seconds. You can sort of see their commands in action as they flash by, if your Taskbar buttons are large enough.

While these particular DOS batch files use only DOS commands, they do something very important to Windows (back up and restore the Windows 95 Registry), and at the same time they look a lot like Windows programs.

DOS batch files are no longer just DOS batch files. They can now contain the Start command, which allows them to start Windows programs. You can run Windows programs and use their internal macro languages to carry out further commands. Batch files can pause until the Windows program has completed its work.

First, the brute-force method: You can use the shareware hexadecimal editor we feature on the *Windows 95 Secrets* CD-ROM to change the string windir to WINDIR in Win.com. If this string is in all caps, DOS batch files can test for it.

But if you'd rather not perform this surgery, you *can* write a batch file that uses the value of *windir* correctly.

The following batch file (Wintest.bat) tests for the existence of the string windir= in the environment, and jumps to the label *nowin* if it isn't found:

```
@Echo off
SET|FIND "windir=">C:\TEMP_1.BAT
COPY C:\TEMP_1.BAT C:\TEMP_2.BAT
IF NOT EXIST C:\TEMP_2.BAT GOTO :NOWIN
C:\TEMP_2.BAT
:NOWIN
DEL C:\TEMP_1.BAT
ECHO Windows 95, where are you?
```

The first line pipes the output of the Set command into Find, which is case-sensitive. Find writes the line it finds into a temporary file. If no line contains *windir=*, this will be a 0-byte file. This will be the case if you booted Windows 95 to the command prompt. It will also be true if you are in MS-DOS mode. It will not be true if you are in a Windows DOS session.

The second line copies the temporary file to a new name. Due to a feature of Copy (which thousands of batch files now rely upon), if the first file is a 0-byte file, the second file will not be created.

The third line, therefore, tests for the existence of the second file. If there is none, no *windir=* was in the environment.

If the batch file was run in a Windows DOS session, however, temp_2.bat will contain a single line:

```
windir=C:\WINDOWS
```

Running temp_2.bat executes this line, which runs a file (which you must create) called windir.bat and feeds it a single parameter: the directory name. (DOS considers a single equals sign to be a blank, so this line looks like windir c:\windows to DOS.)

windir.bat does your *real* work starting with the line as follows:

```
@echo off
SET WIN-DIR=%1
DEL C:\TEMP_2.BAT
```

The replaceable parameter %1 has the value c:\windows. This is just what you want. This batch file leaves an environmental variable, %win-dir%, available for future use (until this DOS session is terminated or the PC is rebooted).

You can then create and use any batch file that uses the environmental variable %win-dir%. Both of these batch files are on the *Windows 95 Secrets* CD-ROM. You might want to copy both of these files to your C:\Windows\Command folder (or wherever you have stored your Windows 95 DOS files).

Using the Clipboard in DOS Sessions

The Windows Clipboard is an extremely useful area of memory for Windows applications. Microsoft almost didn't ship an updated version of the Clipboard with Windows 95, but was persuaded to do so by its beta testers. You'll find it in the \Other folder on the Windows 95 CD-ROM.

DOS applications recognize the Clipboard/Clipbook

In Windows applications, highlighting some text and then pressing Ctrl+Insert copies the text into the Clipboard. Pressing Shift+Delete has the effect of *deleting* the text from the application while moving it to the Clipboard. In either case, moving the insertion point to another location or another application and then pressing Shift+Insert pastes the text into the new location. You can perform the same operations with a mouse by choosing Edit, Copy; Edit, Cut; and Edit, Paste — choices that appear in the menu bar of almost all Windows applications. After performing any of these actions, you can view the contents of the Clipboard memory area by running the Clipbrd.exe program that is included with Windows. This program is actually a *viewer* of the Clipboard, not the Clipboard itself. The Clipboard memory area can contain many types of data other than text — bitmapped graphics, Windows metafile graphics, and so on.

DOS applications vary widely in their support for the Windows Clipboard. Many DOS apps (such as Edit.com) can't use it directly. But other programs, such as Microsoft Word for DOS, have choices right on their menus for copying to and pasting from the Clipboard. (This assumes that Windows is running and, therefore, a Clipboard exists.)

You can copy text *from* a DOS application *into* the Clipboard; simply use the Mark and Copy toolbar buttons in the DOS window. If you are in full-screen text mode in a Windows DOS session, press the Print Screen key to copy text to the Clipboard. If you are in a window, Alt+PrtSc prints your DOS window in graphics mode to the Clipboard.

To paste text *from* the Clipboard *into* a DOS application, run the DOS application in a window, and click the Paste toolbar button. The text is pasted at the location of the cursor in the DOS application.

If the text that appears in your DOS application is missing a few characters, the program may not be able to receive keystrokes as fast as the Clipboard is capable of sending them. In this case, you need to change the DOS application's shortcut to turn the Fast pasting option *off* (click the Misc tab in the Properties dialog box).

End runs around the Clipboard

If you have major problems making a DOS application accept material from the Windows Clipboard (and you've tried the method explained above), there may be a formatting conflict. All three applications involved in a copy-and-paste — the source of the material, the Clipboard, and the recipient of the material — must have *some* format in common in order for the transfer to work.

To get around this, you may have to first save the material into a file on your hard disk. You can then merge this file into your DOS application to transfer the material. You can save text into a plain-text file on disk using the Windows Notepad. If you want to save textual material that has *formatting* you don't want to lose, such as boldface and italic type or different type sizes, try saving it with Windows Write as a Microsoft Word format file. Many DOS programs can import Microsoft Word files, complete with formatting.

A possibility for getting graphics into your DOS application is to save the graphic in a *pcx* format on disk using MS Paint or another format using Paint Shop Pro. Then try to open this file in your DOS application.

Can't start a DOS app? Delete stuff in the Clipboard

If you can't start a DOS session because of low memory, the Clipboard may, surprisingly, be the cause. The Clipboard can handle almost anything, and any large objects that you copy stay in memory until you cut or copy something else.

You might think that the solution to this problem would be to start the Clipboard application, and then choose Edit, Delete. This displays a dialog box asking you to confirm (by clicking OK) that you want to clear whatever is taking up memory in the Clipboard. But there's a better way.

Secret

If you are in a low-memory situation, simply copy *a single character* into the Clipboard from any application. This erases whatever was previously in the Clipboard and releases the corresponding amount of memory, except what's needed for the one character. You needn't leave your current application or answer any dialog boxes.

Now try to run whatever program would not start earlier due to lack of memory.

Using the Print Screen Key in DOS Sessions

We want to emphasize that you can Print Screen to the printer when you're running a DOS application (or Command.com). If you clear the PrtSc check

box in the shortcut associated with the DOS application (located in the Misc
tab of the Properties dialog box), your text (or graphics) goes to the printer
instead of to the Clipboard.

Getting a Directory Listing

It's hard to print out a directory (folder) listing from Windows. You can focus
on a folder using your Explorer or a folder window. You can send this view
of your folder to the Clipboard by pressing Alt+PrtSc. You can then print this
view by pasting it into a new empty MS Paint file and printing from MS Paint.

This will work only if your whole folder view is visible in one screen (unless
you wish to do this multiple times).

DOS gives you a better way.

STEPS

Printing a Directory Listing from DOS

Step 1.   Click the Start button, point to Programs, and then click
MS-DOS Prompt.

Step 2.   Use the CD, or *change directory,* command to move to the folder
or directory whose file listing you are interested in printing.

Step 3.   Type in the command **dir > dir.txt** and press Enter. If you have
redefined your DIR command to pause for each page, type this
instead: **dir /-p > dir.txt**. This transfers the directory listing to a
file that can then be printed.

While you can print the directory listing directly to the printer
with dir > lpt1:, this method will fail to eject the last page from a
laser printer.

Step 4.   Navigate using your Explorer to the directory whose listing you
have just printed. Right-click dir.txt to select this file in the
Explorer. If you can't find dir.txt, press F5 to refresh your file
listing in your Explorer.

Step 5.   Click Print on the context menu.

If you have created a quick way to the DOS prompt using the methods
detailed in the *Connecting a DOS window to the Explorer* section of this
chapter, you'll be able to skip the first two steps above.

Undocumented

While the above method is a good ad-hoc way of printing a directory of a
given folder, you might want to create a permanent method that will always
reside in the context menu. You can do this by creating a directory-printing
batch file and editing your Registry to connect this file to your folders.
Here's how:

STEPS

Printing a Directory Listing from the Context Menu

Step 1.   Using Notepad, create a file with the following two lines:

```
cd %1

dir>lpt1
```

Step 2.   If you have modified your DIR command, you should change the second line as described in step 3 of the Printing a Directory Listing from DOS steps above. If you print to a port other than LPT1, you need to substitute the name of that printer port in step 1.

Step 3.   Save the file in the folder My System (which we suggested you create in Chapter 3) as Printdir.bat.

Step 4.   Using the Explorer, right-click Printdir.bat, click Properties, and then click the Program tab. Mark the Close on exit check box, and choose Minimized in the Run drop-down list. Click OK.

Step 5.   Start your Registry editor (Regedit.exe in the \Windows folder). Navigate to HKEY_CLASSES_ROOT\Directory\shell, highlighting *shell* in the left pane.

Step 6.   Right-click the right pane, and choose New, Key. Type **Print** as the name of the new key, and then press Enter.

Step 7.   Highlight Print in the left pane, right-click the right pane, and choose New, Key. Type **Command** as the new key name and press Enter.

Step 8.   Double-click Default in the right pane, and type **C:\My System\Printdir.bat**.

Step 9.   Close the Registry editor. The changes take place immediately.

These steps add a new Print command to the context menu. When you right-click on a folder, you can choose this command to print the contents to your printer.

Increasing Files in Config.sys versus System.ini

All applications open files when they run. DOS provides a method to set aside enough memory to keep track of the various files that applications may need to read and leave open. This memory area is set aside by a statement in the Config.sys file such as Files=30. This allows DOS to reserve memory for the names that applications use to manipulate files; these names are called *file handles*.

When you start a DOS application in a Windows DOS session that uses a lot of open files, you may see the following error message:

```
Insufficient File Handles, Increase Files in Config.sys
```

This message is in error, and changing the Files= statement in your Config.sys will not cause it to go away. Instead, the message should advise as follows:

```
Add "PerVMFiles=15" to the [386Enh] section of SYSTEM.INI.
If 15 is not enough file handles, increase the number to 20.
```

The number of file handles specified in the Config.sys file relates to the number of file handles that are available to applications. The Pervmfiles= statement in System.ini refers to the number of file handles that can be open per virtual machine under Windows. Without any Pervmfiles= statement in System.ini, Windows defaults to only 10 file handles allowed within a DOS session. This may not be enough for some DOS applications.

Windows recommends 30 file handles in Config.sys. You should change the file handles per virtual machine in System.ini only if you receive an error message. Each file handle requires a very small amount of memory — only a few bytes under DOS.

The number of handles specified by the Files= line in Config.sys and Pervmfiles= in System.ini combined cannot be greater than 255 (although it is unlikely anyone would need to approach this limit).

Summary

Windows 95 provides a better virtual machine for DOS programs. Lots of DOS programs can run in Windows DOS sessions.

▶ Windows 95 takes over even more of the functions formerly provided by DOS. We discuss which is the real operating system.

▶ Windows programs can use conventional memory, which is always in short supply. We discuss the impact of this design flaw.

▶ Windows 95 provides a DOS window for the DOS screen. The DOS screen has access to 20 different fonts and can be extensively manipulated by the DOS window.

▶ DOS programs can have shortcuts to them just like Windows programs. These shortcuts also define the virtual machine that surrounds the DOS program.

▶ If you can't run the DOS program in a Windows DOS session, you should be able to run it in MS-DOS mode (real-mode DOS). Each program can have its own Autoexec.bat and Config.sys files.

▶ Batch files now work with both DOS and Windows programs so that you can use DOS batch files for Windows programming.

Windows 95 Memory-Handling Improvements

The major memory improvement in Windows 95 is the introduction of a broad list of 32-bit protected-mode drivers. These drivers replace 16-bit DOS drivers that had to be loaded in conventional memory (the first 640K of RAM in your system) or upper memory blocks (UMBs, the memory between 640K and 1MB in your system). This reduced the amount of memory available for DOS programs running either stand-alone or in Windows DOS virtual machines. (DOS programs depend in large part on the first 640K of RAM on your PC. To the extent that you have video, SCSI, sound, and network drivers in that memory area, less memory is left to run DOS programs. This partially explains why owners of PCs with multimedia upgrade kits and multiple add-on boards often have trouble running DOS programs under Windows 3.1. To find out more about DOS virtual machines, turn to Chapter 17.)

These new 32-bit drivers are loaded when Windows 95 is loaded. For example, a properly configured Windows 95 computer with a DoubleSpace/DriveSpace hard disk will first load a 16-bit driver in conventional memory. When Windows 95 is loaded, the 16-bit driver is removed from memory and the 32-bit driver takes over.

Tip

You no longer have to load mouse drivers in Config.sys or Autoexec.bat. The Windows 95 mouse drivers are 32-bit and support the mouse both for Windows programs and for DOS programs running in Windows DOS sessions. But 16-bit mouse drivers are not automatically removed from memory, so you need to remove instructions to load them from your Autoexec.bat or Config.sys files.

CD-ROM and sound card drivers that were previously loaded in conventional memory or in UMBs have for the most part been replaced by protected-mode drivers. Your sound card and CD-ROM will work with Windows programs and DOS programs running in Windows DOS sessions (also known as DOS Windows sessions or windowed DOS sessions).

Network drivers that could eat up lots of conventional memory as well as UMBs have been replaced with protected-mode drivers. This is true for Microsft Networks, NetWare, and TCP/IP networks. Other network providers have been encouraged by Microsoft to provide protected-mode drivers for their networks.

In addition, you no longer have to use Smartdrv.exe to provide a RAM cache for your hard disk reads and writes. Smartdrv.exe is a 16-bit driver that takes up conventional memory or UMBs. Disk caching is built into Windows 95 and works for all Windows programs and DOS programs running in Windows DOS sessions.

Starting with Windows for Workgroups 3.11 (WFWG), you no longer had to load Share.exe for those programs that needed it (such as Word for Windows). WFWG 3.11 came with a VxD, a protected-mode version of Share called Vshare.386. Vshare is now part of Vmm32.exe, and it is automatically loaded when Windows 95 starts. Sharing works for all Windows programs and DOS programs running in Windows DOS sessions.

Windows 95 does not provide the benefits of 32-bit protected-mode drivers to DOS programs that need to run in MS-DOS mode or before Windows 95 starts (or if you press F8 and start at the command line). If you run DOS programs that need a mouse or access to a CD-ROM in MS-DOS mode, you need to load those 16-bit drivers in Autoexec.bat or Config.sys (or in Autoexec.bat and Config.sys files that are created on the fly when you run specific DOS programs, as discussed in Chapter 17).

In addition to using these 32-bit drivers, Windows 95 also provides greater Windows resources and better cleanup of abandoned Windows resources. We discuss this in *Windows 95 resources* later in this chapter.

When to Worry about Memory

There are six major memory issues with Windows:

- Configuring your memory so you can run DOS programs that require large amounts of conventional memory and/or expanded memory

- Having enough hard disk space so the Windows swap area for virtual memory is large enough to handle all your active applications as well as the Windows 95 components

- Running out of Windows resources when you have a number of Windows applications open

- Windows applications written for Windows 3.*x* that can (and often do) spring memory leaks, eating up resources until they are all gone

- Windows programs that use significant amounts of conventional memory, which is always limited

- Unrecognized memory address conflicts between video and network cards in upper memory

In this chapter, we concentrate on the first issue, configuring memory for running DOS programs. So let's look at the other issues first.

Hard disk space for virtual memory

To get the full story on virtual memory, turn to Chapter 27. Windows 95, like its predecessor, Windows 3.*x*, uses your hard disk to "swap" programs and data out of RAM when it needs this memory to accomplish your more pressing tasks. Unlike Windows 3.*x*, Windows 95 doesn't ask you to create a permanent swap file for maximum performance. It handles swapping automatically.

It is a very good idea to let Windows 95 have plenty of room on your fastest hard disk for swap space. Depending on the amount of RAM that you have (more RAM calls for more hard disk swap space — see Chapter 27), it is best to have at least 20MB of unused hard disk space available.

If you don't have enough hard disk space and the swap file takes up every bit of it, you will get an error message about not being able to write User.dat, a file that is part of the Registry. Windows 95 produces information about the state of the machine dynamically and every so often writes it out to User.dat in the background. If you don't have enough hard disk space, it can't write the information to disk.

Again, turn to Chapter 27 for more information on swap space.

Windows 95 resources

Windows 3.x often runs out of resources and displays error messages that blame limited memory as the problem. This is very frustrating to users who just purchased 16MB of memory and are quite willing to yell back at their machines that they have plenty of "memory."

If you receive such a message when using Windows 3.x, what is really happening is that one of your applications asked for more system resources and Windows 3.x ran out of them. You may have plenty of unused memory (RAM) and plenty of swap space left, but you just can't use them because of a limitation in the ability of Windows 3.x to assign system resources.

Resources are essentially lists (referred to as *heaps*) of memory. The lengths of the lists under Windows 3.x are quite small. The lists can be much longer with Windows 95. The lists point to areas of memory where user interface elements (and other items) are stored — things like dialog boxes, windows, and so on.

System resources under Windows 3.x employ four 16-bit heaps. Three of the heaps are part of the User resource, which manages the user interface portion of Windows. One is the Graphic Device Interface (GDI) resource, which manages drawing objects to the screen. Because these lists are 16-bit heaps they can address only 64K of memory each—a total of 256K of memory to store the objects used in the user interface and displayed on your screen.

If one of your applications asks Windows 3.x for more objects and one of the heaps has already allocated all the memory on its list, Windows generates the out-of-memory message.

Windows 95 has greatly expanded the lists for the GDI and User resource areas in Windows 95. George Moore from Microsoft has reported that, "In addition to all of the things in User and GDI that were moved to the 32-bit heap, Device Contexts and Logical Font structures in GDI are moved to the 32-bit heap. This means that the old system-wide limit on the number of Device Contexts has been raised from around 150–200 to over 10,000. In addition, you can now also easily load many, many more TrueType fonts than you ever could under Windows 3.1."

In Windows 95, the three heaps in User have been replaced by one 32-bit heap with the ability to address 2 gigabytes of memory — probably enough for the next couple of years. Microsoft maintained the 16-bit heap for the GDI for compatibility reasons. Essentially, some programs managed this heap directly without going through the Windows application program interfaces (APIs), and changing it to a 32-bit heap would break these programs. Some of the elements that were in the GDI heap have been moved to the 32-bit User heap, as George Moore points out.

Table 18-1 shows how system-wide resources have been increased in Windows 95.

Table 18-1	System-Wide Resources Then and Now	
Resource	**Windows 3.1**	**Windows 95**
Window/menu handles	About 299	32K (each)
Timers	32	Unlimited
Listbox items (per listbox)	8K	32K
Listbox data (per listbox)	64K	Unlimited
Edit control data (per control)	64K	Unlimited
Regions	All in 64K	Unlimited
Physical pens and brushes	All in 64K	Unlimited
Logical fonts	All in 64K	750-800
Installed fonts	250-300	1,000
Device contexts	200 (best case)	16K

Windows 3.x programs spring memory leaks

Many applications written for Windows 3.x have the unfortunate habit of asking for system resources and then not giving them back after they quit. The longer you run Windows 3.x, the fewer resources you have until you finally run out of resources and are forced to start Windows again.

These same programs will have the same problems running under Windows 95, but Windows 95 has two new defenses. First, with greater system resources, the problems will show up less frequently. Second, Windows 95 cleans up after Win-16 applications (those written for Windows 3.x), making sure that the resources they were allocated get back in the common pool.

It can do this only after all Win-16 apps (excluding those that have been specifically tagged as Windows 95-aware) have quit. Windows 95 must wait because Win-16 apps can share the same resources. Therefore, you have to be sure that you quit all your old Win-16 applications every now and then to get the resources back.

Windows 95 cleans up the resources used by 32-bit applications if they don't do it properly themselves.

Piggy Windows programs

Some Windows programs, 16-bit drivers, and even 32-bit protected-mode video drivers use up lots of conventional memory. If you tried to run a couple of these oinkers, you would soon see the error message saying you were out of memory when, again, you had plenty of memory. In this case you ran out of conventional memory.

The problem here is poor programming. The writers most likely included fixed memory segments in their programs, which under Windows 3.*x,* have to be allocated out of the limited pool of 640K of conventional memory. Microsoft has fixed most of this problem in Windows 95 by loading these structures in extended memory instead of conventional memory.

One program that tracks the amount of available DOS memory is the Norton System Watch applet that comes with the Norton Utilities version 8 (DOS). Another is the System Information portion of Norton Desktop for Windows 3.1 (and its Windows 95 counterpart). You can use either of these programs to see whether your free DOS memory gets low as you start and use your regular Windows applications.

Windows 95 automatically provides a good deal more DOS memory than Windows 3.*x* because it substitutes 32-bit protected-mode drivers for the 16-bit drivers that work with Windows 3.*x*. These 32-bit drivers reside in extended memory. In many cases, you have to check your Config.sys and Autoexec.bat files, and if you haven't done so yet, remark out the 16-bit drivers.

Under Windows 95, these piggy programs will have more conventional memory available to them. Given that portions of the programs that were previously loaded in conventional memory are now loaded in extended memory, they should be less of a problem than under Windows 3.*x*. We hope that newer 32-bit versions of these applications won't use fixed memory segments to nearly the same extent. You may have to upgrade your applications if this continues to be a problem for you. Just because the program is a newer version doesn't mean its authors have fixed the problem.

In this chapter, we concentrate on increasing conventional memory for DOS programs that require much more than even these piggy Windows programs, although any increases in conventional memory will also help these Windows programs work better.

Conventional Memory Tracker, a component of Microsoft's Kernel Toys, lets you find out which programs and drivers are using up the lower 640K of your memory. Download Kernel Toys from http://www.microsoft.com/windows/software/krnltoy.htm.

Memory Conflicts

Windows 95 should be able to identify most, if not all, potential memory conflicts. These occur when a video, network, or some other card uses a memory address between A000 and FFFF without revealing that address to Windows. This used to cause serious configuration difficulties for Windows 3.*x*. Windows 95 is much better at spotting these cards and not using the forbidden memory addresses.

The Device Manager will highlight any detected memory-use conflicts. You can also use the Device Manager to reserve memory address ranges for use by hardware devices.

Memory conflicts are discussed in detail in the *Troubleshooting Memory Conflicts* section near the end of this chapter. The Device Manager is revealed in all its glory in Chapter 19.

Fatal Exception Errors

If you receive error messages in the form of "Fatal Exception Error 0x:xxxxxxxx" it probably means that you have a bad physical memory chip in your computer. The first thing you can do to try to get rid of these errors is to turn off your external (L2) cache. You can often do this by restarting your computer and pressing the Delete key when prompted to bring up your BIOS setup screen. You then need to follow the instructions on your screen to see how to disable this cache.

If this is not the problem, you can also try increasing the number of memory wait states in BIOS.

If neither of these methods work, you are in the position of replacing SIMMs. You can test RAM using a RAM drive configuration. To see how check out Microsoft's Knowledge Base for the following article: http://www.microsoft.com/kb/articles/q142/5/46.htm.

The Short of It — More Conventional Memory

Before we go into all the gory details, we want to give you some quick tips on how to get the most conventional memory possible if you need it to run your DOS programs or if your Windows programs are running out conventional memory.

DOS programs in Windows DOS sessions

Tip

If you want to have the largest amount of conventional memory for Windows programs and DOS programs that can run in Windows DOS sessions, you'll need to have a Config.sys file that starts off looking like this:

```
Device=Himem.sys
Device=Emm386.exe noems
DOS=High,UMB
```

Pull from your Config.sys and Autoexec.bat files any references to 16-bit drivers that have 32-bit replacements with Windows 95. Load high any DOS TSRs that you want easily available to all DOS virtual machines in your Autoexec.bat as:

```
LoadHigh C:\Windows\Command\Doskey.exe
```

If you need expanded memory for your DOS programs running in Windows DOS sessions, change the *noems* parameter after Emm386.exe to *ram*.

If you still need more free UMBs in order to get drivers or whatever out of conventional memory, and there isn't a memory conflict with your video or network card, change the second line in your Config.sys to:

```
Device=Emm386.exe i=b000-b7FF noems
```

or

```
Device=Emm386.exe i=b000-b7FF ram
```

You can see if this area of memory is available by using the Device Manager as detailed in the *Troubleshooting Memory Conflicts* section later in this chapter.

Pull all unneeded references to FILES, STACKS, and so on in Config.sys and go with the default values (described in the section entitled *Cleaning Up Config.sys and Autoexec.bat*). Don't load the DoubleSpace or DriveSpace compression drivers in UMBs.

DOS programs in MS-DOS mode

Tip

If you need to run DOS programs in MS-DOS mode (that is, you have really tried to run them in a Windows DOS session and they won't work), modify your MS-DOS mode *pif*s to create private Config.sys and Autoexec.bat files. You can associate these private files with each program that runs in MS-DOS mode or with MS-DOS mode in general. They are stored in a *pif* file for that program or in the *pif* for the shortcut icon associated with MS-DOS mode in general. See Chapter 17 for more details.

You don't have to change the values in the Config.sys or Autoexec.bat files associated with Windows (or even have such files) because MS-DOS mode restarts (warm boots) your computer and uses its own set of files. If you start your computer and press F8 to go to the DOS prompt before you go into Windows 95, you won't have the same Config.sys and Autoexec.bat files that start in MS-DOS mode.

Modify the private files using the tips given in the preceding section. Include your 16-bit drivers and DOS TSRs in your private Config.sys and Autoexec.bat files. Otherwise, the DOS programs can't use your mouse, CD-ROM, and so on. Include your DoubleSpace or DriveSpace driver in Config.sys as:

```
Devicehigh=C:\Windows\Command\Drvspace.sys /move
```

Load all the 16-bit drivers high. You may need to fiddle with the order of these drivers to get them all to load in UMBs. You may not have room to put them all there and might have to put some of them in conventional memory. In the *Windows Memory Management* section later in this chapter, we discuss fiddling in more detail.

The PC Memory Map

Before we continue with the issue of configuring memory to run DOS programs, here's an overview of how memory is structured on personal computers. If you already understand this structure, then go right to the next section.

Figure 18-1 shows a memory map that applies to most 386, 486, and Pentium computers with 16MB of memory. 16MB equals 16384K of RAM. The first 640K of the first megabyte of RAM is addressed from 0–640K (0000h–9FFFh), and the next 384K is addressed starting at 1024K (10000h). The rest of RAM starts at 1408K (16000h) and continues through 16768K (106000h).

The Windows 95 Device Manager uses a slightly different memory address notation than is standard for DOS and Windows 3.*x*. For example, the address A000 (the notation used in DOS) is shorthand for 000A0000 (the notation used by the Device Manager).

The first notation recognizes the fact that we were concentrating our attention on a small range of memory below 1MB, so it ignores anything smaller than a paragraph (16 bytes). Therefore, it drops the three higher digits and ignores the first digit.

The second notation points out the fact that Windows can address FFFFFFFF (4,294,967,295) bytes of memory using its flat-memory, protected-mode model. All eight places are used, as in 000A0000. We use the notations interchangeably.

You should be concerned with six types of memory: *conventional memory, UMBs,* and *extended memory* are the first three. You can load portions of DOS into the *high memory area* (HMA), the fourth. DOS applications also use a fifth type of memory, *expanded memory. Virtual memory,* the sixth, is a combination of RAM and swap space on your hard disk.

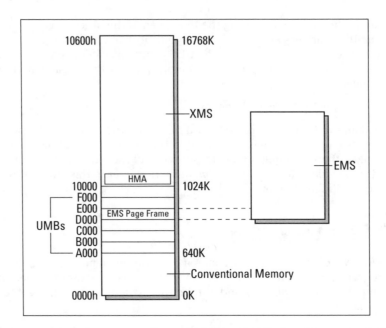

Figure 18-1: This diagram shows a PC with 16MB of RAM (640K of conventional memory plus 15744K of extended memory =16384K plus 384K of UMBs, for a total of 16768K). EMS memory is taken from the extended memory by using EMM386.exe or other third-party memory managers, or is given to DOS programs running in Windows DOS sessions by Windows 95 itself.

■ *Conventional memory* is the first 640K of memory in your PC. DOS applications run in this memory. Real-mode drivers that start before Windows 95 starts use this memory unless they are loaded into UMBs. DOS TSRs that are loaded before Windows 95 starts use this memory. Windows also uses this memory when it switches to V86 mode in order to access some DOS device drivers and PC hardware. Some Windows programs use significant amounts of conventional memory. Windows can put some (or all) of its translation buffers in conventional memory.

■ *UMBs* are memory addresses where hardware devices and software drivers may be accessed by DOS and Windows. Exactly 384K of memory addresses are reserved for UMBs, and it is always located just above the first 640K of conventional memory. Much of this memory can't be used to relocate 16-bit drivers and DOS TSRs from conventional memory, because it is used by the ROM on your video card and/or network card and the system ROM. The 64K EMS page frame, if any, is located here. 16-bit drivers and DOS TSRs can use UMBs if the parameter *ram* or *noems* is present after EMM386.exe in your Config.sys file.

■ *Extended memory* (also called XMS, for eXtended Memory Specification) is the memory above conventional memory and the UMBs. It begins at the 1MB line, which is the same as 1024K (640K plus 384K). If you have 16MB of RAM in your system, the first 640K is conventional memory, and the rest begins at the 1024K line and is counted upward from there.

■ The first 64K of extended memory (minus 16 bytes) is called the *high memory area* (HMA), and it is used by DOS, Windows, and a few other programs. No more than one program can be loaded into HMA, which is typically a part of DOS. Loading DOS in HMA saves about 46K in conventional memory. The DOS buffers also get loaded here.

■ *Expanded memory* (also called EMS, for Expanded Memory Specification) is a special type of memory that requires at least 64K of address space in the UMBs. On a 386 and higher, expanded memory is usually provided by an expanded memory manager, a program that converts extended to expanded memory as required. Expanded memory requires a 64K page frame somewhere below the 1MB line in order to function. The Emm386.exe file provided by Windows 95 is an expanded memory manager. Additionally, QEMM, 386Max, NetRoom, and other products available from other software vendors provide somewhat more functionality than the Microsoft utility.

■ *Virtual memory* is the combination of RAM that can be addressed by Windows 95 and the dynamic swap file space on your hard disk. Windows 95 manages this combined memory to allow you to load a significant number of applications at once without running out of physical (RAM) memory. The programs that are actually doing something are in RAM, while those sitting idly are swapped to the hard disk.

We discuss the UMBs a lot in this chapter. This is because you can increase the amount of conventional memory available under Windows 95 by moving device drivers and DOS itself from conventional memory into UMBs and into HMA.

UMBs from A to F

You can think of the 384K of UMBs as six separate areas, each of which is 64K in size. These six blocks are known as A, B, C, D, E, and F. This is because the address of the first byte of memory in the A block is A000 (pronounced "A thousand") in hexadecimal numbering.

The A block is used for the addresses of the RAM on your VGA or higher video board. When the board is in graphics mode (as opposed to text mode), the 64K of address space at A000 is used by Windows to write information into the RAM on the board. No matter how much RAM is physically installed on the board — 256K, 512K, or more — the same 64K block is used to write to all video memory.

The B block is used for two purposes. The first 32K, which begins at B000, is used when a VGA or higher resolution video board is in monochrome graphics mode. These memory addresses would be used, for example, if you were using a monochrome monitor and the Windows VGA monochrome driver. The second 32K, from B800 to C000, is used for VGA or higher text mode. A portion of this address space is used when you are at a DOS prompt and type a command. The DOS output is written to B800, where it appears on your screen as text characters.

The second line loads Emm386, the real-mode manger for expanded and upper memory, with a parameter (*noems*) that tells it not to set aside a 64K page frame for handling expanded memory and thereby not provide any expanded memory. All upper memory that Emm386.exe marks as available can be used for loading 16-bit drivers, TSRs, and portions of DOS.

The *noems* parameter means that no expanded memory will be available for DOS programs whether they are running in Windows DOS sessions under Windows 95 or in MS-DOS mode. It doesn't matter where you set the EMS value in the DOS *pif*, if *noems* has been specified in Config.sys, no EMS will be available to DOS programs.

If you want to set aside a page frame in upper memory so that you can provide expanded memory for DOS programs, then instead of the parameter *noems*, use the parameter *ram*. This allows both EMS memory and the use of UMBs for 16-bit drivers and TSRs.

Using the parameter *ram* decreases by 64K the amount of UMBs that can be used to store 16-bit drivers and DOS TSRs. If they can't fit in UMBs, they will be loaded in conventional memory.

If you don't include the second line in your Config.sys (or you don't have a Config.sys file), Windows is free to allow EMS memory in DOS sessions under Windows as you see fit. You can set the limit of the EMS memory for each DOS session in its *pif*. See Chapter 17 for further details.

The third line loads a portion of DOS into HMA — a 64K area just above the 1024K boundary — instead of in conventional memory. It also directs DOS to manage the UMBs so that 16-bit drivers and TSRs can be loaded there and still retain their connection to conventional memory and DOS. If UMB is not included in this line (or in a separate line of the form DOS=UMB), no drivers are loaded into UMBs.

You can use a number of specific and esoteric parameters with Himem.sys and Emm386.exe. If you still have DOS 6.2*x* on your computer, you can find out more about them by opening up a Windows DOS session, changing directories to your old DOS directory, and typing **help Emm386.exe** or **help Himem.sys**. Windows 95 doesn't come with a DOS Help command.

Loading drivers in UMBs

If you are going to load your 16-bit drivers into the UMBs, you need to use Devicehigh= in Config.sys and/or Loadhigh in Autoexec.bat. Here's an example Config.sys that loads the real-mode DriveSpace driver in upper memory :

```
Device=c:\Windows\Himem.sys /testmem:off /v
Device=c:\Windows\Emm386.exe noems /v
DOS=High,UMB
Devicehigh=C:\Windows\Command\Drvspace.sys /move
```

You would not want to load this particular driver in upper memory unless you were running DOS programs in MS-DOS mode with no private Autoexec.bat and Config.sys files. This is because Windows 95 automatically unloads this real-mode driver if it is loaded in conventional memory.

An Autoexec.bat that loads Doskey.exe (a DOS TSR) in a UMB would look like this:

```
LoadHigh C:\Windows\Command\Doskey.exe
```

Stack pages

In Brian's Windows Manager column for InfoWorld Magazine, he dealt thoroughly with the setting MaxBPs=768. This setting, added to the [386Enh] section of a Windows 3.1 system, reduces crashes by setting aside an extra 4K of extended memory for Windows "break points."

Windows 95, by contrast, dynamically allocates break points, which are 10-byte chunks of memory used to track virtual device drivers (VxDs). As VxDs use more memory, Windows 95 simply assigns more memory to break points as needed. This is why the MaxBPs line is no longer necessary in Windows 95.

The MaxBPs=768 setting does still work in Windows 3.11 and Windows for Workgroups 3.11, but it is not needed in Windows 95.

It appears that Windows 95 may have its own setting to deal with a similar but different kind of program crashes. This setting deals exclusively with 32-bit software.

The problem that afflicts 32-bit software affects stack pages. *Stack pages* are 4K blocks of memory that Windows 95 sets aside for 32-bit device drivers to use as a stack. (A *stack*, in this case, refers to a scratch area of memory used by programs. This entire discussion of stack pages, by the way, is unrelated to the Stacks= command found in Config.sys, which is used by 16-bit DOS drivers.)

If a 32-bit device driver exceeds 4K of memory for its stack, the program causes an error, but Windows 95 can recover. This is because Windows 95, by default, maintains two extra memory pages known as *spare stack pages*.

Unfortunately, many Windows 95 users are finding that even having two spare stack pages is not enough for some of the drivers they're running. In this case, you'll see a confusing error message similar to the following:

> There are no spare stack pages. It may be necessary to increase the setting of "MinSPs" in System.ini to prevent possible stack faults. There are currently 2 SPs allocated.

The typical user, facing this message, could be forgiven for having a blank look. What's a "MinSPs" and what should it be increased to? Looking in Windows 95's System.ini file doesn't reveal anything that looks like "MinSPs."

The solution is to add a MinSPs (minimum stack pages) line to the [386Enh] section of your System.ini. Start with a value of 4, which doubles the spare stack pages, and restart Windows. If that value doesn't resolve the problem, try 6 and then 8. Each spare stack page consumes 4K of extended memory.

Add the setting to your System.ini file like this:

```
[386Enh]
; Increases stack pages from 2 to 4.
MinSPs=4
```

You can make this change with Notepad or any plain-text editor. You'll find System.ini (in case you haven't looked for it since you installed Windows 95) in your C:\Windows folder.

Just as Microsoft decided to allocate break points dynamically in Windows 95 (so users wouldn't have to guess how many to allocate in System.ini), perhaps Microsoft will eventually update Windows 95 so drivers can't run out of stack space.

How Windows Uses Upper Memory

Windows looks for space in UMBs for two different purposes:

■ It places an expanded memory page frame, 64K in size, in an unused area above 640K. If an expanded memory manager was loaded in Config.sys, Windows "inherits" the settings for that EMS page frame.

■ Windows claims another area, approximately 16K in size, for DOS translation buffers. These buffers are used by Windows to transfer data to and from real-mode devices such as disk drives. If there is not enough space left in UMBs, Windows takes the equivalent amount of space out of conventional memory.

Windows doesn't need EMM386.exe to accomplish these tasks. It has its own built-in expanded and UMB memory manager.

Memory for DOS Programs

You can run DOS programs in a Windows DOS session, in MS-DOS mode, or before Windows 95 starts (if you press F8). Each mode provides a different amount of conventional memory for DOS programs. MS-DOS mode makes available about 3K less conventional memory than starting a DOS program at the DOS command prompt before Windows 95 starts (if they both use the same Autoexec.bat and Config.sys files). See Chapter 17 for more details.

Windows provides each DOS program in a Windows DOS session with a "virtual machine." The memory available to the virtual machine is determined by what was loaded by Io.sys, Autoexec.bat, Config.sys, and Windows. Windows 95 provides protected-mode drivers that are used by DOS programs running in Windows DOS sessions. These protected-mode drivers aren't available to DOS programs that are running in MS-DOS mode or that were started before Windows 95 loaded.

Io.sys automatically loads Drvspace.sys in conventional memory if it detects a DoubleSpace or DriveSpace compressed drive and there isn't a line in a Config.sys file loading the driver in UMBs. This real-mode driver is removed from conventional memory and replaced by a protected-mode driver loaded in extended memory when Windows loads. It is not removed from the UMBs if it was loaded there.

You may need to run DOS programs that can't run in Windows DOS sessions (for whatever reasons) and need resources that require 16-bit drivers. You either have to load these drivers before Windows 95 starts or load them in each MS-DOS mode session. Each DOS program that has to run in MS-DOS mode can have its own private Autoexec.bat and Config.sys files. Again, Chapter 17 provides more details.

If these 16-bit drivers are loaded by Autoexec.bat and Config.sys, you can load them into UMBs. This increases the amount of conventional memory available to DOS programs you do run in Windows DOS sessions and provides more conventional memory for DOS programs you run in MS-DOS mode.

You can load the DoubleSpace/DriveSpace driver into conventional memory and it won't take up any conventional memory in a virtual machine because it is replaced by the 32-bit driver. DOS programs that run outside Windows DOS sessions have less available conventional memory because the real-mode DoubleSpace/DriveSpace is taking up conventional memory.

If you run a DOS program that requires expanded or extended memory in a Windows DOS session, you can configure the *pif* associated with that DOS program to tell Windows to provide the required expanded or extended memory. Windows won't be able to allocate expanded memory to DOS programs if the line

```
Device=Emm386.exe noems
```

or

```
Device=Emm386.exe frame=none
```

is in Config.sys. You don't need a line in your Config.sys file (or even a Config.sys file, for that matter) for Windows 95 to be able to provide expanded memory to DOS programs running in Windows DOS sessions.

Examples of available memory for DOS programs

You can configure Config.sys and Autoexec.bat in different ways to load different drivers and make them available to DOS programs. Here are the consequences of these configurations.

No Config.sys or Autoexec.bat

If you don't have Config.sys or Autoexec.bat and don't have any real-mode drivers or DOS TSRs, and if you used the default values for variables such as Files and Stacks (more about this *Cleaning Up Config.sys and Autoexcec.bat* later in the chapter), you will find that on a representative computer, a Windows DOS session has about 604K of conventional memory available. In MS-DOS mode, 606K is available (if the MS-DOS mode is configured without its own Config.sys and Autoexec.bat).

If the computer has a hard drive compressed with DoubleSpace or DriveSpace, the respective values would be 604K and 556K of conventional memory. Because Windows 95 replaces the real-mode compressed disk driver that was automatically loaded in conventional memory with a protected-mode driver, the Windows DOS session's conventional memory is not reduced at all.

Minimum real-mode drivers in Config.sys

Assume you were to use a Config.sys to allow access into the UMBs to load the real-mode compressed disk driver, as shown previously in the Config.sys file. The respective values for conventional memory would be 612K for a Windows DOS session, and 623K in MS-DOS mode.

Some real-mode drivers that were loaded in conventional memory by Io.sys are now automatically loaded into UMBs. These include Ifshlp.sys, Setver.exe, and Command.com, as well as Drvspace.sys. This accounts for the increased conventional memory across the board.

While the DOS programs have more memory outside of Windows 95, they are without the services of the protected-mode drivers for a mouse, CD-ROM, sound card, network, and so on. If your DOS programs need these services, you can have their 16-bit drivers loaded into the UMBs or conventional memory.

You should be able to load all the real-mode equivalents of the protected-mode drivers mentioned in the previous paragraph (minus the network drivers) into the UMBs, as long as you don't have to provide expanded memory for any of the DOS programs.

Too many 16-bit drivers and expanded memory

Things begin to get tight in conventional memory as you continue to pile on the real-mode drivers or set aside 64K of UMBs for a page frame for expanded memory. There just isn't enough room after a while, so Io.sys places some of the drivers in conventional memory.

Using the following Config.sys and Autoexec.bat files, which include 16-bit drivers for a sound card, mouse, and CD-ROM as well as set aside 64K of UMB for expanded memory, you end up with 562K of conventional memory in MS-DOS mode and 545K in a Windows DOS session. (LH is shorthand for LoadHigh):

```
Devicehigh=C:\Windows\Command\Drvspace.sys /move

Path=C:\Windows;C:\Windows\Command
LH C:\Logitech\mouse
LH C:\Windows\Mscdex.ese /s /d:mscd001 m:10
Device=C:\Windows\Himem.sys /testmem:off
Device=C:\Windows\Emm386.exe ram
DOS=High,UMB
Devicehigh=C:\Sound\Mtmcde.sys /d:mscd001 /p:310 /a:0 /m:64 /t:s /i:5
```

If your DOS programs run in this reduced conventional memory, it is no problem. Unfortunately, many DOS programs want at least 600K of conventional memory plus expanded memory to boot. If they can run in the Windows DOS session, you can quit loading these 16-bit drivers and have plenty of conventional memory.

This example doesn't show the results of loading a 16-bit network driver, which would reduce the conventional memory that much more.

More Memory for DOS Programs

There are numerous ways that you can claim additional UMBs to provide more conventional memory for DOS programs.

Claiming the space used by the page frame

If you have large DOS programs that need lots of conventional memory but don't require expanded memory, you can get more memory for these programs by disabling the creation of a 64K page frame in upper memory when you load EMM386.exe in your Config.sys file.

If you are using Emm386.exe, do this by adding *frame=none* to the command line in Config.sys, as in:

```
device=c:\windows\emm386.exe frame=none
```

This parameter also works with Qemm386, but varies with other memory managers. The parameter *frame=none* does not work in some configurations. It usually frees a little more memory than putting *noems* on the Emm386 command line. But if *frame=none* does not work in your system (Windows 95 won't start, for example), go back to using the *noems* parameter.

If you eliminate the page frame in your memory manager in Config.sys, you should also keep Windows 95 from creating one. To do this, place a line in the [386Enh] section of your System.ini file with Notepad or Sysedit, as follows:

```
[386Enh]
NoEMMDriver=TRUE
```

By preventing the creation of the 64K page frame in Emm386 and in Windows, you open up this much space to load additional device drivers and memory-resident programs into UMBs. Drivers that wouldn't load high before you reconfigured your memory managers may now fit just fine.

Claiming the space used by translation buffers

Windows 95 tries to load approximately 16K of translation buffers in the UMBs. Only if it is prevented from doing so will it take up 16K of conventional memory.

You can see Windows move its translation buffers to conventional memory by taking the following steps.

STEPS

Showing the Memory Used by Translation Buffers

Step 1.   Rename Config.sys and Autoexec.bat to filenames that won't be used by Windows 95.

Step 2.   Reboot Windows 95 and open a Windows DOS session.

Step 3.   Type **mem /c/p** at the DOS command prompt, press Enter, and write down how much conventional memory is available.

Step 4.   Exit the Windows DOS session and then restart Windows 95. When the Starting Windows 95 message appears on your screen, press F8, and then boot to the command prompt.

Step 5.   Type **Win /d:x** to start Windows 95 in the debug mode and exclude it from using the UMBs.

Step 6.   Open a Windows DOS session. Type **mem /c/p** and press Enter. Write down the amount of conventional memory available.

Step 7.   Rename the files that you created in step 1 back to and Autoexec.bat Config.sys.

The difference in the two measurements of conventional memory is the size of your translation buffers. If Windows finds room for these buffers in the UMBs, it will place them there. If there is not enough room, they go into conventional memory.

If you fill up your UMBs with 16-bit drivers, you might be able to get more conventional memory for DOS applications under Windows by loading one of the smaller drivers into conventional memory instead of UMB. Even a 1K device driver might be taking up a 16K address space that could be used for Windows translation buffers.

There is one other thing that might be preventing Windows from finding a free 16K space in UMB. If an expanded memory manager claims all UMBs, Windows may find there are none for it to use. Emm386.exe doesn't do this.

Tip

If Windows is forcing its translation buffers into conventional memory, try setting aside a 16K area of UMBs from your expanded memory manager. Emm386.exe allows you to do this by adding the switch /win to the command line in Config.sys, followed by an equals sign and the exact addresses to exclude. For example, if you want to exclude the last 16K of the D000 block, you would put the following line in Config.sys:

```
device=c:\Windows\Emm386.exe /win=dc00-dfff
```

Getting the best of conventional and upper memory

If you have fit the translation buffers and page frame into upper memory as well as you can and your DOS programs are still not getting enough conventional memory to run, you can add another trick to your arsenal: claiming the monochrome UMB area.

If you run Windows with a VGA or super VGA color driver, it's likely that no program is using the memory area that starts at B000. Additionally, DOS text-mode programs rarely use all of the text-mode memory that starts at B800 and continues to C000. (IBM XGA adapters, however, do use the B000 area to store information, so don't use the following technique with them.)

Even if you have a monochrome monitor or a laptop with a monochrome display, you may be able to use this technique. Instead of using the VGA with Monochrome Display driver that comes with Windows, try switching to the color VGA driver. Many monochrome displays simply use shades of gray when color information is output and will work fine with color VGA drivers.

To find out if your display driver uses this area of upper memory, take the following steps:

STEPS

Determining Memory Usage

Step 1. Click the Start button, point to Settings, and then click Control Panel.

Step 2. Double-click the System icon in the Control Panel. Click the Device Manager tab in the System Properties dialog box.

Step 3. At the top of the tree, Computer should be highlighted. If not, highlight it.

(continued)

Determining Memory Usage

Step 4.   Click the Properties button. Click the Memory option button on
the View Resources tab of the Computer Properties dialog box,
as shown in Figure 18-2.

The memory addresses used by your video card and video driver as well as
the system ROM are shown in this dialog box. As you can see in Figure 18-2,
the memory between 000B0000 and 000B7FFFF is marked "Unavailable for
use by devices." This memory is marked to be used by the monochrome
portion of your video driver.

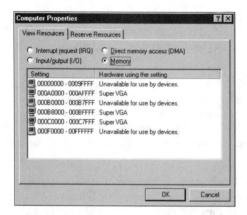

Figure 18-2: The View Resources tab of the Computer Properties dialog box. You can view
the memory addresses used by the display adapter and system BIOS.

You can use this memory range if it is marked "Unavailable for use by
devices." To give your expanded memory manager access to the monochrome B000 area, use an *include* parameter in Config.sys similar to the
following:

```
device=c:\Windows\Emm386.exe i=b000-b7ff ram
```

This statement instructs your memory manager to use the entire block
between B000 and B800 (the address B7FF is one byte lower than B800 in
hexadecimal numbering). Memory managers often avoid this block because
VGA adapters can be switched into monochrome mode by programs at any
time. But if you don't use such programs, your 386 memory manager can
safely manage this area.

If you give access to this area to your memory manager in Config.sys, you
should also specify this to the Windows 386 memory manager. This is not
absolutely necessary, since Windows inherits Emm386.exe settings, but it

makes this memory available if you ever disable Emm386.exe for any reason. To do so, add an *include* line to the [386Enh] section of System.ini with Notepad or Sysedit, as follows:

```
[386Enh]
EMMInclude=B000-B7FF
```

When you restart Windows and run Mem in a DOS session, you may find that a substantially larger amount of conventional memory is now available (if 16-bit drivers couldn't previously be loaded in the UMBs). There is now more room to locate Windows translation buffers, a page frame (if you use one), 16-bit drivers, and DOS TSRs.

Cleaning Up Config.sys and Autoexec.bat

As you can see from the previous sections, after you install Windows 95 on a computer that already has DOS 5.0 or DOS 6.*x* and Windows 3.*x* installed, you will benefit from examining Config.sys and Autoexec.bat files. These files may contain references to 16-bit drivers that you no longer need. You may be able to get rid of these files entirely.

The major functions of Config.sys were to set a series of system values and to load 16-bit drivers. Io.sys now sets most of these values. If it can, Windows will replace 16-bit drivers with 32-bit drivers when it loads.

Io.sys sets the following values that were normally set in Config.sys in Windows 3.*x*:

```
FILES=60
FCBS=4
BUFFERS=30
LASTDRIVE=Z
STACKS=9,256
```

It also sets the path equal to C:\Windows;C:\Windows\Command; the prompt equal to pg; TMP=C:\Windows\Temp; and TEMP=C:\Windows\Temp.

If these values work for you, you don't need to repeat them in Config.sys or Autoexec.bat. The Windows 95 Setup program may have already modified these files, changing your path statement and remarking out redundant lines. You can take out the 16-bit drivers that you don't need anymore if you can run your DOS programs without them.

The DOS buffers get loaded into the HMA, so you may be able to increase their number if needed without affecting conventional memory.

Troubleshooting Memory Conflicts

Windows 95 relocates some extended memory from addresses above 1MB to UMB addresses between 640K and 1MB. Problems occur when Windows relocates memory into a block that is also used by a device such as a video board or a network adapter. Boards such as these require some address space between 640K and 1MB to operate. Windows attempts to identify all UMBs in use, but this attempt may not always be successful.

Conflicts can also occur if the real-mode expanded memory manager loads 16-bit drivers or DOS TSRs into upper memory areas used by other devices. Before you continue troubleshooting, remark out the line in Config.sys that loads Emm386.exe to force all the drivers and DOS TSRs to load in conventional memory.

You can check for memory conflicts between different devices by using the Device Manager. Windows highlights known conflicts in the Device Manager.

STEPS

Checking for Memory Conflicts

Step 1.   Click the Start button, point to Settings, and then click Control Panel.

Step 2.   Double-click the System icon in the Control Panel. Click the Device Manager tab in the System Properties dialog box.

Step 3.   At the top of the tree, Computer should be highlighted. If not, highlight it.

Step 4.   Click the Properties button to display the View Resources tab of the Computer Properties dialog box.

Any memory conflicts that Windows 95 detects are displayed in this dialog box.

The addresses between 640K and 1MB that Windows relocates memory into are referred to in the Device Manager in hexadecimal numbering as 000A0000 to 000FFFFF.

Tip

One way to test whether some form of memory conflict is causing a problem is to force the expanded memory manager built into Windows to stop using these memory addresses. You do this by forcing Windows not to use these blocks. To do so, take the following steps:

STEPS

Excluding Windows from Using UMBs

Step 1.   Shut down and restart Windows.

Step 2.   At the Starting Windows 95 message on your screen, press F8 and then choose to boot to the command prompt.

Excluding Windows from Using UMBs

Step 3.   Type **Win /d:x** to start Windows 95 in the debug mode and
exclude it from using the UMBs.

If you have remarked out the line in your Config.sys that refers to
Emm386.exe (if such a line exists) and are running Windows 95 in this debug
mode, nothing should be loaded into the upper memory area. If the problem
goes away, you know that there was a memory conflict.

Start finding out where the conflict was by unremarking the line in
Config.sys containing Emm386.exe. If it contains a *memory-include* parameter, such as i=b000-b7ff, erase it. Restart Windows in debug mode and see if
the problem is still absent. If it is, you know that Windows is causing the
problem by loading some of itself into an area in upper memory that is used
by a conflicting card.

Now you need to find out just what memory addresses are in conflict. To do
so, take the following steps:

STEPS

Excluding Memory

Step 1.   You use the System.ini file to exclude memory from use by
Windows 95. This may seem old-fashioned now that we have the
Registry and a way to reserve memory using the Device Manager,
but trust us, it is easier this way.

Step 2.   Double-click the Sysedit icon. You'll find it in \Windows\System
if you haven't already put a shortcut to it on your Desktop or in
the System Tools submenu of the Start menu (Start, Programs,
Accessories, System Tools).

Step 3.   Add the following lines to the [386Enh] section of System.ini:

```
EMMExclude=A000-AFF

EMMExclude=B000-B7FF

EMMExclude=B800-BFFF

EMMExclude=C000-C3FF

EMMExclude=C400-C7FF

EMMExclude=C800-CBFF

EMMExclude=CC00-CFFF

EMMExclude=D000-D3FF
```

(continued)

STEPS *(continued)*

Excluding Memory

Step 4.   Save System.ini, shut down, and restart Windows.

If the problem goes away when you restart Windows with these excluded memory addresses, a memory conflict was definitely present in the first half of the upper memory. Only one or two of the reserved address ranges are actually needed to resolve the problem, however — not all of them are needed.

Step 5.   If the problem didn't go away, comment out the lines listed in step 3 (by placing a semicolon in front of EMMExclude) and add these lines.

```
EMMExclude=D400-D7FF

EMMExclude=D800-DBFF

EMMExclude=DC00-DFFF

EMMExclude=E000-E3FF

EMMExclude=E400-E7FF

EMMExclude=E800-EBFF

EMMExclude=EC00-EFFF
```

Shut down and restart Windows.

Step 6.   To determine which ranges are necessary, comment out the bottom half of the lines (by placing a semicolon in front of EMMExclude) and restart Windows. If the problem recurs, comment out only the bottom *two* lines, and so on. By this method, you should be able to isolate the culprit within only about four trials (if just one line is at fault). This is faster than trying the lines one at a time.

Using Mem to Determine Available Memory

If you type **Mem /c/p** within a Windows DOS session, you see something like Table 18-2:

Table 18-2			Results Produced by Mem			
Modules using memory below 1MB:						
Name	**Total**		**Conventional**		**Upper Memory**	
SYSTEM	34,109	(33K)	9,101	(9K)	25,008	(24K)
	1,920	(2K)	1,600	(2K)	320	(0K)
HIMEM	1,120	(1K)	1,120	(1K)	0	(0K)
EMM386	3,200	(3K)	3,200	(3K)	0	(0K)
WIN	2,048	(2K)	2,048	(2K)	0	(0K)
vmm32	79,392	(78K)	3,536	(3K)	75,856	(74K)
COMMAND	7,504	(7K)	7,504	(7K)	0	(0K)
COMMAND	10,016	(10K)	0	(0K)	10,016	(10K)
DRVSPACE	39,472	(39K)	0	(0K)	39,472	(39K)
IFSHLP	2,816	(3K)	0	(0K)	2,816	(3K)
SETVER	688	(1K)	0	(0K)	688	(1K)
DOSKEY	4,448	(4K)	0	(0K)	4,448	(4K)
Free	627,008	(612K)	627,008	(612K)	0	(0K)

Memory Summary:			
Type of Memory	**Total**	**Used**	**Free**
Conventional	655,360	28,352	627,008
Upper	158,624	158,624	0
Reserved	393,216	393,216	0
Extended (XMS)	15,570,016	?	16,744,448
Total memory	16,777,216	?	17,371,456
Total under 1 MB	813,984	186,976	627,008
Largest executable program size	626,976	(612K)	
Largest free upper memory block	0	(0K)	
MS-DOS is resident in the high memory area			

Mem tells you which DOS programs, 16-bit drivers, or TSRs are loaded in memory, how big they are, and where in memory they are loaded (conventional or UMBs). You can see how much conventional memory is available, the size set aside for UMBs, and how much is used. Reserved memory is the memory between 640K and 1024K (384 * 1024 bytes).

This report contains some errors because Mem was run inside a Windows DOS session and not before Windows 95 started. The question mark in the column/row for used extended memory clues you into the fact that free extended and total free memory are incorrectly calculated.

You can also run Mem before Windows 95 starts or in MS-DOS mode. Mem has a number of command line parameters that alter its behavior as follows:

```
MEM [/CLASSIFY | /DEBUG | /FREE | /MODULE modulename] [/PAGE]
```

/CLASSIFY or /C	Classifies programs by memory usage. Lists the size of programs, provides a summary of memory in use, and lists largest memory block available.
/DEBUG or /D	Displays status of all modules in memory, internal drivers, and other information.
/FREE or /F	Displays information about the amount of free memory left in both conventional and upper memory.
/MODULE or /M	Displays a detailed listing of a module's memory use. This option must be followed by the name of a module, optionally separated from /M by a colon.
/PAGE or /P	Pauses after each screenful of information.

Mem is invaluable for determining how well you are doing in placing 16-bit drivers and DOS TSRs into UMBs.

Using MSD to Examine Memory Configuration

Another way to see what programs are loaded into UMBs is to start your PC and press F8 at the Starting Windows 95 message, and then choose menu item 5, Start only the Command Prompt. At the DOS prompt, type **MSD**. This starts the Microsoft Diagnostic program.

The MSD utility provides screens that show the use of upper memory and any devices that are loaded there. Microsoft uses this utility when people call for technical support. Strangely, MSD can provide unreliable information when used in a DOS session under Windows, so run it from a plain DOS prompt instead.

Undocumented

MSD isn't automatically installed by Windows 95 Setup. You'll find it on the Windows 95 source CD-ROM in the Other folder.

Optimizing UMB Usage With MemMaker

You can use MemMaker to place as many 16-bit drivers and DOS TSRs as possible into the UMBs. MemMaker sort of automatically reconfigures Config.sys and Autoexec.bat to place device drivers in upper memory. You can do this yourself by changing Device= to Devicehigh= in your Config.sys, and putting Loadhigh (or LH) in front of any DOS TSRs in Autoexec.bat.

MemMaker won't move the lines around in your files that make the calls to your DOS TSRs and 16-bit device drivers. You can put the largest ones first, and that should help get more of these things into upper memory.

To run MemMaker, edit Msdos.sys and add or change a line so the [options] section reads:

```
BootGUI=0
```

This allows you to keep booting to the DOS prompt automatically during the multiple booting MemMaker process instead of going into Windows 95. You can change this back after you're done.

You'll find MemMaker on the Windows 95 source CD-ROM in the Other\Oldmsdos folder.

Third-Party Expanded/UMB Memory Managers

You can use a third-party expanded/UMB memory manager to get additional space in the upper memory area. Memory managers like QEMM, 386 to the Max, and NetRoom are more aggressive than Emm386.exe in going after this address space.

Windows 95 cuts down on the need to be so aggressive by introducing 32-bit protected-mode drivers that aren't loaded into UMB and don't take up conventional memory. You will need to be extra aggressive only if you have to load 16-bit drivers and large DOS programs.

Managing Memory with Multiple Config.sys Configurations

You can also use a Config.sys that is set up for multiple configurations to allow for different memory setups. Much of the reason for doing this is wiped out by MS-DOS mode and the ability to tailor each private Config.sys and Autoexec.bat file in this mode for each DOS application. See Chapter 17 for details.

Multiple configurations in Config.sys let you set different startup parameters for any number of menu options. You can choose whether to have expanded memory available to DOS programs, whether to load anything high or not, and whether to be on a network or not.

Turn to Chapter 6 for details on how to create a multiconfiguration Config.sys file.

Windows 95 and DOS Games

So let's finally get to the real point of this chapter. How can your get your games to work under Windows 95?

Most games written for PCs are written for DOS. This is because doing so gives the game's author access to the hardware and therefore the best chance at getting the best performance. Since the games market is highly competitive and very technically sophisticated (compared to the business market), game authors really have to know how to deal with the hardware.

Until Microsoft introduced WinG and a games software development kit, games that relied on Windows suffered. Game makers didn't care if their programs even worked with Windows in Windows DOS sessions. They figured that their clients would just exit Windows (or not even start it) to run the game. DOS games often have memory managers that conflict with the Windows memory-management specification.

Microsoft is of course very interested in having games work in Windows and with Windows. They are embarrassed that this "technical" part of the market considers Microsoft and Windows a stumbling block to performance.

Consequently, Microsoft programmers have worked hard to make sure that Windows 95 can run DOS games in Windows DOS sessions. That doesn't mean they have always succeeded. Of course, the fact that it is more difficult to get to DOS in Windows 95 than it was in Windows 3.*x* makes Microsoft committed to getting DOS games to work in Windows DOS sessions.

Try your DOS games first in a Windows DOS session. You may need to provide expanded memory for some games (such as Xwing) or make other changes to the Windows DOS session properties. If they don't work, try the DOS games in MS-DOS mode with their own Config.sys and Autoexec.bat files.

If that doesn't work, you can always start the DOS game before Windows starts. See Chapter 17 for more details.

Summary

When we combined previous versions of Windows with existing DOS programs, we learned to be very careful about how we configure memory. In a lot of cases it was way too difficult.

▶ Windows 95 makes memory management a lot easier by reducing the drain on conventional memory.

▶ We show you how to see if you are suffering from afflictions that could be caused by memory problems.

▶ We give you a lot of ways (and show you the quick and dirty ways) to give your DOS programs more conventional memory.

▶ We also show you how to get more upper memory so you can get more conventional memory.

Part IV

Plug and Play

Chapter 19

Plug and Play — Device Management

In This Chapter

Windows 95 "captures" your PC hardware. Microsoft provides a raft of 32-bit drivers for almost everything under the sun. We discuss:

▶ What's so great about plug and play?

▶ How Windows 95 works with existing hardware and new plug and play devices

▶ Automatic hardware detection during and after setup

▶ Adding new hardware drivers

▶ Untangling resource conflicts

▶ Setting up multiple hardware configurations (profiles)

▶ Why CD-ROMs and sound cards mess with your parallel ports

So What's All the Hoopla?

Microsoft has made a very big deal about plug and play. A consortium of hardware manufacturers and software developers have agreed to a standard that allows easier installation and tracking of PC hardware independent of the operating system. Windows 95 is the first commercial manifestation of an operating system that completely embraces this standard.

Unlike the Apple Macintosh, nobody (not even Microsoft) owns the PC hardware and software standards. Therefore, a great deal of cooperation is required among companies that would like nothing better than to grind each other into the ground to arrive at standards that offer great benefits to the customer.

Everyone knows it is relatively difficult to set up PC hardware (and accompanying hardware drivers), especially when your computer is filled with cards from different manufacturers. The major difficulties are:

■ Assigning hardware interrupts, of which there are only 16 — and some of these are used by the basic computer hardware

■ Assigning non-conflicting I/O addresses so each add-on card can have its own unique address

- Assigning Direct Memory Access (DMA) channels (in non-PCI bus cards) so there is no conflict

- Installing PC Cards (formerly known as PCMCIA cards) that adhere to different standards

- Setting monitor parameters to automatically work with your video card

- Making sure there are no memory blocks used (especially by video and network cards) that conflict with memory assignments, particularly in upper memory

- Recognizing and highlighting conflicts so they can be resolved

- Gracefully handling multiple hardware configurations for one computer; for example, docking stations with portables

- Recognizing when the hardware configuration changes, so that the operating system and Windows 95-aware application software can take the appropriate action

Microsoft realized that many of its support calls had to do with hardware conflicts of the first three types. Hardware manufacturers realized that it was more difficult to sell add-on devices (in particular multimedia kits) when they were so difficult to install.

The first order of business for plug and play was to make it easier to install hardware and resolve any conflicts with the hardware interrupts, the I/O address, the memory ranges used, and the DMA channel used, if any. Windows 95 solves most of these problems automatically and gives you the tools to solve the rest.

32-bit Drivers

Haven't we talked about this elsewhere? Windows 95 is a 32-bit operating system (for the most part) and one big part of that is its 32-bit drivers. All the new device drivers get loaded into extended memory and don't take up conventional or upper memory.

Not only are they 32-bit, but they have lots of new features, features that come about because they have more room to wiggle in extended memory. The Device Manager and the Add New Hardware Wizard install these new drivers for the hardware that they detect. When you run Windows 95 Setup, it casts aside 16-bit drivers for the new 32-bit drivers.

16-bit Drivers

If you need to run 16-bit drivers, you're going to have to use the older installation routines that come from the manufacturers. Only in relatively rare circumstances, however, will you need to run these drivers.

Undocumented

There is a list, Ios.ini, in your Windows 95 folder that contains the names of the hardware driver files that can be (and are) *safely* replaced by 32-bit drivers in Windows 95. *Safe* just means that the 32-bit driver implements at least all of the functionality of the 16-bit driver. If you find that your real-mode driver is on the list but provides functionality missing from the replacement 32-bit driver, you can delete it from the list and reinstall the driver (unremark the call to it in Config.sys).

If you have 16-bit drivers that aren't replaced, you'll find them listed in the Device Manager with a yellow exclamation mark. You can remark out the drivers in Config.sys and Autoexec.bat, install more generic drivers using the Add New Hardware Wizard (details later in this chapter), and reboot your computer.

Plug and Play BIOS and Devices

You may have a computer that doesn't have a plug and play BIOS and has no plug and play cards. That's fine. Windows 95 does its best to search for and identify the hardware you have installed and then install the appropriate drivers.

You may have a computer without a plug and play BIOS, but with some plug and play devices. That's fine also. The plug and play devices give Windows 95 a little more flexibility in configuring the hardware resource usage so there are no conflicts among the devices.

You may have a computer with a plug and play BIOS *and* plug and play cards. Great! Windows 95 can work with the plug and play BIOS to configure your computer automatically so there are no conflicts among hardware devices.

Hardware Detection

Windows 95 Setup detects installed hardware and drivers for a broad range of pre-plug and play hardware as well as the new stuff.

Undocumented

The installation files contain a database of existing hardware and drivers. This database is stored in specific *inf* files and coordinated by the Msdet.inf file. You will find these files in the \Windows\Inf folder. (If you don't see the Inf folder, choose View, Options in the Explorer, and mark Show all files in the View tab.) The detection routines are non-invasive and do their best to determine just what you've installed over the years from one of a zillion different manufacturers.

Undocumented

Hardware detection won't be able to determine what monitor you have unless it is plug and play compatible, so you'll need to pick your monitor from a list.

It may register your modem as generic, so if you know what modem you have, you should go back later and specify that modem. Knowing the right modem assures you that Windows 95-aware (TAPI compliant) communications software will use the correct initialization string.

Undocumented

You'll find references to your hardware under the HKEY_LOCAL_MACHINE key, specifically under the Enum (enumeration) subkey. It's easy to use the Registry editor to view the values stored there.

When you start Windows 95, a dynamic hardware tree is created based on information in the Registry. This tree is stored in RAM, and you can view it using the Registry editor under the HKEY_DYN_DATA key and the Config Manager\Enum subkeys. Looking at this data is not particularly enlightening, as you will quickly see for yourself. It consists of unique keys that enumerate the installed hardware and its current status.

The hardware tree in RAM is updated every time the hardware configuration changes. Microsoft's favorite example is that the tree updates when you plug your portable into a docking station. We assume they have a lot of these over at Microsoft's Redmond campus.

It is a much better idea to use the Device Manager to manage your hardware configuration. The Device Manager's user interface is a lot more informative and understandable. You should use the Registry editor only if the Device Manager is not working for you and you understand the effect of the changes that you are making.

Adding New Hardware Drivers

In a perfect world, you would physically install your new device, such as a printer, in your computer (or perhaps plug it into a port). The drivers for that device would be automatically installed and the device activated. If you install a plug and play compliant device, this *almost* happens.

You may need to turn off the computer first so you don't inadvertently cause any electrical damage when you install a card in a slot (although you can plug in PC Cards without turning off your computer). After you turn your computer back on, you may be asked for a diskette or CD-ROM from the device manufacturer that contains the drivers needed to use the device. If the drivers for that device were shipped with Windows 95, you will be asked to insert a Windows 95 diskette or the Windows 95 CD-ROM. After Windows 95 installs the new drivers, you'll be able to use your new device.

If the device is pre-plug and play, you may need to double-click the Add New Hardware icon in the Control Panel (as shown in Figure 19-1) to inform Windows 95 that it needs to check for the new hardware and add a new driver. You can have the Wizard automatically detect your installed hardware (and thereby find the device that you just installed). Alternately, you can direct the Wizard to install a specific driver by providing it with a manufacturer and model designation or pointing it toward an installation diskette from the manufacturer.

Figure 19-1: The Add New Hardware Wizard. It invokes the hardware detection routines to find your pre-plug and play device. If you know what driver you want installed, you can pick the manufacturer and model yourself.

Getting the Settings Right

Windows 95 can resolve potential conflicts between plug and play devices, setting their IRQ, I/O, memory address, and DMA channel requirements so all these devices can cooperate. It needs your help to do this for pre-plug and play devices (which Microsoft insists on calling *legacy* devices).

We know this is not how plug and play is supposed to work in a plug and play operating system, but Windows 95 has to encompass the past. Pre-plug and play cards and devices can't automatically be configured. You may need to move some jumpers or run a hardware-specific DOS-based configuration program that changes the settings on a given card. You can do this before running the Add New Hardware Wizard or after you determine the conflicts.

Secret

After the Add New Hardware Wizard finds your hardware, or after you direct it to install a driver for a specific device, a dialog box detailing the settings specified for that device appears (see Figure 19-2). The driver settings have been configured by the Wizard to not conflict with any existing settings for other installed hardware. *But these settings may have nothing whatsoever to do with the actual settings or available settings for your device.*

You cannot change these driver settings at this time, even if you know they don't match the actual device settings. The Wizard did not interrogate your device to see what settings you actually have or what settings are possible (unless it's a plug and play device). Understand that the Wizard is not so smart at the moment. You are going to have to provide the smarts to get this process completed.

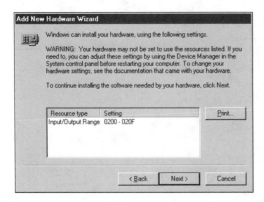

Figure 19-2: The Add New Hardware Wizard's resource settings dialog box. The Wizard has determined the settings that it would like to see you set your device to. You may not be able to do this, given the limitations of your device. These settings will not conflict with any other existing hardware that you have installed. Don't try to change them just yet.

Secret

Continue with the Add New Hardware Wizard, clicking the Finish button in the last dialog box. The drivers for the new device are now installed. You will find them in the Device Manager, as described later in this chapter, if you care to look for them. *Don't use the Device Manager to change the settings at this time, because it will do no good.* We'll get to that in a minute.

You can now reconfigure your device to match the driver settings just assigned to it, change your device to other settings that don't conflict with the driver settings for other hardware, or leave your device settings as they are and change the driver settings for your device in the Device Manager. The actual settings for your device might be determined by jumpers or by device settings stored in ROM on the device. If you need to make changes on your device, you might need to turn off the computer to set jumpers or run a DOS application that allows you to change the device ROM settings.

You can use the Device Manager, as described in the next section, to make sure that the actual settings for your device do not conflict with existing hardware drivers. If they do, you are going to have to change them. Remember, we are talking about the *actual* device settings, not the driver settings that the Add New Hardware Wizard just assigned to your device, which it *took from those available*.

If you need to change ROM settings on the device, open a DOS window and run the device-specific configuration routines on the manufacturer's diskette now. Change the settings on your device so there is no conflict with existing hardware drivers. When you are done, you are ready to shut down Windows 95.

If you need to change jumpers on a device, shut down Windows 95 and turn off your computer. If you change jumpers, be sure the new device settings don't conflict with existing hardware drivers. For details, see the next section, *The Device Manager*. Restart your computer after you have made the changes.

Your device may have a limited range of choices allowed for the various resource settings. Limiting the number of IRQs available to a device is one way that a manufacturer can reduce its price, but this practice causes high user dissatisfaction when conflicts become irresolvable. Do your best to move device resource usage around to avoid conflicts, and keep in mind that you may not be successful. You might have to purchase an improved device, hopefully plug and play enabled.

To get the actual device settings and the driver settings as recorded in the Registry in sync, you need to use the Device Manager. Using the Device Manager now — and not before — you will be able to make changes in the resource settings for your new device driver that match the device's actual settings. After you make these changes, you may need to restart your computer once again to get the new values to take hold.

The Device Manager

The Windows 95 Control Panel is filled with icons that let you manage your computer's hardware and drivers. We outline what some of these icons do in Chapter 16, and the rest in the many hardware-specific chapters in this book. If you have a question about a specific piece of hardware, turn to the chapter that focuses on that hardware.

The Device Manager, which you access through the System icon in the Control Panel, provides a general view of all hardware installed on your computer. Sometimes the Device Manager and the hardware-specific icons overlap in functionality, and sometimes you can do something only in one and not the other.

The Device Manager is a powerful tool. Nothing like this has been available before, even from third-party software developers that created Windows-specific diagnostic tools. The Device Manager supersedes MSD (the Microsoft Diagnostic tool) that came with Windows 3.x but was never documented by Microsoft. It is much easier to use and much more powerful than MSD.

To get to the Device Manager, take the following steps:

STEPS
Starting the Device Manager

Step 1. Click the Start button, point to Settings, and then click Control Panel.

Step 2. Double-click the System icon in the Control Panel, and click the Device Manager tab in the System Properties dialog box. The Device Manager is shown in Figure 19-3.

(continued)

STEPS *(continued)*

Starting the Device Manager

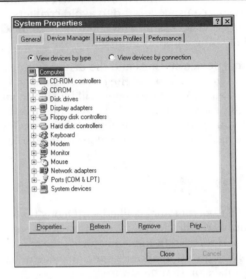

Figure 19-3: The Device Manager. To print your system configuration, highlight Computer and click Print. To view the installed devices of a particular type, click the plus sign next to the type (or double-click it). To view the properties of a specific device, double-click the device.

Devices are listed in the Device Manager. Click the plus sign to the left of a device type to see the installed devices. Double-click a particular device name to display its properties sheets. You can also highlight a device and click the Properties button.

If you mark the View devices by connection option button, the devices are displayed hierarchically by their hardware connection to the mother board.

To get your computer to re-identify the plug and play devices on your computer, click the Refresh button. This button also tells your computer about any SCSI devices that have been newly plugged in.

If there is a yellow exclamation mark over a device name, it means that there is a problem with the device driver. This mostly likely indicates a resource conflict. You may need to set different jumper settings on a non-plug and play device. Use the Device Manager to track down these conflicts.

If you have to hunt for the source of a problem, highlight the Computer icon in the Device Manager, and then click the Properties button. In the View Resources tab of the Computer Properties dialog box, successively click the option buttons to check for interrupt, I/O, memory, and DMA channel conflicts.

The yellow exclamation mark may also indicate a missing device that was previously installed, or a removable device (such as a Zip drive). You can remove the device permanently (until you reinstall it) by highlighting the device and clicking the Remove button.

If there is a red X over your device, the Device Manager is telling you that this device isn't functioning. You may need to install 32-bit drivers, or it may be working with 16-bit drivers and you'll have to just leave it that way.

Click the Print button to generate a report of the devices in the computer. You can specify a summary report, a report on a specific device, or a report for all the devices. The report lists your devices, their properties, and the resources they use. You can print any of these reports to a text file. Be sure to first install the Generic/Text Only printer driver (using the Printers icon in the Control Panel) and then assign it port FILE.

IRQs, I/O, memory addresses, DMA channels

If you double-click Computer in the Device Manager (or highlight it and click the Properties button), you get a wonderfully powerful dialog box that shows all the hardware interrupt request settings for your computer, (see Figure 19-4). You now know just what hardware is using just what interrupt. You'll see what interrupts (between 0 and 15) are available.

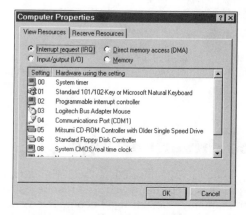

Figure 19-4: The View Resources tab of the Computer Properties dialog box. You can't change anything here, but you do get a consolidated view of interrupt usage.

You can view other resources by clicking the option buttons at the top of the View Resources tab. These buttons let you view consolidated I/O, memory addresses, and DMA channel usage — very helpful.

The Reserve Resources tab lets you set your resources so that Windows 95 won't assign them to a plug and play device.

Specific device drivers

The device drivers installed in your computer are by default displayed by type in the Device Manager. Clicking the plus sign next to a device type displays the device drivers installed. Double-clicking a device driver's name displays its properties sheets, as shown in Figure 19-5.

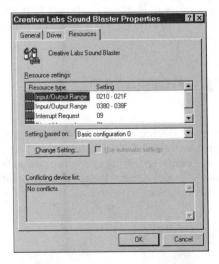

Undocumented

Figure 19-5: The Resources tab of the Properties dialog box for the Creative Labs Sound Blaster. (These values are actually incorrect so don't use them.) You can change them in the Device Manager.

Changing device driver settings

If you have plug and play devices, you should usually let the hardware detection routines in Windows 95 determine what the resources settings should be. If you set them manually, the settings become fixed and Windows 95 can't adjust them to avoid conflicts. You can, however, change the resource settings for plug and play as well as non-plug and play devices.

To change the resources assigned by Windows 95 to a device to match the actual settings for that device and to avoid any conflicts with other devices, take the following steps. If your device driver settings don't match the device's settings, the device driver entry in the Device Manager will have a yellow exclamation sign on it.

STEPS

Changing a Device's Resource Settings

Step 1. Double-click the specific device in the Device Manager.

Step 2. Click the Resources tab in the Properties dialog box for the device.

Step 3. Double-click a resource type in the Resource settings field (or highlight a resource and click the Change Setting button). If the Use automatic settings box is marked, you'll need to clear it first.

   If this resource can be changed, you'll see a dialog box to let you adjust its settings (see Figure 19-6). Use the spin arrows in the Value field to change the values of the resource requested.

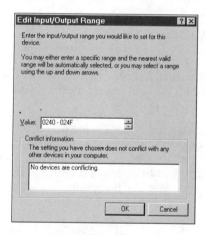

Figure 19-6: The Edit Input/Output Range dialog box. This dialog box is specific to changing an I/O resource. Other resources display different dialog boxes.

   Your device driver may allow different basic configurations, which in turn allow for different resource values and the ability to change some resources in one configuration but not in another. In the Resources tab, display the Setting based on drop-down list to see if there are other configurations. If there are, you can try them to see what difference this makes in allowable resource values.

Step 4. Click OK in the resource settings dialog box to accept the changes that you have made. Click OK again in the Properties dialog box to accept all the changes and close this properties sheet.

Step 5. You may be asked to restart your computer to allow the new resource settings to take effect.

Throughout this process, be sure you haven't introduced any new resource use conflicts. If you printed a copy of the system summary, you will have a ready reference on resource use. Also, the Device Manager will track conflicts for you and warn you when you have created them.

If you have changed settings in the driver for a non-plug and play device, you need to make the same changes to the hardware itself. You may now need to go back and either change the jumpers on the device to match the settings that you just made, or if the hardware device is software configurable, run the manufacturer's software to reconfigure the hardware. This may require opening a DOS window to run the hardware configuration software.

Remember, the process detailed above just changes the device driver settings, and not the actual hardware itself (if it is not plug and play).

Updating device drivers

You can install new device drivers over existing ones for some devices through the Device Manager. You may want to do this when you get a new driver from your hardware manufacturer, perhaps one you have downloaded from a bulletin board.

You could, of course, install the new device driver by using the Add New Hardware Wizard. However, this Wizard is primarily designed to search for new hardware and install the corresponding driver. If you haven't installed new hardware and just want to update a driver, the Device Manager provides a semantically friendlier starting point.

STEPS

Installing an Updated Device Driver

Step 1. Double-click the specific device in the Device Manager.

Step 2. Click the Driver tab in the Properties dialog box for the device, if it has one. If there is no Driver tab, you can't update the driver.

Step 3. Click the Change Driver button to display the Select Device dialog box. You can select from among the drivers that came with Windows 95, or you can click the Have Disk button if you have a new driver on a diskette, a CD-ROM, or your hard drive.

Step 4. Click OK in the Select Device dialog box to accept the new device driver. Click OK in the Driver tab of the Properties dialog box to accept the changes.

Step 5. Restart your computer to allow the new driver to take effect.

Resolving resource conflicts the easy way

There is another way to resolve resource conflicts. Windows 95 help contains a Hardware Conflict Troubleshooter. It gives you a little background on resource conflicts and then promptly leads you to the exact same places that we just covered. It's kind of cute, though.

STEPS

Starting the Hardware Conflict Troubleshooter

Step 1. Click the Start button, and then click Help.

Step 2. Click the Contents tab, and then double-click Troubleshooting.

Step 3. Double-click "If you have a hardware conflict."

Step 4. Follow the suggestions and shortcuts to the Device Manager.

Hardware Profiles

We have *hardware profiles* for different hardware configurations on one computer, *user profiles* for different users on the same computer, and *Windows Messaging profiles* for different mail services. Windows 95 presents us with quite a prolific world.

You don't need hardware profiles if you have a plug and play computer with plug and play devices. Windows 95 can automatically load the hardware drivers that it needs based on the hardware it detects and stores in the hardware tree in RAM. Change the configuration (by pulling the portable from the docking station, for example), and Windows 95 reconfigures itself dynamically.

The static hardware profiles are a bit of a kludge. A menu comes up in DOS full-screen text mode before the Windows 95 Desktop appears and asks you to choose your current configuration.

Tip

You have to set up the hardware profiles manually. You install all the drivers for all the hardware configurations for all the profiles, and then assign the proper set of drivers to each profile. The hardware doesn't have to be installed at the time that you install the drivers. You can just install the drivers, and then make any necessary changes later if there is a difference between the device settings and the resource settings that you choose.

To create multiple hardware configurations, take the following steps:

How you change your computer's BIOS settings varies between BIOS manufacturers. If your portable has an AMI BIOS, press the Delete key when prompted during bootup to display the BIOS setup screen. Choose Power Management Setup, then Primary Display, and then press Ctrl+PgUp to scroll through the display options. After you've chosen CRT, press Esc, press F10, and answer Yes.

After you've changed your BIOS settings, you need to create two Windows 95 hardware profiles. Unless you have a plug and play external monitor and plug and play video chips in the portable, the Windows 95 hardware detection routines won't be able to tell that you have two displays, so you're going to have to force the issue.

STEPS

Creating Two Windows 95 Hardware Profiles for Two Monitors

Step 1. Click the Start button, Settings, then Control Panel. Double-click the System icon, and then click the Hardware Profiles tab.

Step 2. Your original hardware profile should be highlighted. Click the Copy button to make a copy of it.

Step 3. Enter a new name for the new profile — perhaps "External Monitor (800x600)" if the original profile has the LCD screen as the display. (If the original profile has the external monitor as its display, name the new profile "LCD Screen (640x480).")

Step 4. Highlight the original profile and click the Rename button to rename the original profile, perhaps to "LCD Screen (640x480)."

Step 5. Click the Device Manager tab. Click the plus sign next to the Monitor icon and double-click the attached icon for your current display. At the bottom of the Properties dialog box, clear the check box for the hardware profile that doesn't apply for that display. For example, if your current display is an external monitor, clear the check box for the "LCD Screen (640x480)" profile. Click the OK button, and then click OK again.

Step 6. Shut down Windows 95 normally. Restart Windows 95. You will be given the choice between two hardware profiles, as shown here. Choose the new profile.

```
Windows cannot determine what configuration your computer
is in:
Select one of the following:

    1.    External Monitor (800x600)
    2.    LCD Screen (640x480)
    3.    None of the Above

Enter your choice:
```

Creating Two Windows 95 Hardware Profiles for Two Monitors

Step 7.   Right-click the Desktop and choose Properties. Click the Settings tab. Change the color depth (choose it from the Color palette drop-down list), and change the resolution (drag the slider bar in the Desktop area) to match the new display and the new hardware profile.

Step 8.   Click the Change Display Type button, and click the Change button to the right of Monitor Type. (If you don't have a Change Display Type button, click the Advanced Properties button, click the Monitor tab, and click the Change button.) Choose a display that corresponds to your second configuration in the Select Device dialog box. Click OK, click Close, and then click OK again.

Step 9.   Click the Start button, Settings, then Control Panel. Click the Device Manager tab. Click the plus sign next to the Monitor icon and double-click the attached icon for your current display. Clear the check box for the first hardware profile, which doesn't apply for the new display. Click the OK button, and then click OK again.

You have now created two hardware profiles. When you restart your computer, you will be given the choice between them just after the Windows 95 splash screen is displayed and just before Windows 95 starts up.

Just because you have two Windows 95 hardware profiles doesn't mean you've correctly configured your hardware to work with them. Your BIOS has been set to direct the video feed to the external monitor. You need to be able to flexibly override this BIOS setting to direct your internal video hardware to send its signal to the external video port, to the LCD display, or perhaps to both.

Often you can accomplish this with a small DOS utility (or set of utilities) that the portable manufacturer supplies. You can run these utilities in a batch file or in the Autoexec.bat file to switch the video hardware output between displays. You still need to use these utilities to correctly set the video feed to correspond with the hardware profile you choose during bootup.

To do this, you can create multiconfiguration Config.sys and Autoexec.bat files. While Microsoft would prefer that you forget about these files, and in particular forget about their ability to support multiple configurations, it didn't provide strong enough video drivers to make this possible. You still need to use the capability of these files to accomplish your goal of switching somewhat painlessly between displays.

To create multiple configurations for two monitors, take the following steps:

STEPS

Creating Multiple Configurations for Two Monitors

Step 1. Edit your Config.sys file to include the menu items in a configuration menu, as shown here:

```
[menu]
;the two menu items follow
Menuitem=CRT,Display on External Monitor (800x600)
Menuitem=LCD,Display on LCD Screen (640x480)
;next we set which menu item is chosen by default and what
the time delay is
Menudefault=CRT,5
[global]
;we could put some Config.sys entries here
 [CRT]
;we could put in different items for this configuration
here
include=global
[LCD]
include=global
```

Step 2. You can edit this example file to include other Config.sys elements — in the global area, for example.

Step 3. Edit your Autoexec.bat file as shown here to react differently based on the choice that you make in the multiple configuration menu:

```
@echo off
goto %config%
:CRT
rem portable manufacturer's utility for using the external
monitor
c:\util\crt.com
GOTO END
:LCD
rem utility for directing video output to the LCD screen
c:\util\lcd.com
:END
cls
```

Step 4. The Autoexec.bat and Config.sys file edits that we have made will result in the multiple configuration menu shown here:

```
Microsoft Windows 95 Startup menu
=============================
    1.    Display on External Monitor (800x600)
    2.    Display on LCD Screen (640x480)

Enter a Choice: 1        Time Remaining: 05


F5=Safe mode   Shift+F5=Command Prompt
Shift+F8=Step-by-Step  Confirmation [N]
```

Creating Multiple Configurations for Two Monitors

In spite of the heading for this menu, it is not the same as the Windows 95 Startup menu. (You can display that menu before this one appears.) In this menu, Shift+F8 won't work to do a step-by-step startup (even though it's listed), but Shift+F5 will get you to the command prompt.

Step 5. The multiple configuration menu can have a timer. By entering the Menudefault command with a seconds value (as shown in step 1), you can choose which configuration will be chosen by default.

Step 6. After you have created/edited the Autoexec.bat and Config.sys files, restart Windows 95 in the normal fashion.

When Windows 95 restarts, you will first see a menu letting you select your hardware profile, and then you'll see a menu letting you choose between your two configurations. Choosing a hardware profile tells Windows 95 which of the two profiles to use when configuring Windows 95. Choosing between the two configurations tells the hardware which configuration to use. The idea is to choose a profile and a configuration that work together.

You're not done yet. Because you have used a BIOS setting to direct the video output to the external monitor, you may not be able to read the menus when you boot your portable without an external monitor. You can either press a keyboard combination that is particular to your portable (perhaps Ctrl+Alt+.) to switch to the LCD display, or you can enter a choice from the menu without actually seeing the menu (and then press Enter) when your portable stops hitting the hard disk during the bootup process.

When you switch resolutions, the placement of your icons on your Windows 95 Desktop changes. It would be best to be able to save two configurations of icon placement and choose between them depending on your choice of video resolutions. This capability isn't built into Windows 95, but you can use a wonderful little shareware utility that does save your Desktops, EZDesk. You can download a trial version of it from ftp://users.aol.com/EzDesk95/ezdesk17.zip, or get it from the *Windows 95 Secrets* CD-ROM.

When you install EZDesk, it automatically places its shortcut in the Startup folder, but if you'd rather not have the utility start every time you start Windows 95, you can move the shortcut to your Desktop. Make sure you place the shortcut in a place you can get to at either resolution.

We hope that better video drivers for portables will soon make this type of manual configuration unnecessary. Those of you who have entirely plug and play computers don't have to deal with these issues, but if you have older hardware, you may have to contend with things as they are presented here.

Hot swapping and hot docking

A plug and play compatible computer can notify Windows 95 when the connection with a docking station is made or broken. This will trigger a reconfiguration of the hardware tree, which in turn makes Windows 95 aware of the new hardware.

Windows 95-aware applications can respond to messages about hardware changes. Windows 3.*x* programs have no idea what is going on. If you are using a Windows 3.*x* application, you have to save any files you are editing to a remote hard disk before you pull your portable out of the docking station.

Undocumented

You can plug a device into your SCSI controller card (if you have one), and then use the SCSI device (for example, a SCSI-based Zip drive) without having to restart Windows 95. Unfortunately Windows 95 doesn't automatically check that you've installed a new device. You need to give it a hint. To do this, open the Device Manager (double-click the System icon in the Control Panel and click the Device Manager tab), choose the View devices by connection option button, highlight Computer, and click the Refresh button.

Look for the new device by opening up the branches in the Device Manager and looking for your SCSI host adapter. Check to see if the new device is connected to it.

Autorun

Windows 95 can automatically start CD-ROMs and audio CDs when you insert them into your CD-ROM player. In order for a CD-ROM to start automatically, it needs to have a file named Autorun.inf in its root directory.

You can turn off Autorun for audio CDs, CD-ROMs, or both, and the easiest way to do so is to use TweakUI (download the latest version from Microsoft's web site). The option to disable Autorun is in the Paranoia tab.

Before this capability was put into TweakUI, the most common way to turn off Autorun was to disable the Auto insert notification in the CD-ROM settings. Autorun uses the Auto insert notification message to determine whether to run or not. Without the message, Autorun doesn't get to make this decision, so if you want to use the TweakUI method, you'll need to turn on Auto insert notification.

If you don't have TweakUI, you can turn off Autorun in the Device Manager. Highlight your CD-ROM drive, click the Properties button, click the Settings tab, and then clear the Auto insert notification check box.

Sound Cards, CD-ROMs, and LPT Ports

Secret

Windows 95 doesn't flag interrupt conflict between devices such as sound cards and CD-ROMs and the LPT1 and LPT2 ports. LPT1 and LPT2 use Interrupts 7 and 5 respectively. Many sound cards and CD-ROMs are also set by default to use these very same interrupts. In spite of this conflict, the Device Manager doesn't inform us that it exists.

The Device Manager is silent on this conflict because printers connected to these parallel ports really don't use these interrupts. In some ways they are up for grabs.

The problem is that Direct Cable Connection *does* use these interrupts when it is configured to use a parallel cable. DCC is at its fastest when it uses the parallel ports, and it will slow by a factor of three if it finds a sound card or CD-ROM drive using these interrupts. The only way you notice this is by testing the speed of communication across these ports.

Detlog.txt, Setuplog.txt, and Ios.log

Undocumented

If you are using any 16-bit drivers, you have three files — the first two are in your root directory and the third is in your Windows 95 folder — that can give you another look at your hardware. Detlog.txt is a record of the hardware detection process. Setuplog.txt details what files were installed. Ios.log tracks your real-mode drivers.

You can simply read these files with Notepad to get a little added insight into your configuration.

If you inadvertently erase a file that is crucial to the proper running of Windows 95, you can rerun Windows 95 Setup to verify files and install only those that are missing. If you do this, Windows 95 reviews Setuplog.txt during the setup process to see what you originally installed.

Summary

Microsoft has made a concerted effort to bring a new level of standardization to the PC world. By providing an extensive list of 32-bit device drivers and giving manufacturers a new model for creating new ones, it has improved the stability of Windows 95.

▶ Windows 95 deals with both existing and plug and play hardware, providing a way to track it all.

▶ Hardware detection routines built into Windows 95 do a robust job of matching your hardware to Windows 95 needs.

▶ We show you how to add new hardware drivers to match your devices.

- ▶ The major benefit of plug and play is the automatic resolution of hardware conflicts. It isn't automatic with non-plug and play hardware, but it is easier.
- ▶ If you have multiple hardware configurations, you can direct Windows 95 to the current configuration.
- ▶ You will likely find a conflict between your sound card and CD-ROM driver and your parallel ports.

Chapter 20

Fonts

In This Chapter

We examine how text is displayed on the screen and printed on the printer. We show:

- ▶ The differences between screen fonts, printer fonts, TrueType fonts, and PostScript fonts
- ▶ How to view, install, and uninstall fonts using the new Windows 95 font installer
- ▶ The essentials of a bitmapped font
- ▶ The advantages of scaleable fonts such as TrueType
- ▶ How to set the magnification factor for Windows 95 and what it does to your fonts
- ▶ What screen fonts are used for and why
- ▶ Why TrueType fonts are so popular
- ▶ Why PostScript fonts continue to be used by design professionals

What Are Fonts?

Text is displayed on your screen or printer through the medium of typefaces or fonts. The characters look different depending on which font or typeface you use to display the text.

A *font* is a set of character shapes of a given size, weight, style, and design. For example, Courier 12-point regular or Times New Roman 12-point bold are different fonts. A *type family* or *typeface* is a family of fonts of a similar design with different sizes and weights, including italic, bold, condensed, and expanded versions of the same design. In Windows terminology, *font* is often used to mean a font file or a typeface. Following the Windows convention, we use *font* in this book to mean font or typeface, interchangeably.

Most of the fonts available for Windows 95 use the Windows 3.*x* ANSI character set. Symbol and Wingdings, two TrueType fonts that come with Windows 95, are exceptions. If you want to use unusual characters, you may need to purchase additional fonts that include those characters. If you installed Multilanguage Support, your Arial, Courier New, and Times Roman fonts provide a new 652-character set. You can find more details on character sets in Chapter 21.

Using Fonts in an Application

Windows 95 applications have access to a common Font dialog box. You can see what the font looks like in the Sample area of the dialog box, as shown in Figure 20-1.

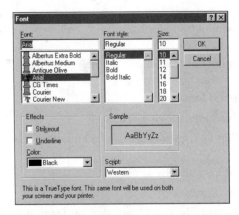

Figure 20-1: The Font dialog box. This dialog box is used by WordPad and can be used by other applications to make it easy to choose a font.

WordPad, a word processing applet that comes with Windows 95, uses the Font dialog box to allow the user to change font style. Choose Format, Font in WordPad to bring it up.

The Script field shown in Figure 20-1 lists the character set used by the font. Western refers to the Windows ANSI character set, DOS/OEM to the IBM PC-8 character set, and Symbol to one of many non-standard character sets. Turkish, Cyrillic, Central European, Greek, Baltic, and so on, refer to other character sets. These designations appear only if you have installed fonts that support these additional characters, which you can do by installing Multilanguage Support while setting up Windows. See Chapter 21.

You can configure the Fonts folder so that applications do not have access to screen or printer fonts. Turn to the *Freedom from screen fonts and printer fonts* section.

Where Are the Fonts Installed?

To see what fonts you currently have installed, click the Start button on the Taskbar, point to Settings, and then click Control Panel. Double-click the Fonts folder icon to display the Fonts folder window. The Fonts folder window shown in Figure 20-2 displays the extended font names and font file icons of the fonts that come with Windows 95.

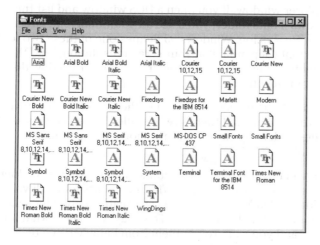

Figure 20-2: The Fonts folder window showing the standard screen (raster) and TrueType fonts that come with Windows 95.

All of the fonts that come with Windows 95 are stored in the \Windows\Fonts folder. To see the Fonts folder, take the following steps:

STEPS

Finding the Fonts Folder

Step 1. Right-click the My Computer icon on the Desktop. Click Explore.

Step 2. Choose View, Options, and make sure that the Show all files option button is selected. Click OK.

Step 3. Click the plus sign to the left of the icon that represents the hard drive that stores your \Windows folder, most likely the C drive.

Step 4. Click the plus sign next to the \Windows folder icon in the Explorer. Click the Fonts folder icon.

STEPS *(continued)*

Installing TrueType Fonts

Step 4. Use the Add Fonts dialog box to browse to find the location of the fonts that you want to install. Select the fonts that you will be installing from the list box and click OK.

If you cleared the Copy fonts to Fonts folder check box, you will notice that only shortcuts are added to the \Windows\Fonts folder.

TrueType fonts and font packs that worked with Windows 3.*x* will also work with Windows 95. The font installers that worked with Windows 3.*x* installed their TrueType fonts in the \Windows\System folder. You can use the above steps to move fonts from the \Windows\System folder to the \Windows\Fonts folder.

Tip

You can install fonts from TrueType font packs using the Windows 95 font installer and ignore the Windows 3.*x* font installers that come with these fonts.

You can also drag and drop fonts to install them. Copy a series of fonts from diskettes or CD-ROMs to your \My System\Fonts folder (or another folder you've created to store your fonts). Right-drag the fonts to \Windows\Fonts in your Explorer. Click Create Shortcut(s) Here. This method installs the fonts and makes them immediately visible to applications that use fonts, while leaving them in your own fonts folder.

Limits on the number of fonts installed

In spite of what it says in the *Microsoft Windows 95 Resource Kit*, there is a limit to the number of TrueType fonts you can install. The total number depends on the length of the font names, but it is about 1,000 fonts — fewer if the average length of the font names is greater than ten characters.

As you install more fonts, your computer takes longer and longer to boot. Font management becomes a problem, and applications accessing the fonts get font drop-down lists that are endless. If you have a large number of installed fonts, you should consider using more sophisticated font-management tools, such as those we make available as shareware on the *Windows 95 Secrets* CD-ROM.

Where are the missing TrueType fonts?

If you upgrade an existing computer to Windows 95, you may notice that some of your TrueType fonts are missing from the Fonts folder, and if you install new TrueType fonts, they may not appear in the Fonts folder. (This can happen if you install too many fonts.) To clear the air and reinstall your fonts, take the following steps.

STEPS

Reinstalling TrueType Fonts

Step 1. Use your Explorer to create a temporary folder, and copy the contents of your Fonts folder to the temporary folder.

Step 2. Start your Registry editor and navigate to HKEY_LOCAL_MACHINE\SOFTWARE\Microsoft \Windows\CurrentVersion

Step 3. You should find a Fonts key in the left pane of the Registry editor. If you do, right-click it and click Delete. Then exit the Registry, and skip to step 5. If you don't find a Fonts key, go to the next step.

Step 4. Highlight the Current Version key in the left pane of your Registry editor. Right-click the right pane and choose New, Key. Type **Fonts**, and press Enter. Exit the Registry.

Step 5. Drag the font files for the fonts that you want installed from the temporary font folder to the \Windows\Fonts folder. Make sure you include the bitmapped fonts (the ones with an A in their font icon) or you may not be able to restart Windows 95 in normal mode.

Remember not to install more than 1,000 fonts. If you want to manage a large number of fonts, we suggest that you use a more sophisticated font handler than the one that comes with Windows 95. You might check out QualiType's Font Handler and Font Sentry at http://www.qualitype.com.

Uninstalling fonts

If you delete a font file that is stored in the \Windows\Fonts folder, it is both uninstalled (the font is no longer available to Windows 95 applications) and deleted (the font file is removed to the Recycle Bin). If you delete a shortcut in the \Windows\Fonts folder for a font file that is stored in another folder, the font is uninstalled but the font file is not deleted.

To uninstall a font by deleting its font file stored in the \Windows\Fonts folder, click the Start button, point to Settings, and click Control Panel. Double-click the Fonts folder icon, right-click the font you want to uninstall, and select Delete from the context menu. If you have another copy of the font file stored in another folder, you can later reinstall it using the Installing TrueType Fonts steps earlier in the chapter.

To uninstall a font by deleting its shortcut in the \Windows\Fonts folder, highlight the font's shortcut and press Delete. Answer Yes to the message asking if you want to uninstall the font. The original font file is not deleted, but the font is no longer available to be used by Windows 95 applications and is not displayed in the \Windows\Fonts folder.

Scaleable fonts are stored in files on your hard disk (or in your printer's ROM) as descriptions of each character. This description includes an outline of the font as well as *rules* (known as *hints*) used to display the font. When scaleable fonts are displayed on the screen (or printed on paper) they are rendered by a font-rendering algorithm that takes this description and turns it into dots. In other words, they are *rasterized.* Your TrueType fonts are scaleable fonts. An example of a scaleable font is Times New Roman, a TrueType font created by Monotype, licensed by Microsoft, and included with Windows 95.

Scaleable fonts have a number of advantages over bitmapped fonts.

■ Scaleable fonts can be displayed over a wider range of point sizes and magnifications and still look good. Keeping enough fixed-sized bitmapped fonts (in different sizes) to cover such a wide range would require significantly more hard disk space. Enlarging bitmapped fonts on the fly to display larger font sizes produces jagged fonts, and Windows can't shrink bitmapped fonts to display sizes smaller than the smallest size font stored in a font file.

■ Scaleable fonts can be used for both your screen and printer. You don't need one set of bitmapped screen fonts (in a limited number of sizes) and another set of bitmapped printer fonts in the same sizes. The rasterizer takes advantage of the highest resolution available on your printer.

■ A scaleable font description method provides a standard that font foundries can use for every printer and font size. This considerably reduces the work required to create a font. At the same time, it vastly expands the market because one font can be used on all printers with Windows printer drivers. Fonts become much less expensive. Printer manufacturers can concentrate on producing printers (and printer drivers for Windows) and not on creating fonts (which they aren't very good at anyway).

■ The likelihood that a font will look the same when it prints as it does on your screen greatly increases with scaleable fonts. Both the printer rasterizer and the screen font rasterizer are reading from the same book (using the same font description).

Bitmapped fonts have one advantage over scaleable fonts. Each font is created by hand to look its best on a video monitor (or a particular printer) at a certain resolution (dots per inch, or dpi). A team of human beings has taken the time necessary to make each sized font the best it can be. Compare the examples of TrueType and screen fonts shown later in this chapter.

Tip

If you want to check out the difference in rendering speed between bitmapped and scaleable fonts, launch the Character Map applet (on the Accessories submenu of the Start menu). Go through each character set, one at a time, and look at bitmapped fonts and TrueType fonts. The first time you view a character set that uses a TrueType font, your computer will take a second to render the characters. In contrast, it can render character sets that use bitmapped screen fonts such as MS Sans Serif instantly. After you view character sets the first time, you won't be able to detect a difference in the time it takes to render characters using a TrueType font versus a screen font.

A crude form of scaleable fonts included with earlier versions of Windows were known as *vector* fonts. The font descriptions for vector fonts are stored as sets of coordinates that make up the letters as stick figures. There are three vector font files — Modern.fon, Script.fon, and Roman.fon. These files have the same *fon* extension as the bitmapped fonts, which makes it difficult to differentiate them. Modern.fon is installed by default, but the other fonts are installed only if you install a plotter.

Screen fonts

Screen fonts are bitmapped fonts used (for the most part) to display icon titles, dialog box text, help files, file and folder names in the Explorer, and so on. Applications assume you won't use these fonts to create text documents. In fact, you can't see them in the font lists in Microsoft Word for Windows.

Unless a printer manufacturer has created matching printer fonts, screen fonts won't print, even if you created a document using these fonts. Instead, the printer driver substitutes printer fonts of the same or similar size, and prints your text using those fonts.

When you first install Windows 95, titles in the title bars of folder windows, titles under the icons on the Desktop, menu items, application and document names on Taskbar buttons, file and folder names in the Explorer and folder windows, and text in dialog boxes use either the screen font MS Sans Serif 8 point or MS Sans Serif 10 point, depending on your screen resolution. You can use TrueType fonts or other screen fonts instead, if you like. See Chapter 22 to learn which fonts you can use for these screen text entities.

Printer fonts

Printer fonts can be either bitmapped or scaleable fonts. They can be stored in your printer's ROM, in cartridges plugged into your printer, or down-loaded from your computer's hard disk to your printer's RAM.

Microsoft does not supply printer fonts with Windows 95 or Windows 3.1, although it did with Windows 3.0. Printer manufacturers supply these fonts. Many laser printer manufacturers provide built-in (ROM) PostScript or PostScript-compatible fonts. Hewlett-Packard provides built-in scaleable TrueType-compatible fonts in its LaserJet 4 and 5 series. The HP 4L fonts are shown in Figure 20-6.

Unlike paper, computer monitors and their associated graphics adapters come in four major nominal sizes and five major screen resolutions. You, the user, can change the size of the display area (the Desktop) just by turning some knobs on the monitor.

Computer screens are usually farther away from our eyes than the distance that we comfortably hold a book or a sheet of paper. To be perceived as being the same size, text on a computer needs to be bigger than its corresponding print on the paper. The "apparent" height of an image decreases as you move back from it.

So, 24-point text on your screen is most likely magnified to display larger than one-third of an inch high.

The logical inch

Undocumented

Enter the logical inch. Twenty-four point text displayed on your Windows Desktop is one-third of a *logical inch* high, although it will be printed at exactly one-third of an inch high on your printer. Text is usually displayed larger than it will be printed, so the logical inch on your monitor is most likely larger than the printed inch.

The logical inch is a magnifier. The size of the logical inch divided by one inch gives the value of the magnification. The actual size of the logical inch depends on the size of your monitor, the resolution of your graphics card, how large you have adjusted your image size, and the value you have chosen for the magnification factor internal to Windows 95. (As you may recall, this is the second meaning of the term *font size*.) The magnification factor values available to you are Small Fonts, Large Fonts, and Custom. Custom allows a wide range of values. You set this value in the Settings tab of the Display Properties dialog box. More details are available in Chapter 22.

So how big is a logical inch? One of the authors has a Compaq 14-inch SVGA monitor connected to one of his computers. While 14 inches is its nominal dimension, the actual diagonal size of the image of the Windows 95 Desktop on the screen is approximately 13 inches.

Most monitors used with PCs that run Windows are constructed to have greater width than height. They use the ratio of 4 (width) to 3 (height). The height of the Desktop image on our 14-inch monitor is $7^7/_8$ inches, and its width is $10^3/_8$ inches.

The screen resolution on this computer is set to Super VGA, or 800 x 600 pixels (notice the 4-to-3 ratio of width to height). Therefore, our dots per inch (dpi) resolution is approximately 76 pixels per inch.

So, do we know how big a logical inch is yet?

We can set the magnification factor to Small Fonts (96 pixels per logical inch), Large Fonts (120 pixels per logical inch), or Custom (a wide range of values). Given these values and our screen resolution of 76 pixels per inch, we can calculate the size of the logical inch.

Secret

For the small font magnification, the size of the logical inch is 96 pixels divided by 76 pixels, or about 1¹/₄ inches. For large font magnification, it is about 1⁵/₈ inches.

We have calculated the size of the logical inch, but to test our calculation, we need to closely examine the characters on our screen to confirm that they display at the correct size.

Windows screen fonts are designed on grids of dots. The screen fonts come in two sets. The large screen font set was designed to be used with a high resolution display (1024 x 768). The fonts are built on a grid of dots assuming 120 dots per logical inch. The small screen font set was designed for VGA resolution (640 x 480). The fonts assume a grid of 96 dots per logical inch. The small screen font set should not be confused with the font typeface Small Fonts, which is provided in both sets.

Windows 95 uses small screen fonts when the magnification factor is set to Small Fonts (96 pixels per logical inch). Not surprisingly, it uses large screen fonts when the magnification factor is set to Large Fonts (120 pixels per logical inch). You can, of course, also display TrueType fonts (which don't come in sets). TrueType fonts are magnified by the same amount as screen fonts.

Figure 20-7 shows the letters *T, f,* and *g* as designed for the MS Sans Serif 24-point screen font from the small screen font set. Figure 20-8 shows the same letters from the large screen font set.

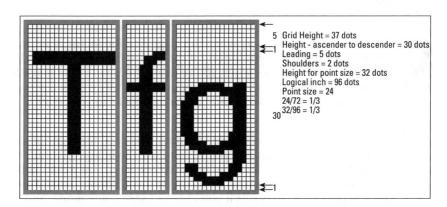

Figure 20-7: Small fonts: MS Sans Serif font at 24 points. You can count the number of dots used to create this font.

The height of the 24-point type using a font from the large screen font set is 40 dots (for MS Sans Serif — 46 dots minus the 6 dots of internal leading). We are assured by Figure 20-8 that the font designers have correctly named and designed this font because 24 points is one-third of a logical inch and 40 dots is one-third of 120 dots.

The size of the font that is used to display text on the Desktop increases when we use the Settings tab of the Display Properties dialog box to change from Small Fonts to Large Fonts, or go to larger sizes with the Custom option. Therefore, we see less text displayed. After all, the Windows 95 Desktop stays the same size. Microsoft Word for Windows has a zoom feature that is equivalent to changing the font size or using custom font sizes, although it changes only the displayed size of the fonts in the Word for Windows client area and not the size of the fonts used in dialog boxes, and so on. Word users often use this feature to shrink the font size enough that the full width of a line of text is visible on screen.

Large monitors with high-resolution display adapters can display more text because they have more logical inches on the display. Go to Chapter 22 for detailed comparisons of different monitor sizes.

Screen Fonts in Detail

Microsoft supplies the screen fonts used in Windows, although other manufacturers can, if they wish, supply screen fonts as well — perhaps ones that match their printer fonts.

Secret

Screen fonts are bitmapped fonts. The screen fonts are stored in screen font files that end in the extension *fon*. These files may contain fonts of one or more font sizes. Windows creates, on the fly, the bold, italic and bold italic versions of screen fonts from the regular bitmapped version, which is the only version that is stored in the bitmapped screen font file.

Table 20-1 lists the screen font files that Microsoft ships with Windows 95.

Table 20-1	Windows 95 Screen Fonts by Font Set
Font Filename	*Somewhat Esoteric Embedded Typeface Name*
	Large screen fonts
8514fix.fon	Fixedsys for the IBM 8514
8514oem.fon	Terminal Font for the IBM 8514
8514sys.fon	System (Set #6)
Courf.fon	Courier 10, 12, 15 (8514/a resolution)
Seriff.fon	MS Serif 8, 10, 12, 14, 18, 24 (8514 resolution)
Smallf.fon	Small Fonts (8514/a resolution)
Sseriff.fon	MS Sans Serif 8, 10, 12, 14, 18, 24 (8514 resolution)
Symbolf.fon	Symbol (8514 resolution)

Font Filename	Somewhat Esoteric Embedded Typeface Name
Small screen fonts	
Vgafix.fon	Fixedsys (Set #6)
Vgaoem.fon	Terminal (US) (Set #6)
Vgasys.fon	System (Set #6)
Coure.fon	Courier 10, 12, 15 (VGA resolution)
Serife.fon	MS Serif 8, 10, 12, 14, 18, 24 (VGA resolution)
Smalle.fon	Small Fonts (VGA resolution)
Sserife.fon	MS Sans Serif 8, 10, 12, 14, 18, 24 (VGA resolution)
Symbole.fon	Symbol (VGA resolution)
DOS fonts	
Dosapp.fon	MS-DOS CP 437

Table 20-2 lists screen fonts by typeface.

Table 20-2	Screen Fonts by Typeface	
Typeface	Font Filename	Character Set
Fixed-pitch fonts		
Fixedsys	8514fix.fon	Windows 3.0 ANSI
	Vgafix.fon	Windows 3.0 ANSI
Terminal	8514oem.fon	DOS/OEM
	Vgaoem.fon	DOS/OEM
	Dosapp.fon	DOS/OEM
Courier	Coure.fon	Windows 3.0 ANSI
	Courf.fon	Windows 3.0 ANSI
Proportional fonts		
System	8514sys.fon	All Windows 3.0 ANSI
	Vgasys.fon	
Sans Serif	Sserife.fon	
	Sseriff.fon	
Serif	Serife.fon	

(continued)

Table 20-2 *(continued)*

Typeface	Font Filename	Character Set
Proportional fonts		
	Seriff.fon	
Small Fonts	Smalle.fon	
	Smallf.fon	
Symbol	Symbole.fon	Symbol
	Symbolf.fon	Symbol

Undocumented

Windows 95 stores the references to the screen fonts (other than the DOS fonts) in the Registry files System.dat and User.dat. This is what the Registry entries look like:

```
[HKEY_LOCAL_MACHINE\SOFTWARE\Microsoft\Windows\CurrentVersion\fontsize]
[HKEY_LOCAL_MACHINE\SOFTWARE\Microsoft\Windows\CurrentVersion\fontsize\96]
"Description"="Small Fonts"
[HKEY_LOCAL_MACHINE\SOFTWARE\Microsoft\Windows\CurrentVersion\fontsize\96\System]
"vgasys.fon"="fonts.fon"
"vgafix.fon"="fixedfon.fon"
"vgaoem.fon"="oemfonts.fon"
[HKEY_LOCAL_MACHINE\SOFTWARE\Microsoft\Windows\CurrentVersion\fontsize\96\User]
"serife.fon"="MS Serif 8,10,12,14,18,24 (VGA res)"
"sserife.fon"="MS Sans Serif 8,10,12,14,18,24 (VGA res)"
"coure.fon"="Courier 10,12,15 (VGA res)"
"symbole.fon"="Symbol 8,10,12,14,18,24 (VGA res)"
"smalle.fon"="Small Fonts (VGA res)"
[HKEY_LOCAL_MACHINE\SOFTWARE\Microsoft\Windows\CurrentVersion\fontsize\120]
"Description"="Large Fonts"
[HKEY_LOCAL_MACHINE\SOFTWARE\Microsoft\Windows\CurrentVersion\fontsize\120\System]
"8514sys.fon"="fonts.fon"
"8514fix.fon"="fixedfon.fon"
"8514oem.fon"="oemfonts.fon"
[HKEY_LOCAL_MACHINE\SOFTWARE\Microsoft\Windows\CurrentVersion\fontsize\120\User]
"seriff.fon"="MS Serif 8,10,12,14,18,24 (8514/a res)"
"sseriff.fon"="MS Sans Serif 8,10,12,14,18,24 (8514/a res)"
"courf.fon"="Courier 10,12,15 (8514/a res)"
"symbolf.fon"="Symbol 8,10,12,14,18,24 (8514/a res)"
"smallf.fon"="Small Fonts (8514/a res)"
```

All the screen fonts whose font filenames begin with 8514 or whose names before the *fon* extension end in an *f*, such as Sserff.fon, are Large Fonts (designed on a dot grid of 120 dots per logical inch). The font files that begin with VGA or whose names end in an *e*, as in Sserfe.fon are the Small Fonts (96 dots per logical inch).

Font point sizes

Point size is a convenient and consistent method of referring to font size across all kinds of fonts. For example, a 9-point font is $^9/_{72}$ of a (logical) inch high. The (small font set) font file Vgafix.fon contains one font of size 9 points. It was created on a grid that is 15 dots high and 8 dots wide. The top 3 dots are line spacing (or internal leading) and are not used to draw the character. The characters are therefore 12 dots high (from the top of the ascender to the bottom of the descender with no shoulder).

A small screen font 12 dots high is a 9-point font because 12 dots times the ratio of 72 points per logical inch divided by 96 dots per logical inch equals 9 points: (12*72)/96 = 9. The arithmetic doesn't always produce integers. For example, the MS Serif font file Serife.fon has a 10-point font that is 13 dots high, so it's actually a 9.75-point font.

Fixed-pitch screen fonts

There are three fixed-pitch screen fonts. Each is designed for a different application or purpose. Two are used in communicating with the world of fixed-pitch font computers and operating systems (Fixedsys fonts and Terminal fonts), and one is used to mimic a typewriter (Courier fonts). These fonts let us reach back into the past.

Tip

Figures 20-10, 20-12 and 20-14 show the lower-case *r* for each of the fixed-pitch fonts. You can use these figures (in conjunction with Extreme CloseUp) to identify which font is being used in Windows 95 to display a given text entity. Start Extreme CloseUp and use it to look at an *r* in the icon titles on your Desktop. For an example, refer to Figure 20-9. Compare what Extreme CloseUp shows you with what you see in the figures for each screen and TrueType font to determine which font is in use on your display for that text entity.

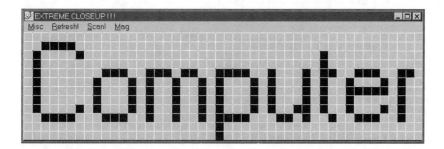

Figure 20-9: Extreme CloseUp view of part of the My Computer icon title in 16x magnification with the grid on. Each grid point represents a pixel (or dot) on the grid used to create the screen font, or a pixel that is the result of the rasterization of the TrueType font.

Fixedsys fonts

The Fixedsys fonts are fixed-pitch fonts used by Notepad to display ASCII (and Windows ANSI) characters. You can also use them in HyperTerminal to display text coming from the host computer. This font is basically a hold-over from the days when Windows 2.x and previous versions of Windows used it as the system font to display the text in menus and dialog boxes.

The font file Vgafix.fon contains a 9-point font, and 8514fix.fon contains an 11-point font. The 11-point large Fixedsys font was designed on a grid 10 dots wide and 20 dots high. The height from the ascender to the descender is 16 dots, and the shoulder is 2 dots above the ascender. The point size calculation is as follows: (16+2) times 72 divided by 120 dots per logical inch, which results in 10.8, or 11 points. See Figure 20-10 for a comparison of weights. Throughout this chapter, we use the *r* character to show differences between various fonts.

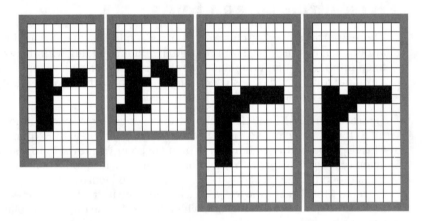

Figure 20-10: Lower case *r* from Vgafix.fon, Vgaoem.fon, 8514fix.fon, and 8514oem.fon font files, from left to right respectively.

Terminal fonts

The terminal fonts use the OEM, or the original IBM PC-8 (bit), character set. This is the standard character set used by DOS programs. For more information about character sets, see Chapter 21.

Like Vgafix.fon, the screen font file Vgaoem.fon contains a 9-point font, and 8514oem.fon contains an 11-point font.

These fonts are used by the Clipboard to display DOS text. You can copy text from a Windows application into the Clipboard, use the Clipboard Viewer to switch the text to the OEM font (choose Display, OEM Text, as shown in Figure 20-11), and then paste the text into a DOS application. Most of the time, there is no point in switching to the OEM font because the actual characters you are copying back and forth are the same in the Windows application as in the DOS application. Characters with an ASCII number greater than 127, however, differ between Windows and DOS applications. See the character set discussion in Chapter 21 for a comparison of the Windows ANSI and the DOS/OEM character sets.

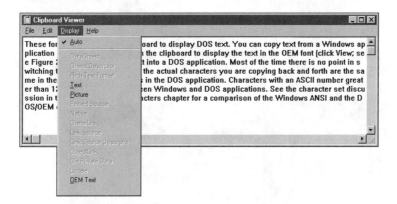

Figure 20-11: You can change from the Windows ANSI to the OEM character set in the Clipboard by using the Display menu in the Clipboard Viewer.

Secret

The Vgaoem.fon file provides one of the DOS fonts, 8 x 12 (which is also found in the Dosapp.fon file) and the 8514oem.fon file provides another DOS font, 10 x 20.

Windows will not boot unless these files are stored in the \Windows\Fonts folder on your computer, and you can't delete them from the Fonts folder.

DOS fonts

The DOS fonts share the typeface name Terminal with the OEM fonts. These fonts are used only in DOS Windows sessions. Your DOS window uses eight bitmapped screen fonts from the Dosapp.fon file. The DOS window can also use the TrueType fixed font, as shown by the letter *r* in Figure 20-12.

One line in the System.ini file determines which DOS screen fonts are used by windowed DOS applications. Find the line woafont=dosapp.fon in the [386enh] section.

Secret

The Dosapp.fon file contains eight fonts. They were designed using a grid of 96 dots per logical inch. The DOS fonts don't have separate sets of large and small fonts. They are the same (pixel) size irrespective of what magnification factor, or font size, you set. The windowed DOS session will be the same physical height on your Desktop irrespective of which font size you choose in the Settings tab of the Display Properties dialog box.

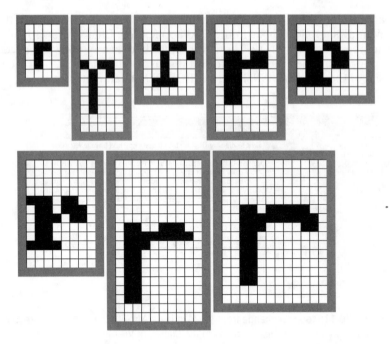

Figure 20-12: DOS fonts 4 x 6, 5 x 12, 6 x 8, 7 x 12, 8 x 8, 8 x 12, 10 x 18, and 12 x 16.

The DOS font size drop-down list on the toolbar of a windowed DOS session (or on the Font tab of the MS-DOS Prompt Properties dialog box, as shown in Figure 20-13) gives the size of the pixel grid that was used to create each of the DOS screen fonts — first their width and then their height. Dosapp.fon contains the screen fonts created on grids of sizes 4 x 6, 5 x 12, 6 x 8, 8 x 8, 8 x 12, 7 x 12, 10 x 18, and 12 x 16 dots. The additional DOS screen font, 10 x 20, is in the 8514oem.font file.

A DOS window can also use a set of fixed-pitch fonts created from the TrueType font Courier New. These fonts are included in the DOS window font drop-down list when you mark the Both font types option button in the Font tab of the MS-DOS Prompt Properties dialog box.

A DOS window using the 8 x 12 font is 300 pixels high (12 pixels x 25 lines), not including the DOS window title bar and toolbar height. On a 14-inch monitor at SVGA resolution, this DOS window is about 4 inches high, or over half of the screen height (600 pixels). This same DOS window on a monitor with 1280 x 1024 resolution is less than 30 percent of the height of the screen.

On a 15-inch inch monitor with a resolution of 1024 x 768, DOS text using the 7 x 12 DOS screen font is smaller (78 percent of the height) than the same DOS text on the same monitor at SVGA (600 x 800) resolution (0.131 inches versus 0.168 inches). A large number of DOS text font sizes are required to make sure that everyone can comfortably read text in windowed DOS sessions, given the wide variety of display resolutions and monitor sizes.

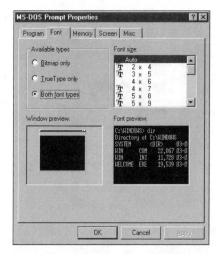

Figure 20-13: The Font tab of the MS-DOS Prompt Properties dialog box.

Courier fonts

The Courier screen font comes in 10, 12, and 15 points, in both the small and large screen size. These Courier font sizes are a subtle joke. Courier is a fixed-pitch font, so you might be tempted to think that these point sizes refer to *pitch*, as in characters per inch. Fifteen characters per inch, a standard size in old-fashioned line printers, requires a small font, while 15-point Courier is bigger than 12-point Courier.

The Windows font developers are having a little fun at our expense. They remember that these three sizes, 10, 12, and 15 pitch, were standards. They encourage us to think in this wrong headed-fashion (by providing Courier in these three sizes, and not, say, 10, 12, and 14 points).

The small fonts stored in Coure.fon were created on grids of 8 x 13, 9 x 16, and 12 x 20 dots for the 10-, 12-, and 15-point fonts respectively. For a comparison, see Figure 20-14. The large fonts in Courf.fon were created on grids of 9 x 16, 12 x 20, and 15 x 25 dots. Courier uses the Windows ANSI character set.

You can use Courier to display fixed-pitch text in HyperTerminal (although you may want to use a font that uses the DOS/OEM character set) or in your personal letters. Almost all printers have a corresponding Courier print font — at least 10 and 12 point.

Just because screen fonts are created and stored on a fixed-size grid doesn't mean that you can't display them in a larger size. Windows contains code that enlarges a screen font and displays it at a larger size. The results aren't very pretty because the code doesn't do any filling and smoothing, but it gets the job done quickly.

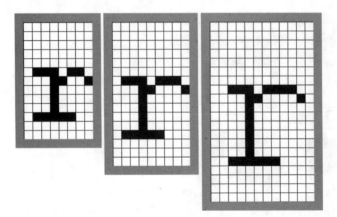

Figure 20-14: Courier screen font in 10, 12, and 15 points. That's 15-point Courier, not Courier at 15 characters per inch.

There is a TrueType font — Courier New — that pretty much replaces Courier. The advantages of using Courier New include better looking fonts at larger than 24 points and perhaps better correspondence between the font size you see on the screen and the font size printed in your letter to Aunt Sally.

Proportional screen fonts

Proportional fonts are used throughout the Windows 95 user interface. You can, if you wish, use a fixed-pitch font such as Courier for your menu items, window titles, and so on, but proportional fonts take up less room. The boxes that the text inhabits adjust to the font size and length of the text within them, so they are smaller and more manageable.

System fonts

The System font comes only in 10-point bold and bold italic. It can be used for text entities such as window titles and menu items. Because it comes only in bold, it can't be used for the finer things in life. While it was once an important font for displaying all sorts of Windows text entities, it has fallen into disuse in Windows 95.

Secret

If all your font files are erased from your hard disk, you cannot boot your computer in Windows and will get a Gdi.exe error message. If, however, the System font files Vgasys.fon and Vgaoem.fon (assuming that you last chose Small Fonts in Settings tab of the Display Properties dialog box) are still in the \Windows\Fonts folder, you can start and use Windows. These two files (or their equivalent Large Fonts files — 8514sys.fon and 8514oem.fon) are the minimum font files needed to make Windows work. Figure 20-15 shows the lower case *r* for the two sizes of System fonts.

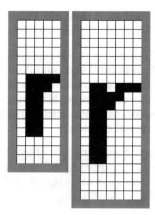

Figure 20-15: Lowercase *r* from Vgasys.fon and 8514sys.fon screen font files. These are the System font files from the small font and large font screen sets.

The Terminal font in the OEM font files (Vgaoem.fon or 8514oem.fon) is needed to give the DOS window a font. The System font (Vgasys.fon) is used for all the text entities in Windows if there is no other font.

MS Sans Serif fonts

MS Sans Serif is the default font for all Windows 95 screen text entities. Depending on your resolution, either 8 or 10 points is used. The MS Sans Serif font files, Sserife.fon and Sseriff.fon, each contain six fonts in 8, 10, 12, 14, 18, and 24 points, as shown in Figure 20-16. The Windows 95 screen-font rasterizer automatically constructs larger MS Sans Serif fonts if you choose to display bigger screen fonts. They will look a bit crude, though.

Figure 20-16: MS Sans Serif in six sizes — 8, 10, 12, 14, 18, and 24 points — from the Sserife.fon file.

TrueType Fonts

One aspect of Windows 3.1 that helped make it a successful product was the addition of TrueType — typeface outlines that Windows smoothly scales to any size on any Windows-supported monitor and printer.

This capability meant that Windows could use the same typefaces to display a document that it used to print the document. It no longer mattered whether a Windows user's printer contained the same typeface as the one used to display the text of a document on the Desktop. Windows prints its TrueType faces to any printer that has the ability to print graphics or download fonts.

TrueType is integrated into Windows 95. When you send a document to another person or company and you use one of the five TrueType typeface families included with Windows 95 that are intended for use in documents — Times New Roman, Arial, Courier New, Symbols, and Wingdings — the recipients of your document can view it on their monitors and print it on their printers exactly the way you saw it on your monitor and printed it.

Microsoft Plus! comes with additional TrueType font files, including Book Antigua, Comic Sans, Lucida Console, Lucida Sans Unicode, News Gothic MT, and OCR-A.

If you install Windows 95 Multilanguage Support (either during initial setup or later using the Add/Remove Programs icon in the Control Panel), the 652-character versions of Arial, Courier New, and Times Roman are installed.

There are great font resources on line. Check out Steve's font warehouse at http://fonts.eyecandy.com/main.html. Or visit http://www.fonthead.com/, and be sure to download GoodDogCool.ttf.

Microsoft has more TrueType fonts that you could possibly download at http://www.microsoft.com/truetype.

Freedom from screen fonts and printer fonts

Before TrueType, Windows required that a font designer build a set of specific fonts for every point size that you might require on your printer. These printer fonts required several megabytes of disk space for a complete set, especially when you needed larger sizes. Furthermore, the font designer had to build a separate set of screen fonts in a different format to display these printer fonts on screen.

TrueType almost completely eliminates this confusion. If you don't like the typefaces included with Windows 95, you can buy TrueType fonts from a variety of vendors. Once you install these fonts, all sizes of that typeface are immediately supported by all applications, displays, and printers.

You can configure the Fonts folder so that applications do not have access to screen or printer fonts. In the Fonts folder, choose View, Options, and click the TrueType tab. Mark the check box labeled "Show only TrueType fonts in the programs on my computer."

The TrueType fonts that come with Windows 95

As shown in Table 20-3, Windows 95 ships with six TrueType font families: Arial, a Helvetica sans serif font; Times New Roman, a Times Roman serif font; Courier New, a fixed-pitch font to replace the Courier screen font; Symbol, a replacement of the Symbol screen font; Wingdings, which uses dingbats as characters, and Marlett, which is used to create Desktop "furniture."

Table 20-3	Windows 95 TrueType Families
Typeface	*Font Filename*
Fixed-pitch fonts	
Courier New	Cour.ttf
	Courbd.ttf
	Couri.ttf
	Courbi.ttf
Proportional fonts	
Arial	Arial.ttf
	Arialbd.ttf
	Ariali.ttf
	Arialbi.ttf
Times New Roman	Times.ttf
	Timesbd.ttf
	Timesi.ttf
	Timesbi.ttf
Non-text fonts	
Marlett	Marlet.ttf
Symbol	Symbol.ttf
Wingdings	Wingding.ttf

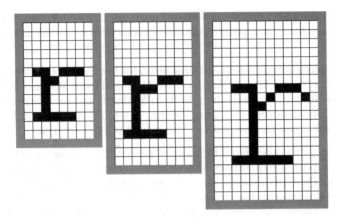

Figure 20-21: The lowercase *r* in Courier New Roman at 10, 12, and 15 points. Compare these r's with those Courier r's in Figure 20-14.

Microsoft sells other TrueType fonts — in particular, Font Packs 1 and 2. More information on some of the unusual characters sets available in those font packs is given Chapter 21.

Marlett

The Marlett font provides some of the "furniture" for the Windows 95 Desktop. You don't want to delete this font. The minimize, maximize, and close buttons on the right end of any Windows title bar are constructed using this font.

The emergence of the Metafile format

For many years, one of the nice features of the Macintosh environment compared to Windows has been its support for Encapsulated PostScript (EPS) graphics files. These files can contain line drawings, photographs, and text — almost any graphical material. When you print an EPS file (which is a vector graphics format that can also contain bitmapped information) to a PostScript printer, you can scale it to any size without it becoming jagged. This is not the case with the more limited *bmp* graphics file (which is a raster, or pixel-based, graphics file format).

Windows, in fact, has long supported its own scaleable graphics format — Windows Metafile, or WMF.

If you specify text in a Windows Metafile as, say, Times New Roman, anyone with Windows can print the file at any size to any device supported by Windows. A recipient of the document could revise the text and save it as a file that would print to any printer. Unlike EPS files, Windows Metafiles do not require a PostScript device.

Send your favorite typeface

TrueType gives you the ability to send TrueType faces to anyone, including typesetting service bureaus, without violating the copyright of the owner of the typeface. This is made possible by a TrueType feature called *font embedding* — you simply include the typefaces required by the document in an encoded form within the document itself.

Font embedding is a response to a serious problem within the PostScript service industry. A PostScript typesetter, such as a Linotronic 300, will not print a PostScript job unless the typesetter contains *exactly* the same typefaces that were used in the preparation of a document. If a document calls for a typeface with a name unknown to the device, it will often substitute a Courier font or not print at all. In either case, expensive service bureau time is wasted.

Many PostScript users, therefore, copy their special PostScript typefaces — Helvetica Black for headlines, say — onto a disk and send them along with their print job to the service bureau. This is a copyright violation (which is widely ignored), it wastes service bureau time in downloading the fonts, and it doesn't always work.

TrueType solves this problem by allowing you to embed typefaces into a document in an encrypted form. This encryption, which is easily supported by any application, prevents the recipient of a document from removing the typeface file and using it without paying for it. But the document can be viewed on any monitor and printed to any device supported by Windows — complete with the exact fonts used by the document's originator.

Microsoft has built three levels of usability into TrueType font embedding.

- At the most restrictive level, a vendor of TrueType faces can choose *not* to allow them to be embedded into documents for transmission. In this case, applications that support font embedding simply refrain from embedding those typefaces. The recipient of the document must purchase the required typefaces or substitute a generic typeface such as Times or Helvetica.

- At the second level, a TrueType vendor can choose to allow *read-only embedding*. A document embedded with read-only typefaces can be viewed and printed, but not edited. (If the document could be edited, the original contents could be deleted and the file used over and over again to produce other documents, with no payment to the owner of the typeface.) This kind of document could be edited if the embedded typefaces were deleted first.

- The third and most useful level of font embedding is *read-write embedding*. When read-write TrueType faces are embedded in a document, that document can be freely viewed, printed, and saved by the recipient, as well as edited. Furthermore, applications are expected to give the user of such a document the option of permanently installing the embedded typefaces into Windows so that other applications and documents can also use the faces. This type of embedding is most appropriate for free and public-domain TrueType faces.

TrueType is included in Windows; PostScript isn't

The most obvious statement, but perhaps the most influential over time, is that TrueType faces are built into Windows, and PostScript faces are not.

Furthermore, Microsoft cites industry studies that show that only 2–3 percent of Windows users in the U.S. have a PostScript printer, while the overwhelming majority have some kind of LaserJet-compatible printer.

Windows users can easily add ATM or another third-party type rasterizer that works with Type 1 outline faces. Adobe encourages this even more by bundling ATM essentially for free with such Windows applications as Lotus's Word Pro and 1-2-3 for Windows, Adobe's PageMaker and Persuasion, Ventura Publisher, Micrografx Designer, and many others.

But many more Windows users employ the TrueType faces that are built into Windows than add separate rasterizer programs.

PostScript is built into typesetters; TrueType isn't

Almost all high-end typesetting is conducted with computerized imagesetters programmed with built-in PostScript interpreters. Most serious graphic arts professionals (especially publication designers) use Macintoshes instead of Windows, and almost all of them prefer PostScript over TrueType because of its dominance in high-end typesetters.

Tip

On the other hand, you can send output containing TrueType fonts (either directly or in the form of a PostScript print file) to a PostScript device. Windows automatically converts TrueType fonts into the exact same fonts in Type 1 format either when creating a print file or before the fonts are sent directly to the printing device. But there appears to be no compelling reason for professional designers to switch from PostScript to TrueType (or from a Macintosh to Windows) since their existing technology is working well.

TrueType fonts are less costly; some are cheap

The battle continues over which fonts have the highest quality, but TrueType fonts have won the war regarding price. Many TrueType fonts are available at a dollar a font or less. You can try out shareware TrueType fonts before you buy. TrueType font packs are sold by Microsoft, Monotype, and many others.

TrueType hints are in the font; PostScript's (mostly) aren't

Hints are instructions in a computer program that make scaleable type look better on displays and laser printers.

These hints are necessary because computer monitors and printers don't have enough dots to truly follow the shape of most typefaces at smaller sizes. The hinting instructions reshape the letterforms so they don't have odd pixels sticking out where curves would normally appear, or have pixels missing where fine strokes in a character would normally be less than one pixel thick.

TrueType and PostScript faces provide hinting instructions in very different ways. But in both cases, hints are most useful with 18-point type and smaller on a computer display such as a VGA monitor, and 12-point type and smaller on a 300-dpi laser printer. Hints aren't necessary, no matter what size the type is, on 600-dpi printers (including high-end laser printers), nor are they necessary on imagesetters, which typically feature resolutions of 1270 or 2540 dpi.

The essential difference between TrueType and PostScript typefaces is where the hinting instructions are placed. TrueType hints are actually part of the typeface file itself. The program that scales TrueType for the screen and printer has little hinting information of its own, but reads what is contained in each typeface file.

PostScript faces, by contrast, contain little hinting information. Rasterizer programs for PostScript faces, such as ATM, are smart enough to use that limited information to figure out exactly how each character should be reshaped to retain a legible design in small screen or printer sizes.

The upshot of this difference is that PostScript typefaces, once perfected, seldom need to change. If better hinting methods are discovered or changes need to be made in order to accommodate new kinds of output devices, these changes can be made to the PostScript rasterizer program in an update. The typeface files themselves should be unaffected.

The inclusion of hinting instructions in the typeface file itself is a boon to typeface vendors, who can compete with each other for sales on the basis of arguments that they have the best-hinted faces available. This also means that type buyers must become aware of the subtle differences between typefaces from competing vendors (all type is definitely not the same).

TrueType and PostScript Type 1 differ on device independence

Device independence means that a printed document looks the same whether it is printed on a 300-dpi laser printer, a 2540-dpi typesetter, or any other resolution device. *Looks the same* means that each printout of the document should have the same number of lines and pages, regardless of the resolution of the printer. The most important factor that allows a document to print out exactly the same way on printers of different resolutions is that the spacing of each individual character is the same at all resolutions.

Device independence has always been a selling point for PostScript typefaces and printers. But PostScript is by no means perfect in this regard. Any experienced typesetting service bureau can tell you horror stories about print jobs that came out perfectly when printed to a PostScript laser printer but were several lines longer or shorter when printed on an imagesetter (ruining the carefully formatted job).

Microsoft states that this happens because PostScript Type 1 characters suffer from rounding errors. Each character in a PostScript typeface counts as a certain width on a line. A character at a small size, such as 10 points, might be 7.5 pixels wide on a computer monitor. But because it is impossible for an application to give a character half a pixel, this character spacing is rounded up, giving the character a whole 8 pixels.

Over the length of a line, these rounding errors add up. When the document is printed on a PostScript printer of a different resolution, this character spacing rounds differently, which can result in different line breaks and a different layout for the whole job.

Some applications, such as Adobe PageMaker, compensate for these rounding errors by allowing the user to specify that the spacing of characters should be performed using the resolution of the ultimate printing device, no matter what the current printer is. But most applications do not include these fine adjustments, and this can result in a different appearance for documents printed on two different PostScript devices.

TrueType attempts to handle these rounding errors by giving applications more information about each character. An application that supports TrueType can add up all the fractional pixel widths of each character on a line. The application then must round off only the pixel count at the end of each line, not the pixel count for each character. This theoretically results in TrueType documents with a rounding error of only one pixel per line, instead of many.

Even this is enough to throw off the word wrap of a line — a difference of a single pixel can mean that a short word such as *a* or *I* will fit at the end of one line instead of wrapping to the beginning of the next line. But the improved spacing information in TrueType faces may lead to an improved portability of documents across all types of printers.

Printing with TrueType and PostScript fonts

Tip

Turn to Chapter 23 to see a further discussion of the interaction between these scaleable fonts and your printer. In particular, we discuss LaserJet- and PostScript-compatible printers in detail.

How Hinting Affects the Look of Your Work

Hinting is such an important component of computer typefaces that it's worth knowing how hinting technology can change what you get when you display or print text.

Hinting affects the process of converting a typeface into a type font. All scaleable, outline typefaces start out as a perfect, ideal shape for a set of characters. Because monitors and printers can handle only squarish pixels, not ideal shapes, these outlines must be converted into bitmaps of the correct size and shape. The ideal outline of a set of characters is called a *typeface*. When a typeface has been scaled to a particular size, the resulting pattern is called a *font*. The program that converts the typeface shapes into recognizable bitmaps is called a *rasterizer* because most printers are raster (bitmap) devices rather than vector-drawing devices, such as plotters.

If the pixels in a monitor or a printer were infinitely small, typeface hints would not be necessary. All type fonts would appear perfect.

In fact, this is exactly what happens on high-end typesetters; 1270-dpi imagesetters and 600-dpi laser printers have enough resolution to print any font and do not need hints.

But this is not the case with most laser printers and monitors. Below 13 points on a 300-dpi laser printer and below 19 points on a 96-dpi VGA screen, a typeface outline can fall in place on the grid of pixels in such a way that not every letter looks the way you would expect it to.

Take as an example the uppercase letter *H* in a sans serif typeface, as shown in Figure 20-23. The letter *H* has only three lines: two vertical lines, called stems, and a horizontal line, called the crossbar. To display these lines on a monitor, the shape of the *H* must turn on a certain pattern of pixels (make the pixels black).

In Figure 20-23, the uppercase *H* is shown superimposed over a grid of pixels on the face of a monitor. A typeface rasterizer program normally turns on a pixel if the center of the pixel falls inside the outline of a letter. But in the case of Figure 20-23, the letter *H* does not fall neatly on the grid.

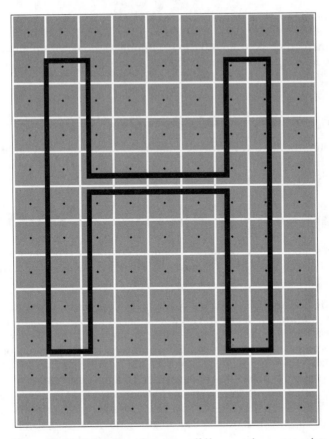

Figure 20-23: The outline of a sans serif *H* covers the center points of several pixels on the face of a computer monitor.

If you turn on pixels using a mechanical system that considers only the center point of each pixel, you get the result shown in Figure 20-24. The right stem of the letter is twice as thick as the left because the outline falls over two center points on the right-hand side. Meanwhile, the crossbar disappears from the image because it does not enclose the center of any pixels. Almost no one would find this bitmap recognizable as the letter *H*.

Hints in the typeface help to correct this problem. The rasterizer, reading the hinting instructions, detects that both stems are supposed to be equal in width, and therefore one stem cannot be two pixels wide while the other is only a single pixel wide. The rasterizer also detects that the crossbar is an essential element of the outline, which cannot earn less than one pixel.

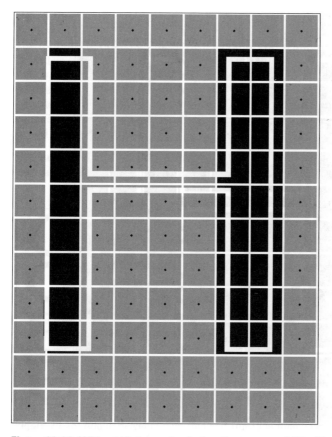

Figure 20-24: Without hinting, only pixels whose centers fall inside the original outline would be turned on, creating a stem on the right that is two pixels wide instead of one pixel, and a crossbar that doesn't show up at all.

Therefore, the rasterizer effectively moves the outline of the character so it is better aligned with the bitmap grid. The result is shown in Figure 20-25. Both stems now turn on only one pixel, and the crossbar turns on one pixel also. This is much more recognizable as the letter *H*. The shape of the letter has been slightly distorted to get this result — the crossbar is no longer at the height it was originally, for example — but at the low resolution of this particular monitor, there was no choice if the character was to be readable at all.

The upper-left serif of the Times New Roman letter *N* is not the same thickness as the upper-right serif of the M, as they are in Adobe Times. The lower stroke of the letter *e* flares outward much more in Times than in Times New Roman, and the % signs in both typefaces are completely different.

No one is going to reject one of your memos or proposals because it is formatted in Arial rather than Helvetica, of course. Based on the differences in design, many people would find the TrueType versions of these typefaces more graceful than the Adobe versions.

Tip

It's simply important to recognize that TrueType faces are *not* the same as PostScript faces. They may act differently, they may space differently, and they may appear differently. There are certainly many reasons to use TrueType faces. But you shouldn't assume that typefaces based on different technologies are interchangeable. You can mix them and match them, but remember that a difference as small as a single pixel can sometimes mean that a block of type will fit on a single line or that it will *not*.

Summary

▶ We show how to use the font installer that is built into Windows 95 to view both installed and uninstalled fonts, as well as to install and uninstall them.

▶ We examine the construction of both bitmapped and TrueType fonts and look closely at each of the fonts that comes with Windows 95.

▶ We detail the differences between screen fonts, printer fonts, TrueType fonts, and PostScript fonts.

▶ We show how to adjust the magnification that Windows 95 uses to size the text displayed on your screen.

▶ We show how you can send your TrueType fonts in a PostScript file to your imagesetting service bureau.

Chapter 21

Keyboards and Characters

In This Chapter

We show you how to type the characters available to you in Windows 95, how to pick a keyboard layout for easier access, and how to use shortcuts to run Windows 95 from the keyboard. We reveal:

▶ The relationship between fonts and characters

▶ What characters and what eight character sets come with Windows 95

▶ The five ways to type (or insert) little-used characters into your documents

▶ Modifying your keyboard layout to more easily enter these little-used characters

▶ Creating multilingual documents

▶ Windows shortcut keys that can speed up your work

▶ Speeding up your keyboard

▶ Changing your keyboard driver if you get a new and different keyboard

Fonts and Characters

There is a relationship (although it is a complex one) between the characters you see on your keyboard's keys and the characters that appear on your screen when you press those keys. For one thing, the appearance of the characters you type depends on which font you are using. For another, you can type characters that may not appear on your keyboard, such as ©, ™, ®, $^1/_4$, $^1/_2$, $^3/_4$, é, õ, ä, ¢, £, and ¥.

The characters that are displayed on your screen are stored on your computer's hard disk in font files. Each font file has at least 224 character definitions (known collectively as a *character set*) stored in it. A *font* is a visual expression of a character set. When you purchase a packet of fonts, the characters come with it at no additional charge (this is a typographer's little joke).

As explained in Chapter 20, TrueType and bitmapped screen fonts ship with Windows 95. The TrueType fonts consist of font descriptions for each character and the ability to scale the font across a wide variety of sizes.

TrueType fonts work with both the screen and the printer. The bitmapped fonts are for display on the screen, and consist of dots on a grid.

For a complete understanding of fonts, you should read this chapter in conjunction with Chapters 20 and 22.

Windows Character Sets

The fonts that ship with Windows 95 are based on these eight character sets:

1. Windows ANSI, Windows 3.1 version (also called ISO-8859-1 or Latin 1)

2. Windows ANSI, Windows 3.0 version

3. DOS/OEM (also called IBM PC-8 or Code Page 437)

4. Symbol

5. Wingdings

6. Marlett

7. Extended Windows ANSI (652 characters)

8. Lucida Sans Unicode and Lucida Console (comes with Microsoft Plus!)

Three of the TrueType fonts (Arial, Courier New, and Times New Roman) use the Windows ANSI character set defined when Windows 3.1 and TrueType fonts were developed. This character set is also known more esoterically as the *ISO 8859-1* or *Latin-1* character set.

Five of the bitmapped screen fonts (Courier, Fixedsys, MS Sans Serif, MS Serif, and System) use the earlier Windows 3.0 version of the Windows ANSI character set, which defined fewer characters between positions 128 and 160.

The bitmapped screen font Terminal and the bitmapped DOS fonts used in windowed DOS sessions all use the DOS/OEM character set. This is also referred to as the *IBM PC-8* (which stands for 8-bit) or *Code Page 437* character set. This character set was developed by IBM when it created the first IBM PC. This same character set is stored in ROM in U.S.-made PCs and used by full-screen DOS programs.

Three additional TrueType character sets ship with Windows 95 — Symbol, Wingdings, and Marlett. They have their own particular characters and don't relate to the previous "standards." Figure 21-1 shows the characters from the TrueType fonts Times New Roman, Symbol, and Wingdings with their corresponding character numbers. The Times New Roman characters display the Windows ANSI character set.

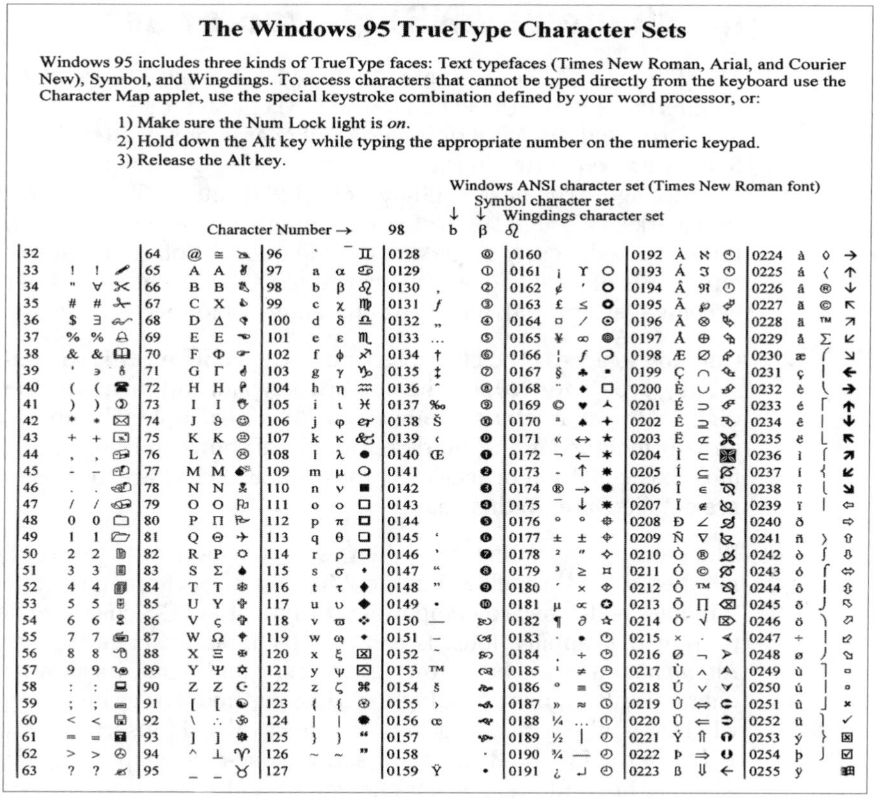

The Windows 95 TrueType Character Sets

Windows 95 includes three kinds of TrueType faces: Text typefaces (Times New Roman, Arial, and Courier New), Symbol, and Wingdings. To access characters that cannot be typed directly from the keyboard use the Character Map applet, use the special keystroke combination defined by your word processor, or:

1) Make sure the Num Lock light is *on*.
2) Hold down the Alt key while typing the appropriate number on the numeric keypad.
3) Release the Alt key.

Windows ANSI character set (Times New Roman font)
Symbol character set
Wingdings character set

Character Number → 98 b β ℒ

32				64	@	≅	🐭	96	`	‾	♊	0128		⊗		0160				0192	À	ℵ	☺	0224	à	◊	→
33	!	!	✏	65	A	Α	🐑	97	a	α	♋	0129		①		0161	¡	ϒ	○	0193	Á	ℑ	☻	0225	á	⟨	↑
34	"	∀	✂	66	B	Β	🐍	98	b	β	♌	0130	‚			0162	¢	′	●	0194	Â	ℜ	☺	0226	â	ⓒ	↓
35	#	#	✀	67	C	Χ	♎	99	c	χ	♍	0131	ƒ		③	0163	£	≤	◉	0195	Ã	℘	☞	0227	ã	ⓘ	↖
36	$	∃	✆	68	D	Δ	♏	100	d	δ	♎	0132	„		④	0164	¤	⁄	⊙	0196	Ä	⊗	♨	0228	ä		™	↗
37	%	%	🔥	69	E	Ε	✉	101	e	ε	♏	0133	…		⑤	0165	¥	∞	⊗	0197	Å	⊕	☜	0229	å	Σ	↙
38	&	&	🕮	70	F	Φ	☞	102	f	φ	♐	0134	†		⑥	0166	¦	ƒ	○	0198	Æ	∅	♣	0230	æ	⎛	↘
39	'	∋	δ	71	G	Γ	♐	103	g	γ	♑	0135	‡		⑦	0167	§	♣	■	0199	Ç	∩	☚	0231	ç		←
40	(	(	☎	72	H	Η	✂	104	h	η	≋	0136	ˆ		⑧	0168	¨	♦	□	0200	È	∪	♥	0232	è	⎝	↑
41	)	)	☜	73	I	Ι	☝	105	i	ι	ℋ	0137	‰		⑨	0169	©	♥	❏	0201	É	⊃	♠	0233	é	⎡	↓
42	*	∗	✉	74	J	ϑ	☺	106	j	φ	☞	0138	Š		⑩	0170	ª	♠	✦	0202	Ê	⊄	✘	0234	ê	⎣	↺
43	+	+	✇	75	K	Κ	☝	107	k	κ	☜	0139	‹		❶	0171	«	↔	★	0203	Ë	⊂	✙	0235	ë	⎩	↻
44	,	,	📇	76	L	Λ	☺	108	l	λ	⬤	0140	Œ		❷	0172	¬	←	✷	0204	Ì	⊆	✚	0236	ì	{	✙
45	-	−	📁	77	M	Μ	✌	109	m	μ	○	0141			❸	0173		↑	✺	0205	Í	∈	☦	0237	í		✚
46	.	.	🗋	78	N	Ν	☙	110	n	ν	■	0142			❹	0174	®	→	✹	0206	Î	∉	✞	0238	î		↘
47	/	/	🗇	79	O	Ο	☜	111	o	ο	□	0143			❺	0175	¯	↓	✶	0207	Ï	∠	♱	0239	ï		⇦
48	0	0	🗁	80	P	Π	✎	112	p	π	□	0144			❻	0176	°	°	⊕	0208	Ð	∇	✠	0240	ð		⇨
49	1	1	🖉	81	Q	Θ	✈	113	q	θ	□	0145	'		❼	0177	±	±	✠	0209	Ñ	®	✝	0241	ñ	∫	⇧
50	2	2	📖	82	R	Ρ	○	114	r	ρ	□	0146	'		❽	0178	²	″	✣	0210	Ò	©	✡	0242	ò	⌠	⇩
51	3	3	📄	83	S	Σ	●	115	s	σ	•	0147	"		❾	0179	³	≥	⌘	0211	Ó	™	☪	0243	ó		⇪
52	4	4	📇	84	T	Τ	✴	116	t	τ	◆	0148	"		❿	0180	´	×	✦	0212	Ô	™	☯	0244	ô	⌡	⇫
53	5	5	📚	85	U	Υ	✱	117	u	υ	◆	0149	•		⓫	0181	µ	∝	○	0213	Õ	∏	⌧	0245	õ	⌡	✍
54	6	6	🏃	86	V	ς	✾	118	v	ϖ	❖	0150	–		⓬	0182	¶	∂	✆	0214	Ö	√	⌦	0246	ö		✎
55	7	7	🖬	87	W	Ω	✚	119	w	ω	•	0151	—		⓭	0183	·	•	♤	0215	×	·	✖	0247	÷		✏
56	8	8	🕯	88	X	Ξ	✖	120	x	ξ	⊠	0152	˜		⓮	0184	¸	÷	♧	0216	Ø	⌐	✗	0248	ø		✐
57	9	9	🕮	89	Y	Ψ	✿	121	y	ψ	⊞	0153	™		⓯	0185	¹	≠	○	0217	Ù	∧	✓	0249	ù		✑
58	:	:	🖳	90	Z	Ζ	✇	122	z	ζ	⌘	0154	š		⓰	0186	º	≡	○	0218	Ú	∨	✔	0250	ú		✒
59	;	;	🖮	91	[	[	◉	123	{	{	⊕	0155	›		⓱	0187	»	≈	○	0219	Û	⇔	☒	0251	û		✓
60	<	<	🖰	92	\	∴	✂	124					●	0156	œ		⓲	0188	¼	…	○	0220	Ü	⇐	⊃	0252	ü		✔
61	=	=	🖲	93	]	]	✿	125	}	}	"	0157			⓳	0189	½		○	0221	Ý	⇑		0253	ý	}	☒
62	>	>	🖱	94	^	⊥	♈	126	~	~	"	0158			·	0190	¾	—	○	0222	Þ	⇒	⊙	0254	þ		☑
63	?	?	🖂	95	_	_	♉	127			✇	0159	Ÿ		•	0191	¿	↵	○	0223	ß	⇓	←	0255	ÿ		

Figure 21-1: The Windows 95 TrueType character sets.

The Marlett font contains the Windows 95 "furniture." The symbols on the minimize, maximize, and close buttons at the right end of Windows title bars are in this font. Because the symbols in the buttons are fonts, it is easy to resize the buttons. Make sure not to delete this font from your \Windows\Fonts folder.

The Windows 95 source CD-ROM comes with a second set of TrueType font files for Arial, Courier New, and Times New Roman. These files contain 652 characters instead of 224. The additional characters are from central European languages, which use the Greek, Turkish, and Cyrillic alphabets. The original 224 characters are the same in the extended multilingual font sets and the original font sets. The extra characters are accessible only when you use the appropriate keyboard driver or software.

Microsoft Plus! includes Lucida Sans Unicode for an even greater number of characters, as well as Lucida Console, which replaces the TrueType DOS fonts that come with Windows 95.

The Windows ANSI character set

The Windows ANSI characters numbered 0 through 127 are identical to their counterparts in the DOS/OEM (IBM PC-8) character set. (These characters are also called the ASCII or lower ASCII character set, after the American Standards Committee for Information Interchange, which codified them decades ago.) The next 32 characters, 128 through 159, are mostly punctuation marks, although some character numbers are left unused. Of special interest are the curly single and double quotes. Following these are 32 characters of legal and currency symbols, then 32 characters of uppercase accented letters, and, finally, 32 characters of lowercase accented letters.

One way to access the characters numbered above 127 is to hold down the Alt key, type a zero (0) on the numeric keypad, and then type the three digits of the character's number — 0189, for example. This extra zero is already included in the character numbers shown in Figure 21-1. This is the most basic method of accessing these additional characters. Better methods are detailed later in this chapter.

You must add a leading zero when using this method to insert characters numbered 128 through 255 in the Windows ANSI character set because Windows is downward compatible with the IBM PC-8 character set, which is used by DOS applications. The IBM PC-8 character set already uses the Alt+*number* method for its own characters, and Windows allows you to enter characters from this set using the same method. For example, regardless of whether you're typing in DOS or Windows, Alt+171 inserts character number 171 from the IBM PC-8 character set, the one-half symbol ($^1/_2$). If you type Alt+0171 in Windows, you get character number 171 from the Windows ANSI character set, which is a chevron bracket («). (Windows ignores characters in the IBM PC-8 character set that do not exist in Windows, such as line-draw characters, or converts them into other keyboard characters.)

The difference between the Windows 3.0 ANSI character set and the Windows 3.1 version is that fewer characters between character numbers 128 and 160 are defined in the older version. Because this character set is not used for TrueType fonts, you don't need to be concerned about it when you're creating documents. In Figure 21-2, the Windows 3.0 ANSI character set is shown in MS SansSerif.

Font designers are supposed to base their TrueType fonts on the Windows ANSI (Windows 3.1) character set or on the extended Windows ANSI 652-character set, which includes the previous 224 Windows 3.1 ANSI characters. That is, their fonts are supposed to be an expression of the same characters as those defined by the Windows ANSI character set. Font designers generally stick to this standard unless they are designing a special-purpose font such as Wingdings.

	!	"	#	$	%	&	'	(	)	*	+	,	-	.	/	0	1	2	3	4	5	6	7	8	9	:	;	<	=	>	?
@	A	B	C	D	E	F	G	H	I	J	K	L	M	N	O	P	Q	R	S	T	U	V	W	X	Y	Z	[	\	]	^	_
`	a	b	c	d	e	f	g	h	i	j	k	l	m	n	o	p	q	r	s	t	u	v	w	x	y	z	{	|	}	~	.
.	.	.	.	.	.	.	.	.	.	.	.	.	.	.	.	'	'	.	.	.	.	.	.	.	.	.	.	.	.	.	.
¡	¢	£	¤	¥	¦	§	¨	©	ª	«	¬	-	®	¯	°	±	²	³	´	µ	¶	·	¸	¹	º	»	¼	½	¾	¿
À	Á	Â	Ã	Ä	Å	Æ	Ç	È	É	Ê	Ë	Ì	Í	Î	Ï	Ð	Ñ	Ò	Ó	Ô	Õ	Ö	×	Ø	Ù	Ú	Û	Ü	Ý	Þ	ß
à	á	â	ã	ä	å	æ	ç	è	é	ê	ë	ì	í	î	ï	ð	ñ	ò	ó	ô	õ	ö	÷	ø	ù	ú	û	ü	ý	þ	ÿ

Figure 21-2: The Windows 3.0 version of the Windows ANSI character set, used by the current bitmapped screen fonts. It is shown in MS SansSerif.

It is important that font designers use the Windows ANSI character set. As computer users, we are interested in easily accessing the ANSI characters no matter what text font we are using. If the copyright symbol is displayed when we use Times New Roman, we would like that to also be the case if we are using Coronet. This will be true only if the copyright symbol is present in the Coronet font, and if it has the same character number as it has in Times New Roman.

The five ANSI accents

One reason that many English-speaking computer users aren't more familiar with the accented letters in the ANSI set is that these letters seem to be a jumble of random, unrelated symbols. Actually, all of the accented letters in the ANSI character set fall into one of five types:

1. Characters with an Acute Accent:

Á É Í Ó Ú Ý á é í ó ú ý

2. Characters with a Grave Accent (*grave* rhymes with "Slav" or "slave"):

À È Ì Ò Ù à è ì ò ù

3. Characters with an Umlaut (also called a *dieresis*):

Ä Ë Ï Ö Ü ä ë ï ö ü ÿ

4. Characters with a Circumflex (also informally called a *hat*):

Â Ê Î Ô Û â ê î ô û

5. Characters with a Tilde, or an Iberian or Nordic Form:

Ã Æ Ç Ð Ñ Õ Ø ¡ ¿ ã æ ª ç ñ õ ø º ß

These accented characters largely occupy the positions numbered 192 through 224 — the uppercase letters start at 192, while the lowercase versions are exactly 32 positions higher. On non-U.S. keyboards, the accented characters that are common in the national language are assigned to keys, so that pressing, say, the ñ key on a Spanish keyboard automatically inserts ANSI character 241 into the document.

international characters and symbols are available in Windows because the ANSI set eliminates the line-drawing and math characters that are part of the IBM PC-8 set. Because it moved IBM's math characters into a new Symbol font and delete the line-draw characters entirely, Windows has room to add several accented letters needed in various languages, as well as copyright and trademark symbols, and the like. (Most Windows word processing applications can draw lines without having to use text characters.)

The IBM PC-8 character set is shown in Figure 21-3. In the U.S. keyboard layout, the main keyboard provides keys for each of the alphabetic characters and punctuation marks, numbered 32 through 127. You access the other characters (number 128 and up) by holding down the Alt key, typing the appropriate character number on the numeric keypad (with the Num Lock light on), and then releasing the Alt key. Alt+157, for example, produces ¥, the Japanese yen symbol. Notice that if you use this method with the DOS/OEM character set, you don't need to type the additional zero for the characters above character number 127, as you would for the Windows ANSI characters.

CTRL & PUNC:		ALPHABETIC:		ACCENTS & LINE DRAW:		MATH:
0 ▪	32	64 @	96 `	128 Ç	160 á	192 └	224 α
1 ▪	33 !	65 A	97 a	129 ü	161 í	193 ┴	225 β
2 ▪	34 "	66 B	98 b	130 é	162 ó	194 ┬	226 Γ
3 ▪	35 #	67 C	99 c	131 â	163 ú	195 ├	227 π
4 ▪	36 $	68 D	100 d	132 ä	164 ñ	196 ─	228 Σ
5 ▪	37 %	69 E	101 e	133 à	165 Ñ	197 ┼	229 σ
6 ▪	38 &	70 F	102 f	134 å	166 ª	198 ╞	230 μ
7 ▪	39 '	71 G	103 g	135 ç	167 º	199 ╟	231 τ
8 ▪	40 (	72 H	104 h	136 ê	168 ¿	200 ╚	232 Φ
9 ▪	41)	73 I	105 i	137 ë	169 ⌐	201 ╔	233 θ
10 ▪	42 *	74 J	106 j	138 è	170 ¬	202 ╩	234 Ω
11 ▪	43 +	75 K	107 k	139 ï	171 ½	203 ╦	235 δ
12 ▪	44 ,	76 L	108 l	140 î	172 ¼	204 ╠	236 ∞
13 ▪	45 -	77 M	109 m	141 ì	173 ¡	205 ═	237 ø
14 ▪	46 .	78 N	110 n	142 Ä	174 «	206 ╬	238 ∈
15 ▪	47 /	79 O	111 o	143 Å	175 »	207 ╧	239 ∩
16 ▪	48 0	80 P	112 p	144 É	176 ░	208 ╨	240 ≡
17 ▪	49 1	81 Q	113 q	145 æ	177 ▒	209 ╤	241 ±
18 ▪	50 2	82 R	114 r	146 Æ	178 ▓	210 ╥	242 ≥
19 ▪	51 3	83 S	115 s	147 ô	179 │	211 ╙	243 ≤
20 ▪	52 4	84 T	116 t	148 ö	180 ┤	212 ╘	244 ⌠
21 ▪	53 5	85 U	117 u	149 ò	181 ╡	213 ╒	245 ⌡
22 ▪	54 6	86 V	118 v	150 û	182 ╢	214 ╓	246 ÷
23 ▪	55 7	87 W	119 w	151 ù	183 ╖	215 ╫	247 ≈
24 ▪	56 8	88 X	120 x	152 ÿ	184 ╕	216 ╪	248 °
25 ▪	57 9	89 Y	121 y	153 Ö	185 ╣	217 ┘	249 ∙
26 ▪	58 :	90 Z	122 z	154 Ü	186 ║	218 ┌	250 ·
27 ▪	59 ;	91 [	123 {	155 ¢	187 ╗	219 █	251 √
28 ▪	60 <	92 \	124		156 £	188 ╝	220 ▄	252 ⁿ
29 ▪	61 =	93]	125 }	157 ¥	189 ╜	221 ▌	253 ²
30 ▪	62 >	94 ^	126 ~	158 ₧	190 ╛	222 ▐	254 ▪
31 ▪	63 ?	95 _	127	159 ƒ	191 ┐	223 ▀	255

Figure 21-3: The IBM PC-8 character set. In addition to nonprintable control codes, punctuation, and alphabetic characters, the PC-8 character set includes accented characters, line-draw characters, and math symbols. You access these last three types of characters using the Alt key and the numeric keypad.

Although the IBM PC-8 character set seems to be a chaotic jumble of letters and signs, there is a natural order of sorts (no pun intended). For instance, the first 32 characters are control codes (including tab and carriage return characters), the next 32 are punctuation and numerals, the next 32 are uppercase letters, and exactly 32 places above that are the lowercase letters.

Easily Typing the Less-Used Characters

As you can see in Figure 21-1, Windows 95 provides a broad array of characters that do not appear on your keyboard. These characters include fractions, footnote superscripts, copyright and trademark symbols, and many others. Even if you are using a French, German or other European-style keyboard, you only get a few different characters defined on your keyboard, mostly for the accented letters.

One standard (but awkward) method of inserting characters that don't appear on the keyboard is to use the Alt+*number* method. You turn Num Lock on, hold down the Alt key, type a number on the numeric keypad, then release the Alt key. For example, typing Alt+0169 inserts the © symbol.

Another (somewhat awkward) method is to use the Character Map applet that comes with Windows 95 (Start, Programs, Accessories). In the Character Map window, you select a symbol (or several symbols), copy it, and then switch to your word processing program and paste it into your document. This method is cumbersome because it requires that you switch between applications, but you might find it useful at times because it lets you preview all the characters before you actually insert them in your document (even if they look pretty small on high resolution monitors).

In addition to these two methods, Windows provides four other more efficient ways of inserting characters that don't appear on the keyboard. If you install the U.S.-International keyboard layout (see the *U.S.-International keyboard layout* section), you can type characters such as © into text in any Windows application by pressing a simple two-key combination.

In the *Switching between keyboard layouts in one language* section, you learn how to type non-standard characters using only one or two keystrokes. You can switch this ability on and off at any time (by switching between keyboard layouts), and you can use it in conjunction with the Character Map applet or the Alt+*number* method whenever you wish.

If you have a full-featured word processing program such as Word for Windows or WordPerfect for Windows, you can also insert many special characters using keyboard shortcuts defined in those programs. See the section entitled *Accessing unusual characters in Word for Windows 95 and 97* for details about typing these characters in Word.

Finally, the *Accessing more hidden characters* section introduces you to a typeface that comes with Windows 95 that contains hundreds of symbols. You also learn about the typefaces from Microsoft and third-party vendors that contain literally thousands of other special characters you can use in your documents.

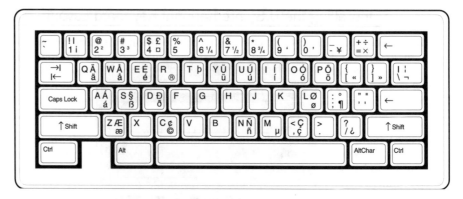

Figure 21-5: The U.S.-International keyboard layout.

The normal character is shown on the left of each key, and the character inserted when you hold down AltChar or Shift+AltChar is shown on the right.

Unusual characters on the keyboard

You gain access to many categories of characters by switching to the U.S.-International keyboard. For clarity's sake, we break them into the following categories:

- Legal characters, such as the copyright symbol (©), the registered trademark symbol (®), the section mark (§), and the paragraph mark (¶) used by lawyers

- Currency symbols, such as the British pound (£), the Japanese yen (¥), the cent sign (¢), and the international generic currency symbol (¤)

- The fractions one-fourth ($^1/_4$), one-half ($^1/_2$), and three-fourths ($^3/_4$), and the degree symbol (°), useful when typing addresses such as $120^1/_2$ Main St. or recipes (300°)

- Superscripts from one to three (^{123}), useful for inserting footnotes into a page of text, or for expressions such as x^2. Windows 95 doesn't offer superscript numbers higher than three, but Windows NT provides a full set of superscript and subscript numbers, from 0 to 9

- True multiplication and division symbols (× ÷), so you don't have to use a lowercase x and a forward slash (/) in your documents

- Open and closed quote marks (' '), also called "smart quotes," which look like the quote marks used in professionally typeset magazines and newspapers

- Accented characters, so you can correctly spell words such as *résumé* and *mañana*

The U.S.-International keyboard actually provides two different ways to insert accented letters into your documents. This ability is becoming more important as more Americans have names that include accented letters, such as Frederico Peña, the nominee for the Secretary of the Department of Energy at the time of this writing.

The first way to insert accented letters is to hold down the AltChar key and press one of the letters on your keyboard that has an accented alternate character. For example, AltChar+E produces the accented é, while AltChar+N produces the accented ñ.

The second way is to use what are called *dead keys*. These are keys that do nothing until you press another key on the keyboard.

On the U.S.-International keyboard, five keys are converted into dead keys. These are:

■ The circumflex or "hat" over the 6 key (^) — used in words such as *crêpes Suzette*

■ The back quote (`) — produces a grave accent in words such as à la carte

■ The tilde (~) — used in words such as jalapeño

■ The apostrophe (') — produces an acute accent in words such as exposé

■ The double quote (") — produces an *umlaut* (or *dieresis*) in words such as *naïve*

When you press one of these dead keys, Windows shows nothing on your screen until you press another key. If the second key you press is a letter that has an accented form, such as most vowels, the appropriate accented letter is inserted into your document. If a letter doesn't have an accented form, the letter *t* for example, both the accent and the *t* are inserted, one after the other. If you want to insert just the accent itself, press the corresponding dead key followed by the spacebar.

This behavior produces a small irritation when you're using the apostrophe and double-quote key on your keyboard. When you press the apostrophe, which is common in contractions such as *don't* and possessives such as *Brian's,* you don't see the apostrophe until the second letter is typed. But you don't get an apostrophe at all if you type an unusual contraction, such as Hallowe'en. With the U.S.-International keyboard, pressing the apostrophe and then *e* produces the letter é, unless you remember to press the spacebar after the apostrophe.

This is a very minor problem, because most English contractions end in *s* or *t,* not in vowels. But it is a more serious problem with the double-quote key, which you use to begin sentences that are quotations, such as "Are you there?" Sentences often begin with *A, E,* and other vowels, and you must remember to press the spacebar after the double-quote key when typing any such sentence.

If you ever use symbols or accented characters, the advantages of using the U.S.-International keyboard far outweigh the slight disadvantage of remembering how to use the apostrophe and double-quote key. But because it *is* irritating, we wish Microsoft hadn't used the apostrophe and double-quote key as a dead key. Instead, they should have used the colon (:) and the semicolon (;). The colon looks like an umlaut, and the bottom of the semicolon resembles an acute accent mark. Because colons and semicolons are always followed by spaces or carriage returns in normal English usage, you wouldn't need to remember to press the spacebar before pressing a vowel after these keys. If a letter immediately followed a colon or semicolon, you could be sure that it was meant to be an accented letter.

In any case, using the U.S.-International keyboard is usually better for users of U.S. keyboards than switching to an entirely different keyboard layout to type in another language, such as French. You can, of course, use the Keyboard Properties dialog box in the Control Panel to add keyboard layouts in addition to (or instead of) U.S. layout. There are 26 available keyboard layouts. But the non-U.S. keyboard layouts almost always move some alphabetical keys to new positions that are customary in those locales. For example, the top row of alphabetical keys on keyboards sold in France starts out with the letters AZERTY, not QWERTY, as on U.S. keyboards. Unless you're a touch typist who learned to type on keyboards in a different country, it's better to stick with the U.S.-International keyboard.

What if you don't have an extended keyboard?

For users with older 84-key keyboards (the ones on the original IBM AT, with 10 function keys on the left side), the U.S.-International keyboard provides another way to access alternate characters. This is necessary, of course, because 84-key keyboards do not have two Alt keys and therefore cannot convert one into an AltChar key.

While the U.S.-International keyboard is in effect, you can hold down Ctrl+Alt while pressing a letter as a substitute for holding down the right Alt key (the AltChar key). Shift+Ctrl+Alt does the same thing as Shift+AltChar.

Unfortunately, these parallel methods are in force even if you are using a 101-key extended keyboard. This means that you must take care when using a macro language in your word processor to redefine Ctrl+Alt keys or Shift+Ctrl+Alt keys to run macros. These macro definitions overrule the meaning of letters that have an alternate form when used with the AltChar key. In other words, a macro that you have defined to run when you press Ctrl+Alt+A takes precedence over AltChar+A. Instead of AltChar+A inserting *á* into your document, the macro will execute.

Switching between keyboard layouts in one language

You can set up two (or more) keyboard layouts and easily switch between them. You can switch back and forth between the U.S. and the U.S.-International keyboard if you like. This can help you avoid the irritation of dealing with poorly defined dead keys (see the *Unusual characters on the keyboard* section earlier in this chapter).

Undocumented

To set up both the U.S. and U.S.-International keyboard layouts, follow the steps in the section entitled *Setting up and using multilingual identifiers* later in this chapter. Choose the language English (United States) and associate the U.S.-International keyboard layout with it, and then choose English (Australian) and associate the U.S. keyboard layout with it. You now have two language identifiers on your Taskbar that are in fact the same language (almost) but refer to two different keyboard layouts. You switch between layouts by choosing one or the other language identifier.

The only problem this can cause occurs if you have two spelling dictionaries in your word processor, one for the U.S. and one for Australia. The text that you type while you are typing Australian English (using the plain U.S. keyboard layout) will be proofed by the Australian spelling dictionary.

Accessing unusual characters in Word for Windows 95 and 97

For an example of how a full-featured word processor handles non-standard characters, see Table 21-2. The elements in this chart were taken directly from the Word for Windows help files (and edited to improve clarity).

Table 21-2	Shortcut Keys for Inserting Accented Letters in Word for Windows 95 and 97
Character	**Keystrokes**
à, è, ì, ò, ù, À, È, Ì, Ò, Ù	Ctrl+`(accent-grave), the letter
á, é, í, ó, ú, ý, Á, É, Í, Ó, Ú, Ý	Ctrl+' (apostrophe), the letter
â, ê, î, ô, û, Â, Ê, Î, Ô, Û	Ctrl+Shift+ ^ (caret), the letter
ã, ñ, õ, Ã, Ñ, Õ	Ctrl+Shift+~ (tilde), the letter
ä, ë, ï, ö, ü, ÿ, Ä, Ë, Ï, Ö, Ü, Ÿ	Ctrl+Shift+: (colon), the letter
å, Å	Ctrl+Shift+@, a or A
æ, Æ	Ctrl+Shift+&, a or A

(continued)

Table 21-2 *(continued)*

Character	Keystrokes
œ, Œ	Ctrl+Shift+&, o or O
ß	Ctrl+Shift+&, s
ç, Ç	Ctrl+, (comma), c or C
∂, Ð	Ctrl+' (apostrophe), d or D
ø, Ø	Ctrl+/, o or O
¿	Ctrl+Alt+Shift+?
¡	Ctrl+Alt+Shift+!
©	Ctrl+Alt+C
®	Ctrl+Alt+R
™	Ctrl+Alt+T
... (ellipsis)	Ctrl+Alt+.(period)
' (single opening quotation mark)	Ctrl+ ` (accent-grave), `
' (single closing quotation mark)	Ctrl+'(apostrophe),'
" (double opening quotation mark)	Ctrl+ ` (accent-grave)," (double quote)
" (double closing quotation mark)	Ctrl+'(apostrophe)," (double quote)

Word for Windows (6.0 and later) is by default set to replace straight quote marks with the typesetter's quote marks. You won't have to use the last four keystroke combinations in the table if you leave this setting at its default.

Undocumented

There are some conflicts between the U.S.-International keyboard layout and Word for Windows. The Word team at Microsoft has chosen to redefine a number of the Ctrl+Alt shortcut keys, so many of the AltChar+*letter* shortcuts don't work as indicated. Fortunately, you have a number of options if you want to use the convenient U.S.-International keyboard layout with Word.

First, many of the keys on the U.S.-International keyboard that conflict with a Word shortcut key have a different shortcut key in Word (refer to Table 21-2). You can just use these shortcut keys instead of AltChar+*letter*. For example, on the U.S.-International keyboard layout, you type AltChar+N to get the letter ñ, but Word defines Ctrl+Alt+N as a shortcut for choosing View, Normal. If you're typing in Word, you can use Word's keyboard shortcut **Ctrl+Shift+~ (tilde),n** to get the letter ñ instead.

Second, you can remove 13 of the 16 keyboard shortcuts in Word that conflict with the U.S.-International keyboard layout. Fortunately, these shortcut definitions are stored in the Normal.dot template. You can easily change or eliminate these shortcut key combinations in Normal.dot or whatever template you use with Word.

STEPS

Easing Use of the U.S.-International Keyboard with Word

Step 1. Double-click your Microsoft Word icon. Choose File, New from the menu.

You can make the changes to the Normal.dot template or to a new template. If you create a new template and then decide you want your new template to be the default template, you can use the Explorer to rename Normal.dot to Normal.old, and then rename your new template to Normal.dot.

Step 2. If you want to make changes to Normal.dot, click the OK button in the New dialog box. If you want to make a new template based on Normal.dot, click the Template option button, and then click OK.

Step 3. Choose Tools, Customize, and click the Keyboard tab (or click the Keyboard button in Word 97).

Step 4. Select the template that you want to change from the Save Changes In drop-down list in the lower-right corner window of the Customize (or Customize Keyboard) dialog box.

Step 5. Choose the categories shown in Table 21-3 in the Categories list, and scroll through the Commands list until you find the ones listed in the table.

Table 21-3   Word for Windows Shortcut Keys That Can Be Removed

Category	Command	Predefined Shortcut	Alternate
File	FilePrintPreview	Ctrl+Alt+I	Ctrl+F2
Edit	GoBack	Ctrl+Alt+Z	Shift+F5
Edit	RepeatFind	Ctrl+Alt+Y	Shift+F4
View	ViewNormal	Ctrl+Alt+N	
View	ViewOutline	Ctrl+Alt+O	
View	ViewPage	Ctrl+Alt+P	
Insert	InsertAnnotation	Ctrl+Alt+A (Word 6.0 and 7.0)	
Insert	InsertComment	Ctrl+Alt+M (Word 97)	
Insert	InsertEndnoteNow	Ctrl+Alt+E	
Format	ApplyHeading1	Ctrl+Alt+1	

(continued)

Table 21-3 *(continued)*

Category	Command	Predefined Shortcut	Alternate
Format	ApplyHeading2	Ctrl+Alt+2	
Format	ApplyHeading3	Ctrl+Alt+3	
Table	TableUpdate AutoFormat	Ctrl+Alt+U	
Window and Help	DocSplit	Ctrl+Alt+S	

Step 6. In the Current Keys field of the Customize (or Customize Keyboard) dialog box, highlight the shortcut key that you want to remove. Click the Remove button.

Step 7. Repeat steps 5 and 6 until you have removed all the shortcut key definitions that you want. The changes are made immediately to your new template or to Normal.dot.

Step 8. If you are creating a new template, choose File, Save when you are done.

The third conflict involves the fact that you can't easily redefine two Word shortcut keys that conflict with the U.S.-International keyboard layout. They are:

Add a command to a menu   Ctrl+Alt+ = (equals sign)

Remove a command from a menu   Ctrl+Alt+ - (minus sign)

Word has defined another keyboard combination, Ctrl+Alt+T, to insert the trademark symbol. You can remove this keyboard shortcut if you so desire. (Choose Insert, Symbol, choose Normal text in the Font drop-down list, click the ™ symbol, click the Shortcut Key button, click Alt+Ctrl+T in the Current keys field, and click the Remove button.) In Word 95 and Word 97, you can very easily insert a trademark symbol without using Ctrl+Alt+T. Simply type **(tm)** in your text. As soon as you continue to type, Word's AutoCorrect feature automatically replaces (tm) with ™.

You can, of course, choose to ignore these three conflicts and choose Insert, Symbol to pick the × and ¥ characters from Word's built-in character map. Another alternative is to define a new AltChar+*letter* shortcut for the three orphan symbols by choosing Insert, Symbol, highlighting them one at a time, and clicking the Shortcut Key button.

Accessing more hidden characters

A little-known benefit of Windows 95 is that it includes a bundled typeface containing several clipart-like characters. This face is called Wingdings, and it can definitely add interest to your documents — once you know what characters it contains.

Every Windows 95 user has access to hundreds of characters that are not visible on any keyboard. And users who have the Lucida Bright and Monotype Sorts fonts have access to more than 1,000 symbols, bullets, arrows, and other designs that printers call *dingbats*. All this, and there is almost no way for the average person to find out what characters are available.

To be fair, we must mention that Microsoft does provide the Character Map applet with Windows 95 to try to help people access these symbols. When you start this map, it displays all 224 characters that appear in a Windows font (but not the 652 characters in a multilingual font). Unfortunately, the Character Map window is small (and it can't be resized, although you can click on one character at a time to see an enlarged view of each character), so it's difficult to use it to browse through your type collection.

To give you a place to see many of these characters and symbols, we've collected all the characters (other than the extended multilingual fonts) available to Windows 95 users into two charts. Figure 21-1, which is at the beginning of this chapter, is for all Windows 95 users, while Figure 21-6 is for users who have the Lucida Bright and Monotype Sorts fonts. You might want to photocopy these charts and tack them on the nearest bulletin board for the next time you need just the right symbol.

You can insert about half of the characters in these figures into a document by pressing a key on your keyboard. Pressing the *w* key, for example, inserts character number 119 into your document. (Refer to Figure 21-1.) If you're using a text typeface, such as Windows 3.1's Arial, the inserted character is, in fact, a *w*. But if you're using Wingdings, the same keystroke inserts a diamond-shaped bullet (◆).

We use many of the higher-numbered special characters all the time. Windows makes it easy for us to use a long dash for emphasis — like this — by typing Alt+0150. A bullet you can use to set off paragraphs is at Alt+0149.

The Wingdings character set takes these special symbols much, much farther. Many Wingdings characters are pictorial. This includes keyboard and mouse symbols (Alt+55 and Alt+56), and electronic mail symbols (Alt+42 through Alt+47).

The Lucida Bright and Monotype Sorts character sets.

To access characters that cannot be typed directly from the keyboard:

1) Make sure the Num Lock light is *on*.
2) Hold down the Alt key while typing the appropriate number on the numeric keypad.
3) Release the Alt key.

Lucida Bright Math Extension character set
Lucida Bright Math Italic character set
Lucida Bright Math Symbol character set
Monotype Sorts character set
↓ ↓ ↓
Character Number → 64 @ @ @ ✣

32				64	@ @ @ ✣	96	` ` ` ✆	0128	(	0160		0192 À À ①	0224 à à à ➡
33	! ! ! ✂	65	A A A ✿	97	a a a ✤	0129	)	0161	¡ ¡ ¡ ❿	0193 Á Á ②	0225 á á á ➥
34	" " " ✄	66	B B B ✛	98	b b b ✥	0130 . , (	0162 ¢ ¢ ¢ ❢	0194 Â Â ③	0226 â â â ➤
35	# # # ✄	67	C C C ✜	99	c c c ✽	0131 ƒ ƒ)	0163 £ £ £ ❣	0195 Ã Ã ④	0227 ã ã ã ➢
36	$ $ $ ✄	68	D D D ✢	100	d d d ✳	0132 „ „ (	0164 ¤ ¤ ♥	0196 Ä Ä ⑤	0228 ä ä ä ➣
37	% % % ✍	69	E E E ✣	101	e e e ✾	0133 … …)	0165 ¥ ¥ ♦	0197 Å Å ⑥	0229 å å å ↪
38	& & & ∅	70	F F F ✦	102	f f f ✿	0134 † † ‹	0166 ¦ ¦ ❡	0198 Æ Æ ⑦	0230 æ æ æ ↬
39	' ' ' ⊗	71	G G G ◇	103	g g g ✺	0135 ‡ ‡ ›	0167 § § § ≋	0199 Ç Ç ⑧	0231 ç ç ç ♦
40	(((✈	72	H H H ★	104	h h h ✼	0136 ˆ (	0168 ¨ ¨ ✦	0200 È È ⑨	0232 è è è ➡
41	))) ✉	73	I I I ☆	105	i i i ✦	0137 ‰ ‰)	0169 © © © ✧	0201 É É ⑩	0233 é é é ⇨
42	* * * ☛	74	J J J ✇	106	j j j ✷	0138 Š Š (	0170 ª ♥	0202 Ê Ê ❶	0234 ê ê ê ⇨
43	+ + + ☞	75	K K K ☆	107	k k k ✿	0139 ‹ ‹)	0171 « « ♠	0203 Ë Ë ❷	0235 ë ë ë ⇔
44	, , , ✔	76	L L L ✫	108	l l l ●	0140 Œ Œ (	0172 ¬ ¬ ⑪	0204 Ì Ì ❸	0236 ì ì ì ➔
45	- - - ✍	77	M M M ★	109	m m m ○	0141)	0173 - - - ⑫	0205 Í Í ❹	0237 í í í ➙
46	. . . ✎	78	N N N ★	110	n n n ■	0142	0174 ® ® ® ⑬	0206 Î Î ❺	0238 î î î ➘
47	/ / / ✏	79	O O O ★	111	o o o ❑	0143	0175 ¯ ¯ ⑭	0207 Ï Ï ❻	0239 ï ï ï ➚
48	0 0 0 ✌	80	P P P ☆	112	p p p ❐	0144	0176 ° ° ⑮	0208 Ð Ð Ð ❼	0240 ð
49	1 1 1 ☞	81	Q Q Q ✹	113	q q q ❒	0145 ' '	0177 ± ± ± ⑯	0209 Ñ Ñ ❽	0241 ñ ñ ñ ➡
50	2 2 2 ●	82	R R R ✹	114	r r r ❒	0146 ' '	0178 ² ² ⑰	0210 Ò Ò ❾	0242 ò ò ò ❍
51	3 3 3 ✓	83	S S S ✳	115	s s s ▲	0147 " "	0179 ³ ³ ⑱	0211 Ó Ó ❿	0243 ó ó ➤➤
52	4 4 4 ✔	84	T T T ✳	116	t t t ▼	0148 " "	0180 ´ ´ ✎	0212 Ô Ô →	0244 ô ô ➡
53	5 5 5 ✕	85	U U U ✳	117	u u u ◆	0149 • ☐	0181 μ μ μ ❶	0213 Õ Õ →	0245 õ õ ➦
54	6 6 6 ✖	86	V V V ✳	118	v v v ❖	0150 — ☐	0182 ¶ ¶ ¶ ❶	0214 Ö Ö ↔	0246 ö ö ↗
55	7 7 7 ✗	87	W W W ☆	119	w w w ▶	0151 — ☐	0183 · · · ❷	0215 × × × ↕	0247 ÷ ÷ ↘
56	8 8 8 ✗	88	X X X ✳	120	x x x ✣	0152 ˜ "	0184 ¸ ¸ ❸	0216 Ø Ø ➡	0248 ø ø ➡
57	9 9 9 ✚	89	Y Y Y ✳	121	y y y ❘	0153 ™ ™	0185 ¹ ¹ ❶	0217 Ù Ù →	0249 ù ù ➡
58	: : : ✢	90	Z Z Z ●	122	z z z ■	0154 š š	0186 º º º ❻	0218 Ú Ú ↗	0250 ú ú ➡
59	; ; ; ✢	91	[[[✳	123	{ { { '	0155 › ›	0187 » » » ➤	0219 Û Û ➤	0251 û û ➡
60	< < < ✢	92	\ \ \ ✳	124	¦ ¦ ¦ '	0156 œ œ	0188 ¼ ¼ ¼ ❽	0220 Ü Ü →	0252 ü ü ➡
61	= = = ✝	93	]]] ✳	125	} } } "	0157	0189 ½ ½ ½ ❾	0221 Ý Ý →	0253 ý ý ➡
62	> > > ✞	94	^ ^ ^ ✣	126	~ ~ ~ "	0158	0190 ¾ ¾ ¾ ❿	0222 Þ Þ →	0254 þ þ ➡
63	? ? ? ✟	95	_ _ _ ✿	127		0159 Ÿ Ÿ	0191 ¿ ¿ ¿ ⑩	0223 ß ß ß →	0255 ÿ

Figure 21-6: The Lucida Bright and Monotype Sorts character sets.

All of these characters are laid out for you in Figures 21-1 and 21-6. Look through them with an eye for a particular character that you might use in your work. Chances are you'll find it.

Microsoft isn't the only source for fonts, of course. More symbols (and even better TrueType faces) are available from a variety of vendors. Casady & Greene offers two font libraries, one for Cyrillic languages and one for Eastern European languages (call 800-359-4920 or fax 408-484-9218). For more details, see the discussion that follows regarding additional special purpose fonts.

Using Multiple Languages

Many North American companies routinely use different languages in their documents. Companies in the southern U.S. often produce documents containing both English and Spanish text, while Canadian documents often include both English and French.

In WordPad, Word for Windows, and other word processors, you can mark text as belonging to a particular language. By default, text in Word documents is marked as the language you have selected using the Keyboard icon in the Control Panel. But you could use the Tools, Language command to mark one section as English (United States), and mark another section as French (Canadian), for example. You can mark text blocks as small as a single word or character as a particular language.

The ability to mark sections of text as different languages is helpful when you're spell-checking, hyphenating, and using a thesaurus in a document with text in multiple languages. If you have installed proofing utilities in another language, Word for Windows automatically uses those utilities when operating on any section of text marked as that language.

This ability to keep track of what text is in what language is part of the operating system in Windows 95, so many applications can take advantage of this capability now.

In addition, Windows 95 makes it easy to switch between different languages and, if you like, between different keyboard layouts. You can set up a number of different language identifiers and choose between them as you write a multilingual document. You just pick the appropriate identifier to tell Windows 95 which language you're going to use for the next section.

Setting up and using multilingual identifiers

You use the Keyboard Properties dialog box (under the Keyboard icon in the Control Panel) to set up multilingual identifiers. Once you've created the identifiers, they appear in the Tray on your Taskbar, as shown in Figure 21-7.

Figure 21-7: Language identifiers in the Tray on the Taskbar.

To create these identifiers, follow these steps:

STEPS

Adding Multilingual Identifiers

Step 1.   Open the Control Panel by clicking the Start button, pointing to Settings, and then clicking Control Panel.

Step 2.   Double-click the Keyboard icon.

Step 3.   Click the Language tab.

Step 4.   Click the Add button to display the Add Language dialog box.

Step 5.   Display the Language drop-down list.

Step 6.   Pick the language that you want, and click OK. The default keyboard layout for that language or location is now displayed next to the language in the Keyboard Properties dialog box.

Step 7.   If you want a different keyboard layout, click the Properties button, and choose a new layout.

Step 8.   Repeat steps 4 through 7 until you have added all the language identifiers that you will be using regularly, and then close the Keyboard Properties dialog box.

Once you have set up a list of language identifiers, you can choose among them by picking them from the Taskbar. Click the language identifier in the Tray (the identifier for the currently selected language). The list of identifiers pops up. Click the identifier of the language that you want to use.

You can also use the Left Alt+Shift key combination to rotate through the list. You have to release the Alt key before you press the next Shift key.

If you prefer, you can change the Left Alt+Shift shortcut key to Ctrl+Shift, or to no shortcut key at all. To do this, select the desired option button in the Language tab of the Keyboard Properties dialog box.

One language/keyboard layout combination is always set as the default. To designate the default combination, highlight it in the Language tab of the Keyboard Properties dialog box, and click the Set as Default button.

Multilingual documents

If you have installed Multilanguage Support, either during the Windows 95 setup process or later using the Add/Remove Programs icon in your Control Panel, you can write documents using Greek, Turkish, Cyrillic, or Central European character sets. Installing Multilanguage Support installs Arial, Times New Roman and Courier New fonts with the extended Windows ANSI character set containing 652 characters.

Once you have set up multilingual identifiers, as described in the previous section, you are ready to start typing in a foreign language. Of course, your keyboard keys often won't have the correct characters engraved upon them (check out Greek, for example), so you'll need to make up a chart that tells you which characters show up in your document when you type specific keys.

All you need to do to switch between languages and keyboard layouts is press Left Alt+Shift. To test this, start WordPad. Type text and then press Left Alt+Shift to switch your language/keyboard layout to Greek (assuming you set up a Greek identifier). The font list box in the WordPad format bar switches from a font identified as Western to one identified as Greek, and Greek letters now appear in your document as you type.

Multilingual proofing tools

If you find yourself using different languages frequently, you should probably obtain one or more of Alki Software Corp.'s Proofing Tools packages. The manual alone is valuable for its extensive charts showing the location of Windows characters and the layout of every different keyboard language supported by Windows. More importantly, each package provides a spelling checker, thesaurus, and hyphenation utility for a different language supported by Microsoft Word for Windows. (Alki offers packages for several versions of Word, including Word 97.)

Alki provides Proofing Tools packages for the following languages: Danish, Dutch, English-British, Finnish, French, French-Canadian, German, Italian, Norwegian, Portuguese, Portuguese-Brazilian, Spanish, and Swedish.

Each package has a list price of $99.95, or $89.95 if you obtain it directly from Alki ($79.95 for the Word 95 package). The company also sells a Comprehensive Thesaurus for Word for Windows (list $79.95, $39.95 from Alki), which contains three times the synonyms of the thesaurus that comes with Word, and a Comprehensive Spelling package (list $79.95, $69.95 from Alki), which adds 84,000 medical, legal, and business terms to Word's spelling checker.

You can reach Alki Software Corp. at 300 Queen Anne Ave. N., Suite 410, Seattle, WA 98109, 800-669-9673 or 206-286-2600.

Using Upper ANSI Characters in E-mail

The Internet and many other e-mail systems handle only the lower ASCII character set (unless you are using MIME or UUENCODE). CompuServe's WinCIM and its internal e-mail system handle the full Windows ANSI character set. You can also use Windows Messaging to send e-mail with these additional characters. Now all your buds in Germany and France will finally appreciate receiving letters from you.

Some Characters Say What You Mean

When you're documenting Windows applications for the average user, you might find yourself wondering how to represent certain keystrokes that the user is supposed to press.

Windows is full of important key combinations that are, frankly, hard to remember. In this book, we indicate key combinations like this by capitalizing the first letter of special keys on the keyboard. For example, to display the Start menu, we write, "press Ctrl+Esc."

But Elizabeth Swoope found that this wasn't enough, and she actually did something about it. She teaches a microcomputer literacy course to beginners, and says, "Some of my students just didn't 'get it' when I used ENTER or [Enter] or <Enter>, no matter how carefully I explained it." So she created her own TrueType and PostScript shareware fonts, which show every key on the keyboard as a tiny keycap.

There are many retail versions of fonts that show the PC keyboard, of course. But Swoope didn't find them useful, because they were too "arty." By rendering each keycap as a three-dimensional object, or with an artistic shadow border, these keycap characters actually became too small to read clearly when inserted into 10-point or 12-point type — the same size as the body copy of Swoope's documentation.

Swoope's fonts, shown in Figure 21-8, are simple, two-dimensional shapes that reproduce well at small sizes.

One font, RRKeyCaps, includes all the "gray keys" on a typical PC keyboard. Certain keys, such as Tab, come in different variations. Sometimes the key shows the word *Tab*, sometimes it shows a double-headed arrow, sometimes both. The variations allow you to choose the Tab key that looks like the one on the keyboards in your company.

Another font, RRKeyLetters, includes keycaps for punctuation marks, such as periods and commas. When you register, you receive a complete set of both fonts, with all the letters of the alphabet.

We have featured the RRKeyCap font and a sampler font with characters from both the Keyletter and Winsym fonts on the *Windows 95 Secrets* CD-ROM. To download the latest versions of these fonts from CompuServe, type

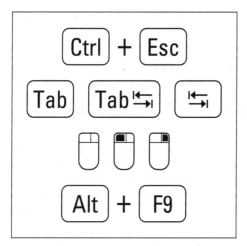

Figure 21-8: Examples of characters in the RRKeyCaps TrueType face.

GO DTPFORUM. Select the PC Fonts library, then download RR-PT#.ZIP (TrueType) or RR-PP#.ZIP (PostScript), where # is greater than 2, representing the latest version number.

To register or to obtain printed documentation by mail, send $49 (Louisiana residents add tax) to: Elizabeth Swoope, RoadRunner Computing, P.O. Box 21635, Baton Rouge, LA 70894; CompuServe: 76436,2426; 504-928-0780.

Using Keyboard Shortcuts

In this section, we examine the many shortcuts Windows and Windows applications assign to key combinations, such as Ctrl+Insert and Ctrl+A. Additionally, we teach you how to redefine key combinations that aren't used by *any* Windows applications in order to support your own macros.

You can specify that you have to press and release the Shift, Ctrl, or Alt keys *before* pressing the letter key of the combination by marking the Use StickyKeys check box in the Keyboard tab of the Accessibility Properties dialog box. You'll find this dialog box under the Accessibility Options icon in the Control Panel.

The most important (and poorly documented) shortcuts

Despite the ease-of-use publicity about Windows, a novice Windows user is confronted with a bewildering array of new objects to click and shortcut keys to learn. These shortcut keys are difficult to memorize, and some

Table 21-4 *(continued)*

Key or Combination	Effect
Print Screen	Copies the entire Windows display to the Clipboard. You can then paste the image into MS Paint or another graphics application and print it if you like.
Alt+Print Screen	Copies only the currently active window to the Clipboard. This could be the current application or a dialog box that has the keyboard focus within that application. This may not work on 84-key keyboards and computers with old BIOS chips. If it doesn't, try Shift+Print Screen instead.
Spacebar	Marks or clears a check box.
Alt+Spacebar	Pulls down the system control menu, the icon in the upper-left corner of an application window that controls that application's size and position, among other things.
Tab	Moves the selection box (the dotted rectangular box) to the next choice in a dialog box.
Shift+Tab	Moves the selection box in reverse order.
Alt+Tab	Switches to the application that was the current application before the application you are presently in. Switches back when pressed again. This may not work on 84-key keyboards and computers with old keyboard BIOS chips.
Alt+Shift+Tab	Switches between applications in the opposite direction as Alt+Tab.
Alt+Tab+Tab	Switches to every application currently running under Windows. Hold down Alt and press Tab repeatedly until the icon of the application you want to switch to is highlighted. Then release the Alt key. This is like Alt+Esc, but it displays only the icon and application names until you release the Alt key. (See the *Alt+Tab+Tab — the task switcher* section below.) This may not work on 84-key keyboards and computers with old keyboard BIOS chips.
Ctrl+Tab or Ctrl+F6	Jumps to the next child window in a multidocument application such as File Manager. (Use Ctrl+F6 in Word for Windows.)
Ctrl+X	Cuts highlighted item.
Ctrl+C	Copies highlighted item.
Ctrl+V	Pastes a copied or cut item.
Ctrl+Z	Undoes a previous action.

Key or Combination	Effect
The following keyboard shortcuts work with the Microsoft Natural keyboard. The Win key is the key with the Windows flag.	
Win	Displays the Start menu.
Win+E	Starts the Explorer.
Win+F	Opens the Find Files dialog box, similar to F3.
Ctrl+Win+F	Opens the Find Computer dialog box.
Win+M	Minimize All Windows.
Shift+Win+M	Undo Minimize All.
Win+R	Opens the Run dialog box.
Win+Tab	Switches between Taskbar buttons.
Win+Break	Opens the System Properties dialog box.
The following keyboard shortcuts let you modify how Windows 95 starts up. You press them before the Windows 95 graphic appears on your screen, while the Starting Windows 95 message is displayed.	
F4	Start the previous operating system. Boot MS-DOS. If Windows 95 has been installed in its own directory on the computer that has the MS-DOS 6.x or previous DOS operating system, then this key will start DOS instead of Windows. This also works for OS/2 and Windows NT.
F5	Safe mode startup of Windows 95. This allows Windows 95 to start with its most basic configuration, bypassing your Autoexec.bat and Config.sys files, using the VGA driver for video, and not loading any networking software. Use this if you have any problems starting Windows 95.
Shift+F5	Command line start. Boots into real-mode version of DOS 7.0. MS-DOS, Command.com and Dblspace are loaded low, taking up valuable conventional memory. Bypasses Config.sys and Autoexec.bat.
Ctrl+F5	Command line start without compressed drives. The Dblspace.bin and Drvspace.bin files are ignored, and double-spaced and drive-spaced drives are not mounted.
F6	Safe mode startup (like F5) but with the addition of the network.
F8	Go to the following menu before startup: 1. Normal 2. Logged (\BOOTLOG.TXT) 3. Safe mode 4. Safe mode with network support 5. Step-by-Step confirmation 6. Command prompt only 7. Safe mode command prompt only 8. Previous version of MS-DOS

(continued)

Table 21-4 *(continued)*	
Key or Combination	*Effect*
Shift+F8	Interactive start that goes through Config.sys and Autoexec.bat one line at a time and lets you decide if you want each line read and acted upon. Also goes through each command that Io.sys initiates before it carries out the commands in Config.sys.

Alt+Tab+Tab — the task switcher

You probably already know two shortcut key combinations that allow you to switch among running applications. Alt+Esc opens a different application every time you press it, and Alt+Tab switches from your current application to the application you previously used, and back.

But the best way to switch among your running applications isn't documented at all. Just *hold down* the Alt key while you press the Tab key several times, pausing slightly between each press. Unlike Alt+Esc, which switches applications and redraws the window for every application in turn, Alt+Tab+Tab switches applications but shows only the application's icon and name. Alt+Tab+Tab is a much faster method than Alt+Esc, because it lets you cycle quickly through all your running applications until you find the one you want. Simply release the Alt key when the desired application's icon is highlighted. The application's window is fully drawn and shifts to the foreground.

Alt+Esc and Alt+Tab+Tab work with both Windows apps and DOS apps running under Windows, whether these apps are running maximized, restored, or minimized as icons on the Taskbar.

84-key keyboards and computers with older keyboard BIOS chips may not recognize the Alt+Tab key combination. IBM's BIOS for its enhanced-AT 101-key keyboard was one of the first to accept the Alt key as a way to modify the meaning of the Tab key. Test your keyboard to see which combinations of keys you can take advantage of. If you have a 101-key keyboard, you shouldn't have a problem with Alt+Tab+Tab or any of the other possible combinations.

Using the humble Shift key

Behold the lowly Shift key. You hold it down while you type, and all you get is an uppercase letter, right? Not quite. Beneath the Shift key's humble reputation lies a world of undocumented functionality.

Many Windows users know the most basic ways the Shift key has been redefined. One of the first lessons for a new Windows user, for example, is that holding down the Shift key in a word processor while pressing an arrow key actually highlights text, instead of just moving the insertion point. And holding down Shift while clicking in text highlights everything between the insertion point and the place you clicked (in most word processors).

Other functions of the Shift key are much less well known. When you use the straight-line tool in MS Paint and many other drawing programs, for example, holding down Shift forces the line you draw to be perfectly horizontal or vertical. Similarly, when you use the box or oval tools, Shift forces these shapes into perfect squares or circles, respectively.

Undocumented

When you press and hold down Shift as you double-click a document icon in a folder or Explorer window, you will most likely put the document into the print queue. The Shift+double-click combination performs the second defined action for that document type (text file or WordPad file, for example) and usually the second action is Print. You can find out just what actions are defined for your document type by choosing View, Options in any folder or Explorer window, and clicking the File Types tab. For more on this topic, see Chapter 13.

If you have redefined any application menu items — by writing a Word for Windows macro to modify the File Print routine, say — you can often force the application to revert to the original, built-in procedure by holding down Shift while clicking that menu choice. (To defeat Word's AutoExec macro, however, you must start the application with the command Winword /m.)

Another great use of the Shift key involves the \Windows\Start Menu\ Programs\Startup folder. If you put shortcuts to applications in this folder, the applications are automatically loaded by Windows every time it starts. But if you hold down Shift when you see the Windows 95 logo — and keep it held down until the Taskbar is displayed on your Desktop — the Startup folder is completely ignored! This is *very* handy if something in the Startup folder is hanging Windows. You might also use this just to get Windows up and running quickly for some short task.

If you hold down Shift as soon as you see the Starting Windows 95 message, your Config.sys and Autoexec.bat files are ignored.

If you are using the File Manager, you can use the Shift key to display subdirectories only when you *care* to see them. For example, clicking the drive C icon (or pressing Ctrl+C) displays the top-level directories of the C drive. If you instead hold down the Shift key when you click the drive C icon, you force the File Manager to display all of the subdirectories on that drive. The Shift key works as a keyboard shortcut, too. When you press Ctrl+Shift+C, File Manager changes to drive C and displays all subdirectories, and so forth. This (undocumented) feature does not work in the Windows 95 Explorer.

Undocumented

If you mark the Restart the computer option button in the Shut Down Windows dialog box and then hold down the Shift key as you click the Yes button, Windows 95 restarts without a warm reboot.

If you want to open a file using an application that is different than the application associated with its file type, you can hold down the Shift key as you right-click the file, and then choose Open With in the context menu.

Do you want to really delete a file instead of sending it to the Recycle Bin? Highlight the file in a folder or Explorer window, and hold down the Shift key as you press Delete.

If you don't want a CD-ROM to start up automatically when you insert it in your CD-ROM drive, hold down the Shift key for a few seconds after you insert the CD-ROM.

A hot key and Desktop shortcut for screen savers

By right-clicking the Desktop, clicking Properties, and then clicking the Screen Saver tab, you can choose which screen saver you want to use.

Screen savers were originally designed to prevent ghostly images from permanently "burning in" on monochrome monitors that displayed the same application day after day. The "rotated-L" of Lotus 1-2-3 spreadsheets, for example, might still be visible even after you had exited the program.

Modern color monitors don't have the severe burn-in problems of mono-chrome monitors. But screen savers still have their uses. If the document you're working on is at all confidential or personal, you might want to blank your screen when you leave the room or when someone walks in. You might even blank the screen just to clear your mind for a few moments without your work staring you in the face.

You can, of course, start your screen saver by right-clicking the Desktop, choosing Properties, clicking the Screen Saver tab, and clicking Test — the saver will then begin. But there is a much faster method, which isn't in the Windows manual. If you've obtained any compatible screen savers from companies other than Microsoft, the following steps should work with them, too.

STEPS

Creating a Hot Key to Your Screen Saver

Step 1.   Use the Explorer to view your \Windows\System folder. Click the Details toolbar button (or choose View, Details), and then click the Type column header button in the right pane to arrange the filenames by type. Scroll down to the screen saver files. You should see Flying Windows.scr and Flying Through Space.scr, and any other screen savers you have.

Creating a Hot Key to Your Screen Saver

Step 2. Right-drag the desired screen saver from the right pane of the Explorer to your Desktop. Choose Create Shortcut(s) Here.

Step 3. Right-click the shortcut to your screen saver and click Properties. Click the Shortcut tab and click in the Shortcut key field.

Step 4. Press a key that you'll combine with Crlt+Alt to form your hot key combination. For example, if you press the letter *s*, the hot key combination Ctrl+Alt+S appears in the Shortcut key field. (In Word for Windows, this is the keyboard shortcut for the Window, Split command.) Click the OK button.

Now you can instantly invoke your screen saver by double-clicking the screen saver shortcut on your Desktop, or by holding down the Ctrl and Alt keys and pressing the associated letter key.

Caps Lock Notification

Tip

If you find yourself accidentally hitting Caps Lock, you can provide yourself with a little notification so you won't end up typing something LIKE THIS. You'll need to install the Accessibility options when you install Windows 95 or later using the Add/Remove Programs icon in the Control Panel.

STEPS

Turning on Caps Lock Notification

Step 1. Click the Start button, point to Settings, and then click Control Panel.

Step 2. Double-click the Accessibility Options icon.

Step 3. Mark the Use ToggleKeys check box. Click OK.

You will now hear a tone every time you press the Caps Lock, Num Lock, or Scroll Lock keys. The tone for enabling the key function is different from the tone for disabling it.

Keyboard Remap

Download Microsoft's Kernel Toys from http://www.microsoft.com/windows/software/krnltoy.htm and try out the keyboard remapper.

The Speed tab of the Keyboard Properties dialog box is, like all properties sheets, part of the user interface to the Registry. The actual Registry information about the keyboard is stored in the User.dat file in the \Windows folder. It is part of the information that is particular to a given user. This is what the exported ASCII file version of it looks like:

```
[HKEY_USERS\.Default\Control Panel\Keyboard]
"KeyboardSpeed"="31"
"KeyboardDelay"="0"
```

This Registry entry states that the repeat delay time is as short as possible, and that the key repeat rate is as fast as possible. We tried entering a number of values greater than 31, and it made no difference. If you set the sliders in the Speed tab of the Keyboard Properties dialog box all the way to the left, the values stored in the Registry are 0 and 3, respectively.

Secret

If you have a portable computer and an external keyboard, the speed and repeat rate settings may not be applied to them when you first start Windows 95. You'll have to open the Keyboard Properties dialog box every time you start Windows 95 and change these settings. You can put a short-cut to the Keyboard Properties dialog box on your Desktop to help with this process. For details, turn to Chapter 10.

If You Get a New and Different Keyboard

Almost all keyboards sold now are based on and compatible with the PC/AT Enhanced Keyboard (101/102-Key) standard. If you have a different keyboard attached to your computer, when you install Windows 95, it should detect the keyboard and install the correct keyboard driver. If you change your keyboard or if the hardware detection procedures in Windows 95 Setup didn't install the correct driver, then you can manually identify the keyboard to Windows 95 and get the correct keyboard driver installed.

To change the keyboard driver:

STEPS
Changing the Keyboard Driver

Step 1.   Open the Control Panel by clicking the Start button, pointing to Settings, and then clicking Control Panel.

Step 2.   Double-click the Keyboard icon.

Step 3.   Click the General tab.

Step 4.   Click the Change button.

Step 5.   Choose a new keyboard driver from the list, as shown in Figure 21-10.

Changing the Keyboard Driver

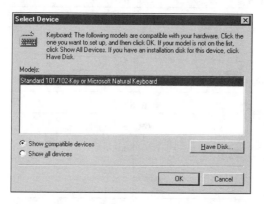

Figure 21-10: The Select Device dialog box. Choose a new keyboard driver here.

Behind the Keyboard Properties Sheets

Information about your keyboard type, layout, and language is stored in the Registry in the System.dat and User.dat files in the \Windows folder. You can start the Registry editor and search on *keyboard* to see how it is stored.

You can find other hardware and driver properties of the keyboard by double-clicking the System icon in the Control Panel, clicking the Device Manager tab, clicking the plus sign next to the Keyboard icon, highlighting your keyboard description, and then clicking the Properties button. There is not much you can change (unless you want to change the keyboard driver, which you can do more easily by following the instructions in the section *If You Get a New and Different Keyboard*).

Keyboard layout definition files are stored in the \Windows\System folder and have the extension *kbd.* Only the files necessary for your keyboard layouts are stored there. If you previously installed other keyboard layouts and have since uninstalled them in the Language tab of the Keyboard Properties dialog box, you can remove their associated files. The files, listed in Table 21-5, are quite small, so there is no need to remove them unless you are tight on hard disk space.

Table 21-5	Keyboard Layout Files It's Safe to Remove
Description	*Filename*
Belgian	kbdbe.kbd
Brazilian	kbdbr.kbd
British	kbduk.kbd
Canadian Multilingual	kbdfc.kbd
Danish	kbdda.kbd
Dutch	kbdne.kbd
Finnish	kbdfi.kbd
French	kbdfr.kbd
French Canadian	kbdca.kbd
German	kbdgr.kbd
German (IBM)	kbdgr1.kbd
Icelandic	kbdic.kbd
Italian	kbdit.kbd
Italian 146	kbdit1.kbd
Irish	kbdir.kbd
Latin American	kbdla.kbd
Norwegian	kbdno.kbd
Portuguese	kbdpo.kbd
Spanish	kbdsp.kbd
Swedish	kbdsw.kbd
Swiss German	kbdsg.kbd
Swiss French	kbdsf.kbd
United States	kbdus.kbd
United States Dvorak	kbddv.kbd
United States International	kbdusx.kbd

Summary

We detail the characters that you can use in Windows 95 and show you how to type characters that are not shown on your keyboard. We also discuss keyboard shortcuts and hot keys. Finally, we tell you how to modify properties of your keyboard driver to, for example, increase the key repeat rate. We provide:

▶ Lists of the character sets that come with Windows 95 and the fonts they are associated with.

▶ Tables of characters, so you can find just the ones you want to spice up your documents.

▶ Four methods of typing characters that don't show up on your keyboard.

▶ Steps for creating multiple keyboard layouts, as well as multilingual documents.

▶ A table of all Windows 95 hot keys.

▶ Instructions on how to fix the Shift key so that it works the way a touch typist would expect it to.

▶ Details on creating a hot key (and shortcut icon) to bring up your screen saver.

▶ Steps for modifying your keyboard speed.

Chapter 22

Displays

In This Chapter

We discuss monitors, video cards, and the Windows 95 software that drives them.

▶ What to look for in monitors

▶ What to look for in graphics cards

▶ Choosing a monitor/graphics card combination

▶ Installing video cards

▶ Changing the screen magnification

▶ Making the Desktop and all the elements on it look the way you want them to by changing their color, size, font, and font color

▶ Creating a fancy Desktop background and picking a screen saver

▶ Setting up Energy Star monitors and cards

First a Little Terminal-ogy

Your fingers are typing on the keyboard and your eyes are looking at the computer screen — no, at the monitor; no, at the display; no, at the image on the computer's screen; no, at the Desktop; no, at the wallpaper; well, how about that big colorful thing that sits on top of your desk. Hey, we've all got to get together on this so that we, the authors, can write something meaningful but not be straight-jacketed by the words.

■ The *monitor* is what sits on your desk or on top of your computer. It contains the display or the screen upon which Windows 95 is displayed. There is most likely a colorful image on the screen, surrounded by a thin black border. The thickness of the border depends on how you adjust your monitor. This image forms the background for everything placed "on top" of it — "on top" in the sense that it obscures the image.

■ The *image* is what appears when you start Windows 95. It can be a single color, even just black, although it's hard to tell the difference between the image and the black borders when it is black. The image can have a pattern such as tiled bricks or it can be a photograph. The image can be just about anything you want it to be — this is an area of great personal freedom. This image is the image of your *Desktop*. Things that obscure it are things on your Desktop.

Speed

If you are going to use a higher resolution card, you need to get a faster card because you don't want to fall behind yourself. The more pixels you push, the slower it goes. If you're now at 800 x 600 pixels, you need a boost to get your performance back to where you were at 640 x 480 pixels.

All video cards today (except the very cheapest) are accelerated. You can follow their ratings in computer magazines if you want to get some idea of their relative acceleration. Many of the video cards sit in a VESA or PCI local bus slot, giving them a fast connection to the processor. The processor is handing the video card the primitive video instructions as fast as it can. It is nice not to have to wait on a slow bus to get these instruction to the video card.

You won't need the fastest cards (and won't have to pay the premium for them) if you are not doing Desktop publishing, imaging, multimedia (video images running as though they were on video tape), or CAD (computer-aided design). Of course, multimedia continues to be a hot button, and it eats computer processing (and high-definition TV bandwidth) alive.

If you are going to have your children spend their formative years looking at Microsoft's Encarta (a CD-ROM based encyclopedia), then a fast card (and a 6X or better CD-ROM drive) may be just what you are looking for. A card that provides video acceleration (as distinct from graphics acceleration) does not, in fact, speed up the display of videos. What it can do is scale up the video size, say from 160 x 120 pixels to 320 x 240 pixels, without losing speed as measured in video frames per second.

Colors

More colors equals more memory required on the video card. More colors at higher resolutions equals even more required memory. Most Windows video cards come with 1MB or 2MB of dynamic RAM (DRAM) or video RAM (VRAM). VRAM is faster and more expensive. One type of DRAM, called EDO, or *extended data-out memory,* is almost as fast as (and is cheaper than) VRAM. Again check the card specifications and see what *color depth* (number of colors) is supported at what resolutions.

Some cards come with 4MB of VRAM. They can handle 24-bit, or 16,777,216 colors, at high resolution. Unless you are doing fancy artwork or color publishing, you don't need more than 256 colors. This is the fat middle of the market. Most CD-ROM videos come in 256 colors. Be sure to get at least 256 colors at the resolution you desire.

Choosing a Monitor/Card Combination

The bigger the monitor, the higher the resolution of the video card, the more they cost. You can easily check out the costs in the mail-order marketplace, but what about the benefits?

If you match a bigger monitor with a video card running at a moderate resolution, then you get the benefit of larger text on the screen. Larger text is easier on the eyes *as long as you can place the larger monitor as close to you as you can place a smaller monitor.*

The closer the monitor is to you, the bigger the text appears to your eyes, and the easier it is to read. If you have the monitor as close as you want and you still want the text bigger (without reducing how much material you see), then you need to get a bigger monitor.

There is a cost to increasing the size of the text on the screen by increasing the magnification factor. For a given size monitor, you see less text if the text is bigger.

If you match a bigger monitor with a video card running at a high resolution, you get the benefit of having more room to put stuff on your Desktop. This is referred to as more *real estate*.

Just what stuff are we talking about here? That depends. If you are just running one application, say at maximum size, more real estate gives you a bigger view of that application with more items in the application showing. For example, you see more text in a word processor, more cells in a spreadsheet, more of the image in a paint package, more of the page in a page-layout package, and more lines in a CAD system.

If you are running multiple applications on your Desktop, you have more room to place the other applications where you can bring them to the top of the Desktop easily. You can tile applications side by side. If you bring up dialog boxes in an application — a Find dialog box in a word processor, for instance — you can place it to the side and not in the way of the words.

Now might be a good time to review the section in Chapter 20 in which we discuss font sizes, in particular the discussion of the "logical" inch (also see the section later in this chapter about the "displayed" inch). The short of it is this: The objects on the screen are magnified. On a 14-inch display with a video card set at 800 x 600 resolution and font size (or magnification) set to 96 pixels per logical inch (Small Fonts), text is 25 percent larger than its printed size. On a 17-inch display with the same video resolution, you see the same amount of text, but now the text is 44 percent larger than its printed size.

Picking a monitor from the list

When you install Windows 95, you can specify which monitor you are using (if it isn't plug and play). Make sure you do so, because this sets the limit on the available video resolutions in the Settings tab of the Display Properties dialog box.

You can always go back and use the Add New Hardware icon in the Control Panel to choose a different monitor later.

Place a physical ruler over the ruler displayed on the screen and see how much bigger (or smaller) the displayed inch is compared to an actual inch. The ratio of the size of the displayed inch to the actual inch is the magnification of the text on your screen. An inch of text is displayed at the size of the displayed inch.

Getting comfortable first

Sit down in front of your system and/or a friend's computer. Adjust the monitor and keyboard to a comfortable position. Is it easy to read the text displayed on the screen? Adjust the text size by using the zoom feature in a word processor or, if you are using Windows 95, by changing the font size in the Settings tab of the Display Properties dialog box. Do you notice an improvement?

Table 22-2 is a comparison of monitors of different sizes paired with video cards of different maximum resolutions and a range of font sizes or magnifications. It gives you the actual increase in the size of the text displayed on the screen over its size on the printed page for each combination. The percentages represent the ratio of the displayed inch to the actual inch.

■ The first monitor size is the nominal (or advertised) diagonal dimension of the display. The second monitor size is the average actual diagonal dimension of monitors in the class.

■ The height and width of the Desktop image is given in inches, assuming a 3-to-4 ratio of length to height.

■ Video card resolution names are by common name or resolution value in pixels.

■ Font size is given in the values used in the Custom Font Size dialog box, and in the Settings tab of the Display Properties dialog box. The first value is dots per logical inch, and the value in parentheses is the magnification factor.

■ NA = Not applicable.

Use your experience working with your computer or your friend's computer and the information in Table 22-2 to see what size monitor, card resolution, and font size are most comfortable for your eyes. Say you find that a 14-inch monitor at SVGA resolution and Large Fonts size is about right. This corresponds to 156 percent magnification. If you later use a 15-inch monitor at 1024 x 768 resolution, set the font size at 150 percent to get the same magnification.

Table 22-2 Magnification by Monitor Size and Video Card Resolution

	Video Resolution				
	VGA	SVGA	1024 x 768	1280 x 1024	1600 x 1280
14-inch monitors (actual size 13 inches — 7.8 inches high x 10.4 inches wide)					
96 (Small Fonts)	156%	125%	98%		
129 (Large Fonts)	195%	156%	122%		
144 (150%)	NA	187%	146%		
15-inch monitors (actual size 14 inches — 8.4 inches high x 11.2 inches wide)					
96 (Small Fonts)	168%	134%	105%		
129 (Large Fonts)	210%	168%	131%		
144 (150%)	NA	202%	158%		
17-inch monitors (actual size 15 inches — 9 inches high x 12 inches wide)					
96 (Small Fonts)	NA	144%	113%	84%	
129 (Large Fonts)	NA	180%	141%	105%	
144 (150%)	NA	216%	169%	127%	
150 (200%)	NA	288%	225%	169%	
21-inch monitors (actual size 19 inches — 11.4 inches high x 15.2 inches wide)					
96 (Small Fonts)	NA	NA	143%	107%	86%
129 (Large Fonts)	NA	NA	178%	134%	107%
144 (150%)	NA	NA	214%	160%	128%
150 (200%)	NA	NA	285%	214%	171%

Use Table 22-2 to put a number on your comfort zone. Given how far away you normally are from the monitor, this number represents how much bigger you want the text on your display. Use this number to gauge the value of using a larger monitor at a higher resolution.

You can also use the table to see how to adjust your monitor, video card resolution, and font size. It doesn't make any sense to set up your monitor in a manner that will give you a value for your magnification, if it is far away from your comfort zone.

by the video card makers. You can still use the older 16-bit drivers from the video manufacturers with Windows 95 if your video card does not have a 32-bit video driver from Microsoft, or if it supports features that Microsoft's drivers don't.

Setup

When Windows 95 is installed, Setup attempts to determine what type of video display adapter is installed in your computer. It examines the chip set on your video adapter. If you already have Windows 3.0 or 3.1 installed, Setup attempts to match your previous video resolution and color depth.

If the video driver that Microsoft supplies with Windows 95 can't run at the settings of your previous version of Windows, then the new video settings will default to VGA values (640 x 480 pixels at 16 colors) or, if possible, 640 x 480 pixels at 256 colors. You can make changes to these settings after Windows 95 is installed.

Wait a minute. Where are the instructions for installing the Windows 95 video drivers? Well, that's it. When you set up Windows 95, the driver for your video card is installed automatically.

You can pick a different driver during the installation process when you are asked to confirm the hardware list as detected. Click the video driver, and then click Change to choose from a list of all the available Microsoft-developed video drivers. See further instructions in the next section.

Installing a new video driver

If you change your video card, or if Setup hasn't correctly detected your video card, you can install another video driver. One way to do this is to first install the new video driver, and then shut down Windows 95, power down the computer, install the new video card, and finally reboot Windows 95. Alternatively, you can change the video driver to the Standard Display Adapter (VGA) driver, shut down Windows 95, power down your computer, install the new video card, reboot Windows 95, install the new video driver, and then reboot Windows 95 again. We suggest that you use the second method.

If you install the new video card before installing the new driver, Windows may boot up in Safe mode, which is VGA, and then you can change the video driver.

STEPS

Changing the Video Driver

Step 1. Right click the Desktop. Click Properties, and then click the Settings tab. Click the Change Display Type button to display the Change Display Type dialog box. (If you don't have a Change Display Type button, click the Advanced Properties button.)

Step 2. Click the Change button in the Adapter Type area of the dialog box to display the Select Device dialog box. (If you clicked the Advanced Properties button in step 1, click the Change button in the Adapter tab of the Advanced Display Properties dialog box.)

Step 3. The Show compatible devices option button is marked by default. Click the Show all devices option button, as shown in Figure 22-2, to get the complete list of video drivers for Windows 95.

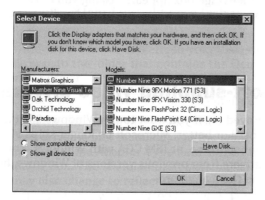

Figure 22-2: The Select Device dialog box listing the video drivers that come with Windows 95.

Step 4. Click the video driver for the card that you have or will install in your computer.

Step 5. If you have a diskette from the video card manufacturer that contains its Windows driver for this card, and if this driver is newer than the one that shipped with Windows 95, insert that diskette into your floppy disk drive and click Have Disk. After you have indicated the correct diskette drive letter, click OK in the Install From Disk dialog box.

Step 6. Click the OK button in the Select Device dialog box. Your video card driver is installed, and the name for the new driver appears in the Adapter Type field in the Change Display Type dialog box.

(continued)

Reinstalling if there are problems

Windows 95 may start in Safe mode or display an error message stating that it can't use the video driver choices you have implemented. If this happens, you can easily go back to the Settings tab of the Display Properties dialog box and install a new video driver. Windows 95 will start in VGA mode if it can't start in any other video mode.

More video card problems

Microsoft makes an effort to get the best performance out of video cards, but this may cause problems with your card. If you experience problems with your mouse pointer or unexplained crashes, you might want to back off on the default setting for hardware acceleration of your video card. Here's how:

STEPS
Changing Video Hardware Acceleration

Step 1.   Click the Start button, point to Settings, click Control Panel, and then double-click the System icon. Click the Performance tab.

Step 2.   Click the Graphics button to display the Advanced Graphics Settings dialog box. Use the slider to reduce hardware acceleration to None.

Step 3.   Click the two OK buttons.

Changing Resolution, Color Depth, and Magnification

A really nifty feature of Windows 95 is that you can change the display resolution of your monitor without having to restart Windows. Windows 95 still has to restart if you change the color depth (the number of colors that can be displayed on the screen at any one time) or the magnification, but it does that automatically.

To change your resolution, color depth, or magnification, right-click the Desktop, click Properties, and then click the Settings tab. The Desktop area slider lets you change screen resolution (in pixels), the Color palette list lets you change color depth, and the Font size list lets you change the magnification (see Figure 22-3).

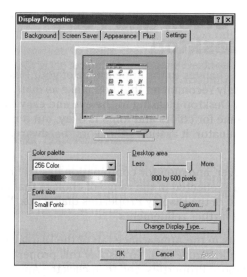

Figure 22-3: The Settings tab of the Display Properties dialog box.

Not all combinations of Desktop area and Color palette will be available to you. What is available depends on how much video memory is installed on your display adapter card, the maximum video resolution of your card and driver, and the capabilities of your monitor.

Choose a new Desktop area by moving the slider to the left or right. As you do so, the monitor graphic in the dialog box changes to give you an idea of the relative changes you can expect at the different resolutions. When you click OK, Windows asks if you want to keep the new values. Click OK, and the Desktop will be rebuilt within a few seconds.

Quickly Changing Video Resolution

The *Windows 95 Secrets* CD-ROM features a video resolution utility called Vidres.exe that you can use to quickly change video resolution without having to go to the Display Properties dialog box. You can use it to change color depth also, but this requires restarting Windows 95.

Microsoft also supplies a simple utility that is essentially a shortcut to the Settings tab of the Display Properties dialog box. Quickres.exe creates a small icon in the Tray on the Taskbar. Double-click this icon to display the Settings tab of the Display Properties dialog box. You can download this utility as a part of PowerToys from the Microsoft web site, at http://www.microsoft.com/windows/software/powertoy.htm.

To see how to create your own shortcut to the Settings tab of the Display Properties dialog box, turn to the *Control Panel icons* section of Chapter 10.

The items

There are 18 Desktop objects in the Item drop-down list (in the Appearance tab of the Display Properties dialog box). Twelve are displayed in the mock Desktop window at the top of the dialog box. Some, such as Icon Spacing (Horizontal) and Icon Spacing (Vertical), would be difficult to show on the mock Desktop.

If you click an object on the mock Desktop, its name appears in the Item field, and its attribute values are shown in the other fields. You can also pick a Desktop object from the Item drop-down list.

Lots of objects on your Desktop aren't listed in the Item drop-down list. Some names in the list refer to something other than what you would expect. And it isn't always obvious which attributes you're affecting when you make changes to a Desktop object. To make certain changes to Desktop objects, you have to edit the Registry.

Table 22-4 lists the attributes associated with every Desktop object in the Item drop-down list. This table not only lists most of the Desktop objects, it also tells you what attributes you can change for each object.

Table 22-4	Attributes of Desktop Objects				
Item	*Color*	*Font*	*Size*	*Font Color*	*Font Size*
3D Objects	x			x	
Active Title Bar	x	x	x	x	x
Active Window Border	x	x			
Application Background		x			
Caption Buttons	x				
Desktop		x			
Icon	x		x	x	
Icon Spacing (Horizontal)	x				
Icon Spacing (Vertical)	x				
Inactive Title Bar	x	x	x	x	x
Inactive Window Border	x	x			
Menu	x	x	x	x	x
Message Box			x	x	x
Palette Title	x		x	x	
Scrollbar			x		
Selected Items	x	x	x	x	x
ToolTip		x	x	x	x
Window		x			x

Table 22-5 lists the Desktop objects in the Item drop-down list and describes what they mean.

Table 22-5	What the Names of Desktop Objects Mean
Name of Item	*What Is It?*
3D Objects	Setting the color for 3D Objects sets the colors for message boxes, title bars, scrollbars, caption buttons, the Taskbar, window borders, and dialog boxes. You can reset the colors associated with some of these items directly by choosing the items from the Item drop-down list.
Active Title Bar	The horizontal strip at the top of an active window. Setting the font style and size here also sets the font style and size used by the Taskbar.
Active Window Border	The thin (sizable) line around the window that has the focus. It is two pixels in from the actual border. Dialog boxes that are active don't get one. As you make it thicker, you also increase the thickness of the inactive window border.
Application Background	The background color of the application window. You see this color in multidocument applications when there are no documents open or they are all minimized.
Caption Buttons	The buttons in the upper-right corner of the window title bar. You can't change their color independently of 3D Objects.
Desktop	The color of the Desktop itself and the background color of the icon titles. If your Desktop is completely wallpapered, you won't see this color except behind the icon titles.
Icon	The size of icons and the font style and size used by the icon titles. You can only change the color to black or white, depending on the Desktop color. The font style and size attributes you set for this object are also used by the Explorer and folder windows.
Icon Spacing (Horizontal)	The space between large icons on the Desktop and in folder windows (measured in pixels). This value changes with the font size setting in the Settings tab of the Display Properties dialog box.
Icon Spacing (Vertical)	The same as horizontal icon spacing, except vertical.
Inactive Title Bar	The horizontal strip at the top of an inactive window. Contains the caption buttons.

Undocumented

Undocumented

(continued)

Table 22-5 *(continued)*

Name of Item	What Is It?
Inactive Window Border	The thin (sizable) line around windows that don't have the focus. See Active Window Border.
Menu	The menu area below the window title bar. You can change all five attributes. The font changes are also reflected in the Start menu and in all other menus.
Message Box	The little messages, often error messages, that pop up on your Desktop. This is not the same as a dialog box.
Palette Title	Unknown, no visible effect.
Scrollbar	You can't set the color of scrollbars through this item.
Selected Items	The block of color around the menu item that you have clicked or pointed to, often a bright color and a contrasting font color to let you quickly see where you are.
ToolTip	Little boxes with text that appear when you leave your mouse pointer over items such as Taskbar buttons. The ToolTip font size also sets the size of the text in status bars.
Window	A major item. The background color of the client window. In your word processor, this sets the background color of your document windows.

Undocumented

Undocumented

Changing the color of disabled text and Explorer items

Secret

One item that you might want to change is the color of disabled menu items. You can this see this element in the mock Desktop window, but you can't get to it in the Item field. You can, however, change it in the Registry. This color not only changes the color of the disabled menu items, it also changes the color of the squares around the plus signs in the Explorer and the color of the dotted lines connecting Explorer items in the left pane. Here's how to change how disabled menu items are displayed:

STEPS

Changing the Color of Disabled Menu Items

Step 1.   Double-click Regedit.exe in your \Windows folder.

Step 2.   Navigate to HKEY_USERS\.Default\Control Panel in the Registry editor window.

Changing the Color of Disabled Menu Items

If you have enabled user profiles, you can choose your name or any user name instead of .Default.

Step 3. Click Colors in the left pane. Click GrayText in the right pane.

Colors will not exist as an item in the Registry unless you have previously changed one of your Desktop colors and saved it. (If you don't see the Colors item, exit the Registry, change the color of an item in the Appearance tab of the Display Properties dialog box, save the change as a new scheme, and then come back to these steps.)

Step 4. Choose Edit, Modify.

Step 5. Type an RGB value for the color you want for disabled menu items. You can check out the RGB values for various colors in the Color dialog box. When you click a color, its RGB value is displayed in the Red, Green, and Blue fields. See the *The Color dialog box* section later in the chapter.

Step 6. Click OK, and exit the Registry.

Step 7. The next time you start Windows, the new colors will be used.

Color

Most of what we say about colors here assumes you have configured your video card driver to display 256 colors. We mention differences related to using 16-color drivers throughout the text.

You can change the color and/or font color of many Desktop objects. For example, you can change the color and font color of the menu bar. In general, you want the font color of an object to contrast with the color of the object itself so that you can read the text.

Changing the color of 3D Objects changes the color of everything but ToolTip, Desktop, Application Background, and Window. The 3D Objects color is also the color used for the Taskbar, status bars, toolbars, dialog boxes, and so on.

If you have wallpaper covering your desk, the color of the Desktop won't show up except as a background to the icon title text.

The major color that you see on your Desktop when you open an application or a document is the one labeled Window. It is the background color for your text. The default color is bright white. This can be quite hard on the eyes, especially if the contrast and brightness on your monitor are turned up, you are in a highly lit room with fluorescent lights, and your monitor's refresh rate is less than 70 Hz. You should try out other Window colors to see how your eyes feel.

The Window color is also dithered (combined) with the 3D Objects color to create the Scrollbar color. The Application Background color is different from the Window color. For example, in Microsoft Word, the Application Background color is the color behind your document windows. You see it when you don't have any documents open, or when they are all minimized. In contrast, the Window color is the background color of the document itself.

The Color pick box

When a Desktop object whose color you can modify is selected in the Item drop-down list and you click the Color button, a Color pick box appears, as shown in Figure 22-5. The pick box contains 20 solid colors. The top 16 are always the same colors. The bottom four can change. If you are using 16-color mode, the bottom colors just repeat four of the other colors. Pick the color that you want for the currently selected Desktop object by clicking it.

Figure 22-5: The Color pick box.

Windows reserves the 20 colors in the Color pick box for use with the Desktop objects. If your video card and video driver support 256 colors, your applications can use the additional 236 colors. For example, the producers of a Video for Windows file can use whatever colors they desire out of these 236 in the palette for the video.

The Color dialog box

The Color pick box has an Other button that opens the Color dialog box, which in some cases allows you to choose from a larger number of colors. This dialog box is shown in Figure 22-6.

If you have set your color depth at 256 colors, the increased colors are created by *dithering*, or combining, the first 16 colors displayed in the Color pick box. The Basic colors grid of the Color dialog box contains 48 colors. Thirty-two of them are dithered colors, and the other 16 are the same 16 solid colors shown in the Color pick box. The last four colors in the Color pick box are not shown in the Basic colors grid.

Undocumented

The Color dialog box includes dithered colors when the selected Desktop object can use a dithered color. These objects include 3D Objects (some items whose colors are set by 3D Objects can also use dithered colors), Active Window Border, Desktop, Application Background, and Inactive Window Border.

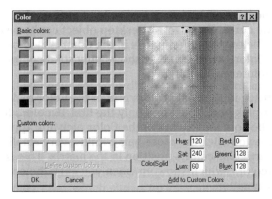

Figure 22-6: The Color dialog box.

If a Desktop object can't use a dithered color, then the Basic colors grid displays only the 16 colors from the Color pick box. The colors are just repeated to fill the 48 slots.

Defining and using custom dithered colors

You can define custom dithered colors for Desktop objects that can use dithered colors. You can't define custom solid colors. The only solid colors that are available are the 20 from the Color pick box.

STEPS

Defining Custom Dithered Colors

Step 1.   In the Appearance tab of the Display Properties dialog box, select the Desktop object for which you want to define a custom dithered color in the Item list, click the Color button, and then click Other to display the Color dialog box.

Step 2.   Create the new color by clicking to place the crosshair on the desired spot in the color matrix, typing the RGB values in the Red, Green, and Blue fields, or typing the Hue, Saturation, and Luminosity values.

Step 3.   Click the Add to Custom Colors button to add your color to the Custom colors grid.

Step 4.   Click the color you just defined in the Custom colors grid.

Step 5.   Click OK.

Step 6.   Your new color is now applied the currently selected Desktop object.

Secret

Changing the button face color (3D Objects) changes the color of many Desktop objects, including status bars, toolbars, scrollbar buttons, caption buttons, and dialog boxes. It doesn't change the other four colors associated with buttons. You can, however, change these four colors in the Registry.

STEPS

Changing the Four Button Colors

Step 1.   Double-click Regedit.exe in the \Windows folder.

Step 2.   Navigate to HKEY_USERS\.Default\Control Panel in the Registry editor window.

If you have enabled user profiles, you can choose your name or any user name instead of .Default.

Step 3.   Click Colors in the left pane. Click ButtonDkShadow or any of the four color names in the right pane.

If you haven't changed the colors of a Desktop object previously, there won't be a Colors item in the Registry. (If you don't see the Colors item, exit the Registry, change the color of an item in the Appearance tab of the Display Properties dialog box, save the change as a new scheme, and then come back to these steps.)

Step 4.   Choose Edit, Modify.

Step 5.   Type an RGB value for that button color, and click OK. Yes, you have to be familiar with RGB values to make sense of this step. To determine the RGB values for various colors, display the Color dialog box (see *The Color dialog box* section earlier in the chapter), and click various colors. The RGB value for the color you click is displayed in the Red, Green, and Blue fields.

Step 6.   Optionally, repeat steps 3 through 5 for other button colors.

Step 7.   Exit the Registry.

Step 8.   The next time you start Windows 95, the new colors will be used.

Undocumented

Windows 95 can easily wipe out the changes you make to the button colors. If you change to another scheme and then go back to your current scheme, your changes will be gone, unless you first save your scheme under a new name.

STEPS

Updating the Four Button Colors

Step 1. Right-click the Desktop. Choose Properties, and then click the Appearance tab. Display the Item drop-down list, and choose 3D Objects. Then choose the color that you want from the Color pick box.

Step 2. Click Apply to apply this button color to your Desktop objects.

Step 3. Click the Save As button, type a name for this scheme, and click OK.

Step 4. Pull down the Scheme drop-down list and choose another scheme. Click Apply.

Step 5. Pull down the Scheme drop-down list and choose the scheme that you just saved. Click Apply.

Step 6. The four button colors are automatically updated to the colors you set in the Registry.

This is not a particularly great way to get these colors to update. Microsoft should have written Windows 95 so it updated these four button colors when you chose the button face color. Unfortunately, it didn't.

Fonts

Windows 3.1 gave you the power to change the colors of the Desktop objects and the sizes of the borders. Windows 95 also lets you change the size of the objects and their fonts. You can choose among screen fonts and TrueType fonts, and you can specify the font point size, font style (regular, bold, or italic), and font color.

These are excellent improvements over Windows 3.1. Given the fact that more people are now using large monitors and high-resolution video cards, it is important for end users to be able to adjust the size of their Desktop objects. We encourage you to make adjustments until you find the right combination.

The font point size multiplied by the ratio of the displayed inch to an actual inch determines the displayed size of text entities on the Desktop. Increasing the font size (magnification) in the Settings tab of the Display Properties dialog box increases the size of the displayed fonts, although their "point size" remains the same.

The default font and font point size on the Desktop and in dialog boxes is 8-point MS Sans Serif (10 points on higher resolutions). MS Sans Serif is a screen font that is specifically designed for VGA-resolution screens. It looks fine on Super VGA screens. MS Sans Serif looks good at 10, 12, 14, 18, and 24 points. It doesn't look so good at other point sizes.

Arial, a TrueType font, looks almost as good on the screen as MS Sans Serif at these point sizes, and it looks better at other point sizes.

Some combinations of font, font point size, and magnification will not work. For example, MS Sans Serif at 8 points and 75 percent magnification does not result in smaller displayed fonts on the Desktop because MS Sans Serif is a screen font, and it isn't displayed below 8 points.

If the font were Arial, then this combination *would* reduce the size of the displayed text.

You cannot change the font in the item labeled 3D Objects, which also means that you don't have control over the dialog box font. (The font used for the text on the Taskbar buttons is controlled through the Active Title Bar font settings.) Because dialog boxes are automatically sized based on the font size, you don't have independent control of dialog box size. Dialog box size is determined by the setting in the Font size drop-down list in the Settings tab of the Display Properties dialog box.

Changing the System font size

You can change the font size used by dialog boxes and the Contents and Index tabs of the Windows 95 help files. Right-click the Desktop, choose Properties, click the Settings tab, and then click the Custom button (or, if you don't have a Custom button, select Other from the Font size drop-down list). Choose a large custom font size, and click OK. Setting a large custom font size increases the size of the dialog boxes and help pages, as well as the size of the font.

When you choose a large custom font size, the displayed size of all the text on your screen is changed, no matter what the point size of its font. If you have a small monitor with a video adapter set to a low or moderate resolution, the dialog boxes may no longer fit on your screen.

Changing the magnification by setting a large custom font size (in the Settings tab of the Display properties dialog box) works well as a way to enlarge text entities whose font point sizes you can't directly control in the Appearance tab. You can use this method in combination with "manually" adjusting font point size settings in the Appearance tab for text entities whose values you can change.

Be sure to read the discussion in Chapter 20 regarding fonts.

Size

Review Table 22-4 earlier in this chapter to see which items can be resized. The vertical and horizontal icon spacing values don't change the size of the icons, just the distance that separates them. You can change the size of the title bars, the menu bar height, the width of vertical scrollbars, the height of horizontal scrollbars, and the thickness of window borders.

Many of the size properties interact with each other, and often with font sizes. For example, if you increase the size of the caption buttons, this in turn increases the height of the title bar. If you choose a bigger font point size for the menu bar, the menu bar height increases so that it can fit the larger menu bar text.

Icons on the Desktop are normally 32 x 32 pixels. You can increase (or decrease) their size in the Appearance tab of the Display Properties dialog box. Because these icons were originally created by hand on a 32 x 32 pixel grid, multiplying them by some factor will produce icons that don't look as sharp as the originals.

When you change video resolution, icon size is automatically changed (in some cases). You can change it back to the original 32 x 32 size easily enough in the Appearance tab.

Changing icon size, icon spacing, and icon font sizes is easy, so you can play with these settings a bit to see what you like. If only it were as easy to change all the text objects on your Desktop!

Registry values

The values you set in the Appearance tab of the Display Properties dialog box are stored in the Registry. To view these values, follow the steps in the section earlier in this chapter entitled *Changing the color of disabled text and Explorer items*. The values are stored in the following areas:

```
HKEY_USERS\.Default\Control Panel\Appearance\Schemes
HKEY_USERS\.Default\Control Panel\Colors
HKEY_USERS\.Default\Control Panel\Desktop\WindowMetrics
```

We have included an exported Registry branch that you can import to change the colors of your Desktop. Its name is Color.reg, and it is stored in the Registry folder on the *Windows 95 Secrets* CD-ROM. If you are using a standard color scheme, or if you have previously saved your existing color scheme, you can easily revert back to your previous colors. To import Color.reg into your Registry, take the following steps:

STEPS

Importing Color.reg into Your Registry

Step 1.   Save your current color scheme if you are not using one of the schemes that comes with Windows 95.

Step 2.   Open an Explorer window focused on the Registry folder on the *Windows 95 Secrets* CD-ROM.

Step 3.   Right-click Color.reg. Click Merge.

Step 4.   Restart Windows 95.

(continued)

STEPS *(continued)*

Importing Color.reg into Your Registry

Step 5. Right-click your Desktop. Choose Properties, and click the Appearance tab.

Step 6. Click the Save As button, enter a name for this color scheme, and click OK.

Changing the size of dialog boxes

Most Windows applications create the dialog boxes for functions such as opening and closing files by taking advantage of a Microsoft common dialog box dynamic link library called Commdlg.dll. (Notable exceptions are the Microsoft Office applications, which don't use Commdlg.dll.) This library makes all of these dialog boxes look consistent, and Microsoft can update it as Windows itself evolves.

The dialog boxes that Commdlg.dll produces for File Open and other functions are a lot smaller than what most monitors today are capable of displaying. Even a bad old DOS character-mode display could show you 25 files per screen (or more than 100 with the *wide* switch on). But the File Open dialog box doesn't even use the full display area of a plain VGA display (640 x 480 pixels). Now that EGA is no longer a supported display type, Windows has no excuse for these dinky dialog boxes.

End users don't have an easy way to resize the common dialog boxes to take advantage of the full resolution of their displays. Fortunately, Commdlg.dll is somewhat extensible for developers. And a version of a shareware utility makes it possible for you to redefine common dialog boxes to almost any size that will fit on your screen.

Let Me See is a $5 utility by Eric Askilsrud, the same developer who created the Icon Corral program. Let Me See redraws your File Open dialog boxes and others that are generated by Commdlg.dll. You can specify the size of the dialog boxes and change the way files are listed — as a plain filename list or with complete details sorted by name, size, and so on.

Many of the items in the common dialog boxes are fixed in size, so how does Let Me See enlarge the dimensions without distorting things? The program enlarges only the "client area" of dialog boxes — the empty box into which the filenames are written. Expanding this area lets you display more information without making the rest of the dialog box look "jagged" due to scaling.

The first time you run Let Me See, it displays its own control panel that lets you specify box size and other options. A Test button lets you see what your choices will do to a typical dialog box. After configuring the program, you place a shortcut to it into your Startup folder. It runs invisibly thereafter. If you need the control panel again, you run Let Me See a second time.

Eric Askilsrud's home page is at http://weber.u.washington.edu/~redlense/ win95.html. Let Me See currently works only on English versions of Windows 95 and NT and only up to 150 percent font magnification. Systems other than these may have different font metrics that can throw off the calculation of dialog box sizes.

The Desktop Wallpaper

Talk about a mixed metaphor — when was the last time you put wallpaper on a real Desktop? Not likely.

You choose the color of your Desktop in the Appearance tab of the Display Properties dialog box. The Desktop is one of the items in the Item drop-down list. If you don't put up any wallpaper, this is the color you get as the background color on your screen. If you do put up some wallpaper, this is the background color of the titles of the icons on the Desktop.

Whatever graphic image you choose as your wallpaper functions as background to your Desktop on your screen. Your Desktop feels like a clear piece of glass on top of this graphical background. The Taskbar and folders appear to lie on the glass.

Right-click the Desktop and choose Properties in the context menu to display the Background tab of the Display Properties dialog box. As shown in Figure 22-7, you can choose a wallpaper or a pattern. (See the next section for more information about patterns.)

Two-color patterned wallpaper

Wallpaper is something of a misnomer. We normally think of wallpaper as patterned paper. There can be all kinds of wallpaper in Windows 95.

Windows 95 comes with lots of graphical patterns that, when repeated across your screen, create a two-color patterned wallpaper. To create this type of wallpaper, choose None in the Wallpaper list, and choose a pattern from the Pattern list. One color in the pattern is your Desktop color, and the other is black.

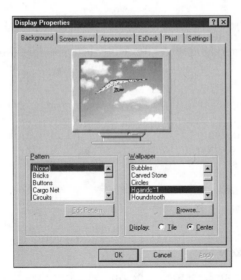

Figure 22-7: The Background tab of the Display Properties dialog box.

Repeated picture element wallpaper

You can create another type of wallpaper by choosing a wallpaper in the Wallpaper list and marking the Tile option button. Windows 95 repeats the picture (a small *bmp* file) across your screen. The wallpaper can contain more than two colors, and it completely covers the Desktop color.

Big-picture wallpaper

If you want to have one non-repeating graphic element as your wallpaper, then choose a *bmp* file in the Wallpaper list and click the Center option button. You can also use the Browse button to find a *bmp* file of your own. If your *bmp* file is the same size as your current display resolution (the same number of horizontal and vertical pixels), then the picture from the *bmp* file will cover the whole Desktop. If it is smaller than the display resolution, you will see a border around the picture made up of your Desktop color.

You can tile a large *bmp* file, but it will be cut off on one or more sides if your screen resolution is not an exact multiple of the *bmp* dimensions. In other words, the *bmp* must be exactly $\frac{1}{2}$, $\frac{1}{3}$, $\frac{1}{4}$ (and so on) the size of the screen resolution.

It is great fun to have a splashy photo up on your Desktop. You can download graphics files from the web, as well as from CompuServe, America Online, Microsoft Network, and many bulletin boards. Using Paint Shop Pro from the shareware on the *Windows 95 Secrets* CD-ROM, you can size your bitmapped graphics to the resolution of your screen.

Using RLE files as graphic backgrounds

The wallpaper list box neglects to display Run Length Encoded *(rle)* files, although you can use them as graphical backdrops.

An *rle* file is just an ordinary bitmap file — like the bitmap wallpaper files included with Windows that are provided as wallpaper, such as Leaves.bmp or Winlogo.bmp — after it has been compressed into *rle* format.

Before compression, monochrome bitmap files contain one bit of data for every pixel displayed on the screen — the first bit is black, the second bit is black, the third bit is white, and so on. Sixteen-color bitmaps require *four* bits of data to represent every pixel, because each pixel could be one of 16 (or 2^4) possible colors.

If you convert a *bmp* file to an *rle* file, it takes up less space on disk. The *rle* file contains such information as "2 pixels of black, 12 pixels of white, 20 pixels of blue," and so on. The file stores the number of pixels (the *run length*) of each color instead of storing the meaning of each individual pixel.

You can convert any *bmp* file that's in the Windows proprietary *bmp* format to an *rle* file by using a graphics program that can read and write both formats. Paint Shop Pro, a program featured on the *Windows 95 Secrets* CD-ROM, is perfectly suited to do just that.

To use an *rle* file as a background graphic, do the following:

STEPS

Using RLE Files as Background

Step 1. Right-click the Desktop, choose Properties, and then click the Background tab.

Step 2. Click the Browse button, type ***.rle** in the File name box of the Browsing for wallpaper dialog box, and press Enter.

Step 3. Double-click various folder names in the Folders list box to navigate to the folder that stores the *rle* file you want to use as a background.

Step 4. Double-click the *rle* file, and click OK in the Desktop Properties dialog box.

Choosing a Screen Saver

Windows 95 comes with a number of different screen savers. You can buy additional ones from third-party software developers.

STEPS

Choosing a Screen Saver

Step 1.   Right-click the Desktop, and select Properties.

Step 2.   Click the Screen Saver tab, and then select a screen saver in the Screen Saver list box, as shown in Figure 22-8.

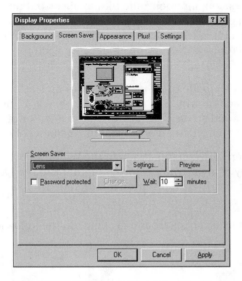

Figure 22-8: The Screen Saver tab of the Display Properties dialog box.

Step 3.   You can view the screen saver in full-screen mode by clicking the Preview button. To stop the preview, just move your mouse.

Step 4.   Optionally, change settings specific to the selected screen saver by clicking the Settings button. When you're done, click OK.

You can download 3D screen savers (pipes, rotating 3D text, and so on) along with Microsoft's OpenGL from Microsoft's FTP site. OpenGL is Microsoft's high-end 3D video driver and application programming interface. The two files to download are: ftp://ftp.microsoft.com/Softlib/MSLfiles/ Oglfix.exe and ftp://ftp.microsoft.com/Softlib/MSLfiles/Opengl95.exe.

You'll find the screen savers in Oglfix.exe. Opengl95.exe has the updated versions of the DLL files you need (Opengl32.dll and Glu32.dll). Use the DLLs in this file and not the ones in Oglfix.exe. Put these two DLLs in your \Windows\System folder, and put the screen savers in either your \Windows or \Windows\System folder.

Energy Star Settings

If both your monitor and video card conform to the VESA specifications for Display Power Management Signaling (DPMS), you can set the timing initiating low-power standby and shutoff. This lets you reduce the power consumption of the monitor if you have not used the keyboard or mouse for a given time period.

The time-out settings for low-power standby and shutoff are in the Screen Saver tab of the Display Properties dialog box. They only show up if you have the appropriate hardware.

Non-Plug and Play Monitors and Cards

When you install Windows 95, it won't figure out what kind of monitor you have if your monitor isn't plug and play compatible. If you have a non-plug and play monitor, you need to choose the appropriate monitor model during the setup process.

If you want to install a new monitor at a later date, right-click the Desktop, click Properties, click the Settings tab, and click the Change Display Type button. In the Change Display Type dialog box, click the Change button under Monitor Type, and select your monitor in the Select Device dialog box. (If you don't have a Change Display Type button in the Settings tab, click the Advanced Properties button, click the Change button in the Advanced Display Properties dialog box, click the Monitor tab, click the Change button, and select your monitor in the Select Device dialog box.)

It is important to tell Windows 95 which monitor you have so that it can use the proper values for the maximum display resolution in the Settings tab of the Display Properties dialog box. Some monitors require that their scan rates be set by a program called from Autoexec.bat. If yours requires such a program, choose your display resolution to match your scan rate.

To set the monitor refresh rate in the Registry, take the following steps:

STEPS

Setting the Monitor Refresh Rate

Step 1. Double-click Regedit.exe in your \Windows folder. Navigate to

HKEY_LOCAL_MACHINE\System\CurrentControlSet\Services\Class\Display\0000\DEFAULT

Step 2. Right-click the right pane of the Registry editor, and choose New, String Value. Enter the name **RefreshRate**.

(continued)

Summary

We provide you with the information that you need to make your computer screen look the way the you want it to.

▶ We discuss the important properties of monitors and video cards — the properties that still differentiate monitors and cards in the marketplace.

▶ We give you a set of tables you can use to define the benefits of a particular monitor and graphics card combination.

▶ We lead you step-by-step through the video card driver installation process.

▶ We show you how to change the size of all the elements on your Desktop.

▶ We show you how to change the color, font, and so on of all the Desktop elements, and how to change Desktop backgrounds and screen savers.

▶ We discuss themes, font smoothing, and full-window drag.

Chapter 23

Printer Drivers

In This Chapter

We discuss the Windows 95 print subsystem, the software that drives physical printers. We go over each area that has been improved since Windows 3.*x* and discuss:

▶ Using the Printers folder to install, configure, and manage your printers

▶ Putting a shortcut to each of your printers on your Desktop

▶ Dragging and dropping documents to any of your printers

▶ Making the drag and drop to a printer icon do anything you want it to

▶ Turning off DOS print spooling or printing Windows files directly to the printer

▶ Printing TrueType fonts correctly on PostScript printers

▶ Printing to a printer that isn't physically connected to your computer

▶ Semi-automatically installing network printer drivers

The Improvements

Windows 95 doesn't introduce any radical changes to the Windows printing subsystem. Printer drivers in Windows 3.*x* were already based on a universal driver that gave printer manufacturers a big head start toward producing specific drivers for their printers. Microsoft later used this approach to write a more complete core video driver and thereby improve the stability of Windows 95.

But lots of incremental improvements increase configuration flexibility and provide faster and more stable printing.

32-bit printer driver

Like all the other drivers that come with Windows 95, the printer driver has been moved to the 32-bit world. This means it spools the print jobs as threads, which Windows 95 can preemptively multitask. The 32-bit driver gives the print subsystem more control over the printing process, including bi-directional communication with the printer.

Each printer has its own print queue. You can have multiple printers connected to different ports, all printing at the same time and all managed by a different queue manager.

The print queue managers do a better job of spooling print jobs to the printers than the Windows 3.1 Print Manager did. They are aware of when the printer is ready for more data and don't send it until it is.

New universal print driver

The new universal print driver that communicates with the printer-specific mini drivers and the rest of the operating system comes with enhanced capabilities in Windows 95. It supports 600-dpi laser printers. It can download TrueType outlines to printers that support the PCL language (the HP LaserJet printer control language) so the printer can rasterize the fonts without using the resources of the computer.

It supports Hewlett-Packard's HPGL/2, a plotter language. CAD and similar applications can send their HPGL output to a printer instead of to a plotter.

Unified printer control interface

Windows 3.x has a Printer icon in the Control Panel (which you use to install and configure printers) and a separate Print Manager icon (which you use to manage your print queue), initially stored in the Main program group in the Program Manager. In Windows 95, printer configuration, installation, and the print-queue management functions have been combined. They are now associated with the individual printer icons in the Printers folder. Instead of one Printer icon for all installed printer drivers, each printer has its own icon.

In Windows 95, each printer icon represents a separate print queue manager and a separate set of printer driver properties sheets. You set the configuration information for each printer separately. Configuration variables that you had to set globally in Windows 3.x can now be set individually. You can manage each print queue separately and simultaneously.

Spooling EMF, not RAW printer codes

When you print a document, the document file has to be translated into the printer's codes that instruct the printer on how to print each character. Microsoft refers to these printer codes as the RAW data. (We capitalize RAW here because Microsoft does in order to contrast it with EMF, or *Enhanced Metafile Format*.) The printer driver/translator/spooler (the Print Manager) that came with Windows 3.x translated your document into the RAW data and created a temporary file, which was then spooled to the printer.

This translation process began as soon as you told your application to print your document. During this process, you couldn't use your application. You couldn't bring up another document and work on it. The Print Manager began printing the document while it was still translating it. When the translation process was complete, you were allowed to return to your application while the Print Manager continued to spool the translated temporary file to the printer in the background.

Translation is a lengthy process. In Windows 95, both translation to RAW data and print spooling have been moved to a background thread. You don't have to wait for the translation to RAW data to finish before you can continue working with your application. Your document is instead translated to Enhanced Metafile Format (EMF), which is a much higher-level and more-compact format than the RAW data. This reduces the initial translation time and returns you to your application more quickly.

The translation from EMF to RAW takes place in the background, leaving you free to continue your work. The temporary EMF file is spooled and translated as it is sent to the printer. EMF is built into the Graphic Device Interface (GDI) module of Windows 95.

If you run into problems spooling EMF files, you can switch to the old way of spooling RAW data files instead. We show you how later in this chapter in the section entitled *Details*.

PostScript printer drivers spool PostScript files to the PostScript printer. There is no EMF translation available for PostScript printers. PostScript is already a high-level page description language like the Enhanced Metafile Format, so there is little or no benefit in translating first to EMF and then from EMF to PostScript. The PostScript printer driver translates your document to a temporary PostScript file, spools this file, and starts sending it to the printer as the driver creates the temporary file.

DOS and Windows printing work together

Under Windows 3.*x*, the Print Manager did not manage the printing of DOS files, which meant that DOS files were not spooled, and there were device contention conflicts if you tried to print DOS and Windows applications simultaneously.

The Windows 95 print subsystem spools DOS print files, so you can print from any application and let the operating system handle the printer. The printer ports are virtualized, so the DOS application thinks it is printing to a real port, when in fact it is printing to the Windows 95 print subsystem. You can turn off DOS print spooling.

DOS print files are not translated into EMF print files. Rather, the translation occurs as the files (as RAW data files) are spooled. This still releases the DOS application faster than would be the case without a spooler. The spooler is not available in MS-DOS mode.

Offline printing

If you don't have a printer currently hooked up to your computer, you can still create print files. They will be printed automatically the next time you get connected to a printer and use the queue manager to put the printer back online. To do this, you must first install on your computer a printer driver that references a printer connected to a network server or to another computer over a peer-to-peer network. This network can be as simple as the Direct Cable Connection (DCC) program, which lets your laptop computer connect to your Desktop computer.

Undocumented

Offline (or *deferred*) printing is useful whenever your computer is not connected to a network printer. Unfortunately, offline printing works only for printing to non-local (network) printers. You can't use it with a local printer that, for whatever reason, is not currently connected to your computer. You can pause printing while you reconnect your local printer, if for some reason it was offline when you started printing, but pausing does not save the print jobs for later printing.

Bi-directional communications

For years, users couldn't have cared less what a printer had to say to them. Now we all realize that things would be a lot easier if the printer were smarter.

Plug and play printers can give the Windows 95 printer installation routines all the information they need to set up the printer, without requiring you to answer any questions about manufacturer, model, and so on.

Some printers can send status reports to the printer driver reporting such things as "paper jam" or "out of paper." This helps if the printer is down the hall. Some sophisticated plug and play printers can supply even more detailed status reports.

Support for enhanced parallel port

There has even been progress in the mundane (to some people) world of parallel ports. The EPP and ECP specifications for parallel ports permit higher speeds and improved bi-directional communication. This is most evident when you use devices that can deal with these new higher speeds. See the section in Chapter 25 entitled *Configuring ECP and EPP Ports*.

PostScript

The Windows 95 PostScript printer driver was jointly developed by Adobe and Microsoft. The fact that Microsoft is willing to credit Adobe with joint development speaks volumes about Adobe's power and prestige, and Microsoft's desire to have a well-respected printer driver.

The PostScript printer driver is used for all PostScript printers. Windows 95 uses a separate *spd* (Simplified PostScript printer description) or *ppd* (PostScript printer description) file to modify the driver to reflect the features of each PostScript printer. These files are stored in the \Windows\System folder. The filenames are shortened versions of the printer name.

The Windows 95 PostScript driver includes PostScript Level 2 support as well as numerous incremental upgrades to better handle more complex PostScript documents.

Printer shortcuts

Because each printer has its own associated icon in the Printers folder, you can place shortcuts to each printer driver on your Desktop (or in any other folder). When you want to print to the printer, drag and drop your document file onto the shortcut.

If you drag a printer icon from the Printers folder, Windows assumes you want to create a shortcut when you drop the icon. You don't need to hold down the Ctrl+Shift keys.

Print without installing printer drivers first

You may have installed a local printer by installing its driver on your computer. You can always print to that printer. If you want to print to another printer on your network, you don't necessarily have to install the driver beforehand. You do need to have a driver for that printer installed on your computer, but the installation process can be semi-automatic. This comes in handy, because there could be all sorts of printers on an extensive network, and it would be a bit of a pain to manually install drivers for all of the 800 printers that Windows 95 supports.

If you print to a shared printer on your network that's on a computer running Windows 95, Windows NT, or Novell NetWare, Windows 95 semi-automatically installs the printer driver for that printer on your computer. Microsoft calls this "point and print."

If the network printer is connected to a Windows 95 computer, all the information about the printer and the location of the files associated with it are stored in the Registry of that computer. Point and print uses this information to change your Registry, copy the appropriate files from the other Windows 95 computer, and install the printer driver on your computer.

See the section later in this chapter entitled *Point and Print* for details on how to set up your computer to use and share this capability.

Network printer management

Both Digital Equipment Corporation and Hewlett Packard provide printer server software that eases the job of managing printers that are connected directly to NetWare, Microsoft, and Digital networks. A Windows 95 computer using this software becomes a network print-management station.

NetWare print services

A computer running Windows 95 can serve as a single-printer, NetWare-compatible print services provider when it's connected to a Novell NetWare print server. A NetWare print server can send print jobs to a printer connected to a Windows 95 computer as long as that computer is also running Microsoft Client for NetWare and Microsoft Print Server for NetWare. The Windows 95 computer providing print services does not need to be running Microsoft's file and printer sharing for NetWare. All of these programs come with Windows 95.

The Windows 95 computer does not need to be a dedicated print services provider, and you can use it to carry out other tasks. It can manage only one local printer for the NetWare server. Microsoft Print Server for NetWare runs in the background and has minimal effect on foreground tasks.

No need for logical port redirection

Windows 3.x required that you assign a network printer to a specific logical port if you wanted to print to it. This is not necessary in Windows 95, as long as your network supports the universal naming convention (UNC) for naming its server, folders and printers. When you install a network printer, Windows 95 retains its UNC name and uses it to direct the output to the correct printer, for example, \\Billserver\HP5.

If your network doesn't support UNC (the 16-bit networks that worked with Windows 3.x do not), you can still redirect printer output to logical ports LPT1 through LPT9 through the Capture Printer Port button (in the Details tab of the Properties dialog box for your printer). Some DOS programs may require that you print to a logical port and not to a printer through a UNC port name.

The Printers Folder

Unlike Windows 3.x, you'll find that most printing functions in Windows 95 are consolidated in the Printers folder. You can get to the Printers folder in four ways:

1. Click the Start button, point to Settings, and then click Printers.

2. Double-click My Computer, and double-click the Printers folder icon.

3. Right-click My Computer, click Explore, and click the Printers folder icon in the left pane of the Explorer.

4. Use any of the above methods, but click the Control Panel folder instead of the Printers folder, and then double-click the Printers folder in the Control Panel.

Your Printers folder window will look something like the one shown in Figure 23-1. You won't have any icons other than the Add Printer icon in this folder until you install some printers (or have them installed for you). Each installed printer driver has its own printer icon in the Printers folder.

Figure 23-1: The Printers folder window. This folder contains the Add Printer icon and icons for each of your installed printers.

You can use the Printers folder and the icons in it for a variety of purposes. Double-click the Add Printer icon to install a new printer. Double-click a printer icon to view its print queue. Right-click a printer icon and click Properties to view a printer driver's properties, or click Set As Default to change the default printer. Right-click the client area of the Printers folder window and click Capture Printer Port to redirect a logical printer port to a network printer.

You'll find most everything to do with printers in the Printers folder. You can

■ Install new printer drivers.

■ Delete printer drivers you are no longer using.

■ Change the characteristics of your printer driver.

■ View and manage the print queues (pause and purge print jobs).

■ Set the default printer.

■ Give LPT*x* names to printers connected to networked servers (redirect logical printer ports to network printers).

Printer driver installation and configuration and print-queue management were combined in Windows 95 to make it easier to get at the important printer functions. So what is outside of the Printers folder that relates to printing?

■ The Fonts folder, where you'll find the fonts that are installed on your computer (See Chapter 30 for details on fonts.)

- Printer and communication port configurations, including the new enhanced parallel port, which you will find in the Device Manager under the System icon in the Control Panel

- The Add New Hardware icon in the Control Panel, which you can use to run the Add Printer Wizard (You can also run this Wizard by double-clicking the Add Printer icon in the Printers folder.)

- The Network icon in the Control Panel, which lets you enable printer sharing

- Shortcuts to printer icons (You can't drag a printer icon out of the Printers folder, but you can drag to create a shortcut to the printer icon on the Desktop.)

- The Print Preview capability, a systemwide dynamic link library (DLL) that developers can incorporate into their applications (An example of Print Preview is found in WordPad.)

- The common print dialog box, which developers can use in their applications (An example of this dialog box is found in WordPad.)

- Shared printers attached to servers on your network, which you can view by double-clicking their icons in the Explorer (The shared printers also appear in your Printers folder if you print to them, drag and drop them to the Printers folder, or double-click them.)

- Network printer management tools from DEC and HP

Tip   The Device Manager tracks most of the hardware attached to your computer, but it doesn't track your printers. Only the properties sheets associated with a particular printer store the parameters of that printer driver. The Device Manager does track the printer port parameters.

Drag and Drop to a Printer Icon

You can drag and drop a file icon in a folder window or the Explorer (or on the Desktop) to a printer's shortcut icon on the Desktop, to a printer icon in the Printers folder, or to the printer's queue window. With this action, you are telling Windows 95 to invoke the application that is associated with the print command for this file type and then execute the application's print command.

If you want to quickly print a file or a group of files, this is an easy way to do it. The associated application starts, and you may see the document in the application window on the Desktop while the document is spooled to the printer. The application is closed as soon as the document is completely spooled.

This is the same action that would take place if you right-clicked a document file and chose Print from the context menu. The actions listed at the top of this menu are the ones defined for the file type in the Registry and listed in the File Types tab of the Options dialog box. We discuss file types in detail in Chapter 13.

If you drag and drop a file to a network printer icon in a shared folder, and your computer doesn't have that printer's driver installed, you are instructing Windows 95 to start installing the driver on your computer.

You can define an action named Print for a given file type, and then associate that action with a specific application's print command. This connects the user action of dragging and dropping a file of that type onto the printer icon with the specified application's print command. You define the Print action using the method detailed in Chapter 13.

Undocumented

You can define the "Print" action to be something other than Print, if you like. This will let you drag and drop a file to a printer icon to invoke a different action. For example, you can define the Print action to invoke a file translator that converts the specified file type into another file type. If you do this, you can convert files of the specified type by simply dragging and dropping them onto any printer icon.

The Print action is defined by default for many file types. This happens when you install the Windows application associated with the file type (after you've installed Windows 95).

Installing a Printer Driver

The Add Printer Wizard pretty much installs the printer driver for you. You just have to respond to its not-too-difficult questions.

Windows 95 documentation often refers to *installing a printer*. That really means *installing a printer driver,* in other words, installing software. This is confusing, because the intuitive meaning of installing a printer is to physically place a printer next to a computer and connect them with a printer cable. You'll have to do a little translation in your head when you see the words *install a printer*.

If you install Windows 95 into your existing Windows 3.*x* directory, Windows 95 Setup automatically installs the printer drivers for the printers that you previously installed. On the other hand, if you install Windows 95 to a new folder, you will be asked during setup to install a new printer. You'll see the Add Printer Wizard, and you just need to answer the questions.

After Windows 95 is installed, you can invoke the Add Printer Wizard (to add more printer drivers) by opening the Printers folder and double-clicking the Add Printer icon. If your printer is plug and play compatible, the Add Printer Wizard can communicate with it, find the correct printer driver, and install the correctly configured printer driver itself.

Otherwise, the Add Printer Wizard asks you for the manufacturer's name and printer model before it proceeds to find the correct files from the Windows 95 source diskettes or CD-ROM. To do this, it uses the *inf* files Msprint.inf and Msprint2.inf in the \Windows\Inf folder. (This folder is only visible if the Show all files option button is selected in the View tab of the Options dialog box, which you display by choosing View, Options in any Explorer or folder window.)

If you have a printer that isn't covered in these two *inf* files and you have a printer setup diskette from your printer manufacturer, you can click the Have Disk button in the Add Printer Wizard. This diskette has to include an *inf* file for the new printer.

If the printer is connected to a serial port and is not plug and play compliant, the Wizard will let you change the port's baud rate, and so on. The Wizard also lets you choose a meaningful name for your printer, so if you share it on a network, others will know where to find their output.

When the Add Printer Wizard has finished installing the driver, it asks if you want to print a test page. You should do this if you're setting up the printer for the first time. Printing a test page lets Windows 95 check out the printer, and if Windows 95 finds a problem, it leads you to a Windows 95 help-based printer troubleshooter. This troubleshooter asks you questions about the test page and other printer items to help you track down glitches in your printer driver configuration.

You can also invoke the printer troubleshooter from the Contents tab of the Windows 95 Help Topics window. Click the Start button, click Help, click the Contents tab, double-click Troubleshooting, and then double-click "If you have trouble printing," the first topic under Troubleshooting.

You can install a printer driver for a network printer in the same manner that you install a driver for a local printer. The only difference is that you will be asked for the server and printer name. Type the name using the UNC. Your network must support this convention if you install a network printer this way.

You can install a printer driver on your computer for a printer on a network in a few other ways, a couple of which are a little more automated. See the section entitled *Point and Print* later in this chapter for details.

Printer Driver Properties Sheets

Each printer driver has its own icon in the Printers folder. Attached to each printer icon is a raft of properties sheets for the numerous properties that you can customize for each type of printer.

Properties that were previously global for all printer drivers have been moved to each printer driver's properties sheet. For example, you can determine for each printer whether to print directly to the printer or through a print queue.

Getting to a printer's properties sheets

You get to a printer driver's properties sheets by right-clicking its icon in the Printers folder and clicking Properties in the context menu. You can also highlight a printer icon in the Printers folder and choose File, Properties. If a printer's print queue window is open, you can choose Printer, Properties in that window.

You can't get to a printer's properties sheets by right-clicking a shortcut icon for the printer on your Desktop and clicking Properties. This will just get you to the properties of the shortcut. You need to double-click the shortcut icon and then choose Printer, Properties in the print queue window.

You can also get to some of the printer properties sheets through the printer setup options in your application, usually through the Print or Print Setup command in the File menu. New 32-bit applications can use the common print dialog box DLL to get to the printer properties sheets. The properties sheets you access through your applications will not exactly match the ones connected to the printer's icon in the Printers folder.

Basic printer properties sheets

There are too many printer properties sheets to go through all of them in this book. Besides, we want to focus on the undocumented aspects of printer drivers, not those features that are obvious.

You can find out what the various option buttons and fields on these properties sheets do by right-clicking them and then clicking the What's This? button that appears. You can also click the question mark in the upper-right corner of the properties sheet and then click an area of interest.

Here, we'll go over a few properties sheets to give you an idea of the range of things you can set. After that, we give you some guidance on how to deal with some of the less well-explained printer driver properties.

The Graphics properties sheets for a LaserJet compatible printer and a PostScript compatible printer are shown in Figures 23-2 and 23-3. The specific graphics properties depend on the features available in the printer and the printer driver.

Separator page

The General properties sheet is the same for all printers. One of the options on it lets you print a separator page between print jobs so that you can easily separate them. Separator pages are useful if many different people print to one printer.

The separator page can be blank, or it can contain a graphic that more easily identifies it. The graphic needs to be in the Windows Metafile format. Files of this type have the extension *wmf*.

Undocumented

Microsoft doesn't ship any applications with Windows 95 that can produce Windows Metafile files. You have to purchase an application that creates such files if you want to be able to create a separator page with a graphic on it. We feature Paint Shop Pro on the *Windows 95 Secrets* CD-ROM, which allows you to create *wmf* files or convert them from *bmp* files.

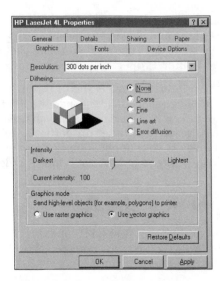

Figure 23-2: The Graphics properties sheet for a Hewlett Packard 4L printer. You get to determine the quality of the graphics output (traded against time to produce the output and per-sheet costs). Resolution doesn't affect text unless you print the text as a graphic (a setting on another sheet).

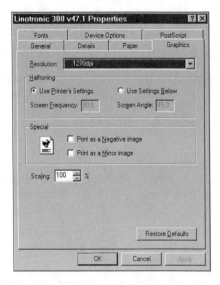

Figure 23-3: The Graphics properties sheet for a Linotronic 300. The Linotronic is often used at service bureaus to produce film and other high-end output. You send PostScript from your application to a file using this driver, and then send the file to the service bureau. If you're printing to film, you can use the two check boxes in the Special area to flip or reverse the image.

Details

All Windows 95 printer drivers have the same Details properties sheet, which is shown in Figure 23-4. Use the Print to the following port drop-down list to change the port to which you are printing (after you physically reconnect your local printer) or to print to a file.

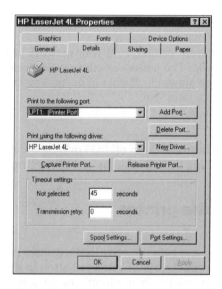

Figure 23-4: A printer driver's Details properties sheet.

Click the Capture Printer Port button if you want to redirect output from a named LPT port to a network printer. Use the Port Settings button if you need to turn off the spooling of DOS print jobs. You can even switch to one of the other printer driver properties sheets by using the Print using the following driver drop-down list (this overwrites your existing driver). You can also update your printer driver from a diskette using the New Driver button.

Undocumented If you change the Print to the following port field to a network printer path, and that printer is of the same type as the printer whose properties you are currently viewing and editing, you will switch the current printer to the network printer as soon as you click Apply or OK. This is probably not what you want to do, as you lose your driver to your current printer. It's better to add a separate driver for the network printer than to switch connections in this field.

If you move the network or local printer, you can use the Add Port button to specify the new path to the printer.

You can adjust the time interval that your applications wait before Windows 95 reports a printer time-out error. Change the number of seconds in the Not Selected field to a higher value if you find that you continually get the "Windows will retry in 5 seconds" message box when you try to print.

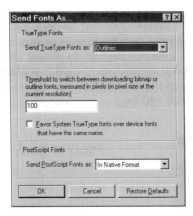

Figure 23-6: The Send Fonts As dialog box. Choose Outlines from the Send TrueType Fonts as drop-down list.

One thing that you can't do with a printer driver that is configured to print to a file is share the printer (because there isn't any printer there to share). If you have an actual printer connected locally and you've enabled print sharing (using the Network icon in your Control Panel), you have a Sharing properties sheet in the printer driver's Properties dialog box that lets you specify whether or not to share the printer.

You can also get to the Sharing properties sheet by right-clicking a local printer's icon in the Printers folder and clicking Sharing in the context menu. For more details, see the section later in this chapter entitled *Sharing a Printer*.

PostScript

The PostScript driver has its own PostScript-specific properties sheet, as shown in Figure 23-7. The Advanced options let you do such wonderful things as getting rid of the Ctrl+D at the beginning or end of your PostScript output so you don't have to manually edit them out if you run over a Unix network to a PostScript printer.

You can choose among several PostScript output formats. The default format, Optimize for Speed, is fine for local printers. If you're printing to a file for off-site printing, you might want to try Optimize for Portability - ADSC. (ADSC stands for Adobe Document Structuring Conventions.) Choose Encapsulated PostScript (EPS) if you're printing to a file that will be incorporated into another file.

Defining your own printer

If you have installed the Generic/Text Only printer driver, you can define escape sequences (printer commands) that control your specific printer and set the various font sizes and types. In most cases, you don't have to do

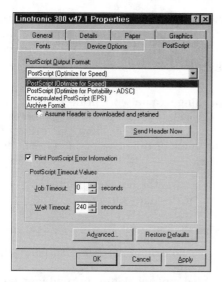

Figure 23-7: The PostScript properties sheet. Use the PostScript Output Format drop-down list to specify an output format, and click the Advanced button for more options.

this, because Microsoft has included printer drivers for 800 different printers with Windows 95. But the capability is there if you run into the 801st.

Use the Device Options and Fonts properties sheets associated with the Generic/Text only printer driver to define the printer codes for your particular printer.

Tip

Installing the Generic/Text Only printer is a great way to produce text-only output from applications that don't have an option to save unformatted text-only files.

Deferred Printing

You can print documents using a printer driver for a network printer that isn't currently connected through the network to your computer. The print jobs will be spooled, and you can print them later when you reconnect to the printer through the network. The print jobs are tracked in the print queue for that printer, and when you put the printer online, they are automatically printed.

One way you can use deferred printing is to create documents on a portable, print them to the print queue, and then print them later when you connect your portable to a computer with a printer (perhaps your desktop computer). The portable has to have a printer driver for the desktop's printer installed as a network printer. The portable and the desktop computer need to be connected with Direct Cable Connection (DCC) or through another network connection. See Chapter 30 for more on connecting laptops and desktops.

You can also use Dial-Up Networking (DUN) to phone in from the portable to the desktop computer and print your documents at the office while you are on the road or at home. You need to have the desktop computer configured as a DUN server. (See the *Setting Up Your Windows 95 Computer at Work as a Host* section of Chapter 28.)

If you are on a network and printing to a network printer and you lose the connection to that printer, your print jobs will be spooled until the connection is reestablished and you place the printer online. The printer driver for the network printer will display itself as offline as soon as the network connection is broken.

Even if you are presently connected to the network printer, you can take it offline (for you) by right-clicking its icon in your Printers folder and clicking Work Off-line.

Undocumented

If you take a network printer offline by right-clicking its icon in the Printers folder and clicking Work Off-line, the icon in the Printers folder is ghosted. If you have a shortcut to that icon on your Desktop, however, it is not ghosted when the printer is offline. If you double-click the shortcut icon on the Desktop, you will see a message stating that the printer is offline in the title bar of the print queue window.

Printing to a file

Tip

You can always create a print file for a specific printer and manually send this file to the printer later. To do this, change the Print to the following port field in the Details properties sheet for that printer's driver from a specific port to FILE. When you print your document, a new file will be created that contains the document formatted with the printer codes for that specific printer.

When you later connect to the printer, you can copy the file to the printer port. You actually need to use the DOS Copy command. You can't drag and drop the print file to the printer icon. This method would make the most sense (visually), but it doesn't work.

Undocumented

You can run the DOS Copy command from the Run dialog box if you like (click the Start button, and click Run). Assuming that the name of your print file is File1.hp, you would type the following command in the Run dialog box:

```
command /c copy /b file1.hp lpt2:
```

This copies the file of print commands to the second parallel port (which could also be redirected to a network printer). The /c parameter tells Command to execute the following command and then return to the DOS prompt. The /b parameter tells Copy to copy the file in binary mode. For some trickier approaches to printing files, turn to the *Printing to an offline Postscript printer* section coming up next.

The whole point of deferred printing is to get around this tiresome technique of manually copying print files to the printer port. Unfortunately, deferred printing works only for network printers and not for local printers that are presently offline.

Printing to an offline PostScript printer

You can also use the above technique to print to an offline (off-premises) PostScript printer. You can install a PostScript driver on your computer for your target PostScript printer. You can have the PostScript driver print to a file. Then you transfer this file via diskette or over the phone lines to the location with the PostScript printer. Using the DOS Copy command, you can then print the PostScript file on the printer.

Printing PostScript files

You can create a print file of PostScript output on a computer that doesn't have a PostScript printer connected to it (or to the network that the computer is connected to). You then take this PostScript output file, which usually has a *ps* extension, to a computer with a PostScript printer and copy the file to the printer. (The PostScript output file is just a series of ASCII commands and parameters.)

Copying a file to the printer is a DOS-based function, but we can configure Windows 95 to carry out this function without using the Start, Run dialog box or opening a DOS window and issuing the DOS Copy command.

Undocumented

There are two ways to do this. First, you can create an association between the *ps* file extension and a command that copies the file to the printer. Second, you can create a batch file (and a shortcut to it) that consists of the DOS commands to send the file to the printer. Then you can place the shortcut to the PostScript printing batch file in the SendTo folder. The batch file is generic, so it will send any file to the printer, not just PostScript files.

To create an association to the *ps* file type, take the following steps:

STEPS
Create a Print Command Associated with PostScript Print File

Step 1. Open your Explorer, choose View, Options, and click the File Types tab.

Step 2. Click the New Type button.

Step 3. Type **PostScript Print Output File** in the Description of type field, **ps** in the Associated extension field, and **PostScript Commands** in the Content Type (MIME) field.

(continued)

Create a Print Command Associated with PostScript Print File

Step 4. Click the New button, and the type **Copy to Printer** in the Action field and **C:\Windows\Command.com /c Copy /b %1 Lpt1:** in the Application used to perform action field. Click OK.

Note that you can replace *Lpt1:* in this command line with another printer port designator, or with the UNC name of a network printer.

Step 5. Click the Choose Icon button, and browse to find an appropriate printer-type icon. Click OK.

Step 6. Click OK, and then click Close.

You can now double-click any file with a *ps* extension to print it on your PostScript printer. Unfortunately, the DOS window will flash briefly when you use this method.

To create a batch file and an accompanying shortcut that will print any file (and not flash a DOS window) take the following steps:

STEPS

Create a Print Batch File

Step 1. Double-click Edit.com in your \Windows\Command folder (if you haven't already made a shortcut to this nifty DOS editor).

Step 2. Type **C:\Windows\Command.com /c Copy /b %1 Lpt1:**

Step 3. Choose File, Save As, and save the file as Ps.bat.

Step 4. Right-drag and drop Ps.bat to your Desktop to create a shortcut to it. (You could also try another method to create a shortcut on your Desktop. Right-click Ps.bat, and click Create Shortcut. Right-click the shortcut, which appears in the same folder as Ps.bat, and click Cut. Then right-click the Desktop and click Paste.)

Step 5. With the new shortcut on the Desktop highlighted, press F2 and rename the shortcut something like Print Files.

Step 6. Right-click the shortcut, choose Properties, and then click the Program tab.

Step 7. Choose Minimized in the Run drop-down list, and mark the Close on exit check box to enable it. Click the Change Icon button and find an appropriate icon for this shortcut that prints files. Click OK.

Step 8. Right-click a PostScript print output file in a folder or Explorer window, and click Copy in the context menu.

Create a Print Batch File

Step 9. Right-click the new shortcut on the Desktop and click Paste. The PostScript file will be copied to the PostScript printer. A button will appear briefly on the Taskbar as the file is copied.

The file is treated as a DOS file, and it will be spooled to the printer if you haven't turned DOS print spooling off.

You can place this shortcut in the \Windows\SendTo folder. If you do this, you can right-click the PostScript (or text) file, point to Send To in the context menu, and then click the shortcut in the Send To submenu to copy the file to the printer.

Troubleshooting with Windows 95 Help

If you are having trouble printing, you can use the Troubleshooting section of the help system to track down the problem. Windows 95 help is not just a semi-meaningless collection of statements of the obvious; it is actually useful in the real world. The printer troubleshooter can pinpoint a problem for you, as long as you answer the questions correctly.

To get to the printer troubleshooter, click the Start button, click Help, click the Contents tab, double-click Troubleshooting, and then double-click the topic "If you have trouble printing." (Notice that the printer troubleshooter is the first item. This placement lets you know what causes the most problems.)

Undocumented

The CD-ROM version of Windows 95 contains an enhanced printer trouble-shooter. You'll find it in the \Other\Misc\Epts folder. Just double-click Epts.exe to start it.

Graphics Fail on Hewlett Packard Printer

If you are attempting to print a complex graphic to a Hewlett Packard laser printer and it doesn't want to print, you might not have enough memory in the printer to print the graphic. Take the following steps to get your graphic to print:

STEPS

Printing Complex Graphics on HP Printers

Step 1. Click the Start button, point to Settings, and then click Printers. Right-click the printer icon for your HP printer. Click Properties.

(continued)

Actually sharing your printer

To share a printer, take the following steps:

STEPS

Sharing a Printer

Step 1. Click the Start button, point to Settings, and then click Printers.

Step 2. Right-click the icon of the printer that you want to share, and then click Sharing in the context menu.

Step 3. You'll see the Sharing properties sheet, as shown in Figure 23-9. Click Shared As.

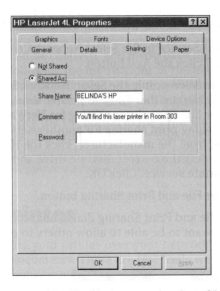

Figure 23-9: The Sharing properties sheet. Click Shared As to allow your printer to be used by others. You can give a useful comment and name to help others decide if they want to use your printer and determine where to find the output.

Step 4. Fill out the three Shared As fields.

Step 5. Click OK.

Your computer is now a full-fledged print server. If you are using a NetWare network, you can use the Windows 95 computer as a complete print server and off-load the extra resource use from your NetWare server.

If you are using a Windows NT or NetWare server to provide user-level security, you won't see the Password field that appears in Figure 23-9. The users who can access your printer will be determined by the database of users to whom you have granted access to your resources. This list of groups and users is kept on the Windows NT or NetWare server.

To specify which server the list of users is kept on, take the following steps:

STEPS
Specifying User-Access Control

Step 1. Click the Start button, point to Settings, and then click Control Panel.

Step 2. Double-click the Network icon. Click the Access Control tab.

Step 3. Click the User-level access control option button.

Step 4. Type the name of the server that has the list.

Slow network printing with MS-DOS programs

If you print a document from a DOS program or press the Print Screen key while in a DOS window and it takes from 60 to 90 seconds for the printing to begin, the DOS program might not have closed the printer port. The Windows 95 default setting is to wait 45 seconds after the DOS program stops sending information to begin printing if the printer port isn't closed by the DOS program, so this can mean some rather long waits.

To solve this problem, add the following lines to your System.ini file:

```
[Network]
    PrintBufTime=10
[IFSMGR]
    PrintBufTime=10
```

If these lines aren't already in your System.ini file, create them after the [386Enh] section. They set the print buffer time at 10 seconds (instead of the default 45 seconds). If you experience problems, you should try increasing the values.

Microsoft Print Server for NetWare

If you are on a NetWare network, you can configure your Windows 95 computer as a print services provider for a NetWare server. Instead of setting up your computer to be an independent print server, you use

STEPS

Installing a Network Printer by Drag and Drop Printing

Step 1. Open a folder window containing a document file or a shortcut to a document file.

Step 2. Make sure you have the shared resources folder window open for the server whose printer you are going to install.

Step 3. Drag and drop the document icon to the printer icon in the shared resources folder window. The message box shown in Figure 23-10 will appear.

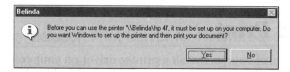

Figure 23-10: A message box telling you that you have to set up the printer driver on your computer.

Step 4. Click the Yes button. The Add Printer Wizard (network printer installation version) appears, as shown in Figure 23-11. If you want to assign a logical printer port to your network printer, click the Yes option button to indicate that you want to print from MS-DOS programs, and then click the Next button. (MS-DOS programs often require that you print to an LPT port.)

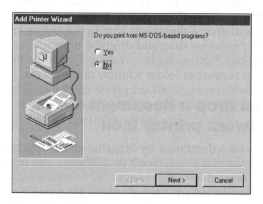

Figure 23-11: The network printer installation version of the Add Printer Wizard. If you don't want to capture a printer port, click Next. Otherwise, click the Yes option button, and then click Next.

Step 5. Finish answering the Wizard's questions. Give the printer a name that reminds you which one it is when you print to it.

The printer driver for the network printer is now installed. When you open your Printers folder window, you'll see an icon for the network printer.

Undocumented

Now that you have installed the network printer, you can drag and drop documents to either of its icons to print documents. The network printer's icon in the shared resources folder and in your local Printers folder behave in the same way. Double-click either and you will see the same print queue window. One minor difference is that only the icon in the Printers folder is ghosted if the network printer is offline.

Undocumented

You can put a shortcut to a network printer on your Desktop, just as you can a local printer. If your network connection is DCC, you can't invoke the connection by double-clicking the network printer's icon if it isn't already set up. You have to make the connection first before the network printer can be seen.

Drag and drop a network printer icon

The network printer icon should be visible to you in the Explorer or in a shared resources folder window that is focused on the network server computer. You can drag and drop the network printer's icon from the Explorer or folder window to your Desktop or to your Printers folder window or folder icon.

Double-click the network printer icon

If you can see the icon that represents the shared printer on the network computer, just double-click it. That moves its printer drivers over to your computer and puts its icon in your Printers folder. (As an alternative, you can also right-click the network printer's icon and click Install.)

Enabling point and print

You can install printers that are shared on networked Windows 95, Windows NT, and NetWare servers with point and print. If you are printing to a Windows 95 print server, all the information about the printer drivers and the drivers themselves are stored there. You don't have to do anything to allow the drivers to be transferred to the client Windows 95 computer. The Windows 95 printer server must be running file and printer sharing for NetWare Networks or file and printer sharing for Microsoft Networks.

Point and print to a NetWare server

If you want to be able to have Windows 95 client computers point and print to your printers managed by a NetWare printer server, you're going to need to do a little more work. You have to copy the driver files that are used for each of the printers managed by that server to a directory on the server. It turns out that this is more akin to the Add Printer Wizard than to point and print.

Set up a NetWare print server for point and print

If you have administrative privileges on the NetWare server that you are logged onto, you can configure the server to store the needed printer drivers and auxiliary files. Take the following steps to do so:

STEPS
Configuring a NetWare Server to Store Point and Print Files

Step 1. Right-click a NetWare print queue icon displayed in the NetWare Shared Resources window. Click Point and Print Setup in the context menu.

Step 2. Click Set Printer Model. In the Select dialog box, highlight the manufacturer and model of the printer associated with the print queue on the NetWare server. Click OK.

Step 3. Right-click the same NetWare print queue again, and then click Set Driver Path.

Step 4. Type a path and folder name that is valid for the NetWare server and in which you will store the printer driver files for this printer.

Step 5. Open Msprint.inf or Msprint2.inf in your Inf folder with Notepad. See which files are going to be copied when you install this printer. Extract these files from your Windows 95 CD-ROM or diskette source cabinet files and copy them into the directory you just created on your NetWare server.

You now have the printer driver source files on your NetWare server. This makes it somewhat easier to point and print to a NetWare printer from a Windows 95 client computer.

Point and print to a NetWare printer

Now that you have set up your NetWare server to allow point and print (after a fashion), you can use it to install printer drivers on a Windows 95 client computer. To do this, take the following steps:

STEPS
Installing a Printer Driver from a NetWare Server

Step 1. Log onto a NetWare server from a client Windows 95 computer.

Step 2. In the Network Neighborhood on the client computer, double-click the NetWare server's icon to display a folder window listing the resources of the NetWare server.

Installing a Printer Driver from a NetWare Server

Step 3.   Drag and drop a printer icon from the NetWare window to your local Printers folder window. This activates the Add Printer Wizard.

Step 4.   Type the name of the new printer.

Your NetWare network printer driver is now installed on your local Windows 95 computer.

Summary

Windows 95 arrives with a significant number of improvements in printing capabilities. We describe them for you.

▶ We discuss how the new Printers folder unites almost all of the print functions in Windows, making it easier for you to manage your printers.

▶ Because each printer has its own icon, you can put a shortcut to each printer on your Desktop. Now you can drag and drop documents to the particular printer that you want without having to change the default printer.

▶ You can define drag and drop to a printer to be any possible action, not just printing.

▶ DOS files are, by default, spooled to the printer through the Windows 95 print spooler. This alleviates printer device contention.

▶ We show you how to print TrueType fonts correctly on PostScript printers.

▶ You can print to a print queue and have your files printed later when you actually connect to your printer.

▶ You can have the appropriate printer drivers semi-automatically installed when you print to network printers.

Chapter 24

The Mighty Mouse (Other Pointing Devices, Too)

In This Chapter

Mouse support has improved significantly in Windows 95, giving you a mouse that is friendlier, more powerful, and more useful. We describe:

▶ The improvements in the 32-bit protected-mode mouse driver

▶ Improving mouse responsiveness and making it easier to double-click

▶ Turning your mouse pointer into a nifty animated pointer

▶ Turning your middle button into a double-click button

▶ When to use double-click and how to get around using it

▶ The power of the right mouse button and why you'll want to use it often

Mouse Basics

In this chapter, we don't mean *mouse* exactly, but whatever pointing device you use that acts like a mouse, be it a trackball, BallPoint, InPort, pen and tablet, or one of the other devices that are variants on these themes. The purpose of all these devices is to move the mouse pointer about the screen.

The Windows user interface is a point-and-click interface. The mouse is the instrument you use to point and click. Windows 95 has made the mouse more important than it was in Windows 3.*x* by making it more powerful.

Windows 95 supports, right out of the box, a broad variety of mice from different manufacturers. All Microsoft mouse-compatible mice, of course, are supported as though they were, in fact, manufactured by Microsoft. Specifically named are mice manufactured by Logitech, Kensington, Compaq, and Texas Instruments (TI). Windows 95 also offers generic support for various "standard" mice.

Among the mouse models that Windows 95 supports are serial mice, bus mice, PS/2 mice, the TI QuickPort BallPoint mouse, the Compaq LTE trackball, and the Kensington Serial Expert mouse, as well as all models compatible with these models.

STEPS *(continued)*

Changing an Existing Mouse Driver

Step 5.   Click OK until you have exited all the dialog boxes.

Step 6.   Restart Windows 95 to have the mouse driver take effect.

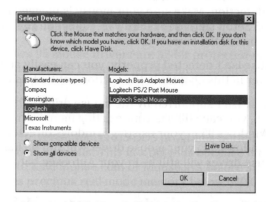

Figure 24-1: The Select Device dialog box. Highlight a manufacturer and then a mouse model. Click OK. You will have to restart Windows after you choose a new mouse driver.

Adding a mouse driver

You can add a mouse driver if you add a mouse after you have installed Windows 95:

STEPS

Adding a Mouse Driver

Step 1.   Click the Start button, point to Settings, and then click Control Panel. Double-click the Add New Hardware icon. Click Next.

Step 2.   Windows 95 asks if you want it to search for new hardware. Click Yes if you aren't sure what kind of mouse is physically installed on your computer, and be prepared to wait for a few minutes. If you know what type of mouse you have, click No, and then click Next. Click Mouse in the list of hardware types. Click Next.

Step 3.   Choose a mouse manufacturer and model from the Select Device dialog box. If the mouse you have isn't listed and you know that it is not compatible with the models listed and you have a mouse driver diskette, click the Have Disk button.

Adding a Mouse Driver

Step 4.   Put your mouse driver diskette in the disk drive and click the OK button if the correct path to your diskette drive is shown. Otherwise, type the correct path before clicking OK.

Step 5.   Click Finish.

Step 6.   Restart Windows 95 to have the mouse driver take effect.

You can install mouse drivers that were written for Windows 3.*x* if you don't find one that works with your mouse. Try to install one of the new ones first before you install an older driver. Just because your mouse and the mouse driver don't have the same names doesn't mean one of the new drivers won't work — try a few first.

Undocumented

To install a Windows 3.*x* mouse driver or a mouse driver that didn't come with Windows 95, click the Have Disk button in step 3 of the Adding a Mouse Driver steps above. You need to have a diskette with the mouse driver on it. The diskette needs to include a mouse setup file. This file has an *inf* extension and defines how to install the mouse drivers.

IntelliPoint

Microsoft released new IntelliPoint drivers after the initial release of Windows 95. They continue to release updates to these drivers. If you have an IntelliPoint device, you can download the latest drivers at http://www.microsoft.com/kb/softlib/default.htm. Download Pnt32upd.exe.

Configuring Your Mouse Driver Properties

Use the Mouse Properties dialog box to set the properties of the mouse driver. You can use this dialog box to change the responsiveness or speed of the mouse pointer relative to your movements of the mouse. You can switch the function of the right and left mouse buttons for left-handed operation. You can also change the double-click time interval. A longer interval counts two separate mouse clicks that are separated by a longer period of time as a single double-click.

You get to pick from a collection of mouse pointer icons, including animated pointers that correspond to a range of mouse functions. You can turn the hourglass pointer into a spinning world, for example. Since Windows 95 uses the same *ani* file format as Windows NT, you can select from a wide variety of shareware and freeware animated icons available on online services such as CompuServe, as well as on the *Windows 95 Secrets* CD-ROM. And if you're using an LCD screen, you can add mouse pointer trails by setting the number of ghost images that get left behind (briefly) at the mouse pointer's former location.

Follow these steps to change the properties of your mouse:

STEPS

Configuring the Mouse Driver

Step 1. Click the Start button, point to Settings, and then click Control Panel. Double-click the Mouse icon (it looks like a white right-handed bar of soap).

Step 2. The Buttons tab of the Mouse Properties dialog box, as shown in Figure 24-2, lets you switch the "handedness" of the mouse buttons and set the speed at which you have to click the mouse twice in order to get the two clicks to count as a single double-click.

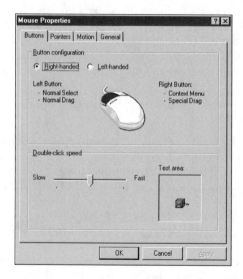

Figure 24-2: The Buttons tab of the Mouse Properties dialog box. You can swap the left and right mouse buttons and adjust the time interval between mouse clicks that will count as a double-click.

Changing the handedness of the mouse buttons

Click the Left-handed option button to switch the left and right mouse buttons. On a three-button mouse, these are the two outside buttons. If you are left-handed, swapping the function of the left and right mouse buttons lets you use your index finger to single- and double-click when you're controlling the mouse with your left hand.

Changing the double-click speed

To adjust how fast you need to double-click, do the following:

STEPS

Changing Double-Click Speed

Step 1. Move the double-click speed slider to the left to increase the time interval allowed between two mouse clicks that are counted as one double-click. Move the slider to the right to increase the speed with which you must twice click the left mouse button (assuming a right-handed configuration) in order for it to count as a double-click.

Step 2. To test your double-click agility, click twice in the test area. If your two clicks count as one double-click, the jack-in-the-box goes up or down.

Secret

The range of the slider is between 900 milliseconds (nine-tenths of a second) at the left end and 100 milliseconds (one-tenth of a second) on the right end. This makes the middle of the slider equal to half a second.

Changing the double-click height and width

Secret

Windows 3.*x* allowed you to determine the size in pixels of an invisible box around the location of the mouse pointer where the first click of a double-click takes place. The mouse pointer must be located within this box for a second click to count as part of the double-click. You could insert the variables DoubleClickWidth and DoubleClickHeight in the [Windows] section of the Win.ini file to do this. If you didn't add these variables to Win.ini, the default size of the box was four pixels on a side.

To change the size of the double-click box (which defaults to four pixels) under Windows 95, you have to edit the Registry. You might want to do this if you find that Windows 95 is missing a lot of your double-clicks (because you are moving the mouse a bit between clicks). Here's how:

STEPS

Changing the Size of the Double-Click Box

Step 1.   Double-click the Registry editor icon on your Desktop (or double-click Regedit.exe in the \Windows folder in an Explorer window).

Step 2.   In the left pane of the Registry editor, click the plus signs to navigate to

HKEY_CURRENT_USER\Control Panel\Desktop

Step 3.   Highlight desktop in the left pane, right-click in the right pane, away from any of the entries. Choose New, String Value.

Step 4.   Type the name **DoubleClickWidth,** and press Enter.

Step 5.   Double-click the entry you made in step 4. Type the desired width (in pixels) of the double-click box. Click OK.

Step 6.   Repeat steps 3-6, but this time type **DoubleClickHeight** and specify the desired height in pixels.

Step 7.   If you misspell either of the names, highlight it and press F2, and then retype the name.

Step 8.   Exit the Registry editor, and then restart Windows 95 to have these new values take effect. You can test them using the jack-in-the-box in the Buttons tab of the Mouse Properties dialog box.

You can use TweakUI to set the size of the double-click box (it assumes you want a square box). Just open TweakUI in your Control Panel, and in the Mouse sensitivity area of the Mouse tab, increase the number in the Double-click field to increase the size of the double-click box. You test the sensitivity by double-clicking on the gear icon.

Desensitizing dragging

If you find that you are often inadvertently moving folder icons around in your Explorer, you can widen the area that you have to drag an icon before it begins moving. Signs that accidental dragging is a problem for you include folders disappearing when you click on them and error messages stating that you can't move a folder when you weren't trying to move one to begin with.

The default Windows 95 setting for initiating a drag is two pixels. That is, if you highlight an icon, press and hold down the left mouse button, and move the mouse pointer just two pixels, then the icon begins to move. The hand movement required to do this is comparable to a slow left click with a slight movement of your wrist.

You can increase the distance that you have to move an icon before dragging starts by using TweakUI. Open TweakUI in your Control Panel, and increase the number in the Drag field (in the Mouse tab) to something like five or ten pixels. Test it using the gear icon. If you're still having problems, increase the size again.

High-resolution displays with high-density mice are the source of this problem. The Microsoft's defaults are for VGA resolution screens. Two pixels is much too small a distance for high-resolution displays, and high-density mice take only the slightest movement to move this far.

Using different mouse pointers

You can (and we feel should) use some of the newer static and animated mouse pointers created for Windows 95. They are a lot of fun, and they are often better designed than the Windows standard ones.

Microsoft Plus! comes with lots of animated pointers. Some are stored in the \Windows\Cursors folder and some in the \Program Files\Plus!\Themes folder. Only a few animated pointers come with Windows 95; these pointers are stored in the \Windows\Cursors folder.

You must have your display card driver set to at least 256 colors in order for animated cursors to work. See Chapter 22 for details about display cards.

Secret

Some cards that can display 256 colors have video drivers that don't work with animated pointers. The Diamond Viper is one such video card. You'll need to test your card and driver with one animated pointer to make sure that it works.

Secret

Animated pointers don't work if you use 16-bit real-mode hard disk drivers instead of the 32-bit protected-mode drivers that come with Windows 95. Your Config.sys file references these drivers if you are using them. You can also check to see if you are using 32-bit hard disk drivers by double-clicking the System icon in your Control Panel, and then clicking the Performance tab. If File System and Virtual Memory are marked as 32-bit, you are not using 16-bit hard disk drivers.

If you did a custom Windows 95 installation, as is our recommendation, you need to install the mouse pointers initially (as an accessory) if you want to have them available to you now. If you didn't install them during setup, you can double-click the Add/Remove Programs icon in the Control Panel, click the Windows Setup tab, click Accessories, and mark the Mouse Pointers check box to install them.

Secret

Table 24-1 *(continued)*	
Pointer	*Function*
Move	When you click the Move command in the system menu of a window, this pointer appears. When you see it, you can move the window with your arrow keys.
Alternate Select	The only place we have seen this pointer is in the FreeCell solitaire card game.

A very important cursor not included in this list shows the insertion point in text editors and word processors. This cursor, aptly called the *insertion point*, tells you where your text will get inserted if you start typing.

If you use the Display Properties dialog box to change the background color of your windows to something other than the default stark white, you'll need to set the color of the insertion point so that it shows up well on top of the background color. For more details, see Chapter 22.

Microsoft Plus! comes with its own sets of pointers that work with various themes. You can edit these pointers (revise the graphic images used for the pointers) and also use them independently of the themes. To change themes (and therefore pointers), double-click the Desktop Themes icon in the Control Panel. The pointers associated with themes are stored in the \Program Files\Plus!\Themes folder.

Changing mouse pointer speed

Undocumented

Speed is a bit of a misnomer. What you are determining is how much *faster* the mouse pointer moves as you move the mouse faster. This is a semi-complicated multiplier of the already-set ratio of mouse pointer movement to mouse movement.

The ratio of mouse pointer movement to mouse movement has already been set by your mouse and video driver. The pointer speed values multiply this ratio so that the mouse pointer moves even faster if you move the mouse faster. Each one of the tick marks in the Pointer speed slider, shown in Figure 24-4, corresponds to a different set of values for Mouse Speed, MouseThreshold1, and MouseThreshold2. These values are shown in Table 24-2.

Table 24-2		**The Pointer Speed Values**					
Slider Position	*1*	*2*	*3*	*4*	*5*	*6*	*7*
MouseSpeed	0	1	1	1	2	2	2

Slider Position	1	2	3	4	5	6	7
MouseThreshold1	0	10	7	4	4	4	4
MouseThreshold2	0	0	0	0	12	9	6

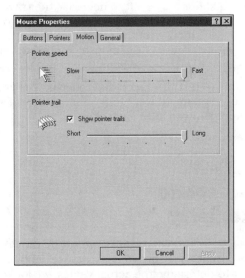

Figure 24-4: The Motion tab of the Mouse Properties dialog box. Change the responsiveness of the mouse pointer to movements of the mouse. Add trails to the mouse pointer on LCD screens. The units for MouseThreshold1 and 2 are pixels.

If you move your mouse slowly, the mouse pointer moves slowly. If you move the mouse quickly, the mouse pointer moves even more quickly if the MouseSpeed is greater than zero.

Windows compares the number of pixels the mouse pointer has moved during the time interval between mouse interrupts against the mouse thresholds. The mouse sends out interrupts periodically. If you move the mouse quickly, the mouse pointer movement exceeds the number of pixels of one or both of the mouse thresholds.

If the MouseSpeed is set to 1 and the mouse pointer movement exceeds the number of pixels given by the value of MouseThreshold1, the mouse pointer speed is double the normal rate. If the MouseSpeed is set to 2 and the mouse pointer movement exceeds MouseThreshold2, the mouse pointer speed is quadrupled. If it exceeds MouseThreshold1 it is doubled, the same as if MouseSpeed is set to 1.

Play with this mouse speed slider a bit to see what you are comfortable with. The optimal setting will vary depending on whether you have a trackball or a mouse, among other things.

STEPS

Changing the Mouse Pointer Speed

Step 1. Click the Motion tab in the Mouse Properties dialog box. Move the Pointer speed slider to the left to decrease the travel of the mouse pointer across the screen relative to the speed of travel of the mouse across the mouse pad. Move the slider to the right to increase the responsiveness of the mouse pointer movement on screen to the speed of mouse travel on the mouse pad.

Step 2. You won't be able to test the speed difference unless you click the Apply button. You might want to try a few different speeds and click the Apply button after each change.

Changing mouse speed values in the Registry

Secret

You may wonder how we figured out what values are set by the Pointer speed slider. They turn out to be the same values as those set by the mouse driver in Windows 3.*x*. But to determine the actual values, we looked in the Registry. The way we did it is generally quite useful and bears detailing:

STEPS

Seeing Your Registry Values Change

Step 1. Display the Motion tab of the Mouse Properties dialog box. (Double-click the Mouse icon in the Control Panel and click the Motion tab.)

Step 2. Also display the Registry editor, Regedit.exe. You can do this from the Explorer by double-clicking \Windows\Regedit.exe.

Step 3. Open the Registry editor to HKEY_CURRENT_USER \Control Panel\Mouse. Highlight Mouse, as shown in Figure 24-5. If you don't see this Mouse branch in the Registry, check the undocumented feature at the end of this section.

Step 4. Click the Motion tab of the Mouse Properties dialog box. Move the Pointer speed slider. Click Apply.

Step 5. Click the Registry editor and press the F5 key. You will see the values of MouseSpeed, MouseThreshold1, and MouseThreshold2 change.

Step 6. Repeat steps 4 and 5 to check all the values assigned by the Pointer speed slider. You can do the same thing with the Double-click speed slider (in the Buttons tab).

Seeing Your Registry Values Change

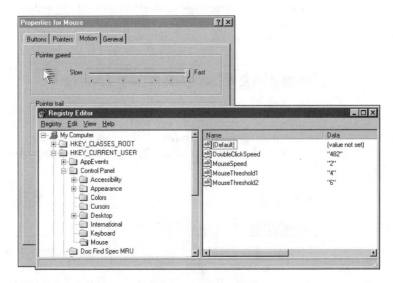

Figure 24-5: The Motion tab of the Mouse Properties dialog box and the Registry editor working together.

Step 7.   Exit the Registry editor.

Secret

The values set in a user interface to the Registry (in this case the Mouse Properties dialog box) are immediately reflected in the Registry, and used by the applications that rely on them.

Undocumented

You can also edit the values directly in the Registry. If you use this method, these new values aren't used by the mouse until you restart Windows. Until you do, the mouse uses 0, 0, 0 instead, meaning no acceleration.

If you have user profiles enabled for your computer, there is a separate mouse setting for each user. If you edit these values in the Registry, you need to change them in the branch that applies to the particular user.

You have to make some changes in your mouse speed values (through the Mouse Properties dialog box) before the Mouse branch will show up in the Registry. You may need to make these changes and quit Windows 95 before you see the branch, because it takes Windows a while to write these changes back out of memory to the disk files that contain the permanent copy of the Registry.

Undocumented

If you have made changes to mouse speed, you will find the Mouse branch in HKEY_CURRENT_USER, as well as in HKEY_USERS. If you have disabled user profiles in the Passwords Properties dialog box (under the Passwords icon in the Control Panel), these branches are the same. The

HKEY_CURRENT_USER branch is an alias for the current user found in the HKEY_USERS branch.

Numerous values are not stored in the Registry unless they are different than the default values. For example, if you don't make any changes in the mouse double-click speed, you won't find an entry for it in the Registry.

Changing the pointer trails

Pointer trails, which leave "ghosts" of the mouse pointer in the mouse pointer's former position, are really useful only on LCD screens where the mouse pointer is hard to find. Otherwise, they are just a distraction. (The default is no pointer trails at all.) Here's how to modify them:

STEPS
Changing the Number of Pointer Ghosts

Step 1.   On the Motion tab of the Mouse Properties dialog box, click the Show pointer trails check box and then move the Pointer trail slider to the left and right. You will see the effect immediately.

Step 2.   To apply the change that you have made to the mouse pointer trails, click OK.

Creating Your Own Mouse Pointers

Windows 95 comes with a number of static and animated mouse pointers that you can assign to different mouse pointer functions. Microsoft Plus! comes with more, and the *Windows 95 Secrets* CD-ROM has more still.

You can use these mouse pointers, you can edit them to create your own pointers, or you can create your own static and animated pointers. The Windows 95 source CD-ROM contains two programs that help you create pointers and string pointers together to create animated pointers.

These programs, Imagedit.exe and Aniedit.exe, are stored in the \Admin\Reskit\Apptools\Aniedit folder on the Windows 95 CD-ROM. You can copy them to your \Program Files\Accessories folder (or any folder you like) on your hard disk. They have an accompanying setup *(inf)* file, so you can use the Add/Remove Programs icon in your Control Panel to "install" them if you like. Use the Windows Setup tab, click the Have Disk button, and then browse to the folder on the hard disk that holds these applications. (Installing sets up an association of Aniedit.exe with the file type *cur.*)

Use both of these programs to look at existing animated and static pointers to get an idea of how they are created.

You can have even more fun tracking the distance that your mouse has traveled with Odometer for Windows 95. You'll find it at http://www.windows95.com.

What Is Missing in Mouse Configuration?

You can't set the mouse pointer to *snap to* the active button or item in a dialog box, as you can with some other mouse drivers, including the ones that come with the Windows 3.*x* Microsoft mouse. *Snap to* can substantially cut down on mouse movement — although it can also be annoying because the mouse moves to unexpected places.

The mouse doesn't wrap around the edge of the screen. When it goes off the left edge, you can't make it come in the right edge.

Undocumented

Microsoft doesn't give you a straightforward way to define the middle mouse button to function as a keystroke of your choice. (We discuss the only definition that you can make later in this chapter.)

All of these missing features and more are available in software provided by mouse manufacturers, and by Microsoft for Microsoft mice.

Built-in Trackballs and Mice

Undocumented

If you have a built-in trackball in your portable, you can use a plug-in serial mouse along with it without having to disable the trackball. Both mice are detected by Windows 95 and both are functional at the same time.

If you add a serial mouse later or enable the internal trackball (using your BIOS setup) after Windows 95 is installed, you have to force Windows 95 to detect the "new" hardware (unless these are plug and play devices). Use the Add New Hardware icon in the Control Panel, and follow the steps in the section earlier in this chapter entitled *Adding a mouse driver*.

A generic built-in trackball is most likely supported by the Microsoft PS/2 Port Mouse or Standard PS/2 Port Mouse drivers in Windows 95.

The Mouse in a DOS Box

If you have a DOS program that is mouse-aware — that is, it can accept and use mouse movements and mouse button presses — Windows 95 automatically allows you to use your mouse with the DOS program in a DOS Windows session. You don't have to do anything special to let it know that you are using a mouse; Windows 95 passes along mouse movements and button presses to the DOS program.

In previous versions of Windows, if you wanted to have your mouse available for your DOS programs, you had to load a DOS real-mode mouse driver with calls in your Autoexec.bat or Config.sys files. The mouse drivers that ship with Windows 95 are clever enough to handle both Windows and DOS (in DOS Windows sessions), so you don't need to load your old mouse driver.

On the other hand, if you run DOS programs that use a mouse in MS-DOS mode, you do need to load a real-mode mouse driver when you enter that mode. You are able to do this because MS-DOS mode gives you the option of creating specific Autoexec.bat and Config.sys files for that mode. See Chapter 17 for details.

You have two options for modifying how the mouse works with your DOS programs while running in a Windows DOS session. You can specify these in the Misc tab of the Properties dialog box for a given DOS application or for your general DOS Windows sessions. (To display the Properties dialog box, right-click the shortcut icon for a specific DOS program or, if you want to change these options for all DOS Windows sessions, right-click the Dosprmpt shortcut in the \Windows folder. Then click Properties.)

First, you can select the QuickEdit option, which disables the mouse functions of the DOS program (if it has any) and dedicates the mouse to marking, copying, and pasting between the DOS program and Windows programs or other windowed DOS programs. This is particularly useful if the DOS program is not mouse-aware. Second, you can choose the Exclusive mode option to force the mouse to work only within the DOS client window area and only under control of the DOS program. Turn to Chapter 17 for more details on how to set these options.

Double-Clicking with the Middle Mouse Button

Logitech builds and sells more mice than Microsoft (although not more at retail) and most of its mice (and trackballs, for that matter) have three buttons. If the mouse that came with your computer has three buttons, it is very likely a Logitech mouse. Look on the underside of the mouse for a label.

Logitech sells a piece of software — the Mouse Control Center — that lets you define, among other things, the function of the middle button as well as the right button. The default setting for the Logitech middle button is double-click, and we prefer to use this button rather than double-clicking the left mouse button.

Secret

You can set the middle button of the Logitech mouse to double-click even if you don't have Logitech's Mouse Control Center. By editing the Registry, you can define this mouse behavior using only the Logitech mouse driver that Microsoft ships with Windows 95:

STEPS

Making the Middle Mouse Button Double-Click

Step 1.   Install the Logitech mouse driver that comes with Windows 95 first. See the steps in the earlier section entitled *Setting Up Your Mouse Driver*.

Step 2.   Use the Explorer to find Regedit.exe in the \Windows folder. Double-click it to start the Registry editor.

Step 3.   Click the plus signs to navigate to

HKEY_LOCAL_MACHINE\SOFTWARE\Logitech\MouseWare\ Current Version

Figure 24-6 shows the Registry editor at this location for a particular mouse (in this case, the Logitech MouseMan).

Step 4.   Click the plus sign next to your Logitech mouse type. Click the 0000 key in the left pane.

Step 5.   Double-click the DoubleClick key in the right pane. Change the value from 000 to 001.

Step 6.   Exit the Registry, and restart Windows 95 to have this change take effect.

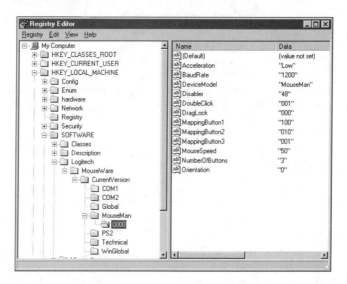

Figure 24-6: The Registry editor. Edit the DoubleClick value in the right pane by double-clicking it. To get the middle key to be a double-click, change this value to 001.

This double-click definition doesn't work with Microsoft Edit. We use Edit all the time to edit Autoexec.bat, Config.sys, and other text files.

This double-click definition also doesn't work if you have configured the mouse to be a left-handed mouse.

Placing the Mouse Icon on the Desktop

You can have ready access to the properties controlling the way your mouse behaves if you place a shortcut to the Mouse Properties dialog box on your Desktop:

STEPS

Putting the Mouse Icon on the Desktop

Step 1.   Click the Start button, point to Settings, and then click Control Panel.

Step 2.   Right-drag the Mouse icon to the Desktop.

Step 3.   Drop the Mouse icon on the Desktop and click Create Shortcut(s) Here.

Step 4.   Press F2, and type a new name for the shortcut to the Mouse Properties dialog box.

If you have a Logitech mouse and want to have Logitech's purple mouse icon on your Desktop (Microsoft provides only the soap-bar-like icon in the Control Panel with its Logitech driver), you can change the shortcut icon you just created. Here's how:

STEPS

Putting the Logitech Purple Mouse Icon on the Desktop

Step 1.   Right-click the Mouse shortcut on the Desktop. Click Properties, and click the Shortcut tab.

Step 2.   Click the Change Icon button. Click the Browse button and search for the folder for your old Logitech driver (Lmouse, perhaps?).

Step 3.   Look for a Logitech executable file in this folder, such as Wmousecc.exe. When you find it, double-click it.

Step 4.   Choose the mouse icon you want, and click OK.

Step 5.   Click OK.

Your Mouse in the Device Manager

If you double-click the System icon in your Control Panel and then click the Device Manager tab, you'll see an entry for Mouse, and one for Ports. These two entries list the driver files for the mouse and serial ports, and they display the characteristics of the serial ports.

The Ports section of the Device Manager stores the address and interrupt of the serial port to which your mouse may be attached. If there are conflicts between these assignments and other port hardware in your computer, they will be highlighted. For details on dealing with ports, turn to Chapter 25.

Double-Clicking versus Single-Clicking

It is not always clear when you are supposed to double-click to initiate an action and when a single click is sufficient. Windows 95 was designed to cut down on the use of the double-click. While double-clicks are not now required, they are often the easiest way to initiate an action.

A *click* means a press and release of the left mouse button. A *double-click* is two clicks within a set time interval. A *right-click* is a click of the right mouse button.

Tip

What is the keyboard equivalent of a double-click? Move the highlight to the icon with the arrow keys. When the item that you want to open is highlighted, press Enter.

Double-clicking to open

You can open all icons on the Desktop by double-clicking them. *Open* has multiple meanings. If the icon is a folder, it means open a folder in a window to display its contents. If the icon represents an application, it means start the application. If the icon represents a document, it means start the application associated with the document and open the document within the application.

Open is often the default action associated with a double-click, but you can choose or define other actions that will take place instead. For example, you could choose the Explore action, a variation on Open that opens the item in an Explorer window. If you set this action as the default action, then double-clicking an icon on the Desktop initiates the Explore action. See Chapter 13 for more details.

Double-clicking a filename or icon in a folder window often opens it. Double-clicking a filename or folder name in a common file dialog box (a dialog box associated with File Open) opens it within the associated application.

If a folder icon appears in the left pane of the Explorer, you only have to single-click it to open it and display the folder's contents in the right pane. If a folder icon appears in the right pane, you have to double-click it.

The Taskbar displays buttons for running applications or folders; you single-click a Taskbar button to bring the associated application or folder to the top of the Desktop. Right-clicking the Taskbar lets you:

1. Cascade the open windows on the Desktop

2. Tile the open windows horizontally or vertically

3. Minimize all open windows (or undo the previous minimization)

4. Edit the properties of the Taskbar

Turn to Chapter 7 for more details on using the Taskbar.

Right-clicking the time

Right-clicking the time at the right end of the Taskbar gives you the same options as right-clicking the Taskbar itself, and it also lets you adjust the settings for the date and time.

Right-clicking a file icon

Right-clicking a file icon lets you open the file with its associated application, and if a document has an associated Quick Viewer, you can quickly view the document's contents by choosing Quick View (assuming you have installed the Quick View component of Windows 95).

When you right-click a file icon, you can also access all the standard file-management commands, including Cut, Copy, Delete, and Rename.

Shift+right-clicking a file icon

If the file is of a registered file type, Shift+right-click adds the Open With command to the context menu. Open With lets you open the file with an application other than the one associated with that file type.

Right-clicking a folder icon

The context menu for a folder is similar to that of a file. Choosing the Open command in a folder's context menu displays the contents of that folder in a folder window (if the icon is in a folder window) or in the Explorer (if the icon is in the Explorer). You can also use the context menu to move, share, create a shortcut to, rename, or delete a folder, and to bring up its properties sheets.

Right-clicking a shortcut

Right-clicking a shortcut brings up the same context menu that appears when you right-click the target of the shortcut. The difference is that the Properties command in the context menu for a shortcut brings up the Properties dialog box for the shortcut itself, not for the target.

You can get to the application or document to which the shortcut points by installing the Target dynamic link library file that comes with Microsoft's PowerToys (download PowerToys from http://www.microsoft.com/windows/software/powertoy.htm). Target.dll adds the Target command to the context menu for a shortcut. When you point to Target, a submenu appears that includes, among other things, an Open Container command, which opens a folder window with the focus on the target, and a Properties command, which displays the Properties dialog box for the target.

Right-clicking the Desktop

If you right-click the Desktop itself (staying clear of icons and the Taskbar) you display the Desktop's context menu. This context menu lets you:

1. Arrange (line up) the icons on the Desktop

2. Create a new folder, file, or shortcut on the Desktop

3. Open the Display Properties dialog box

The last item is the same as double-clicking the Display icon in the Control Panel.

Right-clicking the client area of a folder window

The options you get when you right-click the client area of a folder window are similar to those you get when you right-click the Desktop, with two differences. You don't get a Properties command for bringing up the Display Properties dialog box, and you do get commands for changing how the icons are displayed in the folder window: Large Icons, Small Icons, List, and Details.

Right-clicking the title bar of the active application

If you right-click the title bar of the application window with the focus, you display the system menu for that window. (The title bar of a window with the focus is blue if you are using standard Windows colors.)

The system menu is programmable, so it can change from application to application. The standard functions that are available in this menu include moving, sizing, and closing the window.

You can also right-click the title bar of a folder window to display its system menu, or right-click a Taskbar button to display the system menu for the associated folder or application.

Right-clicking in a dialog box

Dialog boxes are a little different than most windows that show up on your Desktop. You may see common resource dialog boxes used by 16-bit Windows 3.*x* applications or common dialog boxes used by 32-bit Windows 95 applications. Many Windows applications also have their own unique dialog boxes.

Many Windows 95-compliant dialog boxes have a question-mark button in the upper-right corner. If you click that button and then click an item in the dialog box, you get an explanation of the item. As an alternative to using the question-mark button, you can right-click an item, and then click the What's This? button that appears.

Right-clicking in a 16-bit
File Open dialog box

Common resource dialog boxes for 16-bit Windows 3.*x* applications include the File Open and Fonts dialog boxes. If you right-click within one of these dialog boxes, a What's This? button appears.

Right-clicking in a 32-bit
File Open dialog box

Right-clicking a filename in a 32-bit Windows 95 common File Open dialog box highlights the filename and displays a context menu with options to open the file and perform other file-management tasks. Right-clicking in other places gives you other context menus appropriate to the item you clicked. In some areas, you get the What's This? button.

Figure 24-7 shows the 32-bit File Open dialog box with the context menu for the first filename displayed.

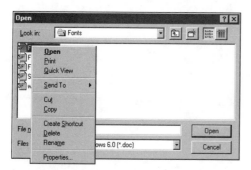

Figure 24-7: The File Open dialog box. Right-click a filename to display its context menu.

Right-clicking in the client area of an active application

You can right-click within the application, on a document in your word processor for example. If the application is Windows 95-aware, a context menu appears with options appropriate to the place you clicked. In a word processor, the context menu might give you commands for copying, cutting, and pasting text. The context menu gives you quick access to frequently used commands.

Summary

The nice thing about the mouse in Windows 95 is that it is a lot more useful. You need to know what its new functions are so that you can take advantage of its enhanced power.

▶ A new Mouse Properties dialog box lets you easily change the responsiveness of the mouse pointer to mouse movements.

▶ You can use animated pointers in place of some of the duller mouse pointers.

▶ You can turn the middle button on your Logitech mouse into a double-click button.

▶ You don't need to double-click as much as you had to in Windows 3.*x*.

▶ The right mouse button has been empowered.

Chapter 25

Modems, Serial Ports, and Parallel Ports

In This Chapter

Modems and ports (serial and parallel) are communications devices. Windows 95 automatically detects them and helps you set them up. We discuss:

▶ Configuring your modem driver

▶ Getting behind the configuration routines and changing modem driver parameters

▶ Manually controlling which ports can be used by Direct Cable Connection (DCC) and adding ports that were inadvertently removed

▶ Configuring your serial and parallel ports

▶ Testing for the presence of an advanced serial port chip

Hello, World

When the personal computer was envisioned and designed, the focus of its communication facilities was the monitor, the keyboard, and the printer — the electronic typewriter model. Serial ports and modem communications were peripheral considerations, so to speak. This legacy has hung on.

Computer-mediated communication is now a central concern. The widespread use of laptop and portable computers in business has increased the demand for reliable, easy to use, fast communications links. Inexpensive high-speed fax/modems, the advent of commercial Internet service providers, and the adoption of graphical user interfaces for online services all speak to a popular interest in electronic communications.

Windows 3.x was not up to the task of effectively handling these communications demands. High-speed communications (over 9600 bits per second, or *bps*) required third-party replacements to the Windows 3.x serial port driver (Comm.drv). Personal computers required a new chip, the 16550A Universal Asynchronous Receiver/Transmitter (UART), to keep up with the data flow through the serial port or modem.

Configuring a Modem

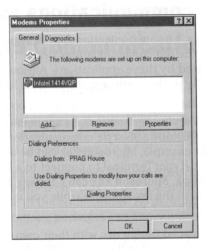

Figure 25-1: The General tab of the Modems Properties dialog box.

Step 2. If you haven't yet configured a modem, the Install New Modem Wizard automatically starts (see Figure 25-2). Choose your modem type and click Next.

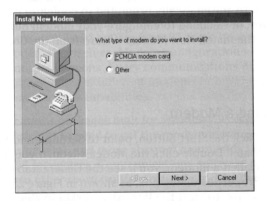

Figure 25-2: The Install New Modem Wizard.

Step 3. You can have the Windows 95 hardware detection routines look for your modem or you can select it from the list of explicitly supported modems. You can change the selection during this configuration process, so it doesn't hurt to let Windows 95 try to

Configuring a Modem

detect your modem. Make sure you are not running any communications programs, because they won't allow the detection routines to access the modem. If you want to specify the modem yourself, mark the check box labeled "Don't detect my modem; I will select it from a list" (see Figure 25-3). Click Next.

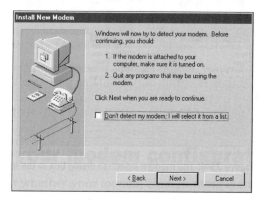

Figure 25-3: Choose whether to have Windows 95 detect your modem.

Step 4. If you choose to have Windows 95 detect the modem, it will take a few seconds to query the modem to determine its type and which communications port it is using. Windows 95 can't detect all modems. The fall-back position for the detection routines is Standard modem at a certain speed, such as 9600 bps. Click Change if you don't think the modem that has been detected is correct or you think you can do a better job.

Step 5. If you are choosing your own modem, or if you clicked Change, you will see a list of modem manufacturers in the next Install New Modem dialog box, as shown in Figure 25-4. Scroll the left box to find the manufacturer of your modem. Highlight its name. Scroll the right box and select the model of your modem. Click Next.

If you have a diskette from a modem manufacturer that includes a Windows 95 setup routine for the modem, click Have Disk instead. Modems manufactured after the release of Windows 95 may have these diskettes. Microsoft also publishes setup files for new modems on its web site.

(continued)

Changing Modem Driver Settings

Step 2.   Click Properties to display the General tab of the Properties dialog box for your modem, as shown in Figure 25-5.

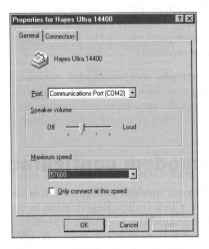

Figure 25-5: The General tab of the Properties dialog box for a modem. You have already selected the port, so unless you move the modem, you shouldn't change that. You can set a global volume for the speaker and the maximum speed your computer/modem combination can handle.

Step 3.   An alternate and equivalent way of carrying out steps 1 and 2 is to click the System icon in the Control Panel. Then click the Device Manager tab, click the plus sign next to the Modem icon, click the icon associated with your modem, click Properties, and click the Modem tab.

Step 4.   If necessary, change one or more values in your modem's General tab. The maximum speed at which your modem can receive data depends on what kind of error correction protocol it has and the speed of your CPU. For instance, a 14.4 Kbps modem that implements the V.32bis standard when combined with a 486 processor may be able to sustain 57.6 Kbps with compression. If you find your communications applications are reporting high error rates, reduce this maximum value.

Changing the basic modem connection properties

Each connection — each bulletin board, Internet service provider, friend with a computer and a modem, or server at work that you connect to using your modem — requires unique connection settings. You can follow these steps to set the default choices that your modem will use until you modify them for a given connection:

STEPS

Setting Modem Connection Properties

Step 1.   Carry out steps 1-3 in Changing Modem Driver Settings in the preceding section. Click the Connection tab to display the connection properties for the specific modem, as shown in Figure 25-6.

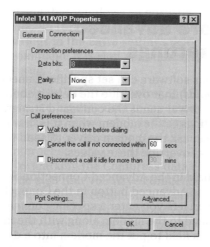

Figure 25-6: The Connection tab of the Properties dialog box for a modem. You can set global default values for the data bits, parity, and stop bits.

Step 2.   The values of 8, None, and 1 for data bits, parity, and stop bits are probably just fine. Change them only if you are attaching to a new service that regularly calls for other values.

Step 3.   By default, Windows 95 waits for the dial tone before dialing. If you are calling outside the U.S., you should clear the check box labeled "Wait for dial tone before dialing" to turn off this U.S.-specific behavior. You may also need to clear this check box if you purchased a modem in a country other than the one you are presently calling from.

(continued)

Setting Advanced Connection Properties

Step 6.   If you are using a cellular modem, mark the Use cellular protocol check box to reduce errors over multiple cellular connections. This box is only enabled if you're using a CDPD (Cellular Digital Packet Data) modem and the TCP/IP protocol.

Step 7.   The default setting in the Modulation type drop-down list is Standard. This is the fall-back low-speed communications standard if two modems can't communicate at a higher speed. If you experience trouble while trying to communicate with a given site at 300 and 1200 bps, switch from Standard to Non-standard (Bell, HST).

Step 8.   Mark the Record a log file check box if you want to keep a log file to help with debugging a connection. The file, Modemlog.txt, will be in your \Windows folder.

Step 9.   Click OK.

Changing 16550A UART settings

If your serial port uses a 16550A UART, you have the option of adjusting the size of its receive and transmit buffers. You might want to do this if you are dropping characters during transmissions or if you want to increase your throughput. To change these settings, click the Port Settings button in the Connection tab of the Properties dialog box for your modem.

The same Port Settings button is associated with each connectoid. To verify this, right-click a connectoid, for example in the HyperTerminal folder. Then click Properties, click the Configure button, click the Connection tab, and there it is. Each connectoid can have its own Advanced and Port Setting values.

Changing any modem settings

The file Modems.inf and the files starting with Mdm in the \Windows\Inf folder contain the modem manufacturer and model information displayed when you click the Have Disk button in the Install New Modem Wizard. (The Inf folder is only visible if you have chosen View, Options in an Explorer or folder window and marked the Show all files option button in the View tab.) Modem manufacturers can ship a file with their modem on a diskette that provides equivalent information about their new modem. Plug and play modems contain the pertinent information on a ROM chip.

Secret

Each modem model has an associated initialization string or set of initialization strings that are defined in the modem setup files. Additional strings for
hanging up the modem, setting it in auto-answer mode, turning on or off the
speaker and setting its volume, data compression, tone or pulse dial, and so
on, are provided in the modem's setup, or *inf*, file.

You can edit the information in these files if you want to change the values
Windows 95 uses when you configure a modem. You do this by changing the
inf file before you add the particular modem driver. From the Explorer,
double-click the *inf* file that has a name resembling the manufacturer of
your modem. You can then edit it with Notepad. Be sure to make a backup
file first.

After you have added a modem driver to your Windows 95 configuration
(using the associated *inf* file), you can change any of the settings associated
with the modem by using the Registry editor. This is a bit easier than editing
the esoteric *inf* file directly. Turn to Chapter 15 if you are not familiar with
how to edit the Registry.

Go to the following branch of the Registry:

HKEY_LOCAL_MACHINE\System\CurrentControlSet\
Services\Class\Modem

There may be a number of modems specified on this branch, each designated as a branch and starting with the branch key numbered 0000. This
area of the Registry is shown in Figure 25-8.

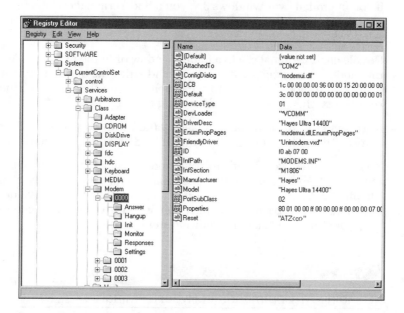

Figure 25-8: The Registry editor displaying the area of the Registry that contains the
modem configuration information. Click the plus signs next to the names in the branch to
get to this area. (The names on the branch now have minus signs in front of them.)

Find the branch that corresponds to your modem driver by checking the DriverDesc field (in the right pane of the Registry editor) for its familiar name as you highlight each key starting with 0000. If you have set up DCC, you will see modems in the DriverDesc field labeled Serial cable between 2 PCs. Expand the branch for your modem by clicking the plus sign in front of its designated number to see the keys that you can edit.

If you want to change the initialization string for your modem in the Registry, click the Init folder for your modem in the left pane of the Registry editor. The initialization string is displayed in the right pane. Double-click the 2 in the right pane and edit the string. You might want to edit the Answer, Hangup, Fax, and Settings values. (You may see other values and variables as well, depending on what items your modem manufacturer chose to place in the Registry.)

It's a good idea to make a copy of System.dat and User.dat in your \Windows folder before you make any changes to your modem configuration in the Registry.

Test and Interrogate Your Modem

You can find out if your modem is working and what values are stored in its registers. To do this, you can use Terminal, the Windows 3.*x* communications package, because it makes it easy to talk directly to your modem. Alternatively, you can configure HyperTerminal.

If you upgraded over Windows 3.*x*, you'll find Terminal.exe still in your \Windows folder. Otherwise, you may need to retrieve it from your Windows 3.*x* diskettes.

Double-click Terminal.exe in a folder window or in the Explorer. To check if the modem is working, type the command string **atz** or **ath** or **ate1m1v1**. (Check your modem manual to see which one you should use.) If the modem returns *OK*, then it is there and listening to you.

Next, send the **ati?** command, replacing the ? with the numbers **2** through **9**, one at a time. This should tell you what kind of modem you have.

You can send AT commands to your modem using HyperTerminal. Just follow the steps detailed in the *Answering Incoming Data Calls* section of Chapter 29. You can also send AT commands from a terminal window associated with a particular connection. If you have created a connectoid for HyperTerminal, take the following steps:

STEPS

Sending AT Commands in HyperTerminal

Step 1.   Right-click a HyperTerminal connectoid. Click Properties.

Sending AT Commands in HyperTerminal

Step 2. Click the Configure button, and then click the Options tab.

Step 3. Mark the Bring up terminal window before dialing check box.

Step 4. Click OK. Click OK again.

Step 5. Double-click this connectoid. Click Connect.

Step 6. A terminal window appears on your Desktop. Type the AT commands and see what response you get.

Step 7. Press F3 to cancel the attempted connection when you are done.

Step 8. Click Cancel.

You can invoke a modem diagnostic dialog box by double-clicking the Modems icon in the Control Panel, clicking the Diagnostics tab, highlighting the port to which your modem is attached, and then clicking the More Info button. Windows 95 sends various AT commands to your modem and reports the responses in the dialog box, as shown in Figure 25-9. It's not too interesting unless you know from looking in your modem's manual what the correct responses are supposed to be.

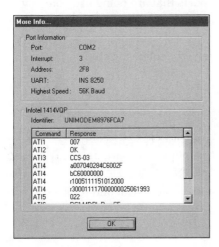

Figure 25-9: The More Info dialog box.

Serial and Parallel Ports as Modems

In Chapter 30, we discuss DCC, which lets you hook two computers together using a serial or parallel cable.

DCC keeps track of your serial and parallel ports as though they were modems. When you first click DCC, hardware detection routines determine which serial and parallel ports are available. They create modem designations for each of these ports and allow you to choose between Serial Cable on COM*x* and Parallel Cable on LPT*x*. The modem descriptions and properties of each port are stored in the Registry in the area referred to in the *Changing any modem settings* section of this chapter.

These are not real modems, but the Modems area of the Registry is a convenient place to keep track of the fact that these ports are available to be used by DCC. These port connections do not show up on the list of modems when you double-click the Modems icon in the Control Panel.

There are two ways to see which ports the hardware detection routines have found. You can click the Start button, point to Programs, then Accessories, and then click Direct Cable Connection. If you click the Change button and then click Next, you'll see a list of ports available for DCC.

The other way to see the list of ports is to click the Start button, point to Settings, and then click Control Panel. Double-click the System icon, and then click the plus sign next to the Modem icon. A list of all "modems" will appear, including your serial and parallel cables on ports if you have previously run DCC.

If you use this second method, you can remove certain ports that you won't be using with DCC — perhaps ports that are being used only by your mouse, for instance. If you remove a port/cable that you decide later to use with DCC, you must restore it manually.

To add back a removed port, take the following steps:

STEPS

Adding a Removed Port

Step 1.   Click the Start button, point to Programs, then Accessories, and finally click Direct Cable Connection.

Step 2.   Click the Change button, click Next, and then click Next again.

Step 3.   Click the Install New Ports button.

Configuring Serial Ports

You can change a serial port's settings as well its address and interrupt values. You make all changes to serial and parallel ports through the Device Manager, found under the System icon in the Control Panel.

Changing serial port settings

Windows 3.*x* included a Ports icon in the Control Panel. The functions of this Ports icon are now included in the Device Manager. You can use the Device Manager to change a serial port's speed, data bits, stop bits, parity, and flow control (handshaking). If you are using this serial port for a connection, the settings for that particular connection override these settings.

STEPS

Changing Serial Port Settings

Step 1. Click the Start button, point to Settings, and then click Control Panel. Double-click the System icon to display the System Properties dialog box, and click the Device Manager tab.

Step 2. Click the plus sign to the left of the Ports icon in the Device Manager. You will see a listing of all the serial and parallel ports connected to your computer.

Step 3. Highlight the serial port you want to change and click the Properties button. Click the Port Settings tab.

Step 4. Using the Port Settings properties sheet, as shown in Figure 25-10, you can change the values for speed, data bits, stop bits, parity, and flow control (handshaking).

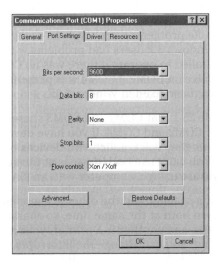

Figure 25-10: The Port Settings tab of the Communications Port (COMx) Properties dialog box.

Changing Serial Port Addresses and Interrupts

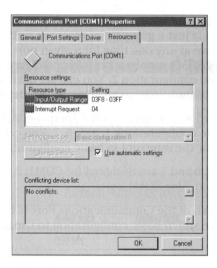

Figure 25-11: The Resources tab in the Communications Port (COM*x*) Properties dialog box.

Step 6. If the address in the currently selected basic configuration can be changed, when you highlight Input/Output Range and click the Change Setting button, you'll see the Edit Input/Output Range dialog box, as shown in Figure 25-12. You can give the port a new address if the documentation for the port hardware indicates support for the new address.

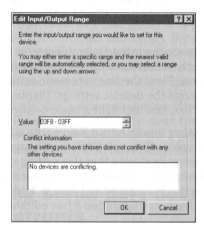

Figure 25-12: The Edit Input/Output Range dialog box. Change the value of the port address by scrolling through the available addresses. The lower field reports whether a hardware device driver is already using this address.

Changing Serial Port Addresses and Interrupts

Step 7. Scroll through the various available addresses to set a new address for this port. You are warned if there is a conflict with another hardware device driver.

Step 8. If the interrupt in the currently selected basic configuration can be changed, you can highlight Interrupt Request in the Resources tab, click the Change Setting button, and then change the interrupt value in the Edit Interrupt Request dialog box. You will be warned if there is a conflict.

Step 9. Click OK. Click OK again.

Step 10. Restart Windows 95.

Better Serial Ports

Over the lifetime of PC-compatible architecture, the UART chip that controls serial ports has evolved. It began in the IBM PC as the 8250. In the AT class machines, it was upgraded to a 16540. The current chip of choice in Intel 486 and Pentium-based PCs is the 16550A.

Undocumented

The 16550A has two advantages over its predecessors. First, it incorporates a 16-byte buffer. By buffering incoming and outgoing data, the 16550A UART can accumulate characters without losing them while waiting for its interrupt request to be serviced by the CPU. Second, the 8250 and the 16540 UARTs send an interrupt to the CPU whenever they receive a character. The 16550A can send one interrupt to service all the characters in the buffer.

By accumulating characters while waiting for the CPU to be available, the 16550A greatly enhances the reliability of high-speed communications, which is a very important feature, given our increased usage of the serial port as a networking device.

Undocumented

Windows 3.*x* didn't take much advantage of this buffering capability of the 16550A UART. It didn't use it to transmit data and used only a single byte of the buffer in the receive mode. This allowed third-party software developers to find a niche in the market by creating additional COM port drivers to replace Comm.drv.

Windows 95 takes full advantage of the 16650A UART, enabling the full 16 bytes of the receive and transmit buffers.

Testing Your Internal Modem for a 16550A UART

You can test whether your internal modem includes a 16550A UART:

STEPS

Testing an Internal Modem

Step 1.   Set up your modem driver, as described in the steps in the *Configuring Your Modem* section earlier in this chapter.

Step 2.   Click the Start button, point to Settings, and click Control Panel. Double-click the Modems icon.

Step 3.   Click the Diagnostics tab. Highlight the port with your modem attached. Click More Info. The More Info dialog box will tell you which UART you have.

Configuring Parallel Ports

The Windows 95 user interface for configuring parallel ports is almost the same as that used for serial ports. Unlike the nine basic configurations available for a serial port, there are only four basic configurations available for a parallel port. Basic configurations 0 and 2 do not have interrupts.

Tip Windows 95 by default does not assign an interrupt to a parallel port. The interrupt is rarely needed for printing. The previous standard was to assign Interrupt 7 to LPT1 and LPT3, and Interrupt 5 to LPT2. Here's how to change addresses and interrupts:

STEPS

Changing Parallel Port Addresses and Interrupts

Step 1.   Click Start, point to Settings, and click Control Panel. Double-click the System icon to display the System Properties dialog box. Click the Device Manager tab.

Step 2.   Click the plus sign next to the Ports icon in the Device Manager tab to see a listing of all serial and parallel ports connected to your computer.

Step 3.   Highlight the parallel port that you want to change, and click Properties. Click the Resources tab.

Changing Parallel Port Addresses and Interrupts

Step 4. You can change the Input/Output Range or the Interrupt Request settings. Each of these settings is stored with a numbered basic configuration. Display the Setting based on drop-down list to see the possible basic configurations. Highlight a basic configuration.

Step 5. Highlight either Input/Output Range (the address of the parallel port) or Interrupt Request. Clear the Use automatic settings check box to allow settings other than the default ones. Click the Change Setting button.

Step 6. If you highlighted Input/Output Range in step 5, you can change the port address setting with the arrow buttons.

Step 7. If you highlighted Interrupt Request in step 5, you can change the interrupt value. You will be warned if there is a conflict. There isn't an interrupt displayed with every basic configuration.

Step 8. Click OK. Click OK again.

Step 9. Restart Windows 95.

Configuring ECP and EPP Ports

Windows 95 Setup detects whether you have an *extended capabilities port* (ECP) or an *enhanced parallel port* (EPP), but it won't set up the port for you. Both of these port types provide you with high-speed and bi-directional communication capabilities. If you want high-speed communication, you have to enable ECP or EPP support yourself. Here's how:

STEPS

Configuring ECP or EPP Support

Step 1. Click the Start button, point to Settings, and then click Control Panel.

Step 2. Double-click the System icon in the Control Panel, and then click the Device Manager tab.

Step 3. Click the plus sign next to the Ports icon (or double-click it).

Step 4. If Windows 95 Setup detected an ECP or EPP parallel port in your computer, you will find it under the Ports icon. Double-click it (or highlight it and click the Properties button), and then click the Resources tab.

Step 5. Clear the Use automatic settings check box, display the Settings based on drop-down list, and select Basic configuration 0002.

(continued)

Null Modem Cables

If you are going to use Direct Cable Connection across serial ports, you should use null modem cables to connect two Windows 95 computers. When you ask for a *null modem*, sometimes the sales people at the computer store will know what you're talking about, and sometimes they won't. This is not exactly a brand name. It's easier to pick these items out of a mail order catalog. If you need to be specific, Tables 25-3 and 25-4 describe the connections for null modem cables.

Table 25-3	Serial 9-Pin to 9-Pin Null Modem Cable	
Signal	*Host Serial Port Pins*	*Guest Serial Port Pins*
Transmit Data	3	2
Receive Data	2	3
Request to Send	7	8
Clear to Send	8	7
Data Set Ready and Data Carrier Detect	6, 1	4
Signal Ground	5	5
Data Terminal Ready	4	6, 1

Table 25-4	Serial 25-Pin to 25-Pin Null Modem Cable	
Signal	*Host Serial Port Pins*	*Guest Serial Port Pins*
Transmit Data	2	3
Receive Data	3	2
Request to Send	4	5
Clear to Send	5	4
Data Set Ready and Data Carrier Detect	6, 8	20
Signal Ground	7	7
Data Terminal Ready	20	6, 8

Summary

Windows 95 gives you a great deal of control over your ports and modems:

▶ You can change the address and interrupt value for serial or parallel ports to avoid conflicts with other hardware devices.

▶ You can configure your modem once, and this configuration will be used by all Windows 95-aware communications software.

▶ You can determine whether your internal modem has an advanced serial port (UART) chip.

Chapter 26

Telephony and the Phone Dialer

In This Chapter

Windows 95 provides a powerful resource to aid in telephone communications. Among other features, TAPI (the Telephone Application Programming Interface) indicates to TAPI-compliant communications applications the characteristics of the location you are dialing from. We show you how to use the Dialing Properties dialog box for:

▶ Entering the numbers that you have to dial to get an outside line or a long-distance line

▶ Automatically using calling cards to bill calls correctly from out-of-town locations

▶ Defining alternative dialing methods for unusual situations

▶ Formatting phone numbers so you can dial them from anywhere

▶ Designating the first three digits of a phone number in your area code as requiring long-distance dialing

▶ Setting up speed dialing with Phone Dialer

Where Am I Calling From?

Microsoft provides a resource in Windows 95 for keeping track of where you are. What problem are they trying to solve?

Consider for a moment your garden-variety communications package. You know that it keeps track of the phone numbers of the computer services that you use. That is, it keeps track of the area codes and local numbers. It also knows that if you place an area code in a phone number, it has to dial a 1 to make a long-distance call.

If you stay in one place (say, your office) and have your calls billed to one number (most likely the number you are calling from), your communications software only needs to know the number that you are dialing. It knows how to complete the call because the billing and other information required are implicit.

If, on the other hand, you and your computer travel around at all, your computer needs to know not only where you are calling *to* but the special features of the phone system you are dialing *from*. In addition, you need to be able to easily choose the long-distance carriers that handle your calls and determine how they will bill you.

Different locations have different means of accessing outside lines or long-distance carriers. For example, calling from the office may require that you preface your phone numbers with a 9, while calling from home does not. If you call from a hotel, you might have to use a credit card and dial into a specific long-distance carrier. A phone number may be local when you call from home and long-distance when you call from the office. Some phones have only pulse dialing services. Some locations require special calling methods.

You can handle all these situations with the Dialing Properties dialog box.

Preliminary Location Information

The first time you set up your modem (see Chapter 25 for details) you encounter the Location Information dialog box as part of the Install New Modem Wizard (shown in Figure 26-1). At this point, all you need to do is type your area code.

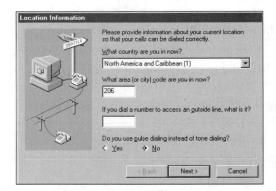

Figure 26-1: The Location Information dialog box.

You have the option of changing the country code, typing a number required to get an outside line, and choosing whether or not to use pulse dialing. You can change all these values later in the Dialing Properties dialog box.

Dialing Properties

The Dialing Properties dialog box lets you define the characteristics of the (perhaps numerous) locations you will be calling from. You will most likely define your office and/or home location right away. Define others as you need them.

One of the easiest ways to go to the Dialing Properties dialog box is through the Modems icon in the Control Panel. Double-click the icon, and then click the Dialing Properties button.

You can also access the Dialing Properties dialog box in these Windows 95-aware communications programs: Phone Dialer, Dial-Up Networking, HyperTerminal, and Windows Messaging. Here is how to get to the dialog box using Phone Dialer:

STEPS

Accessing the Dialing Properties Dialog Box

Step 1. Click the Start button, point to Programs, and then Accessories. Click Phone Dialer.

Step 2. Choose Tools, Dialing Properties to display the Dialing Properties dialog box, as shown in Figure 26-2.

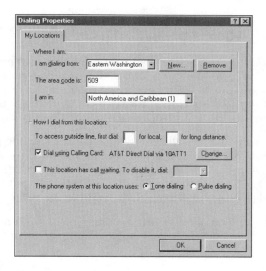

Figure 26-2: The Dialing Properties dialog box.

The Dialing Properties dialog box is independent of the application that you use to call it up. It works the same for all Windows 95 TAPI applications. All of the features discussed in this chapter are applicable to any TAPI-compliant communications software.

Setting up a new location

The particular characteristics of each location are stored by location name. Location names can be anything: Grandma's house, Home Office, HO with ATT, Michigan - direct, Timbuktu - pulse. When you set up a new location, choose a name that is unique and meaningful to you.

A location name stands for a location and for the unique dialing sequence used to make the phone call. This includes whether you use a calling card, have to dial a number to get an outside line, and so on. If the number you're dialing is in the international format (see the section later in this chapter entitled *Format for the Numbers That You Dial Out*), the information stored in the location is used to create the sequence of numbers needed to place the call correctly.

Click the New button to define a new location. Then type the new location name.

Each location should have an area code. The area code field can accommodate a number up to 29 digits in length, but your entry will most likely be no more than 5 digits in length. A location should also have a country code. The drop-down list contains 242 country codes, so you will probably be able to find yours.

Defining how to dial out

Your location may require that you enter a number to get an outside line. You might also have to enter a long-distance access number to get a line that is used for special billing purposes. You may have multiple such billing numbers at work. If this is the case, you could set up separate locations for each number.

Tip

Call waiting can interfere with modem access. If the line you are using at a given location has the call waiting feature, you need to turn it off for the duration of your call when you are using a modem. In the U.S., you normally disable call waiting by dialing *70, 70#, or 1170. These three choices are displayed in the drop-down list to the right of the call waiting check box.

You have the choice of pulse or tone dialing with your modem. If the local telephone office can handle only pulse dialing, you need to mark that option button.

Credit card calls

The procedures for making credit cards calls (or for using a specific long-distance carrier) are uniform enough in most cases for you to automate them. Windows 95 includes specific phone numbers for some long-distance carriers (AT&T, British Telecom, MCI, U.S. Sprint, and others), and you can add more to the basic list. Information on long-distance carriers and calling card numbers is a part of the location definition, so you can have different location names for the same physical location but with different calling cards.

To specify a specific long-distance carrier or bill your calls from the location that you are defining to a calling card, mark the Dial using Calling Card check box. When you mark this check box for the first time for a given location, the Change Calling Card dialog box appears, as shown in Figure 26-3. If you have previously marked this check box, you can click the Change button to display the Change Calling Card dialog box.

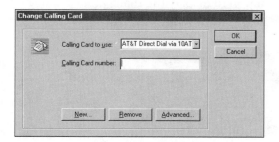

Figure 26-3: The Change Calling Card dialog box.

The Calling Card to use drop-down list by default contains 22 calling card numbers from numerous long-distance vendors, including AT&T, British Telecom, Carte France Telecom, MCI, Telecom Australia, U.S. Sprint, and others. If the drop-down list includes one of the long-distance carriers that you want to use, select it, type your calling card number, and click OK. Your card number will be encrypted when it is stored on your hard disk in the Telephon.ini file. If you want to add a calling card that's not on this list, see the next section.

Adding a long-distance carrier/method to your list

If your long-distance carrier is not on the list in the Change Calling Card dialog box, or if you want to access your carrier through another method, you can use the steps below to create a new carrier listing. You can also use these steps to define another dialing method to match your situation. The Dialing Rules dialog box is not only useful for entering information about calling cards and accessing long-distance carriers, you can also use it to dial a string of numbers that you need for other purposes.

STEPS

Adding a New Long-Distance Carrier

Step 1. Click the New button in the Change Calling Card dialog box to display the Create New Calling Card dialog box. Type a name to identify a carrier and a method. Click OK.

Step 2. The Change Calling Card dialog box now shows the new long-distance carrier number in the Calling Card to use field. Click the

(continued)

Adding a New Long-Distance Carrier

Advanced button to display the Dialing Rules dialog box, as shown in Figure 26-4.

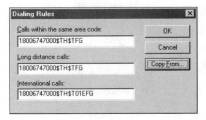

Figure 26-4: The Dialing Rules dialog box. When you first display this dialog box, the fields are empty. This figure shows the dialog box after the fields have been filled.

Step 3. In the three fields in the Dialing Rules dialog box, you enter the access phone number of the long-distance carrier, as well as a series of instructions about how to dial local, long distance, and international calls. You can start with blank fields and type the entries from scratch. The easiest method, however, is to start with a set of rules for an existing similar long-distance carrier. Click the Copy From button to display the Copy Dialing Rules dialog box, as shown in Figure 26-5.

Figure 26-5: The Copy Dialing Rules dialog box. There are 21 calling card dialing rule sets in this list.

Step 4. Click a calling card name/method in the list, and click OK. The dialing rules associated with that calling card and method are copied into the three fields in the Dialing Rules dialog box.

Adding a New Long-Distance Carrier

Step 5.   Edit the fields in the Dialing Rules dialog box to work for your specific carrier/method. Notice that in most cases, at least the long-distance and international calls fields start with a phone number for the long-distance carrier (perhaps just a five-digit prefix) and then include instructions on how to dial the remaining numbers. The dialing rules are explained in the next section.

Step 6.   Click Close and then click OK twice to return to the Phone Dialer. You have defined the properties of a given location as well as a new long-distance carrier.

The dialing rules

Each of the long-distance carriers/methods has a set of three templates of dialing rules: local, long-distance, and international. You can add a long-distance carrier to your list and edit the dialing rules to match those required by that carrier. The templates are not associated with particular long-distance carriers; you can use them to define any dialing method.

The templates of dialing rules are a series of numbers, letters, and punctuation marks that you type in the fields in the Dialing Rules dialog box. When a number is dialed, these rules are read and carried out.

Here is an example template of dialing rules:

1 - (800) 674-7000 THT01EFG

This is a variation on the template for international dialing shown in Figure 26-4. The rules in this template are as follows:

1. Dial the number 1 - (800) 674-7000.

2. Wait for the "bong" tone ($).

3. Using touch tone, send the calling card number (TH).

4. Wait again for the "bong" tone ($).

5. Using touch tone, send 01 (T01).

6. Send the country code, area code, and local number (EFG).

Spaces, hyphens, periods, and parentheses are ignored.

The dialing rules shown in Table 26-1 let you complete a phone call throughout much of the world.

Table 26-1	Dialing Rules
Code	**Represents**
0-9	Number to be dialed
#	Touch tone pound sign
*	Touch tone star
!	Hook flash
,	Pause for two seconds
@	Wait for a ringing tone followed by five seconds of silence
$	Wait for the calling card tone — the "bong" tone
?	Prompt user for input
E	Country code
F	Area code
G	Local phone number
T	Dial the following number using touch tone
P	Dial the following number using pulse dialing
W	Wait for a second dial tone
H	Your calling card number

Waiting for the "bong"

Undocumented

Your modem may not support the option of waiting for the "bong" tone. If it doesn't, it will ignore the $ and dial your calling card number before the phone company is ready to receive it.

If this happens, try substituting the @ symbol for the $ in your version of the dialing rules. Your modem may respond to this. If not, you can also substitute commas (,,,, instead of $) to force an eight-second wait until the calling card number is sent.

Suppressing the 1 prefix

Your company's phone system may dial the prefix 1 for you when you dial long-distance numbers. You can use the Change Calling Card dialog box to create a set of dialing rules that suppresses the prefix 1 for all of the calls you make from work:

STEPS
Creating Dialing Rules to Suppress the 1 Prefix

Step 1. Click the Start button, point to Settings, and click Control Panel. Double-click the Modems icons, and then click the Dialing Properties button.

Step 2. Click the New button, and type a name that describes your office location and phone system.

Step 3. Mark the Dial using Calling Card check box. Click the New button. Type a description for the dialing method used at your office, perhaps a name that describes the dialing rules. Click OK.

Step 4. Click the Advanced button, and then type the following rules in the three fields of the Dialing Rules check box:

Calls within the same area code   G

Long-distance calls   FG

International calls   011EFG

Step 5. Click the Close button, click the OK button, and then click OK again.

The MCI dialing rules

Secret

The default dialing rules for MCI that come with Windows 95 may be wrong. If you use MCI, you should check to make sure that they are correct for you. For example, the long-distance dialing rule for one of the MCI numbers is:

18006747000THTFG

This rule sends your calling card number before the phone number. If this doesn't work, you might try a rule that dials the MCI number, waits for the bong, dials 0, dials the area code and phone number, waits for a second bong, and then enters the calling card number. To do this, create a new MCI listing that includes this long-distance dialing rule:

18006747000$0TFG$TH

Format for the Numbers That You Dial Out

Windows 95-aware communications applications use certain styles to designate numbers that can be dialed out. The most flexible style is the international style:

+CC (AC) LocalNumber

The plus sign, spaces, and parentheses are all required elements of this format. CC is the country code, which in the U.S. is 1. AC is the area code. There is a space between the country code and the area code and a space between the area code and the local number. The local number can have hyphens in it.

If you enter a number in this format, you can call it from anywhere. If you are calling it from the same area code in the same country, TAPI-compliant software won't use the area code and country code (unless you specify to dial this number as a long-distance number — see the next section).

If you want to dial a number such as 911 or an extension number within your company, you shouldn't put the number in the international format. Just type it as is.

You can type phone numbers in Phone Dialer, as shown in the section entitled *Setting up speed-dial numbers* later in this chapter.

Undocumented

Dial-Up Networking and HyperTerminal connectoids (a word coined at Microsoft) automatically format phone numbers in the international format. You can change this by clearing the Use country and area code check box in any connection's Properties dialog box. To get to this check box, right-click the appropriate connectoid in the Dial-Up Networking or HyperTerminal folder window and click Properties.

If you clear the Use country and area code check box, the software sends only the phone number as you have entered it. It doesn't use any of the location properties from the Dialing Properties dialog box to format the sequence of numbers sent when you make this call.

Which local prefixes require long-distance dialing

Undocumented

Windows 95-aware communication applications assume that all phone numbers with the same local area code as your location's area code are local numbers; that is, they can be reached without dialing a 1 followed by the area code. This may not be the case, however, so you need a way of telling applications which numbers are not really local to a given location.

Windows 95 keeps track of which prefixes (the first three numbers of a local phone number) are long-distance numbers with respect to a given location, and it assumes that all the local numbers you enter with this prefix require the long-distance dialing rules, that is, 1+area code+phone number.

You can tell Windows 95 which prefixes in the area code of a given location require long-distance dialing, although this process is not that straightforward. You can do it in Phone Dialer, Dial-Up Networking, or HyperTerminal. All of these communications packages are TAPI-compliant, so setting up these prefixes in one package sets them up for all TAPI-compliant packages. To use Phone Dialer, take the following steps:

STEPS

Identifying a Prefix that Requires Long-Distance Dialing

Step 1. Click the Start button, point to Programs, then Accessories, and then click Phone Dialer.

Step 2. Choose Tools, Dialing Properties. Change the I am dialing from field to the location with which you want to associate the prefixes for the phone numbers that require long-distance dialing. Click OK.

Step 3. Type a local phone number in the Phone Dialer's Number to dial field that is a long-distance call from the location in the Dialing Properties dialog box but in the same area code.

Step 4. Choose Tools, Dialing Properties to display the Dialing Properties dialog box, as shown in Figure 26-6. The number you just typed is listed to the right of the "Number to be dialed" label at the bottom of the dialog box, directly above the Dial as a long distance call check box. Mark this check box, and click OK.

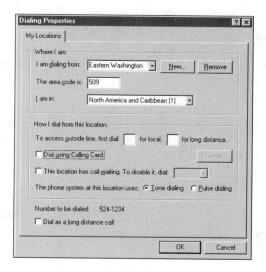

Figure 26-6: The Dialing Properties dialog box with the number to be dialed. You can force this and all other numbers with this prefix to be dialed as long-distance numbers.

Now whenever you call from the location that was specified in the Dialing Properties dialog box when you marked the Dial as a long-distance call check box, TAPI-compliant applications will automatically dial phone numbers with this prefix as long-distance calls. You can reverse this change by repeating these steps again with the same prefix and clearing this check box.

You can also do this with phone numbers that you use in HyperTerminal and Dial-Up Networking. If you select the designated connection phone number before displaying the Dialing Properties dialog box in these applications, the phone number will appear at the bottom of the dialog box.

The list of prefixes that require long-distance calls is stored in the Telephon.ini file. See the section entitled *Telephon.ini* later in this chapter to find out how to read this file.

10-digit phone numbers

You may live in an area that requires that you dial the area code and the phone number even to make a local call. In these areas, the prefix 1 is not used, and local calls may have different area codes.

Undocumented

You can make the Dialing Properties dialog box handle this situation in some limited cases, but Microsoft doesn't currently provide a general solution to this problem. We can give you a workaround.

When you are entering a phone number to call, use the international style to enter the area code in the area code field. In the local number field, enter the area code again as part of the local number, for example:

+1 (214) 214555-1234

If the area code for your location is 214, the full 10-digit number will be dialed. Unfortunately, if you are in another area code, the area code for this number will be dialed twice, unless you have cleared the Use country and area code check box in the Properties dialog box for your connectoid. Even in this case, you need to add the prefix 1 to get the number dialed correctly.

If your location is in a different area code, but the phone number is still local, you can enter *your* area code as its area code, and include *its* area code in the local phone number. For example, if your area code were 713, you would create the following number:

+1 (713) 214555-1234

Dialing from the location in the 713 area code would just dial a local 10-digit phone number. Again, this method is restricted to the 713 area code and will not work if you try to call from another area code.

You can also create dialing rules that apply to these situations. For example, you can follow these steps to create dialing rules that dial all phone numbers that have the same area code as your own with 10 digits (in other words, include the area code):

STEPS

Creating Dialing Rules to Dial 10-Digit Numbers

Step 1. Click the Start button, point to Settings, and then click Control Panel. Double-click the Modems icon, and then click the Dialing Properties button.

Step 2. Mark the Dial using Calling Card check box. Click the New button. Type a description for the dialing method that describes these dialing rules, perhaps **10-digit dialing**. Click the OK button.

Step 3 Click the Advanced button, and then type the following rules:

Calls within the same area code	FG
Long-distance calls	1FG
International calls	011EFG

Step 4. Click the Close button, click the OK button, and then click OK again.

As this is a bit of a kludge, we await further developments from Microsoft concerning the TAPI feature set.

Phone Dialer

If ever there was an application that is in fact an applet, it is Phone Dialer. This program uses your modem to dial your phone for you. You then pick up the phone and speak with the person whose number your modem dialed.

Microsoft didn't intend Phone Dialer to be a serious application. It is just an example to developers of how they can use the facilities provided by Windows 95 to create full-fledged communications applications. Unless you have a shortcut to Phone Dialer on your Desktop so that you can get at it quickly, or you have to dial a long string of numbers to place a call (as you might if you're using a calling card), you won't use Phone Dialer, because it is more work than just dialing the number on your phone.

Phone Dialer uses the information in the Dialing Properties dialog box to make phone calls. It can store up to eight phone numbers on its speed-dial buttons, and it keeps a record of the last 20 numbers you called. It can prompt you to keep a record of the phone numbers of calls coming in and/or going out. Phone Dialer is shown in Figure 26-7.

Figure 26-7: Phone Dialer. Click a speed-dial button, and Phone Dialer will dial the number for you if your modem is hooked up to your phone line.

Setting up speed-dial numbers

You can define the eight blank speed-dial buttons to dial a number when you click the button, just like on a real phone. This is the productivity benefit of Phone Dialer.

STEPS

Setting Up the Speed Dialer

Step 1.   Click the Start button, point to Programs, then to Accessories, and then click Phone Dialer.

Step 2.   Choose Edit, Speed Dial.

Step 3.   Click the button that you want to define in the Edit Speed Dial dialog box. Type the person's name and phone number. Repeat this step for all the buttons that you want to define.

Step 4.   Click the Save button when you are done.

Step 5.   If you want to quickly define a single blank button in Phone Dialer, just click the button, enter the person's name and phone number in the Program Speed Dial dialog box, and click Save or Save and Dial.

When you're entering numbers for the speed-dial buttons, use the international style if you want the numbers to be dialed correctly from any location.

Undocumented

The speed-dial phone numbers and the last 20 phone numbers you have dialed with Phone Dialer are stored in the Dialer.ini file in the \Windows folder. You can edit this file with Notepad if you like. Dialer.ini also stores the position of Phone Dialer on the Desktop and log book information.

Toby Nixon, a program manager in Microsoft's Internet Platform and Tools Division, replied to a question on the Windows 95 beta testing forum about whether you could use command line parameters with Phone Dialer by stating that Phone Dialer doesn't take command line parameters. However, he went on to say that you could write a little program that does take command line parameters, and then pass the parameters to Phone Dialer. He attached a little program that he wrote to do just that. We have included his program, Dial.exe, on the *Windows 95 Secrets* CD-ROM. Put it in your \Windows folder. Because it takes a phone number as a command line parameter, you can use it to dial a phone number from the Start, Run dialog box by typing a command such as **dial 62792** or **dial +1 (206) 882-8080**.

Telephon.ini

The Telephon.ini file is stored in the \Windows folder. It stores data about your locations and calling cards, as well as pointers to applications that use the telephony services provided by Windows 95. Using an *ini* file is quite unusual for Windows 95, because it stores most of its data in the Registry, and Microsoft tries not to use Win.ini, System.ini, or any other *ini* file.

If you don't have any stored locations or calling card data, you may have a damaged or missing Telephon.ini file. You can create a new one (which will be missing your special edits) by double-clicking the file Tapini.exe in the \Windows\System folder.

The sections in Telephon.ini of interest to us are [Locations] and [Cards].

Locations section

Here is an example of a line in the Locations section:

Location1=1, "Home," "9","","206",1,0,0,1,"357,847",0," "

Here is how to interpret the line:

Location*x*=ID, "location name", "# (number) for outside line", "# (number) for long-distance line", "area code", countrycode, card ID, previous card ID, use area codes, "LD prefixes"

These and other variables are listed in Table 26-2.

Table 26-2	Location Variables
Variable	*Stands for*
x	Ordered sequence of location numbers
ID	The location's identification number

(continued)

Table 26-2 *(continued)*

Variable	Stands for
location name	Your name for the location
# for outside line	The prefix you have to dial to get an outside line
# for LD line	The number you have to dial to get a long-distance line
area code	Area code
countrycode	Country code
card ID	If a calling card is used, this is its ID, otherwise it is 0 for direct dialing
previous card ID	The previous calling card ID before its last modification
use area codes	If 1, then dial local phone numbers with prefixes listed in the LD prefixes (next variable) using the area code. This is true only in North America, only if the country code and the area code for the number being dialed are the same as the current location, and only if the prefix of the number being dialed is listed in LD prefixes. If 0, then don't include the area code before the local call number.
LD prefixes	List of prefixes that are long-distance calls from Location*x*

Cards section

The Cards section stores the data about the calling card methods. These methods don't have to be calling cards exactly, but they can include any alternative dialing methods that can use a special phone number and/or a user code number. You can define these calling methods yourself using the methods detailed in the *Adding a long-distance carrier/method to your list* section. Here's an example:

Card12=1, "AT&T Direct Dial via 10ATT1","55041111938112", "102881FG","102881FG","10288011EFG",1

The format of this line is as follows. These and other variables are shown in Table 26-3.

Card*x*=ID, "card name", "encrypted card", "local call", "long-distance", "international", hidden

Table 26-3	Card Variables
Variable	Stands for
x	Ordered sequence of card numbers
ID	Card ID

Variable	Stands for
card name	Your dialing method name
encrypted card	Your card number encrypted
local call	The dialing rules for making a local call
long-distance	The dialing rules for making a long-distance call
international	The dialing rules for making an international call
hidden 0,1,2,3	Whether or not this calling card method is displayed as an available dialing method
0	Not hidden
1	Not hidden — values can only be set up by an application
2	Hidden
3	Hidden — values can only be set up by an application

Changes in international dialing access codes

Since the original version of Windows 95 was released, the international dialing access codes have changed for forty countries. You dial these codes to access international long distance in other countries.

Microsoft has prepared a Knowledge Base article that lets you easily update your Telephon.ini file to incorporate these changes. You can download the file at http://www.microsoft.com/kb/articles/Q142/3/28.htm. Just copy the last part of the article into your Telephon.ini file, which is stored in the \Windows folder.

Summary

We focus on how to work with the Dialing Properties dialog box to define the properties of each location you dial out from. The Dialing Properties dialog box is used by all Windows 95-aware communications applications.

▶ We show you how to define each of your dialing locations.

▶ We describe how to use calling cards or alternative dialing methods with your modem or voice calls.

▶ We show you how to tell communications applications just which local phone prefixes require long-distance dialing.

▶ We show you how to use Phone Dialer as a speed dialer.

Chapter 27

Disk Tools and File Systems

In This Chapter

Windows 95 provides new, powerful tools to give you lots of hard disk space while keeping your files safe and your disk fast. We discuss:

▶ Navigating through Windows to find all the tools

▶ Repairing your disks when trouble comes knocking

▶ Speeding up your disk drives

▶ Doubling the size of your hard disk and floppy drives

▶ Compressing very large drives to store much more data

▶ Letting weird programs have direct disk access

▶ Setting your disk cache parameters for optimum performance

▶ Choosing from new characters in long filenames

▶ Repartitioning your drives

▶ Creating super-high-density diskettes

The Real Changes

If you want to look at the changes that have been made to the fundamentals of an operating system, look at how it works with files that are stored on disk drives. They don't call it the Disk Operating System (DOS) for nothing.

The Microsoft personnel who handled the Disk Tools section of the Windows 95 beta forum on CompuServe (for the most part Brian Emanuels, William Keener, and Gregg Rivers) asked probing questions and provided detailed answers to beta tester queries and reports. They set a very professional tone. It was clear to those of us who followed this section that Microsoft was quite interested in getting its new disk tools thoroughly tested.

Most of the changes Microsoft has made to the "disk operating system" affect what is under the hood — speeding up access to your hard disk, diskettes, and CD-ROM drive. Microsoft also reduced the amount of user interaction required to set obscure performance parameters — such as permanent swap files and disk cache size — while at the same time improving the performance that tuning these parameters is supposed to provide.

These advances vastly increase the amount of available conventional memory and improve the responsiveness of your computer to multiple tasks. New compression drivers let you double (more or less) your hard disk (and diskette) space. In this chapter, we look at the major changes and additions.

VFAT

In Windows for Workgroups 3.11, the Virtual File Allocation Table (VFAT) is called *32-bit file access*. You get to it through the Enhanced icon in the Control Panel. In Windows 95, it's called the *32-bit protected-mode* VFAT file system. Microsoft released the prebeta version of this code when it produced Windows for Workgroups 3.11. It worked, except for numerous software and hardware incompatibilities. And it sped up read and write operations, at least when you didn't have to turn it off because of these incompatibilities.

The code has been much improved, and it now actually works reliably. It provides fast access to files. It improves multitasking by reducing the amount of time that it blocks other tasks. It is compatible with existing DOS partitions — the original FAT — on your disks. Because your processor doesn't have to switch to real-mode to read and write to the disk, everything gets faster.

VFAT 32

The OEM Service Release 2 version of Windows 95 comes with FAT 32, a version of the standard FAT file system that supports drives bigger than 2GB and cluster sizes of 4K (instead of 32K at 2GB partitions). FAT 32 is not compatible with earlier programs that directly access the hard disk, including all disk utilities. Microsoft also removed the capability to dual boot with this version of Windows 95.

Most computer manufacturers have ignored FAT 32 and instead continue to configure their hard drives as FAT-16 volumes. Of course, as computer disks continue to increase in size, this will become a less tenable solution.

If you have OEM Service Release 2, you have the capability of reformatting your hard disk for FAT 32. Of course, you lose all your data and programs. Partition Magic (http://www.powerquest.com) lets you go back and forth between FAT 16 and FAT 32 if you have OEM Service Release 2, without destroying your setup.

Vcache

Windows 95 comes with a 32-bit protected-mode dynamic cache. It replaces 16-bit, real-mode SmartDrive (Smartdrv.exe). Vcache doesn't take up conventional or upper memory space. It does a much better job than

SmartDrive does of caching disk reads and writes. It also caches CD-ROMs and networked drives.

You don't have to specify how much memory should be set aside for Vcache (unlike SmartDrive). It sizes itself based on available free memory and disk read/write activity. (That's the dynamic part of Vcache.)

Direct CD-ROM support

No more messy ducks (Mscdex.exe) in your Config.sys file. Windows 95 provides another one of its 32-bit protected-mode drivers, CDFS (CD-ROM file system), to support CD-ROM drives. This driver replaces the 16-bit real-mode Mscdex.exe driver that comes with Windows 3.1*x* and MS-DOS.

You get a dynamic CD-ROM cache that works with Vcache. No conventional or upper memory is used by the driver. It isn't an add-on afterthought called by a line in Config.sys. (Consequently, there is even less need for Config.sys.) CDFS is also quite a bit faster than Mscdex.exe.

Long filenames

You can type filenames up to 255 characters long. The names can include spaces. Windows 95 can read and write long filenames supported by other operating systems, such as Windows NT, NetWare, Unix, and OS/2.

Files with long filenames also have short filenames that are recognized by applications that can't handle long filenames (including DOS). Windows 95 manages these short names to ensure that only unique names are created.

The unique short filenames consist of the first six characters of the long filename, plus ~1 or additional ordinals. See the section entitled *Long Filenames* later in this chapter for details.

Windows 95-based disk tools

Earlier versions of Windows and DOS required that you quit Windows and go to DOS if you needed to work directly with your disk drive at a low level. While you can still do this, it's a lot harder to "get out of" Windows 95.

Windows 95 comes with very powerful Windows-based disk tools that help you manage and protect your files. ScanDisk finds and repairs problems with your disks. Defrag makes your files contiguous. These are both Windows 95 programs, although you can also run ScanDisk from DOS and in batch files.

Compression disk drivers

Windows 95 comes with a 32-bit protected-mode compression disk driver that works with both DoubleSpace and DriveSpace disks. Instead of taking 50K of conventional memory, it is loaded into extended memory.

You can approximately double your disk space with, in many cases, minimal or no loss of file-access speed. You can also approximately double the room available on your diskettes.

Microsoft Plus! adds more disk compression with its DriveSpace 3 utility for computers with 486 or faster processors. DriveSpace 3 further compresses files (quite often at a ratio greater than 2.5-to-1) to free up more room on your hard disk. The file volumes can be up to 2GB in size. You can also use a Microsoft Plus! utility called System Agent to schedule compression, error scanning, and defragging to take place during idle times.

DriveSpace 2 and 3 do not work with FAT 32 volumes. This may not be much of an issue, however, because you have less need for compression with large drives, and you most likely have large drives if you have FAT 32.

Built-in SCSI hard disk support

Earlier versions of DOS and Windows didn't support SCSI drives without special drivers from hardware manufacturers that you loaded in Config.sys. Windows 95 has built-in support for SCSI devices.

Installable File System Manager

Both the VFAT and the CDFS are installable file systems managed by the Windows 95 Installable File System Manager. You can add other file systems, and you will if you connect your computer to network servers. Windows 95 can manage multiple file systems, which makes it much easier to connect to many different networks at once.

Windows 95 doesn't support HPFS (high performance file system), which is native to OS/2, or NTFS, the Windows NT file system, on local hard disks, but it does over a network. Third-party vendors provide solutions that can handle these file systems on local hard disks.

Dynamically sized swap file

Virtual memory no longer requires a permanent swap file for the fastest operation. Windows 95 can dynamically size the required swap file. This cuts down on the user decisions required to optimize Windows. The swap file can even be on a compressed drive without incurring a performance hit.

Support for enhanced IDE devices

Windows 95 supports the enhanced IDE (EIDE) specification, so it can handle drives larger than 1GB directly. In fact, Windows 95 supports EIDE hard disks as large as 137GB.

Windows 95 also supports IDE-based CD-ROMs. You can hook these drives to the existing IDE card used by your hard disk without buying a separate SCSI card to support the CD-ROM.

Multitasked floppy drive formatting

No longer does everything grind to a halt while you format a diskette. A Windows 95 32-bit driver now handles multitasked access to your floppy drives.

Finding Your Disks and the Disk Tools

You've got to be able to find the disk tools if you're going to use them. Fortunately, you can easily reach this collection of programs through several different routes.

The Start button

The easiest way to find the disk tools is to click the Start button, point to Programs, then Accessories, and finally click System Tools. If you haven't edited your Start menus, the System Tools submenu will contain Disk Defragmenter, ScanDisk, and DriveSpace, as well as Backup, System Monitor, and Net Watcher, if you installed them.

A drive icon

Another way to display the disk tools that is almost as easy is to double-click My Computer, right-click one of the hard drive icons, click Properties, and then click the Tools tab. Windows 95 displays the dialog box shown in Figure 27-1. You now have access to ScanDisk, Backup, and Disk Defragmenter.

You can right-click any drive icon in any folder or Explorer window and click Properties to get to this Tools tab.

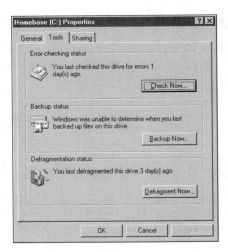

Figure 27-1: The Tools tab of the Properties dialog box for a hard drive. Click Check Now to launch ScanDisk, Backup Now to launch Backup, or Defragment Now to launch the Disk Defragmenter.

Using help

There are many ways you can access the disk tools through shortcuts in the help system. Click the Start button, click Help, and then try any of the following:

- Double-click the How To book in the Contents tab of the Help Topics dialog box. Double-click Maintain Your Computer. You now have numerous options for reaching various disk tools. For example, you can choose "Detecting and repairing disk errors" to get to a shortcut to ScanDisk.

- Double-click Tips and Tricks in the Contents tab. Double-click For Maintaining Your Computer, followed by "Defragmenting your hard disk regularly." You can now click the shortcut to Disk Defragmenter.

- Click the Index tab in the Help Topics dialog box. Type **disk tr**. Double-click "disk troubleshooter" and then click the button next to "Create more disk space by using DriveSpace disk compression." You now see a shortcut to DriveSpace, as well as some help on how to use it.

In a DOS window

You can type **Scandisk**, **Defrag**, or **Drvspace** in a DOS window. Each of these commands invokes the Windows 95 graphical version of these programs. You can run Windows programs from your DOS window.

Tip

If you type **Scandisk /?** in a DOS window and press Enter, you'll see the following instructions for finding the section of the Windows 95 help system that tells you how to use command line parameters with ScanDisk:

For information about the command line parameters supported by ScanDisk for Windows, look up 'checking for errors, in disks' in the Windows Help index. Then view the topic 'Checking your disk for errors every time your computer starts.'

You can run a DOS 7.0 version of ScanDisk from MS-DOS mode or from the DOS command prompt before Windows 95 starts. You can't run Disk Defragmenter or DriveSpace in MS-DOS mode.

Device Manager

The Device Manager lets you look at the basic resources used by your devices, including your disk drives and controller card(s). You can get to the Device Manager (a tab in the System Properties dialog box) in at least two ways:

- Right-click My Computer, click Properties, and then click the Device Manager tab.

- Click the Start button, point to Settings, and then click Control Panel. Double-click the System icon and choose the Device Manager tab.

Once you're in the Device Manager, click the plus signs next to the icons labeled Disk drives, Floppy disk controllers, or Hard disk controllers. Highlight the controller or drive name that is displayed, click the Properties button, and then click the Resources tab. The resources used by an IDE hard disk controller are shown in Figure 27-2.

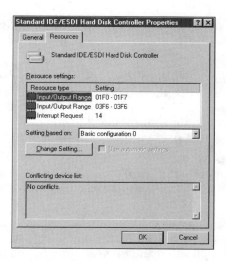

Figure 27-2: The Resources properties sheet for an IDE/ESDI controller. If you clear the Use an automatic settings check box, you can choose between the two basic configurations in the Setting based on drop-down list.

File system performance

The Performance tab of the System Properties dialog box lets you disable all sorts of 32-bit file access settings as well as optimize your disk caching scheme.

Use the same steps to get to the System Properties dialog box as described in the preceding section, but click the Performance tab instead of the Device Manager tab. Click the File System button to display the File System Properties dialog box.

To see how to optimize file system performance, turn to the *Setting disk cache parameters* section of this chapter.

Virtual memory performance

Windows 95 can manage your swap file without any input from you. If you want to change its location and set a minimum or maximum size, you can do so.

Use the same steps to get to the System Properties dialog box as described in the earlier section entitled *Device Manager*, but click the Performance tab instead of the Device Manager tab. Click the Virtual Memory button to display the Virtual Memory dialog box. See the *Managing Your Swap Space* section of this chapter to learn about changing your swap file size.

System Monitor

You can use System Monitor to track how your hard disks (or hard disks on other computers on your network) are being used. You'll find System Monitor in the Start menu.

Click the Start button, point to Programs, Accessories, System Tools, and then click System Monitor. It won't be there unless you did a custom installation of Windows 95 and specifically chose to install it. You can use the Add/Remove Programs icon in the Control Panel to add it. Click the Windows Setup tab, and look under Accessories.

Gary Tessler of TNT (Tessler's Nifty Tools) has developed a replacement for System Monitor. It's called SuperMonitor, and it displays different resources in separate windows. You can use it to determine usage by individual applications.

To determine an application's memory usage with SuperMonitor, you start a window on memory and then stop that window's monitoring. (This "freezes" the figures.) Then start your application and open another SuperMonitor window. The difference between the two readings is the amount of memory used by the application or any combination of applications you choose.

SuperMonitor can display continuous, average, or maximum values in different windows. You can set the timing interval SuperMonitor uses, and you can log the figures to a disk file.

You'll find the latest version of SuperMonitor at
http://ourworld.compuserve.com/homepages/nifty_tools/tnt.htm.

Disk Tools

You use ScanDisk and Disk Defragmenter to fix your hard disks, diskettes,
and other removable media (not CD-ROMs) when your files get corrupted or
are stored in too many pieces. If parts of the surface of your hard disk are
bad, ScanDisk marks them so files won't be stored there. ScanDisk also
moves the data off of these spots if it can.

ScanDisk

ScanDisk does an excellent job of analyzing your hard disk and repairing
errors. Microsoft has taken great pains to make sure it works under all
circumstances.

ScanDisk reviews and repairs errors on compressed drives as well as on
physical drives. It repairs problems with long filenames, the FAT, the
directory and file structure, the drive surface, and the internal structure of
compressed volume files (CVFs). It can find and fix errors on diskettes and
hard drives, and, as if you really cared, RAM drives and memory cards that
are treated as drives.

ScanDisk can find and repair problems on both DriveSpace and DoubleSpace
drives (but not on Stacker or SuperStor drives). The CVFs don't have to be
mounted (have a drive letter associated with them) for ScanDisk to work
with them, although in most cases they will be.

ScanDisk can't find or fix errors on CD-ROMs, networked drives, or pseudo
drives created by using Assign, Subst, Join, or Interlnk (all of these are DOS
commands).

*If one of your applications reports disk problems when reading a file, run
ScanDisk immediately to repair the file.* If Windows 95 crashes while you are
editing a file and the file is damaged, it is very likely that ScanDisk can fix it.

ScanDisk options

As stated earlier in this chapter, you can start ScanDisk by right-clicking a
drive icon in a folder or Explorer window, choosing Properties, clicking the
Tools tab, and then clicking the Check Now button. If you do this, you are
presented with a ScanDisk dialog box containing buttons labeled Options
and Advanced, as shown in Figure 27-3.

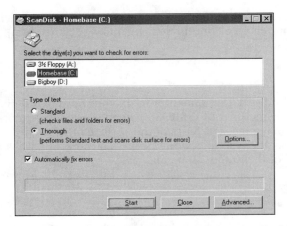

Figure 27-3: The ScanDisk dialog box.

To find out what all these options do, take the following steps:

STEPS

Exploring ScanDisk Options

Step 1. Start ScanDisk and mark the Thorough option button (see Figure 27-3), and then click the Options button.

Step 2. Right-click any item in the Surface Scan Options dialog box. Click the What's This? button to see what the option really does.

Step 3. Click the Cancel button in the Surface Scan Options dialog box, and then click the Advanced button.

Step 4. Right-click any item in the ScanDisk Advanced Options dialog box, and click What's This? to learn more about what it does. Click the Cancel button when you're done.

ScanDisk command line parameters

You can run ScanDisk from a batch file or from the DOS prompt. You can also create a shortcut to ScanDisk and include it in your Startup folder so that it will check your hard disk every time you start your computer. You may want to add some command line parameters to the command line of the shortcut. (Right-click the shortcut, choose Properties, click the Shortcut tab, and type the command line in the Target field.)

ScanDisk can take the following parameters:

```
Scandisk {x:} {options}
```

or

```
Scandisk x:\drvspace.nnn
```

or

```
Scandisk x:\dblspace.nnn
```

x: is the drive letter for the drive you want to check. It can be the drive letter assigned to a compressed volume file.

ScanDisk can take the following options:

/all or /a	Checks all your local, nonremovable hard disks
/noninteractive or /n	Starts and finishes ScanDisk without user input
/preview or /p	Prevents ScanDisk from correcting errors that it finds
dblspace.*nnn*	Name of compressed volume file (CVF) to check
drvspace.*nnn*	Name of compressed volume file (CVF) to check

Hidden CVFs reside on host drives and are named by their type of compression (DoubleSpace or DriveSpace) and a number (*nnn*) as the file extension. If you want to scan an unmounted compressed drive, include dblspace.*nnn* or drvspace.*nnn* on the command line. The drive letter in this case would be the host drive letter.

Put ScanDisk in the Startup folder

The Windows 95 help system can tell you how to put ScanDisk into your Startup folder. We don't need to repeat these instructions here, but you might like to know how to find them. Here's how:

STEPS

Learning How to Put ScanDisk in the Startup Folder

Step 1. Click the Start button, click Help, and then click the Index tab.

Step 2. Type **chec** to highlight the phrase *checking for errors*. Double-click *in disks*.

Step 3. Click the Display button in the Topics Found dialog box while the first item is highlighted.

Step 4. Click the Shortcut icon (the small button with the red arrow).

Follow the steps in Windows 95 help for creating a shortcut to ScanDisk.
You might want to add a command line parameter or two from the ones in
the preceding section.

Running ScanDisk from DOS

Undocumented

There are really two ScanDisk programs, Scandskw.exe and Scandisk.exe.
The Windows 95 version is Scandskw.exe, an executable stub, which calls
code located in the dynamic link libraries Shell.dll and Dskmaint.dll.

Scandskw.exe is called when you click the Check Now button in the Tools
tab of the Properties dialog box for a hard drive, or ScanDisk in the System
Tools submenu of the Start menu. It is also called when you type **Scandisk**
at a DOS prompt in a Windows DOS session. You can also type **Scandskw** at
the command prompt in a Windows DOS session, although there is one
exception to this. If you type a command of the form **Scandisk C:/
dblspace.000** in a Windows DOS session, the DOS version of ScanDisk is
executed because the Windows version works only with mounted drives.

If you boot your computer to the DOS command prompt or start an MS-DOS
mode session, type **Scandisk** at the DOS command prompt to run the DOS
version of ScanDisk. If you dual boot into your previous version of DOS, you
can still run the DOS 7.0 (Windows 95) version of ScanDisk. This comes in
handy when you are setting up Windows 95.

Scandisk.ini

Undocumented

Scandisk.ini, the ScanDisk configuration file, is stored in your \Windows
folder. This file works only with the DOS version of ScanDisk and is not used
if you run ScanDisk from Windows or from a Windows DOS session.

Scandisk.ini is internally well documented, and you can edit it to change the
way the DOS version of ScanDisk operates. Open it with Edit.com, and you
will find plenty of documentation explaining how to change ScanDisk's
parameters.

ScanDisk and your FAT

Undocumented

The DOS version of ScanDisk always uses the primary copy of your FAT
(unless it finds a physical disk error). The primary FAT replaces the backup
FAT when ScanDisk repairs errors.

The Windows 95 version of ScanDisk checks both of your file allocation
tables, and, if they are out of sync, determines which FAT is "better" and
uses that one.

ScanDisk and Setup

The DOS version of ScanDisk is run automatically when you run Windows 95
Setup. If you start Setup from the DOS prompt, you can see ScanDisk;
otherwise, it is hidden behind a Windows face. If ScanDisk finds problems
with your hard disk, you can fix them before you continue with the setup
process.

If you run Setup from Windows 3.1*x* and there are problems, exit Setup and run the DOS 7.0 version of ScanDisk from the DOS prompt.

Setup runs ScanDisk to put everything in order and to cut down on the number of variables before you install this very complex operating system. ScanDisk is discussed in more detail in Chapter 3.

Defrag, the disk defragmenter

As you probably know, DOS and Windows (all versions) don't necessarily keeps the contents of your files stored in contiguous sectors of your hard disk. Your files become more fragmented as they are rewritten, and fragmented files take longer to read and write. You can speed up disk access by occasionally defragmenting the files on your hard disk.

Defrag is a Windows program. You can run it from the DOS prompt in a Windows DOS session, but unlike ScanDisk, you can't run it in an MS-DOS mode session.

You can run Defrag while you are running other programs. In fact, it is running as one of the authors types these words. Disk reads and writes interrupt the defragmentation process, but Defrag is always operating and continues to defragment where it left off, after the read or write is complete.

Defrag in details view

Defrag is a fun program to watch if you put it into details view. Here's how:

STEPS

Running Defrag in Details View

Step 1. Click the Start button, point to Programs, Accessories, System Tools, and then click Disk Defragmenter.

Step 2. In the Select Drive dialog box, display the drop-down list to show the available drives. You can defrag your floppies if you want to (but why?). Highlight the hard drive that you want to defragment (or select All Hard Drives to defragment all of them), and click OK. (You can select multiple drives to defragment by Ctrl+clicking them.)

Step 3. Click the Start button in the Disk Defragmenter dialog box, click the Show Details button, and then click the Legend button. The Defrag Legend dialog box appears on top of the Defragmenting window, which contains rows and rows of little colored squares that represent disk clusters (see Figure 27-4).

(continued)

Running Defrag in Details View

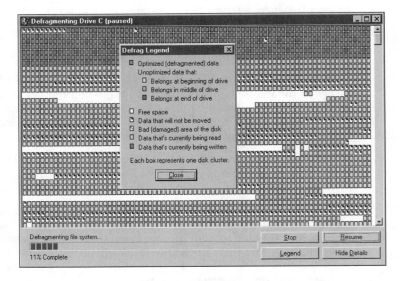

Figure 27-4: The disk defragmenter in details view with the Defrag Legend showing.

Showing details slows down the defragmentation process a little, but what you lose in speed you make up for in visual interest.

Before you click the Start button in the Disk Defragmenter dialog box, you can choose how extensive you want the defragmentation process to be. To see these options, click the Advanced button. To find out what each option does, right-click the text next to each option and click the What's This? button.

Data that will not be moved

Secret

You may notice that some or many sectors on your hard disk are marked "Data that will not be moved" in the details view of the Defragmenting window. Defrag doesn't move files that are marked *both* hidden and system. Some copy protection schemes put a file or two in certain locations and mark them as both system and hidden. If they are moved, the copy protection scheme fails.

Defrag takes the conservative approach. In reality, almost all files that are marked both system and hidden are, in fact, not related to any copy protection schemes. Windows 95 marks many of its files as both system and hidden. Of course, they are easy enough to see in a folder or Explorer window, so they are not really all that hidden.

If you have a CVF on a host drive, it will probably appear as a large block of contiguous sectors and will be marked as "Data that will not be moved." If you view the compressed drive itself, you'll see that data in these clusters can indeed be moved. Both views are right.

Secret

The CVF shouldn't be moved, and you can defragment the files within it by defragmenting the compressed drive directly.

Your dynamically sized swap file is also marked as unable to be moved, but it doesn't have the hidden or system attribute.

You can have Defrag move the files marked both system and hidden by changing their attributes. You (not Defrag) are taking the responsibility for the consequences.

To remove the system and hidden attributes from a file, type the following command at any DOS prompt:

```
attrib -s -h {drive:\pathname\filename}
```

Unfortunately, the Windows 95 Find dialog box doesn't let you collect all the files that have a certain attribute turned on (or off). If it did, you could search for all the files with the attributes system and hidden, and decide for yourself whether to turn these attributes off for each file displayed in the Find dialog box.

If you want to find out more about the attrib command, type **attrib/?** at the DOS prompt.

It's very important to reset any CVFs back to hidden and system so that they are not moved by Defrag. To do this, type the following command at the DOS prompt:

```
attrib +s +h c:\Drvspace.nnn
```

or

```
attrib +s +h c:\Dblspace.nnn
```

In the preceding command line, *nnn* is the number of the CVF volume.

DOS 6.*x* versions of Defrag would not move files if they were marked either hidden or system or both. The Windows 95 Defrag is a little less reluctant to move files.

Never use earlier versions of Defrag from MS-DOS 6.*x* because they will destroy long filenames.

Tip

The disk defragmenter will not work with Stacker or SuperStor compressed drives. If you have these types of compressed drives, get a third-party disk defragmenter program, such as the one included in Symantec's Norton Utilities for Windows 95. You also can't use Defrag over a network. It has real trouble with CD-ROMs, which are read-only. Don't try it on drives that are created by Assign, Subst, or Join.

You can run Defrag on the host drive and/or on the compressed drive if you have DoubleSpace or DriveSpace drives.

Defrag in the Startup folder

Like ScanDisk, you can run Defrag every time you start your computer. This can get pretty tedious if you start your computer frequently.

You can create a shortcut to Defrag.exe (it's in the \Windows folder), and put it in your Startup folder. Edit the Target line of the shortcut (right-click the shortcut, click Properties, and click the Shortcut tab) to change the command line parameters (see the next section). You might want to designate only one drive to defragment, for example.

Defrag command line parameters

If you run Defrag from a DOS prompt, from the Run dialog box (Start, Run), from a batch file, or from a shortcut, you can change the way it runs by adding command line parameters.

```
Defrag {x: or /all} {options} {/noprompt} {/concise or /detailed}
```

The command line parameters are as follows:

x:	Drive letter designator for drive to be defragmented
/all	Defragment all local, nonremovable drives
{*options*}	
/f	Defragment files and free space
/u	Defragment files only
/q	Defragment free space only
/noprompt	Do not display confirmation message boxes
/concise	Don't show the details view (this is the default)
/detailed	Show the details view

Disk-Related Functions

Numerous commands and functions affect the drive performance and file-access speed.

Disk space

When you select a folder in the left pane of the Explorer, the status bar displays the total size of the files stored in the folder. It also lists the amount of free space available on the drive partition that contains the highlighted folder.

Another way to find the size and available disk space on a particular drive is to take the following steps:

STEPS

Displaying Disk Size

Step 1.   Double-click My Computer.

Step 2.   Right-click a drive icon, and then click Properties.

These steps display the General tab of the Properties dialog box for the selected drive, as shown in Figure 27-5.

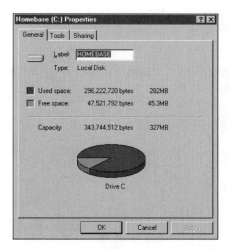

Figure 27-5: The General tab of the Properties dialog box for a hard drive. You can type a new name for the disk in the Label field.

File size and attributes

The status bar of the Explorer (or any folder window) tells you the size of the files you have highlighted or, if you have highlighted a folder in the left pane, the number and total size of all the files in the folder.

Right-click a file in an Explorer or folder window and click Properties to display the file's General properties sheet, as shown in Figure 27-6. This sheet tells you the size of the file as well as its attributes (Read-only, Archive, Hidden, System).

If you select a group of files and then right-click the group and choose Properties, the General properties sheet shows the total size of all the files. This is handy if you are dragging these files to your floppy disk drive. The total size of the selected files is also displayed in the status bar of the Explorer or folder window.

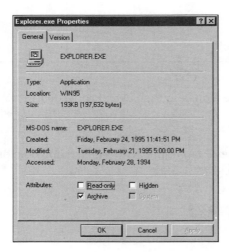

Figure 27-6: A file's General properties sheet. You can change a file's attributes by marking or clearing the Attributes check boxes.

Undocumented

Do you want to know the total size of all the files on a hard disk? Take the following steps:

STEPS

Finding the Total Size of All Files on a Disk

Step 1. Highlight a drive icon in the left pane of an Explorer window.

Step 2. Highlight the top entry in the right pane.

Step 3. Scroll down the right pane, and Shift+right-click the last entry.

Step 4. Click Properties.

The total number of files and their accumulated size will be displayed. It may take a few seconds to count all the files.

Format

You can format a hard disk, diskette, or other removable media by right-clicking the icon representing the drive in either a folder or Explorer window and choosing Format from the context menu.

Undocumented

You can't format a compressed diskette in this manner. If you try to format the compressed volume or the host drive, you'll receive error messages. If you want to format such a diskette, you'll need to uncompress it first (which may require that you erase the files on it).

You can format a compressed drive using DriveSpace. See the *Other DriveSpace options* section later in this chapter for details.

Thankfully, clicking Format in the context menu does not immediately begin the formatting process. You're given the opportunity to determine some format parameters. If you accidentally click Format after you right-click your boot drive, you will have a chance to back out.

Diskcopy

Tip

Do you want to make a copy of a diskette? Put the diskette in the diskette drive, double-click My Computer, right-click the diskette drive icon, and then click Copy Disk.

Sharing

If you are on a network (even if you just have Direct Cable Connection installed), you can give other computers access to files on your disk drives. To share access to all the files on a drive, right-click the drive icon in a folder or Explorer window, and click Sharing in the context menu to display the Sharing properties sheet shown in Figure 27-7.

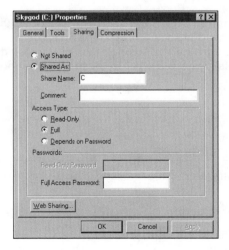

Figure 27-7: The Sharing properties sheet for a hard disk drive. Choose the Shared As option button to share your drive with other computers on the network.

Recycle Bin size

Just because you delete a file doesn't mean it is gone. The files sit in your Recycle Bin, taking up disk space until you empty it. The free space on your disk doesn't increase until you empty the trash. (An exception to this is if you right-click the Recycle Bin on the Desktop, choose Properties, and mark the check box labeled "Do not move files to the Recycle Bin. Remove files immediately on delete.")

If you like, you can adjust the maximum amount of space the Recycle Bin can occupy on your drive(s). By default, the maximum size is set to 10 percent of each drive. To change this setting, right-click the Recycle Bin on the Desktop and choose Properties. If you want to use the same size setting on each drive, mark the Use one setting for all drives option button, and drag the slider on the Global tab. If you prefer to set different maximum sizes for each of your drives, mark the Configure drives independently option button, and then use the tabs for each drive to configure the maximum Recycle Bin size on each drive individually.

Chkdsk /f

Chkdsk (Check disk) is an outdated DOS command that deletes bad files when you specify the /f parameter. It doesn't work anymore, and you should instead use ScanDisk to fix files or the DOS command Mem to give you a memory usage breakdown.

Troubleshooting disk access

Even though the 32-bit disk and file access provided by Windows 95 is much better than what came with Windows for Workgroups 3.11, there may still be incompatibilities. You can turn off various portions of the disk driver to track down problems with disk access. To get to these troubleshooting options, take the following steps:

STEPS

Troubleshooting Disk Access

Step 1.   Right-click My Computer. Choose Properties, and click the Performance tab.

Step 2.   Click the File System button.

Step 3.   Click the Troubleshooting tab.

Disk Compression

Windows 95 supports two versions of disk compression: DriveSpace and DoubleSpace. They are slightly different because of a legal settlement with Stac Electronics, the manufacturer of Stacker disk compression software. Windows 95 creates DriveSpace compressed drives.

Microsoft Plus! comes with DriveSpace 3, an upgrade to DriveSpace compression, and the Compression Agent, which gives you even higher levels of compression, as well as control over which files are compressed to what levels when. None of the restrictions that we discuss later in this chapter regarding compressed volume size apply if you use DriveSpace 3.

Starting with Windows 95, Microsoft provides a unified driver that handles both DoubleSpace and DriveSpace. The files Dblspace.bin and Drvspace.bin, the disk compression drivers in the root directory of your host drive, are exactly the same.

Undocumented

You shouldn't erase either Drvspace.bin or Dblspace.bin. Only Drvspace.bin is needed for drives you compressed while running Windows 95. Dblspace.bin (which is the same as Drvspace.bin but with a different name) is used when you mount old volume files compressed with DoubleSpace, such as when you place a DoubleSpace diskette in your diskette drive.

When you start your computer, either Dblspace.bin or Drvspace.bin is loaded in conventional memory if you have a mounted compressed drive. Once Windows 95 starts, the real-mode D??space.bin driver is unloaded, the conventional memory is reclaimed, and the 32-bit driver takes over.

Windows 95 can work with five disk compression schemes: DoubleSpace, DriveSpace, Stacker, SuperStor, and AddStor. Microsoft provides 32-bit drivers for DoubleSpace and DriveSpace compressed drives. You can use the existing Stacker or SuperStor real-mode drivers in conventional or upper memory to access drives compressed with these products. 32-bit drivers are available for these disk compression schemes (but not from Microsoft). The discussion in this chapter refers to the Microsoft-supplied disk compression schemes.

A *compressed drive* is not a physical drive or a volume (a DOS FAT partition), but rather a file stored on a disk drive. Windows refers to a compressed drive as a *compressed volume file* (CVF) and gives it a disk drive letter designator just as though it were a volume. Application software (and most of the operating system, including Defrag and ScanDisk) treats it as though it were a volume.

The CVF is stored in the root directory of an uncompressed drive, which is referred to as the *host drive*. The CVF has the attributes read-only, hidden, and system. Defrag doesn't move it. If it is a Microsoft CVF, its name will be something like Drvspace.000 or Dblspace.002. CVFs created by Windows 95 use the Drvspace name.

Because the compressed drive is actually a file on a host drive, you can cause all sorts of mischief if you erase the file or in other ways fool with it. You might consider refraining from messing with this file.

You can compress an existing uncompressed volume or create a compressed drive from the free space on an existing partition. If you compress an existing volume, DriveSpace creates a CVF and stores the existing files and free space in the CVF. If you are creating a compressed drive from free disk space, DriveSpace creates an empty CVF.

Compressed disk size

You can divide a disk partition or volume into at least two logical drives, one for the host drive and one for the compressed drive. Compressed drives can't be larger than 512MB (unless you are using DriveSpace 3). The size of the CVF will depend on how compressible the files in the CVF are. If you create a compressed drive from free disk space, the CVF will be half the reported size of the compressed drive.

The Explorer displays the uncompressed size of files stored on a compressed drive. Their actual file size can be (and most often is) less than the size that's reported. If you compress a file on a physical drive, using WinZip, for example, the file size reported by the Explorer is the compressed size. Because DriveSpace can't further compress a WinZip file (at least not very much), its actual size when stored on a compressed drive is about the same as its reported size. You don't get any benefit from storing zipped files on a compressed drive.

A compressed drive isn't actually compressed, of course; it is the *files* on the drive (in the CVF) that are compressed. VFAT and FAT report the uncompressed size of the files, so it appears as though you have a bigger drive when you actually have smaller files.

When you create a new compressed drive from free disk space, VFAT doubles the amount of reported free disk space so that the reported drive size is twice the size of its CVF on the physical disk. The size of the compressed drive decreases if you start filling it with files that can't be compressed at a 2-to-1 ratio.

Secret

If you create a compressed drive from free disk space, the CVF won't be any larger than 256MB because the estimated compression ratio is 2 to 1, and the maximum size of a compressed drive is 512MB. If you fill the compressed drive with 512MB of highly compressible files, there will be unused (and unusable) space in your CVF. You can go back and reduce the size of the CVF, which will give you more space on your host drive to create another CVF.

Secret

If you have an existing physical disk with more than 512MB of files (in one partition) you won't be able to compress it (unless you are using DriveSpace 3 from Microsoft Plus!).

Undocumented

One way around this is to create a compressed drive from the free space (if any) on your physical drive. Move files from the host drive (your drive has now become a host drive) to the newly created compressed drive. Adjust the free space between the host and compressed drive, taking advantage of the newly released free space on the host drive to increase the size of the compressed drive (up to 512MB).

Continue moving files and increasing the size of the compressed drive until you have moved most (but not all) of the files from the host drive to the compressed drive.

Secret

If you have a drive partition (or a physical drive that isn't divided into multiple partitions) that is larger than 256MB and has no files on it, you won't be able to compress the volume into one compressed drive. You'll need to compress it into multiple compressed drives.

You can create multiple compressed drives (from free disk space) on a large drive, all up to 512MB in size. On a 1GB drive, you could have up to four 512MB compressed drives.

So why does a compressed drive that reports, for example, 100MB free before you copy 40MB of files to it report only 40MB free afterward? Because 100MB free is an estimate based on the anticipated compression ratio of the files yet to be copied to the compressed disk (defaulted at a 2-to-1 ratio). It turns out, in this example, that the files could be compressed only at a 1.5-to-1 ratio. They therefore took up 30MB of the CVF, or 60MB of the estimated space.

DriveSpace 3 can create CVFs that are as large as 2GB. You won't have to divide your large drive into multiple volumes if you purchase Microsoft Plus!.

Creating a compressed drive

It is quite easy to experiment with disk compression, so there is no reason not to create a compressed drive out of some of the free space on your existing drive and play with it a bit. You can always uncompress the drive as long as the total file size isn't greater than what will fit on your drive uncompressed.

You can compress an existing uncompressed volume or create a compressed drive from the free space on an existing partition. Compressing an existing volume creates a CVF and stores the existing files and free space in the CVF. Creating a compressed drive from free disk space creates an empty CVF.

Remember that compression doesn't work with FAT-32 volumes.

Compressing existing files and free space

You have to have at least 2MB of free disk space on a boot hard drive to compress it. Non-bootable hard drive partitions (and diskettes) require at least 768K of free space.

To create a compressed drive with existing files, take the following steps:

STEPS

Compressing a Drive

Step 1. Click the Start button, point to Programs, Accessories, System Tools, and then click DriveSpace to display the DriveSpace window, as shown in Figure 27-8.

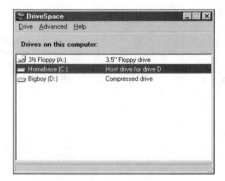

Figure 27-8: The DriveSpace window. Highlight a drive you are going to examine. You can compress, uncompress, mount, or unmount a drive from here.

Step 2. Highlight an existing physical drive.

Step 3. To compress both the files and the free disk space on an existing drive, choose Drive, Compress. The Compress a Drive dialog box appears, as shown in Figure 27-9.

Compressing a Drive

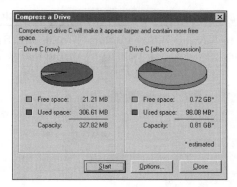

Figure 27-9: The Compress a Drive dialog box. Your only option is the letter designator for the host drive.

Step 4.   Click the Start button to begin the compression process.

DriveSpace will figure out how to compress your drive based on its size and the total size of the files on your drive. If the drive is too big to compress into one CVF, it leaves the extra space on the host drive, which you can then compress into a new CVF.

While a host drive is a physical drive, you can always change the host drive's letter designator. Your physical drive may start out as C, but after you put on a bunch of compressed drives, it will be set by DriveSpace to H (or a letter greater than the last drive on your computer). You can change the host and compressed drive volume letter designators, although you can't change the letter designator for the drive that contains the \Windows folder.

The CVF might be larger than 256MB if the compression ratio is less than 2 to 1 and the total reported size of the files in the CVF is less than or equal to 512MB.

Compressing free space

To create a compressed drive out of free disk space, follow these steps:

STEPS

Creating a Compressed Drive Out of Free Disk Space

Step 1.   Click the Start button, point to Programs, Accessories, System Tools, and then click DriveSpace.

Step 2.   Highlight an existing physical drive.

(continued)

Creating a Compressed Drive Out of Free Disk Space

Step 3. Choose Advanced, Create Empty to display the Create New Compressed Drive dialog box, as shown in Figure 27-10.

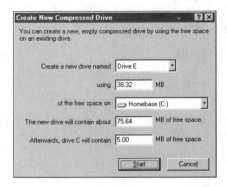

Figure 27-10: The Create New Compressed Drive dialog box. You can give the compressed drive a new drive letter designator, but that is about all you can change in this dialog box.

Step 4. Click the Start button to begin the compression process.

The new compressed drive will be as large as it can be (up to 512MB) taking all the free space that is available (up to 256MB). A CVF will be created on the physical drive that contains the free space, and you can choose the letter designator for the new compressed drive.

Later, you can adjust the size of the compressed drive and the amount of free space left on the host drive (see the next section for details).

Changing the size of the compressed drive

You can increase the size of a compressed drive if there is free space available on the host drive. You are just increasing the size of the CVF that is stored on the host drive, and thereby taking up more free space. You can't increase the size of the compressed drive beyond 512MB (unless you have DriveSpace 3).

If there is free space on your compressed drive, you can increase the amount of free space on the host drive by decreasing the size of the compressed drive (CVF).

To change the size of the compressed drive, take the following steps:

STEPS

Changing the Size of the Compressed Drive

Step 1. Click the Start button, point to Programs, Accessories, System Tools, and then click DriveSpace.

Step 2. Highlight an existing drive.

Step 3. Choose Drive, Adjust Free Space to display the Adjust Free Space dialog box, as shown in Figure 27-11.

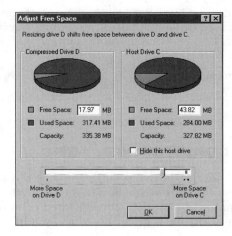

Figure 27-11: The Adjust Free Space dialog box.

Step 4. Drag the slider to move the free space from the host to the compressed drive, and vice versa. If you move the slider into the red area, Disk Defragmenter will be called to defragment the drive.

When you adjust the free space, the amount of used space on the compressed drive and the capacity of the host drive does not change.

The amount of space you can adjust on the compressed drive is determined by the sum of the free disk space on the compressed drive and the host drive. If you need to make larger changes, you must first delete files.

Problems with changing the size of the compressed drive

Steve Bernhard found out about an interesting bug when he called Microsoft support. Here is his story:

> Those of you who use DriveSpace and have used the Advanced, Change Ratio command to alter the ratio know that Windows 95 switches temporarily to a special mode — and then switches back to standard Windows 95 mode. Yesterday I got a dreaded message: "DriveSpace cannot complete this task. If Windows does not start properly, contact Product Support." This was accompanied by a black MS-DOS screen.

> The Windows 95 techie was a genius. Within 5 minutes he had told me what to do, and I was back in Windows 95 mode — in full color. The compressed drive had failed to remount because of a bug in Microsoft Plus! — and the instruction line you should type at the DOS prompt to fix this is:

> Scandisk /mount=000 c:

> Apparently, I was very lucky; 50 percent of the time this fix does not work!

Estimated compression ratio

The size of the compressed drive is determined by the size of the CVF and the actual compression ratio of the files in the CVF. When DriveSpace creates a CVF, it automatically sets the estimated compression ratio to 2 to 1. This is before any file is compressed and put in the CVF.

After DriveSpace copies files to the compressed drive, it reports the actual compression ratio, as well as the estimated compression ratio for the remaining free space on the compressed drive. The estimated compression ratio is, by default, set to 2 to 1.

Some files compress to a greater extent than others. Just because the files that you have copied to your compressed drive have a certain average compression ratio doesn't mean that the next group of files will have a similar compression ratio.

DriveSpace uses the estimated compression ratio to report the size of the free space available on the compressed drive. If this ratio is higher than the average for files that you subsequently copy to the compressed drive, the actual amount of free space available will be less than what was reported.

If you believe your actual compression ratio is a better estimate of the compression ratio of the files you will be adding to your compressed drive, you can change the estimated ratio to match your actual ratio (as long as it doesn't make the compressed drive greater than 512MB). This will give you a more realistic idea of the free space available on your compressed drive.

To change the estimated compression ratio, take the following steps:

STEPS

Changing the Estimated Compression Ratio

Step 1. Click the Start button, point to Programs, Accessories, System Tools, and then click DriveSpace.

Step 2. Highlight a compressed drive.

Step 3. Choose Advanced, Change Ratio to display the Compression Ratio dialog box, as shown in Figure 27-12.

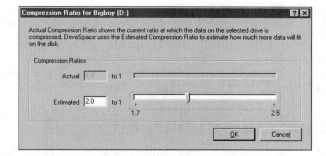

Figure 27-12: The Compression Ratio dialog box.

Step 4. Move the slider to change the estimated compression ratio.

Other DriveSpace options

DriveSpace gives you numerous other ways to manage your compressed drives.

You can use the Drive, Format command in the DriveSpace window to format a compressed drive, thereby erasing all the files within the CVF.

You can hide the host drive. You can do this regardless of how much free space it has, although you'll most likely want to hide the host drive if the CVF takes up almost all of it. You don't need to see an extraneous letter designator for the host drive if there isn't any space to store files on it. To hide the host drive, highlight it in the DriveSpace window, choose Drive, Properties, and mark the Hide this host drive check box.

Compressed drives, like physical drives, volumes, and drive partitions, are automatically mounted when you start your computer. You don't even think about the process because the drives are always there. With compressed drives that weren't there when you booted your computer (a compressed diskette, for example), you can choose whether you want to mount them automatically. One example of when you should turn off auto-mounting is if a removable drive doesn't always have a cartridge in it.

You can turn off auto-mounting for new compressed drives by choosing Advanced, Settings in the DriveSpace window, and then clearing the Automatically mount new compressed devices check box in the Disk Compression Settings dialog box. If you want to subsequently mount a compressed drive (or unmount one) choose Advanced, Mount or Advanced, Unmount.

You can change the letter designator of a host drive and/or a compressed drive by choosing Advanced, Change Letter. You can't change the letter designator for the drive that contains the \Windows folder.

Tip

Your application configuration files and/or the Registry quite probably contain references to the drive letters that you are contemplating changing. You have to make changes to these files and to the Registry if you want your applications to track the "new" location of their files.

Compressing a diskette

One of the great things about disk compression is that you can increase the capacity of your diskettes by compressing files as they are copied to them. Of course, DriveSpace must be on any computer that is going to read the diskettes you create on your computer.

Tip

Windows 95 computers can read diskettes with DoubleSpace and DriveSpace compression. Computers with DOS 6.*x* and Dblspace.bin in their root directories can read DoubleSpace diskettes. Computers with Drvspace.bin in their root directories can read DriveSpace diskettes.

Compressing a diskette is the same as compressing a hard disk. The diskette will contain the compressed drive and the host drive. The host drive will start off with zero free space. The letter designator for the compressed drive will be either A or B. The host drive letter designator will be a letter greater than the last drive on your computer.

You can't hide the letter designator for a host drive for removable media. The host drive shows up in your Explorer or My Computer window as soon as you click on the diskette drive icon (if the drive is automatically mounted).

If you haven't mounted a compressed diskette (auto-mounting is turned off), you will find a file on the diskette named Readthis.txt. Use the command dir /a in a Windows DOS session to find this file. This file explains how to mount the diskette. You will also see a CVF, Dblspace.000, when you use the dir /a command.

You cannot compress a diskette unless it has at least 512K of free space. Also, it cannot contain a single file that is greater than half the uncompressed size of the diskette.

The amount of file compression

You can see how much an individual file is compressed by using the Dir command in a Windows DOS session. At the DOS command prompt type:

```
dir /c
```

This command reports the actual file compression ratio for each file in the current directory.

Compression safety

You can turn off your computer in the middle of compressing a physical drive. When you turn it on again, compression will continue where it left off without any problems with the files being compressed. Microsoft made safety its number one design priority when developing disk compression.

Dblspace.ini

The parameters that define your DriveSpace or DoubleSpace drives are kept in a hidden, system, read-only file called Dblspace.ini, which is stored in the root directory of your host drive(s). If you change these file attributes (by right-clicking the file in the Explorer, choosing Properties, and then clearing these Attributes check boxes), you can edit this file. Here are some sample parameters:

```
AutoMount=1
FirstDrive=D
LastDrive=E
MaxRemovableDrives=1
MaxFileFragments=241
ActivateDrive=D,C1
```

For example, to change the drive letter designator for the compressed drive from D to E, make the following changes:

```
ActivateDrive=E,C1
LastDrive=F
```

DriveSpace speed

This file compression is all fine and good, but doesn't it take longer to access your files from a CVF?

Secret

Small files should load more quickly because they are being loaded from a sector instead of from a cluster. (Files on compressed drives are allotted space one sector, or 512 bytes, at a time.) Large files, such as Windows 95 files or big applications, should load slightly more slowly because of the DriveSpace overhead as DriveSpace sorts out sectors and reports them as clusters.

If you are running a system with only 4MB of RAM, you'll see some slow-down because you have less disk cache space. But then, on a 4MB system, everything is slow.

DriveSpace command line parameters

DriveSpace is not a DOS program. You put the command line parameters in the Target field in a shortcut to DriveSpace (right-click the shortcut, choose Properties, and click the Shortcut tab). You can also use them in batch files. You can't run DriveSpace in MS-DOS mode. All of the parameters you can add to the Drvspace command have equivalent commands in the more friendly DriveSpace menus, so you may opt to start the program and then use the menu commands instead of adding command line parameters.

```
Drvspace {options}

{options}

/compress e: {/reserve=n} {/new=f:}
    Compress an existing physical drive e:, reserve a certain amount
    of space (n) uncompressed, and give the host drive the letter
    designator f:.

/create e: {/size=n or /reserve=n} {/new=f:} {/cvf=nnn}
    Create a new compressed drive (CVF) from the free space on
    physical drive e:. Set the amount of uncompressed space on the
    host drive for the CVF, reserve an amount of uncompressed space
    on the host drive, give the compressed drive the letter designa-
    tor f:, and report the CVF extension.

/delete e:\d??space.nnn
    Delete the named CVF.

/format e:\d??space.nnn
    Format the named CVF.

{/info} e:
    Report the amount of free and used space on the compressed drive
    e: and other information.

/interactive
    Coupled with an operation switch (/ratio, /mount, and so on),
    tells DriveSpace to display the interactive path for the
    particular operation switch. If you don't specify a drive letter
    or volume file, DriveSpace prompts you for additional input.
```

```
/mount {=nnn e: or e:\d??space.nnn} {/new=f:}
    Mount the named or extension numbered CVF.

/move e: /new=f:
    Change the letter designator of the e: compressed drive to f:.

/ratio{=n} e:
    Change the estimated compression ratio of the e: drive.

/noprompt
    Prevent the display of confirmation dialog boxes. You can add
    this to any command but /info and /settings.

/size{=n or /reserve=n} e:
    Change the size of the compressed drive e:.

/uncompress e:
    Uncompress the compressed drive e:.

/unmount e:
    Unmount the compressed drive e:.

d??space.nnn
    The CVF filename, either Drvspace.nnn or Dblspace.nnn.
```

Compressing with DriveSpace 3

After you install Microsoft Plus!, you should upgrade your existing
DriveSpace or DoubleSpace CVFs to DriveSpace 3 drives. You get an opportunity to do this as soon as you restart Windows 95 after you complete
setting up Plus!. If you don't choose to upgrade immediately, you can do so
later by clicking DriveSpace in the System Tools menu (Start, Programs,
Accessories), and then choosing Drive, Upgrade in the DriveSpace window.

By default, DriveSpace 3 uses Standard compression, which is the same
compression method as the one used by the previous version of DriveSpace.
You can also set DriveSpace 3 to use HiPack compression, which compresses
your files an additional 10 to 20 percent. To do this, choose Advanced,
Settings in the DriveSpace 3 window to display the Disk Compression
Settings dialog box, and then click the HiPack compression option button
(see Figure 27-13).

If you have upgraded to DriveSpace 3 and you want to compress files on a
compressed drive even further, you can run Compression Agent, which
comes with Microsoft Plus!. You will find this agent on the System Tools
menu. (Compression Agent does not work with the previous version of
DriveSpace.)

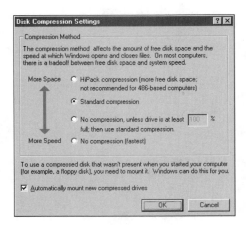

Figure 27-13: The Disk Compression Settings dialog box in DriveSpace 3.

Compression Agent gives you two levels of compression that are higher than Standard compression, called HiPack and UltraPack. (Choosing HiPack in Compression Agent is the same as choosing it in DriveSpace 3.) The trade-off for using one of these higher compression levels is that it takes some-what longer to read and write compressed files, and it takes a lot longer to compress them in the first place.

System Agent is a scheduling program that comes with Plus!. You can reach it through Start, Programs, Accessories, System Tools. By default, System Agent runs Compression Agent every day after 8 p.m., assuming that your computer is idle. (It checks to see if your computer is idle every 20 minutes after 8 p.m.) You can set System Agent to run Compression Agent whenever it is convenient for you. If you leave your computer on, you might want to run Compression Agent while you're sleeping or away from work.

Once you have created a CVF, DriveSpace continually compresses files as you write them to the compressed drive. The DriveSpace window is just a front end for the behind-the-scenes, on-the-fly file compression that is always going on if you have a CVF.

You can turn off this on-the-fly file compression and just write the uncompressed file to your compressed drive, of course. While this speeds up file writes, it also eats up disk space more quickly. To turn off compres-sion, choose the No compression option button in DriveSpace 3's Disk Compression Settings dialog box (Advanced, Settings), as shown in Figure 27-13.

Tip

If you set DriveSpace 3 to no compression in the Disk Compression Settings dialog box, set the Compression Agent to use HiPack, and set System Agent both to warn you when you're low on disk space (the default setting) and to run Compression Agent at night, you can speed up your disk access to compressed drives (by not compressing files on-the-fly), and still compress your newly written files at night.

You can choose the option button labeled "No compression, unless drive is at least [   ]% full; then use standard compression" in the Disk Compression Settings dialog box to turn off on-the-fly file compression until the drive starts to fill up. If you do this, you can still set Compression Agent to compress files at night, which will give you more room by morning.

Even if you have set Compression Agent to compress files in UltraPack format, DriveSpace doesn't store your files in this format during the day. Instead, it writes your files back to the compressed drive using the compression format you specified in the Disk Compression Settings dialog box (Standard compression, HiPack compression, or No compression). At night, Compression Agent gets to work recompressing the files to HiPack or UltraPack (or a combination of the two), depending on the compression settings you choose in Compression Agent (shown in Figure 27-14).

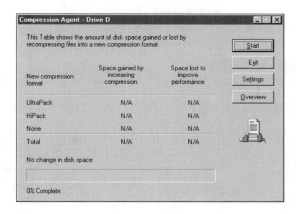

Figure 27-14: The Compression Agent.

To specify the compression format in Compression Agent, click the Settings button, and select the desired option buttons in the Compression Agent Settings dialog box, as shown in Figure 27-15. You can configure Compression Agent to UltraPack all of your files (not recommended if you have a 486), not to UltraPack any files at all or to only UltraPack files that you haven't used in a specified number of days. For all of the files you've chosen not to UltraPack (which may be all of them) you can tell Compression Agent to HiPack them or to store them uncompressed.

To view the results of all these different levels of compression on a CVF, right-click the drive icon of a compressed drive in an Explorer or folder window, choose Properties, and click the Compression tab. You will see something similar to Figure 27-16.

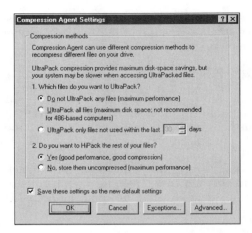

Figure 27-15: The Compression Agent Settings dialog box.

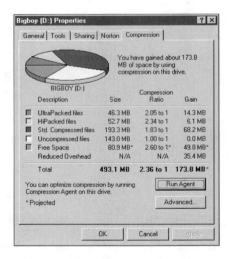

Figure 27-16: The Compression tab of a Properties dialog box for a compressed drive.

Why would you create a CVF (a compressed drive) and then not compress any of the files that you store in it?

Secret

If you have a 1GB disk partition, then the minimum cluster (and therefore file) size is 32K. Even a small file with only a letter to your aunt in it will be stored as though it contained 32,768 characters — a lot of slack space here.

If you store these small files in a CVF, they don't take up a cluster apiece. Space for files on compressed drives is doled out one sector (512 bytes) at a time. The letter to your aunt may now take up only 1024 bytes — a 32-to-1 "compression" ratio without any compressing at all.

Why is there a 2GB limit to a DriveSpace 3 CVF? Let's not get greedy here. Plus! quadruples the size of any one compressed drive.

Secret

Chad Petersen at Microsoft tells us that the 2GB limit is imposed by the maximum number of clusters and the largest cluster size supported by the FAT-16 (and therefore VFAT-16) file system. The FAT file system is limited to 65,525 clusters. The size of a cluster must be a power of 2 and less than 65,536 bytes — this results in a maximum cluster size of 32,768 bytes (32K). Multiplying the maximum number of clusters (65,525) by the maximum cluster size (32,768) equals 2GB.

Windows NT allows a volume size of up to 4GB and 4K clusters. FAT-32 also supports 4GB drives and cluster sizes of 4K.

You might want to see just how much space you are currently wasting on your hard disk. You can download a little $5 shareware package that measures this for you. Waste for Windows 95 reports how much space is wasted due to the disk's cluster size, and how much more or less would be wasted with other cluster sizes. You'll find Waste for Windows 95 at http://www.windows95.com.

Virtual File System

Starting with Windows for Workgroups 3.11, Windows significantly reduced its use of DOS for disk/file access. In WFWG 3.11, the file access subsystem was called *32-bit file access*. In Windows 95 it is called the Virtual File Allocation Table (VFAT).

VFAT is compatible with the existing DOS file allocation system. All DOS disks that were partitioned and formatted as FAT partitions can be read and written to by VFAT. This includes hard disks and removable media, including diskettes.

Both VFAT and CDFS (CD-ROM file system) are installable file systems that are automatically loaded by Windows 95. When the DOS portion of Windows 95 (Io.sys) loads, it calls a real-mode installable file system helper file (Ifshlp.sys) that gets the whole virtual file system going.

Lock and unlock

All disk access is directed through VFAT, so you don't normally access the disk directly or through DOS or your BIOS. If you have programs, usually pre-Windows 95 disk utilities, that access the hard disk directly (using Interrupts 25 and 26), Windows 95 prevents them from accessing the disks.

You can use the Lock command to allow direct disk access. After you are done, you use the Unlock command to prevent direct disk access again. You can do this in batch files or at the DOS prompt. You can't access the disk directly even in MS-DOS mode unless you use Lock and Unlock. No access by other programs is allowed when a drive is locked.

If you have a DOS program that requires direct disk access, create a batch file that runs Lock and Unlock around the program. It is not a good idea to run pre-Windows 95 disk utilities because they can destroy long filenames. You should update your disk utilities to ones that are compatible with Windows 95.

Disk utilities provided with Windows 95 (including Defrag and ScanDisk) use the Microsoft-developed *volume locking* API. The commands in this application programming interface lock and unlock the disk drive. All third-party disk utilities should use this API.

Real-mode disk drivers

You may have a hard disk drive that requires a 16-bit driver. Microsoft has made a special effort to provide 32-bit protected-mode drivers for almost all disk drives available, but it didn't cover all of them.

You may be tempted to keep your 16-bit driver because some disk manufacturers boast that they shipped "fast" 16-bit drivers. These drivers are not as fast as the 32-bit drivers from Microsoft. Comment them out of your Config.sys file.

You can check if your hard disk is running in MS-DOS compatibility mode (16-bit) by double-clicking the System icon in your Control Panel, and then clicking the Performance tab. If File System is listed as 16-bit, you may be able to upgrade to 32-bit mode.

Microsoft provides a troubleshooting guide to determine how to fix this problem. You'll find it in the Knowledge Base at http://www.microsoft.com/kb/articles/Q130/1/79.htm.

Compatible drives

Microsoft provides 32-bit protected mode VFAT drivers for these drive types:

- ESDI
- Hardcards
- IDE
- EIDE

Microsoft also provides 32-bit protected mode VFAT drivers for drive controllers of these types:

- MFM
- PCI
- PCMCIA

- RLL
- SCSI
- SCSI 2

In addition, VFAT supports these types of removable media:

- Floppy disk
- Iomega Bernoulli, Jazz, and Zip drives
- CD-ROM

Secret

Microsoft originally planned to provide drivers for Floptical disks and Syquest drives, but these drivers were not included on the Windows 95 diskettes, nor were drivers for BackPack drives. Windows 95-compatible 32-bit drivers should be available directly from the manufacturers of these devices.

IDE drives in the 2.5GB range were available at retail in early 1997 for around $250. Windows 95 provides 32-bit protected-mode drivers for IDE drives up to 137GB in size.

The Windows 95 drivers can support up to two IDE controllers in one computer. You can add a CD-ROM to your IDE controller, and Windows 95 will support it.

Windows 95 provides 32-bit protected-mode drivers for Adaptec, Future Domain, Trantor, and UltraStor SCSI adapters.

Disk Caching

You don't need SmartDrive for disk caching. The Windows 95 Vcache dynamically adjusts the size in memory of your disk cache.

Vcache caches on a per-file basis, unlike SmartDrive, which caches on a per-contiguous-sector basis. If your hard disk is fragmented, SmartDrive won't store your files together (in contiguous sectors), so it isn't as smart as Vcache when it comes to caching a complete file.

Vcache can read-cache removable media, although it can't cache their disk writes.

Setting disk cache parameters

You can give Vcache a few suggestions about how to optimize caching the file system on your hard disk and, separately, on your CD-ROM.

Secret

You have three options that affect how fast Windows 95 displays filenames and folders: Desktop computer, Mobile or docking system, and Network server. If you choose Network server, Vcache caches 64 directory paths and 2729 filenames in memory. If you choose Desktop computer, it caches 32 paths and 677 files. The Desktop computer setting uses 8K of memory as cache and the Network server setting uses 16K. You can mostly likely spare the additional 8K to speed up access to your files and folders.

To modify your file system cache, take the following steps:

STEPS

Modifying Your Hard Disk File System Cache

Step 1. Right-click My Computer. Choose Properties to display the System Properties dialog box, and click the Performance tab.

Step 2. Click the File System button to display the File System Properties dialog box.

Step 3. In the Hard Disk tab, choose from among the options in the Typical role for this computer field.

To optimize caching the CD-ROM, click the CD-ROM tab in the File System Properties dialog box, and specify both a cache memory size and the CD-ROM drive's speed. This cache should be sized like this:

Your Computer's RAM	*CD-ROM Speed*	*Cache Size*
8MB or less	Single	64K
8-12MB	Double	626K
12MB or more	Quad or more	1238K

The Windows 95 memory manager wants to page your loaded applications to the hard disk and manage your RAM for caching the latest applications and data. You can restrict its ability to assign your RAM to cache by fixing the size of the cache. If you want to do this, take these steps:

STEPS

Fixing the Size of Your Cache

Step 1. Double-click System.ini in your \Windows folder.

Fixing the Size of Your Cache

Step 2. Add the following two lines to the [vcache] section (add the section if it's not there):

```
MinFileCache=4096
MaxFileCache=4096
```

Step 3. If you have more than 16MB of RAM, set the above values to about 25 percent of your installed RAM.

Step 4. Save the edited System.ini file, and restart Windows 95.

Managing Your Swap Space

You don't need a permanent swap file because Windows 95 dynamically sizes your swap file space.

Windows 95 manages your dynamically sized swap space for you, so you don't have to assign the volume or minimum and maximum size parameters. If you want to change these parameters, take the following steps:

STEPS

Managing Your Swap Space

Step 1. Right-click My Computer. Choose Properties, and click the Performance tab.

Step 2. Click the Virtual Memory button to display the Virtual Memory dialog box (shown in Figure 27-17).

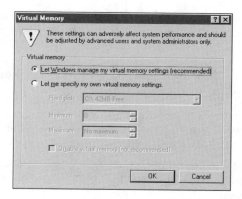

Figure 27-17: The Virtual Memory dialog box. You decide where to place your swap file, and its minimum and maximum size.

(continued)

STEPS *(continued)*

Managing Your Swap Space

Step 3. Choose Let me specify my own virtual memory settings.

Step 4. Choose volume and size parameters.

When you let Windows 95 manage your swap space and your memory, it will take every opportunity to page your loaded applications to the swap space on your hard disk. It uses the freed-up RAM to cache your data and most recently used application code. You might find your hard disk chattering away as this paging occurs in the background.

You can reduce this paging and caching by fixing the size of your swap space. To do this, first defragment your drive to set up a contiguous area on your hard disk big enough for your fixed-size swap space. See the *Defrag, the disk defragmenter* section of this chapter for instructions on how to do this.

Next, set the swap space at 2.5 times the size of your total RAM. To do this, set the minimum and maximum size to the same value in step 4 above, choosing a value in megabytes that is 2.5 times the size of your RAM in megabytes.

Swap space on a compressed drive

Your swap drive can be on a compressed drive (CVF). It is stored in an uncompressed form on the compressed drive to ensure that writing to the swap space will never fail.

A swap file is not particularly compressible, so it doesn't hurt to write it out in an uncompressed form. There is an advantage to putting the swap space on a compressed drive. You don't have to set aside enough unused uncompressed disk space for the maximum amount of space that the swap space might occupy because much of the time this space will never be used.

Windows 3.x permanent swap file

Windows 95 and Windows 3.x can share the permanent swap file space. If you have both Windows 3.x and Windows 95 on your computer and Windows 3.x has a permanent swap file, you may get an error message stating that the swap file has been corrupted when you start Windows 3.x.

To fix this problem, add MinPagingFileSize= to the [386enh] section of your System.ini file in your Windows 95 folder. Set the value to the size of your Windows 3.x swap file.

Undocumented

If this doesn't help, do the following:

- Allow Windows 95 to manage virtual memory settings. (Right-click My Computer, choose Properties, click the Performance tab, click the Virtual Memory button, and choose Let Windows manage my virtual memory settings.)

- While running Windows 95, delete the files 386spart.par (in the root directory), and Spart.par and/or Win386.swp from the Windows 3.*x* directory.

- Open the System.ini file in the Windows 3.1 directory, and comment out these lines in the [386enh] section:

```
PermSwapDOSDrive= {a drive letter}
PermSwapSizeK= {size in K}
```

- Add these lines to the [386enh] section of System.ini in the Windows 3.*x* directory:

```
MaxPagingFileSize={max swapfile size in K}
PagingFile={drive letter}:\{Windows 95 directory}\Win386.swp
```

Long Filenames

A major new feature provided by the VFAT file system is the ability to handle long filenames — up to 255 characters. Every file has two names, the new long filename and a short filename that is compatible with the FAT file system. The backward compatible short filename complies with the 8.3 filename rules.

You see the long filename in Explorer and folder windows. If you open a DOS window, you see both names. VFAT creates a short filename using the long filename as a template, and it makes sure that the all the short filenames in a folder are unique.

Valid filenames

A filename that obeys the 8.3 filename rules can contain any alphanumeric character, any ASCII character greater than 127, and these special characters:

$ % ' - @ ~ ` ! { } ( ) ^ # & _

In addition to these characters, a long filename can contain spaces, and it can also contain the following characters:

+ , ; = [ ] .

A null (one of the ASCII control characters) is included at the end of the long filename, so the total length of the filename, including the null, can be 256 characters. With DOS 6.22 and previous versions, the maximum length of a path and filename combined is 80 characters. It is now 260 characters, including the null. Filenames and folder names obey the same rules.

You can mix case throughout the filename. Filenames are not case sensitive, but the case you choose is preserved and displayed on screen. You can't have two files in the same folder with the same name except for the case of the letters. For example, ToDo.txt and TODO.txt are seen by VFAT as the same filename.

The double quote mark is not a valid character to use in a filename. You use double quote marks to demarcate long path and/or filenames that contain spaces. For example, if you want to copy a file that has spaces in the filename from the DOS prompt, use this format:

```
Copy "File with a long name" "A new name for the long name file"
```

Short filenames

The default method VFAT uses to create a short filename is to take the first six characters of the long filename (ignoring spaces), add ~1 (or a later number), and then set the extension as the first three letters after the last period in the long filename. For example:

```
longfilename.txt -> longfi~1.txt
```

This is also the method that Windows NT uses for drives partitioned to use the NTFS (Windows NT file system).

Undocumented

You can do this in another way — using the friendly short filename scheme. If you use this method, the short filename in the above example will be longfile.txt, assuming there are no other files with this filename in the same folder.

STEPS

Turning On Friendly Short Filenames

Step 1. Using Explorer, double-click Regedit.exe in your \Windows folder. This invokes the Registry editor.

Step 2. Click the plus signs to navigate to this branch:

HKEY_LOCAL_MACHINE\System\CurrentControlSet\control

Step 3. Highlight FileSystem.

Step 4. Right-click the right pane of the Registry editor. Choose New, Binary Value.

Turning On Friendly Short Filenames

Step 5.   Type the value name **NameNumericTail.** Press Enter.

Step 6.   Double-click NameNumericTail. Type **0** as the single entry for the binary value. Click OK.

Step 7.   Exit the Registry editor, and reboot your computer.

If you want VFAT to go back to the old scheme, set the binary value for NameNumericTail to 1.

Because of a bug in the MSN install routine, if you install MSN after changing to friendly short names, MSN cannot find some of its files. The MSN install routine is hardwired to use Progra~1 and TheMic~1 as the short filenames for the MSN folders.

If, after setting NameNumericTail=0 to change to friendly short names, you encounter this problem with MSN or run into similar problems with other programs installed under the Program Files folder, take these steps:

STEPS

Turning Off Friendly Short Filenames

Step 1.   Using the Explorer, double-click Regedit.exe in your \Windows folder. This invokes the Registry editor.

Step 2.   Click the plus signs to navigate to this branch:

HKEY_LOCAL_MACHINE\System\CurrentControlSet\control

Step 3.   Highlight FileSystem.

Step 4.   Delete the value NameNumericTail=0.

Step 5.   Using Explorer, rename the Program Files folder to ProgramFilesfolderhasaproblem.

Step 6.   Rename ProgramsFilesfolderhasaproblem to Program Files. This forces Windows to create a new short name for Program Files.

Microsoft states that NameNumericTail=0 is not supported in Windows 95. It does work, but it might cause problems with Windows 95 components. If you want to use it, you can fix everything in your Registry to work correctly.

You need to edit all entries in your Registry that use the old convention — in other words, all entries that have ~1 hardwired in their names. Search through the Registry and change each name to its new friendly short name or long filename. Most programs created after the release of Windows 95 use long filenames in the Registry.

DOS commands and long filenames

Undocumented

The DOS commands that come with Windows 95 have been updated to handle long filenames (and the short filenames that must go with them). If you use versions of these commands from DOS 6.22 or earlier, you lose the long filenames. If the long filename and the short filename are the same, it doesn't matter.

If you copy files from a Windows 95 computer to a diskette, take that diskette to a computer running DOS 6.*x* or Windows 3.*x,* and then edit those files on the diskette, the long filename is preserved when you copy those files back to the Windows 95 computer. If, on the other hand, you copy the files off the diskette onto the hard disk of the DOS computer, edit those files, and then copy them back onto the diskette, you will lose the long filenames. Only the short 8.3 filenames will be preserved.

Windows 3.*x* Norton Disk Editor

Undocumented

Pre-Windows 95 versions of Norton Disk Editor can work with Windows 95 files, but it's better to use ScanDisk or Windows 95-specific disk utilities. Pre-Windows 95 versions of Norton Disk Doctor have an incompatibility with how Windows 95 uses the file size field, so you shouldn't use them.

Long filenames across the network

Windows 95 32-bit network clients give you long filenames over the network if the server supports them. Earlier 16-bit real-mode network clients can only provide short filenames. This includes NetWare NETX and VLM drivers. You'll need to use Microsoft's Client for NetWare Networks or a 32-bit client provided by Novell instead if you want to support long filenames.

Other file systems on the servers create different short filenames from the long filenames. No big deal. They are still compatible with Windows 95.

You have to configure NetWare servers to use the OS/2 namespace (which emulates the native OS/2 HPFS file system) in order for Windows 95 to see long filenames on them. Doesn't it seem a little weird that Windows 95 would rely on an OS/2 standard? Well, the OS/2 standard is the past, after all.

To configure the NetWare server to use the OS/2 namespace, take the following steps:

STEPS

Enabling Long Filenames to Be Seen on a NetWare Server

Step 1. On the NetWare server, type these commands at the prompt:

Enabling Long Filenames to Be Seen on a NetWare Server

```
load OS/2
add name space os2 to volume sys
```

Step 2. Add this line to the file Startup.cnf:

```
load os2
```

Step 3. Shut down the NetWare server. Copy the file Os2.nam from your NetWare diskettes or CD-ROM to the disk and directory on the NetWare server that contains the file Server.exe.

Step 4. Reboot the NetWare server.

Turning off long filename support

Undocumented

You can turn off long filename support completely. You shouldn't do this unless you have applications that don't work when long filenames are enabled. If you need to disable long filenames, first remove all the long filenames from your hard disk. The utility Lfnbk.exe lets you do this (you'll find it in the \Admin\Apptools\Lfnback folder on Microsoft's Windows 95 CD-ROM). Then follow these steps:

STEPS

Turning Off Long Filename Support

Step 1. Using the Explorer, double-click Regedit.exe in your Windows 95 folder to invoke the Registry editor.

Step 2. Click the plus signs to navigate to this branch:

HKEY_LOCAL_MACHINE\System\CurrentControlSet\control

Step 3. Highlight FileSystem.

Step 4. Double-click Win31FileSystem in the right pane.

Step 5. Press the Delete key, and then replace the 00 binary value with **01**. Click OK.

Step 6. Close the Registry editor, and reboot your computer.

Changing Drive Letters for Removable Media

Unlike your floppy and hard drives, you can set the drive letter designator for your CD-ROM drive, Zip drive, or Syquest drive. You must be using the native Windows 95 32-bit drivers for this to work. Older CD-ROM drives may still be using 16-bit Windows 3.1 drivers, even under Windows 95. (If you're using a 16-bit driver for your CD-ROM drive, you'll see a reference to Mscdex.exe in your Autoexec.bat.) Here's how to change your drive letter if you are using a 32-bit driver:

STEPS

Designating Your Drive Letter

Step 1. Right-click My Computer, choose Properties, and click the Device Manager tab.

Step 2. For your CD-ROM, click the plus sign next to CDROM, highlight your CD-ROM drive, and click the Properties button. For Syquest and Zip drives, click the plus sign next to Disk drives, highlight your Zip or Syquest drive, and then click the Properties button.

Step 3. Click the Settings tab.

Step 4. Select the letter you want for this drive in the Start drive letter and End drive letter fields (choose the same letter in both fields).

Step 5. Click both OK buttons. You will be prompted to reboot your computer.

Disk Drive Partitioning

You have to partition physical drives before you can format them into FAT (or VFAT) volumes. A physical drive can have just one partition, in which case the partition must be bootable, or it can have multiple partitions, including one bootable partition. You assign a drive letter to each partition, and refer to each one as a *drive*.

Windows 95 works with third-party disk partitioning schemes, including Disk Manager, SuperStor, and Golden Bow. These schemes were created to let you partition hard drives that were larger than what Fdisk, which Microsoft supplies, could handle. Windows 95 also works with Fdisk-partitioned drives on removable media.

Windows 95 comes with Fdisk, which you can use to partition your drives. In most cases, the computer manufacturer will have already set up disk partitions on your hard drive when you get a new computer. You can use Fdisk.exe to change these partitions, but you will lose any files stored on them unless you back them up first.

You shouldn't use Fdisk if your hard disk is already partitioned with a third-party scheme. Use the third party's tools instead. You can determine if your hard disk was partitioned with a third-party product by examining Config.sys. You are using a third-party disk partitioner if you find references to the following files: Dmdrvr.bin, Sstor.sys, HarDrive.sys, or Evdisk.sys.

If you want to change the partition structure on your hard disk and you'd rather not go through the pain of redoing your Windows 95 and software installation, you'll need to get Partition Magic. You'll find it at http://www.powerquest.com.

DMF Diskettes

If you purchased Windows 95 on diskettes, you have diskettes that contain 1.7MB of compressed data. Since the data was already compressed before the files were copied to the diskette, it wouldn't have done any good to make these diskettes into compressed drives. Microsoft found a way to store more data (in whatever form) on $3 \frac{1}{2}$-inch diskettes.

These 1.7MB formatted diskettes are referred to as Distribution Media Format (DMF) diskettes.

If you want to copy files from the DMF diskettes onto your hard disk, use the Extract command as follows:

```
extract /c a:filename.cab d:\filename.cab
```

You can find out more about the Extract command in the Microsoft Knowledge Base. Turn your Internet Explorer to http://www.microsoft.com/kb/articles/q129/6/05.htm.

If you want to format DMF diskettes and write files to them, you'll need to use the WinImage package featured on the *Windows 95 Secrets* CD-ROM. To format a DMF diskette with WinImage, take the following steps:

STEPS

Running WinImage to Format a DMF Diskette

Step 1.   Double-click Winmaint.exe in a folder or Explorer window.

Step 2.   Choose Option, Preference. Clear the Use only standard formats check box. Click OK.

(continued)

STEPS *(continued)*

Running WinImage to Format a DMF Diskette

Step 3.   Choose File, New. Drag and drop some files into the new image file.

Step 4.   Choose File, Save, and give the image file a name.

Step 5.   Choose Disk, Format, and then choose Write Disk. Select the 1.7MB format when prompted, and click OK.

The diskette in your diskette drive is now formatted to store 1.7MB of data. You can write more data to it later using WinImage.

Summary

The people staffing the Microsoft support lines want to quit hearing from you about problems with your disk drives. Windows 95 provides you with a set of tools to keep everything in working order.

▶ We show you how to find all the disk tools in all the little corners of Windows 95.

▶ We show you how to repair your disks when you experience a problem, and how to keep an eye on your disks to prevent trouble.

▶ Microsoft includes a great little disk defragmenter that can speed up disk access. We show you how to get the most from it.

▶ Do you want to double your hard disk space at little or no cost in disk access speed? Try DriveSpace or DriveSpace 3.

▶ We show you how to create super-high-density diskettes.

Part V

Communications

Chapter 28

Calling Your Computer at Work from Your Computer at Home

In This Chapter

Windows 95 includes the capability to dial up another computer, whether that computer is running Windows 95, Windows NT, LAN Manager, NetWare, or Unix. It can also let you access the Internet through an Internet service provider. We discuss:

▶ Calling and connecting over a modem to a computer running Windows 95, Windows NT, Unix, or NetWare

▶ Setting up a Windows 95 computer to receive modem phone calls from another Windows 95, Windows 3.1, Windows NT, or other computer

▶ Setting up your Windows 95 computer as a guest and calling into other computers

▶ Configuring the Windows 95 Dial-Up Adapter for the correct protocols

▶ Printing on a printer at work and faxing from a fax/modem at work while directing these operations from your computer at home

Networking? Over a Modem?

Many of you use your computer and modem for communications purposes. Those of you who can remember back to the days before the World Wide Web can probably picture this typical scenario: You started some communications software, perhaps the Terminal emulator software that comes with Windows 3.1. You dialed into a bulletin board, a commercial online service such as CompuServe, or an Internet service provider (using a dial-up shell account). Once connected, you did whatever — downloaded files, sent e-mail, cruised the forums, looked at the news. (See Chapter 29 for more on this subject.)

Many of you have also used software that allows you to connect two computers in close proximity, either through a serial or parallel cable. You run software such as LapLink on both computers, which facilitates file transfer between the computers using a point and click interface. (See Chapter 30 for more about this.)

And if your computer is connected to a local area network, you have experienced high-speed communications with other computers located in your general vicinity. Double-clicking the Network Neighborhood icon in Windows 95 gets you quickly to the shared resources available to you on the network. You can print your files on printers connected to other computers or servers on the network. You can quickly copy files, send e-mail, chat, and so on over the LAN. (Turn to Chapter 36 for more details.)

Dial-Up Networking (DUN) is a mixture of all three of these communications modes — using a modem to dial into another computer or network, connecting two computers in close proximity (through Direct Cable Connection, which uses DUN), and sharing resources with other computers as though you were networked to them.

DUN lets your computer at home or on the road use a modem to access the resources of a computer at work and/or the resources of the network connected to a computer at work, including shared disk drives, folders, printers, NetWare servers, NT servers, and much more. You can also use DUN to connect your home computer to the Internet and the World Wide Web through an Internet service provider.

DUN allows your computer to communicate with a network (or a computer on a network) as though it were on the network directly, even though it's in fact only connected to the network through a modem and another computer on the network. The one difference is that a DUN connection is slower than a direct network connection through a dedicated network card or port.

Undocumented

You can use DUN in a whole host of ways. You can get your e-mail from work. You can send a file from your computer at home to a printer at work. You can send out fax files from your computer at home using the fax/modem on the computer at work. You can run programs that are stored on the computer at work on your computer at home. You can copy and update files between computers. You can copy programs from work. You can be a client of a client/server application running on a computer at work.

With DUN, you get what the computer business calls *remote access*. In other words, you have access to the resources on the remote, or dialed-up, computer or network. You don't have *remote control*, which is the ability to run your computer at the office as though you were typing on its keyboard while you are sitting in front of your computer at home.

Once you get everything set up (which is somewhat tricky), DUN is actually easy to use. It's easy because it uses standard Windows 95 user interface objects such as Explorer and folder windows.

We use *computer at work* and *computer at home* to cut down on the level of abstraction that you have to deal with. By *computer at work*, we mean any computer that you dial into, and by *computer at home* we mean the computer that does the dialing. You can, of course, substitute anything that makes more sense to you — computer A and computer B, computer connected to a network and remote computer, desktop computer and portable computer, guest and host, client and server, mobile and remote, or user and Internet service provider.

Dial-Up Networking

You need to configure your Windows 95 computer at home as the Dial-Up Networking *client*. You learn how to do this in the *Setting Up Your Computer at Home As a Guest* section later in the chapter. If you are calling into a Windows 95 computer at work, you need to configure that computer as a Dial-Up Networking *host*. We show you how in *Setting Up Your Windows 95 Computer at Work As a Host*.

To make the connection between the two computers you need:

1. Properly configured computers at home and work

2. A shared dial-up protocol (to establish the connection)

3. A shared network protocol (to allow communication between the two computers)

In September, 1996, Microsoft released a new version of Dial-Up Networking (version 2.0) as a part of its ISDN Accelerator 1.1 update. If you have the original version or the Service Pack 1 version of Windows 95, you may not have the latest Dial-Up Networking client software. You can download it from http://www.microsoft.com/windows/software/isdn.htm. You should download the ISDN update even if you don't have an ISDN connection, because you can use the DUN 2.0 part of the update and ignore the ISDN part.

Undocumented

DUN 2.0 works with System Monitor to let you see how fast your uploads and downloads are. Once you've installed the ISDN Accelerator 1.1 update, you'll notice an addition to the list of categories in the Add Item dialog box in System Monitor. The new item is Dial-Up Networking Adapter.

Dial-up servers

You can connect your Windows 95 computer at home over the phone lines to another computer or server running:

- Windows 95 Dial-Up Server (if you have installed Microsoft Plus! or the ISDN Accelerator Pack 1.1 on the server, including the DUN server)
- Windows NT Remote Access Server (RAS) or PPP
- Windows for Workgroups 3.11 RAS
- Microsoft LAN Manager
- NetWare Connect
- Unix with SLIP or PPP protocols
- TCP/IP with PPP protocol (especially for connections to the Internet)

You can also connect to a dedicated modem server such as the Shiva LanRover or a compatible device, or to an Internet service provider (if you have a SLIP or PPP account).

Network protocols

Windows 95 supports in native 32-bit mode the following network protocols:

- NetBEUI (Microsoft's networking protocol)
- IPX/SPX (Novell's NetWare protocol)
- TCP/IP (the Unix, Internet, and Intranet standard protocol)

Dial-up protocols

To connect to the computer at work, the Windows 95 DUN client can use any one of the following dial-up protocols:

- PPP (Point-to-Point Protocol)
- NRN (Novell NetWare Connect)
- RAS (Windows NT and Windows for Workgroups 3.11 Remote Access Server using Asynchronous NetBEUI)
- SLIP (Serial Line Internet Protocol)
- CSLIP (SLIP with IP header compression)

Point-to-Point Protocol is the default dial-up protocol used by Windows 95 computers. You can use PPP to connect to a network or computer running any one of the three network protocols included with Windows 95. Many Internet service providers also use PPP. You can also use PPP to call into Unix, Windows 95, or Windows NT servers.

Novell NetWare Connect allows you to dial into a NetWare Connect server.

RAS allows a Windows 95 computer to call into a Windows NT computer running RAS or into a computer running Windows for Workgroups 3.11, and vice versa.

SLIP is an older dial-up protocol, but it is often used by Internet service providers, and it's used on some Unix servers as well.

Setting Up Your Windows 95 Computer at Work As a Host

If you have a significant network at work, then you will want to provide dial-up services through a Windows NT server, which can handle up to 256 dial-up connections, a LAN modem server, a NetWare Connect server, or perhaps a Unix computer. Another option is the Shiva LanRover, which is built for handling large-scale dial-in communications in conjunction with a corporate-sized NetWare, NetBEUI, or TCP/IP local area network.

If your network isn't that big (maybe it just consists of your desktop computer) and only a few people need dial-up access, then calling into a Windows 95 computer at work may fit the bill. The Windows 95 Dial-Up Server can take calls from and connect to Windows 95 clients, computers running RAS on Windows for Workgroups or Windows 3.1, and other computers running the PPP dial-up protocol. The Windows 95 Dial-Up Server can't act as an IP router. That is, you can't call into a Windows 95 computer using only the TCP/IP networking protocol, and access a TCP/IP network through that Windows 95 server.

The Windows 95 Dial-Up Server can handle NetBEUI and IPX/SPX network protocols and allow you to connect to network resources using these protocols. If your network at the office uses both TCP/IP and NetBEUI, you'll be able to connect and see other servers on the network.

The Windows 95 Dial-Up Server software comes with Microsoft Plus! and the ISDN Accelerator Pack 1.1. You have to get one of these packages if you want to configure your Windows 95 system as a DUN server. However, you don't need Microsoft Plus! or the ISDN Accelerator Pack 1.1 if you just want to configure your system as a DUN client.

Microsoft Plus! contains some other communications-related components as well. When Windows 95 was first released, Microsoft's 32-bit TCP/IP stack only came with Microsoft Plus!. Later, Microsoft made it available for download at its web site. The 32-bit TCP/IP stack is required for Microsoft's Internet Explorer (and is included with it). The OEM Service Release 2 version of Windows 95 included it along with the Internet Explorer 3.0.

We are going to assume that you want to call in from home — or from a hotel when you are on the road — to your Windows 95 computer (and your network) at work. You must do four things to set up your Windows 95 computer at work as a host:

1. Install a modem driver (this may have occurred if you had your modem installed when you set up Windows 95).

2. Install the Microsoft Dial-Up Adapter and the accompanying network software/drivers (this may also have occurred during setup).

3. Install Microsoft Plus! or the ISDN Accelerator Pack 1.1 update.

4. Set the Windows 95 Dial-Up Server to allow caller access.

Undocumented

The Dial-Up Adapter will be automatically installed (if it is not already) the first time you choose Connections, Dial-Up Server from the menu bar of the Dial-Up Networking folder window. If you do this and you haven't yet installed your modem, you will be prompted to do so. You can separately install the Dial-Up Adapter (see the section later in this chapter entitled *The Dial-Up Adapter*) and the modem before you install the Dial-Up Server.

STEPS

Setting Up a Windows 95 Computer
As a Host for Dial-Up Networking

Step 1.   If it is not already, set up your modem using the Modems icon in the Control Panel. Click the Add button in the Modems Properties dialog box, and then follow the steps in the Install New Modem Wizard. See Chapter 25 if you need additional instructions. You will be prompted to do this if you take step 4 below first.

Step 2.   If you haven't already done so, set up the Dial-Up Adapter by double-clicking the Network icon in the Control Panel. Click the Add button, highlight Adapter in the Select Network Component Type dialog box, and click the Add button. Follow the steps in the section entitled *The Dial-Up Adapter* later in this chapter. This is an optional step and will happen automatically if you take step 4.

Step 3.   Install Microsoft Plus! or the ISDN Accelerator Pack 1.1, including the DUN server, on the computer at work.

Step 4.   On the computer at work, double-click the Dial-Up Networking folder icon in the Explorer, or choose Dial-Up Networking from the Start, Programs, Accessories menu.

Step 5.   Choose Connections, Dial-Up Server in the Dial-Up Networking folder window. The Dial-Up Server dialog box will pop up, as shown in Figure 28-1.

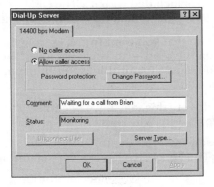

Figure 28-1: The dial-in options in the Dial-Up Server dialog box. You want to allow caller access if this Windows 95 computer is going to be the host and receive calls from the home computer.

Step 6.   Click the Allow caller access option button. You want people (perhaps just yourself) using other computers to be able to call into your host computer (the Windows 95 computer at work).

Setting Up a Windows 95 Computer
As a Host for Dial-Up Networking

Step 7.   To require a password to access your computer at work, click the Change Password button.

Step 8.   Click the Server Type button if you want to change the dial-up protocol used when the server answers the phone. We suggest that you leave it on Default, which starts with PPP and switches to RAS if PPP fails. This makes it easy for computers with Windows 95, Windows for Workgroups, Windows 3.1 RAS, Windows NT, as well other operating systems that support PPP to call into your server.

Step 9.   Click Apply or OK to begin monitoring for phone calls. (Apply leaves the dialog box on the Desktop. OK minimizes the dialog box.) The computer at the office will now pick up the phone line attached to its modem when that line is called. You don't have a way of telling it how many rings to wait until it picks up the line.

You now have a computer at work (or a computer at a friend's house) that will respond to calls from your computer at home or on the road. You need to set the computer at work into this answer mode before you can call into it. You will normally want to leave it in this mode when you are away from the office.

Remember to share some resources (disk drives, folders, printers) if you want to be able to do anything on your computer at work when you call in. See the *Sharing your resources* section in Chapter 36.

Secret

Under most circumstances, the DUN server computer can't act as a fax machine at the same time. That is, you can't set up Windows Messaging on the computer at work to automatically answer the phone and receive faxes if it is operating as a DUN server.

Microsoft released the Unimodem V driver and the Operator program in November, 1995. The driver is supposed to allow simultaneous voice and data communications when you use it with modems that have this capability. Operator, when you use it with Unimodem V, can distinguish between a fax call, a voice call, and a data call. It has a bug that allows it to work only if you have a voice program such as Microsoft Phone active. Microsoft Phone is only available when you purchase a new computer or a new modem that supports its capabilities.

If you use Microsoft Phone, Operator, a modem that can use the Unimodem V driver, and the DUN server, you can configure a server that answers both your modem calls and your fax calls. Nathan A. Curtis told us how.

If the Dial-Up Networking server is running, it has control of your phone line until you load Operator. As soon as you do, Operator takes over from all other running TAPI applications that are monitoring the line. Of course, if any of these applications is connected, Operator waits.

Once Operator starts monitoring your line and provides an initial spoken greeting, it routes incoming calls to your other TAPI applications properly unless you make one of the following false moves:

- Turn off your voice software (Microsoft Phone, for example) or worse, you don't have any. A bug in Operator will not allow it to answer the phone if you aren't running TAPI voice software.

- Turn off Operator's initial greeting, and configure Operator to answer the call and route it to some TAPI software other than voice. If you do this, your fax or data (DUN) program (depending on which application has the priority) will attempt to connect, and it will not release the line until the connection times out (usually in about 60 seconds). By then, the calling party will have hung up, and Operator will not be able to route the call to the next software.

- Turn off the initial greeting and set Operator to route to voice first. Microsoft Phone (or other 32-bit TAPI voice software) takes over the line, but it doesn't know about the DUN server. It can answer a fax call without Operator's help, but not a data call.

To correctly configure your TAPI software, take the following steps:

STEPS

Setting up Dun Server, Operator, and Microsoft Phone

Step 1.   Load Microsoft Phone (with fax receive enabled), the DUN server, and Operator.

Step 2.   Set Operator to answer on one ring, set Microsoft Phone to answer on two rings, and set your fax software to answer on three rings. You can't set the DUN server.

Step 3.   Set Operator to answer with the following order for call routing: voice, fax, and then data.

Step 4.   Record Operator's initial greeting with instructions in the same order given in step 3: "Press one for voice, two for fax, or three to make a DUN connection."

Step 5.   Enable Operator's initial greeting (which gives Operator time to determine what type of call is coming in).

Of course, a better way to do this is to order distinctive ring service from your local phone company, and purchase a modem that supports it. If you use a modem that can handle distinctive ring service and use different phone numbers for each service, the modem can route the incoming calls to the correct service without using Operator.

Disallowing dial-in access

You (or your system administrator) can determine whether a Windows 95 computer has the capability of serving as a host. You can use the System Policy Editor to permanently disable dial-in to Dial-Up Networking. If you do this, the Allow caller access option button in the Dial-Up Server dialog box will be grayed out. Obviously, if you only want to temporarily prohibit people from calling in, you can just choose the No caller access option button. The System Policy Editor is available only on the CD-ROM version of Windows 95.

Security

Security is an issue because anyone with the right password (if even that is required) can gain access to a company's network by calling into its Windows 95 DUN server. System administrators are justifiably wary of allowing users to configure their computers as servers because it leaves the whole network vulnerable.

If the Windows 95 server is on a network that includes NetWare or Windows NT servers, the system administrator can use (and may already be using) the NetWare or Windows NT servers to provide user-level, centrally controlled password protection.

Setting Up Your Computer at Home As a Guest

If you want to set up your computer at home to make the phone call and initiate the modem communications, you need to make sure that:

1. Your modem driver is configured.

2. You have set up your Dial-Up Adapter.

3. You have set up a specific dial-in connection (or *connectoid*) for your computer at work.

Undocumented

You don't have to set up the modem driver first. If it is not set up yet, a Wizard will guide you through the setup process.

STEPS

Setting Up Your Computer at Home

Step 1.   Double-click the Dial-Up Networking folder icon in the Explorer, or choose Dial-Up Networking from the Start, Programs, Accessories menu.

(continued)

STEPS *(continued)*

Setting Up Your Computer at Home

Step 2.   Double-click the Make New Connection icon in the Dial-Up Networking folder window.

Step 3.   The Make New Connection Wizard will start. If you have not set up your modem driver yet, the Install New Modem Wizard will pop up on top of the Make New Connection Wizard and ask that you do this first. Follow the steps in the Install New Modem Wizard on your own, or turn to Chapter 25 for more information.

Step 4.   In the first Make New Connection Wizard dialog box, enter a name for the computer that you will be dialing into, such as **Computer at Work**. Click Next.

Step 5.   Type the area code and number for the computer at work. Click Next.

Step 6.   Click Finish.

Step 7.   If you do not have a Dial-Up Adapter set up in your network configuration (or you have no network configured), you will be asked to install it now.

Step 8.   The Dial-Up Adapter will now be installed, along with the network protocols NetBEUI and IPX/SPX and network support software, if they have not already been installed.

You should leave these network protocols bound to your Dial-Up Adapter if you are going to use Direct Cable Connection, as discussed in Chapter 30, or if you will connect to a Windows network or a NetWare network. If you are going to connect to an Intranet at work or the Internet, you should add the Microsoft TCP/IP protocol. This is discussed in Chapter 33.

An icon for the new connectoid will appear in the Dial-Up Networking folder window with the name you entered in step 4 above. It represents your connection to the computer at the office. When you double-click the connectoid, the Connect To dialog box (shown in Figure 28-2) appears to let you initiate the phone call.

When you're connected, your DUN connectoid has an accompanying Taskbar button. To end the connection, click the Taskbar button and then click the Disconnect button. (If you have DUN 2.0, you won't have a Taskbar button; you disconnect by right-clicking the DUN icon in the Tray and clicking Disconnect.)

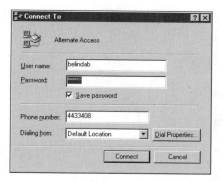

Figure 28-2: The Connect To dialog box for your Dial-Up Networking connectoid. To initiate the phone call, type your password if necessary, and then click the Connect button.

Secret

If your Save password check box is grayed out in the Connect To dialog box for your Dial-Up Networking connectoid, check to make sure that you have installed Client for Microsoft Networks. You can use the instructions provided in the *Network Installation* section of Chapter 36. There are also other reasons why the Save password check box might be dim. Refer to the *Saving your DUN connectoid passwords* section of Chapter 33 for more details.

To change the server type and other properties associated with this connectoid, right-click it in the Dial-Up Networking folder window, select Properties, and click the Server Type button. (If you have DUN 2.0, click the Server Types tab.) The Server Types properties sheet, as shown in Figure 28-3, allows you to determine, among other things, whether you will log on-to the network when you dial into the server. If you don't log onto the network, you won't have access to the resources shared by other servers on the network.

PPP is the default dial-up protocol, and if you set your Windows 95 host computer at work to use this protocol, both computers will be in sync. In the Allowed network protocols area of the dialog box, you can clear any of the protocol check boxes for protocols that you don't use. See the *Dialing into another operating system* section later in the chapter for further guidance.

Your Window 95 client computer uses your modem as a network interface card. You have to bind the proper networking protocols to the Dial-Up Adapter. If you are calling into a Unix or Windows NT TCP/IP server, you need to bind the TCP/IP protocol to the Dial-Up Adapter. To see how to do this, check out the *Bind TCP/IP to your Dial-Up Adapter* section in Chapter 33.

If you have any problems with these instructions, you can find additional help in the Microsoft Knowledge Base (of course, that assumes that you can connect to it, which is likely the problem to begin with). If you can connect to the Internet, point your browser at the document "How to Connect to a Remote Server" at http://www.microsoft.com/kb. (The article is numbered Q145843.)

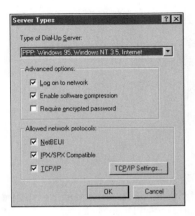

Figure 28-3: The Server Types properties sheet (in Dial-Up Networking 1.0).

General connectoid settings

You can set your connectoids to redial automatically if they don't make a connection on the first try. In the Dial-Up Networking folder window, choose Connections, Settings to display the General tab of the Dial-Up Networking dialog box, as shown in Figure 28-4. This dialog box lets you choose how often to try and how long to wait between tries.

Figure 28-4: The General tab of the Dial-Up Networking dialog box (in Dial-Up Networking 1.0).

If you connect to the Internet through a remote logon, many Internet (Winsock) applications call the connectoid specified in the Connection tab of the Internet Properties dialog box (under the Internet icon in the Control Panel) when you start the application. After launching the program, you'll see the Connect To dialog box before the application's main window is displayed. You can also double-click the connectoid (or a shortcut to it) to establish the connection first, and then load the application you'll use with the connection.

Secret

DUN connectoids have a bit of a redial problem. If you start an application such as Internet Explorer that calls the connectoid, the connectoid won't redial if it can't connect on the first try. Only if you start the connectoid first will it redial.

Microsoft released an update to Dial-Up Networking (version 2.0) in September, 1996 as part of its ISDN Accelerator Pack 1.1. If you upgraded to this software or have a later version of Windows 95, you'll have a different General properties sheet in your Dial-Up Networking dialog box, as shown in Figure 28-5.

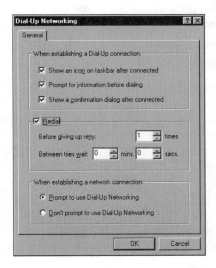

Figure 28-5: The General tab of the Dial-Up Networking dialog box (in Dial-Up Networking 2.0).

This new properties sheet allows you to dial into your computer at work without clicking the Connect button in the Connect To dialog box. In fact, if you clear the Prompt for information before dialing check box, you won't even see the Connect To dialog box (unless you haven't saved your password). You can also get rid of the connection confirmation dialog box and the connection icon in the Taskbar Tray.

Preparing for server dial-back

The server that you are dialing into might need to call you back before you can properly connect to it. This is a security feature. If server dial-back is implemented, each user has an assigned phone number (his or her home phone, for example). The server dials the phone number of the person who supposedly just tried to log in. If someone else is using your name and password, you still get the phone call at home, not the other person. Of course, this does make things difficult if you are in a hotel.

Secret

Windows 95 Dial-Up Networking wasn't built with the server dial-back feature in mind, but you can kludge it in if you are using the PPP protocol to communicate with the server. You'll need to create an additional modem string to properly set the state of your modem when making the connection.

STEPS

Configuring DUN for Dial-Back Servers

Step 1. Click the Start button, point to Settings, and click Control Panel. Double-click the Modems icon.

Step 2. Highlight your modem and click the Properties button.

Step 3. Click the Connection tab, and then click the Advanced button.

Step 4. In the Extra settings field, enter **&C0 S0=1**. Click OK twice, and then click Close.

If there are already settings in the Extra settings field, just add the new string to the end of the existing ones.

The &C0 setting keeps the PPP client active. The S0=1 setting sets your modem to auto-answer after one ring.

Dialing into another operating system

Dial-Up Networking lets you connect over the phone to a whole variety of networks, including the Internet. You can call into a computer running Windows NT Advanced Server, which allows up to 256 connections and supports IPX/SPX, NetBEUI, and TCP/IP protocols. You can also call into computers running Unix and the SLIP or PPP protocols.

If you are calling into a Windows NT, NetWare, Shiva Netmodem/LanRover, Windows for Workgroups, LAN Manager, or Unix server instead of a Windows 95 computer, you need to change the server type associated with the connectoid you created in the Setting Up Your Computer at Home steps earlier in this chapter. Right-click the new connectoid icon in the Dial-Up Networking folder window, click Properties, and then click the Server Type button (or click the Server Types tab if you have DUN 2.0).

You get to choose from PPP: Windows 95, Windows NT 3.5, Internet; NRN: NetWare Connect; SLIP Unix Connection; Windows for Workgroups and Windows NT 3.1; or CSLIP (Unix Connection with IP Header Compression).

Your Unix computer server (in some cases a remote Unix server at an Internet service provider) will use either PPP or SLIP. You need to find out which protocol it uses from your computer support staff (or ISP).

You can use Dial-Up Networking to connect to the Internet if you are calling into a dial-in Internet service provider. See Chapter 33 for more details.

Copying your DUN connectoids to another computer

You'll notice that there is nothing behind the curtain when you look for your DUN connectoids on your hard disk. The Dial-Up Networking folder looks like a regular folder, but there are no files there. This makes it a bit difficult to copy all the connectoid properties to another computer. There is no *there* there.

The connectoid values are stored in your Registry. You'll find them under HKEY_CURRENT_USER\RemoteAccess. You can export this whole branch of the Registry and take it with you to a new computer, or you can just take the parts that you need under Addresses and Profiles.

Unfortunately, this won't quite do it, because these values are associated with modem and COM port settings that are stored not in the User.dat but in the System.dat part of the Registry. The modem and COM port settings on one computer are not necessarily the same as those on another.

We suggest you use a shareware utility called Dial-Up Magic that enables you to export and import DUN values from one computer to another. You can also use Dial-Up Magic to clone a DUN connectoid and use it to create another. You'll find this shareware utility at http://ourworld.compuserve.com/homepages/techmagic/.

SLIP Server Type

Tip

The SLIP and CSLIP server types won't be available unless you install SLIP support. To do so, take the following steps:

STEPS

Installing SLIP Support

Step 1. Click the Start button, point to Settings, and then click Control Panel. Double-click the Add/Remove Programs icon, and click the Windows Setup tab.

(continued)

STEPS *(continued)*

Installing SLIP Support

Step 2. Click the Have Disk button.

Step 3. Put your Windows 95 CD-ROM in the CD-ROM drive and point to E:\Admin\Apptools\DScript (using the appropriate drive letter for your CD-ROM). If you don't have Windows 95 on a CD-ROM, you can download the SLIP support from Microsoft's web site (http://www.microsoft.com/windows/software/admintools.htm).

Step 4. Click the Install button, and then click OK.

To connect to a server using the SLIP dial-up protocol, you need to bind the TCP/IP protocol to your Dial-Up Adapter. To do so, take the steps in the *Bind TCP/IP to Your Dial-Up Adapter* section of Chapter 33.

After you have bound the TCP/IP protocol, you need to create a SLIP connection. Here's how:

STEPS

Creating a SLIP Connectoid

Step 1. Double-click the Dial-Up Networking folder icon in the Explorer, or choose Dial-Up Networking from the Start, Programs, Accessories menu.

Step 2. Double-click the Make New Connection icon in the Dial-Up Networking folder window.

Step 3. The Make New Connection Wizard starts. Give the computer that you will be dialing into a name, perhaps something like **Internet**. Click Next.

Step 4. Type the area code and phone number for the SLIP computer. Click Next.

Step 5. Click Finish.

Step 6. Right-click the new connectoid, and select Properties. Click the Configure button to display the Properties dialog box for your modem, and then click the Options tab.

Step 7. Mark the check box labeled "Bring up terminal window after dialing." This allows you to log onto your SLIP account. You will need to type your name and password when you log on. (You can avoid having to enter your name and password if you use Windows 95's scripting utility, as described in Chapter 33.) Click OK.

Creating a SLIP Connectoid

Step 8. Click the Server Type button (or click the Server Types tab if you have DUN 2.0), and display the Type of Dial-Up Server drop-down list.

Step 9. Highlight either SLIP or CSLIP depending on the capabilities of your Internet service provider or Unix server.

Step 10. If you want to change the IP address of your computer (or how it is obtained), click the TCP/IP Settings button. See Chapter 33 for more details.

Step 11. Click the OK buttons until you are back to the Dial-Up Networking folder window.

Refer to Chapter 33 to learn more about the properties of TCP/IP and connectoids to the Internet. You need to bind to the Dial-Up Adapter the protocol appropriate to the network you are dialing into. If you are dialing into different networks, you may need to bind all three protocols — IPX/SPX, NetBEUI, and TCP/IP.

Setting up your basic telephone information

Windows 95 can keep track of telephone information for multiple locations. For example, for each location you dial from, it can remember whether you have to dial an access number to get an outside line, whether your phone has call waiting, and whether the connection is local or long distance.

To edit this location-specific information, double-click the Modems icon in the Control Panel, and click the Dialing Properties button to display the Dialing Properties dialog box. Turn to Chapter 26 for a discussion of the options in this dialog box.

Your modem

Your modem was originally set up by the Install New Modem Wizard. This most likely happened automatically when you first set up Windows 95, when you set up your computer at home as a guest, or when you double-clicked the Modems icon in the Control Panel, but if you need to, you can change the properties for your modem now.

Right-click your connectoid icon in the Dial-Up Networking folder window, and choose Properties. Click the Configure button to display the Properties dialog box for your modem. Turn to Chapter 25 for details about what changes to make.

The Dial-Up Adapter

To call into your computer at work over your modem, you need to have the Dial-Up Adapter set up on both computers. It is automatically set up on your home computer when you create a new connection. It is also automatically set up on your Windows 95 computer at work when you configure it as a host. You can, however, set it up directly by following these steps:

STEPS

Setting Up the Dial-Up Adapter

Step 1. Click the Start button, point to Settings, and then click Control Panel. Double-click the Network icon.

Step 2. If you don't see Adapter in the list of network components in the Network dialog box, click the Add button.

Step 3. In the Select Network Component Type dialog box, click Adapter, and then click the Add button.

Step 4. In the Select Device dialog box, select Microsoft in the manufacturer list.

Step 5. Select Dial-Up Adapter in the Network Adapters list. Click OK twice.

The Microsoft Dial-Up Adapter and the network software component necessary to carry out remote communications are now installed. You will be asked to reboot your computer.

The default networking protocols that are bound to the Dial-Up Adapter are NetBEUI and IPX/SPX. If you need additional or different protocols, you need to install them directly. If you are going to call into an Internet service provider, you need to bind the TCP/IP protocol to your Dial-Up Adapter. See the *Bind TCP/IP to Your Network Adapter* section in Chapter 33.

After you have rebooted you computer, go back to the Control Panel and double-click the Network icon. Highlight the Dial-Up Adapter and click the Properties button. You'll see the Dial-Up Adapter Properties dialog box, as shown in Figure 28-6.

Undocumented

Microsoft has written an NDIS (Network Driver Interface Specification) 3.1 level driver for the modem/serial port. This is a low-level driver most often associated with network cards. The Dial-Up Adapter treats the modem as though it were a network card using this driver. NDIS 3.1 is a superset of NDIS 3.0, which allows multiple protocols to run on a network interface card (or, in this case, a modem) simultaneously.

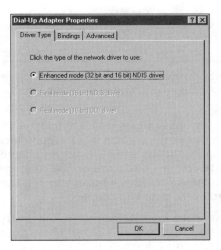

Figure 28-6: The Dial-Up Adapter Properties dialog box.

The default protocol of the Dial-Up Networking communication between two Windows 95 computers is either NetBEUI or IPX/SPX. Both of these protocols were installed when you set up the Dial-Up Adapter and are bound to it. *Bound* means that they are used to carry out the communication between the two computers. You can find out whether one or both of the protocols are bound by clicking the Bindings tab. Which protocol is actually used depends on the configuration of the computer at work.

Dialing into the Office

After you have connected your home computer's modem to your phone line, you can dial into the computer at work. Of course, the computer at work could actually be a networked modem server that acts like a Windows 95, Windows NT, or NetWare Connect server set up as a host.

STEPS

Dialing In from Home

Step 1. Double-click the Dial-Up Networking folder icon in an Explorer window, or choose Dial-Up Networking from the Start, Programs, Accessories menu.

Step 2. Double-click the connectoid for your computer at work in the Dial-Up Networking folder window. If you call work often, you might want to right-drag this icon onto the Desktop or Start button

(continued)

and choose Create Shortcut(s) Here from the context menu. That way, you will have a convenient way of accessing the computer at work.

Step 3.   The Connect To dialog box appears (unless you have DUN 2.0 and have turned off this option, which is not a good idea if you're making a connection for the first time). Type your name and password if you have set up a password on the computer at work. Mark the Save password check box if you don't want to type your password every time you connect.

Step 4.   If necessary, you can click the Dial Properties button to edit your (at home) location information at this point. There are other entry points for editing this information, but this is as good as any. See the previous section entitled *Setting up your basic telephone information* for more on this.

Step 5.   Click the Connect button.

Your computer will dial your modem and attempt to make a network connection across the phone lines to your computer at work. If all goes well, you will be networked to your work computer.

If you are in fact connected to a computer at work, you'll see its shared drives, folders, and printers in a folder window on the Desktop of your home computer.

If you have chosen the Log on to network option in the Server Types properties sheet, you will also be logged onto the network that is connected to the server you dialed into. In this case, you can access other servers on the network by following the steps in the *Accessing shared resources* section later in this chapter.

Notice in step 5 above that you had to click the Connect button. Wouldn't it be nice if Windows 95 did this for you after you double-clicked your connectoid?

There are little utilities that push the Connect button for you: Dunce, RAS+ 95, and RtvReco. You can download the latest version of RtvReco from http://www.clearlight.com/~rtvsoft.

RtvReco lets you define a button or menu item for it to click whenever it detects *any* window that might appear on your display. To suppress the dialog box that appears when you rename a file extension, for instance, you can tell RtvReco to click the Yes button when it sees a dialog box with *Rename* in its title bar that contains the string *If you change*.

You can also upgrade to the latest version of Dial-Up Networking, and you won't have to see the Connect To dialog box at all, much less click the Connect button. You'll find it hidden in the ISDN Accelerator Pack 1.1 update at http://www.microsoft.com/windows/software/isdn.htm.

Dialing In Manually

You can dial into the host computer manually. Once you make the connection, perhaps through an operator or using your credit card, you turn over the phone line to your computer. You might want to do this if you are having trouble defining an automated dialing procedure in a new location.

STEPS

Dialing In Manually

Step 1. Double-click the Dial-Up Networking folder icon in the Explorer, or choose Dial-Up Networking from the Start, Programs, Accessories menu.

Step 2. Right-click the connectoid for your computer at work in the Dial-Up Networking folder window. Click Properties.

Step 3. Click the Configure button, and then click the Options tab.

Step 4. Mark the Operator assisted or manual dial check box. Click OK twice.

Step 5. Double-click the connectoid. You will be prompted to pick up the receiver and dial the number.

Step 6. When you hear the tone from the computer, click Connect, and then hang up the phone.

Networking over a Modem

Once you have made the connection, you are another node (albeit a slow one) on the network at work. If you are just hooking two computers together, then they are networking over the modem, and that is the only network.

Undocumented

If you are calling into a Windows 95 computer acting as the host, you won't see the shared resources in your Network Neighborhood. In order to reduce the overhead on a slow link such as a modem connection, Windows 95 by default turns off the ability to browse the host computer. We show you how to turn this back on in the section entitled *Seeing shared resources*.

Accessing shared resources

You access the shared resources of the computer at work (folders, printers, and drives on the host computer) by explicitly naming the resource. Once you're connected, click the Start button, and then click Run. Type the name of the computer at work followed by the shared resource name, using the universal naming convention (UNC) — \\WorkComputer\C, for example. (When you attempt to access a shared resource, you might be required to enter a password if it is not already stored in the user-password cache on your computer, or if this is the first time you have accessed a resource that is protected by a password.)

For this method (or any method) of accessing a shared resource to work, you first need to share your resources on the host computer. See *Sharing your resources* in Chapter 36.

The UNC allows you to access resources by name, without having to map them to a drive letter on your computer. It uses two backslashes before the name of the server, host, or computer at work, and a single backslash before the resource name.

A folder window containing the resource you specified will open up on the Desktop of your home computer. You can then browse the resource to find the files or programs that you are interested in. To access other computers connected by a network to your computer at work, you can type their UNC names in the Run dialog box.

Seeing shared resources

You can configure the computer at work so that its shared resources are automatically visible to your computer at home through the Network Neighborhood. That way, you don't have to use the Run command. (To enable file and printer sharing, you need to take the steps in *Choosing network services* in Chapter 36.)

STEPS

Turning On the Browse Master

Step 1.   On the computer at work, click the Start button, point to Settings, and then click Control Panel. Double-click the Network icon.

Step 2.   Click File and printer sharing for Microsoft Networks in the network components list. Click the Properties button.

Step 3.   Browse Master should be the first item in the Properties dialog box. Its default value in the Value drop-down list is Automatic. Change this to Enabled.

Turning On the Browse Master

Step 4.   Click OK.

Step 5.   Restart Windows 95.

Step 6.   On the computer at home, double-click the connectoid for the computer at work.

Step 7.   When you're connected, double-click the Network Neighborhood icon. You'll see the shared resources of the computer at work.

Getting your e-mail when you're on the road

Using Windows Messaging to get your e-mail is the same whether you are away from the office or sitting at your desk. You can set up your portable or home computer to automatically call in so that you can check for new messages. The connection is made by Windows Messaging. You don't have to double-click the connectoid to your office computer, because you can configure Windows Messaging to use this connectoid automatically.

You need to create a Windows Messaging profile on your computer at home. If your office computer is on a network that uses Microsoft Mail, this profile should use Microsoft Mail to connect to a workgroup postoffice at work. See Chapter 32 for details.

Even if you have only one computer at work, you can configure it and the computer at home (no doubt someone else's computer) to use Microsoft Mail as your mail delivery system. The person who calls into your office computer picks up his or her e-mail from the Microsoft Mail postoffice on your computer at work.

Printing on the printer at work from home

You can print a document on a printer at work while calling in from your computer at home or on the road. The printer at work must be shared and you need to have it in your Printers folder on your home computer.

The first step is to share the printer at work. If the printer is on a Windows 95 computer, you share it by clicking the Start button, pointing to Settings, and clicking Printers to display the Printers folder window. Right-click the printer that you want to share, and click Sharing. Click the Shared As option button, and type a name for the shared printer in the Share Name field. (If the Sharing command doesn't appear, see Chapter 23.)

You also need to put the printer at work in the Printers folder on the computer at home. Double-click the Add Printer icon in the Printers folder on the computer at home. Tell the Add Printer Wizard that the printer is a network printer, and give it the pathname to the printer using a UNC name such as \\server\HP. Windows 95 will semi-automatically install the printer driver on your computer at home (if you have access to your Windows 95 CD-ROM or diskettes). See Chapter 23 for more information.

Once the printer at work is shared and you have it in your Printers folder on your computer at home, then you can simply print to it.

Faxing from work while on the road

You can use Windows Messaging to send a document from your computer at home over your modem to a shared fax/modem on your network (or computer) at work, and have that document faxed out from work. You might do this if your modem doesn't have a fax capability, if your fax/modem on your computer at home isn't compatible with Microsoft Fax, or perhaps if the company is paying the bill for faxes you send from work.

The first task is to share the fax/modem at work. The second is to configure a Windows Messaging profile on your computer at home that uses the shared fax/modem at work. For details on how to do this, turn to the section entitled *Sharing a fax/modem on a network* in Chapter 32.

Summary

You can call into a server computer over a modem from your computer at home or on the road. The server can be a Windows 95 computer, a Windows NT computer, a LAN Manager server, a NetWare server, a Unix computer, an Internet service provider, or a dedicated networked modem server. We show you:

▶ How to set up a Windows 95 computer as a host at work so you can call into it from home.

▶ How to set up your computer at home so you can call into various servers, including your Windows 95 computer at work.

▶ How to access and use shared resources on the network with Dial-Up Networking.

▶ How to use your computer at home to print on your printer at work and fax via your fax/modem at work.

Chapter 29

Calling the Bulletin Boards

In This Chapter

Windows 95 provides a way to communicate with bulletin boards and other computers over telephone lines. This terminal-to-computer style of communication, while going out of style, is still prevalent among people who use bulletin boards. We discuss:

▶ Setting up different bulletin board connections

▶ Dialing into a bulletin board

▶ Downloading a file

▶ Modifying the parameters of your bulletin board connection

▶ Capturing text to a file

▶ The differences between HyperTerminal in Windows 95 and Terminal in Windows 3.*x*

A Flash from the Past

This chapter is about using HyperTerminal, a wonderful little application that comes with Windows 95. Communication between computers comes in many different modes. Each type of communication has different applications that are best suited to its mode, and HyperTerminal is an excellent program for occasionally communicating with bulletin boards.

It wasn't too many years ago (perhaps for some readers, just a few months ago?) that using a personal computer to communicate meant working with a program such as HyperTerminal. Now, there are many other options for each communications niche.

HyperTerminal has the word *terminal* in it because it is designed around the metaphor of a terminal calling into a multi-user computer. The *hyper* part of its name means that it can do more than act as a dumb terminal. For example, you can't download files using a binary file transfer protocol such as Zmodem with a dumb terminal, but you can with HyperTerminal.

Terminal-computer communication has been around since the late '60s. It was created because computers then were expensive and needed to be shared to be cost-effective. This type of computer communication is still useful. For example, your hardware vendor may provide certain files on its computer bulletin board that you need to download. Or you might want to call into a community bulletin board hosted on another computer so that you can read messages or post your own.

When you call into a bulletin board, you are typically presented with a screen full of options. You, the user, simply send keystrokes to the remote computer that determine how the bulletin board program presents information to you. The remote computer doesn't care what kind of computer you are using. You might as well be using a terminal — that is, until you want to download or upload a file.

HyperTerminal lets you upload and download files to the bulletin board using one of six file transfer protocols. This is a handy feature that works well.

You can also use HyperTerminal to call into a commercial service provider such as CompuServe — although using CompuServe's WinCIM navigation software is a much easier approach. After all, service providers such as CompuServe are just big bulletin boards. In addition, you can use HyperTerminal to call into your local Internet service provider and run programs on the service provider's Unix computer if you have a shell (console or terminal) account. For example, you can use your service provider's Unix e-mail program to send and receive mail on the Internet.

HyperTerminal also lets you communicate with another computer over a Direct Cable Connection (DCC) — a connection through a cable on your serial or parallel port. Depending on what the other computer is, you can send files or use the computer's multi-user operating system. DCC works best if you are connecting to a Windows 95 computer.

Terminal, HyperTerminal's predecessor, was widely ignored — probably because it was too hard to use for a program that did so little and had so few file transfer protocols. Most people used other communications packages because they did quite a bit more.

HyperTerminal is not the most powerful package of its type. The authors of HyperTerminal, Hilgraeve, Inc., have more sophisticated communications software they would be happy to sell you. They assume that you will like the ease of use and features in HyperTerminal and hope that once you have gotten used to it you will want more.

HyperTerminal is easy to use and reliable. It is powerful enough for a significant percentage of the Windows user population. It doesn't have scripting, so you can't automate your sessions or your logon sequences. It won't store your passwords. It doesn't have built-in auto-answer. It doesn't have all the file transfer protocols that you might want. But it does have the basic features that make it easy to call into a bulletin board and upload or download a file occasionally.

HyperTerminal, Private Edition

Hilgraeve has made available at no cost an upgrade to HyperTerminal. You can download it from their site at http://www.hilgraeve.com. The upgrade includes three major features: automatic re-dial of busy phone numbers, Zmodem crash recovery for resuming interrupted file transfers, and better support for foreign characters.

The Private Edition makes it easier to send characters and commands directly to your modem to transfer files over a Direct Cable Connection. It supports Telnet over TCP/IP connections, and it uses the Terminal font for better compatibility with ANSI characters.

Creating Connections (Connectoids)

Most communications packages for terminal-computer communications store the names and phone numbers of the bulletin boards you call into in a list. To access this list, you have to first start the communications package and then issue a menu command.

One nifty feature of HyperTerminal is that instead of storing this information in a list, it creates an icon (and an associated file) for each bulletin board or connection that you want to call, and then displays these icons in the HyperTerminal folder window — ready for easy access. You can create a shortcut to any of these connections and place it on the Desktop. Just double-click the icon and you're off and running. (Terminal, the communications package that came with Windows 3.x, created a separate connection file for each bulletin board, but it didn't present them in as straightforward a fashion as HyperTerminal does.)

Because HyperTerminal puts the connection (referred to internally at Microsoft as a *connectoid*) in a separate file, it can store the data specific to that connection within the file. You can create a separate icon to represent each bulletin board in the HyperTerminal folder window, and then customize each connection with the settings appropriate for that bulletin board.

Here's how to create a new connectoid:

STEPS

Creating a New Connection

Step 1. Click the Start button, point to Programs, then Accessories, and then click HyperTerminal.

(continued)

Creating a New Connection

Step 2.   Double-click the icon labeled Hypertrm.exe in the HyperTerminal folder window. In the Name field of the Connection Description dialog box, type a name for the bulletin board that you want to connect to, and then choose an icon. Unlike almost all other applications in Windows 95, you can only choose icons for Hyper-Terminal connectoids from the ones shown in this list. Click OK.

Step 3.   The Phone Number dialog box, as shown in Figure 29-1, appears next. Enter the area code and the phone number (and the country code if necessary) for the bulletin board.

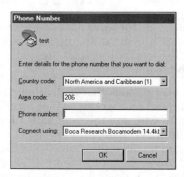

Figure 29-1: The Phone Number dialog box.

If you are going to create a connection between two nearby computers using a serial cable, don't worry about the phone numbers.

Step 4.   The default device for your connection is the modem that you have already installed and configured. You can change to another device, but if you are going to call into a bulletin board over the phone lines, you don't need to change the Connect using field. Click OK.

Undocumented

If you do want to communicate through one of your serial ports, display the Connect using drop-down list and choose which serial port to use. You need to have a null modem serial cable to connect the two computers.

Step 5.   If you are using a modem and not a serial cable, you will see the Connect dialog box shown in Figure 29-2. You can click the Dial button if you want to make a connection immediately. If you just want to save the new connection information, click Cancel, and then choose File, Save.

Creating a New Connection

Figure 29-2: The Connect dialog box.

The Modify button in the Connect dialog box lets you change the phone number and settings for the connection, as well as the modem settings. See the section entitled *Changing the Properties of a Connectoid* later in this chapter for information on changing connection settings. Turn to Chapter 25 for information on modem settings.

The Dialing Properties button lets you choose a new originating location or edit the properties associated with the phone system at the location you are dialing from. Turn to Chapter 26 for more details about location settings.

Making a Connection

If you have already created a connectoid, dialing into a bulletin board is pretty easy.

STEPS

Making a Connection

Step 1. Click the Start button, point to Programs, then Accessories, and then click HyperTerminal.

Step 2. In the HyperTerminal folder window, double-click the connectoid icon for the bulletin board that you want to call.

Step 3. Click the Dial button in the Connect dialog box. If the Connect dialog box isn't showing, click the Connect toolbar button in the HyperTerminal application window (it shows a phone). If the toolbar isn't showing, choose Call, Connect.

(continued)

Making a Connection

Undocumented

If you are connecting two Windows 95 computers through a serial cable, you don't have to take this step. After you double-click the connectoids that use the serial ports on both computers, you are connected.

Downloading a File

The ability to download files is one of the main reasons people call bulletin boards. Unfortunately, downloading a file from a bulletin board is a two-step process. In contrast, if you use a web browser such as Internet Explorer to download files from FTP (file transfer protocol) servers on the Internet, the process is quite a bit easier. When you use Internet Explorer to connect to an FTP server, you can download a file by simply clicking its name and then giving the file a name and location on your computer.

STEPS

Downloading a File

Step 1.   Call into a bulletin board (see the previous section, *Making a Connection*).

Step 2.   On the bulletin board, use the onscreen menus to choose a file to download and specify a file transfer protocol. If the Zmodem file transfer protocol is available on the bulletin board, it is a good choice. The file transfer protocols supported by HyperTerminal are 1K Xmodem, Xmodem, Ymodem, Ymodem-G, Zmodem, and Kermit. (These protocols are described after these steps.)

Step 3.   Issue whatever command is necessary on the bulletin board to begin sending the file from the bulletin board computer.

Step 4.   Click the Receive toolbar button in the HyperTerminal application window (or choose Transfer, Receive File). In the Receive File dialog box, specify the location for the file on your computer, and choose the file transfer protocol that matches the one you told the bulletin board to use in step 2. (If you are using HyperTerminal to download files from CompuServe, you have to use a binary file format such Xmodem, Ymodem, or Kermit instead of CompuServe B, because HyperTerminal doesn't support this protocol.) Click OK.

Downloading a File

Step 5. If the file transfer protocol requires a filename on your computer for the downloaded file, you will be prompted for it. The file transfer then completes automatically.

You can also send (upload) a file to a bulletin board using a slight variation on these steps. The Send button is just to the left of the Receive button on the toolbar.

Among HyperTerminal's file transfer protocols, Xmodem is the most basic. This standard and somewhat slow protocol transfers files in 128-byte blocks. 1K Xmodem transfers files in 1024-byte blocks. This protocol is really the same thing as Ymodem. You can use Ymodem-G, a variation on Ymodem, if your modem and modem driver support hardware error correction. Zmodem is the file transfer protocol of choice for most bulletin boards. It is relatively fast and reliable, and it uses a variable block size. Kermit is used at academic computer centers and on Digital Equipment Corp. VAX systems and some IBM mainframes. It is slow.

Changing the Properties of a Connectoid

The properties associated with a given connection include the phone number, the type of terminal emulation, how many lines of text are buffered (allowing you to scroll back to display them), and how text files are transferred between your computer and the bulletin board.

You can get at these values in four different ways:

1. Right-click the icon for the connectoid in the HyperTerminal folder window, and choose Properties.

2. Double-click the connectoid icon, and then choose File, Properties.

3. Double-click the connectoid icon, click the Connect toolbar button (the phone), and then click the Modify button.

4. Double-click the connectoid icon, and then click the Properties button at the right end of the toolbar.

All of these steps take you to the Properties dialog box for your connectoid.

Changing the phone number and modem properties

HyperTerminal stores the properties for a connectoid in the Properties dialog box, as shown in Figure 29-3. The Phone Number tab duplicates much of what you see in the Phone Number dialog box, which appears when you are creating a new connection. Two additional options are the

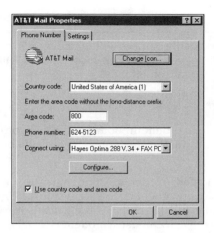

Figure 29-3: The Phone Number tab of the Properties dialog box for a connectoid.

Change Icon button, which lets you change the icon for the connectoid, and the Configure button, which brings you to the Properties dialog box for the modem. (See Chapter 25 for a detailed discussion of modem properties sheets.)

Setting terminal emulation and buffer size

The Settings tab of the Properties dialog box for a connectoid, shown in Figure 29-4, lets you change how the function keys are used in terminal emulation, which terminal you are going to emulate, how large a backward scroll buffer to maintain, and the ASCII properties values.

Various terminal emulations can use the Ctrl, arrow, and function keys to control how text is displayed and manipulated on the bulletin board computer. If you want these keys to operate in this fashion, choose Terminal keys.

You can choose from seven terminal emulation types: ANSI, Auto detect, Minitel (common in France), TTY, Viewdata (common in the UK), VT100, and VT52. You can change some terminal settings in all the terminal emulation modes other than Auto detect. Click the Terminal Setup button after you choose a terminal emulation to change terminal-specific settings. For most connections, you should set terminal emulation to Auto detect, VT100, or ANSI.

The Backscroll buffer lines field determines how many lines of an ongoing communication you can review in the HyperTerminal application window by scrolling back with the vertical scrollbar or by pressing the up arrow or Page Up key. The maximum is 500.

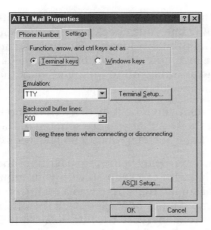

Figure 29-4: The Settings tab of the Properties dialog box for a connectoid. Choose whether the Ctrl, arrow, and function keys are sent to the bulletin board or used by Windows. Pick a terminal to emulate, set how many lines back you can scroll, and choose whether your speaker beeps three times when the bulletin board sends a Ctrl+G.

If you want your computer to notify you when it successfully connects or disconnects from a bulletin board, mark the "Beep three times when connecting or disconnecting" check box.

ASCII text handling

Click the ASCII Setup button in the Settings tab of the Properties dialog box for a connectoid to set the parameters for sending and displaying text information. The ASCII Setup dialog box is shown in Figure 29-5.

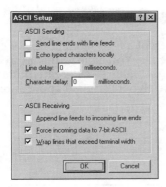

Figure 29-5: The ASCII Setup dialog box. Different bulletin boards send text to you in different ways. Use this dialog box to make up for ASCII miscommunication.

Tip

If the text you are receiving from a bulletin board is writing over itself, mark the Append line feeds to incoming line ends check box. If you want to display only ASCII text — just the printable lower 128 characters in the ANSI character set — mark the Force incoming data to 7-bit ASCII check box. If the lines of text you're receiving are going off to the right, mark the Wrap lines that exceed terminal width check box.

If you are not seeing your text when you type it in, mark the Echo typed characters locally check box. If the text that you are sending to the bulletin board is writing over itself, mark the Send line ends with line feeds check box.

You set the Line delay and Character delay values to make sure that the computer you are communicating with can keep up with your input. Some older time-sharing computers assumed that there was a real person typing the text, so they couldn't take rapid input of ASCII data. If the other computer is not receiving all of your text, increase the line delay (if the other computer is line-oriented) and/or the character delay.

Capturing Incoming Text to a File

You might want to keep a record of your communications sessions or just capture text that you're receiving from a bulletin board. To do this, start by choosing Transfer, Capture Text in the HyperTerminal application window. The default capture file is C:\Program Files\Accessories\HyperTerminal\ CAPTURE.TXT. A Notepad icon appears in the HyperTerminal folder window as soon as you click the Start button in the Capture Text dialog box.

You can close the capture file at any time by choosing Transfer, Capture Text, Stop in the HyperTerminal application window.

If the bulletin board computer echoes your keystrokes (that is, sends them back to you), these echoed keystrokes are also captured in the capture file.

Answering Incoming Data Calls

HyperTerminal doesn't really have much of a host mode, but you can tell your modem to answer incoming data calls. You have to tell it directly by typing the commands **ATA** or **ATS0=1** (or higher for a greater number of rings before the modem picks up) in the HyperTerminal application window. Here are the steps:

STEPS

Answering the Phone

Step 1.   Click the Start button, point to Programs, then Accessories, and then click HyperTerminal. Double-click HyperTrm.exe icon in the HyperTerminal folder window. HyperTerminal starts and displays

Answering the Phone

the Connection Description dialog box to ask you for a name for the new connectoid.

Step 2. If you have the standard version of HyperTerminal, you have to type a name in the Name box before you can click the Cancel button. Just type any name to create a phony connection, click Cancel, and then click Cancel again when the Phone Number dialog box appears. If you have the Private Edition, you can click Cancel in the Connection Description dialog box without typing anything.

Step 3. Choose File, Properties. In the Connect using drop-down list, choose Direct to Com X (where X is the port your modem is connected to).

Step 4. Click the Configure button. Verify the settings in the Port Settings tab, and then click OK.

Step 5. Click the Settings tab, and then click the ASCII Setup button.

Step 6. Mark the check boxes labeled "Send line ends with line feeds" and "Echo typed characters locally."

Step 7. Click OK, and then click OK again. You can now type AT commands. You can use **AT** or **ATS0=x** to answer the phone.

Step 8. Quit HyperTerminal. When you are prompted "Save session *name*?," click Yes if you want to save the session so that you can use AT commands at another time.

If you create a connectoid in step 2, you can save all settings for the next time you want to answer the phone manually with HyperTerminal (either version). There are more than 50 articles in the Microsoft Knowledge Base referring to HyperTerminal. You can check them out by going to http://www.microsoft.com/kb.

HyperTerminal versus Terminal

Microsoft shipped Terminal with Windows 3.1*x*. You would expect that HyperTerminal would be an upgrade of Terminal. It is, but it is also a newly designed product.

Terminal gave you three terminal emulations: TTY (very basic hard-copy terminal), VT100, and VT52 (these last two are Digital Equipment Corp. standards). HyperTerminal gives you six terminal emulations (or seven if you count Auto detect). Terminal supported three modem types in addition to letting you type your own initialization strings. HyperTerminal supports hundreds of modems directly. Once you set up your modem, these settings can be used by any communications package that knows enough to take advantage of this capability, which is built into the operating system.

Terminal gave you two binary file transfer protocols, Xmodem/CRC and Kermit. HyperTerminal comes with six: 1K Xmodem, Xmodem, Ymodem, Ymodem-G, Zmodem, and Kermit. Zmodem is the protocol used most widely to transfer files between personal computers and bulletin boards.

The scrollback buffer size can be 500 lines in HyperTerminal. Its maximum size in Terminal was 399 lines.

HyperTerminal creates separate files/icons for each connection. Double-click the icon for a given bulletin board and you are ready to connect. Terminal created a file for each different connection, but it was difficult to set up a folder of icons that allowed you to quick access to the files. You had to create a program group and then drag and drop the *trm* files that Terminal created for each connection into the group. Windows 95 makes this interface obvious.

In Terminal, you could define function keys (buttons at the bottom of the Terminal window) to carry out a series of commands, such as logging in and sending your name and password. HyperTerminal doesn't let you define function keys. HyperTerminal has a toolbar, which gives you a one-click interface to frequently used menu commands. Terminal only gave you a menu bar.

Terminal allowed you to send commands directly to your modem for troubleshooting. Windows 95 has a help-based modem troubleshooter. You have to create a connectoid in order to be able to send commands to your modem with HyperTerminal.

Summary

Communicating with bulletin boards requires that, for the most part, you turn your computer into a terminal that can upload and download files.

▶ You can use HyperTerminal, a little application that Microsoft bundles with Windows 95, to communicate with bulletin boards.

▶ We show you how to set up HyperTerminal for each bulletin board that you want to dial into.

▶ We show you how to download files from a bulletin board.

▶ We compare HyperTerminal with its previous incarnation — Terminal.

Chapter 30

Laptop to Desktop

In This Chapter

▶ Easily connecting two computers using a serial or parallel cable

▶ LapLink — the software that set the original standard for transferring files

▶ DOS Interlnk — Microsoft's first attempt at serial/parallel cable networking

▶ Direct Cable Connection — Windows 95 serial/parallel cable networking

▶ What to expect in the way of file transfer rates between Windows 95 computers

▶ Using a serial or parallel cable to give your laptop or other computer direct access to your network

▶ Setting up a parallel cable network that gives you much faster communication speeds than you would expect from ordinary parallel ports

▶ Comparing LapLink for Windows 95 with Direct Cable Connection

Connecting Two Computers

You can physically connect two computers using a serial or parallel cable, or even infrared transmitters/receivers. Depending on the software you use to drive the connection, the two computers may be limited to just transferring files. With more powerful software, one computer can use the resources (such as hard disk, files, and printers) of the other as though these resources were directly connected to it.

LapLink for DOS — a history

For years, Traveling Software has "owned" the file-transfer franchise with its LapLink program. LapLink was the first popular software that allowed you to connect two computers using an inexpensive serial or parallel cable and easily transfer files back and forth.

All computers have a parallel port built in (some have two or three) and almost all have one or two serial ports. These ports are communication devices. Add a cable and file transfer software that's both quick and simple to use, and you've got yourself a winner.

LapLink's competition in the file-transfer business was the floppy diskette. Traveling Software's first task was to make LapLink quicker and easier to use than a floppy diskette. That was a technical hurdle, but not a high one.

One of LapLink's strengths (in addition to its speed) was its intuitive user interface. You got to see your directories and files in full-screen view. You could simply click a file to copy it from one computer to the other. No typing commands. No searching around with a one-line-high window (such as a DOS command line) to find your file.

Traveling Software did not develop a network based on the serial or parallel port. Perhaps company officials felt that the speeds of these communications devices were too slow. Perhaps they didn't want to dilute their marketing message. But while the DOS version of LapLink competed well against the floppy diskette, competing against Ethernet was a different story.

Interlnk — Microsoft's cable network

Operating systems such as MS-DOS and Windows 95 already have the built-in ability to transfer files between the hard disk and floppy diskette, between directories, between hard disks, and between RAM and the hard disks. You might think an obvious extension of the operating system would be to allow file transfer between two computers — especially when the communications ports are already built into the computers.

Microsoft's first foray in this direction was the Interlnk program. (Interlnk is the DOS eight-character mode spelling for Interlink.)

Interlnk is a DOS program (actually two DOS programs — Interlnk.exe for the guest computer and Intersrv.exe for the host computer) that allows you to connect two computers using a serial or parallel cable and then treat the host computer's hard disks as though they were additional local hard disks belonging to the guest computer. This allows the guest computer to treat the connected computers as if they were one system.

Unlike LapLink, which allows either computer to be in charge, Interlnk defines one computer as a *guest* and one as a *host*. The guest runs the show. The host simply provides the guest with its hard disks to be used as the guest determines. It sits there passively responding to the guest's commands. You type all of the commands on the guest computer.

Treating two computers as one is a much more powerful metaphor than the file-transfer metaphor. You can do anything with two computers that you can with one. The only problem is that the hard disks of the host computer are available only through a relatively slow connection. Microsoft apparently felt this speed penalty was not significant enough to offset the benefit of the networking model.

Unlike LapLink, Interlnk can run programs on the guest that are stored as executable files on the host. You can also transfer files. There isn't a nice user interface built in, just DOS, but you can use any DOS shell, even DOSSHELL, which comes free with DOS 6.*x*. This gives you a front end for file transfers that is similar to LapLink, and at no additional cost.

Interlnk is a network. Specifically, it's a *zero slot network*, that is, a network without a network card. And because it doesn't have a dedicated network card, it is a relatively slow network.

Here are some of Interlnk's downsides:

■ You have to install Interlnk.exe in the guest computer's Config.sys file — where it stays in memory.

■ Interlnk doesn't offer any security.

■ Interlnk is quite a bit slower than LapLink if you use the serial ports and a serial cable.

Microsoft never heavily promoted Interlnk, and it came out after the company's emphasis had shifted to Windows. Still, it's a useful and very inexpensive product. Too bad you never heard about it. You might call it a DOS 6.*x* secret.

Undocumented

You can use Interlnk to connect a DOS computer and a Windows 95 computer. You just use Intersvr in MS-DOS mode (it doesn't run in a DOS window). Interlnk.exe and Intersvr.exe are stored on your Windows 95 CD-ROM in the \Other\Oldmsdos folder.

You need to reconfigure Interlnk to run in a DOS window. Right-click it, choose Properties, click the Program tab, click the Advanced button, and clear the MS-DOS mode check box.

You can get help on how to run Interlnk in the DOS help file, which is stored in the same Oldmsdos folder on your CD-ROM. You can run the DOS help program from the CD-ROM if you like. You need to open up a DOS window focused on this folder, and then type Help and press Enter. You can use your mouse to navigate to the Interlnk help entry.

Direct Cable Connection

Windows 95 makes it easy to directly connect two computers using a serial or parallel cable. That's because Windows 95 comes with Direct Cable Connection (DCC), which is a serial and parallel port network.

DCC is Interlnk taken to the next level. Like Interlnk, one computer is the guest (presumably a laptop computer that you've brought into the office) and the other is the host. DCC adds the ability to connect not only to the host but to the other computers or servers on the network to which the host is attached.

Because DCC is a network, it uses the built-in Windows 95 network protocols to provide the communications link between the guest and both the host and the network connected to the host. You can use NetBEUI (Microsoft's peer-to-peer networking protocol), IPX/SPX (Novell's NetWare protocol), and/or TCP/IP (the protocol used in Unix networks and/or with dial-up Internet connections). Both IPX/SPX and TCP/IP are routeable, so you can communicate across network routing systems to the wider network.

DCC's user interface is a folder window that displays the shared resources (drives, folders, or printers) on the host. You don't have to learn how to use a different set of conventions. The beauty of integrating this kind of capability into the operating system is that you already know how to use it.

When you use DCC, Windows 95 treats other computers and servers networked to your computer like close friends. You can see the files and folders on hard drives that are shared. On your guest computer, you can run programs that reside as executable files on other computers. These programs are loaded into your computer's memory.

Your computer can easily find documents that are stored on other computers. And, of course, you can easily transfer files back and forth, updating older files to the latest versions.

Speed

DCC's speed varies depending on whether you are using serial or parallel port communications. Serial communications can be quite slow, to say the least. If your computer has the older or less expensive serial ports that use the 8250 or 16450 universal asynchronous receiver/transmitter (UART), you are limited to speeds of up to 57,600 bits per second (bps). (A UART is the chip that drives the serial port.) Most new computers come with 16550 UARTs or better. These chips can be driven at up to 115,200 bps.

Unfortunately, DCC can't give you the 14 kilobytes per second (Kbps) file transfer speed that the 115,200 bps rate would imply (115,200/(1024 x 8)). DCC is slower than LapLink for Windows 95 on a serial cable.

Undocumented

Parallel ports come in a number of varieties. New computers have incorporated enhanced standards for parallel ports, known as EPP or ECP (see the *Parallel ports and cables* section later in this chapter for a full explanation). EPP/ECP ports can facilitate very high speed communications between computers — approaching the speed that is available from dedicated networking cards. You can reach speeds of 120 Kbps with the appropriate cable and automatic data compression that is built into Windows 95 for parallel ports. At these speeds, networking over parallel cables is about a third as fast as dedicated 10 megabit (Mb) Ethernet cards, without the cost of an Ethernet card.

Although they don't have a reputation for speed, the older parallel ports still have better speed performance than serial ports. Windows 95 has enhanced parallel port software drivers that allow computers with standard parallel ports (4-bit unidirectional and 8-bit bi-directional) connedted with a standard bi-directional parallel cable to network at speeds that are often quite acceptable — not just for file transfer, but for data and program sharing, too.

Setup

Direct Cable Connection is not installed unless you did a Custom setup when you installed Windows 95 or you installed DCC through the Add/ Remove Programs icon in the Control Panel. During a Custom setup, you must choose Communications in the Components dialog box and then specifically mark the Direct Cable Connection check box.

If you didn't install Direct Cable Connection when you set up Windows 95, you can take the following steps to do so now:

STEPS

Installing Direct Cable Connection

Step 1.   Click the Start button, point to Settings, and then click Control Panel.

Step 2.   Double-click the Add/Remove Programs icon, and then click the Windows Setup tab.

Step 3.   Click Communications, and then click the Details button.

Step 4.   Mark the Direct Cable Connection check box.

Step 5.   Click the OK button in the Communications dialog box and in the Add/Remove Programs Properties dialog box.

If you install Direct Cable Connection, you will also automatically install Dial-Up Networking (DUN) and networking in general. Direct Cable Connection is really just a variant of Dial-Up Networking. It is a dial-up network that doesn't require that you dial up (or have a network card).

DUN is discussed in Chapter 28. Installing DUN during Windows 95 Setup or later from the Add/Remove Programs icon automatically configures the network protocols necessary to run DCC. You can always change these protocols to reconfigure DUN, and thereby also reconfigure DCC.

Secret

The Network Neighborhood icon appears on your Desktop when you install DCC. If you remove it by using TweakUI or the System Policy Editor, or directly by editing the Registry, you can no longer use DCC.

Configuration

To access Direct Cable Connection, click your Start button, point to Programs, then Accessories, and finally click Direct Cable Connection.

The first time you use DCC, the Direct Cable Connection Wizard pops up, as shown in Figure 30-1, and helps you configure DCC.

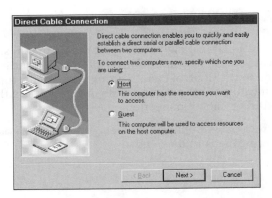

Figure 30-1: The Direct Cable Connection Wizard. Run the Wizard on both your host and guest computer.

The DCC Wizard identifies the serial and parallel ports that are not already in use and can be used for communication, as shown in Figure 30-2. You can pick from among the available ports. If you add ports later, you can rerun the Wizard and ask it to check for new ports.

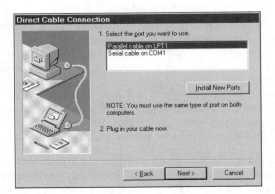

Figure 30-2: Click the Install New Ports button if you have installed new serial or parallel ports since the last time you ran the DCC Wizard.

After you click Next in the dialog box shown in Figure 30-2, the Wizard either brings you to the final Wizard dialog box (shown in Figure 30-3), or, if you haven't yet enabled file and printer sharing, it brings you to a dialog box that contains a File and Print Sharing button. Click this button to configure sharing (see the *Sharing your resources* section of Chapter 36), and then click Next. (If you click Next without enabling sharing, the Wizard warns you that you're setting up DCC without sharing.) In the final Wizard dialog box, you can set a password that is required to connect the guest to the host computer. You can also click Cancel at any time during the process to forget the whole thing.

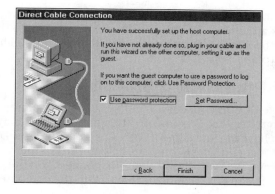

Figure 30-3: Mark the Use password protection check box to require a password to get access to the host computer.

Network configuration

When DCC is installed, Dial-Up Networking is also installed. The default installation is shown in Figure 30-4. If your host computer isn't connected to a network, you will not need to add other protocols or change this configuration.

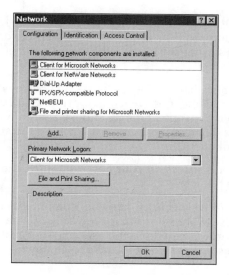

Figure 30-4: The Dial-Up Networking network configuration. All the components of Dial-Up Networking have been installed. The network configuration must be the same on both the guest and the host computer. By default, it will be.

If you want your guest computer to be a full-fledged member of the network to which your host is attached, you may need to add protocols to the Dial-Up Adapter. Turn to the *Network Installation* section of Chapter 36 for instructions on how to do this.

Installing all of the right protocols

If you are trying to use DCC to connect a Windows 95 guest computer to a Windows 95 host computer that is connected to a network, you may experience problems if you haven't bound the IPX/SPX protocol to your Dial-Up Adapter on both the host and guest computer. If you see the messages "Verifying Username and Password" and then "Disconnect" on the guest computer, the NetBIOS may not have been able to find the computer names on the host.

To correct this problem, install and bind the IPX/SPX protocol to the Dial-Up Adapter on both the host and guest computer. You can find further discussion about this and other DCC issues on the Windows95 Direct Cable Connect Problem Page at http://www.tecno.demon.co.uk/dcc.htm.

Sharing comes first

If you want your guest computer to see anything on the Windows 95 host computer or on other computers on the network, you have to share their resources. When the guest computer connects to the host, a folder window displaying the shared resources of the host appears on the guest computer's Desktop.

To enable the host to share its resources, file and printer sharing for Microsoft Networks (or file and printer sharing for NetWare Networks) must be installed. File and printer sharing for Microsoft Networks is installed by default when you install DCC.

Furthermore, you must actually share some resources on your host computer. To do this, right-click the folder, drive icon, or printer icon you want to share, choose Sharing from the context menu, choose Shared As in the Sharing tab of the Properties dialog box, and type a name for the shared resource (and an optional comment).

Once you have shared some resources on your host computer, the guest computer will be able to see them.

If the host computer has user-level security (the host computer is connected to a Windows NT or NetWare server that keeps a user database), you need to both share the resources and add to the user list the guest user(s) who will be allowed to access them. To do this, take the following steps:

Sharing with User-Level Security

Step 1. On the host computer, open an Explorer or folder window that contains your shared drive, printer, and/or folder.

Step 2. Right-click the resource, and then click Sharing in the context menu.

Step 3. Click the Sharing tab in the Properties dialog box for the resource, mark the Shared As option button, type a name (if different) for the resource, and then click the Add button.

Step 4. In the Add Users dialog box, click the names of the guest(s) who will be allowed to access the resources on the host computer.

Step 5. Choose the desired access type.

Step 6. Click OK buttons until you are out of the Properties dialog box for the resource.

Browsing the host

Secret

By default, the Windows 95 host computer doesn't show up in your Network Neighborhood if you double-click the Network Neighborhood icon on your Desktop. You also won't be able to see other computers on the network in the Network Neighborhood. If you want to get to them (and their shared resources) you have to type their UNC names in the Find Computer dialog box (click the Start button, point to Find, and then click Computer).

Microsoft turned off the capability for DCC (and Dial-Up Networking) to see or *browse* the host or the network because they felt this would slow DCC down too much. If you browse, your Windows 95 computer must update lots of information about disks, folders, and files that are on the host computer and on the network connected to the host computer.

You can turn the browsing feature back on and see for yourself if it is too slow for you. To do this, take these steps on your host computer:

Forcing Browsing with DCC

Step 1. On your Windows 95 host computer, click the Start button, point to Settings, and then click Control Panel.

Step 2. Double-click the Network icon, highlight File and printer sharing for Microsoft networks, and then click the Properties button. This will bring up the dialog box shown in Figure 30-5.

(continued)

Forcing Browsing with DCC

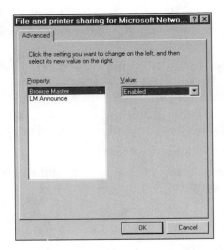

Figure 30-5: The Properties dialog box for file and printer sharing for Microsoft Networks.

Step 3. Highlight Browse Master and then choose Enabled in the Value drop-down list.

Step 4. Click the OK button in this dialog box and in the Network dialog box.

Step 5. Restart your computer for the change to take effect.

Now you will be able to "browse" the Windows 95 host and the network from your guest computer. There is one problem, however. If the Windows 95 host is also configured as a Dial-Up Networking server, you can dial in from a Dial-Up Networking client computer, and the host computer will pick up the phone. When you do this, the Browse Master function will still be enabled to let you browse the host and the network, but it will be enabled for a dial-up connection, which is much slower. A serial DCC connection is also slow, but it isn't slow enough to cause a problem with browsing, at least when the Windows 95 host is not connected to another network.

Secret

You can't see the guest from the host, even if you enable the Browse Master on the guest. The host will only find the network the guest is attached to, and it won't recognize the fact that there is a guest computer networked to it.

Microsoft has prepared a document to help you troubleshoot your connection to your host computer. You can find it in the Knowledge Base at http://www.microsoft.com/kb/articles/q134/3/04.htm.

Connected to what?

The fact that DCC is a network has manifold implications. While you might be interested in just hooking your laptop to your desktop computer, you can actually accomplish much more.

You can use DCC to connect directly to a computer running Windows 95. You can also connect indirectly through the network to a NetWare server computer, to a Windows NT server, to other computers running Windows 95, or to other computers on the network.

If you want to connect through the network to the NetWare server, be sure to bind the IPX/SPX protocol to the Dial-Up Adapter on your guest computer — your laptop perhaps. IPX/SPX and NetBEUI are the protocols that are initially bound to the Dial-Up Adapter when you install DCC.

You can also connect indirectly to a Windows NT server through a Windows 95 computer if the Windows 95 computer is connected to the Windows NT computer on a network. Just use DCC and whatever protocol your Windows 95 host computer is using to talk to the Windows NT computer — probably NetBEUI, but it could be IPX/SPX.

Running Direct Cable Connection

You run DCC (if you have already set it up) by clicking the Start button, pointing to Programs, then Accessories, and then clicking Direct Cable Connection. (If you use DCC a lot, you can easily put a shortcut to it on your Desktop.) Starting DCC displays the Direct Cable Connection dialog box, as shown in Figure 30-6. You can also configure (or reconfigure) DCC in this dialog box, which really means that you can change it from guest to host (or host to guest) and change which port it is using. Click Connect to send a request over the cable to connect to the computer at the other end. You need to run DCC on both the guest and the host computer.

Click the Listen button on the host computer to begin polling for the guest. Click the Connect button on the guest to begin trying to connect to the host. Once the connection is made, the host's shared drives and folders, as well as the shared resources of whatever other network the host is connected to, are available to the guest in the shared resources window. Furthermore, if you double-click the Network Neighborhood icon on the guest's Desktop, you will be able to see the resources available to you if you have set the Browse Master to Enabled on the host computer. (See the Forcing Browsing with DCC steps in the *Browsing the host* section earlier in this chapter.)

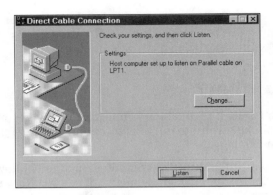

Figure 30-6: The Direct Cable Connection dialog box. On the host computer, the dialog box contains a Listen button. On the guest computer, it contains a Connect button. If you want to invoke the DCC Wizard, click the Change button.

The guest is treated as any other node on the network (except for the fact that the host can't see it). The security provisions of the network are enforced, and the guest may be required to provide a password to connect to the Windows 95 host computer.

Accessing the host

As soon as you make a successful connection with DCC, you will see the host's shared resources in a window on the guest computer. You can double-click any of the shared folders (or drives) to display the contents of the resource in a folder window.

You won't see drive icons in the shared resource window, even if you have shared the whole disk drive on the host. You'll see folder icons used to represent drives instead. This is true even if you browse the host with the Network Neighborhood.

Undocumented

You can map a networked resource (which may be a complete drive or perhaps just a folder) to a local drive letter. A networked drive icon will then appear in the Network Neighborhood if you enabled Browse Master on the host computer.

Undocumented

If you disconnect from the host, the folders or folder views of the host that are displayed on your guest don't automatically close. They just aren't connected to anything anymore. As soon as you reconnect to the host, these folders become active again.

You can drag a shortcut to a file, folder, or application from the host to the guest's Desktop or to any folder on the guest computer. Double-click the shortcut icon to open its target. If you double-click the shortcut icon, but there is no active connection to the host, you won't force DCC to activate and connect to the host. Instead, you will get the message shown in Figure 30-7.

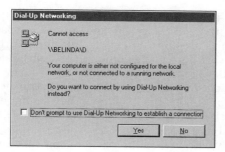

Figure 30-7: The Dial-Up Networking error message. You can see the connection between Dial-Up Networking and DCC. DCC doesn't automatically make a connection, and neither does Dial-Up Networking.

As soon as you click No, the message shown in Figure 30-8 appears to remind you that you need to make the network resource available.

Figure 30-8: The Problem with Shortcut message box. The shortcut can't find the connection to the host.

Serial ports

You can use DCC with a null modem serial cable or a LapLink serial cable. (See Chapter 25 for a discussion of null modem cables.)

LapLink comes with a blue serial cable and a yellow parallel cable. Both of the LapLink cables are about 8 feet long. Traveling Software sells these cables separately and bundled with its LapLink software. You can use them with DCC and Interlnk without any problem. You might want to get some longer cables, but they will be heavier to carry around.

Parallel ports and cables — one-third the speed of 10Mb Ethernet

There are five types of parallel ports: 4-bit, 8-bit, semi 8-bit, EPP, and ECP. Most PCs have 4-bit or 8-bit parallel ports. Many portables with the Intel 386 SL chipset have EPP ports. Computers that support the full IEEE 1284 parallel port specification (this includes all new computers) have ECP parallel ports.

- **Standard parallel ports: 4-bit, 8-bit, semi 8-bit.** Almost every PC since the IBM PC-1 has come with an ordinary, 25-pin D-connector parallel port. These low-speed ports are fine for sending output to a printer (which is usually the slowest device in a computer system). But when you're transferring data between two PC parallel ports — using a LapLink cable or something similar — the speed of data transfer varies. While 4-bit ports can output data 8 bits at a time, they can input data only 4 bits at a time, which is about 40 kilobytes per second (KB/sec.). Eight-bit ports can output and input 8 bits (80 KB/sec. or more). Semi 8-bit ports can too, but only with more sophisticated software and peripherals.

- **EPP ports.** The *enhanced parallel port* (EPP) was developed by Intel, Xircom, Zenith, and other companies that planned to exploit two-way communication with external devices. Some laptops built since mid-1991 have EPP ports. One source estimates that 80 percent of Intel 386SL and 486SL portables support EPP version 1.7, the first widely used version.

- **ECP ports.** At the same time that Intel and others developed the EPP port, Microsoft and Hewlett-Packard were developing a spec called ECP — the *extended capabilities port*. It has about the same high-speed, two-way throughput as an EPP port, but it can use DMA (direct memory access) and a small buffer to provide smoother performance in a multitasking environment, which is why Microsoft supports ECP over EPP.

Both the EPP and the ECP specs were defined by the IEEE 1284 committee in 1993. Chipsets that support 1284 (and therefore can operate in ECP mode or in a EPP 1284 mode) started appearing in PCs in 1994.

Four-bit ports are capable of effective transfer rates of 40–80 KB/sec., while 8-bit ports can handle between 80–150 KB/sec. ECP/EPP ports can sustain rates of 300 KB/sec. Unfortunately, just because a port can sustain this speed doesn't necessarily mean you will get file transfer rates at these speeds.

If your computers have ECP or EPP parallel ports, they can sustain about one-third of Ethernet link speeds when networked together with DCC. (Standard 10Mb Ethernet networks commonly deliver an actual throughput of 350–400 KB/sec.) This means that with a proper cable, you may not need to buy Ethernet cards to link together two computers with ECP or EPP parallel ports.

If you have the LapLink cable package (about $15.95), you already have an 8-foot basic bi-directional parallel cable. This cable is fine for 4-bit ports found on most older computers.

Another type of cable, known as a *universal cable module* (UCM), contains active electronics that speed two-way communications through the ECP/EPP enhanced parallel ports. Because there are several incompatible enhanced parallel ports in the market, the universal cable is key. It detects your port hardware and software and automatically transfers data at the highest available rate.

Microsoft has licensed software code to support the UCM technology
from a small firm called Parallel Technologies Inc. and incorporated it into
Windows 95 as part of Direct Cable Connection. To purchase Parallel
Technologies' UCM cable (called the DirectParallel™ Universal Cable),
contact Parallel Technologies Sales at 800-789-4784 or visit their web site,
http://www.lpt.com/lpt.

More on speed

Undocumented

We have made an effort to quantify the file-transfer speeds that you can
obtain using the various cables and ports and to compare them with
LapLink for Windows. The results are shown in Table 30-1. File transfer
speeds depend greatly on the compressibility of the files and the speed of
the computers to which you connect. We transferred only already zipped
files to eliminate compression efficiency as a variable. The file transfer tests
used one 486-66 computer with 16MB of RAM and an IDE drive and one
Pentium 166 MHz computer with 32MB of RAM and SCSI drives.

Table 30-1	File Transfer Speeds	
Port	*LapLink for Windows 95*	*DCC*
Serial	22 Kbps	11.5 Kbps
4-bit parallel	46 Kbps	76 Kbps
ECP/UCM	N/A	120 Kbps

Undocumented

We used the Device Manager to set the serial ports at 115,200 bits per
second, both in the port settings and in the modem settings. Serial ports
default to 9600 bits per second, and you have to change these defaults in
order to speed up a serial DCC connection. LapLink defaults to setting the
ports to 115,200 bits per second.

Notice that LapLink for Windows 95 is quite a bit faster than Direct Cable
Connection over a serial cable. It is our understanding (from Microsoft
support personnel) that Traveling Software has a patent for a particularly
fast method of transferring data for a serial cable using more than the
normal data lines. Microsoft does not use this technology. No wonder
Microsoft strongly encourages you to use the parallel port for DCC.

The ECP ports with the UCM cable are quite a bit faster than the other
means of file transfer, but only a third as fast as the potential speed of the
ECP ports. This makes file transfer over ECP ports and a UCM cable slower
than dedicated Ethernet cards.

Watch the interrupts

Secret

DCC over parallel ports uses the interrupts assigned to those ports. LPT1 most often uses Interrupt 7, and LPT2 most often uses Interrupt 5. Parallel printers don't really use these interrupts, so it usually doesn't matter if something else in your computer grabs them first.

Sound cards and CD-ROMs often use these interrupts. Because the parallel ports don't really use them, Windows 95 doesn't report a conflict between the ports and the sound card or CD-ROM.

If you use DCC over a parallel port and there is a conflict with that port's interrupt, DCC will be slowed down by a factor of three. To prevent this from happening (if you can), you need to be sure that Interrupt 7 is not used by some other card if you are using LPT1 for DCC. The same holds for Interrupt 5 and LPT2.

To find out if there is a conflict, take the following steps:

STEPS

Determining If an Interrupt Conflict Exists

Step 1.   Click the Start button, point to Settings, and then click Control Panel.

Step 2.   Double-click the System icon, and then click the Device Manager tab.

Step 3.   While Computer is highlighted in the Device Manager, click Properties.

Step 4.   From the list of interrupt requests in the Resources tab, you can determine if 7 or 5 is used.

You may be able to change the interrupt used by the card(s) that conflict with DCC. If your card is plug and play compatible, you can do this using the Device Manager (see Chapter 19). If not, you may need to change some jumpers on the card or run a piece of setup software from the card's manufacturer.

Troubleshooting DCC

If you experience problems getting DCC to work, a troubleshooter dialog box appears that gives you some guidance on how to proceed. Answer the questions and carry out the actions it suggests based on your answers.

You can invoke the DCC troubleshooter manually by taking the following steps:

STEPS

Getting to the DCC Troubleshooter

Step 1. Click the Start button, click Help, and then click the Contents tab.

Step 2. Double-click the Troubleshooting book.

Step 3. Double-click the topic "If you have trouble using Direct Cable Connection."

Step 4. Answer the questions in the DCC troubleshooter help window by clicking the gray buttons next to the questions.

DCC to Windows NT

Undocumented

You can use DCC to connect a Windows 95 computer to a Windows NT computer. The Windows NT computer will run NT Remote Access Server (RAS) and the Windows 95 computer will run DCC.

On the Windows NT computer, use the Null Modem 19200 driver, because DCC defaults to 19200 speed. Windows NT won't let DCC go any faster than 19,200 bits per second over serial lines. Windows 95 computers can communicate with each other using DCC at 115,200 bits per second over serial lines. Either computer can be the guest or the host (referred to as the *server* in Windows NT-speak).

Windows NT uses user-level security. Your Windows 95 computer needs to log into the NT domain if the Windows NT computer is the host. You can set the NT domain by double-clicking the Network icon in the Control Panel, highlighting Client for Microsoft Networks, clicking the Properties button, marking the Log on to Windows NT domain check box, and then typing the domain's name.

To connect the Windows 95 computer to the Windows NT computer, you need to install a null modem driver. For information on this, look at http://www.vt.edu:10021/K/kewells/net/index.html.

Administering the Host Computer's Print Queue

Tip

Let's say you are connecting your laptop to your desktop computer using DCC. Let's assume that the desktop computer (the DCC host) has a printer connected to it. You might want to be able to delete or pause print files that you are printing from your laptop onto the desktop's printer. Unfortunately, the desktop computer's print queue isn't automatically available to you unless you move over to the desktop computer and administer it there.

To administer the desktop computer's print queue from the laptop, you need to set your desktop computer to permit remote administration. To do this, double-click the Passwords icon in the Control Panel of the desktop computer, click the Remote Administration tab, and then mark the "Enable Remote Administration on this server" check box.

So What About LapLink for Windows 95?

LapLink for Windows 95 is not a network on a serial or parallel cable. It doesn't give you full remote access. It does give you easy-to-use file transfer and file synchronization capabilities across a cable, network, modem, or radio modem. It also provides chat and remote control facilities. Remote control lets you run the other computer from your computer. Traveling Software has incorporated a Windows 95 Explorer-like front end to its file transfer software. This cuts down on the cognitive dissonance that you would experience if they had stayed with their old File Manager-like front end. LapLink's serial cable file-transfer speeds are much higher than what is available under DCC on a serial port.

Windows 95 provides file synchronization in the Briefcase applet, which we describe in Chapter 31. LapLink for Windows 95's file synchronization is automatic. When you copy the files back over the originals, LapLink only copies the files that have been modified, updating the originals for you. This is much faster than using the Briefcase.

For more information about Traveling Software and LapLink for Windows 95, call 800-343-8080 or visit http://www.travsoft.com.

Summary

Windows 95 comes with a built-in network called Direct Cable Connection, which lets you connect two computers with a serial or parallel cable, or through infrared devices.

▶ We show you how to configure Direct Cable Connection.

▶ We discuss what kinds of network connection speeds you can expect from different serial and parallel ports.

▶ We show how Windows 95 has taken the next step toward making the parallel port connection a true networking connection with close to network-standard speeds.

▶ We compare the file-transfer standard — LapLink for Windows 95 — with the offerings built into Windows 95.

Chapter 31

Synchronized Filing — the Briefcase

In This Chapter

Windows 95 provides the Briefcase to help you keep the same files on two computers up to date on both.

▶ Using the Briefcase to move files between a computer at the office and one at home, between a portable and a desktop computer, or across a network

▶ Creating and moving a Briefcase

▶ Moving files and folders into and out of the Briefcase and updating files on different computers

---

Why a Briefcase?

Let's take a look at the metaphor of a briefcase before we incorporate its Windows 95 version into our mental framework.

You use a briefcase to take documents with you so that you can work on them outside the office. The documents in a briefcase might be copies, or they might be the originals. All of the changes that you make to these documents are written into the documents as you work on them.

Having two computers with local storage capacity presents a problem. Which document is the most up to date — the one on your computer at the office or the one on your portable? Changes you make to documents stored on computers are not as easily recognizable as those you make to documents on paper. You can quickly lose track.

The Windows 95 Briefcase helps you keep track of files you are using two computers to work on. Like a real briefcase, it moves from place to place. Unlike a real one, you carry only copies of your original documents. You can put the Briefcase on a floppy disk, or you can move it from computer to computer over a network. You can use copies in the Briefcase that have been updated to overwrite the originals.

Tip

The Briefcase relies on the date and time stamp of the file to determine whether it is the latest copy, so be sure to match the date and time on both computers.

The following scenarios describe three common ways you might use the Windows 95 Briefcase.

Scenario 1

You have a desktop computer at work and a desktop computer at home. You want to work at home on some documents that you normally work on at work.

You have a Briefcase on the Desktop of your computer at work. You copy files from folders on your work computer into the Briefcase. You move the Briefcase to a floppy disk.

You take the floppy disk with the Briefcase on it home, perhaps in your actual briefcase. At home, you view the floppy disk using the Explorer or My Computer. You copy files from the Briefcase on the floppy disk into folders on your hard disk. You open the documents in their folders on the hard disk and edit them.

Before returning to work, you click Update All in the Briefcase on your floppy disk, which copies the edited files from their folders on the hard disk in your home computer into the Briefcase on your floppy disk.

At work, you put your floppy disk in your computer and open the Briefcase using My Computer or the Explorer. You then click Update All to update the documents in their original folders on your computer at work. The most recent versions of the files in the Briefcase are copied over their original files in the folders on the hard disk of the computer at work.

Both your computer at home and the computer at work now have the latest versions of the documents. Your Briefcase on the floppy disk also has the latest versions.

Scenario 2

You have a laptop and a desktop computer at work. You want to work on documents on your laptop while you are away from the office.

You have a Briefcase on the Desktop of your desktop computer. You copy documents that you are working on into the Briefcase on your desktop computer. You then continue working on these documents in their original folders.

When you are finished working on your documents at the office, you click Update All in the Briefcase to update all the copies of your documents in the Briefcase based on the originals on your desktop computer.

You connect your laptop to your desktop computer with Direct Cable Connection (DCC) or over the office network. You move the Briefcase from the Desktop of your desktop computer to the Desktop of your laptop computer.

The files in the Briefcase remember their relationship with the original files in the folders on the hard disk of the office computer. While you are away from your office, you edit the documents in the Briefcase on your laptop *without copying or moving them out of the Briefcase.*

The next day at work, you connect the two computers with DCC and move the Briefcase from the laptop to the desktop computer. You then click Update All in the Briefcase to update the original documents on the desktop computer.

Scenario 3

You want Janice, whose computer is on your network, to work on your files. She will return the files to you after working on them.

You copy your files into your Briefcase on your Desktop, and then move the Briefcase to Janice's Desktop across the network.

Janice works on your files, *never copying them out of the Briefcase.* Later, when she is done, she moves your Briefcase back to the Desktop of your computer.

You update all your original files by clicking Update All in the Briefcase on your Desktop.

What Does a Briefcase Do?

After you create a Briefcase and copy a file into it, the Briefcase maintains a synchronization relationship, called a *sync link*, between the original file and its copy in the Briefcase. After you have established this sync link, you can edit either the copy in the Briefcase or the original file. If you want to ensure that both the original and the copy are the latest version, choose Update All from inside the Briefcase. Briefcase copies the later version over the earlier version so that both the original and the Briefcase copy are the latest version.

The idea is that you edit either the Briefcase copy or the original copy, but not both, before you perform an update. If you edit both files without an update, you need to manually edit a combination of the files to create a latest version. See the section later in this chapter entitled *Both the original and the Briefcase copy have been modified* for details on how to do this.

The Briefcase can travel. If it couldn't, it wouldn't be of much use. Microsoft assumes you will edit or work on files in different places sequentially — that you will edit files in one place, carry the Briefcase with the files in it to another location, edit the files in this new location, and later return the Briefcase to the original location. Updates and edits happen sequentially.

Creating a Briefcase

If you chose to install Briefcase during Windows 95 Setup, the Briefcase icon (by default named My Briefcase) is on your Desktop. You can set up this feature when you're installing Windows 95 if you do a Custom or Portable setup. If you do a Custom setup, you need to choose to install the Briefcase when given the option.

To create a new Briefcase on the Desktop (assuming that you have installed the Briefcase during Setup), right-click the Desktop, point to New, and then click Briefcase. You can also create Briefcases in any folder. Just right-click in the folder window and issue the same command.

You can create as many Briefcases as you like. You can name the Briefcases anything you like. You can change the names of any of your Briefcases. This can quickly get out of hand because you have to remember which Briefcase contains the copies of which files. We suggest that you stick to one or two Briefcases, or name your Briefcases for projects.

Putting the Briefcase on the Desktop makes it easy to drag files from the Explorer or other folder windows to the Briefcase, assuming you can see the Briefcase icon on the Desktop. If you can't easily get at the Briefcase on the Desktop, you can also drag files into it in the Explorer. The Briefcase appears in the left pane of the Explorer window, connected by a dotted line to the Desktop at the top of the pane, as shown in Figure 31-1. You can drag files from the right pane of the Explorer into the Briefcase in the left pane.

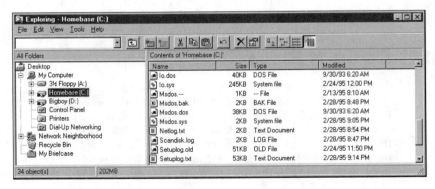

Figure 31-1: An Explorer view that includes a Briefcase. You can drag and drop files from the right pane into the Briefcase in the left pane.

The first time you create a Briefcase or when you open your Briefcase for the first time during a session, the Welcome to the Windows Briefcase dialog box appears to introduce you to the basic steps of working with the Briefcase (see Figure 31-2). In addition to the quick overview provided in this dialog box, you can find further assistance in the Windows 95 help files.

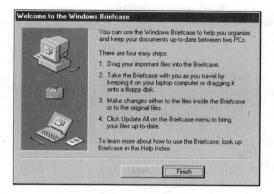

Figure 31-2: The Welcome to the Windows Briefcase dialog box.

Undocumented

You can create a Briefcase on a floppy disk or in a folder other than the Desktop folder. After you create a Briefcase, you can move it into any other folder that you like. For additional information, see the section entitled *Moving a Briefcase* later in this chapter.

Copying Files or Folders into a Briefcase

You can use the Explorer to copy files and folders to a Briefcase. And if the Briefcase is on the Desktop, you can also drag and drop a file or folder from a folder window onto the Briefcase icon.

When you copy files or folders to a Briefcase, they are copied with a *sync link*. The copy in the Briefcase is connected to the original file or folder. If there is a change in the copy or the original, the status of the copy in the Briefcase changes from Up-to-date to Needs updating.

You copy every document that you want to work with on another computer into your Briefcase. The originals stay put, and you take the copies in the Briefcase with you. You can delete the copies from the Briefcase without affecting the originals.

Moving a Briefcase

Once you copy all the files and folders that you want into a Briefcase, you can move it to another computer. You don't want to do this until you have finished editing the original documents for the day because you need to move a fully updated Briefcase to the new computer.

Make sure to close the Briefcase before you try to move it. Otherwise, you will get an error message saying that you have to close it first. It may not be obvious that you have the Briefcase open if you are viewing it in the Explorer. The Briefcase is open if you can see its contents in an Explorer or folder window.

Moving a Briefcase to a floppy disk

One option is to move the Briefcase to a floppy disk. You can drag and drop the Briefcase icon from the Desktop to the floppy disk drive icon in your Explorer. If none of the files in the Briefcase is larger than the capacity of the floppy disk, the Briefcase and the files that it contains will be moved to the floppy disk. You won't be able to copy any files that are too big to fit on the floppy disk.

Secret

If there are more files than will fit on one floppy disk, you will be asked to put in additional floppy disks. Unfortunately, the files on the second and later floppy disks will be marked as *orphans*, which means there will be no sync link between these copies and the original files. Because of this feature, a Briefcase that is copied to a floppy disk cannot be any bigger than one floppy disk and still operate as a Briefcase.

The whole point of a Briefcase is to maintain the sync link. While Briefcases can contain orphans, these are no better than regular copies of the original files. This limits Briefcases transported on floppy disks to floppy-disk size, which is one reason for creating multiple Briefcases.

Secret

You should not move the Briefcase off of the floppy disk onto the computer at home. If you want to work on the files in the Briefcase at home, copy the files out of the Briefcase on the floppy disk into folders on your home computer's hard disk. This allows you to edit them more quickly because they are now stored on the hard disk. Just don't copy the Briefcase itself.

When you copy the files from the Briefcase on the floppy disk into folders on the hard disk, a new and additional sync link is developed between the files in the Briefcase and the new files on the computer at home. The files in the Briefcase now have two sync links: one with the original files on the computer at work and one the copies on your hard disk at home.

If you move the Briefcase from the floppy disk to the Desktop (or to another folder) of the home computer, you will not be able to create the second sync link. If you copy files out of the Briefcase after you move it to the home computer, there will be no connection between these copies and the copies in the Briefcase, although the files in the Briefcase will still maintain a sync link with the original files on the computer at work.

If you want to maintain two sync links, don't move the Briefcase off of the floppy disk. Copy the files from the Briefcase into folders on your home computer's hard disk and update the Briefcase on the floppy after you have edited the files at home. Then take the Briefcase on the floppy back to work to update the files there.

You can move the Briefcase from one computer to another across a network. You can do this over a Dial-Up Networking, DCC, or LAN connection. You won't run into the same size limitations if you move the Briefcase over a network that you would using a floppy disk.

Moving a Briefcase to a portable computer

Secret

When you move the Briefcase from the Desktop of your desktop computer to the Desktop of your portable computer, only one sync link is maintained — that between the files in the Briefcase and the files in the folders of the desktop computer. You need to keep the files in the Briefcase on the portable computer and edit them within the Briefcase in order to maintain the sync link.

Moving the Briefcase to the Desktop of the portable is the same as moving the Briefcase from a floppy disk to the Desktop of the home computer. Once you do this, you need to work with the files on the portable or on the home computer only while they are in the Briefcase.

The Briefcase and its Update All command let you copy files back and forth without explicitly copying them or to having to remember which is the latest version. You can still copy files yourself without using the Briefcase if it is easier for you.

Opening a Briefcase

In some ways, the Briefcase is like any other folder. Double-click its icon on the Desktop and it opens into a folder window. Click its icon in the Explorer, and its contents appear in the right pane. Right-click the Briefcase icon on the Desktop and choose Explore to open an Explorer view of the Briefcase.

Secret

Say you have moved the Briefcase from the Desktop of your desktop computer to the Desktop of your portable computer. When you open the Briefcase on the portable, a message window may appear asking if you want to reconnect with the desktop computer. Just click No. This message window appears because Windows 95 is automatically trying to reestablish the link in the Briefcase with the original files across a network that is no longer connected.

Copying Files or Folders from a Briefcase

You have copied your Briefcase from your desktop computer to your portable computer. You should leave your documents in the Briefcase on the Desktop of your portable computer. If you copy them out of the Briefcase, then the copies in the folders on the hard disk of the portable have no relationship to the files in the Briefcase.

On the other hand, you should copy the files from the Briefcase on a floppy disk to the hard disk of your computer at home. The second sync link is created and you can edit your files on the hard disk.

Tip

Update the Briefcase on the floppy disk before you take it back to the office. Update the files on the office computer from the Briefcase on the floppy disk. You can then leave the Briefcase on the floppy disk where it is, or move it back onto the Desktop on the office computer.

Determining the Status of Files or Folders in Your Briefcase

Copying files and folders to the Briefcase establishes a sync link between the original files and the copies in the Briefcase. If you modify any of the files (either the originals or copies), the Briefcase tells you that the files are out of sync and need to be updated.

When you have just finished copying files or folders into a Briefcase, their status is shown as Up-to-date because the files in the Briefcase haven't yet been modified. If you now edit the original files or the files in the Briefcase, you need to update both the originals and the copies to the latest version, that is, get them in sync.

STEPS

Determining Briefcase File Status

Step 1.   Double-click the Briefcase icon on your Desktop. If the Briefcase isn't showing details view, choose View, Details.

Step 2.   The status of each file and folder is displayed in the Status column. The possible listings in this column are Up-to-date, Needs updating, Orphan, or Unavailable.

Step 3.   The Sync Copy In column lists the location of the original file or folder. An open Briefcase displaying these columns is shown in Figure 31-3.

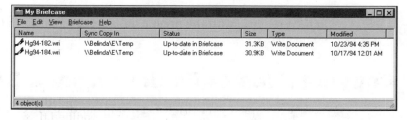

Figure 31-3: An open Briefcase. The Name column lists the file names, the Sync Copy In column shows the name of the folder where the synched file is stored, and the Status column gives the current status of the link between the two files.

Step 4.   You can get further details about a particular file or folder by right-clicking it, choosing Properties, and then clicking the Update Status tab. The Update Status properties sheet for a file in the Briefcase is shown in Figure 31-4.

Determining Briefcase File Status

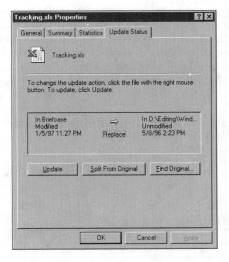

Figure 31-4: The Update Status properties sheet for a file in the Briefcase.

Updating Files and Folders

If you edit your original files after you have placed them in the Briefcase, you need to update them before you move your Briefcase.

When you bring your Briefcase back from home to your computer at work with the original files, you need to update your original files based on their new modified versions in the Briefcase.

If you have copied your files or folders from the Briefcase on a floppy disk onto your portable or home computer, you need to update the files in the Briefcase on the floppy after you have modified them on the computer.

The files are marked Needs updating if you have edited or modified either the file/folder outside the Briefcase or the copies inside. Updating the files/folders will ensure that both the originals and the copies in the Briefcase are the latest version.

The default action of the Briefcase is to replace the file that has an earlier date with the file that has a later date. You can override this action if you so desire.

STEPS

Updating Files and Folders

Step 1. Double-click the Briefcase to open it, and then click the file or folder in the Briefcase that you want to update. Use Ctrl+click or Shift+click to select multiple files and/or folders. If you are going to update all the files and folders in the Briefcase, you don't need to highlight any of them.

Step 2. Display the Briefcase menu.

Step 3. Click either Update All (to update all the files and folders in the Briefcase) or Update Selection (to update only the highlighted files and folders).

Step 4. The Update dialog box, shown in Figure 31-5, appears to let you continue the update as indicated or make some changes.

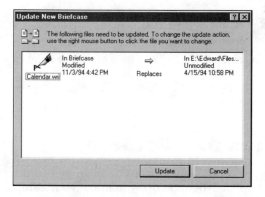

Figure 31-5: The Update dialog box. This dialog box appears when you choose either Update All or Update Selection from the Briefcase menu.

Step 5. Right-click near the horizontal arrow between file names to see how you can change the default action. A small context menu appears to let you choose which action to take. You can change the direction of the Replace action to switch which file updates the other, or you can choose Skip to skip this particular update. The context menu may also occasionally contain a Merge command. This command appears if the selected files include any that are associated with an application for which the developer has implemented a merge feature.

Step 6. Click the Update button.

You have now synched the files and their copies in the Briefcase. You may not have synched the files in the Briefcase with the originals or, conversely, with the files on the portable or home computer. You need to move the newly updated Briefcase to the other computer and then update the files once again. The default action is to update the older files on the computer from the newly updated Briefcase.

Multiple syncs

Undocumented

The Briefcase can keep a sync between the original files on the computer at the office and the copies in the Briefcase as well as between the copies on the home computer and the Briefcase. It is this ability to keep multiple sync links for each file, depending on where the Briefcase is stored, that allows you to copy files out of the Briefcase on the floppy disk into other folders on the home computer.

You can see this feature in action when you open the Briefcase. The Sync Copy In column in the Briefcase shows the relationship of the copies inside the Briefcase to the files outside the Briefcase. When you copy files from your desktop computer into a Briefcase and then move the Briefcase onto a floppy, the Sync Copy In column shows the original folders on your desktop computer. If you then copy the files from the Briefcase on the floppy to folders on another computer, the Sync Copy In column changes to the file folders on the second computer. Moving the Briefcase back to the original computer causes the Sync Copy In column to change back to the original folders.

Both the original and the Briefcase copy have been modified

The Briefcase doesn't really solve all the problems of keeping your files up to date. For example, the merge feature has to be implemented by third-party developers so that their applications can, with some action from you, intelligently update their files.

It is quite easy to modify the original files on your computer at work and forget to update their copies in the Briefcase. Later, you modify these non-updated copies in the Briefcase on the computer at home. You now have two files with different modifications to them and no easy way to sort out those modifications.

The Briefcase does give you fair warning. If you modify your file outside the Briefcase, the file is marked as Needs Updating in the Briefcase. If you edit both the copy in the Briefcase and the file outside, then the Briefcase keeps track of the fact that both have changed. When you go to update, you are informed of this sad fact.

If you now try to update your original files you may be wiping out important modifications that you made to them.

STEPS

Dealing with Multiple Modifications

Step 1. Select the files in the Briefcase that you want to update. Use Ctrl+click or Shift+click if you have more than one file. If you are going to update all the files in the Briefcase, you don't need to highlight any of them.

Step 2. Display the Briefcase menu.

Step 3. Choose either Update All (to update all the files and folders in the Briefcase) or Update Selection (to update only the highlighted files and folders).

Step 4. When you try to update the files, Skip (both changed) appears in the Update dialog box.

Step 5. Right-click the file in the Briefcase that has been updated on both computers. If the application that you used to created these files has the ability to merge files, you'll see the Merge command in the context menu. Click this command.

Step 6. If Merge is not an option on the menu, you can still capture both sets of changes and merge the files manually. To do this, create a third file (using the appropriate application) and copy the original file and the Briefcase file into this third file.

Step 7. Edit or modify this third file to get rid of the redundant information, and manually choose which updates to keep.

Step 8. Copy this third file over the original or over the Briefcase copy, and then perform an update.

Breaking the Sync Link

You can break up the sync relationship between the original file and its Briefcase copy. You might want to do this in order to create a new document and leave the older version as a backup.

STEPS

Orphaning a Briefcase File or Folder

Step 1. Right-click the file in the Briefcase, and choose Properties.

Orphaning a Briefcase File or Folder

Step 2. Click the Update Status tab.

Step 3. Click the Split From Original button.

If you change the name of the file outside the Briefcase, you will orphan the file inside the Briefcase. To find the copy of the file outside the Briefcase, click Find Original in the Update Status tab.

Data Files

One of the potential scenarios for using the Briefcase involves salespeople keeping track of and updating customer files while out in the field. Back at the office, the customer files are also being changed. When the salesperson comes back to the office, the customer files on the office computer have to be updated, but data files on both the salesperson's computer and the office computer have been modified.

The Briefcase doesn't solve this problem, but rather provides a standard method for others to solve the problem. Database developers are encouraged to use the Briefcase facility and combine it with a means of merging data files. This type of merge feature highlights changed records in the data and allows the salesperson (or someone else) to manually decide which modifications to accept.

The Briefcase doesn't provide any means of copying a file over multiple floppy disks. This means that you need to move large data files in the Briefcase over a network instead — across a DCC, Dial-Up Networking, or LAN connection, for example.

Summary

In this chapter, we describe how to create and use the Briefcase to "carry" files and folders between computers.

▶ If you want to make sure that the files on your desktop computer at the office and your home computer are the same, the Briefcase is for you.

▶ If you use a portable and a desktop computer, the Briefcase can help you make sure that your computers are in sync.

▶ If you have someone else work on your files, you can send that person a Briefcase full of your files.

▶ We describe how to avoid losing the sync relationship between your master files and your copies.

Chapter 32

E-mail (And Faxes) Everywhere

In This Chapter

We discuss the ins and outs of Windows Messaging (formerly called the Microsoft Exchange client), a heavy duty e-mail and faxing application. If you need help using the strictly Internet/Intranet mail tool, Microsoft Internet Mail, turn to Chapter 35. In this chapter, we discuss:

▶ Quickly configuring Windows Messaging to send and receive a fax

▶ Sending and receiving e-mail over the Internet, CompuServe, and the Microsoft Network

▶ Dealing with the funny ways Windows Messaging behaves, which are different from the rest of Windows 95

▶ Using command line parameters to view message headers and begin composition of new messages

▶ Using message stores to manage your documents

▶ Renaming message stores and address books

▶ Composing mail from many different sources

▶ Creating a Microsoft Mail postoffice for your workgroup

▶ Configuring Windows Messaging to continuously monitor your phone line for incoming faxes without requiring that you exit the program to send and receive e-mail messages from your Internet service provider

But, I Just Want to Send a Fax

You may have imagined Microsoft as a bunch of wildly individualistic nerds overseen by a boy genius (and the world's richest man). Nice image, but the Microsoft Exchange client (which is now called Windows Messaging to differentiate it from the Microsoft Exchange Server), demonstrates that Microsoft is also a corporation — ponderous (it takes its own sweet time loading up in memory), thick (you really have to drill down to find what you want), and reliant on hidden human experts (postoffice managers).

Five months after the release of Windows 95, Microsoft produced Service Pack 1, which came with a new version of the Microsoft Exchange client. Ten months after Windows 95 was released, Microsoft updated the Microsoft Exchange client version 4.0 with Windows Messaging version 4.0. Microsoft changed the name because you continually had to say all three parts of the name, *Microsoft Exchange client*, to differentiate it from Microsoft Exchange Server. (Exchange Server runs on Windows NT servers and manages e-mail, documents, and discussion forums in corporate settings.)

Windows Messaging is an improvement over the Microsoft Exchange client. It loads faster, sends mail four times faster, and gets rid of a bunch of annoying bugs related to the Internet Mail drivers. Windows Messaging (which Microsoft calls its "universal messaging client") was built assuming you are connected to a vast empire of corporate mail (just like at Microsoft). Microsoft felt that what you needed most was a means to control and view this sea of memos and documents. The ability to quickly and easily send and receive a bit of e-mail (or fax) got lost in the design process (requiring one Wizard to bring back some ease of use and another to ease installation).

Windows Messaging is both an e-mail and fax tool. You use it to send, receive, and store e-mail and faxes from numerous different sources (mail delivery services). We'll use this chapter to blast through all the armor surrounding Windows Messaging and get you up and running quickly with this tank of a product. Once the steady stream of messages begins pouring in, you'll learn to appreciate its gift for mail (and document) management.

In June, 1995, Microsoft stripped out a good chunk of the functionality of the Windows 95 Microsoft Exchange client. It took out some very useful features such as signatures, shared folders (found in Microsoft Mail 3.2 and since restored in Windows 95 Service Pack 1 and Windows Messaging), message filters, mark all messages as read, message threading, and form composition. This reduced significantly Microsoft's claim for the Windows 95 version of Microsoft Exchange client as a "universal messaging client." Throughout 1996 and into 1997, Microsoft was delivering six different e-mail clients:

- The original Microsoft Exchange client

- A slightly updated version of the Microsoft Exchange client that came with Windows 95 Service Pack 1 (http://www.microsoft.com/windows/download/exchupd.exe)

- Windows Messaging, the updated version of the Microsoft Exchange client

- The Microsoft Exchange client that comes with Microsoft Exchange Server

- Microsoft Internet Mail (combined in 1997 with Internet News into Outlook Express)

- Outlook (a PIM/e-mail tool that comes with Office 97)

The first four clients are similar enough that we can discuss them in this chapter. We cover Internet Mail in Chapter 35, and we don't discuss Outlook in this book, although we do discuss Outlook Express (the combination of Internet Mail and Internet News). Outlook uses the Windows Messaging technology for its e-mail delivery and can read and write Windows Messaging files.

Unless we make a clear distinction, when we refer in this chapter to Windows Messaging, we are also referring to the original Microsoft Exchange client and the Service Pack 1 version. While Windows Messaging contains improvements to the Microsoft Exchange client, it still looks very similar. The capabilities that Microsoft stripped from the original Windows 95 version of Microsoft Exchange client are present in the Microsoft Exchange client that comes with Exchange Server.

If you have an early version of Windows 95 (before OEM Service Release 2), you can use the instructions in the next section to set up the Microsoft Exchange client. If you have a later version, or if you have downloaded Windows Messaging from Microsoft's web site, http://www.microsoft.com /windows/software/exupd.htm, you can use the instructions to set up Windows Messaging. If you would like to get the Microsoft Exchange client that comes with the Exchange Server so that you can use its additional capabilities, you can download it from the Microsoft Exchange web site, http://www.ms-exchange.com.

Don't use or download Windows Messaging if you are using the Microsoft Exchange client that comes with Exchange Server. There are some naming and Registry incompatibilities between Windows Messaging and this version of the Microsoft Exchange client. If you want to use Windows Messaging with the Exchange Server, uninstall the Microsoft Exchange client first.

Yes, but, I *Still* Just Want to Send a Fax

At the end of the Windows 95 Custom setup, the Inbox Setup Wizard takes over and steps you through the process of setting up the Windows Messaging or Microsoft Exchange client (if you have chosen to install one of them). It sets up a default "profile" with the information and mail delivery services that you desire. You'll most likely need to change the properties of your profile and information services after you go through Windows 95 setup to correctly configure a profile with a fax delivery service. We'll show you how to do that.

STEPS

Installing, Setting Up, and Running Windows Messaging or the Microsoft Exchange Client to Send a Fax

Step 1. If you haven't yet installed Windows 95, be sure to choose the Custom option in Windows 95 Setup. When you are presented with the Select Components dialog box, click the Microsoft Exchange (or Windows Messaging) and Microsoft Fax check boxes. This will install the software that you need to send faxes. Jump to Step 5.

(continued)

Installing, Setting Up, and Running Windows Messaging or the Microsoft Exchange Client to Send a Fax

Step 2.   If you have already installed Windows 95, but you didn't install Microsoft Exchange (or Windows Messaging) and Microsoft Fax, click the Start button, point to Settings, and then click Control Panel. Double-click the Add/Remove Programs icon.

Step 3.   Click the Windows Setup tab, and then click the Microsoft Exchange (or Windows Messaging) and Microsoft Fax check boxes. Click OK. You'll need to restart Windows 95 when prompted to do so.

Step 4.   Click the Start button, point to Settings, and then click Control Panel. Double-click the Mail and Fax icon in the Control Panel. (If you have installed Windows Messaging, the icon will be named Mail.) This starts the Inbox Setup Wizard if the previous steps haven't already done so.

Step 5.   The Inbox Setup Wizard will tell you if Windows 95 Setup has correctly detected your fax modem. Otherwise, this Wizard will run the Modem Detection Wizard. You'll need to step through the modem detection process to be sure that your modem can deliver faxes (for details turn to Chapter 25).

Step 6.   You will be asked by the Inbox Setup Wizard to select information services. Since you just want to send a fax, go ahead and choose Microsoft Fax when given the opportunity. Step through the Inbox Setup Wizard and accept the default values. You will need to type your phone number at one point. Click Finish.

If you have previously installed Microsoft Exchange or Windows Messaging, you will be asked for a profile name. FAX would be an appropriate name for a profile that contains only the Microsoft Fax mail delivery service.

If you have previously created a profile, you can add Microsoft Fax to that profile by double-clicking the Mail (or Mail and Fax) icon in the Control Panel, clicking the Add button, and then highlighting Microsoft Fax.

Step 7.   Click the Start button, point to Programs, Accessories, Fax, and then click Compose New Fax. This starts the Compose New Fax Wizard.

Step 8.   Click Next in the first dialog box of the Compose New Fax Wizard. Enter a known fax number in the third field on the second dialog box (changing the area code if necessary). Click the Add to List button. Click the Next button, and the following Next button as well.

Installing, Setting Up, and Running Windows Messaging or the Microsoft Exchange Client to Send a Fax

Step 9. Enter a subject and a message. This dialog box isn't much of a fax editor, and in fact, there are much better ways to compose a fax, which we cover later in this chapter in the section entitled *Microsoft Fax*. Click Next to display a dialog box that lets you attach a file (document) to your fax. Click the Next button, and click the Finish button.

A fax with your message will now be sent to the number that you typed in step 8.

If you want to receive a fax, carry out steps 1 through 6, and then double-click the Inbox icon on your Desktop. If your current profile includes the Microsoft Fax, a small yellow phone will appear in the Tray on your Taskbar. You can determine just how the phone is answered by double-clicking the Mail (or Mail and Fax) icon in your Control Panel. See the rest of this chapter for more details.

Windows Messaging Features

Here are some of the features included with Windows Messaging:

- Send, receive, view, and store e-mail, faxes, and other documents using a variety of mail delivery services including Microsoft Mail (over your local area network), CompuServe, the Internet or an Intranet, Microsoft Fax, the Microsoft Network, and any centralized mail system that includes an appropriate MAPI driver

- Include files, documents, and OLE 2 objects in your messages

- A complete workgroup version of the Microsoft Mail Server (the Microsoft Mail postoffice that is identical to the one created by WFWG 3.11, so that WFWG 3.11 users and Windows 95 users can share the same postoffice)

- The workgroup version of Microsoft Mail Server, which is upgradable to the enterprise-wide version of Microsoft Mail Server or the Microsoft Exchange Server

- Create and store multiple Windows Messaging configurations (profiles)

- Universal address book (that is, an address book that can be used by and incorporated into many different applications, for example, Microsoft Phone)

- Customizable Windows Messaging toolbar

- Remote access and remote message header preview (call your Microsoft Mail postoffice at work from your computer at home and decide which messages to download)

- Send formatted documents over the Internet transparently using MIME or UUENCODE

- Send editable files through Microsoft Fax with binary file transfer (attach a Word for Windows document to a fax message and ship it to someone with Microsoft Fax running on his or her computer)

- Send e-mail or faxes from Windows applications that enable the Send function

- Print (send) faxes from all Windows applications that can print

- Exchange public-key encrypted faxes

- Send faxes over a shared fax modem on your local area network

- Create fax cover pages with a cover page designer/editor

- Send a note on the fax cover page without having to send another fax page

- Use a really cool fax viewer

- Retrieve, without having to use a touch tone phone, faxes (and files) from fax-on-demand systems

- A general OLE 2 data store that can be used to store, organize, find, and view any of your documents — a much more powerful version of a file-management system than FAT or VFAT

- Share an address book with Microsoft Phone, which uses Windows Messaging to send and receive faxes

Or Lack Thereof

So what features are missing from Windows Messaging?

- You can't transparently store messages that come from the Microsoft Network bulletin boards, CompuServe forums, and Internet newsgroups (turn to Chapter 35 for a review of Microsoft Internet News)

- No online conferences, forums, or conference message threading except when used with Exchange Server

- No optical character recognition (Windows Messaging can't turn a Group 3 type fax into an editable document; you need add-on OCR software to accomplish this.)

- No fax annotations (Use the add-on Wang Imaging for Windows 95.)

- Only one e-mail or fax address per address-book entry

- No automated distribution of faxes received by a shared fax across a local area network to the intended recipients

- No ">" symbols around quotes in replies (We show you how to add this.)

- No automated signatures (We show you how to add this. You can also use the Exchange client that comes with Exchange Server.)

- No message filtering (except if you use the Exchange client that comes with the Exchange Server)

- Limited message organizing

- No spelling checker (If you have installed a 32-bit word processor with a spelling checker, such as the one that comes with Microsoft Office, that spelling checker *will* be used by Windows Messaging. You'll find it in the Tools, Options menu.)

Tip

Windows Messaging can eat up resources and swap space. If you experience trouble running it, be sure that you have 20MB of free disk space on the hard disk that includes the Windows 95 dynamic swap file. Also, Microsoft recommends a minimum of 8MB of RAM. We recommend at least 16MB.

Windows Messaging Is Its Own Product

The people who wrote Windows Messaging were not the same ones who wrote the rest of Windows 95. They were part of the Microsoft Exchange Server/client team, and they had their own ideas of what such a product should look and feel like.

As an example of a difference in the interface, in Windows Messaging, a little triangle appears on the button in the column that orders your messages when you're using details view. The triangle points up or down depending on which sort order you use. There is no such triangle in the details view of a folder or Explorer window.

Windows Messaging is a large and complex application. It includes a complete workgroup edition of Microsoft Mail Server and e-mail drivers for MSN, the Internet, and CompuServe. (You can find the CompuServe driver on the Windows 95 CD-ROM under the \Drivers\Other\Exchange\CompuSrv folder, or you can download the latest version from CompuServe — GO CSMAIL). Windows Messaging includes Microsoft Fax as just a part of the product. Windows Messaging serves as a client of Internet Mail as well as a sophisticated mail-management system and universal address book.

You can find the latest information about Windows Messaging at the Exchange Center, http://www.slipstick.com/exchange. Be sure to download the Exchange client and Windows Messaging help file. It's incredible. The author of this site, Sue Mosher, is also writing a book on Exchange Server and Windows Messaging. If you want to know a lot more about it than we can cover here, get her book.

Installing Windows Messaging

You can install Microsoft Exchange or Windows Messaging (depending on your Windows 95 version) during your Windows 95 setup process. You just click the Microsoft Exchange (or Windows Messaging) and Microsoft Fax check boxes. If you want to add these programs later, use the Add/Remove

Programs icon in the Control Panel to rerun Windows 95 Setup, and mark the same check boxes. Turn to Chapter 3 for more details about setting up Windows 95.

Tip

You can't install the Microsoft Network (MSN) and Microsoft Fax unless Microsoft Exchange (or Windows Messaging) is already installed, or you're installing it at the same time. If you want to uninstall Microsoft Exchange, you will be warned that MSN and Microsoft Fax can't operate without it and will be uninstalled also.

If you have a version of Windows 95 prior to OEM Service Release 2, you can download Windows Messaging from the Microsoft web site, at http://www.microsoft.com/windows/software/exupd.htm.

If you have previously installed the Microsoft Exchange client and have downloaded Windows Messaging, you can install Windows Messaging without first uninstalling Microsoft Exchange. Windows Messaging installs into its own folder under the Program Files folder. The setup procedures for both products are similar, and where they differ, we will point out the differences.

If you try to install Windows Messaging after previously installing the Microsoft Exchange client for Exchange Server, you will be notified that you need to uninstall the Microsoft Exchange client. Don't do this. Just abort the install for Windows Messaging.

Secret

Windows Messaging installs itself in the \Program Files\Windows Messaging folder. The Microsoft Exchange client installs in the \Programs Files\Microsoft Exchange folder. The Windows Messaging setup files don't delete this folder when you install Windows Messaging after previously installing Microsoft Exchange. They leave some references to the Microsoft Exchange client in the Registry untouched. To fix this problem, choose View, Options in the Explorer, and click the File Types tab. Select Mail Message, and click the Edit button to change the action that occurs when you click on a file with a *msg* extension. If you feel comfortable editing your Registry, you can change all references to the old location of Exchng32.exe to \Program Files\Windows Messaging.

Don't uninstall Exchange (using the Add/Remove Programs icon in the Control Panel) after you have installed Windows Messaging. This will uninstall Microsoft Fax and the Microsoft Network. You can instead delete the \Program Files\Microsoft Exchange folder (and all of its contents).

Upgrading to Windows Messaging installs Microsoft Mail as a mail delivery service, even though you might not want this service (if you're not on a local area network with a Microsoft Mail postoffice). You can delete Microsoft Mail by double-clicking the Add/Remove Programs icon in the Control Panel, and then clicking the Windows Setup tab.

If you downloaded the updated version of Windows Messaging, you won't be able to uninstall it using the Control Panel, Add/Remove Programs, Install/Uninstall tab, Add/Remove Windows Messaging Update 1. This is a bug that Microsoft has chosen not to fix. To uninstall Windows Messaging, you need to run exupdusa.exe and choose the remove option.

You can uninstall the Microsoft Exchange client by double-clicking the Add/Remove Programs icon in the Control Panel, clicking the Windows Setup tab, and then clearing the Microsoft Exchange check box.

If you have installed the Windows 95 Service Pack 1 version of Microsoft Exchange, you can't install Microsoft Fax from the original Windows 95 CD-ROM if you now want to install it. You need to install the original Exchange and the original Microsoft Fax, and then after it is all set up and working, reinstall the Service Pack 1 version. Windows Messaging comes with a new version of Microsoft Fax (no bug fixes though), so if you install Windows Messaging you don't have to worry about this problem.

The Inbox Setup Wizard

When you first install Windows Messaging, it invokes the Inbox Setup Wizard. This Wizard creates a *profile* for you. (We get into profiles in the *Windows Messaging Profiles* section later in this chapter.) You choose which information and mail delivery services will be part of your default profile. Let the Inbox Setup Wizard configure a profile for you and don't click "Manually configure information services" in the Wizard's first dialog box, at least not until you've gone through this process a few times.

Microsoft Exchange names the default profile MS Exchange Settings. Windows Messaging names the default profile with your name (the Registered Owner's name). These names are stored in the Registry at HKEY_CURRENT_USER\Software\Microsoft\Windows Messaging Subsystem\Profiles.

The Inbox Setup Wizard doesn't let you configure all the properties of the services associated with a profile. You'll need to go back later and review and perhaps change the numerous properties associated with each profile and each mail delivery service. The Wizard will prompt you for different properties depending on which mail delivery services you have chosen to include in your profile.

We discuss how to respond to the various Inbox Setup Wizard dialog boxes in, among other sections, *Choosing mail delivery services* and *Message Stores* later in this chapter.

Windows Messaging command line parameters

After you install Windows Messaging, you'll find an Inbox icon on your Desktop. After you have configured Windows Messaging, you'll find that when you double-click this icon, Windows Messaging displays the contents of the folder that you had open when you last quit the program.

You can't change what double-clicking the Inbox icon does, but you can add a Windows Messaging shortcut to your Desktop that opens Windows Messaging with its focus on something other than the Inbox (see Chapter 10 for instructions on creating shortcuts).

Undocumented

You can change the Windows Messaging menu item on the Start menu. To do this, right-click the Start button, click Explore, click the Programs menu folder in the left pane, right-click Windows Messaging in the right pane, choose Properties, and click the Shortcut tab. You can add a command line parameter after Exchng32.exe in the Target field (outside the double quote marks). If you add /n, you will open the New Message window of Windows Messaging when you start the program (see *Creating and Sending Mail* later in this chapter).

Other legitimate command line parameters for Exchng32.exe are /f and /p (for opening and printing a file, respectively), but they work only if the name of a message file (a file with the *msg* extension) is specified in the command line. For example: Exchange32 /f *filename*.msg.

The /s command line parameter will open a search window. We discuss the address book command line parameter, /a, later in this chapter.

You can also invoke Windows Messaging with a shareware application named Exchange Profile Selector. This application feeds Windows Messaging a particular profile name. You can place a shortcut (or multiple shortcuts) to Exchange Profile Selector on your Desktop.

Once you place these shortcuts on your Desktop, you can use TweakUI to remove the Inbox icon without losing any Windows Messaging functionality. See below for more details.

Changing the Windows Messaging User Interface

You can make a few quick changes to the Windows Messaging user interface that can really improve its usability.

First, click the Show/Hide Folder List button on the left side of the Windows Messaging toolbar. This button switches between single- and dual-pane view. Dual-pane view lets you easily display the contents of your message folders. Navigating through your store of messages in single-pane view requires that you click the Up One Level button on the left end of the toolbar and pay attention to the folder name displayed in the title bar.

Customize your toolbar by clicking Tools, Customize Toolbar. Highlight the Compose - New Message button in the right pane of the Customize Toolbar dialog box and click the Remove button to move it to the Available buttons box.

Next, do the same for the Go to Inbox button. With the highlight on the separator after Tools - Address Book, highlight Compose - New Message in the left pane and click the Add button, and then highlight Tools - Deliver

Now and click the Add button again. This puts three commonly used buttons next to each other by moving two buttons from the Available buttons box onto the toolbar.

If you use Windows Messaging to log on remotely (to your office or to your Internet service provider), you may want to use the Tools, Remote Mail command to download file headers and choose which messages to download. Unfortunately, there isn't a toolbar button for this function.

You can reset the toolbar to the default settings by clicking the Reset button in the Customize Toolbar dialog box.

Windows Messaging Profiles

Windows 95 uses hardware profiles, user profiles, and Windows Messaging profiles. You can set up user profiles (for different users) on the same computer and also set up different Windows Messaging profiles for each of these users. Logging onto Windows 95 as a given user (using user profiles) connects you to that user's default profile.

The Inbox Setup Wizard steps you through the configuration of a default profile. This may be the only profile you ever need. You can edit this profile at any time to reflect the way you want to send and receive e-mail and faxes. You can ignore profiles if you only use this one.

You'll want additional profiles if:

■ More than one person uses the same computer, so each user can have his or her own personal message store

■ Your computer is sometimes locally connected to a network, and sometimes calls into a network from a remote location using a modem and connects to a Microsoft Mail postoffice on the network

■ You want different profiles in order to keep different information or mail delivery services separate

Tip

You can't change the name of the default profile during the Windows 95 Setup or when you run the Inbox Setup Wizard for the first time (unless you click the Manually configure information services button). Later, you can make a copy of this profile, change its name to something meaningful, and erase the original profile.

If you find Windows Messaging attempting to connect to a second mail delivery service without first closing the connection with the first service, create separate profiles for each mail delivery service you use. Next create a profile containing two mail delivery services and see if they get along, and then try a profile with three, and so on.

There is a major problem with using multiple Windows Messaging profiles with one user. If you open and close Windows Messaging repeatedly (say to switch between profiles) you may find that you are unable to switch to different profiles and that you have to reboot Windows 95 altogether.

This problem is caused by a bug in MAPI (Messaging Application Programming Interface), a Microsoft DLL that runs in the background while you are running Windows Messaging. MAPI isn't swept out of memory when you exit Windows Messaging, but hangs around for a minute or two. If you repeatedly invoke and exit Windows Messaging, MAPI gets confused and Windows Messaging quits working.

Windows Messaging has a little trouble with profiles that contain both Internet Mail and a fax delivery service. You may get the error message "The port is already open." Sometimes outgoing faxes are never sent. The problem occurs if you click Deliver Now while Windows Messaging is trying to set up Microsoft Fax right after you invoke Windows Messaging. If you have Windows Messaging set to poll Internet Mail on a schedule, it can also try to dial out while Microsoft Fax is in the process of initializing the modem.

As a partial fix, you can wait to click Deliver Now until you see the Fax icon appear in the Tray. If you are using Microsoft Phone, it is best to combine your fax and other mail delivery services into one profile that is used by Microsoft Phone. If you do this, you can send/receive faxes and send e-mail to your Internet service provider while Microsoft Phone is running.

Undocumented

If you have both the Internet and Microsoft Network mail delivery services in one profile, you should set the Internet Mail delivery to happen first. In the Windows Messaging menu bar, choose Tools, Options, and then click the Delivery Tab. Highlight Internet Mail and move it up with the arrow buttons.

The point of putting Internet Mail first is that the Microsoft Network mail delivery service tries to deliver Internet Mail also (it assumes that it is the Internet service provider). If you want your Internet Mail to go by way of your Internet service provider, then its delivery service should go first.

A Windows Messaging profile is just a specific set of information services. These services include:

- Message store(s)
- Your personal address book and perhaps other address books
- E-mail (and fax) delivery service(s)
- The location of your postoffice (which Microsoft insists on spelling as one word) if you are connected to Microsoft Mail

If you configure your default profile with the information services that work for you, you don't have to do anything else. You can forget about Windows Messaging profiles and just double-click the Inbox on your Desktop to use Windows Messaging.

Personal Information Store

A *message store* is a database of messages (stored in one file). It includes your message Inbox , Outbox, and Sent Items, as well as other message folders you have created. The default filename for the message store is Mailbox.pst (although you can name it anything you like). By default, Windows Messaging places Mailbox.pst in the \Windows folder (which we consider a very poor place to store this file). Microsoft Exchange creates the Exchange folder and suggests placing the message store in that folder.

A much better place to keep your message store and your personal address book is the My Documents folder, or a subfolder of that folder. If multiple people use the computer, create subfolders for them under the My Documents folder.

The message store starts with the default name Personal Information Store — although you can rename it if you like — and Windows Messaging refers to it in dialog boxes as Personal Folders (referring to your collection of message folders). You only need one message store, because you can store all your messages from all information services in this single store.

You can, however, create additional special-purpose message stores if you choose. For instance, you might create different message stores for:

- Archival messages
- Messages from different information services
- Messages for different users
- Documents unrelated to messages

Each message store you create is a separate *pst* file, and you can put your various message store files in different Windows 95 folders if you like.

A profile can have multiple message stores, although only one message store can be active at a time. The active message store includes the Inbox, Outbox, and Sent Items folder. If you include multiple messages stores in one profile, you can easily copy messages from one store to another.

Your message store is compressed automatically after you delete messages. For this to occur, Windows Messaging has to be running, the amount of recoverable space has to be at least 4 percent of the total size of the message store, and the processor must have idle time. If you have heard your hard disk clicking away while you have Windows Messaging running, now you know why.

You can manually start a compression of your message store. In Windows Messaging, choose Tools, Services. Highlight your message store name (Personal Folders is the default), click Properties, and then choose Compact now.

Address books

Your *address book* is a database and, like your message store, it is stored in one file. Your default address book has the default filename Mailbox.pab (again you can name this file anything you like). Windows Messaging stores your address book in the \Windows folder (poor choice) and Microsoft Exchange stores it in the Exchange folder. Its default name is Personal Address Book. You can name your address book anything you like and store it wherever you want.

If you are connected to a local area network, you will find address books tied to the postoffice(s) found on network servers. If you are using Microsoft Mail, you will find a postoffice address list on the computer that houses your workgroup postoffice.

You may want to store the addresses of your regular e-mail correspondents in your personal address book if you are not always connected to the post office server. A system or workgroup administrator may maintain the postoffice address list. You can send mail to correspondents on the postoffice list by choosing names from it.

Other information services also maintain mailing lists. For example, the Microsoft Network maintains a list of all the people who have accounts on it. You can associate your existing CompuServe address book with a profile that contains a personal address book and the CompuServe mail delivery service.

A profile can have only one personal address book attached to it at a time. The CompuServe address book is not considered a personal address book, even though it is your personal CompuServe address book.

If you don't have Microsoft Mail and you want to use a shared address book in addition to your personal address book, you can purchase the Exchange Server. If Exchange Server is a bit much for you, you might want to check out the shared address book feature in OpenSoft's ExpressMail software. You can explore OpenSoft's software at http://www.opensoft.com/products/expressmail. They also provide a POP3/SMTP mail server that works with Windows Messaging.

Mail delivery services

Using Windows Messaging, you can connect to the following e-mail and fax delivery services:

- Microsoft Mail
- The Microsoft Network (MSN)
- CompuServe
- Internet Mail

■ Microsoft Fax

■ Other third-party e-mail delivery services compliant with MAPI

The MAPI drivers that these mail delivery services use to connect to Windows Messaging are considered by Microsoft to be personal gateways — gateways that connect Windows Messaging to another mail system. Microsoft sells other server gateways that link the Microsoft Mail Server and the Exchange Server to other e-mail systems.

Microsoft Mail

Windows 95 (like Windows for Workgroups 3.11) comes with a workgroup version of Microsoft Mail. You can create and administer a workgroup postoffice that can be shared by all the members of a workgroup whether they are running Windows 95 or WFWG 3.11. In most cases, you will want to have only one postoffice for your workgroup.

If you want to exchange mail using the Microsoft Mail connection with postoffices outside your workgroup, you need to upgrade the computer with the postoffice to the Microsoft Mail Server by installing the Microsoft Mail Postoffice upgrade or the Microsoft Exchange Server. Gateways to other mail systems are available and work with Microsoft Mail Server or Microsoft Exchange Server.

The Microsoft Network

The Microsoft Network (MSN) is Microsoft's online information service. You can send and receive e-mail to and from other Microsoft Network subscribers or over MSN's Internet connection to and from anyone with an Internet e-mail address. MSN provides Internet access as well as its own interest areas.

The Microsoft Network didn't provide POP3 and SMTP mail servers until November, 1996. Therefore, you had to use the MAPI driver specific to MSN to connect Windows Messaging to MSN. This driver is included on the Windows 95 CD-ROM.

Note that Windows Messaging is not used for messages on the MSN bulletin boards.

CompuServe

If you have a CompuServe account, you can have Windows Messaging call your account (using its TAPI-compatible dialer) and check if you have any mail. Of course, you can also send mail through CompuServe.

You can send and receive mail to and from CompuServe subscribers, or to and from anyone with an Internet e-mail address (using CompuServe as your Internet connection).

Secret

Unfortunately, you can't send and receive messages that are posted on CompuServe forums, even if the messages are addressed to you. You'll still need to use WinCIM or some other CompuServe interface program to manage your forum message traffic.

CompuServe is revamping its system architecture to use the Normandy software from Microsoft, which is based on Internet standards. Therefore, it may begin providing Internet-standard connections in 1997.

CompuServe Mail version 1.1 (version 1.0 came with the original Windows 95 CD-ROM) can't handle the Windows Messaging version of Remote Mail. You'll need to download a later version from CompuServe (GO CSMAIL).

Internet

If you have an account with an Internet service provider, you can use Windows Messaging as your e-mail client. You can send and receive regular ASCII Internet e-mail, and you can send messages in either MIME (Multipurpose Internet Mail Extensions) or UUENCODE format.

The Internet client will connect to SMTP (Simple Mail Transport Protocol) and POP3 (Postoffice Protocol version 3) mail boxes. You'll need to bind Microsoft's TCP/IP protocol to your Dial-Up Adapter if you call into an Internet service provider, or to your network card if you access the Internet through a server on your local area network. You'll find details about TCP/IP and Dial-Up Networking in Chapter 33.

Microsoft provides an update to the original SMTP Internet Mail driver that fixes numerous bugs. You can find it at http://www.microsoft.com/windows/software/updates.htm. Don't install the Microsoft Plus! Internet components after you install this update unless you want to write over it.

You can use the Internet Setup Wizard to configure Windows Messaging for Internet Mail. Whether or not this Wizard is available depends on which version of Windows 95 you have. If you have the original version, you'll have to either install Microsoft Plus! or download the Internet Explorer from Microsoft's web site, http://www.microsoft.com/windows/software.htm. Later versions of Windows 95 include the Internet Explorer, so the Internet Setup Wizard is available by default.

You'll want to use the Internet Setup Wizard after you have installed Windows Messaging (which you may have already accomplished during your Windows 95 installation). To access this Wizard, click the Start button, Programs, Accessories, Internet Tools, Get on the Internet.

Microsoft Fax

You can send and receive faxes if you install the Microsoft Fax delivery service in one of your profiles. Windows 95 can send faxes through the fax/modem card in your computer or over a shared fax modem in your workgroup on a computer running Windows 95.

Third-party MAPI mail delivery systems

Other companies can provide MAPI interfaces to their mail systems. If you have other MAPI drivers, you can configure a Windows Messaging profile to use these mail delivery services just as you would any other delivery service.

Tip

You can't use Windows Messaging to receive e-mail from or deliver e-mail to services that don't have MAPI drivers. This includes almost all the bulletin boards without Internet services.

Windows Messaging works with Netscape Navigator. You can also use Windows Messaging to connect to AT&T mail. WinFax Pro works with Windows Messaging, and it can use the Windows Messaging address book. If you want to use the cc:Mail server with Windows Messaging, you can get a MAPI interface for cc:Mail from Transend Corporation at http://www.transendcorp.com.

You'll find other third-party software that works with Windows Messaging at the Exchange Center, http://www.slipstick.com/exchange.

Creating Windows Messaging Profiles

You don't necessarily have to create Windows Messaging profiles, because you already created one profile when you first configured Windows Messaging. You can edit that profile, if you like, so it matches your needs. See *Editing Windows Messaging profiles* later in this chapter.

If you want to create a new Windows Messaging profile, you have two entry points. To add a new profile when you only have one, take the following steps:

STEPS

Creating a New Windows Messaging Profile

Step 1. Click the Start button, point to Settings, and then click Control Panel.

Step 2. Double-click the Mail (or Mail and Fax) icon.

Step 3. Click the Show Profiles button.

Step 4. Your current profiles are displayed in the list box of the Mail dialog box, as shown in Figure 32-1. Click Add to start the Inbox Setup Wizard or click Copy to make a copy of the highlighted profile. You can edit it later.

(continued)

Creating a New Windows Messaging Profile

Figure 32-1: The Mail dialog box.

Undocumented

If you have more than one Windows Messaging profile and you have chosen the option that lets you pick a profile when you start Windows Messaging, you can start the Inbox Setup Wizard from the Inbox icon on your Desktop. Double-click the Inbox icon to display the Choose Profile dialog box, and instead of selecting an existing profile, click the New button. To find out how to configure Windows Messaging to prompt you to choose a profile, see *Picking among profiles at Windows Messaging startup* later in this chapter.

Windows Messaging profiles for multiple users

If you have configured your Windows 95 computer for multiple users, you can associate a default Windows Messaging profile for each user. To do so take the following steps:

STEPS

Configuring Multiuser Windows Messaging Profiles

Step 1. Click the Start button, point to Settings, and click Control Panel. Double-click the Passwords icon.

Configuring Multiuser Windows Messaging Profiles

Step 2. Click the User Profiles tab, choose the option button labeled "Users can customize their preferences and desktop settings. Windows switches to your personal settings whenever you log in," and then click the OK button.

Step 3. Click the Start button, and click Shut Down. In the Shut Down Windows dialog box, choose Close all programs and log on as a different user, and click Yes.

Step 4. Log on as a new user. Run the Inbox Setup Wizard by double-clicking the Mail (or Mail and Fax) icon in the Control Panel. The Inbox Setup Wizard will guide you through the process of setting up a default user profile for the new user.

Editing Windows Messaging profiles

You can edit your Windows Messaging profile(s), not just to change the properties of a given profile, but also to change the properties of an address book, a message store, or a mail delivery service.

You can start editing a Windows Messaging profile in one of two ways. First, you can double-click the Mail (or Mail and Fax) icon in the Control Panel and click the Show Profiles button (if you have more than one profile). Highlight a particular profile in the Windows Messaging Profiles dialog box, and then click the Properties button.

Second, you can double-click the Inbox icon on your Desktop, choose a profile (if you're given this option), and then click Tools, Options in the Windows Messaging window.

The first method allows you to pick which profile you are going to edit before you edit it. The second method lets you select a profile to edit, but only if you have previously configured Windows Messaging to give you this choice (see the next section). In addition, the second method gives you access to more properties to edit than the first.

Picking among profiles at Windows Messaging startup

If you want to configure Windows Messaging to let you choose a profile when you start Windows Messaging (assuming you have already created more than one profile), take the following steps:

STEPS

Picking Your Own Startup Profile

Step 1.   Double-click the Inbox icon on your Desktop.

Step 2.   Click Tools, Options to display the General tab of the Options dialog box, as shown in Figure 32-2. (You won't have the Idioms tab unless you have installed Internet Idioms.)

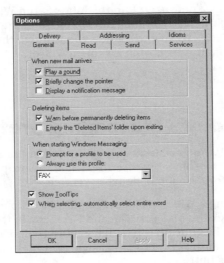

Figure 32-2: The General tab of the Options dialog box. If you want to choose which profile to use when you start Windows Messaging, mark the option button labeled "Prompt for a profile to be used."

Step 3.   Mark the "Prompt for a profile to be used" option button under When starting Windows Messaging.

Step 4.   Click OK. Choose File, Exit and then restart Windows Messaging to have the changes take effect.

The next time you double-click the Inbox icon on your Desktop, the Choose Profile dialog box will appear to let you choose among different profiles.

Adding or removing information services

When you originally create a profile, you can choose which mail delivery services you want to include in it. You can later go back and remove or add additional mail delivery services and message stores, or change to another personal address book.

To add or remove information services, you have two options:

STEPS

Adding or Removing Information Services

Step 1. Click the Start button, point to Settings, and then click Control Panel.

Step 2. Double-click the Mail (or Mail and Fax) icon.

Step 3. If you want to add or remove information services in the profile that normally starts when you double-click the Inbox icon on your Desktop, click the Add or Remove button. If you want to add or remove services from another profile, click the Show Profiles button first, highlight the desired profile, and then click the Properties button to display the Services tab of the Properties dialog box for the profile, as shown in Figure 32-3.

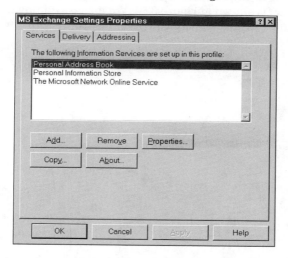

Figure 32-3: The Services properties sheet for profile. Click Add or Remove to add or remove an information service.

Step 4. Click the Add button to add a new information service or the Remove button to remove the highlighted service.

You can also get to the Services properties sheet for a profile by double-clicking the Inbox icon on your Desktop, choosing Tools, Options in the Windows Messaging window, and then clicking the Services tab. The properties sheet shown in Figure 32-3 appears, allowing you to add or remove information services.

When adding a mail delivery or other information service, you may be prompted to configure the service. To do this, you'll need to edit the properties sheets associated with that service. We discuss editing the properties of individual mail delivery services in the *Choosing mail delivery services* section later in this chapter.

Editing information services

Each information service — mail delivery services, message stores, and personal address book — has associated properties sheets. To edit these properties sheets, you just highlight the information service in the profile's Services properties sheet and click the Properties button.

Each mail delivery service has its own unique set of properties sheets as determined by the characteristics of the mail delivery system. The first of eight tabbed properties sheets for Microsoft Mail (the Connection properties sheet) is shown in Figure 32-4. We discuss editing the individual properties of the different mail delivery services in the section later in this chapter entitled *Choosing mail delivery services*.

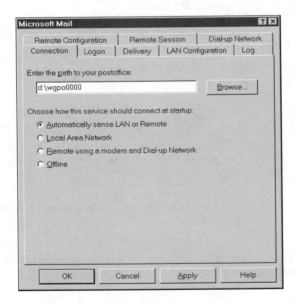

Figure 32-4: The Connection properties sheet for Microsoft Mail. Enter the path for your postoffice in the first field.

You can set the properties for the message store by highlighting the name of the message store in a profile's Services properties sheet, and then clicking the Properties button. We discuss these properties in the *Message Stores* section later in this chapter.

Not only can you change the properties of your address book, you can also change the properties of each address (or individual) in the address book. On the Windows Messaging toolbar, click the Address Book button, then double-click a name in your address book. We discuss address books further in the *Address Book* section later in this chapter.

Opening Windows Messaging with a specific profile

You can use a shareware program called Exchange Profile Selector to open Windows Messaging with a specific profile, allowing you to bypass the Choose Profile dialog box. Say you have one profile for faxing, another for Internet e-mail, and a third for CompuServe e-mail. You can place three shortcut icons on the Desktop, each of which calls Windows Messaging and uses the appropriate profile.

You'll find the Exchange Profile Selector on the *Windows 95 Secrets* CD-ROM or on the web at http://ourworld.compuserve.com/homepages/jsijm. You'll need version 1.3 or later to work with Windows Messaging. You can use TweakUI to get rid of the Inbox icon from your Desktop. After you place shortcuts to the Exchange Profile Selector on your Desktop, you won't need to keep the Inbox icon around.

Edit each shortcut's Target field to include the profile's name. Be sure to include the pathname and Eps.exe in the Target field, and enclose them in double quote marks if there is a space in the pathname. Enclose the profile name in a separate set of double quote marks (if there is a space in its name). Separate the two sets of names with a space.

Using these shortcuts is also a handy way to tell Windows Messaging which folder to open by default when you choose Insert, File in a New Message window. To do this, edit the shortcut (right-click it, click Properties, and click the Shortcut tab) and change the Start in folder to the one you want to use as the default for attachments.

Choosing mail delivery services

The first step in creating a profile is choosing the mail delivery service(s) that will be included in the profile. Each mail delivery service has a specific set of dialog boxes that get included in the Inbox Setup Wizard if you chose that mail delivery service for inclusion in the profile when you created it.

Each mail delivery service will have its own set of properties sheets. Figure 32-4 shows the first of eight properties sheets for Microsoft Mail delivery service. Most of the values in these properties sheets are not accessible when you're creating a profile. To change these values, you need to edit them after you've created the profile.

You can have multiple mail delivery services in a single profile. In fact, this is the default when you first install Windows Messaging and run the Inbox Setup Wizard. If you have multiple mail delivery services in one profile, Windows Messaging accesses them one at a time. For example, if you have MSN, Internet and CompuServe mail delivery services in your profile and you ask Windows Messaging to deliver your e-mail (Tools, Deliver Now), it will call each service in turn and send and receive e-mail from each of them.

If you get an error message stating that no transport was available, it's probably because you are trying to send a message that doesn't have the appropriate mail delivery service in your current profile. For example, you may be trying to send a message to a Microsoft Network user and addressing it with a Microsoft Network name, but there is only an Internet Mail delivery service in your current profile.

If you put multiple mail delivery services in one profile, you can avoid or reduce this problem. You can always check the recipient's address (right-click the name in the To field, and click Properties) to see that it is in the correct format for the current mail delivery service.

To edit the properties of a mail delivery service, you need to focus on it. Here's how:

STEPS

Choosing a Mail Delivery Properties Sheet

Step 1. Click the Start button, point to Settings, and then click Control Panel.

Step 2. Double-click the Mail (or Mail and Fax) icon.

Step 3. Highlight a profile. Click the Properties button. Highlight a mail delivery service. Click Properties.

Internet Mail properties sheets

Microsoft originally placed its Internet Mail delivery services on the Microsoft Plus! CD-ROM. Later, Microsoft made it available for download from Microsoft's web site at http://www.microsoft.com/kb/softlib/MSLFiles/ Inetmail.exe. Windows 95 Service Pack 1 included the updated Internet SMTP driver portion of the Internet Mail delivery service, and the Internet Mail delivery service has been available with every version of Internet Explorer. It is included on the all Windows 95 CD-ROMs that Microsoft released starting with Service Pack 1.

In the Internet Mail server field in the General tab of the Internet Mail dialog box (shown in Figure 32-5), you can enter either the IP address or the name of your POP3 mail server. Be sure to get the name of your POP3 and your SMTP mail servers from your Internet service provider when you contact them to establish an account. Typically, the names of these servers are the same and are mail.*yourserviceprovider*.com.

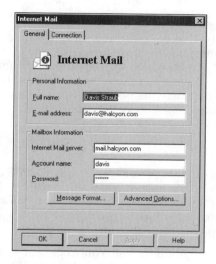

Figure 32-5: The General tab of the Internet Mail dialog box.

Enter the name that you use to log onto your e-mail account in the Account name field. Account name is a synonym for your user ID or host name. The e-mail account name could be different than your logon name (the name you use to log onto your Internet service account), but your ISP will probably set these names to be the same. We describe the differences in Chapter 33.

Your password is the password for your e-mail account. This is usually the same as your password for logging onto your account with your Internet service provider.

The SMTP server handles outgoing mail, and the POP3 server handles incoming mail. If your SMTP mail server has a different name than your POP3 server, click the Advanced Options button and type the name of your SMTP mail server. You can type friendly names if your Internet service provider has a DNS (Domain Name Server) server. Otherwise, type IP addresses.

Click the Connection tab in the Internet Mail dialog box to set how Windows Messaging connects to the Internet. If your computer is connected to the Internet (or to an Intranet) through a local area network, choose Connect using the network. If you're calling into your Internet service provider, choose Connect using the modem, and then choose the Dial-Up Networking connectoid that you'll use to make the connection to your service provider. (See the *Dial-up connection to your service provider* section in Chapter 33.) You'll also want to mark the Work off-line and Use Remote mail options if you are calling in.

If you dial in to log onto your Internet account, click the Login As button in the Connection tab. Type your logon or Internet service provider account name and password. They may be different than your e-mail account name and password.

It is possible, although not likely, that your Internet service provider (or the POP3 mail server on your Intranet) has been set up to use a different port ID than the agreed upon standard 110. If so, you will experience difficulties sending and receiving e-mail messages. To find out more about this problem and how to edit your Registry to change the port address, use your Internet Explorer to find the following Microsoft Knowledge Base article: http://www.microsoft.com/kb/articles/Q133/1/88.htm.

Message format

You have the option of sending outgoing messages in either MIME or UUENCODE format. You choose which format you want to use by clicking the Message Format button in the General tab of the Internet Mail dialog box. If everyone who you are writing to has an e-mail reader that can handle the MIME format, you'll want to use this higher level format.

The UUENCODE format is a tagged ASCII format. Your recipient will need an UUDECODE program to translate your message into a formatted text message. Windows Messaging and Microsoft Internet Mail automatically decode MIME or UUENCODED messages. If your recipient has one of these two programs, no worries, mate.

Windows Messaging allows you to send richly formatted messages to any or all of your recipients. To send such messages, you need to specify this preference for your recipient by marking the "Always send to this recipient in the Microsoft Exchange rich-text format" check box in the properties sheet for the recipient's address in your address book.

If your recipient can't read rich formatted text, but you have the rich-text box checked, he or she will receive attachments from you that contain unreadable (but ASCII) characters.

Secret

If your recipients are getting messages from you that contain an = sign at the end of your lines, click the Message Format button in the General tab of the Internet Mail dialog box, click the Character Set button, and choose US ASCII instead of ISO-8859-2. You can also try clearing the MIME check box.

Secret

If a recipient is getting e-mail messages from you with lines that are too long, you should turn off rich text formatting for that recipient.

Windows Messaging encodes attachments to your messages using whichever method you have chosen for encoding your messages. Some of your recipients may not be able to read attachments if their e-mail clients do not automatically decode encoded messages. They will have to use separate decoder programs to read your attachments.

Don't encode a file before you attach it to a message. Windows Messaging automatically encodes the attachment, so if you do it, it will be encoded twice. Your recipient will then have to decode it twice.

If you want to know more about MIME, check out: http:/www.mathcs.carleton.edu/students/pollatsd/MIME/index.html or gopher://atlas.acpub.duke.edu/00/email/mime or http://www.cis.ohio-state.edu/text/faq/usenet/mail/mime-faq/.

CompuServe properties sheets

The CompuServe mail delivery service comes with its own unique set of properties sheets. You can find the CompuServe MAPI driver on the Windows 95 CD-ROM under the \Drivers\Other\Exchange\CompuSrv folder, or you can download the latest version from CompuServe at GO CSMAIL. Double-click the Setup.exe file in this folder on the CD-ROM to install the CompuServe driver on your hard disk.

You'll be asked a number of questions about your CompuServe account after you double-click Setup.exe. You will be asked to give your CompuServe folder, user name, CompuServe ID number, password, and phone number. If you have been using WinCIM for a while, it's easy to forget your password, and WinCIM just displays it as a bunch of asterisks. Let's hope that you wrote it down someplace.

CompuServe's WinCIM keeps a separate address book. You can use this address book and your personal address book when sending message through CompuServe (either to people on CompuServe or to Internet addresses through CompuServe). You can also easily move people from your WinCIM address book to your personal address book once you start Windows Messaging with a profile that includes CompuServe.

Message Stores

Windows Messaging refers to a message store as your Personal Information Store or Personal Folders. Messages that you receive and create are stored in folders in a message store file, which is a database.

You can have multiple message stores, although one is plenty. The default message store (Mailbox.pst) is created for you when you set up Windows Messaging.

A message store comes with a standard set of folders: Inbox, Outbox, Sent Items, and Deleted Items. You can add additional folders to conveniently order your messages.

Undocumented

You can easily move a message store. Just use your Explorer to move the corresponding *pst* file to a new location. When you open Windows Messaging with a profile that uses that message store, you will be asked to provide a new message store. You can simply browse to the new location.

Adding a message store to a profile

A profile can have only one personal address book. It can have only one Internet Mail delivery service (although it can have other types of mail delivery services). But any profile can have multiple message stores. You can create a message store that will be an archive for your old messages or one for messages of a certain type.

You can create a profile that doesn't have any mail delivery services or a personal address book, just message stores. You can use this profile to move messages from your regular message store to archive message stores.

Windows Messaging loads faster if you keep your message store small. By using archive message stores and a separate profile to archive messages, you can reduce the size of your regular message store.

A message store is one of the Windows Messaging information services. You can follow the steps detailed in the section earlier in this chapter entitled *Adding or removing information services* to add a new message store to a profile. Then take the following steps:

STEPS

Adding a Message Store to a Profile

Step 1. When the Add Service to Profile dialog box (shown in Figure 32-6) is displayed on your Desktop, double-click Personal Folders in the Available Information Services list.

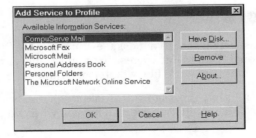

Figure 32-6: The Add Service to Profile dialog box. Double-click the information service you want to add to the profile. In this case, double-click Personal Folders.

Adding a Message Store to a Profile

Step 2. You'll be asked to provide a name and location for the message store file. You can put a message store file wherever you like. You can name it whatever you want to, but make sure that its extension is *pst*.

Step 3. You now have the option of renaming this particular message store, as shown in Figure 32-7. You can also protect this message store with a password.

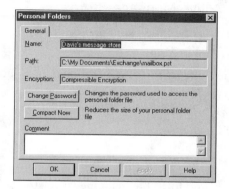

Figure 32-7: The dialog box that appears when you're creating Personal Folders. You can give the message store a password if you like. If the message store file is on a compressed drive and you want to encrypt it, choose Compressible Encryption.

Step 4. Click OK.

Changing a message store's name

You can change the long descriptive name of an existing message store by taking the following steps:

STEPS

Changing a Message Store's Name

Step 1. Double-click the Inbox icon on your Desktop.

Step 2. Click Tools, Services on the Windows Messaging menu bar. Double-click the name of the message store you want to change.

Step 3. Type a new name in the Name field and click OK.

Which message store?

If you have only one message store, all the messages go there. If you have more than one, you can specify which one you want to store new messages in by taking the following steps:

STEPS

Specifying the Active Message Store

Step 1.   Double-click the Inbox icon on your Desktop.

Step 2.   Choose Tools, Options.

Step 3.   Click the Delivery tab in the Options dialog box.

Step 4.   Choose one of the message stores in the drop-down list at the top of the dialog box.

Step 5.   Click OK.

You can switch back and forth between message stores, making first one then another the active store. You can also drag and drop messages between folders in a given message store and between message stores. This works well if one of the message stores is for archival storage.

If you have multiple message stores contained in a profile, they show up in the left pane of your Windows Messaging window. The active message store contains the Inbox and Outbox.

Sorting message headers

Undocumented

Each message in your message store has a header. There are 47 fields — Subject, From (sender), Received (date), Conversation Topic, and so on — in the message header (44 in Microsoft Exchange). When you're using the dual-pane view in the Windows Messaging window, the message headers appear in the right pane, and the window looks like an Explorer window in details view, as shown in Figure 32-8. (Click the Show/Hide Folder List button at the left end of the Windows Messaging toolbar to switch between single- and dual-pane views.)

Unfortunately, in the May, 1995 beta of the Exchange client, Microsoft pulled Exchange's capability to let you filter and group your message headers to give you different message header views. You could define custom header views, store these views, and apply them to any of the folders. This capability is available in the Microsoft Exchange client that comes with Microsoft Exchange Server.

Tip

A message store doesn't have to store just messages. It is a general document storage, sorting, viewing, and retrieval system. If you store OLE documents in a message store, summary and other information about the documents is available to you as fields you can use to sort document headers.

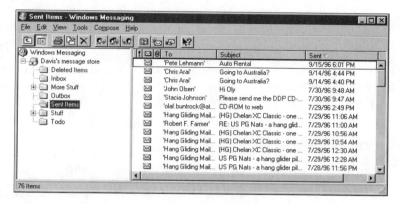

Figure 32-8: Windows Messaging. The message store and its folders are in the left pane. The message headers in a given folder are in the right pane.

Messages outside message stores

You can store messages outside your message stores by saving them as separate files with the *msg* extension. Simply double-clicking a message header in Windows Messaging and then choosing File, Save As will do it. You can also drag and drop messages from the message store onto the Desktop or into a folder in your regular Windows 95 file system.

If you double-click on the name of a message file stored on your hard disk as a separate file and display in an Explorer window, the message-composition portion of Windows Messaging will be invoked. Your message will be loaded, ready to be edited or sent.

Importing Other Messages

In the *Upgrading your Microsoft Mail message store* later in the chapter, we show you how to import your existing Microsoft Mail message store into a Windows Messaging message store.

You can also import messages from Eudora and from just about any other mail client that exports text files by using a utility called E2M. Hal Hostetler, a senior engineer in MIS at KVOA TV 4 in Tucson, turned us on to this utility. You'll need to use it with Microsoft Internet Mail. Download E2M from http://www.mindwave.com.au/freestuf.htm.

E2M can turn a Eudora mailbox into a Microsoft Mail mailbox. If you have installed Microsoft Internet Mail and News, you'll find Internet Mail's mailboxes in your \Program Files\Internet Mail and News*YourLogonName*\Mail folder. Each Internet Mail folder has a separate mailbox (an *mbx* file) and a separate index (an *idx* file).

E2M only needs to use the Eudora *mbx* file (yup, Eudora uses the same extension for its mailbox — *mbx* — as Microsoft), not the *toc* file. Hal moved his messages into Windows Messaging by constructing a Eudora-like *mbx* file that contained all the mail messages he wanted to import. The general procedure is simple: You first save your mail messages from other mail readers to text files with headers. Next, you add a Eudora "start of message" line to the beginning of each text file. Finally, you concatenate them all together! The exact process is as follows:

STEPS

Importing Messages into Windows Messaging

Step 1. Use your existing mail client to save the messages to be moved as text files with headers. You should do this on a "by folder" basis and place the files in a temporary folder.

Step 2. Use your favorite text editor to insert the line **From ???@??? Tue Jan 23 18:04:27 1996** into each message before the first line of the header. This is the Eudora "start of message" marker that the E2M utility looks for; the date in this line is unimportant and isn't used.

Step 3. Open a DOS box in this temporary folder and type **copy /a *.txt** *filename***.mbx** at the command prompt. The *filename* is whatever you want the mailbox to be called. This concatenates all the separate messages into a single mailbox file.

Step 4. Start E2M, and give its input as the *filename*.mbx file you just created. Name its output file an appropriate name for a new Internet Mail and News mail folder. Click the Convert button. This creates the new Internet Mail and News mailbox/folder. Be sure to place the new mailbox/folder file in the Mail subfolder.

Step 5. Start Internet Mail. Choose File, Folder, Compact and select the new folder. You'll get an error message stating that the folder is damaged. Click OK to repair it. You get this error message because you have a *mbx* file without a companion *idx* file. When you click OK, Internet Mail will rebuild the *idx* file.

Importing Messages into Windows Messaging

Step 6.   In Internet Mail, choose File, Export, Messages. You can now send the messages to Windows Messaging.

Address Book

The really cool thing about the Windows Messaging address books is that they are (almost) full featured. For example, you can assign up to eight phone numbers to each person in a book, as shown in Figure 32-9, and dial them by clicking any one of eight Dial buttons. You can also store a person's address, title, assistant's name and number, notes about the person, and so on.

Funny thing though, there is only one e-mail address or fax number per entry. This causes a lot of problems.

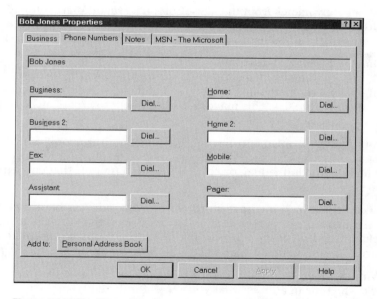

Figure 32-9: The Phone Numbers properties sheet for Bob Jones. Click the Dial button to call any of the numbers.

It's not like you can start printing labels from your Windows Messaging address book, but it does provide a name, address, and phone number database upon which third parties can build other applications. You can use Word for Windows to create labels and print envelopes from the address book.

Undocumented

Each profile can only use one personal address book at a time. In addition to the personal address book, you can attach a CompuServe address book to a profile that includes the CompuServe mail delivery service, and you can associate a Microsoft Network address book (maintained in Redmond, not on your computer) with a profile that uses MSN. You can also associate address books stored on various mail servers with Microsoft Mail delivery services. The same personal address book can be used by numerous different profiles.

You must remove a personal address book from a profile before you can add another. Removing an address book does not delete the address book file. If you rename or move an address book file, Windows Messaging will prompt you to create a new connection to an address book. You could have a number of address book files that aren't currently attached to any profile and therefore not able to be viewed, edited, or added to.

Undocumented

You can create "personal distribution lists" made up of selected members of your address book. You can then send e-mail (or faxes) to any one of these lists.

You can copy names from the MSN, CompuServe, or Microsoft Mail server address books into your personal address book. You can also create personal distribution lists from names stored in these other address books.

If you use a personal distribution list as the address in a message, you can't edit out a few names on a one-time basis for that message. The address field contains just the personal distribution list name and not the names contained within the list. This makes it a bit difficult to create an ad hoc selection of addresses.

Undocumented

If you right-click on an entry in your personal address book, a context menu appears. Choose Properties from the menu to display/edit the properties of the highlighted individual, or choose Delete to remove that entry from the address book.

You can compose a message starting from your address book by highlighting the name of the person that you want to send the message to, and then clicking the New Message button in the Address Book toolbar. The person's address is automatically loaded into the To field in the new message.

If Windows Messaging is running, you can enter names into your address book. The type of address that you can enter depends on the mail delivery services in your current profile. If you have included all the possible mail delivery services in the profile, Windows Messaging will ask whether you want to enter a fax address, an Internet address, a Microsoft Network address, an Internet address reached through Microsoft Network, a Microsoft Mail address, a CompuServe address, or an Internet address reached through CompuServe. You will only be able to enter addresses that work with the mail delivery services in the current profile.

Changing the name of the address book

Undocumented

While the personal address book will always be named Personal Address Book (unlike the Personal Information Store, whose name you can completely change), you can add another name to identify a particular address book. To do so, take the following steps:

STEPS

Changing the Name of Your Personal Address Book

Step 1. Double-click the Inbox icon on the Desktop.

Step 2. Click Tools, Services, highlight Personal Address Book, and then click the Properties button.

Step 3. Type a new name in the Name field. This new name will be added to the name Personal Address Book. For example, type in **Brian's Address Book** and the new name becomes "Personal Address Book (Brian's Address Book)."

The address book's big problem

Each entry (record) in the address book can have only one e-mail address or one fax number (despite the fax and phone number fields displayed in Figure 32-9). This means you must have two records for a given individual if you wish to reach them both by fax and by e-mail using Windows Messaging — two entries that repeat all the same information except for the e-mail or fax number.

This is nuts. Microsoft apparently hasn't been able to figure out how to solve this problem. It is the fax number or e-mail address and the display name that is the "live" portion of the record, that is, the part of the record that connects to the rest of Windows Messaging. You could easily end up with three or four records for the same person with display names as follows:

Bill Smith - Internet

Bill Smith - Fax

Bill Smith - MSN

Bill Smith - CompuServe

Not only do you need a different record for each e-mail or fax address for a given person, but you need different records for the different methods you use to connect to the Internet to reach that person. For example, assume you have an account with a local Internet service provider and an account with MSN. If you have separate profiles for your service provider and MSN, and you want to send e-mail to a person with an MSN address independently of whether you are logged on to MSN or to your Internet service provider, you need to have one record with the MSN-to-MSN connection and another with the Internet-to-MSN connection.

Opening the address book from the Desktop

Undocumented

You can create a shortcut to Exchng32.exe, the Windows Messaging executable file, and get to your address book with a double-click. Here's how:

STEPS

Shortcut to the Address Book

Step 1.   Open your Explorer to C:\Program Files\Windows Messaging.

Step 2.   Drag and drop Exchang32.exe onto your Desktop. Press F2 and rename the new shortcut Address Book. Press Enter.

Step 3.   Right-click the new shortcut, and click Properties. Click the Shortcut tab. At the end of the Target field, add a space followed by **/a** . Click the OK button.

Creating and Sending Mail

You create and send e-mail and faxes from within Windows Messaging using the compose feature. You can also print or send faxes from other Windows applications. Microsoft Fax has the ability to act like a printer driver. If you print to it from a Windows application, it can take whatever it is you are printing and send it out as a fax.

If you have MAPI-enabled applications (such as Word for Windows), you can compose e-mail and faxes from within these applications. To send e-mail or faxes, choose File, Send on the application's menu bar. The current document is sent as an attachment to a message over your active mail delivery service. If Windows Messaging isn't running when you click Send, it will be invoked.

To compose a message while using Windows Messaging, click the New Message button in the toolbar, or choose Compose, New Message. This will bring up what feels like a whole new application, your e-mail message composition application. New Message should remind you a lot of WordPad, as can be seen in Figure 32-10.

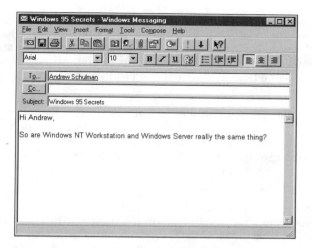

Figure 32-10: The New Message window. Create and send messages from here. Click the Send button (the envelope) on the left end of the toolbar to send a message.

Sending mail

To send a message after you have composed it, click the Send button (the envelope) on the left end of the New Message toolbar. Your message will be placed in the Outbox of your message store. If you are not currently connected to your mail delivery service, your message will sit right there until you do get connected.

You can just drag and drop a message from a Windows Messaging folder to the Outbox. It seems like you should be able to use this method to send your messages, but messages you move to the Outbox with drag and drop aren't actually ready to be delivered. If you look inside the Outbox folder, you'll notice that messages you have placed in the folder via the Send command are displayed in italics. If you use drag and drop to move a message to the Outbox, its name is displayed in a regular font, indicating that it's not ready to be sent. If you want your messages to be delivered when you click the Deliver Now button, you have to move them to the Outbox with the Send command instead of with drag and drop.

You can keep messages in your Outbox and send them later by double-clicking on their headers in the Outbox, and then closing the New Message window without clicking the Send button. If you find a message header in your Outbox that isn't italicized and you want to send it, double-click the header and click the Send button on the toolbar. Of course, if you have configured Windows Messaging to send messages immediately (which you would normally do if you work online), then your messages don't spend too much time sitting around in the Outbox.

Undocumented

If you are connected to a LAN, *and* your active Windows Messaging profile is configured to use Microsoft Mail, *and* you are sending a message to another person on your Microsoft Mail mailing list, your message will automatically be delivered from your message store's Outbox to your Microsoft Mail postoffice. At the same time, it will be moved to the Sent Items folder of your message store.

Undocumented

If you're using a dial-up connection to an Internet service provider, you should configure your Internet Mail delivery service to allow you to compose messages off-line. (Choose Off-line instead of Automatic in the Internet portion of the Inbox Setup Wizard.) After you send messages to the Outbox, you can choose Deliver Now to call up your service provider and deliver the messages.

If you have chosen to work off-line, your e-mail messages are sent to the Outbox when you click the Send button on the toolbar. They aren't really sent on their way, and your Internet service provider is not called when you click the Send button. This is not particularly intuitive. Not only do you have to send the message, you have to deliver it too.

If you are on an Intranet or you access your service provider through your local area network, you can choose to stay on-line and your messages will be delivered automatically from your Outbox.

The Internet Mail delivery service that came with the original Windows Exchange client placed messages in the Sent Items folder even if it encountered a problem connecting to your service provider and was unable to send the messages. Windows Messaging cleans up this error.

To configure your Internet Mail service for one or the other of these connection options, take the following steps:

STEPS

Configuring the Internet Mail Delivery Service

Step 1. Click the Start button, point to Settings, and then click Control Panel. Double-click the Mail or (Mail and Fax) icon in the Control Panel.

Step 2. Click the Show Profiles button first if the Internet Mail delivery service is not included in the default profile. Otherwise, highlight Internet Mail and click the Properties button.

Step 3. Click the Connection tab. In the Transferring Internet Mail section, mark the Work off-line and Use Remote mail options if you access your service provider by dial-up modem.

Step 4. Click OK.

If you are sending e-mail via the Microsoft Network, mail will be sent to the Outbox and stay there until you connect to MSN. You can use Tools, Deliver Now on the Windows Messaging menu bar to connect to MSN and send and receive e-mail.

If you are sending a fax and you have configured your fax mail delivery service to send faxes immediately, Windows Messaging will initialize your fax modem and send the fax as soon as you click the Send button. It will also deliver the fax later (at a time you specify) without further input from you. You can set up faxes for later delivery by choosing Tools, Microsoft Fax Tools, Options.

Undocumented

When you compose a message, you must provide an address to send the message to. This address identifies the mail delivery service that will transport the mail. Even if you have multiple mail delivery services attached to your active Windows Messaging profile, each message will be sent through the correct mail delivery service.

Receiving mail

If you are connected to an Exchange or Microsoft Mail Server over a local area network, messages will be delivered to your Inbox automatically (if Windows Messaging is running on your computer). You have to configure your Microsoft Mail delivery service to notify you of incoming messages by choosing Tools, Services, Microsoft Mail, Properties, Delivery, and Immediate Notification.

If you have dial-up (remote) access, you need to call in and get your messages. The easiest way to do this is to choose Tools, Deliver Now or click the Deliver Now toolbar button.

If you want to see how big your messages are before you download them, or if you want to only download the most important messages, you can choose Tools, Remote Mail, Connect. This automatically downloads the message headers so that you can view the message title, author, date, time, size, and so on. You can then choose which messages you want to download. After downloading a message, you can either delete or keep the original message on the server.

Windows Messaging can't notify you that you have new mail unless it is running. If you don't have enough memory to comfortably run Windows Messaging constantly, there are some shareware products that can do this for you. Check out the *Windows 95 Secrets* CD-ROM.

You can choose the font of incoming non-formatted e-mail if you use WordMail (see the next section) and an add-on applet. Go to http://www./halcyon.com/goetter.

Using Word to create e-mail messages

You can use Microsoft Word for Windows as your e-mail message composition tool instead of the one that comes built in with Windows Messaging.

First you have to configure Windows Messaging and Word to work together. If you installed Windows Messaging before you installed Word, choose Compose, Enable Word in the Windows Messaging window.

If you installed Windows Messaging after Word — for example, you may have upgraded from the Microsoft Exchange client after you installed Microsoft Office — then you need to take a different tack. Insert your Microsoft Office CD-ROM, click the Start button, click Run, and type **d:\Setup /y**, where d: is the volume label for your CD-ROM.

This will set up WordMail. After the installation process is complete, start Windows Messaging and choose Compose, Enable Word. You can find out more about this by turning to the Microsoft Knowledge Base, http://www.microsoft.com/kb/articles/q135/2/95.htm.

WordMail makes it easy to create a signature file without using Internet Idioms. Format the text that you want to use as signature file, and save it as an AutoText entry with the name *signature*. There are macros available at http://miso.wwa.com/~sam/macro.html that allow you to have multiple signatures as well as set your own the Internet quoted reply character, > for example.

WordMail is a pig; even at 16MB you're going to feel the hit. If you thought Microsoft Exchange was bad, well this is what "full featured" really adds up to. If you have a fast computer, lots of memory, and you want it all, then give WordMail a try. Of course, WordMail has now been superseded by Microsoft Outlook. You might want to use Outlook instead if you have Microsoft Office 97 or later.

Internet Explorer and Windows Messaging

Windows Messaging includes a new fast send capability that invokes a less filling version of Windows Messaging and thereby comes up more quickly. It works well with File, Send menu commands from other Windows applications, and with the Microsoft Internet Explorer. This fast send note doesn't invoke the spelling checker, and its window borders are fixed.

You can specify fast send mode by choosing Tools, Options from the Windows Messaging menu bar, and clicking the Send tab. Mark the option labeled "Use simplified note on Internet 'mailto:' and File, Send," and then click OK.

In 1996, Netscape's Navigator came out with an integrated Internet e-mail capability. At first, Microsoft had no response because while the Microsoft Exchange client could be called from the Internet Explorer (1.0 and 2.0), it took a long time to load into memory, and didn't really deliver the mail. If you had configured your computer to work off-line, the e-mail just sat in the Outbox, even if you were on-line at the time that you created your e-mail message. Only if Windows Messaging was already running could you then click the Deliver Now button and send the mail.

Internet Explorer now has a built in e-mail client. You can choose which e-mail client to use with Internet Explorer by clicking View, Options, Programs in the Internet Explorer menu bar. Microsoft Internet Mail is the default, but you can pick Windows Messaging as well. When you click a mailto: e-mail address in a web page, either Microsoft Internet Mail or Windows Messaging will start. Internet Mail delivers the mail when you click the Send button (if you have chosen the Send immediately option in the Internet Mail configuration). Windows Messaging does not deliver the mail immediately (if you have configured it to work off-line); you have to invoke the complete application and then click the Deliver Now icon.

Signatures and ">" indents

As we have pointed out previously, the original Microsoft Exchange client and Windows Messaging are stripped-down versions of the Microsoft Exchange client that comes with Microsoft Exchange Server. There are a couple of add-on utilities you can use to spruce up Windows Messaging by adding signatures and reply quoting. These utilities were written by Ben Goetter, who created them when he was writing a book about programming using Windows Messaging. You can download the latest versions from his web site at http://www./halcyon.com/goetter.

Ben's Internet Idioms include the Inetxidm.dll and Inetxidm.inf files, which let you add a signature and indent characters (using whatever character you like) to your e-mail. When you reply to someone's e-mail message, you use indent characters to offset the text you're quoting from the original message. The ">" character is the standard method of marking quoted text in Internet e-mail.

Internet Idioms only lets you have one signature, so it is difficult to "wear different hats." If you have installed an older version of it to work with the Microsoft Exchange client, you'll find that it doesn't work with Windows Messaging. When you open a New Message window, you get an error message stating that you are using an older version of Internet Idioms and that it might not work.

You should download the latest version of Internet Idioms if you want it to work with Windows Messaging. Also, make sure that all your references in your Registry refer to Windows Messaging and not to Microsoft Exchange. It is generally a good idea to edit your Registry in this fashion after you have installed Windows Messaging if you previously had Microsoft Exchange installed. Follow these steps to get rid of the old references to Microsoft Exchange in your Registry:

STEPS

Cleaning Up after Microsoft Exchange

Step 1.   Delete the folder C:\Program Files\Microsoft Exchange.

Step 2.   Using your Registry editor, search for *exchng32.exe*.

Step 3.   Change each pathname associated with exchng32.exe that includes *Progra~1\Micros~1* to *Program Files\Windows Messaging*.

Ben has a utility that lets you empty the Deleted Items folder by simply choosing File, Expunge Deleted Items. Another utility of his lets you set the default font for incoming unformatted (plain text) e-mail. His utilities can also be found on the *Windows 95 Secrets* CD-ROM.

Sending mail without using an address book

Undocumented

You don't have to put someone in your address book before you can send that person mail. You just have to identify the mail delivery service that you are going to use and write a proper address in the To field. Table 32-1 contains examples of what you can type in the To field:

Table 32-1	Sample Addresses
Address	*Mail Delivery Service*
[FAX:+1 (*nnn*) *nnn-nnnn*]	fax
[MSN:*msn alias*]	Microsoft Network
[MSNINET:*internet address*]	Internet address through MSN
User name from the postoffice	Microsoft Mail (local area network)
[CompuServe: *nnnnn,nnnn*]	CompuServe
[SMTP:*Internet address*]	Internet service provider

If you are sending mail to an Internet address through your Internet service provider, you can just type the Internet address without the SMTP prefix and square brackets.

The New Message window doesn't default to sending a blind courtesy copy or to displaying this field. If you want to send a blind copy to someone, click View and then Bcc Box.

It's more than e-mail

When you think of e-mail you normally think of ASCII text notes — a short note with little or no formatting. With Windows Messaging, Microsoft is attempting to change that whole perception.

You can use Windows Messaging to create and send fully formatted documents. In addition, you can insert documents into plain or formatted text messages as attachments (either by dragging and dropping or by choosing Insert, File). When your message is received, the recipient can double-click the attachment symbol for the document to open the document using the associated application (if the recipient has an application that is associated with the document type — see Chapter 13 for details on document types). Windows Messaging is a full OLE 2 application. You can insert OLE 2 objects in a message and mail or fax them.

To see how to edit OLE 2 objects in Windows Messaging, take the following steps:

STEPS

Editing OLE 2 Objects

Step 1. Click the New Message button in the Windows Messaging toolbar.

Step 2. In the New Message window, choose Insert, Object.

Step 3. Scroll through the Object Type list box and highlight the type of object that you want to create. Click OK.

Step 4. The New Message window will be transformed to incorporate the tools needed to edit the new object. Figure 32-11 shows the window created for a bitmapped object.

(continued)

Editing OLE 2 Objects

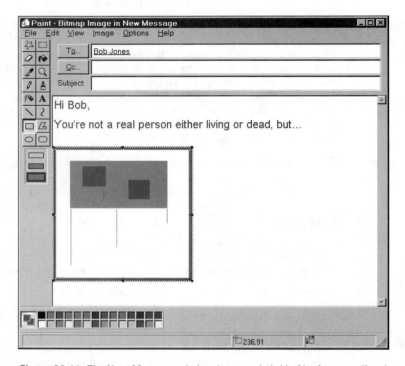

Figure 32-11: The New Message window is now a hybrid of its former self and MS Paint.

Step 5. You can send the message with the enclosed object(s).

Sending pointers to attachments

If you send mail over your LAN using Microsoft Mail, you can send pointers to files instead of the sending the files as attachments themselves. This is just a fancy way of sending someone a file without actually sending it. By sending a pointer to the file (which is itself stored in a shared folder) you cut down on the amount of space used in your postoffice, especially if you are sending a document to a number of people.

STEPS

Sending a Pointer to a File

Step 1. Click the New Message button in the Windows Messaging toolbar.

Step 2. Click the Insert File button in the New Message toolbar.

Step 3. Mark the Link attachment to original file check box.

Step 4. Browse to the file (in a shared folder) you want to link to the message. Double-click a shared folder (or if the volume is already shared, click the file) and then click the filename.

Step 5. Click OK.

The pointer is just a shortcut to the document.

If you are sending mail over the Microsoft Network, you can send shortcuts to documents and folders stored on MSN to other MSN users. This is a handy way to point out how to get to a given location, or to send a document without making a copy.

You can send shortcuts to web sites. Your recipients can just click on the shortcut and it will call up their browser and go to the web site.

Microsoft Mail Workgroup Postoffice

Before you create a profile that includes the Microsoft Mail delivery service, you should either have the name and location of your workgroup's shared Microsoft Mail postoffice, or you need to create such a postoffice. If you included Microsoft Mail as a mail delivery service in the default profile created when you installed Windows 95, you may not have had the opportunity to create a postoffice first. You can go back and do that and then edit your Windows Messaging profile.

If your computer is connected to a LAN and you are using Microsoft Mail, all of the users in your workgroup should use the same postoffice. When you set up Windows Messaging, you need to tell it only the name and location of the shared postoffice.

To create a Microsoft Mail postoffice, double-click the Microsoft Mail Postoffice icon in your Control Panel. This will create a workgroup postoffice. You'll need to decide which computer you are going to store the postoffice on, and who is going to look after it. You'll need to mark the postoffice folder as shared among the members of your workgroup. You'll want only one postoffice for your workgroup so that everyone will be able to send mail to everyone else in the workgroup.

If you want to send mail (using Windows Messaging) to people in other workgroups, you'll need to have Microsoft Mail Server, Microsoft Exchange Server, or some other company's Microsoft Mail-compatible server.

Clicking the Microsoft Mail Postoffice icon in your Control Panel will start the Microsoft Workgroup Postoffice Administration Wizard, which will guide you through setting up a postoffice.

Upgrading your Microsoft Mail message store

Windows Messaging comes with its own form of a message store. If you install Windows 95 over your existing Windows 3.x directory, your existing message stores (files with the extension *mmf*) will be converted to Personal Information Store format (files with *pst* extension). If you have additional older message stores that weren't converted, you can do it manually.

STEPS

Converting Older Message Stores

Step 1.   Double-click the Inbox icon on your Desktop.

Step 2.   If you need to create a message store to store these converted messages, follow the steps detailed in the *Adding a message store to a profile* section earlier in this chapter.

Step 3.   If you have more than one message store and you want to store the converted messages in a secondary message store, click Tools, Options, click the Delivery tab, and then choose the appropriate message store. Click OK.

Step 4.   Click File, Import on the Windows Messaging menu bar.

Step 5.   Browse to find the older message store and then double-click it.

Your older messages will be added to the new message store you chose. You original *mmf* file is not altered by the conversion process. You cannot convert the *mmf* file, if it is located on the postoffice server. To create a new message store from a *mmf* file on your postoffice server, you can log onto your mail account using Microsoft Mail, then click Mail, Options, Server and give the *mmf* file a local name. Exit Microsoft Mail, start Windows Messaging, and use File, Import to create a new message store from the *mmf* file.

Remote access to a Microsoft Mail postoffice

If you use CompuServe, MSN, and/or the Internet as mail delivery services, you are already familiar with remotely accessing your mail delivery service. You need to access them through a modem. This is not the case if your LAN has server access to the Internet.

If you have Microsoft Mail running on your office network, you can also set up your portable computer or computer at home to access your e-mail account at the office over the phone. You can call either your computer at work or your company's network, depending on how these computers are set up.

Any of the remote mail delivery connections give you a number of options. One option is to review just the message headers and decide which messages to download. Outgoing messages are queued in your portable's Outbox until the next time you connect with the office. You can create a schedule that tells your computer (if it is turned on) when to call into the office (or other mail delivery service) and check for e-mail.

If you have a portable computer that you use at the office and on the road, you will most likely want to set up two different profiles, both of which use the Microsoft Mail delivery service, but one that uses it over the phone lines. To configure a new profile for remote access to your Microsoft Mail postoffice, take the following steps:

STEPS

Creating a Profile for Remote Access to a Microsoft Mail Postoffice

Step 1. Click the Start button, Settings, and then Control Panel.

Step 2. Double-click the Mail (or Mail and Fax) icon in the Control Panel, and then click the Show Profiles button.

Step 3. Highlight a profile that contains your Microsoft Mail delivery service. If you don't have such a profile, click the Add button to create a new profile using the Inbox Setup Wizard.

(continued)

Creating a Profile for Remote Access
to a Microsoft Mail Postoffice

Step 4. Once you have a profile that uses Microsoft Mail, highlight that profile and click the Properties button. Highlight the Microsoft Mail information service and click the Properties button in the Services properties sheet.

Step 5. Click the Connection tab and then choose Automatically sense LAN or Remote, as shown in Figure 32-12. If you want to force a remote connection, click Remote using a modem and Dial-up Network.

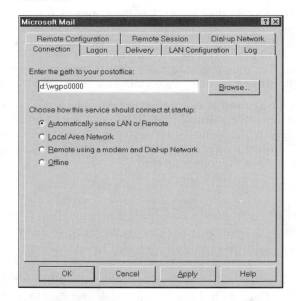

Figure 32-12: The Connection tab in the Microsoft Mail dialog box. Enter the server name and folder name for your Microsoft Mail postoffice. Click one of the two option buttons that allows for a remote connection.

Step 6. Click the Remote Configuration tab and choose the options that you want.

Step 7. Click the Remote Session tab. If you want to dial up your Microsoft Mail postoffice as soon as you double-click the Inbox icon, mark the When this provider is started check box, as shown in Figure 32-13.

Creating a Profile for Remote Access to a Microsoft Mail Postoffice

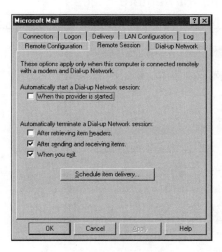

Figure 32-13: The Remote Session tab of the Microsoft Mail dialog box. You determine when the computer at the office will be called up and when it will be terminated.

Step 8.   To create a schedule for regular connections with the office Microsoft Mail postoffice, click the Schedule item delivery button. You'll need to already have a Dial-Up Networking (DUN) connection defined, so you might want to do the next step first.

Step 9.   Click the Dial-up Network tab to define how to make a connection with your office. If you don't already have a DUN connection for your office, you can create one by clicking the Add Entry button, as shown in Figure 32-14.

(continued)

STEPS *(continued)*

Creating a Profile for Remote Access
to a Microsoft Mail Postoffice

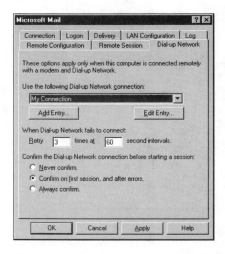

Figure 32-14: The Dial-up Network tab of the Microsoft Mail dialog box. Click the Add Entry button to create a new connection to your office.

It is not a simple one-step operation to create a new Dial-Up Networking connection. You should review Chapter 28 if you are unfamiliar with how to do it.

Step 10. Click OK when you are done.

You can create a DUN connection to a computer running Windows 95 (if you have installed the DUN server on it), a Windows NT server, a Novell NetWare server, Shiva LanRover, an Internet service provider, or other servers. Check Chapter 28 for more details.

Troubleshooting Windows Messaging

Secret

Terri Bronson at Microsoft gives the following advice when you have big general problems with Windows Messaging:

STEPS

Troubleshooting Windows Messaging

Step 1. Delete the Windows Messaging profile you are having problems with (perhaps your *only* one). Double-click the Mail (or Mail and Fax) icon in the Control Panel, click Show Profiles, highlight the bad profile, and click Delete.

Step 2. Create a new profile (click Add).

Step 3. Click the Start button, then Run, type **Awadpr32.exe,** and then press Enter.

Step 4. Make sure there are no files left in your \Windows\Spool\Fax folder due to prior crashes that are "stuck."

Step 5. Make sure there are no "stuck" messages in your Outbox.

Step 6. If you also run Microsoft Mail, make sure it is not the first mail delivery service in your profile.

You may find that Windows Messaging hangs or generates a Mapisp32 error message when you start it. These are symptoms of a damaged Outbox. To see how to removed damaged files from the Windows Messaging Outbox, go to http://www.microsoft.com/kb/articles/Q137/3/64.htm.

If you repeatedly start and exit Windows Messaging, you may also run into Mapisp32 errors. The symptoms include the inability to restart Windows Messaging using anything but the previous profile. The best way of preventing these problems is to have enough memory (16MB or more) to start Windows Messaging and to leave it active throughout the day.

Microsoft Fax

Windows Messaging treats faxes printed from other applications as attachments to messages. The messages are stored in your Windows Messaging message store, and you can view the stored faxes by double-clicking the attachment symbols in their messages. The fax message header contains the pertinent information identifying the fax.

A message store is an OLE 2 container. It can store all sorts of different kinds of files and objects. Faxes printed from other applications just happen to be another kind of document.

With Microsoft Fax, you can send editable documents as faxes to recipients, who can then open them using compatible applications. Microsoft Fax utilizes the Microsoft-developed *binary file transfer* (BFT) capability to fool the fax transport into sending documents instead of dots to Class 1 fax/

modems. Of course, you can't send these editable documents as editable documents to a fax machine or Class 2 fax/modems. Microsoft Fax sends documents as faxes to Group 3-compatible fax machines.

Faxing from the Start button

Click the Start button, point to Programs, Accessories, and then Fax. You'll find four options in the Fax menu: Compose New Fax, Cover Page Editor, Fax Viewer, and Retrieve File.

Compose New Fax

Clicking this menu item starts the Compose New Fax Wizard and Windows Messaging. The Wizard lets you compose a little fax or send a file. Windows Messaging has a much better composition window than the little dialog box that the Wizard gives you. To compose and send a fax from Windows Messaging, take the following steps:

STEPS
Composing and Sending a Fax

Step 1. Double-click the Inbox icon on your Desktop and choose a profile with a Microsoft Fax mail delivery service if you have more than one profile.

Step 2. Choose Compose, New Message (or click the New Message button on the toolbar).

Step 3. In the New Message window, click the To field to choose someone to send the fax to.

Step 4. Compose the fax, and then click the Send button (the envelope) on the left end of the toolbar to send the fax.

Undocumented Faxes you compose within Windows Messaging or through the Compose New Fax Wizard are messages and not attachments to messages, as is the case with faxes printed from Windows applications.

Undocumented Faxes sent by Microsoft Fax will come out as short faxes if you send them to thermal fax machines. These machines cut the paper after the last bit of text. To get around this problem, put footers (date or page number, for example) in the documents that you fax.

Undocumented You can place a shortcut to the Compose New Fax Wizard on your Desktop. Open your Explorer to \Windows\Start Menu\Accessories\Fax. Copy and paste a copy of the Compose New Fax Wizard onto your Desktop. This is a shortcut to the file Awsnto32.exe. You can drag and drop a document that you want faxed onto this Desktop icon.

Cover Page Editor

The Cover Page Editor is a standalone application that you use to create and edit fax cover pages. Cover pages can be fairly complex and rich documents in and of themselves. The editor allows you to place fax information fields as well as graphics. It is an OLE 2 application, so you can use MS Paint to create graphical items.

You don't need to send cover pages with your faxes or edit any of the existing cover pages before you send your first fax. Cover pages are a frill. The Cover Page Editor is quite a powerful utility that shows off the capability of OLE 2 and reusable code and objects (from WordPad), but it's still just an accessory.

The original Cover Page Editor has a bug. If the Archive bit on a cover page file is cleared (turned off), the cover page is no longer visible. Archive bits are routinely turned off by backup programs. Also, if you created a cover page in some other format (and the file had a *cpe* extension) the cover pages disappear.

Microsoft has fixed this in later versions of Windows 95. If you have the original version (Faxcover.exe in the \Windows folder is dated 7/11/95), download http://www.microsoft.com/kb/softlib/MSLFiles/Coverpg.exe. Save this file to a temp folder and then double-click it in your Explorer.

Fax Viewer

Double-click a fax attachment in a message to invoke the Fax Viewer and view the fax. Once you are in the Fax Viewer and viewing a fax, you can save the fax in a file outside of the message store. You can then use the Fax Viewer in standalone mode to view the fax file (a file with the *awd* extension).

Double-click a file with an *awd* extension to invoke the Fax Viewer. You can also just drag and drop a fax file onto your Desktop to copy it outside of the message store. Microsoft supplies a general image viewer on its Windows 95 CD-ROM starting with OEM Service Release 2. You can use this viewer to annotate faxes. Wang developed the viewer — entitled Imaging for Windows 95 — for Microsoft, and then released its first version in December, 1995. A second version was released in October, 1996. If you don't have the latest version, you can download it from http://microsoft.com/windows/software.htm.

This viewer replaces the Fax Viewer that comes with the Exchange client. After you have installed Wang's Imaging for Windows 95, double-click a fax image inside Exchange or Windows Messaging. Imaging displays the fax. You can also try highlighting sections of your fax or attaching yellow sticky notes.

Request a Fax

Do you want to call a fax-on-demand service and download a fax or two? This is what the Request a Fax menu item is for (Start button, Programs, Accessories, Fax, Request a Fax). It invokes a Wizard that makes the call and retrieves the fax (or a document, file, or software update from a fax server that supports BFT).

Click the Retrieve whatever is available option button in the Request a Fax Wizard dialog box to get a fax that gives you the names of the other fax/ documents that are available on the service. You can then call the fax service again and ask for specific faxes (or files).

Request a Fax is also available from the Windows Messaging menu bar. Double-click the Inbox icon on your Desktop and choose a profile that includes Microsoft Fax if you have multiple profiles. Click Tools, Microsoft Fax Tools, Request a Fax to start the same Wizard that launches when you choose Request a Fax on the Start menu.

Receiving faxes

You can set your computer to answer the phone when a call comes in and receive incoming faxes. You first need to double-click your Inbox icon and then choose a profile (if you have multiple profiles) that includes Microsoft Fax as a mail delivery service.

A little icon that looks like a fax/phone combination will appear in the Tray on the Taskbar. You can click this icon to see the Microsoft fax status. Click Options, Modem Properties in the Microsoft Fax Status menu bar to display the Fax Modem Properties dialog box, as shown in Figure 32-15. Using this properties sheet you can change how Windows Messaging will answer your phone. If you choose Answer after 2 (or more) rings, Windows Messaging will automatically answer the phone and begin to make the fax connection if you don't pick up the phone before two rings. You can't set the automatic answer for fewer than two rings.

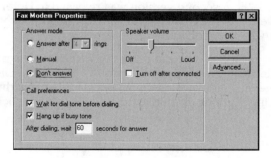

Figure 32-15: The Fax Modem Properties dialog box. Choose how Windows Messaging will answer incoming phone calls.

If you want to use your phone primarily for voice communication, set the Answer mode to Manual. The phone status box does appear when a phone call comes in, and you can click Answer Now if you think a fax is coming in.

Tip

You can't use Windows 3.*x* or DOS communications packages while Windows Messaging is waiting for a fax phone call unless you click Don't answer in the Fax Modem Properties dialog box. These other packages will report being unable to use the serial port that is assigned to your modem.

Other Windows 95 TAPI-aware communications packages (including HyperTerminal) can use the modem at the same time Windows Messaging is waiting for a fax phone call. Of course, only one communication can be going on at a time, so you can't use HyperTerminal while you are sending or receiving a fax.

Tip

Fax machines are on all the time. Computers often aren't. If you want your computer to operate as a fax machine and to be always ready to receive faxes, you'll need to run Windows Messaging with a profile that includes Microsoft Fax at all times and leave your computer on.

Microsoft Phone creates a profile for Windows Messaging or Microsoft Exchange the first time that you run it. This profile will include both fax and Internet Mail delivery services if they are available. It is best to install Windows Messaging before you install Microsoft Phone, so that it will configure a profile for Windows Messaging.

You can add an application that will print your faxes as they come in, ship them to another Windows Messaging user, or both. You can download Print Fax at http://home.istar.ca/~anthony/add-ins/printfax.html.

Fax type

You can send faxes as editable files, as regular Group 3 faxes, or as either—depending on the capabilities of the recipient hardware. You can determine how a particular fax is sent by taking the following steps:

STEPS

Determining in What Format a Fax Is Sent

Step 1. Double-click the Inbox on your Desktop.

Step 2. Choose a profile that has Microsoft Fax as a mail delivery service if you have more than one profile.

Step 3. Choose Compose, New Message in the Windows Messaging menu bar.

Step 4. Choose File, Send Options in the New Message menu bar. The Message Options dialog box, as shown in Figure 32-16, will be displayed on your Desktop.

(continued)

Determining in What Format a Fax Is Sent

Step 5.   Choose Editable, if possible; Editable only; or Not editable.

Figure 32-16: The Message Options dialog box. Choose the type of fax that you are going to send. Click Paper to set image quality.

You can set numerous other send options. To set these same properties for all faxes, clicking Tools, Microsoft Fax Tools, Options in the Windows Messaging menu bar.

Sharing a fax/modem on a network

A fax/modem board in a sufficiently powerful Windows 95 computer at work can be shared with Dial-Up Networking guests, as well as with other computers on a local area network. If you are calling into the Windows 95 computer at work using a modem in your computer at home, the fax/modem that is shared at work must be different than the modem that is answering your call and also be on a different phone line.

If the fax-server computer is dedicated to that task, it needs 8MB of RAM; if it's used for other tasks as well, it needs 12MB. In addition, at least a 486 processor is required.

Share the fax/modem on the network by taking the following steps:

STEPS

Sharing a Fax/Modem

Step 1. Double-click the Inbox icon on the Desktop of a Windows 95 fax-server computer. If you are set up to choose among multiple Windows Messaging profiles, choose a profile that includes Microsoft Fax. If you haven't previously set up a profile that contains Microsoft Fax as a mail delivery service, step back to the *Adding or removing information services* section and do so.

Step 2. Click Tools, Microsoft Fax Tools, Options in the Windows Messaging menu bar. Click the Modem tab (see Figure 32-17).

Figure 32-17: The Modem tab of the Microsoft Fax Properties dialog box. Clicking "Let other people on the network use my modem to send faxes" enables fax/modem sharing.

Step 3. Choose "Let other people on the network use my modem to send faxes."

Step 4. Type a shared fax name in the Share name field, choose a volume on which the NetFax folder will be stored, and click the Properties button.

Step 5. Define the characteristics of the shared folder (NetFax) that will store the faxes. Enter a password if you want to password-protect this folder and you are using share-level protection.

Step 6. Click the next two OK buttons.

Connecting to a shared fax/modem server

Whether you are calling in from your computer at home or accessing the networked fax server from another computer on the network, you need to create an Windows Messaging profile on your computer that will let you use the shared fax/modem on the Windows 95 fax server.

If you are going to connect to the fax server at work from a computer at home, be sure to create a Dial-Up Networking connectoid first before you begin these steps. For details on creating connectoids, see Chapter 28.

To create a connection to a shared fax server, take the following steps:

STEPS

Creating a Windows Messaging Profile to Use a Shared Fax Server

Step 1. Double-click the Mail (or Mail and Fax) icon in the Control Panel of your computer. Click Show Profiles.

Step 2. Click the Add button. Choose only the Microsoft Fax services in the Inbox Setup Wizard. Click Next.

Step 3. Type a name for this profile, such as **Shared fax.** Click Next.

Step 4. Click Network fax service or other type of device and then Next.

Step 5. Click the Add button (if necessary). Highlight Network fax server and click OK.

Step 6. Type the name of the shared fax-server computer preceded by two back slashes, followed by the name of the shared fax/modem (given to the shared fax in step 4 of the Sharing a Fax/Modem steps earlier), preceded by a single back slash. Click Next.

If the shared fax is on a remote computer (perhaps your computer at work and you are setting this up on your computer at home) and you enter the name of the computer at work and the name of the shared fax when you are not presently connected to the work computer over the phone lines, you will be asked if you want to connect to the fax server using Dial-Up Networking. Click Yes. Go to step 8.

Step 7. Enter your phone number and click Next. Continue clicking Next until you have completed the Inbox Setup Wizard. You're done.

Step 8. We assume you have previously created a connectoid to connect to the fax server computer. Choose the name of the connectoid after completing step 7.

Step 9. Enter a password for connecting to the shared fax/modem if needed. Click Cancel unless you want to connect to the fax server at work now.

Tip

If you are sending a fax to a Group 3 fax machine, use 14-point Arial (if you have only the basic fonts that come with Windows 95) for the text in your fax. This will significantly improve the readability of your fax, because fax printers are often of poor quality and low resolution (200 x 100 or 200 x 200). If you have additional fonts (such as Lucida Fax from the Microsoft True Type Font Pack), you can use them instead of Arial.

Troubleshooting Microsoft Fax

Secret

Terri Bronson at Microsoft once again provides help. If you have received a fax successfully, but it never appeared in your Inbox, take the following steps:

STEPS

Faxes Don't Appear

Step 1.   Exit Windows Messaging.

Step 2.   Locate the received files in the fax spool folder. This folder is typically \Windows\Spool\Fax. The files have the following form:

RCV*xxxxx*.MG3

or

RCV*xxxxx*.EFX

where *xxxxx* is a 5-digit hex number. Each of the files contain one fax message.

Step 3.   Copy these files to another folder, just as a backup.

Step 4.   Open the following key in the Registry:

HKEY_LOCAL_MACHINE\SOFTWARE\Microsoft\At Work\Fax\LocalModems\Received

This key may have several values all of type *string* (REG_SZ)), with the format: R*nn* and F*nn,* where *nn* is a two-digit decimal number starting with 00. The F*nn* entries contain filenames (the RCV*xxxx*.mg3/.efx files referred to in step 2). The R*nn* entry contains the result code for the transmission. A value of 001 indicates a successful receive.

Example: F00 = RCV3edd0.MG3

   F01 = 001

   R00 = 001

   R01 = 001

(continued)

STEPS *(continued)*

Faxes Don't Appear

Step 5. Add entries for all the files identified in step 2 to this list if they are not already on the list, making sure that each F*nn* has a corresponding R*nn* (you can set all R00 values to 001), and that the *nn* numbers are consecutive, starting from 00 (so we have F00, F01, F02 . . . R00, R01, R02 . . .).

Step 6. Restart Windows Messaging. If all went well, the messages should soon show up in the Inbox, and the Received key above will get cleared.

You can also take the steps that Terri provided in the *Troubleshooting Windows Messaging* section, especially if you are having problems rendering faxes. In addition, if you are having trouble sending faxes, click Tools, Deliver Now to force the Outbox to empty. Check the Outbox and if there is anything in it, delete the messages. A message with a non-fax address will cause problems. You can also create a new profile with just the fax delivery service.

Want to see what the faxes that you send out look like? Sue Mosher at Slipstick Systems, http://www.slipstick.com/exchange, comes up with a great solution. It won't work to check problems with your modem, but you do get to see your faxes.

STEPS

See What Your Faxes Look Like

Step 1. Double-click the Inbox icon and choose a profile with a fax delivery service.

Step 2. Choose Compose, New Message. In the To field type [fax:me]. Pretty cool, huh!

Step 3. Choose Tools, Microsoft Fax Tools, Options, and in the Message Format area choose Not editable. (After all, you want to receive it as a regular fax.) Click OK.

Step 4. In a few moments you should have a fax in your Inbox.

If you want to see what faxes look like when you use the Compose New Fax Wizard, click the Start button, Programs, Accessories, Fax, Compose New Fax. In the second dialog box, choose (None - Dial as Entered) which is the first entry in the Country Code list. Enter **me** in the fax number field and click the Add button. Continue on as normal. In a few seconds you will see what your fax cover page and fax look like.

Further help on problems with faxing can be found in the Microsoft Knowledge Base at http://www.microsoft.com/kb/articles/q140/4/32.htm.

Summary

Windows Messaging provides full e-mail and fax connectivity.

▶ You can send and receive e-mail using the Internet, CompuServe, the Microsoft Network, or Microsoft Mail servers.

▶ Windows 95 comes with a complete workgroup version of Microsoft Mail for local e-mail and document exchange.

▶ You can send a fax or e-mail message without putting someone in your address book.

▶ With Windows Messaging, e-mail is not just an ASCII text message, but can include all types of attached files and OLE 2 objects.

▶ You can edit OLE 2 objects within Windows Messaging.

▶ If you are sending e-mail over the phone lines, you have to tell Windows Messaging to connect to the remote e-mail service; you can't just send the mail.

Chapter 33

Connecting to the Internet

In This Chapter

Want to get on the Internet? We show you how to do it using the tools built into Windows 95. Windows 95 comes with a TCP/IP stack and a dialer to connect your computer to an Internet service provider (ISP).

▶ Getting the right kind of account (PPP, SLIP, or TIA) from your Internet service provider

▶ Asking your service provider for the right information about your account

▶ Setting up Dial-Up Networking (DUN) to make the connection to your service provider

▶ Getting your TCP/IP stack and your Dial-Up Adapter to work together

▶ Connecting to your service provider

▶ Verifying that you've got a good connection

Microsoft and the Internet

Millions of Windows 3.x users accessed the Internet before the end of 1995 without any help from Microsoft. Numerous companies, individuals, universities, government agencies, and loose associations created a solid body of Internet applications that take advantage of the Windows 3.x interface.

These applications started becoming available in 1993, both as retail packages and as shareware distributed over the Internet, or sometimes as a combination of both. The academic culture (and sometimes government-financed research) encouraged the authors to make their applications freely or cheaply available.

Microsoft has not been a pioneer in cyberspace, although when it released Windows 95 it started to catch up. Even when general Internet awareness was rising in 1993 and 1994, Microsoft's presence was limited to an Internet e-mail connection to its local network and later a file transfer protocol (FTP) site. In late 1994, the company cobbled together its web site.

Why was Microsoft so late to the Internet party? The Internet used to be a strictly Unix kind of thing. Microsoft's culture is not a Unix culture, nor is it an academic culture. Microsoft has been doing what it can to defeat Unix in the marketplace and has not been interested in developing software to give away, until forced to in late 1995 by competition from Netscape.

Windows software for the Internet didn't really get going until 1994, so people didn't see Windows machines as Internet clients. The Internet gets a lot better with faster modems, and the mass market didn't have a critical mass of 14.4 Kbps modems until 1993-94. Microsoft just didn't see a demand for Internet-based services. Before 1994, few Internet service providers allowed ordinary businesses and individuals to purchase access to the Internet at competitive rates.

The Internet's first killer app was a program named Mosaic. Written by a group of college students at the University of Illinois at Champaign-Urbana's National Center for Supercomputing Applications, Mosaic is a *browser* — a program you can use to view files on the Internet's World Wide Web (the web). Mosaic was created in 1993. Windows versions of the browser followed the initial versions written in Unix in late 1993. The Unix version was developed first because it was written at a university (universities are Unix strongholds). Academic sites also have access to fast Internet connections, which puts them ahead of the general public in demanding high-level web tools. In 1994, the original authors of Mosaic formed their own company to create Netscape, which quickly captured 80 percent of the web browser "market."

At the same time, Microsoft was providing product support and receiving e-mail from customers electronically through CompuServe. Because CompuServe pays a royalty of 8 to 10 percent of connect-time charges on their service to software vendors, Microsoft and other software vendors found CompuServe to be an attractive addition to their support programs. There was no way to charge on the Internet in 1994. This explains in part why Microsoft and other software vendors were slow to use the Internet to provide product support.

When Windows 95 was about to be released, Microsoft's strategy was to connect everyone to the Microsoft Network (MSN), and through MSN to the Internet. It wanted to provide on MSN the electronic services found on the Internet, and a lot more. Microsoft also wanted to capture a very large client base (potentially, all Windows users). It saw MSN as a competitor to the Internet. At the same time, Microsoft wanted MSN to be the Internet service provider of choice.

This strategy meant that Microsoft chose to use its resources (in early 1995) to make it easy for Windows 95 users to access the Microsoft Network and, through it, the Internet. Few Microsoft resources went toward making it easier for everyone to go to their local Internet service provider for Internet access. It wasn't until very late in the beta test cycle (June of '95) that Microsoft finally acknowledged the need for a scripting utility that would allow easy access to many Internet service providers.

Microsoft's strategy has, of course, changed considerably since the first days after the release of Windows 95. Now Microsoft wants Windows 95 to be your integrated interface to the Internet and to erase the differences between the Desktop, your local resources, and those resources available on the Internet.

Microsoft first released its own 32-bit TCP/IP stack on Microsoft Plus!, and then later placed it, along with the Internet Explorer, on the Microsoft web site for free download.

On December 7 "a day that will live in infamy," 1995, Bill Gates announced Microsoft's commitment to turning the company into an Internet company. Microsoft unveiled the new integrated Windows 95/Internet Explorer interface for the first time.

With the release on August 13, 1996 of Internet Explorer 3.0, computer industry journalists (other than Nichols Petrelli) agreed that Microsoft had equaled, or slightly exceeded, Netscape in browser functionality. We began alpha testing Internet Explorer 4.0 in July, 1996.

Your First Point of Internet Attachment

There are two fundamentally different ways to gain access to the Internet from your computer — retail and wholesale. You can call through the modem connected to your computer to a local or national Internet service provider. Or you can communicate over your local area network (LAN) to a server that is connected by a phone line to an Internet service provider. The connection can vary from a dial-up 28.8 Kbps service to a fast, dedicated leased-T1 line.

Service providers that offer call-in modem access to the general public are a relatively new phenomenon. Before 1994, most users accessed the Internet through their Unix workstations on campus or on the job at defense contractors. They didn't have to worry about how to get access. The system administrator took care of those details. Once the rest of us were allowed to join the party, *we* became the system administrators for our own computers.

CompuServe, America Online, Prodigy, and other online services have turned themselves into Internet service providers (although not completely) while maintaining some or all of their online services. These national online services have offered connections to Internet mail (although not connections to Internet mail POP3 and SMTP servers) since 1993, and in 1995 they began providing almost full Internet access, like their Internet service provider competitors.

When Microsoft offered MSN with Windows 95 in 1995, it also purchased partial interest in a nationwide service provider named UUNET. MSN provides a connection to Internet mail (but it didn't install a direct connection to POP3 and SMTP Internet e-mail servers until early 1997) and full access to Internet newsgroups with an NNTP news server (although it didn't provide access to Internet news servers outside of MSN until early 1997). As a nationwide service provider, MSN provides dial-up access that supports both Internet TCP/IP protocol and MSN networking protocol.

Tip

You should look for a service provider that has enough phone lines so you won't get a busy signal too often. The Internet works best at the highest speed you can afford. If the service provider has 28.8 Kbps (V.34) modems and so do you, great. Some service providers are very small and may not have adequate technical support to keep their lines up and functioning. Move on to another one if this is the case.

Some service providers let you connect with ISDN. This will give you 56 Kbps transfer rates. See if your telephone company will install an ISDN line to your home or business. If so, purchase an ISDN card with a Windows 95-compatible driver for your computer (now available from Microsoft), and you are ready to really cruise the Internet.

Microsoft's TCP/IP Stack

Windows 95 comes with tools that allow you to access the Internet either over a modem or through a network. At the lowest level, Microsoft provides a TCP/IP stack. TCP/IP (Transfer Control Protocol/Internet Protocol) is the Internet protocol (or language). It can be spoken over your modem, network card, or through the Windows 95 Direct Cable Connection (see Chapter 30 for more on DCC).

When Microsoft first released its TCP/IP stack, you had to purchase it on the Microsoft Plus! CD-ROM. Later, Microsoft made it available on its web site. If you have an earlier version of Windows 95 and don't have Microsoft's TCP/IP stack, you can download the upgrade to Windows 95 that includes the integrated Internet Explorer and TCP/IP from the Microsoft web site (http://www.microsoft.com/windows/software.htm).

You can associate (bind) the TCP/IP stack to your Dial-Up Adapter and/or your network card. If you bind it to your Dial-Up Adapter, you can use Windows 95's Dial-Up Networking to call your service provider and connect to the Internet using TCP/IP.

If you bind the TCP/IP stack to your network card, and your network is connected to a Unix server or Windows NT server, or to a Windows 95 computer with WinGate software, you can communicate with that server using Internet (or Internet-related) applications compatible with Winsock. The server can provide the gateway to the Internet.

If you use the TCP/IP protocol on your local area network, your network becomes an Intranet. (An *Intranet* is a local area network that uses Internet standards.) If you do this, you can configure Windows 95, Windows NT, NetWare, and, of course, Unix servers as web servers and POP3 and SMTP e-mail servers.

Installing an Internet dial-up connection

To gain Internet access through your modem, you need to carry out the following tasks:

- Install and configure your modem.

- Sign up for an Internet account with your service provider or online service.

- Obtain from the service provider the information you need to successfully connect your computer to their computer.

- Install Dial-Up Networking on your Windows 95 computer.

- Install and bind the Windows 95 TCP/IP stack to the Dial-Up Adapter (your modem).

- If you have a SLIP (Serial Line/Internet Protocol) account at your service provider, install the SLIP connection software and the connection scripting utility.

- Define and configure a Dial-Up Networking connection for your service provider.

- Configure the TCP/IP settings specific to your service provider using the information they provide.

- Write a connection script if your Internet service provider doesn't provide PPP with CHAP or PAP.

The Internet Explorer comes with the Internet Connection Wizard (Get on the Internet) that can help you create a dial-up connection to your Internet service provider. We discuss how to use this Wizard later in this chapter.

Installing and configuring your modem

We discuss how to install and configure your modem in Chapter 25. The Windows 95 Setup program's hardware detection routines may already have correctly identified your modem and installed the appropriate driver for it. Even if you installed your modem after you installed Windows 95, similar hardware detection routines may have correctly detected it and installed the right driver.

To check if your modem has been detected, double-click the Modems icon in your Control Panel to display the Modems Properties dialog box. If your modem has been detected, it will be listed in the General tab of the dialog box. You can also click the Dialing Properties button to review or edit the properties that characterize your calling location. If your modem driver isn't yet installed, you can do so at this point by clicking the Add button.

An Internet service provider account

To connect to the Internet, you need an account with an Internet service provider. Service providers give you access to the Internet through their computers, which are connected to fast, dedicated telephone lines. The service provider maintains a bundle of dial-in phone lines attached to racks of modems, which are in turn attached to the service provider's computer(s).

Tip

If you are opening a new account, you should obtain a PPP (Point-to-Point Protocol) account from the service provider. If you already have a different type of account, you should change it to a PPP account. In addition, you should find a service provider that provides either PAP (Password Authentication Protocol) or CHAP (Challenge-Handshake Authentication Protocol), if possible. If your account supports PAP or CHAP, you don't have to type your logon name and password after you connect to the service provider. If your PPP account doesn't have one of these types of authentication, you have to either type your logon name and password each time you connect or create a script file (using a scripting utility that comes with Windows 95) that enters this information for you.

When you connect to the Internet, your computer is assigned an IP address to identify it to other computers. Most Internet service providers assign IP address dynamically, that is, at logon time. In some cases you can obtain a static IP address. If you have a SLIP (Serial Line/Internet Protocol) account instead of a PPP account, and you have a dynamically assigned IP address, your SLIP script will need to capture the dynamically assigned IP address and send it back to the service provider.

Some service providers don't offer PPP or SLIP accounts directly, but require that you first connect to a shell account, and then send a message once you're online to switch to a PPP or SLIP connection. A *shell account* is the most basic account type available from a service provider. It treats your expensive computer as a dumb terminal and requires that you run Unix software on the service provider's computer to do anything on the Internet. You can use your script to send a command to switch from the shell to SLIP or PPP.

Tip

If you just want to maintain a low-level shell account, you can use HyperTerminal (see Chapter 29) to call into your service provider. HyperTerminal doesn't come with scripting to automate the logon process, but it will still work fine as a tool for connecting to a Unix computer.

Tip

Your service provider may offer a TIA (The Internet Adapter) account, which allows you to switch to a SLIP-type account after you log on in your shell account. The Windows 95 scripting utility works with TIA accounts to switch to SLIP.

Service provider account information

The first step, of course, is to find a service provider. If you live in a metropolitan area, you should be able to find a free local computer newspaper at computer stores that lists service providers.

A local service provider will have a local number and perhaps an 800 number. A national service provider will provide local numbers, an 800 number, or a number in the closest town. You can find ads for national service providers in national computer magazines or in national newspapers such as *The New York Times* (especially the Tuesday *Science Times* section). If you have access to a friend's Internet account, you can check out online databases of server providers such as http://thelist.com.

You need some specific information from your service provider. The staff at local service providers much prefer to talk to other people (sometimes known as customers) by way of their computers. This can be quite difficult when you don't have an e-mail account (which is one of the reasons that you're trying to contact the service provider to begin with). If you already have an e-mail account with a national online service such as AOL or CompuServe, you can use that account to send e-mail to a local service provider, assuming you can find their e-mail address.

You can always just call an ISP on a voice line, but it is often difficult to reach anyone. You can fax them your questions, and hope that they fax you back the answers. This poor "out-of-the-box" experience with some service providers has been a major bottleneck in their growth. Many are very small companies run by one or two technically minded people; no glad-handing sales types are allowed. On the other hand, ISPs are independent businesses with a self interest in serving their local customers, so some do indeed make every effort to give you the assistance you need.

The major online services and the Microsoft Network are attempting to simplify the process of getting online. Microsoft is very smart to make it so easy to connect to MSN (although some would say it is unfairly using its monopoly position).

You need the following information from your service provider to configure your Windows 95 TCP/IP stack:

- Dial-in phone number you'll use to connect to the service provider's modems
- Account type
- If it is a SLIP account, whether it is compressed SLIP (CSLIP) or not
- If it is a PPP account, whether it has either PAP or CHAP
- If it is a PPP account without PAP or CHAP, whether it supports software compression and encrypted passwords
- User name (or *logon name*), for example, something like *billsmith* or *nancyf*

- Password
- Your host name (which can be the same as your user name)

    You can think of your host name as your computer's name, or as your name on the Internet. It will be appended to the service provider's domain name to become your address on the Internet. Since this will become your address, you should tell the service provider what you want as a host name, and see if they can swing it without any conflicts.

- The service provider's domain name (for example, *netters.com*)

    Your Internet address will be a combination of your host name and the service provider's domain name, as in *billsmith.netters.com*. Your e-mail address will be *billsmith@netters.com*. You can have as many different e-mail addresses on the Internet as you have accounts.

- Domain Name System (DNS) server's IP (Internet Protocol) address

    DNS servers translate (from a lookup table) the somewhat user-friendly domain names into the underlying IP addresses (for example, 207.182.15.50). Get the IP address of the DNS server that you'll be automatically accessing when you use your service provider's services. Your service provider may automatically assign the IP address of the DNS server, in which case you won't have to get this address.

    You can also register your own domain name and have it translated by a DNS server. You'll need to set up a web server (or rent a spot on a virtual server at an Internet service provider) to take advantage of the name. The address for your web site will be something like www.yourname.com, and people will be able to send you e-mail at yourname@yourname.com. Talk to your service provider about registration and costs.

In most cases, your service provider will assign a different IP address to your computer every time you log on. When other people use your Internet address to contact your computer, your service provider will automatically translate your Internet address into this dynamic IP address.

If your service provider doesn't automatically assign you an IP address, you'll need to get:

- Your own IP address (a fixed IP address)
- An IP subnet mask
- A gateway IP address

It can be quite useful to have a fixed IP address. It's almost like having your own domain name. Internet routers can find your computer using your IP address, so you can give out your IP address to all your "friends" and they can contact you there whenever you are connected to the Internet. Also, if you have a fixed IP address, you can put up web pages on your own Windows 95 computer. People will be able to access your pages when you're connected to your service provider over your 28.8 modem.

Of course, the Internet routers won't have a way of finding your computer by looking for a domain name such as www.yourcomputer.com (instead of your fixed IP address) if you haven't registered one. And if you aren't online pretty much all the time, putting a web site on your own computer, while technically feasible, wouldn't be that useful. It's a better idea to put your web site on the service provider's computers because they are online 24 hours a day, they have a fast connection to the Internet, and you won't be bothered with people connecting to your computer while you're using it.

Microsoft offers the Personal Web Server for Windows 95, which allows you to publish HMTL pages and make them available to others on your local area network or over the phone lines. You can download it from http://www.microsoft.com/msdownload/personalweb.htm.

The above information is all you need to be able to connect to your service provider. To be able to access e-mail and newsgroups, you'll need the following information:

- Your e-mail address (most likely the combination of your host name and the service provider's domain name)
- POP3 mail server's address
- SMTP mail server's address
- News server's address
- Mail gateway's address (needed only for some mail readers)

Your service provider should have no problem giving you this information (assuming you can actually talk to someone). In fact, many service providers have all of the information compiled into one document, which they can fax or mail to you. Or, if you have access to a computer connected to the web, you can download it from their web site.

The Internet Connection Wizard

The Internet Connection Wizard can help you through the processes detailed in this chapter. And for select Internet service/online providers, it can actually set you up with an account automatically.

Starting with OEM Service Release 2, Microsoft allowed other Internet service providers a place in a folder called Online Services on the Desktop in exchange for their commitment to promoting Internet Explorer as their preferred Internet user interface. You can sign up automatically for AOL, AT&T World Net, or CompuServe, as well as the Microsoft Network.

If you want to sign up with another national or local Internet service provider, you have to manually provide to the Internet Connection Wizard the information that the Wizard supplies automatically for the favored service providers. If you connect to your service provider using a SLIP account, you also have to manually edit the service provider's DUN connectoid to switch from the default PPP protocol to SLIP (or CSLIP), and you might have to create a SLIP script.

We give you all the information that you need to create a connectoid to your service provider either manually or by using the Internet Connection Wizard in this chapter and in Chapter 28. The Internet Connection Wizard automatically starts the first time you install Internet Explorer. If you want to run it again, you'll find it in your Start menu, under Programs, Accessories, Internet Tools. The executable file for the Internet Connection Wizard is Iwconn1.exe, and it's stored in the \Program Files\ICW-Internet Connection Wizard folder.

Dial-Up Networking

If you installed Direct Cable Connection (DCC) during Windows 95 Setup, Dial-Up Networking (DUN) is already installed. You may also have chosen to install DUN if you ran a Custom setup.

To find out if DUN is installed, click the Start button, point to Settings, and then click Control Panel. Double-click the Network icon in the Control Panel and see whether Dial-Up Adapter is listed in the Network dialog box.

If it isn't, you can install DUN by taking the following steps:

STEPS

Installing Dial-Up Networking

Step 1. Click the Start button, point to Settings, and then click Control Panel.

Step 2. Double-click the Add/Remove Programs icon. Click the Windows Setup tab.

Step 3. Highlight Communications, and then click the Details button.

Step 4. Mark the Dial-Up Networking check box, and click the OK button in the Communications dialog box.

Step 5. Click the OK button in the Add/Remove Programs Properties dialog box. You may be asked to insert your Windows 95 source CD-ROM. DUN is now installed.

Bind TCP/IP to your Dial-Up Adapter

Adding Dial-Up Networking to your Windows 95 configuration doesn't automatically add the TCP/IP stack to the list of protocols bound to the Dial-Up Adapter. You need to do this separately.

Binding Your TCP/IP Stack to Dial-Up Adapter

Step 1.   Click the Start button, point to Settings, and then click Control Panel.

Step 2.   Double-click the Network icon. Click the Add button.

Step 3.   Highlight Protocol in the Select Network Component Type dialog box and click the Add button.

Step 4.   In the Select Network Protocol dialog box, highlight Microsoft in the Manufacturers list, and highlight TCP/IP in the Network Protocols list. Click the OK button.

Step 5.   Click OK in the Network dialog box. You may be asked to insert your Windows 95 source CD-ROM.

You now have a TCP/IP stack and a dialer, both of which will be encompassed in your DUN connectoid. After you configure your connectoid for your service provider account, you will be able to make an Internet connection. The default TCP/IP settings are described in the next section.

Tip

If you double-click the Network icon in your Control Panel, you will notice that other protocols have been installed and bound to your Dial-Up Adapter by default. You can remove these other protocols, such as NetBUEI, if you like. However, you shouldn't remove them if you are going to use Direct Cable Connection, connect to a local area network, or connect to Windows NT servers running Microsoft Networks over the Internet.

Configuring the TCP/IP stack

The default settings for the TCP/IP stack are:

■ Obtain an IP address automatically

■ Use DHCP for WINS resolution

■ No gateways

■ Disable DNS

You don't need to change these settings if you are going to connect to the Internet only through a server provider and you don't use TCP/IP on a local area network. You can just set the TCP/IP settings that are specific to your service provider when you create a connectoid, as shown in the *Dial-up connection to your service provider* section later in this chapter.

You do need to change the default TCP/IP settings if you are connected to a single LAN through TCP/IP and you don't connect to the Internet except through the LAN. The DNS settings you configure in the TCP/IP Properties dialog box (see the steps below) override those you set in a DUN connectoid for a specific Internet service provider. You don't want to set your DNS values in the TCP/IP Properties dialog box if you can at all help it.

If you have both a LAN TCP/IP connection and a DUN TCP/IP connection, you need to make other provisions to deal correctly with DNS routing. Turn to the section entitled *Which DNS is used?* later in the chapter.

If you have a LAN connection over a network card to a TCP/IP network, you should also turn to Chapter 36 for additional information on local area networks.

You can configure the TCP/IP stack for a LAN connection using the following steps:

STEPS

Setting the Default TCP/IP Properties for a LAN Connection

Step 1. Click the Start button, point to Settings, and then click Control Panel.

Step 2. Double-click the Network icon. Highlight TCP/IP in the Network dialog box and click the Properties button.

Step 3. Click the DNS Configuration tab. In the DNS Configuration properties sheet (shown in Figure 33-1), type your host name, your service provider's domain name, and the IP address of the DNS server you will use. Click the Add button to put the DNS server's IP address in the list. If you have multiple addresses, enter them in the order that you want them searched. Be sure to click the Add button after you type each one.

Step 4. Click the OK button, and then click the IP Address tab.

Step 5. In the IP Address properties sheet (shown in Figure 33-2), mark the Obtain an IP address from a DHCP server option button if your network has a DHCP server that provides you with a dynamic IP address. If you have a fixed IP address, mark the Specify an IP address option button, and enter the IP address and the subnet mask.

Step 6. If you have a fixed IP address, click the Gateway tab, enter your Gateway IP address, and click the Add button.

Step 7. Click the WINS Configuration tab and make sure that the Disable WINS Resolution option button is marked unless your network has a WINS server. If you have a WINS server, but not a DHCP server, mark Enable WINS Resolution and type the IP addresses for your WINS servers. If you have a DHCP server, mark the Use DHCP for WINS Resolution option button.

Setting the Default TCP/IP Properties for a LAN Connection

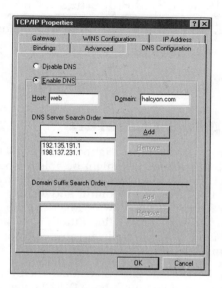

Figure 33-1: The DNS Configuration properties sheet. Fill in the fields for your host name, your service provider's domain name, and the DNS server's IP address.

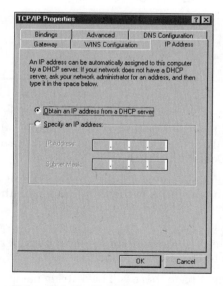

Figure 33-2: The IP Address properties sheet. Mark Obtain an IP address from a DHCP server if your network has a DHCP server.

(continued)

STEPS *(continued)*

Setting the Default TCP/IP Properties for a LAN Connection

Step 8.   Click OK to close the TCP/IP Properties dialog box.

Step 9.   Restart your computer.

Speeding up file transfers

If your file transfer rates are in the neighborhood of 1000 to 1500 bytes per second on a 28.8 Kbps modem, you might be able to speed things up by adding the MaxMTU value to your Registry. One way to check out your file transfer rates is to use the System Monitor and display the bytes written to your hard disk per second as you download a large file. Also, CuteFTP reports its file transfer rates. (You'll find CuteFTP on the *Windows 95 Secrets* CD-ROM.) You should expect file transfer rates of around 3000 bytes per second on 28.8 Kbps modems.

If you have Dial-Up Networking 2.0, you can use the System Monitor to display transfer rates. If you don't have DUN 2.0 yet, go to http://www.microsoft.com/windows/software/isdn.htm and download and install the ISDN Accelerator 1.1 pack. You can just use the DUN component and ignore the rest of the package.

STEPS

Setting a MaxMTU Value

Step 1.   Double-click Regedit.exe in your \Windows folder. Navigate down to HKEY_LOCAL_MACHINE\Enum\Root\Net.

Step 2.   Net will have one or more subkeys numbered 0000, 0001, and so on. Highlight each subkey until you find the one that has DeviceDesc set to "Dial-Up Adapter".

Step 3.   In the left pane, highlight the subkey Bindings under the subkey you found in step 2. In the right pane, note the four-digit number immediately to the right of MSTCP\.

Step 4.   Navigate to HKEY_LOCAL_MACHINE\Enum\NetWork\MSTCP. Highlight the four digit number subkey under MSTCP that corresponds to the one you found in step 3.

Step 5.   In the right pane there will be a string named Driver with a four-digit number to the right of NetTrans\. Note this number.

Step 6.   Navigate to HKEY_LOCAL_MACHINE\System\CurrentControlSet\ Services\ Class\NetTrans\.

Setting a MaxMTU Value

Step 7.   Under NetTrans, highlight the key whose value matches the one you found in step 5.

Step 8.   Right-click the right pane. Choose New, String Value. Type the string name **MaxMTU**.

Step 9   Double-click the string name MaxMTU in the right pane. Enter the value **576**. Click OK, and exit the Registry.

Step 10.   Restart Windows 95.

Undocumented

The default value for MaxMTU is 1500. John Navas, at the Navas Group, recommends setting the MaxMTU parameter to a value of 576 for PPP connections. You can check out his site, which specializes in information about modems at http://www.aimnet.com/~jnavas/modem/faq.html.

Undocumented

You can also set the value of RWIN to further speed up transfer rates under some circumstances. Take the following steps:

STEPS

Setting RWIN

Step 1.   Double-click Regedit.exe in your \Windows folder. Navigate down to HKEY_LOCAL_MACHINE\System\CurrentControlSet\Services\ VxD\MSTCP\.

Step 2.   Right-click the right pane. Choose New, String Value. Type the string name **DefaultRcvWindow**.

Step 3   Double-click the string name DefaultRcvWindow in the right pane. Enter a value. 2144 is the default value. Click OK, and exit the Registry.

If you want further information about how to set RWIN and other parameters for speeding up file transfers, visit http://www.cerberus-sys.com/~belleisl/mtu_mss_rwin.html.

Multiple TCP/IP settings for multiple connections

You can provide different TCP/IP settings for different connections if you have multiple Internet service providers.

The only TCP/IP settings that can be specific to a given connection to an Internet service provider are:

■ Your IP address (fixed or dynamically assigned)

■ IP address for DNS or WINS server (fixed or dynamically assigned)

■ Use IP header compression or not

■ Use default gateway at Internet service provider or not

Follow the steps in the *Dial-up connection to your service provider* section below to set these TCP/IP settings for each of your connections.

Dial-up connection to your service provider

Now that you have installed DUN and bound the TCP/IP stack to the Dial-Up Adapter, you are ready to create a DUN connection (a connectoid) that will call your service provider and establish the connection to your account. To do this, take the following steps:

STEPS

Creating a Service Provider Connection

Step 1.   Click the Start button, point to Programs, then Accessories, and then click Dial-Up Networking. (You can place a shortcut to DUN on your Desktop or in any other folder if you like. For details on creating and using shortcuts, see Chapter 10.)

Step 2.   Enter the name of your service provider in the first dialog box of the Make New Connection Wizard. If you want to change the modem-specific characteristics for this connection, click the Configure button to display the Properties dialog box for the selected modem, make the desired changes, and click OK. Click the Next button, and enter the phone number your modem will dial to connect to the ISP. Click Next again, and then click Finish.

Step 3.   Right-click the new connectoid in the Dial-Up Networking window. Click Properties to display the Properties dialog box for your connection to this service provider.

Step 4.   If you are using DUN 2.0, click the Server Types tab, as shown in Figure 33-3. (If you're using DUN 1.0, click the Server Type button to display the Server Types dialog box.)

You don't need to mark the Log on to the network check box in a connectoid for an Internet service provider unless you are logging onto a Windows network over the Internet. Otherwise, it just slows things down.

Creating a Service Provider Connection

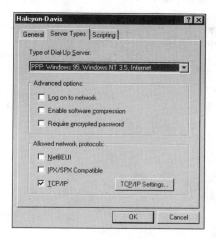

Figure 33-3: The Server Types properties sheet (in Dial-Up Networking 2.0).

Checking Enable software compression tells your connection software to negotiate compression with the remote computer. If your modem already handles hardware compression, then you don't really want to do this. Your modem may have already negotiated hardware compression with the server's modem (most do), so adding software compression slows things down.

If you mark the Require encrypted password check box, your computer sends an encrypted password directly to your server provider's computer. The ISP has to be able to decode the password before you can connect, and your password doesn't go out on the Net (where passwords can be stolen).

Require encrypted password only works with PPP. Many service providers can't deal with encrypted passwords, so check with yours before you mark this check box.

Step 5. Choose the server type (from the Type of Dial-Up Server drop-down list at the top of the dialog box) that describes your account. If you have a SLIP account, you need to select either CSLIP: Unix Connection with IP Header Compression or SLIP: Unix Connection, depending on which type of SLIP account you have.

Step 6. Clear the NetBEUI and IPX/SPX Compatible check boxes under Allowed network protocols. You only need TCP/IP to connect with your service provider, and clearing these boxes will speed things up a bit at connect time.

(continued)

Creating a Service Provider Connection

If you choose SLIP or CSLIP, these check boxes will be grayed out. You only use the TCP/IP protocol to communicate to a Unix server.

Step 7. Click the TCP/IP Settings button to set the specific TCP/IP settings for this connection. The values that you enter in the TCP/IP Settings dialog box (see Figure 33-4) are those that you received from your Internet service provider.

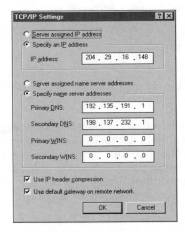

Figure 33-4: The TCP/IP Settings dialog box. These settings are specific to this connection to an individual Internet service provider.

Step 8. If your computer's IP address is fixed, mark the Specify an IP address option button, and then type your IP address in the IP address field. If your IP address is dynamically assigned, mark the Server assigned IP address option button. (If you have a TIA account, your IP address will be fixed. If you have a PPP account, it will be dynamically assigned. If you have a SLIP account, it could be either fixed or dynamically assigned.)

Step 9. If your service provider gave you one or more IP addresses for their DNS or WINS server(s), mark the Specify name server addresses option button, and enter the IP addresses in the four fields in the middle of the dialog box. If your service provider dynamically assigns the IP addresses of their servers, mark the Server assigned name server addresses option button.

Creating a Service Provider Connection

Step 10. If you have a TIA account, clear the Use IP header compression check box. Click OK in the TCP/IP Settings dialog box. If you have DUN 2.0, click OK again in the Properties dialog box. If you have DUN 1.0, click OK to close the Server Types dialog box, and then click OK to close the Properties dialog box.

Step 11. Click the Configure button in the General tab of the Properties dialog box for your service provider. This brings up the Properties dialog box associated with your modem and this connection. Click the Options tab to display the Options properties sheet, as shown in Figure 33-5.

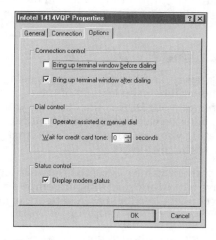

Figure 33-5: The Options properties sheet. Mark the option button labeled "Bring up terminal window after dialing" if you have a SLIP account or a PPP account without PAP or CHAP and you are not using the scripting utility.

Step 12. If your service provider requires that you manually log in before you start your session, you will need to check Bring up terminal window after dialing. This will be the case if you have a SLIP account or a PPP account without PAP or CHAP and you are not using the scripting utility.

If you are going to use the scripting utility, you normally want to leave this check box cleared because the scripting utility doesn't need the terminal window opened by this setting. However, when you are opening a new account at a service provider that requires a manual log on, you might want to mark this check box temporarily. That way, you can make sure that the commands that you enter are correct before you try using the script that you have edited to contain these commands.

(continued)

STEPS *(continued)*

Creating a Service Provider Connection

Step 13. Make any other changes you think are necessary in the Properties dialog box associated with the modem and this connection.
Then click the OK button, and click OK again to close the Properties dialog box for the service provider connection.

You are now ready to connect to your service provider. If you have a SLIP
account or a PPP account without PAP or CHAP and you want to automate
the connection with the scripting utility, you still have a little bit of work to
do. See the section entitled *Installing SLIP and automating your logon* later in
this chapter.

Which DNS is used?

If you set the DNS, gateway, and IP address values using the Network icon in
the Control Panel, they will be used instead of the corresponding values that
you set when you created your DUN connectoid for your service provider. If
you're connected to your service provider and you get an error message in
Internet Explorer stating you can't open a web site that you know exists, this
might be the source of the problem.

You don't need to set these values using the Network icon in the Control
Panel unless you have a network card in your computer and you are using
the network card to connect to a local area network using the TCP/IP
protocol.

This is a bug in Windows 95, although you can work around the problem. It
becomes an issue if you are connected to a LAN at the same time that you
are calling up your service provider. It will also show up if you have multiple
service providers, each with their own connectoids, and each with their own
DNS values.

Undocumented

One fix is to double-click the Network icon in your Control Panel, double-
click the TCP/IP protocol bound to your Dial-Up Adapter, click the DNS
Configuration tab, and change the DNS server values to the ones stored in
your service provider's connectoid. If you do this, you won't be able to
resolve names of resources on the local TCP/IP network while you are
connected to your service provider. One way around this is to create a
Lmhosts file that specifically assigns IP addresses to NetBIOS-type names
for any local resources.

Undocumented

Another option is to check out the Route command (a DOS program found in
the \Windows folder). If you are connected to a TCP/IP network locally
through a network card and you are calling out through a modem to an
Internet service provider, you can have two default routes. You can use the
Route command to delete the local route or the PPP route so that you use
only one at a time.

Netswitcher and TCP Switcher

If you have two different Internet service providers and they both require different DNS addresses, you'll need to get a little utility that keeps track of the two separate addresses and reconfigures your Registry to let you call one or the other. If you access your TCP/IP local area network through a network card and a separate Internet service provider through your modem, you'll likewise run into problems with DNS routing.

Because you can create separate DUN connectoids for each service provider, you would think that you could have separate DNS addresses. You can assign them, but one address interferes with the other, unless the service providers automatically assign the DNS addresses for you. To get around this problem, download Netswitcher at http://www.bysnet.com/netsw.html.

You can also use Netswitcher if you are connecting up to different LANs through a network card. For example, you might have a portable that you use to dock into different networks. You can use Netswitcher to track the different IP addresses, netmasks, gateways, hostnames, and so on.

TCP Switcher is a slimmed down version of Netswitcher that lets you change a Windows 95 Dial-Up Networking connectoid's hostname, domain name, and DNS server values. It is the DNS server values that concern us because that is where the conflict in Microsoft's TCP/IP stack occurs. You'll find TCP Switcher at http://www.bysnet.com/tcpsw.html.

Saving your DUN connectoid passwords

You may find that the Save password check box is grayed out when you double-click a DUN connectoid. This means that you can't save your password for this service provider connection, so you have to type your password every time you call them up. This can be quite irritating.

Undocumented

There are three possible causes for this problem. One, you haven't installed either Client for Microsoft Networks or Client for NetWare Networks. Two, your Windows startup is configured to ask you for a password (to identify you to the computer), and you clicked Cancel or pressed the Esc key when the logon dialog box was displayed. Three, you have a corrupted password file.

The cure to the first problem is easy. Install one of the above named clients using the Network icon in your Control Panel.

Windows 95 won't save your DUN passwords unless it knows who you are. If you log on with a Cancel, it won't save your passwords. You should log on as yourself, that is, type a user name in the logon dialog box.

If you think your password file is corrupted, rename the *pwl* files in your \Windows folder, and then shut down and restart Windows 95. You will have to build your list of passwords from scratch. The earliest version of the Windows 95 Service Pack 1 corrupted password files. If you installed this version, download the fix at http://www.microsoft.com/windows. You can also check Don Lebow's Generic DUN Password Saving Advice web page at http://www.maui.net/~dml/dunpass.html for the latest approach to the problem.

Calling Your Service Provider

Now that you have created a connection to your service provider, you are ready to make the connection.

STEPS

Connecting to Your Service Provider

Step 1. Double-click the new connectoid in your DUN folder window. The Connect To dialog box appears on your Desktop, as shown in Figure 33-6. If you have DUN 2.0, you can make this dialog box disappear by choosing Connections, Settings in the Dial-Up Networking folder window and clearing the Prompt for information before dialing check box.

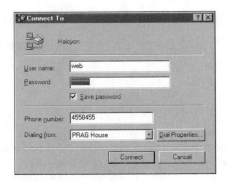

Figure 33-6: The Connect To dialog box. You don't need to use the User name and Password fields unless you have a PPP account with PAP or CHAP. Click the Connect button to have the modem start dialing up your service provider.

Step 2. Enter your logon name and password and click the Save password check box if you would rather not type your password every time. User names and passwords are case sensitive. Be sure you type them correctly.

Step 3. Click the Connect button to direct your modem to dial into your service provider and make a connection. Once the connection is made, you are on the Internet and ready to run Winsock-compatible Internet applications. If your account requires that you manually log in, a terminal window will be displayed first, as shown in Figure 33-7.

Connecting to Your Service Provider

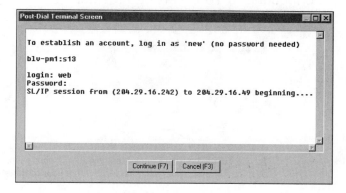

Figure 33-7: The Post-Dial Terminal Screen. Type PPP or SLIP and press Enter if your service provider requires that you first specify your account type. Type your logon name and password when prompted. If you have a SLIP account, wait for your dynamically assigned IP address to be displayed and write it down so that you can remember it for a few seconds.

Step 4. If you need to specify your account type to your service provider, type **PPP** or **SLIP** and press Enter. When prompted by your service provider's computer, type your logon name and password. Again, your logon name and password are case sensitive. If you have a TIA account, you will log on first and then type **TIA** at the shell prompt.

Step 5. If you have a SLIP account with dynamically assigned IP addresses, your IP address will appear. Write it down; you will need it in the next step, and this terminal window is going to disappear. Click the Continue button or press F7.

(If you configured your TCP/IP stack for a fixed IP address that matches the first two or three numbers of your dynamically assigned one, you will only have to worry about typing the last number or two in the next step.)

Step 6. If you have a SLIP account, the dialog box shown in Figure 33-8 will be displayed after step 5 to let you enter your IP address. Make sure you type your IP address exactly as it was displayed in the terminal window. If you get it wrong, your Winsock-compatible Internet applications will not work.

(continued)

Connecting to Your Service Provider

Figure 33-8: The SLIP Connection IP Address dialog box. Type your dynamically assigned IP address exactly as displayed in your terminal window.

Step 7.   If you have a TIA account, you will see the dialog box shown in Figure 33-8. If you earlier specified a fixed IP address in the TCP/IP Settings dialog box, this address will be displayed here. You need to change this IP address if you were prompted to do so after you typed **TIA** in the terminal window.

If you are using the scripting utility, you can omit steps 4 through 7.

If you are using Windows Messaging, you can make the connection with your service provider just by double-clicking the Inbox icon on your Desktop (if you have configured the mode for transferring Internet messages as Automatic — see Chapter 32). If you have configured Windows Messaging for Remote Mail, you need to double-click the Inbox icon, and then choose Tools, Deliver Now.

You can configure Microsoft's Internet Explorer, Netscape's Network Navigator, Microsoft's Internet Mail, Internet News, Net Meeting, and other Internet-specific applications to automatically call your service provider by invoking your DUN connectoid. To do this, double-click the Internet icon in the Control Panel, and click the Connection tab in the Internet Properties dialog box. Under Dialing, select the connection you want to use in the drop-down list, and mark the Connect to the Internet as needed check box.

Notice in step 3 above that you had to click the Connect button. Wouldn't it be nice if Windows 95 did this for you after you double-clicked your connectoid (or a shortcut to it)?

There are three little utilities (two of them freeware) that push the Connect button for you: Dunce, RAS+ 95, and RtvReco.

Installing SLIP and automating your logon

The Windows 95 scripting utility can run a script that you create for a specific connection. This script can send your logon name, password, and account type. It can also capture a dynamically assigned IP address and send it back to your Internet service provider.

You can install SLIP and the scripting utility during Windows 95 Setup by clicking the SLIP and Scripting for Dial-Up Networking check box. If you didn't set it up then, you can do so by following the steps given in the *SLIP Server Type* section in Chapter 28.

Once you install SLIP and the scripting utility, you will be able to choose the SLIP or CSLIP server type from the drop-down list at the top of the Server Types properties sheet. (To display this properties sheet, right-click your connectoid, click Properties, and click the Server Type button if you have DUN 1.0, or click the Server Types tab if you have DUN 2.0.) The script interpreter and sample script files will be stored in your \Program Files\Accessories folder. You can edit a copy of one of these script files (they have an extension of *scp*) to meet the requirements of your Internet service provider. To do so, double-click the file to open it in Notepad.

Undocumented

Notice that Microsoft doesn't use the *scr* extension for its script files, like everyone else in the world does. This is because they already use this extension for their screen saver files. Windows 95 creates an association with the *scr* extension and the screen saver tester. Double-click a script file with an *scr* extension, and Windows 95 will try to play it as a screen saver. (In Chapter 13 we show you how to solve this problem for any script file you have that ends in *scr*.)

DUN 2.0 incorporates the scripting interpreter front end into the Properties dialog box for DUN connectoids. You still create script files, but they are associated with the given connectoid. To edit a script, right-click the connectoid, click Properties, and then click the Scripting tab. You then browse to find the script file.

To associate the edited script with your Internet service provider's connectoid using DUN 1.0, you need to choose Start, Programs, Accessories, and then Dial-Up Scripting Tool. You can place your script files anywhere you like, and you can erase the example script files from the \Program Files\Accessories folder. Just highlight the name of your service provider's connectoid in the Connections box of the Dial-Up Scripting Tool, and then browse for the actual script file.

The Microsoft Plus! CD-ROM provides a more sophisticated version of the scripting tool. If you have an earlier version of Windows 95 and if you need the Integer command, you'll need the scripting tool from Plus!. You can download the Plus! version at http://www.microsoft.com/windows/software/admintools.htm.

If you would like more detailed instructions on how to create scripts, go to http://www.ora.com/catalog/netpc/ch06-04.htm.

Making sure you have a good connection

You can check out your connection to your service provider. If you are having connection problems, you can try a few things in the Server Types properties sheet. Make sure you have the correct account type specified in the drop-down list, disable software compression, and, if you have a SLIP account, switch from CSLIP to SLIP or vice versa.

You can also try using the Unix ping command. Ping sends out a request to see if a certain computer at a given address is indeed there. After you have dialed up your server provider, open a Windows DOS session. Type **ping 198.105.232.1**. This is the IP address for ftp.microsoft.com (the FTP server at Microsoft). If ping works, your TCP/IP stack and connection to the Internet is working.

Tip

You can also use ping to test your DNS server connection. To do this, try to ping to an IP address, and then ping the name that goes with that IP address. For example, type **ping 198.105.232.1** and, if that works, type **ping ftp.microsoft.com**. If both pings work, you know that you are correctly connected to a DNS server.

If the first case works but the second doesn't, then your DNS is set up wrong. If the first fails, either you are not talking to the network or the network doesn't know who you are.

Creating a connection log file

You can generate a log file that will record the progress of your attempt to connect to your service provider. This file can help pinpoint problems. To generate a log file, take the following steps:

STEPS

Creating a Connection Log File

Step 1. Click the Start button, point to Settings, and then click Control Panel.

Step 2. Double-click the Network icon. Highlight Dial-Up Adapter, and click the Properties button.

Step 3. Click the Advanced tab, highlight Record a log file in the Property field, and choose Yes in the Value field.

Step 4. Click OK in both the Dial-Up Adapter Properties dialog box and the Network dialog box.

Step 5. Double-click your connectoid in the Dial-Up Networking folder window.

A file named Ppplog.txt will be created in your Windows folder when you take step 5. You can review this file after you attempt to make your connection.

Disabling IP header compression

If you have a PPP account, you might experience connection problems that you can cure by disabling IP header compression. To do this, take the following steps:

STEPS

Disabling IP Header Compression

Step 1. Click the Start button, point to Settings, and then click Control Panel.

Step 2. Double-click the Network icon. Highlight Dial-Up Adapter, and click the Properties button.

Step 3. Highlight Use IP header compression in the Property field. Choose No in the Value field.

Step 4. Click both OK buttons.

Connecting to CompuServe

Undocumented

You can use Internet Explorer and your CompuServe account to connect to the Internet. H&R Block, CompuServe's corporate owners, paid $100 million in 1994 to purchase Spry, the makers of Internet-in-a-Box, and used their technology to quickly get a web browser front end and a TCP/IP stack. You can completely ignore their expenditure of this vast amount and use the better 32-bit TCP/IP stack that comes with Windows 95, and, of course, the more advanced web browser, Internet Explorer.

CompuServe used to use a version of Air Mosaic that comes with its own Winsock.dll file. If you installed Air Mosaic, make sure that its accompanying Winsock.dll hasn't overwritten the one that comes with Windows 95. You can look in the \Windows\System folder and check the file dates to be sure you have the right one.

The problem of incompatible Winsock.dll files used to be quite common, and you want to be sure your Winsock-compatible Internet applications are not using the wrong Winsock.dll. You only want one Winsock.dll (plus the backup copy in \Windows\Sysbckup) on your computer, and you can search your hard disks with Find to make sure this is the case.

To make a connection to your CompuServe account, take the following steps:

Connecting to CompuServe with Internet Explorer

Step 1.   Click the Start button, point to Programs, then Accessories, and then click Dial-Up Networking.

Step 2.   Double-click the Make New Connection icon to start the Make New Connection Wizard.

Step 3.   Type **CompuServe** as the name of the connectoid, and click the Next button.

Step 4.   Type your regular local CompuServe connection number. CompuServe has added 28.8 Kbps lines, so if you have a 28.8 Kbps modem, you might try that number. Click Next. Click Finish.

Step 5.   Right-click your new connectoid in the Dial-Up Networking folder window, and click Properties.

Step 6.   Click the Configure button, and click then the Connection tab. Under Connection preferences, make sure the communication parameters are the default choices — 8, None, 1. Click OK.

Step 7.   Click the Server Type button (or the Server Types tab if you have DUN 2.0), and then click the TCP/IP Settings button.

Step 8.   Choose the following parameters in the TCP/IP Settings dialog box:

>   Server assigned IP address

>   Specify name server addresses

>>   Primary DNS - 149. 174.211.5

>>   Secondary DNS - 149.174.213.5

>   Use header IP compression

>   Use default gateway on remote network

>   Click OK.

Step 9.   In the Server Types properties sheet, make sure the server type is PPP (the default). Under Advanced options, clear all three check boxes: Log on to network, Enable software compression, and Require encrypted password. Under Allowed network protocols, mark TCP/IP, and clear NetBEUI and IPX/SPX Compatible. Click OK.

Step 10. Edit the sample script file Cis.scp in the \Program Files\Accessories folder to make any changes necessary for your connection to CompuServe. If you haven't installed the scripting facility, follow the steps in the *SLIP Server Type* section of Chapter 28.

Connecting to CompuServe with Internet Explorer

Step 11. Click the Start button, point to Programs, then Accessories, and then click Dial-Up Scripting Tool. Highlight your CompuServe connectoid and browse for Cis.scp. Click OK.

Step 12. Double-click the Internet icon in the Control Panel. Click the Connection tab, and then select CompuServe in the drop-down list. Click OK. This connects the Internet Explorer to the CompuServe connectoid.

Step 13. Double-click your CompuServe connectoid in the Dial-Up Networking folder. Enter your CompuServe account number in the User name field, and your CompuServe password in the Password field. Click the Save password check box.

You have created a connectoid that logs you into CompuServe as an Internet service provider. You can just double-click the connectoid to make the connection, or you can double-click the Internet icon on your Desktop to make the connection and start the Internet Explorer.

The CompuServe connection is similar to other Internet service provider connections, except that it lacks a POP3 and SMTP mail server, and — in our experience— it is quite a bit slower. You can run other Internet application software on it using the Windows 95 Winsock.dll. You could run Netscape if you like; you don't have to run Internet Explorer or Air Mosaic. Microsoft gave you in Windows 95 what CompuServe paid $100 million for.

Creating a DUN connectoid for your Netcom account

You can use the instructions in the *Dial-up connection to your service provider* section earlier in this chapter to create a new DUN connectoid with the name Netcom. To make it specific to your Netcom account, you'll need to set the following properties:

Server type is PPP (the default)

IP address is dynamically assigned (as is true of all PPP accounts)

Assign the primary DNS server address as 199.182.120.203

Assign the secondary DNS server address as 199.182.120.202

Put a pound sign (#) before your user name

Internet through Your LAN

As we mentioned at the beginning of this chapter, you can also access the Internet through your local area network. In fact, you can have Unix, NetWare, Windows 95 and Windows NT servers on your LAN and access them through your TCP/IP stack — no need to dial them up. Your LAN becomes an Intranet.

Tip

You can place a World Wide Web server on a local server and publish your own home pages internally. Computer users throughout your business can surf the local net, using copies of Internet Explorer, Mosaic, or Netscape to access local home pages that are updated to provide corporate information. If you install a POP3 and SMTP mail server, you can handle e-mail as though it were any other Internet mail.

Of course, your system administrator can provide access to the Internet (in addition to the Intranet) through a server over any level of telephone access to some type of Internet service provider. (When companies do this, they often set up a firewall to keep overly inquisitive outsiders from accessing internal corporate information.)

You or your system administrator will configure your computer in a manner similar to that described earlier in this chapter in the section entitled *Installing an Internet dial-up connection*. If you have a LAN connection, your TCP/IP stack is bound to your local area network card instead of to your Dial-Up Adapter (local modem). Your system administrator can set up a local DHCP server to resolve addresses. You won't need a Dial-Up Adapter, except for Direct Cable Connection.

If you have TCP/IP bound to your Dial-Up Adapter and your network card and there is no DHCP server in your local area, your computer will pause every now and then when it's trying to find something or somebody. If this gets annoying, you will need to unbind TCP/IP from your network card (or get a DHCP server locally).

Tip

A Windows 95 computer set up as a Dial-Up Networking server can't route TCP/IP. So you can't call in from home (to this computer) by using the TCP/IP protocol bound to your Dial-Up Adapter at your home computer and expect to be able to connect over TCP/IP to your Intranet on your LAN at work.

A Windows NT server set up as RAS (or DUN) server can take your TCP/IP call and connect you to your company's Intranet, and, through one of your company's servers, to its Internet service provider.

Undocumented

If you have two Internet connections — a LAN and an Internet service provider — and if you have a DNS server on your local area network, you should list your DNS server second in the DNS Configuration tab of the TCP/IP Properties dialog box (double-click the Network icon in the Control Panel, highlight TCP/IP, and click the Properties button). The local DNS server won't have the IP address of your Internet service provider. If you are dialing out to the Internet, the Internet DNS server can resolve your IP addresses if it is first on the list. If you are connecting locally, the Internet DNS server won't reply and the local DNS server will be contacted next.

You can find further instructions for connecting a Windows 95 computer through a local area network to the Internet at http://www.windows95.com/connect/lan.html.

Connecting a Windows 95 network to the Internet

You can configure a peer-to-peer network of Windows 95 computers to connect to the Internet without using a Windows NT, Unix, or other type of server. One of the Windows 95 computers acts as the Internet connection server.

Qbik Software's WinGate (available at http://www.windows95.com) provides the gateway to the Internet and runs on the Windows 95 computer that provides the Internet connection for the rest of the computers on the network. You have to connect all the computers using network cards and configure the TCP/IP stacks on the other Windows 95 computers to the gateway computer.

You can download specific instructions on how to configure this type of Internet connection from http://www.windows95.com/connect/lansing.html.

Microsoft Network over the Internet

The Internet is a TCP/IP network. An Intranet is a TCP/IP local area network. You can treat the Internet as though it were a local area TCP/IP network. It's a really slow local area network if you are connecting to it through anything other than a T1 line.

There are Windows NT and Windows 95 computers connected to the Internet that you can access as though they were connected to a Microsoft Windows network. There is a Winserver that provides DCHP name resolution so that you can connect to these other computers.

To find out more about using the Internet in this semi-strange manner, check out http://www.windows95.com/connect/peercon.html and http://www.winserve.com/.

TCP/IP Utilities

Microsoft ships some low-level TCP/IP utilities with Windows 95. Most of these utilities are DOS-based — which is kinda weird. Well, Unix and DOS are text-based, and TCP/IP is down there below the user interface, so it makes some sense. Microsoft also provides one Windows-based TCP/IP utility.

Table 33-1 lists the TCP/IP utilities you get with Windows 95:

Table 33-1	TCP/IP Utilities
Command	*What It Does*
DOS Utilities	
Arp	Displays and modifies the IP-to-Physical (Ethernet card) address translation tables used by address resolution protocol (ARP). If you're dialing into the Internet over your own modem, you won't be using this utility.
Ftp	File Transfer Protocol. Allows you to log onto other computers on the Internet (perhaps as anonymous) and download or upload files. We feature much better Windows-based FTP programs on the *Windows 95 Secrets* CD-ROM and suggest that you use them instead.
Nbtstat	Displays protocol statistics and current TCP/IP connections using NBT (NetBIOS over TCP/IP).
Netstat	Displays protocol statistics and current TCP/IP connections.
Ping	Checks for a connection to a remote computer. For example, type **ping ftp.microsoft.com**. We suggest you use our featured shareware, Ws_ping, instead.
Route	Manually controls network routing tables. Routes added to the table are dynamic and need to be re-established every time your reboot the computer. You can create a batch file with the proper commands and then put a *pif* file that points to it in your Startup folder.
Tracert	Displays the route taken to a remote computer. For example, type **tracert ftp.microsoft.com**. If you aren't connected, your default DUN connectoid is called. Use Ws_ping instead.
Windows Utility	
Winipcfg	Displays current TCP/IP network configurations. You don't use it to change these configurations; for that, you go to the TCP/IP Properties dialog box (accessed through the Network icon in the Control Panel).

To find out how to use the DOS-based TCP/IP applications, open a DOS Windows session and type the command name followed by **-?**. Winipcfg is stored in the \Windows folder. You can create a shortcut to it and put the shortcut in a folder you use for Internet utilities. (You can also do this for the DOS-based utilities. You'll find them in the \Windows folder as well.)

Displaying your TCP/IP settings

You can easily use Winipcfg to display your current TCP/IP configuration. Winipcfg.exe is by default stored in your \Windows folder. If you haven't created a shortcut to it, just run it by clicking your Start button, clicking Run, typing Winipcfg, and clicking the OK button. The results are shown in Figure 33-9:

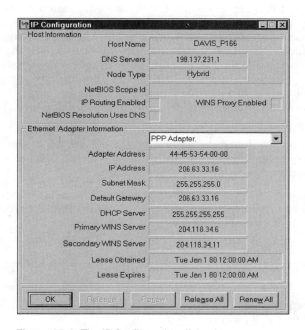

Figure 33-9: The IP Configuration dialog box.

Your adapter address is a number hard coded into a network card if your TCP/IP protocol is bound to a network card. If your TCP/IP protocol is bound to your Dial-Up Adapter (your modem, in other words), the number is meaningless because modems don't have an address hard coded in.

If your IP address is dynamically assigned, this field and the subnet mask field will be filled with zeros. If you have a dynamically assigned IP address from a DHCP server, you can get a new one by clicking the Renew All button.

Telnet

Windows 95 comes with a reasonably good Telnet client. Telnet lets you log onto a remote computer (or even your service provider's computer) as a terminal (like HyperTerminal). You can then run the Unix software running on that remote computer.

This might seem like a step backwards, but it is handy at times to be able to get the Internet out of the way of talking to a specific computer. Telnet.exe is stored in the \Windows folder. Create a shortcut to it and place it in an Internet folder.

Network file system

Tip

Windows 95 doesn't include a network file system (NFS) such as the installable file system for Unix or Spry's Air FTP. The directories and file systems on Unix computers don't look like the file systems on Windows 95 computers. It's nice to have a translation layer that both makes them look like VFAT, the Windows 95 file system, and adds drag and drop between file systems. That way, you can just drag a file from a remote Unix computer and drop it in your local folder. You can use FTP Explorer found at http://www.windows95.com to provide some of this functionality.

A no-cost program called Samba that runs on a Sun server allows Windows 95 computers to access the files on the Sun server as though they were FAT-type files. You can get information about Samba at http://lake.canberra.edu.au/pub/samba/samba.html.

You might also try ICE NFS, which provides a virtual drive for Windows 95. It allows Windows 95 to mount drives on other machines. You'll find it at http://www.jriver.com/ice.nfs.html.

Summary

Windows 95 supports three networking protocol stacks, one of which is TCP/IP (the protocol used by the Internet).

▶ Combine TCP/IP support with Dial-Up Networking, and Windows 95 gives you the tools you need to connect to the Internet.

▶ We help you secure the right kind of account with an Internet service provider.

▶ You need to get the right information from your service provider; we tell you what to ask for.

▶ We explain each of the steps for setting up your Windows 95 computer for Dial-Up Networking and TCP/IP support.

▶ We show you how to connect to your service provider and make sure that you've got a good connection.

Chapter 34

Internet Explorer

In This Chapter

We've referred to Internet Explorer throughout this book. In this chapter, we delve into the depths of Microsoft's web browser. If you have installed Internet Explorer 4.0, you'll see that the browser is integrated into the Windows 95 Desktop user interface. If you have Internet Explorer 3.01, most of what we say in this chapter still applies.

▶ If you want 128-bit encryption, Internet Explorer comes in a special U.S.- and Canada-only version

▶ Organize and move your Favorites folder

▶ Convert Netscape Navigator bookmarks

▶ Find a URL even in a frame

▶ Move your Internet files cache folder

▶ Add the Edit button to the Internet toolbar

▶ Filling in forms causes an error

▶ Cool Windows 95-related web sites

The Internet Explorer and the Windows 95 User Interface Are One

If you have installed the integrated shell version of Internet Explorer 4.0, you'll notice that an upgraded Internet Explorer 3.01 with some modifications is now integrated into the Windows 95 user interface. Now we all know why Microsoft did this: They want to preserve their monopoly position in personal-computer operating systems. The Netscape Navigator browser has threatened to turn Windows into the equivalent of your computer's BIOS — a necessary component, but hardly sufficient for getting your work done, and getting less necessary by the minute.

But just because Microsoft has a very strategic interest in "embracing" the web browser interface and technology and "extending" it into its operating system doesn't mean that there aren't benefits for us lowly users. Microsoft has to sell their vision and their software, and even though they are a near monopoly, they aren't going to sell their products if they don't provide us with some compelling reasons to want them.

In this chapter, we give you all sorts of tricks and undocumented features that you can use to more easily work with both Internet Explorer 3.01 and 4.0. Integrating the Internet Explorer with the Explorer and the Windows 95 Desktop decreases the barriers between applications and between different kinds of data and their locations.

Internet Explorer 4.0 disappears as a separate application, and its functionality is included in and transforms the Windows 95 user interface. While the Internet icon still sits on the Desktop and in the Control Panel, the Internet toolbar is now available in any Windows 95 window (and appears when you type a URL in the Address field, for example). Any Explorer or My Computer window can now look like Internet Explorer.

When we refer to Internet Explorer throughout this chapter, we usually refer to both 3.01 and 4.0. When we are speaking of only one of the versions, it will be clear. You can download the latest version of Internet Explorer from http://www.microsoft.com/ie.

Active or standard Desktop

Active Desktop, an Internet Explorer 4.0 feature, gives you a web page-like view of your Desktop, as shown in Figure 34-1. You get icons you can single-click, and "live" continuously updated information from the Internet in *active windows* as you work. Web view gives you an active window in your Explorer or My Computer window.

If you have set Web view to single-click (an option in the View tab of the Options dialog box), you can activate applications and open folder windows by single-clicking them. Whenever we tell you to double-click an icon on the Desktop, you can single-click instead.

To switch in and out of the Active Desktop, right-click the Desktop and click Active Desktop in the context menu to place/clear the check mark next to it. You can also switch in and out of Web view in any Explorer or folder window. In the Explorer, right-click in the right pane. In a folder window, right-click an empty part of the window. Then point to View in the context menu, and choose Web View.

In the Explorer (or in My Computer), you can focus on a file or folder that's stored on your computer (or on the network), or you can focus on a URL. To jump to any location, you can simply type the address in the Address box of the toolbar (or choose it from the Address drop-down list). You can enter addresses of documents or folders on your own computer or network — such as C:\My Documents — or addresses of web pages — such as http://www.windows95.com. All this works regardless of whether you're using Web view or the standard Desktop view.

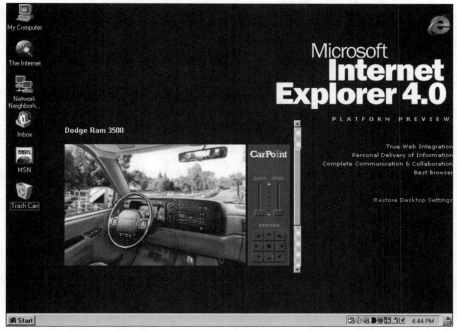

Figure 34-1: The Active Desktop.

If you click an HTML document in the left pane of the Explorer, its content is displayed in the right-pane. If you click a URL, the Explorer initiates a call to your Internet service provider if necessary, and then opens the target site/document in a new window.

It's on your Desktop, your Start menu, your Explorer

Microsoft built Internet Explorer as a *control*, an object that can be integrated into other applications. Internet Explorer 4.0 users experience it as an extension to and a part of the user interface.

Internet Explorer adds Web view, a new view of your folder windows, and Active Desktop, a new view of your Desktop . It adds the Favorites command to the Start menu. It adds active windows to the Desktop. It adds the Internet toolbar to the Explorer and My Computer windows. It adds the Internet Explorer icon to the second level of the tree in the left pane of the Explorer.

This may actually seem a little strange after you use Internet Explorer 4.0 for a while. When you click an HTML document in the Explorer, the document is displayed in the Explorer window (see Figure 34-2), effectively transforming the Explorer into a viewer. Viewing an HTML document in a window works just fine. You can't, however, view a web page directly on the Desktop itself.

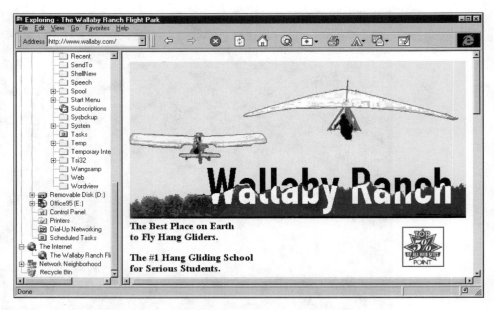

Figure 34-2: Viewing an HTML document in the Explorer.

Setting up the Internet Explorer

You can use both versions of Internet Explorer with any Internet service provider, including the Microsoft Network, America Online, and CompuServe. You can download the latest version of Internet Explorer from the Microsoft web site, http://www.microsoft.com/ie. To install Internet Explorer, just double-click the self-installing downloaded executable file that contains Internet Explorer. You will be asked where you want to install it and whether you want to install all of the options.

Internet Explorer comes with the Internet Connection Wizard, which automates many of the steps required to create an Internet connection (explained in Chapter 33). You can use the Wizard to create a connection, and then go back and manually check what the Wizard did by following the steps we detailed in Chapter 33.

The Internet Connection Wizard creates a Dial-Up Networking connectoid for you if you connect to the Internet through a dial-up connection to an Internet service provider. This connectoid is automatically associated with Internet Explorer, and it is called every time you double-click the Internet icon on your Desktop.

The Wizard also installs and configures the Internet icon in your Control Panel. Double-clicking this icon displays the Internet Properties dialog box. The Dial-Up Networking connectoid that the Internet Connection Wizard created for you is specified in the Connection tab of this dialog box. If you have another connectoid that you want to use to call another Internet service provider instead of the one you originally created using the Internet Connection Wizard, you can specify it in this dialog box.

Undocumented

You can install Internet Explorer 3.01 without having to answers any questions. It will also reboot your computer for you and finish the install. The following example of how to do a "quiet" install is for Internet Explorer 3.01, but you can change the numbers in the filenames for later versions. This doesn't work if you download a file that contains Internet Explorer and additional add-on programs.

To install quietly and reboot your computer, type these command line parameters in a shortcut's Target field: **msie30.exe /q /c:"infinst.exe /q"**. To install quietly and not reboot, type **msie30.exe /q /c:"infinst.exe /q /r:n"**. You'll have to include the path to msie30.exe in these commands. Change 30 to 40 in the filename (msie40.exe) to install Internet Explorer 4.0 quietly.

Internet Explorer, the 128-bit version

Internet Explorer comes in two flavors. One supports 40-bit (or weaker) encryption, and the other supports 128-bit (very strong) encryption. Because of federal government regulations restricting the export of products that incorporate 128-bit encryption, Microsoft normally ships the 40-bit version. You can, however, download the 128-bit version from the Microsoft web site (http://www.microsoft.com/ie/download/) if your IP address indicates that you live in the United States or Canada.

If you want to find out more about 40-bit versus 128-bit encryption, check out http://wellsfargo.com/nav/encryp/B. You can get more information about the 128-bit version of Internet Explorer at: http://xcom.www.conxion.com/questions.htm.

Can't download the 128-bit version?

The Microsoft web server checks to see if you have a valid IP address (that is, one in Canada or the U.S.) before it will ship the 128-bit version of Internet Explorer. If it does not get a valid DNS address return from its query of your Internet service provider, it won't let you download this version. You know that this is the case if the DNS entry on the query-form is blank.

Secret

Many Internet service providers keep their domain name servers behind firewalls for security reasons. The service provider's domain name server may not send your IP address to Microsoft's web server when requested. If you have this problem, contact your service provider and ask them to reconfigure their firewall to permit DNS address queries without compromising security.

English as a second language

With the spread of the web, more and more sites are using character sets other than US ASCII. To display these sites correctly, you need to have the expanded character set installed on your computer. You can download the Internet Explorer international character add-ins from http://www.microsoft.com/ie/ie3/multilang.htm.

Favorites and URL Shortcuts

A URL (Uniform Resource Locator) is a unique identifier for a web page or other resource on the Internet. Both versions of Internet Explorer maintain a list of the URLs for your favorite sites. Your *favorites* are actually shortcuts to URLs that Internet Explorer stores in the Favorites folder, which is located by default in your \Windows folder.

You can divide your Favorites folder into subfolders organized around common topics, and then place shortcuts to your favorite sites in these subfolders. To create Favorites subfolders, click the Favorites button in the Internet toolbar, and then choose Organize Favorites. Right-click an empty part of the Organize Favorites window, and then choose New, Folder from the context menu. (You can also click the Create New Folder button on the Organize Favorites toolbar.)

All Favorites are shortcuts to URLs; you can put copies of these shortcuts on your Desktop and start Internet Explorer by double-clicking the shortcut's icon. You can also create shortcuts to URLs on the fly as you're browsing. See *URL shortcuts* later in this chapter for more information.

You can drag and drop your Favorites folder wherever you like (say, on a drive other than the drive that contains the \Windows folder), and Internet Explorer should track its location. Nonetheless, we found that if you do move your Favorites folder, it's a good idea to edit your Registry to change any references to the previous Favorites location to its new location.

Converting Netscape Navigator bookmarks

When you first install Internet Explorer, it looks to see if you have Netscape Navigator installed. If you do, it shaves 5 percent off the speed of your processor. No, no, just joking. It automatically converts the Netscape Navigator bookmarks to Internet Explorer favorites.

Undocumented

If you want to convert Netscape Navigator bookmarks after you've already installed Internet Explorer, you need to invoke the applet that does this job automatically during installation. You can download this applet from ftp://ftp.microsoft.com/Softlib/Mslfiles/WINBM2FV.EXE.

You can also use shareware package called Navex to move favorites and bookmarks back and forth between browsers. Download it from http://144.118.4.17/navex/.

URL shortcuts

Internet Explorer keeps track of web sites and web pages through shortcuts to URLs. These shortcuts have an extension of *url* instead of the standard *lnk* extension for Windows shortcuts.

If you have Internet Explorer 4.0, your URL shortcuts store more information about the URLs than just their values. (See Figure 34-3.) Internet Explorer uses this additional information to help you manage your shortcuts as well as to let you view web sites offline.

Figure 34-3: The Properties dialog box for a URL shortcut created by Internet Explorer 4.0. Notice the tabs for additional properties.

You can create URL shortcuts to local documents or HTML pages just by displaying the document in Internet Explorer, clicking Favorites, choosing Add to Favorites, and then clicking OK. If you would rather put the shortcut directly on the Desktop, right-click an area on a web page that doesn't include a graphic or a link to another location, and choose Create Shortcut from the context menu (or choose File, Create Shortcut).

To create a shortcut to a link (a jump to another URL) in a web page, drag the link to the Desktop. You can later double-click this shortcut to start Internet Explorer and go to the indicated location on the Web.

Capturing URLs in a frame

Normally when you display a web page or site, its URL appears in the Address box in Internet Explorer. However, if you open a web page that uses frames (panes within the Internet Explorer client window), and then navigate within the main, or largest, frame to a page on another site, the Address box may not update to show you the URL for the page you're currently viewing. This happens because web designers often use frames as a way to let you view other people's pages without leaving their own site. This allows them to keep their text, logos, navigational buttons, and graphics in view (in smaller frames around the main frame) even as you're viewing pages at other locations.

Undocumented

You may want to know the new URL for a page you're viewing in a frame, if for no other reason than to get out of the frame at the original site and onto the new site of the page you're viewing. Here's how to capture the URL:

STEPS

Finding the URL for a Site That's Been "Framed"

Step 1. Right-click an open spot in the frame that contains the web page whose URL you want to know. Select Properties.

Step 2. You'll now see the URL. If you want to jump to the site, highlight the URL, and press Ctrl+C to copy it.

Step 3. Click in Internet Explorer's Address box, press Ctrl+V to paste the URL, and then press Enter.

Save As

You can save a web page just by navigating to it and then choosing File, Save As on the menu. You can also save a target page by right-clicking its link in the source page and choosing Save Target As.

Tip

If you would prefer to name a web page you're saving with its title (the name that appears at the top of the document) instead of its filename, first highlight the title and press Ctrl+C to copy it to the Clipboard. Then issue the File, Save As command, click in the File name text box, and press Ctrl+V to paste in the title.

You create web pages using a markup language called HTML (Hypertext Markup Language). It's called a *markup language* because you use it to mark up the plain text of a web page with *tags* that tell web browsers such as Internet Explorer how to format the page and what links to include where. The term *HTML document* (or *HTML page*) refers to the file that contains the plain text and HTML tags (or *source code*) required to display a web page. These files have an extension of *htm* or *html*. You place a graphic image in a web page by inserting a tag in the underlying HTML document that tells the browser the name of the graphics file to display, and its location on the web server.

Unfortunately, when you save a web page, Internet Explorer saves the text in the page (the HTML document itself), but not the graphic images displayed in the page, because these are actually separate files. You can save individual graphics files one at a time by right-clicking the graphic and then choosing Save Picture As. This can get tiresome, however, and even if you save all the graphics in a web page this way, you probably still won't be able to open the saved HMTL document at a later date and see both its text and graphics.

The reason for this is that graphic images are usually stored in a subdirectory of the directory on the host computer that stores the HTML page, and the graphics tags in the HTML page usually (although not always) contain relative pointers to that subdirectory (which is often called Images).

Undocumented

If you have saved the graphics from a web page in the same folder as the HTML page itself on your hard disk, Internet Explorer probably won't be able to find the graphics when you open the HTML page because the graphics tags in the page most likely contain pointers to a subdirectory that doesn't exist on your computer. If you are familiar with HTML, you could use an HTML editor (or a plain text editor such as Notepad) to view the HMTL source code for the page, and, if you see relative references to a particular directory, move the graphics files to a subfolder of the same name on your own hard disk. This would be quite a pain, however. It sure would be great if you could just grab a site and have it display correctly after you store it on your hard disk.

There are numerous third-party applications that save the contents of web pages and let you redisplay them in their entirety (both text and graphics) without having to connect to the Internet (see http://www.windows95.com). You can also use a shareware application called Microsoft Internet Explorer Cache Viewer to redisplay sites that you have previously visited without going online. It lets you do this by organizing and displaying the Temporary Internet Files cache (where Internet Explorer caches content from previously visited sites). You'll find this application at http://ourworld.compuserve.com/homepages/M_Wolf.

Internet Explorer 4.0 does a good job of displaying a previously cached web site. If the web site is on your list of favorites, you can click its name when you are offline, and remain offline while you view the page. Internet Explorer displays the site for you by retrieving the last downloaded instance of this site from the cache.

New link, new window

If you want to open a new window when you jump to a new site, hold down the Shift key when you click the link. You'll then be able to see both the target site and the source page in different Internet Explorer windows.

Organizing the Favorites folders

If you have installed Internet Explorer 4.0, the Favorites folder icon has a star burst graphic on it. The fact that the folder icon has a graphic should give you a clue that this is a special folder. It is indeed special, but only because the system keeps track of its location. This is why you have to have to edit your Registry to specify its new location if you move it.

Your favorites are stored in the \Windows\Favorites folder. You can create subfolders for your Favorites folder in any Explorer or My Computer window. You can move these folders around (after all, they are just folders containing shortcuts). You can further subdivide the Favorites folder's subfolders, and you can drag shortcuts from folder to folder. You can also rename shortcuts. This is helpful because the default name of a shortcut is often not that meaningful. (The default name is whatever the webmaster came up with for the document at the specific URL to which the shortcut is linked.)

Tip

You can also open a folder window to display the contents of your Favorites folder by holding down the Shift key when you click the Organize Favorites command. This gives you another not-so-clever way to organize your Favorites. We say not so clever because it doesn't display a dual-pane window to help you move things around.

Shortcuts to URLs don't have to be in the Favorites folder tree

Tip

You don't have to put URL shortcuts in the Favorites folder or one of its subfolders. If you do, then the shortcuts are accessible from the Favorites button on the Internet toolbar and from the Favorites menu. But you are free to put them wherever you like. You can create many folders of URL shortcuts, and place shortcuts to these folders on your Desktop.

When you capture a URL, you can either choose Favorites, Add to Favorites to store the shortcut in a Favorites folder or subfolder, or you can simply put the shortcut on the Desktop, perhaps with the intent of moving it somewhere else later. To create a shortcut to the current web page, right-click the page (stay clear of graphics and links) and choose Create Shortcut from the context menu. A shortcut is created on the Desktop. You can drag and drop this shortcut to whatever location you like.

Shortcut to your Favorites folder(s)

Right-drag and drop your Favorites folder onto your Desktop. Choose Create Shortcut(s) Here. If the folder contains a nameable set of shortcuts to URLs, right-click the shortcut icon on your Desktop, choose Rename, and give it a new name. Otherwise, leave it as Favorites.

Click this shortcut to your Favorites folder to open an Internet Explorer window displaying your Favorites subfolders. If you have Internet Explorer 4.0 and are using Web view, the window looks like a web site of your favorite folders and sites. When you're connected to the Internet, you can click a shortcut to a URL displayed in the Internet Explorer window to jump to one of your favorite sites.

Multiple Favorites folders

Undocumented

You can have multiple Favorites folders and Favorites folder trees. By using TweakUI and the Registry editor, you can switch back and forth on the fly between different Favorites folders.

One way to start this off is to make a copy of your existing Favorites folder. To do this, right-click the folder, choose Copy, highlight another folder, say your My Documents folder, right-click it, and choose Paste. You now have a copy of your original Favorites folder under your My Documents folder. Next, edit the two Favorites folder trees to create separate and distinct sets of shortcuts.

The copy of the Favorites folder is a special folder (you can tell because it has a star burst on it) but it isn't recognized as *the* Favorites folder by the system. You use TweakUI and the Registry editor to choose which one of the two folders is the actual system-recognized Favorites folder. First, change all of the references to the Favorites folder in the Registry to point to one of the two Favorites locations. You can change the main references using TweakUI; others you'll need to change "by hand" using the Registry editor. Then use the Registry, Export Registry File command in the Registry editor to create a *reg* file that incorporates these changes. Repeat this process to create a another *reg* file that contains a version of the Registry that refers to the second Favorites location. Run the *reg* files to switch back and forth between the two Favorites folders.

Saving graphics off the Internet

Images can take a long time to download if you are connected to the Internet through a 14.4 or 28.8 Kbps modem. Internet Explorer loads graphics in the background and lets you scroll down beneath the graphics to read the text while you're waiting for them to load.

Do you want to save a graphics file you are viewing in Internet Explorer? Right-click it, choose Save Picture As, and then give it a path and a name. If you don't save a graphics file as you're viewing it, you can save it later from the cache. When Internet Explorer first downloads a graphics file, it automatically caches (saves) it in the \Windows\Temporary Internet Files folder. You can find the file in this folder and save it permanently by copying it to another location. (Internet Explorer periodically deletes old files from the cache folder.)

If you want to turn a graphic in a web page into wallpaper on your Desktop, right-click the graphic, and choose Use As Wallpaper.

Internet Cache Folder

Tip

Internet Explorer caches quite a bit of the material you gather off the Internet. This makes it faster to go back to a web page you've recently visited, because Internet Explorer can open it from your disk instead of retrieving it from the Internet again. Internet Explorer always checks to see if it has the latest version of a web page in its cache before it opens it. If it discovers that the page has been updated on the web site since it was cached, it retrieves the updated version instead of using the cached copy. To make sure that you have the latest information from a site, you can force Internet Explorer to retrieve a new copy of a web page instead of using a copy from the cache. Just choose View, Refresh or press the F5 key.

You can set the size of the Internet cache folder (\Windows\Temporary Internet Files) by right-clicking the Internet icon on your Desktop, choosing Properties, clicking the Advanced tab, and clicking the Settings button. Slide the Cache size slider to a percentage of the hard disk that you are willing to use for caching these Internet files.

Want to view what is in your cache? Choose View, Options in Internet Explorer, click the Advanced tab, and then click the View Files button. If you order the files by Internet address, all the files from the same site will show up next to each other.

You can also use a specialized cache-viewing program such as Mathias Wolf's MSIE Cache Explorer. It lets you view the web sites stored in the Internet Explorer cache when you are offline. You can find this shareware at http://ourworld.compuserve.com/homepages/M_Wolf.

Changing where cached files are kept

When you download web pages, Internet Explorer stores them in C:\Windows\Temporary Internet Files. You determine the maximum storage area available for this folder (see the previous section). You can also tell Internet Explorer to store its cached files in a different folder. This might be a good idea if you have limited space on the drive that contains the \Windows folder.

To specify a different folder for your cached web pages, right-click the Internet icon on your Desktop, click Properties, click the Advanced tab, click the Settings button, and then click the Move Folder button. In the Browse for Folder dialog box, highlight the desired folder and click OK. You have to restart Windows for the change to take effect. Note that when you specify a new cache folder, Internet Explorer deletes all the cached files from the original folder. Furthermore, the four cache subfolders (described in the next section) are automatically visible in the new cache folder.

The cache folder subfolders

The Temporary Internet Files folder is a special folder. A shell extension has been added to it to customize its characteristics. When you display this folder in details view, it gives you additional information, such as the URL and the expiration date, which you don't see in the details view of ordinary folders.

Like other special folders, the Temporary Internet Files folder contains a hidden file, Desktop.ini, which specifies the class object (special type) for this folder. The Desktop.ini file in this folder points to Cachevu.dll. This DLL contains the code that creates this special view of the Temporary Internet Files folder.

Undocumented

There are actually four separate subfolders (cache1, cache2, cache3, and cache4) under the Temporary Internet Files folder, as shown in Figure 34-4. Microsoft split the cache into four separate folders so that Windows 95 could better manage all the files stored there and more quickly access cached web pages. If you want to see the four folders, you can change the hidden attribute of the Desktop.ini file in a DOS window to unhidden (attrib -h desktop.ini). Rename the Desktop.ini file to Desk.ini. Now you'll see the four subfolders in your Explorer.

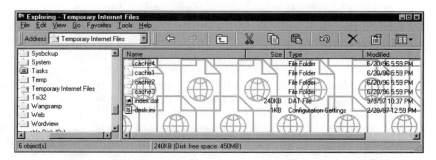

Figure 34-4: The hidden cache folders. If you have Internet Explorer 4.0, you'll notice that it displays these folders as half transparent to remind you that they are hidden.

Rename Desk.ini back to Desktop.ini and hide it again when you are done.

Deleting typed URLs in the Address box

If you type a URL in the Address box in Internet Explorer, you can go back later and choose that URL from a drop-down list attached to the Address box. This list lets you scroll through previously typed URLs to pick the one you want. (Sometimes URLs are put on this list that you didn't type — they get "typed in" automatically.)

Undocumented

You can edit this list or delete it using your Registry editor. Just navigate to HKEY_CURRENT_USER\Software\Microsoft\Internet Explorer\TypedURLs. You'll notice a list of URLs in the right pane of the Explorer. To delete an entry, select it (click its URL*x* name in the Name column) and press Delete. To edit an entry, double-click its URL*x* name.

Creating Custom Versions of the Internet Explorer

Microsoft makes its version of Internet Explorer. You can make your own version. Download the Internet Explorer Administration Kit. With this program, you can set up the default start and search pages, the pages for the Quick Links in the Links toolbar, the logos and title bars, and so on. How about your own animated icon in the upper-right hand corner? To apply for the IEAK CD-ROM, sign up at http://www.microsoft.com/ie/ieak.

You can customize your links, including your start page, your search page, and the Quick Links displayed as buttons on the Links toolbar (located directly beneath the Internet toolbar) without having to use the IEAK. You can change the names of the Quick Links and the URLs for all of the links. By making these adjustments, you can actually make these links useful, and not just ways for Microsoft to draw you into their fold.

To change your links, right-click the Internet icon, click Properties, and click the Navigation tab. Display the Page drop-down list, and select the link you want to modify. The Quick Links are numbered 1 through 5 (Quick Link #1 corresponds to the leftmost button on the Links toolbar, Quick Link #2 corresponds to the next button to the right, and so on.) If you're modifying a Quick Link, enter a name for the link in the Name field. The name you type will appear on the corresponding button in the Links toolbar. (You can't change the names of the start page and search page.) Then type the address for the target of the link in the Address field. The address does not have to be a URL for a web page. You can make it an executable file on your hard disk, as long as you enter the full path and filename.

You can find custom replacements for Microsoft's spinning globe at http://home.cdsnet.net/~suicide/Replacements.zip.

Changing the toolbar background graphic

Undocumented

You can choose your own graphic for the background of the toolbar. It needs to be a *bmp* file, and if it is too big, the toolbar will revert to its default graphic.

STEPS

New Background Graphic for the Toolbar

Step 1. Right-click the Internet icon, click Properties, and click the General tab. Clear the Background bitmap check box. Click OK. Make sure no windows displaying the Internet toolbar are open or active.

Step 2. Open your Registry editor. Navigate to

HKEY_CURRENT_USER\Software\Microsoft\ Internet Explorer\Toolbar.

Step 3. Double-click BackBitmap in the right pane of the Registry editor. Type the path and filename for a smallish (let's say 64K) *bmp* file.

Step 4. Double-click the Internet icon. You should see your graphic in the background if you have set Internet Explorer to display the Internet toolbar.

No underlines for hyperlinks

By default, hyperlinks on web pages are underlined. As you move your mouse pointer over the icons on your Desktop in Web view, you'll notice that they become underlined, mimicking hyperlinks in web pages.

Undocumented

You can turn off the underlining of hyperlinks (but not of the icons on the Desktop) and view other Internet Explorer Registry settings by following these steps:

STEPS

Getting Rid of the Underlines

Step 1.   Double-click Regedit.exe in your \Windows folder.

Step 2.   Navigate to

H_KEY_CURRENT_USER\Software\Microsoft\
Internet Explorer\Main

Step 3.   Double-click Anchor Underline in the right pane. Change
yes to no.

Step 4.   Exit the Registry editor and restart Windows 95.

No home page

One way to open your Internet Explorer is with no home page at all. Choose
Go Home Page in an Explorer or folder window. The Explorer tries to go to
your home page, or to the default start page that Microsoft chose for you
(http://www.msn.com).

Undocumented

You can choose to open to a "no page" home page if you like. Right-click the
Internet icon on your Desktop, click Properties, and then click the Navigation tab. The Page field should say Start Page. Clear the Address field and
enter C:\Windows\System\Blank.htm instead. Click the OK button.

Now right-click the Internet icon on your Desktop and click Open Home
Page, and you'll get no further than your blank page.

Make your own Blank.htm page

If Internet Explorer has trouble connecting to a site, it displays the
C:\Windows\System\Blank.htm page. You can ask it to display another page
when it has similar problems. Of course, you can also just edit Blank.htm if
you like.

STEPS

A New Blank.htm Page

Step 1.   Start Regedit.exe in C:\Windows. Navigate to

HKEY_CURRENT_USER\Software\Microsoft\Internet
Explorer\Main.

A New Blank.htm Page

Step 2.   Double-click LocalPage in the right pane of the Registry editor. Type the path and filename for a new web page that you want to be your default blank page.

The backgrounds and graphics on the Desktop

Undocumented

You'll find the graphics and HTML files that make up the displays in the active window on the Desktop in the \Windows\Web folder. The image that is used for the background of the active window is Dskwmark.gif. You can make a copy of this file (right-click it, click Copy, click the client area of the Explorer next to this filename, click Paste). If you want a new background, create a new *gif* file and name it Dskwmark.gif.

Glen Flinch told us about this previously undocumented feature, and he also pointed out that the background graphic for Web view in Explorer or My Computer windows is the Wmark.gif file. You can look through the HTML files and *gif* files in the \Windows\Web folder and see which graphics files you might want to change.

Edit on the Internet toolbar

Undocumented

If you have installed FrontPage or other Microsoft HTML editors, you'll notice that the Internet toolbar has an additional button — the Edit button. If you click this button, you can edit the page that you are currently viewing in Internet Explorer.

If you don't have the Edit button and wish you did, here's how to get it:

STEPS

Putting the Edit button on the Internet Toolbar

Step 1.   Double-click My Computer. Choose View, Options and click the File Types tab.

Step 2.   Scroll down to Internet Document (HTML). You'll have this document type if you have installed any version of Internet Explorer. Click Edit, New.

(continued)

Putting the Edit button on the Internet Toolbar

Step 3.   In the Action field, type **&Edit**. In the Application used to perform
action field, either click the Browse button or type the path to
your HTML Editor. If you don't have one, type
C:\Windows\Notepad.exe.

Step 4.   Double-click the Internet icon on the Desktop. You'll see the Edit
button in the Internet toolbar.

If you are using Notepad to edit HTML documents and you install FrontPage,
it will change the action associated with the Edit button to call FrontPage.
You can switch it back to Notepad using the steps above.

Stop dialing up my Internet service provider

If you connect to the Internet through one of your Dial-Up Networking
connectoids, you can automatically start up the connectoid whenever you
choose to browse the Internet. You can also turn off this capability and
connect to the Internet manually by double-clicking the appropriate
connectoid when you want to connect.

Double-clicking the Internet icon on your Desktop and choosing a non-local
web address or clicking the Start button and choosing any of the options in
the Browse the Web submenu automatically calls the connectoid that is
connected to your Internet Explorer. You can disconnect the connectoid
from Internet Explorer by taking the following steps:

STEPS

Disconnecting the Connectoid to the Internet Explorer

Step 1.   Right-click the Internet icon on the Desktop, click Properties, and
then click the Connection tab.

Step 2.   Clear the check box labeled "Connect to the Internet as needed."

Step 3.   Click the OK button.

If you lost your auto-dial capability

If you connect to the Internet through a dial-up connection to an Internet service provider, it's nice to have your DUN connectoid automatically start and try to connect after you double-click the Internet icon. If you lose this capability (which is automatically created when you use the Internet Connection Wizard), you can get it back by following these steps:

STEPS

Getting Back to Auto-Dial

Step 1. Right-click the My Computer icon, click Explore, and click the Dial-Up Networking folder icon in the left pane.

Step 2. Double-click the connectoid for your Internet service provider in the right pane. Click the Connect button if it appears.

Step 3. After you are connected to your service provider, double-click the Internet icon on your Desktop.

Step 4. When a web page appears, exit Internet Explorer, and then disconnect from your service provider. (If you have DUN 2.0 or later, right-click the DUN icon in the Tray and click Disconnect. If you have an earlier version of DUN, click the Disconnect button in the Connected to dialog box.)

Step 5. Double-click the Internet icon on the Desktop again. Your connectoid should now appear and attempt to dial up your service provider.

If this doesn't work, try the steps in the *Can't find an Internet site* section later in this chapter.

ActiveX documents

Drag and drop a Word document, Excel spreadsheet, or any other OLE 2-enabled document onto the Internet toolbar.

The document gets displayed in Internet Explorer window as it would appear inside the associated application (see Figure 34-5), toolbars and all. You can edit the document in Internet Explorer as you would in the application itself.

In Internet Explorer, navigate to a similar document on your hard disk, or type the full path and filename in the Address box. Again, the document is displayed in the Internet Explorer window along with the application's toolbars.

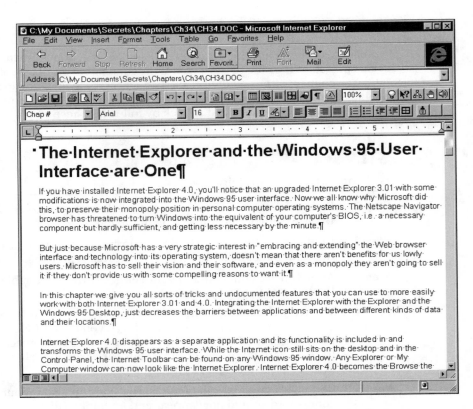

Figure 34-5: In-place word processing with Microsoft Word in Internet Explorer.

If you are an Intranet webmaster, you can see that you don't have to convert all the documents you want to put up on the Intranet into HTML. People will be able to view the original documents quite easily in the Internet Explorer window.

Want to know just what ActiveX controls you have on your computer? You know they get downloaded without saying much. You'll find Active XCavator at http://www.winmag.com/software/xcavate.htm.

Active XCavator lists ActiveX controls installed by Internet Explorer 3.0 or later. It lists the control's name, size, and location. You can use Active XCavator to delete any control. If you delete a control by mistake, you can return to the original web site from which the control was installed, and it will be automatically installed again.

Commands to Connect to the Internet

Undocumented

You can start Internet Explorer just by typing the address of the place you want to go in the Run dialog box. Click the Start button, and then click Run. Type a location such as the following:

ftp://ftp.microsoft.com

or

http://www.windows95.com

Tip

Want to send e-mail while you're using Internet Explorer? Click the Address box in Internet Explorer or click the Start button and then click Run. Type the following:

mailto:brian_livingston@infoworld.com

Then press Enter.

This will start Internet Mail, Microsoft Exchange, or Windows Messaging, depending on your configuration.

You can send a document to a friend that contains the shortcuts to your favorite places. You can put shortcuts in Word or WordPad documents, and you can send these documents as e-mail MIME attachments. You can also put shortcuts in Windows Messaging or Internet Mail e-mail messages. Just copy and paste them from your Favorites folder.

Where Are the Cookies?

The companies that webmasters work for like to keep track of who visits their sites and just what it is that they looked at or did there. One way webmasters can do this is to store a little bit of information on your hard disk that is accessible to them the next time you come around. If you fill out a form when you are at a site, the information goes into the company's transaction-processing database, but some or all of it might also get placed back on your computer, in the form of a *cookie*.

Tasty bits of data, or cookies, are stored on your computer, ready and able to be used by the companies and individuals who own the web sites you visit. Microsoft likes to cite its MSN web site as an example of a web page that is customizable. It can present you with the types of information you have selected (from an rather anemic menu) the next time you go to the site. MSN does this by storing your preferences on your computer as a nice big cookie.

Where's the cookie jar? \Windows\Cookies. The cookie filenames are usually your host name followed by an @ symbol, and then the name of the web site. The files have a *txt* extension and they are readable, but they don't make much sense.

If you have your Internet Explorer set to warn you about incoming cookies, you'll get a cookie alert message. You can choose whether to take the cookie or not. If you want to just take the cookies, you can turn off this warning mechanism by choosing View, Options, clicking the Advanced tab, and clearing the Warn before accepting "cookies" check box.

Mail and News with the Internet Explorer

There are many ways to get Internet Explorer and the accompanying Internet Mail and Internet News applications. You may already have them loaded on your computer when you bought it. You may have downloaded Internet Explorer from the Microsoft web site. If you downloaded it, you had the option of installing the Internet News and Internet Mail add-ons.

Installing these add-ons automatically connects them to Internet Explorer. If you have Internet Explorer 4.0, you'll find that Internet News and Mail have been combined to create Outlook Express. The Outlook Express News and Outlook Express icons can be found on your Start menu.

If you click an e-mail address on a web page while viewing the web page in Internet Explorer, the Internet Mail (or Outlook Express) application is automatically started. You can determine which mail and news clients are associated with Internet Explorer.

Right-click the Internet icon, click Properties, and click the Programs tab. If you have installed other e-mail and news reader programs, you can choose them to work with Internet Explorer. For example, if you have installed Windows Messaging, you can choose it in the Mail drop-down list. If you click an e-mail address on a web page, Windows Messaging will now start instead of Internet Mail or Outlook Express.

Problems with the Internet Explorer

There continue to be little problems with Internet Explorer. Some affect older versions and some are still with us. Given that the Internet is a community effort, not everyone is going to be playing by the same "rules." Be flexible and relax. You didn't do anything wrong.

Filling in forms gives me an error

If you get an error message when you click the Submit button on a simple web-based form, you've run into an incompatibility between Netscape Navigator's extensions and those used by Internet Explorer. The web site author used an Netscape Navigator extension that allows Netscape Navigator to send e-mail disguised as a form.

Presently, there isn't a way around this other than to tell the web site designer to quit using this extension. Of course, it's tough to tell the author unless he or she gives you an e-mail address, which is specifically what the author is trying to hide with the use of this extension. You can find more information on this problem at http://www.microsoft.com/kb/articles/Q154/8/64.htm.

Corrupt History folder

Undocumented

If you open your History folder (Go, Open History Folder) and find that there are no URLs listed, you have a corrupted History folder (or you haven't started using Internet Explorer). To solve this problem, click the Start button, click Run, type **Regsvr32 Cachevu.dll**, and click OK.

Undocumented

If you get error messages stating that there is not enough memory when you try to view the History folder, you might have too many entries for Internet Explorer to handle correctly. If your Clear History button (View, Options, Navigation, Clear History) won't work, take the following steps:

STEPS

Fixing a History Folder That Is Too Big

Step 1. Click the Start button, choose Shut Down, select Restart the computer, and click Yes. When the Starting Windows 95 message appears, press F8, and then choose the DOS prompt option.

Step 2. Use Deltree to remove the \Windows\History and \Windows\Temporary Internet Files folders.

Step 3. Press Ctrl+Alt+Delete and reboot to Windows 95.

Step 4 Click the Start button, choose Run, type **Regsvr32 Cachevu.dll**, and click OK.

Regsvr32 registers applications in your Registry. It finds the target code in Cachevu.dll. It creates the History and Temporary Internet Files folders if they are not present, and then initializes them by creating a copy of Desktop.ini with the proper pointer to the registered objects. It also creates the history index files (Mm*.dat).

After you run Regsvr32, you might discover that the Desktop.ini file in your History folder has been deleted. As a precaution, you might want to put a copy of it in your personal \My System folder before you run Regsvr32. To create a copy of the Desktop.ini file that's stored in the History folder, use Notepad to create a text file with the following contents:

```
[.ShellClassInfo]
UICLSID={FF393560-C2A7-11CF-BFF4-444553540000}
CLSID={FF393560-C2A7-11CF-BFF4-444553540000}
```

Save this file as History Desktop.ini. When and if you need to put it back in your History folder, copy it there, rename it as Desktop.ini, and set its attribute to hidden.

Defrag hangs

Undocumented

If you have URLs in your History folder whose names are longer than 256 characters, Defrag will choke. ScanDisk won't find any problems. You can get around this problem by deleting the History folder.

If you find that Internet Explorer is crashing, try deleting all the contents of the History folder and the folder itself.

Where does the memory go?

In the early versions of Windows 95, there was a memory leak in the Windows 95 kernel. You'll notice it when you run Windows sockets applications such as Internet Explorer. If you have an early version of Windows 95 (Kernel32.dll is dated 7/11/95), you should download the new self-installing Kernel32.dll file. You find it at http://www.microsoft.com/windows/software/krnlupd.htm.

Download this file to a temporary folder. (By *temporary folder*, we're referring to a folder, perhaps named Temp, where you store stuff temporarily. The Temp folder itself can be pretty permanent, but you use it to hold temporary stuff.)

Double-click the downloaded executable file and it does all the work, quietly updating the Kernel32.dll file with a new one put out in February 1996.

Internet security

If you see a little padlock on the right side of your status bar, you know that you are on a site that has some sort of security. If you want to know just what sort, right-click in a clear area of the page you are viewing, click Properties, and then click the Security tab.

Err Msg: MPREXE caused an invalid page fault in Kernel32.dll

Numerous problems with the Windows 95 interface can be traced to a corrupted password file. This file can get corrupted when you're installing Internet Explorer over previous versions. If this happens, you may get this error message: MPREXE caused an invalid page fault in module Kernel32.dll. If you get this message, delete or rename the files in the \Windows folder with the extension *pwl*.

Can't find an Internet site

You are trying to view your own start page, and you get an error message stating that Internet Explorer can't find the site. Or auto-dial quits working, and the steps detailed in the *If you lost your auto-dial capability* section didn't fix the problem.

You may have an old, missing, or corrupted Url.dll file. When you uninstalled earlier beta versions of Netscape Navigator, they didn't restore the original Url.dll file.

STEPS

Fixing Url.dll

Step 1. If you can find Url.dll file in the Windows\System folder, remove or rename it.

Step 2. Type the following command at a DOS prompt, and then press Enter:

```
copy C:\Windows\Sysbckup\Url.dll C:\Windows\System
```

Step 3. Click the Start button, choose Shut Down, choose Restart the computer, and then click OK.

Step 4. Click the Start button, point to Settings, click Control Panel, and double-click Add/Remove Programs. Remove Internet Explorer. Double-click the Internet Explorer setup executable file to reinstall it.

In step 2, if you can't find Url.dll in Sysbckup, you can download it (of course, you'll have to use another computer because yours won't let you download) from http://MEMBERS.AOL.COM/danvegso/software/w95.htm.

What happened to my Save As dialog box?

It is easy to clear the "Always ask before opening this type of file" (IE 3.0) or "Don't ask me any more for this type of file" (IE 4.0) check box in the dialog box that Internet Explorer displays when you start to download certain types of files, such as executables. If you do this, you lose your ability to decide what to do with the file type (open the file or save it to disk) because Internet Explore no longer displays the dialog box, with its Open it and Save it to disk option buttons, when you start to download a file of that type. Instead, it automatically opens or saves the file, based on the option that was selected in the dialog box when you cleared the check box. You can get this capability back. You may really want to get it back if you left the dialog box set to open files of a particular type, and now you want to save them to disk.

One way to download a file that always lets you choose whether to open or save is to right-click the filename, and then click Open or Save to disk in the context menu. If you want to get the dialog box back (maybe just to change the default to Save to disk), you need to edit the Registry.

If executable files (files with *exe* extensions) are the problem, use the Registry editor to navigate to exefile in HKEY_CLASSES_ROOT. Highlight exefile in the left pane, double-click EditFlags in the right pane. Change **d8 07 01 00** to **d8 07 00 00**. Click OK. Your dialog box will now come back.

Keyboard Shortcuts for Internet Explorer

You can use the keyboard shortcuts listed in Table 34-1 to navigate with Internet Explorer:

Table 34-1	Keyboard Shortcuts for Internet Explorer
Key or Combination	**Effect**
Enter	Goes to the highlighted link
Backspace and Shift+Backspace, or Alt+Left Arrow and Alt+Right Arrow	Same as Back and Forward arrow buttons on the Internet toolbar
Shift+F10	Displays a context menu for a link
F5	Reloads the current page from the server
Esc	Stops downloading a page
Ctrl+O or Ctrl+L	Goes to a new location (URL)
Ctrl+N	Generates a new window
Ctrl+S	Saves the current page
Ctrl+Shift+Tab	Cycles between frames
Tab and Shift+Tab	Cycles between links on a page
Ctrl+B	Opens the Organize Favorites window
Ctrl+D	Adds current web page to Favorites (immediately and silently)
Ctrl+H	Opens the History folder
Ctrl+R	Reloads the current page (F5)
Ctrl+W	Closes the active Internet Explorer window

One thing that is cool about Tab and Shift+Tab is that they highlight the active areas on an image map. An *image map* is a (usually large) graphic on a web page. The graphic is generally divided into active areas that point to different URLs. When you press Tab or Shift+Tab, you can see an outline around each active area.

Where Does the Search Start?

The Internet toolbar contains a Search button. It connects to http://home.microsoft.com/access/allinone.asp. This is the search page at Microsoft's web site. You can use Microsoft's search page to change your default search engine and to perform searches.

You can change what the Search button connects to by specifying for yourself what the button does. Right-click the Internet icon on your Desktop, click Properties, and then click the Navigation tab. Choose Search Page from the Page drop-down list, and in the Address field, type a URL for the search engine that you want to use.

You can also modify the Search button by first using Internet Explorer to navigate to your favorite search engine. Then display the Navigation tab (see previous paragraph), select Search Page in the Page field, highlight the Address field, and click the Use Current button.

Here are some URLs for search sites:

Site	Address
AltaVista	http://www.altavista.digital.com/cgi-bin/query?pg=q&q=%s
Excite	http://www.excite.com/search.gw?search=%s
InfoSeek	http://guide-p.infoseek.com/Titles?qt=%s
Lycos	http://www.lycos.com/cgi-bin/pursuit?query=%s
Magellan	http://searcher.mckinley.com/searcher.cgi?query=%s
Yahoo (plain search)	http://search.yahoo.com/bin/search?p=%s
Yahoo (IE autosearch)	http://msie.yahoo.com/autosearch?p=%s

Finding web sites

Do you want to find a specific web site?

Double-click the Internet icon. Click the Address box, type **find**, **search**, or **?**, type a space, and then type the name of the company or organization whose site you want to find. If the name has a space in it, forget typing the **find**, **search**, or **?** and just put double quote marks around the name.

This will automatically start a search on your default search engine. The original default is Yahoo.

What Internet Explorer won't do is go to a web site after you just type in the web site's name without the *www* and the *com*.

Getting on the Internet Explorer Newsgroup

You can visit the Internet Explorer newsgroup at msnews.microsoft.com. Its name is microsoft.public.internetexplorer.win95. Follow the instructions in the *Configuring Internet Mail and News* section of Chapter 35 if you want to join the newsgroup.

Windows 95 Home Pages

See Table 34-2 for some interesting Windows 95-related sites you can visit on the web:

Table 34-2:	Windows 95-Related Web Sites
Site	*Address*
Windows 95 Secrets	http://www.halcyon.com/davis/secrets.htm
IDG Books	http://www.idgbooks.com
Brian's InfoWorld Column	http://www.infoworld.com/cgi-bin/ displayNew.pl?/livingst/livingst.htm
Windows Sources	http://www.zdnet.com/~wsources/
Windows95.com	http://www.windows95.com
Windows 95 Annoyances	http:// www.creativelement.com/win95ann/ index.html
My Desktop.com	http://www.clearlight.com/~visanu/
Andrew Schulman	http://www.ora.com/windows/
The Microsoft Exchange Center	http://www.slipstick.com/exchange/
Bob Cerelli's Windows Page	http://www.halcyon.com/cerelli/
Gordon Carter's Exchange help site	http://ourworld.compuserve.com/homepages/ G_Carter/default.htm
The Internet Starting Point for Windows 95	http://www.total.net/~bklein/win/
Animated Cursor Schemes	http://www.islandnet.com/~wwseb/cursors.htm
The Windows 95 Answer Center	http://www.lpdsoft.com/jturner/
Stroud's Windows 95 Applications	http://www.stroud.com/
Ed Tiley's Windows 95 Home Page	http://www.supernet.net/~edtiley/win95/
Internet Mail and News Tips	http://home.sprynet.com/sprynet/edm/

Site	Address
Dale's Windows 95 Themes Page	http://www.bitshop.com/~dale/
Windows 95 Startup Logos	http://www.nucleus.com/~kmcmurdo/ win95logo.html
Download.com	http://www.download.com/PC/Win95/
#Windows Home Page	http://www.windows95.org/
Software for the Internet	http://tucows.tierranet.com/window95.html
Microsoft Windows 95	http://www.microsoft.com/windows/
Internet Explorer	http://www.microsoft.com/ie
Microsoft's Windows 95 Games Pages	http://www.microsoft.com/windows/games/
Windows 95 Tip Sheet	http://www.cs.umb.edu/~alilley/win.html
Club Internet Explore	http://www.clubie.com/
Windows 95 FAQ	http://www.primenet.com/~markd/ win95faq.html
Costa's Tips for Windows 95	http://www-na.biznet.com.gr/sail/isa/tipfrm.html
Herb's Windows 95 answers	http://people.delphi.com/evillage/
WindoWatch Magazine	http://www.windowatch.com/
Dylan Greene's Windows 95 Starting Pages	http://www.dylan95.com/
The 32-bit Software Archive	http://www.32bit.com/software/index.phtml
Windows 95 Help Desk	http://www.southwind.net/faq/help/win95/
The Computer Paper	http://www.tcp.ca/

Summary

Internet Explorer is integrated into the Windows 95 Desktop. This chapter is devoted to helping you make this integration work for you.

▶ We show you how to view web pages with non-US ASCII characters sets.

▶ With the Internet Explorer Administration Kit, you can create your own Internet Explorer.

▶ You don't have to translate your documents into HTML to view them over an Intranet.

▶ You'll find out how to fix resource leak problems.

▶ Internet Explorer has lots of keyboard shortcuts.

Chapter 35

Internet Mail and News (and Outlook Express)

The Basics

Microsoft Internet Mail and News (and Outlook Express) are basic tools. Like many Microsoft operating system extensions, they provide a level of functionality that will work for most people. And they do introduce newcomers to the intricacies of newsgroups and Internet mail. Those who find them too limiting can go on to other vendors or, in the case of Internet Mail, on to Windows Messaging or Outlook.

Internet Mail and News are designed to be easy to understand and easy to get going. In contrast to Windows Messaging, Internet Mail doesn't include separate service profiles (although we show you how to use user profiles to create separate mail boxes), it doesn't do faxes, and it doesn't require a complete chapter of this book just to tell you how to set it up (see Chapter 32). It works easily with Internet Explorer, using the same window if you have Internet Explorer 4.0 and the Outlook Express version of Mail.

With a few configuration changes, Internet News enables you to easily peruse and contribute to newsgroups. Starting with its first version, Internet News could connect to multiple different news servers, something few other newsgroup clients could do at the time. Microsoft included this feature because it wanted you to be able to read Microsoft's own news server, which is limited to Microsoft support groups, as well as the Usenet news server maintained by your own Internet service provider. One drawback of Internet News is that it doesn't have a search facility to let you quickly scan the message headers (although Outlook Express does have this capability).

Microsoft released Outlook Express with Internet Explorer 4.0. It combines Microsoft Internet Mail and News into one program (although you can still have two separate icons to start Outlook Express with its focus either on News or Mail).

Outlook Express is the next iteration of Microsoft Internet Mail and News, and it adds some of the features that users of the 1.0 versions of these programs have been asking for. For example, it has a Find command that searches for messages based on text strings found in the From, To, Subject, or Message body fields. Also, Outlook Express can handle multiple mail accounts.

Tip

Much of what we say in this chapter about Microsoft Internet Mail and News applies to Outlook Express. Where this is not the case, we point out the differences.

Where to find more help

You can download the latest versions of Internet Mail and News (or Outlook Express) from Microsoft's web site at http:/ / www.microsoft.com/ ie/ download/. For more information about Internet Mail and News, visit the Knowledge Base at http:/ / www.microsoft.com/ kb/articles/ Q154/8/80.htm.

Check out Eric Miller's Microsoft Internet Mail & News User Tips at http:/ / home.sprynet.com/ sprynet/edm/. You'll find obscure information about Windows 95 in general as well as Internet Mail and News at Costas Andriotis' site, http:/ / www-na.biznet.com.gr/ sail/ isa/ tipfrm.html. You'll also find the latest information about Outlook Express at these two sites. Microsoft produces a nice list of tips and tricks for Internet Mail and News at http:/ / www.microsoft.com/ ie/ imn/ tiptrick.htm.

Microsoft provides some help with troubleshooting Internet Mail. Check out http:/ / www.microsoft.com/ kb/articles/ Q154/9/10.htm. If you have trouble receiving mail with Internet Mail, try http:/ / www.microsoft.com/ kb/ articles/ Q154/9/09.htm. If you have trouble sending attachments with either Internet News or Mail, try http:/ / www.microsoft.com/ kb/articles/ Q154/8/ 79.htm.

Configuring Internet Mail and News (and Outlook Express)

If you are connected to the Internet through a dial-up connection, you'll need to properly configure a DUN connectoid as described in Chapters 28 and 33 before you can connect to the Internet with Internet Mail or Internet News (or Outlook Express).

To use Internet Mail, you need to get the names of the SMTP and POP3 servers at your Internet service provider, as well as your e-mail address, and your account name and password for your e-mail account. Choose Mail, Options in the Internet Mail window. Click the Server tab, and enter this information in the appropriate fields. In Outlook Express, choose Tools, Accounts, Add, Mail to start a version of the Internet Connection Wizard that will help you create an entry for your Internet mail account.

By default, Internet Explorer uses Internet Mail (or Outlook Express) as the mail tool when you click an e-mail address while viewing a web page in Internet Explorer. If you want to use another e-mail client (such as Windows Messaging or Eudora) you can change this default behavior. Double-click the Internet icon in your Control Panel, click the Programs tab, and then display the Mail drop-down list. If you have another e-mail program installed on your computer, you can choose it here.

To read the articles (also called *messages* or *postings*) in newsgroups, you need to connect to a news server. Most likely, your Internet service provider maintains a Usenet news server. You can also connect to other news servers. The most likely name for your service provider's news server is news.*serviceprovidername*.com. We provide a list of places where you can find news servers near the end of this chapter in the *Access to public news servers* section.

To connect to a news server, choose News, Options in Internet News, click the Server tab, click the Add button, and then enter the news server name. If you are using Outlook Express, choose Tools, Accounts, Add, News to start a version of the Internet Connection Wizard that will help you set up a news server account.

Changing Mail and News options right away

We don't like the default configurations for Internet Mail and News (or for Outlook Express, for that matter) — especially for the first time user. We suggest that you make a number of changes along with us.

In Internet News, choose News, Options (or choose Tools, News Options in Outlook Express). Click the Send tab, and clear the check boxes labeled "When selecting, automatically select entire word" (Outlook Express doesn't have this option) and "Include original message in reply." On the Read tab, mark the Auto expand conversation threads check box, as shown in Figure 35-1. Now you won't have to click the plus symbol repeatedly to follow a discussion thread, at the slight cost of seeing multiple entries in a thread that you might not be particularly interested in.

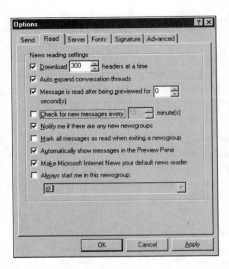

Figure 35-1: The Read tab of the Options dialog box in Internet News.

Enter a 0 in the field for "Message is read after being previewed for [   ] seconds." You can set this back to 5 seconds later if you find it useful. We never did. Clear "Check for new messages every [   ] minutes" if you use a Dial-Up Networking connectoid and are only online for a limited amount of time during any one session.

Use the Server tab to add additional news servers to your list. You'll want to add the msnews.microsoft.com news server. This is Microsoft's support news server. You'll find a basic level of supervision from Microsoft support personnel, peer-to-peer support, and help from Microsoft volunteers. The microsoft.public.internet.mail and microsoft.public.internet.news newsgroups provide the latest information about Internet Mail and News.

Highlight a server in the Server tab, and click the Properties button. You can choose which server is the default, or first-accessed server, by clicking the Set as Default button in the General tab of the News Server Properties dialog box. In Outlook Express, choose Tools, Accounts, highlight your news server account, and click Set as Default.

If you want people to contact you directly from your postings in newsgroups, type your address in the Email Address field of Server tab in the Options dialog box. On the Internet News toolbar, you will find a Reply to Author button, which lets you send a response directly to the author of a message when you don't feel the need to respond on the newsgroup. You won't be able to send a private message if the author hasn't placed his or her e-mail address in the Email Address field. If you leave the Reply Address field blank, the address in the Email Address field is used. If you send mail from one address but want replies to go to another, then enter the second address in the Reply Address field.

Undocumented

If you don't want your address picked up by Usenet bots that scan Usenet newsgroups for addresses, then put a fake address in the Reply Address field, such as fakename@fakenet.net.

Click the Signature tab and put in at least a rudimentary "signature," your name at least. You can make a more elaborate signature later, but we suggest that you don't get carried away. Mark "Add signature to the end of all outgoing messages." You can choose a command from the menu bar to insert your signature when you write a message, but it's easier and more consistent to let the computer do it for you.

Make similar changes in the default settings in Internet Mail (choose Mail, Options in the Internet Mail window, or Tools, Mail Options in Outlook Express). Make sure that the Send messages immediately check box in the Send tab is marked if you work online or want to have messages sent as soon as you finish writing them. If you work off-line, clear this check box, and click the Send and Receive button on the toolbar when you're ready to send your mail. (Internet Mail will prompt you to connect to the Internet and then send and receive messages.)

If you are browsing the Internet online and click an e-mail address on a web page to send a message, you normally want that message to go as soon as you've written it. If Internet Mail is your default e-mail client, it does this for you automatically, whether the Send messages immediately check box is marked or not. Outlook Express pops up a dialog box when you send a message and quite nicely asks if you want to deliver it now.

If Windows Messaging is your default e-mail client, clicking an e-mail address on a web page can be quite a bother because Windows Messaging takes a long time to load (unlike Internet Mail or Outlook Express). If you use Windows Messaging as your main e-mail client, it's a good idea to mark the check box labeled "Make Internet Mail your default e-mail program" in the Send tab of the Mail, Options dialog box so that you can quickly send messages while browsing the web.

More Mail and News changes

The Mail and News windows are divided into two panes. The message header pane (the one on the left or the top) lists the message headers, and the preview pane (the one on the right or the bottom) displays the contents of whatever message you have selected in the message header pane. You can arrange the two panes either horizontally or vertically. To do this, choose View, Preview Pane, and click Split Horizontally or Split Vertically from the submenu.

When you single-click a message header, you can view its contents in the preview pane. This works just fine most of the time. If you want to view a message in a new (and bigger) window instead of the preview pane, double-click the message header. If you want to get rid of the preview pane and only view messages in separate message windows, choose View, Preview Pane, None. On low-resolution video cards with small monitors, this may be the way you want to go.

In Internet News, if you want news messages to appear in the preview pane as soon as you select them, choose News, Options (or choose Tools, News Options in Outlook Express), click the Read tab, and mark the "Automatically show messages in the Preview Pane" check box. When this option is turned off, you have to press the spacebar after selecting a message to display its contents in the preview pane.

If you don't like the column order in the message header pane in the News or Mail window, drag the gray column header buttons to the desired position. You can also change the width of the columns by resting your mouse on the spacer line between column header buttons and dragging to the right or the left. To sort your messages by a particular column (the Subject column, for example), click the column header button. To sort by the same column in reverse order, click the button again.

The Internet Mail window has a Folders drop-down list box that displays your mail folders, and the Internet News window has a similar Newsgroups drop-down list box that contains your subscribed newsgroups. Using list boxes is not a very convenient way to display and select your mail folders and newsgroups. Outlook Express solves this problem by creating a large pane for these lists.

If you right-click the Internet Mail or News (or Outlook Express) toolbar, you'll notice that you can keep the toolbar above the two panes in the Mail and News window, or you can align it to the left. We found the left side to be preferable. It's your choice.

Undocumented

If you leave the toolbar on top, you can swap the position of the toolbar and the Newsgroups box (in Internet News) or the Folders box (in Internet Mail). By default, the Folders/Newsgroups box is underneath the toolbar. To move it above the toolbar, first drag the double vertical lines at the far left end of the Folders/Newsgroups box up until the box moves onto the same row as the toolbar. The box shortens to only show its label to the left of the toolbar (see Figure 35-2). Then drag the bottom edge of the toolbar down. As soon as you've increased the height of the toolbar area enough, the Folder/Newsgroup box expands across the window above the toolbar. If you want to put the box back underneath the toolbar, drag the toolbar (using the double vertical lines on its left edge) up so that it shares the row with the Folders/Newsgroups box, and then drag the bottom edge of the box down.

The toolbar gets a lot smaller if you take out the text under the icons (right-click the toolbar and choose Icons Only from the context menu), but then it also gets less understandable (although you do get ToolTips to replace the text). If you have a low-resolution video card on a small monitor, you may want to reduce its size. You can also get rid of it altogether by choosing View, Toolbar.

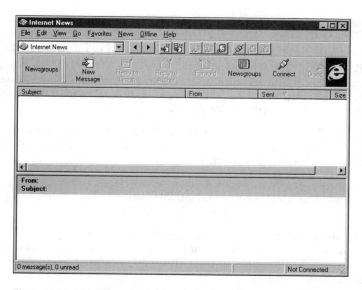

Figure 35-2: The Newsgroups box is temporarily truncated to the left of the toolbar.

You can customize the buttons in the Mail and News toolbars. To do so, right-click the toolbar, and choose Customize Toolbar from the context menu (in Outlook Express, choose Buttons). We find the default buttons in the News Icon Bar (the News toolbar) to be pretty useless (the toolbar in Outlook Express switches between Mail and News depending on whether you have selected a newsgroup or a mail folder). We added Mark All as Read and Reply to All. We got rid of Forward and Reply to Author. We wish that View All Messages and View Unread Messages Only were available as buttons (unfortunately this didn't get fixed in Outlook Express). If you go to the default folders (Sent Items, Posted Items, and so on) often enough, you might want to put their buttons on the toolbar. With regard to the Mail Icon Bar (the Mail toolbar), you might want to add the Print, Go to Inbox, and Address Book buttons, and remove the Delete button (you can simply press Delete to delete messages instead).

In Internet News, when you choose News, Reply to Newsgroup and Author (or click the Reply to All button if you have added this button to the toolbar) to reply to a posting in a newsgroup, your message gets sent to the newsgroup and to the author of the message to which you are replying. By default, a copy of the message to the author is stored in the Sent Items folder in Internet Mail. If you want to disable (or enable) this feature, choose Mail, Options in the Internet Mail window (or Tools, Mail Options in Outlook Express), click the Send tab, and clear (or mark) the Save copy of sent messages in 'Sent Items' folder check box. (If you disable this feature, Internet Explorer will no longer save any messages, regardless of whether you send them from Internet Mail or Internet News.)

If you need to view mail or news articles in a foreign language, you may need to use other character sets. To see how to install these characters sets, turn your browser to http://www.microsoft.com/kb/articles/Q154/6/54.htm.

POP3, SMTP, and XOVER required

Internet Mail (and Outlook Express) requires that your Internet service provider (or your local area network) have a SMTP server if you want to send mail and a POP3 server if you want to receive mail. Some service providers use only a SMTP server to send and receive mail. This configuration won't work with Internet Mail.

As of early 1997, CompuServe still didn't have a POP3 mail server. The Microsoft Network didn't have one as of March, 1997, although they claimed that they would have one soon.

Your Internet service provider's news server needs to support the XOVER extension of the NNTP protocol (Network News Transfer Protocol). Most likely it does. If not, give your service provider a call, or find a new provider.

Undocumented

You can send mail with Internet Mail even if you don't have a POP3 server to receive mail. Just choose Mail, Options, click the Send tab, and mark the "Send messages immediately" box. This way, Internet Mail won't check for incoming mail.

Outlook Express lets you deal with this problem a bit more gracefully. Click Tools, Accounts, highlight a mail server, and click Properties. You can choose whether to use this account when doing a full Send and Receive.

If you don't want to send messages as soon as you click the Send button and you don't have a POP3 mail server, use this workaround. Don't click the Send button when you're done with the message. Close the New Message window by clicking the Close box in the upper-right corner of the window. When Internet Mail asks if you want to save changes to the messages, click Yes. Internet Mail will store the message in your Inbox. When you do want to send the message, double-click it in your Inbox and click the Send button.

If you don't have a POP3 server, you can put a bogus entry in the POP3 server field. If you have mail in the Outbox, don't click Mail, Send and Receive. Just leave it there until you exit Internet Mail. You will be asked if you want to send the mail in your Outbox. Internet Mail won't check for new mail. Outlook Express lets you deal with this problem a bit more gracefully. Click Tools, Accounts, highlight a mail server, and click Properties. You can choose whether to use this account when doing a full Send and Receive.

Where is everything stored?

You'll find your mail and news storage files in the Mail and News subfolders, which are stored in \Program Files\Internet Mail and News*yourusername* (or in \Program Files\Plus!\Microsoft Internet\Internet Mail and News*yourusername*). If you don't have a user name, you won't have a *yourusername* folder. In the Mail subfolder, the messages are stored in the *mbx* (mailbox) files. The *idx* files store the indexes of their associated *mbx* files. The *mbx* files are for the most part text files, so you can read them with Notepad or WordPad. If you have Outlook Express, you'll find these folders under \Program Files\Outlook Express.

In the News subfolder, you'll find the names of the newsgroups to which you are subscribed (or were previously subscribed). The *nch* files contain the subject headers and downloaded messages that are stored on your hard disk.

Your Internet Mail address book is stored in your *yourusername.wab* file. You'll find it in the \Windows folder. If you don't have a user name, the file will be called UserMPS.wab.

If you like, you can compress (or compact) these files to get rid of the deleted records. To do this for Internet News, choose News, Options, click the Advanced tab, click the Clean Up Now button, and then click the Compact button in the Local File Clean Up dialog box. In Internet Mail, choose File, Folder, Compact, and choose the desired option on the submenu (All Folders, Deleted Items, Outbox, and so on). In Outlook Express, choose File, Clean Up Files if you are focused on a newsgroup, and Files, Folder, Compact if you are focused on a mail folder.

Connecting with the DUNs

Internet News and Internet Mail (and Outlook Express) let you connect to your news servers and mail servers in three different ways. To see these options in Internet News, choose News, Options, and click the Server tab. Highlight a news server, click the Properties button, and then click the Connection tab (see Figure 35-3). To see them in Internet Mail, choose Mail, Options, and then click the Connection tab. With Outlook Express, choose Tools, Accounts, highlight a news or mail server, click Properties, and then click Connection.

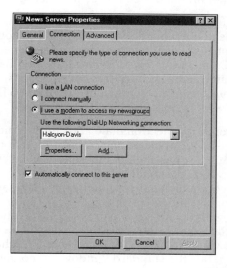

Figure 35-3: The Connection tab of the News Server Properties dialog box.

If you are connected over a local area network, mark the I use a LAN connection option button.

If you want to connect to the server after you have connected to the Internet by other means (say using a Windows 95 DUN), mark the I connect manually option button. You should select this button if you want to use your standard Windows 95 DUN connectoid to connect to the Internet before you invoke Internet News or Internet Mail, regardless of whether you start the connectoid by double-clicking the connectoid itself (or a shortcut to it) or by double-clicking the Internet icon on the Desktop. (Most likely, double-clicking the Internet icon just calls the standard Windows 95 DUN connectoid for your service provider.) If you have DUN 2.0, you won't see the DUN Connect To dialog box and you won't have to click the Connect button if you have highlighted your connection in the Dial-Up Networking folder window, chosen Connection, Settings, and cleared the check box labeled Prompt for information before dialing.

If you want to launch Internet News or Internet Mail directly and then use the Connect To dialog box that serves as a front end to your standard Dial-Up Networking connectoid to connect to the Internet, choose the option button labeled "I use a modem to access my newsgroups" (or "I use a modem to access my e-mail"), and then select your connectoid from the drop-down list. If you have Internet Explorer 3.0, you can create shortcuts for the Internet Mail and News programs on the Desktop by right-dragging Internet Mail or Internet News from the \Windows folder onto the Desktop. (Alternatively, you can start the programs by choosing them in the Start, Programs menu.)

Even if you choose "I use a modem to access my newsgroups" (or e-mail), you can still access the Internet first and then invoke Internet Mail or News (or Outlook Express).

If you are not currently connected to your service provider and you issue a command in either the Mail or News window that requires a connection, you will see a dialog box named Connect to *name of service provider* that prompts you for your user name and password. This dialog box is different than the Connect To dialog box associated with your Windows 95 DUN connectoid.

Why Microsoft created a different connection dialog box for Internet Mail and News (and Outlook Express) is not clear. The connection that is established when you use this dialog box has slightly different properties than the ones for a connection created by a standard Windows 95 DUN connectoid. Unlike the Connect To dialog box, which you can bypass if you have Windows 95 DUN version 2.0 and later, this dialog box requires that you click the OK button to log onto your service provider. One other difference is that if you use this connection dialog box, you will be asked if you want to disconnect after you exit Internet Mail or News (whichever you started first). If you manually start the standard Windows 95 connectoid, you won't receive this prompt.

Internet Mail allows you to connect and disconnect by choosing Mail, Send and Receive (or by clicking the Send and Receive toolbar button or pressing Ctrl+M). If you have configured your connection to disconnect when finished sending and receiving (click Mail, Options, the Connection tab, and then mark the "Disconnect when finished sending and receiving" check box), and you dialed up your service provider using the connection dialog box that comes with Mail, you will get disconnected automatically (although you still can't connect without clicking the OK button).

None of the DUN connectoids allow you to automatically connect or disconnect without further intervention after you invoke Internet Mail or News. If you want to do this, you should download DUNCE from http://windows95.com.

You can set up Internet Mail to automatically retrieve new mail. Choose Mail, Options (or Tools, Mail Options in Outlook Express), and click the Read tab. Mark the Check for new messages every [   ] minute(s) check box. This works when you invoke Internet Mail, regardless of whether you have chosen "I connect manually" or "I use a modem to access my e-mail" in the Connection tab of the Options dialog box. If you use "I connect manually," Internet Mail does not ask whether you want to disconnect after it's checked for mail. If you use "I use a modem to access my e-mail," Internet Mail prompts you to disconnect after sending and receiving mail.

No SOCKS

Secret

Internet Mail and News won't work if you are behind a firewall that uses a SOCKS proxy to get your news and mail through the firewall. This is because the Microsoft TCP/IP stack (the Wsock32.dll file) doesn't support the SOCKS protocol. You can find out more about firewalls and SOCKS at http://www.osa.com/products/openweb/demo/firewal.htm.

You can replace the Microsoft TCP/IP stack with a stack that does handle the SOCKS protocol. Point Internet Explorer at http://www.windows95.com/apps and search for Hummingbird.

Spell Checking

Internet Mail and News both use the Microsoft Office 95 or 97 spell checker. If you don't have Microsoft Office 95 or later, Microsoft Works 4.0 or later, or a compatible 32-bit spell checker, you can download AutoSpell from http://www.pygmy.com/autospell/ver41/download.htm.

Undocumented

Internet Mail and News looks in the registry to find the dictionary and the spelling engine. It goes to HKEY_LOCAL_MACHINE\Software\Microsoft\SharedTools\ProofingTools\Spelling\languageID\Normal. The LanguageID is a 4-digit number. For example, US English is 1033, Australian is 2057, British English is 3081. You'll find two string values under the Normal key that name the dictionary and the engine.

If you still are having trouble getting spell checking to work, check out http://www.microsoft.com/kb/articles/Q154/8/78.htm. You can also look through Eric Miller's Microsoft Internet Mail & News User Tips at http://home.sprynet.com/sprynet/edm/.

Messages Formatted in HTML

Internet Mail and News (and Outlook Express) allow you to format your posts using HTML. Open either News or Mail, and choose News, Options or Mail, Options (or Tools, Mail Options or News Options in Outlook Express). On the Send tab you'll find the option to format messages with HTML.

Marking the HTML or Plain Text option button in the Send tab sets the default. You can always override this setting for the current post or e-mail message. Just choose Format in the New Message window, and click HTML or Plain Text. If you're using HTML, you get a formatting toolbar that lets you choose the font, font size, font color, and so on.

Lots of newsgroup and e-mail clients aren't able to display HTML-formatted text. If they can't, your correspondents will see the HTML tags embedded in the plain text of your messages.

Eric Miller mentions an error that you may run into with HTML-formatted messages:

> If you have selected HTML formatting as your default under Mail or News, Options, the Send tab, HTML, and you have set Internet Mail and News to automatically add your signature to the end of new messages or posts, you may be unable to use the HTML formatting toolbar to choose font settings other than your defaults at the beginning of a new message. Even if you change the font settings, when you tab into the body of the message and start typing, the settings will automatically change back to your defaults. The workaround is to tab into the body of the message, type a character or insert a space and then change the font settings. The changes you make will then stick.

Colored backgrounds

Undocumented

You can set the background color for your HTML-formatted messages. You'll need to edit the Registry to add this capability. Eric Miller provided this neat little trick, and he credited Brett M. with finding it.

STEPS

Adding Color to the Background of Your HTML Messages

Step 1. Double-click Regedit.exe in your \Windows folder.

Adding Color to the Background of Your HTML Messages

Step 2   In Internet Mail and News, navigate to HKEY_CURRENT_USER\
Software\Microsoft\Internet Mail and News; in Outlook Express,
navigate to HKEY_CURRENT_USER\Software\Microsoft\Outlook
Express.

Step 3.   Right-click the right pane of the Registry editor. Choose New,
DWORD Value. Name the new value **ColorCycle**.

Step 4.   Double-click ColorCycle in the right pane. Enter its value as **1**,
and click OK. Exit the Registry editor.

You can now use Ctrl+Shift+Z to cycle through sixteen background colors as
you create HTML messages (see Figure 35-4).

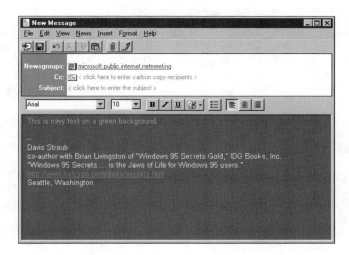

Figure 35-4: An HTML-formatted message with a colored background.

Undocumented   Eric Miller also found a way to disable background colors in incoming
messages. Use the above steps to add the ColorSucks value and set it
equal to 1. Check Eric's site for more colorful backgrounds at
http://home.sprynet.com/sprynet/edm/.

Adding Internet Mail and News Messages to the New Menu

Undocumented   In earlier chapters, we have discussed ways to add items to the New menu.
If you like, you can create a New menu item for Internet Mail. Here's how:

Step 1.   Right-click your Desktop, point to New, and click Text Document.

Step 2.   Rename the text document **New.eml.** Click OK.

Step 3.   Click the Start button, point to Settings, and click Control Panel. Double-click your TweakUI icon. (We assume that you've installed TweakUI. If you haven't, you can download it from http://www.microsoft.com/windows/software/powertoy.htm.) Click the New tab.

Step 4.   Drag and drop New.eml into the New tab. You'll notice that there is now a new checked entry on the list of new documents in TweakUI: Internet E-mail Message.

Undocumented

Do you want to add an item for Internet News postings to the New menu? Follow these same steps, but in step 2, rename the new text document **New.nws**. Or, instead of following steps 1 and 2, click the New Message button while you're using Internet News, click the Save As button in the New Message toolbar, and save the blank news document with the name New.nws on your Desktop. Then continue with steps 3 and 4.

Not Sending Yet

You can pause while writing a message in either Internet News or Mail. To save the message so that you can edit and send it later, click the Close box in the upper-right corner of the New Message window. Click Yes when prompted to save changes to the message. If you're using Internet Mail, the message is saved in your Inbox. If you're using Internet News, the message is saved in your Sent Items folder.

Internet Mail won't save your message if you haven't specified a recipient yet. Internet News automatically inserts the address of the currently selected newsgroup in the Newsgroups field. You don't have to type a subject in the New Message window of either Mail or News in order to save the message when you click the Close box.

Saving Attachments

To save an attachment to a message you received, double-click the message header in the message header pane to display the message in a separate window. Then drag and drop the attachment icon from the bottom of the window into a folder or onto the Desktop. You can also right-click the attachment icon and click Save As.

To view an attachment in the main Internet Mail or News window, single-click the message header. The attachment will appear in the preview pane. If you want to save the attachment you're viewing, click the yellow paper clip icon in the upper-right corner of the preview pane. A context menu listing the attachments in that message appears. Hold down the Ctrl key as you click the name of the attachment you want to save to display the Save Attachment As dialog box. (If you click the attachment name without using the Ctrl key, Internet Mail or News opens the associated application and then opens the document within it.)

You can send graphic files in GIF and JPEG format (as well as others) as attachments in Internet Mail messages. Internet Mail encodes the graphics in UUENCODE or MIME format. After you receive a message with a *gif* or *jpeg* attachment and it is decoded (which Internet Mail does automatically) you can read the file with the helper application that it's associated with. (To check what applications are associated with *gif* and *jpeg* files, choose View, Options in the Explorer, click File Types, and look through the Registered file types list for these file types.)

UUENCODE or MIME

Both Internet Mail and News (and Outlook Express) allow you to choose which encoding scheme (MIME or UUENCODE) to use when sending messages. The options for MIME are somewhat different then those available with Windows Messaging, as detailed in the *Message format* section of Chapter 32. There is no setting for the character set, for example. You have to wonder if the different development teams (which have since combined) for Microsoft Exchange and Internet Mail and News ever exchange Internet e-mail. Probably not.

Undocumented

You can change the character set used by Internet Mail and News. With your Registry editor, navigate to HKEY_CURRENT_USER\Software\Microsoft\Internet Mail and News*yourusernname*\Mail. Double-click Default Charset in the right pane. Change to US ASCII if you like. You can also do this for News.

You might want to change to the US ASCII character set if your correspondents receive messages from you with the = symbol at the end of your lines. When you use the default Windows ANSI (ISO-8859-1) character set, you can select different font settings. If you switch to US ASCII, the only font options that Internet Mail accepts are Arial, 10-pt, black (even if you select different ones).

Another way to get rid of the = at the end of your lines is to set your word wrap to less than 76 characters. Choose Mail, Options, click the Send tab, click the Plain Text option button, click the Settings button, and change the entry in the "Automatically wrap text at [   ] characters, when sending" field to a number less than 76. Finally, you can also get rid of the = signs by encoding your messages with UUENCODE instead of MIME (the default).

To change your coding scheme, choose News or Mail, Options, click the Send tab, and then click the Settings button for the selected format, HTML or Plain Text. The Settings button for HTML doesn't let you use UUENCODE, just MIME. The Settings button for Plain Text lets you choose either UUENCODE or MIME.

If you choose MIME, you can choose None, Quoted Printable, or Base 64 from a drop-down list. These options only apply to the text portion of your message and not to the attachments. The attachments are coded in MIME at Base 64.

Internet Mail and News automatically encode and decode attachments. It's best just to attach files and not encode them first. If you receive an attachment that was encoded before it was attached (you wonder why the person sending it to you went to the trouble), you'll have to decode it using another application. WinZip 6.2 (and later) can decode such files. You'll find WinZip at http://www.winzip.com. To make the attachment available to WinZip or to other decoding programs, you need to save it as a separate file. Use the methods described in the previous section, *Saving Attachments*.

If you need to decode an e-mail or news message, you can also use File, Save As to save it as a separate file and then decode it with a separate application.

Undocumented

Apparently, Internet Mail and News can automatically decode attachments that were encoded with UUENCODE. Internet Mail has trouble with MIME attachments, either Base 64 or Quoted Printable. You may have to use another decoder to handle these. The same is true for BinHex-encoded attachments.

You can read more about encoding and decoding in Internet Mail and News at Eric Miller's site at http://home.sprynet.com/sprynet/edm/. Be sure to look under Issues Affecting both Mail and News, Encoding Information.

You can find encoders and decoders at http://www.windows95.com or ftp://ftp.andrew.cmu.edu/pub/mpack/ for munpack (MIME decoding), http://www.texoma.com/mirror/tucows/catalog.html#w for Wincode (UUdecoding), and http://www.aladdinsys.com/ for StuffIt (BinHex). Microsoft has agreed that there are problems in these areas and has promised to address them in an updated version of Outlook (the PIM that comes with Microsoft Office). Hopefully, the changes it makes in Outlook will also migrate to Outlook Express.

Multiple Users and User Profiles

Unlike Windows Messaging, Internet Mail doesn't let you easily switch between different e-mail accounts (this is not true of Outlook Express). You set up Internet Mail for one mail server and stick with that one. Likewise, all the news messages are stored under one user name.

There are a number of ways to track multiple e-mail accounts and different user preferences related to newsgroups and news servers. The official Microsoft-approved way is to use user profiles. Each user logs on under his or her name, and Internet Mail and News keeps track of each person's mail and newsgroups in separate subfolders under a folder with the user's name. Users set up their own mail servers by logging onto their Windows 95 Desktop, starting Internet Mail, choosing Mail, Options, clicking the Server tab, and entering their SMTP and POP3 mail server information. They set up news servers by starting Internet News and following similar steps (choose News, Options, click the Server tab, and click the Add button).

If you have multiple users on one Windows 95 computer, you can configure Windows 95 to use user profiles, by following the steps detailed in *Whose Desktop Is This Anyway?* in Chapter 12. Each user can then have a different Internet Mail address book, newsgroups, and mail folders. Remember that these files are stored under each user's user name.

If you set up multiple users after you install Internet Mail and News, all of your mail and news will go to the original user. You have to edit your Registry to tell Internet Mail and News that there are now multiple users and that Internet Mail and News should use multiple user folders when sorting and delivering the mail and news.

You will need to add to the Registry a Mail, News, and address book branch for each new user. Follow the specific instructions at Eric Miller's site at http://home.sprynet.com/sprynet/edm/. Go to Issues Affecting Both Internet Mail and News, and read the instructions under Multiple Users.

This method requires that you log off and log on again to get e-mail first for one user and then another. This is obviously a bit cumbersome. Some users want to be able to switch mail accounts without all this hassle.

Multiple accounts/users without using user profiles

You can fool Internet Mail and News into placing e-mail and newsgroup messages into different user folders. It requires editing your Registry on the fly using *reg* files.

Patrick Freeman has created a little utility called SwitchIt! that accomplishes this task for you. It allows you to keep separate Internet Mail and News Registry configurations stored under different user names and switch back and forth between them. You can download SwitchIt! from http://www.oz.net/~patrickf/patrick.html.

If you would rather create the necessary *reg* files by hand, follow the instructions at Costas Andriotii's site at http://www-na.biznet.com.gr/sail/isa/tipfrm.html, under How to get mail from multiple accounts with MS Internet Mail.

If you have more than one e-mail account on the same server, you can edit your Lmhosts file to create local aliases for the mail server name. Costas gives you step-by-step instructions for carrying this out.

Internet Mail and News within the Internet Explorer Window

You can either run Internet Mail and News in separate windows — as though they were stand-alone applications — or you can run them inside of an Internet Explorer window. The fact that they are Explorer extensions doesn't really affect how they can appear to the user.

Undocumented

If you are using Internet Explorer 3.01, you can still run Microsoft Internet Mail and News inside of Internet Explorer.

STEPS

Internet Mail and News Inside Internet Explorer 3.0

Step 1.   Right-click My Computer and click Explore. Navigate to C:\.

Step 2.   Right-click the right pane, point to New, and then click Folder. Rename the folder:

Internet Mail.{89292102-4755-11cf-9DC2-00AA006C2B84}

Click OK.

Step 3.   Right-click the right pane, point to New, and then click Folder. Rename the folder:

Internet News.{89292103-4755-11cf-9DC2-00AA006C2B84}

Click OK.

Step 4.   Open Internet Explorer. Type **file://c:\Internet Mail.{89292102-4755-11cf-9DC2-00AA006C2B84}** in the Address box and press Enter. You'll see Internet Mail within Internet Explorer.

Step 5.   Click the Favorites button and click Add to Favorites to create a shortcut to the Internet Mail address.

Step 6.   Open Internet Explorer. Type **file://c:\Internet News.{89292103-4755-11cf-9DC2-00AA006C2B84}** in the Address box and press Enter. You'll see Internet News within the Internet Explorer.

Step 7.   Click the Favorites button and click Add to Favorites to create a shortcut to the Internet News address.

Internet Mail and News Inside Internet Explorer

Step 8. You might want to use the Quick Link buttons instead of (or in addition to) favorites shortcuts for Internet Mail and News. Double-click the Internet icon in the Control Panel, and then click the Navigation tab. In the Page drop-down list, choose a Quick Link to rename, type a name in the Name field (you'll probably want to label these buttons Internet News and Internet Mail) and insert the complete addresses (shown in steps 4 and 6) in the Address field.

If you open an Explorer window, you can run Internet Mail or News in the right pane. Just click the folders that you just created in steps 2 and 3 above.

Internet Mail and News on the context menu

Undocumented

You can put the Internet Mail and News options on the context menu that appears when you right-click the Internet icon on your Desktop. Costas Andriotis came up with this little gem.

STEPS
Internet Mail and News on the Context Menu

Step 1. Double-click Regedit.exe in your \Windows folder.

Step 2. Navigate to HKEY_CLASSES_ROOT\CLSID\{FBF23B42-E3F0-101B-8488-00AA003E56F8}\Shell

Step 3. Highlight Shell, click the right pane of the Registry editor, choose New, Key, type **Mail**, and press Enter.

Step 4. Highlight Shell, click the right pane of the Registry editor, choose New, Key, type **News**, and press Enter.

Step 5. Highlight Mail, double-click the Default value in the right pane, and type **Explorer.exe /root,C:\windows\Internet Mail.{89292102-4755-11cf-9DC2-00AA006C2B84}**. Click OK.

Step 6. Highlight News, double-click the Default value in the right pane, and type **Explorer.exe /root,C:\windows\Internet News.{89292103-4755-11cf-9DC2-00AA006C2B84}**. Exit the Registry editor.

Internet Mail and News on the Desktop and in the Explorer

If you have Internet Explorer 3.01, you can integrate Internet Mail and News into your Desktop and Explorer.

Undocumented

Costas Andriotis has a file, Intdsk.inf, on his site, http://www-na.biznet.com.gr/sail/isa/tipfrm.html, that will put Internet Mail and News on your Desktop and in your Explorer. Download the file, right-click its name in your Explorer, and click Install. After you install this utility, Internet Mail and Internet News icons appear in the left pane of Explorer.

Microsoft Internet (And Outlook Express) Mail

It's easy to keep going, and not too easy to get going. Hooking up to the Internet with e-mail is the most difficult task for most people. Once you get over that, the rest comes naturally. Internet Mail was built to be easy. It's got a powerful address book, and it will work well for most of you.

Internet Mail (or Outlook Express) versus Windows Messaging

Windows 95 comes with two tools for Internet mail. What are the differences?

The Internet Mail address book lets you store multiple e-mail addresses in one record. You have to set one address as the default address, but you can still have one record with multiple e-mail addresses. You can't store multiple e-mail addresses in one record in Windows Messaging. And unlike Windows Messaging's address book, the Internet Mail address book has fields for both business and home addresses and phone numbers.

Windows Messaging lets you send faxes (Internet Mail doesn't). Windows Messaging's address book is shared with Microsoft Phone (Internet Mail's isn't).

Unlike Internet Mail, Windows Messaging can connect to MSN and CompuServe accounts directly. This won't matter as soon as MSN and CompuServe shift to Internet-standard POP3 and SMTP mail servers.

Windows Messaging supports Microsoft's Messaging Application Programming Interface (MAPI). Internet Mail does not. (Outlook Express does.)

You can't create a hierarchy of mail folders in Internet Mail, like you can in Windows Messaging. (You can in Outlook Express, as well.)

You can use rules in Internet Mail (choose Mail, Inbox Assistant, Add). The *rules* in Internet Mail let you sort incoming mail into different folders depending on who it was sent to, who sent it, and what words the subject line contains. You need an add-on or Exchange Server to use rules with Windows Messaging.

Windows Messaging can handle multiple (Windows Messaging) profiles, although it only allows one Internet mailbox per profile. You have to fool Internet Mail into using multiple e-mail boxes without creating Windows 95 user profiles.

Monitoring multiple e-mail accounts

You can get e-mail from one account and then another just by telling Internet Mail which POP3 server to use. You need to do this for each e-mail account you want to collect mail from. A better option is to upgrade to Outlook Express.

In Internet Mail, choose Mail, Options, and then click the Server tab. Enter the appropriate server, account, and password information. Click Apply. Quit and restart Internet Mail. Click the Send and Receive toolbar button on the Internet Mail toolbar. Go through this process again for the next account.

Remember, you are using this method to download e-mail sent to you. It is stored on different POP3 servers in various e-mail accounts. You haven't changed your SMTP e-mail server account information, so your e-mail is still sent out on the same server.

If you want an easier way to monitor multiple POP3 accounts, check out POPIt at http://theweeds.smxcorp.com/popit.htm. POPIt monitors up to ten POP3 accounts and notifies you when you have mail.

MultiPOPer can change your Internet Mail configuration to allow you to check and receive mail from multiple POP servers simultaneously. You'll find it at http://www.i1.net/~birchsw/projects/. There are other shareware utilities that notify you if you have received mail, such as New Mail at http://www.sis.pitt.edu/~ketil/newmail.html. Check for still more at http://www.stroud.com/95mail.html.

Internet Mail (or Outlook Express) as the default mail program

When you install Internet Mail, it sets itself up as the default e-mail client. Windows Messaging still works, but it is no longer used to send e-mail from the Internet Explorer. If you install other e-mail clients or somehow mess up your settings, Internet Mail may not appear when you click e-mail addresses embedded in web pages. To get it back, you'll want to check out your system.

First, choose Mail, Options (or Tools, Mail Options in Outlook Express), and click the Send tab. Make sure that the check box labeled "Make Microsoft Internet Mail your default e-mail program" is checked. To do the same for Internet News, choose News, Options (or Tools, News Options), click the Read tab, and mark the check box labeled "Make Microsoft Internet News your default news reader."

Undocumented

Second, on your Explorer menu, choose View, Options, and click File Types. Select URL:MailTo Protocol from Registered file types. Click the Edit button, highlight Open, and click Edit. For Internet Mail and News, make the Application used to perform action field rundll32.exe C:\WINDOWS\SYSTEM\ mailnews.dll,Mail_RunDLL; for Outlook Express, make the field "C:\\Program Files\Outlook Express\msimn.exe" /mailurl:%1. Clear the Use DDE box. Click OK three times.

Third, double-click the Internet icon in the Control Panel. Click the Programs tab. Make sure that Internet Mail and Internet News are selected in the Mail and News drop-down lists.

If Internet Mail is the default e-mail program, Internet News uses it to send a copy of your news message to the author when you select a message and choose Reply to All (or choose News, Reply to Newsgroup and Author). Internet Mail puts a copy of the outgoing e-mail message in the Sent Items folder, although it doesn't pop up on your Desktop when it does this.

Urgent or not

You can set the priority of an Internet Mail message by choosing Mail, Set Priority in the New Message window, but what is the fun in that? Instead, click the postage stamp in the upper-right hand corner of the New Message window and select your message priority (low, normal, or high).

If you see a little red exclamation point next to a message you receive, you'll know that the sender thinks the message is urgent. Maybe, maybe not.

Undeleting deleted messages

If you delete an Internet Mail (or Outlook Express) message, it goes to the Deleted Items folder. It's not exactly deleted — more like moved.

If you delete the message from the Deleted Items folder, you'll no longer be able to find its header in any of your Internet Mail folders. This doesn't mean it's gone though. It's still there, somewhat intact in the Deleted Items folder. Specifically, it's still in the mailbox file called Deleted Items.mbx.

Secret

If you compact the Deleted Items folder, it's history.

If you haven't compacted the Deleted Items folder, you can quickly retrieve missing messages. Here's how:

STEPS
Restore Your Deleted Items Folder

Step 1. Quit Internet Mail.

Restore Your Deleted Items Folder

Step 2. Delete the Deleted Items.idx file in \Program Files\Internet Mail and News*yourusernname*\Mail (or Program Files\Outlook Express\yourusername\Mail).

Step 3. Restart Internet Mail. Click Deleted Items in the Folders box. You'll get an error message stating that the folder has been damaged and that it will now be repaired. Click OK. Internet Mail rebuilds the index from the mailbox file.

Your Deleted Items folder has been restored with the missing items back in it. Now you can delete again those messages that you really did want to delete.

Deleted Items.mbx is for the most part a text file. (This is also true for the other mailbox files.) You can easily read it with Notepad or WordPad. If you want to retrieve a piece of text from any of these files, just open them with either text editor.

You can use two methods to compact the Deleted Items folder. The first is to choose File, Folder, Compact, Deleted Items. The second is to choose Mail, Options, click the Read tab, and mark the check box labeled "Empty messages from 'Deleted Items' folder on exit." This method automatically compacts the Deleted Items folder when you exit Internet Mail.

Error message referring to the Outbox

Secret

It appears to be quite easy to corrupt your Internet Mail's Outbox. If you get error messages complaining about your Outbox, you're going to have to delete it and its accompanying index. Internet Mail will construct a new clean empty one for you.

First exit Internet Mail. Use your Explorer to navigate to \Program Files\Internet Mail and News*your username*\Mail (or \Program Files\Outlook Express\yourusername\Mail). Delete Outbox.mbx and Outbox.idx. Restart Internet Mail.

Waving when the mail arrives

You can make your computer play a tune (play a *wav* file) when your mail arrives. To do this, choose Mail, Options (or Tools, Mail Options), click the Read tab, and mark the Play sound when new messages arrive check box. This only makes sense if you have marked "Check for new messages every [ ] minute(s)" in the same tab. If you dial up to your Internet service provider, download your mail, and then disconnect, what's the point of doing this? Internet Mail (or Outlook Express) must be running for the tune to play. (And if you receive your mail from the Internet and not an intranet, you have to be connected to the Internet as well.)

You can, if you like, set your own sound to play when new messages arrive. Use the steps detailed in the *Applying sounds to application events* in Chapter 16. Find the New Mail Notification event under the Windows events, and choose among the listed *wav* files, or browse for another one.

When Internet Mail is running and you're connected to the Internet (or your intranet), an envelope appears in your Tray when mail arrives.

Leaving mail on the server

If you are traveling, you might want to leave mail messages on your mail server until you get back, even though you want to read them now. That way, you can download them to your office computer when you return.

To do this, choose Mail, Options, click the Server tab, click the Advanced Settings button, and mark the Leave a copy of messages on server check box. With Outlook Express, choose Tools, Accounts, highlight your mail server, click Properties, and then click the Server tab.

You can take a copy of your address book with you on your portable just by copying your *username.wab* file from the \Windows folder on your desktop computer onto your portable computer. We are assuming that you have already set up Internet Mail on your portable and that the *wab* files have the same name and location on your portable and desktop computer. You are just overwriting your portable's version with your desktop's version.

Internet Mail (and Outlook Express) address book

You can import addresses from your Windows Messaging (or Microsoft Exchange) address book into your Internet Mail address book. You can choose which Windows Messaging profile to use when importing, so this lets you choose which personal address book to import.

The problem is that you could quite easily have multiple entries for the same person in your Windows Messaging address books. Windows Messaging is unable to correctly handle multiple e-mail addresses and fax numbers in one record. As you import the addresses, Internet Mail asks you (by default) whether to overwrite an address that it just imported when it encounters the next record with the same name. You don't know which record is the correct Internet address and which is a CompuServe or MSN address.

To solve this problem, it is best to first make a copy of your Windows Messaging *pab* file. Create a new Windows Messaging profile that points to this new copy. Open up Windows Messaging using this profile and delete the names with fax numbers or non-Internet addresses. Use this profile when importing names into your Internet Mail address book. The Internet Mail address book import process is supposed to keep out the fax addresses, but just to be sure, delete them first.

Internet Mail (build 1160 and later) allows you to import addresses from Microsoft Internet Mail for Windows 3.1, Netscape Navigator, and Eudora. This is also true for Outlook Express. If you want to import addresses from other databases, you can use a Word macro that first imports them into *pab* files. Go to the Exchange Center at http://www.slipstick.com/exchange to find and download the macro.

There is a Registry entry that corresponds to your Internet Mail (or Outlook Express) address book. Each address book uses your user name as its filename and adds the *wab* extension. If you move your Internet Mail address book to a new computer, make sure to update the Registry on the new computer so that it knows where to find the address book and what its name is. Look for an entry at HKEY_CURRENT_USER\Software \Microsoft\ WAB\Wab File Name. If you don't have this entry, add this key, double-click the Default value in the right pane of your Registry editor, and type the path and filename for your address book.

If you have user profiles, the current user changes depending on who has logged in, so you can have multiple Internet Mail address books. If you are not using user profiles, you can use SwitchIt! to switch between different user address books. You can download SwitchIt! from http://www.oz.net/~patrickf/patrick.html.

Printing a list of addresses from your Internet Mail address book

With build 1160 of Internet Mail and Outlook Express, all you need to do to print the contents of your Internet Mail address book is choose Files, Print after you have opened an Address Book window. There isn't a simple way to do this if you have build 1155 or earlier. However, you can still fool the earlier versions of Internet Mail into creating a list of everyone in your address book. Richard B. Merren from Puerto Jimenez, Costa Rica came up with this not-so-elegant, but practical means of printing the names and addresses from earlier versions.

STEPS

Print Your Internet Mail Address Book

Step 1.   Open Internet Mail, choose Mail, Options, and click the Send tab. Clear the Send messages immediately check box, and click OK.

Step 2.   Click the New Message button. Click the Rollodex icon in the To field, scroll to the bottom of the Select Recipients dialog box. Hold down the Shift key and click the last name in your address book. Click the To button. Click OK.

Step 3.   Type anything in the Subject field of your new message and click the Send button on the toolbar.

(continued)

STEPS *(continued)*

Print Your Internet Mail Address Book

Step 4.   In the Folders box, select your Outbox. Highlight the new message and click the Forward toolbar button. This creates a new message. Within the body of that message you'll find your list of addressees.

Step 5   Copy and paste this list to Word or some other powerful word processing program that will allow you to format the list easily.

Step 6.   Quit the forwarded message and delete the original message from your Outbox.

You can also print one page of addresses from your address book at a time using a freeware package, Hard Copy, which you'll find at http://ourworld.compuserve.com/homepages/sweckman/Hardcopy.htm.

Converting the mail

In Chapter 32, we give you a way to convert Eudora and similar e-mail messages into Windows Messaging format. The process first converts these messages into an Internet Mail folder file (a file with an extension of *mbx*). If you want to convert messages to Internet Mail format, you can obviously stop part way through the process. Turn to the *Importing Other Messages* section of Chapter 32 to see how to do this.

You'll find a program called E2M that helps with this conversion at http://www.mindware.com.au/freestuf.htm. (We tell you how to use this utility in Chapter 32.) You can find out more about Eudora, which uses the same message format as Internet Mail, at http://mango.human.cornell.edu/kens/MoreFAQ.html.

You can download a demo version of Eudora at ftp://ftp.eudora.com/eudora/windows/3.0/eu30demo.exe or go to Qualcomm's Web site at http://www.eudora.com/, where you can also download a freeware version of the program.

Microsoft Internet (And Outlook Express) News

It's your basic Internet news reader. If you want fancy, there are plenty of other products available that will do a lot more. But Internet News is well-designed and sleek. Simple, straightforward, obvious. We show you the less obvious parts.

Multi-part files

In some newsgroups, you might come across find postings that are in fact large files, most likely binary files. These files are often broken into several parts that are identified as such. In order to successfully discover the contents of these files, you need to recombine them and decode them. You can use Internet News to do just that.

Holding down your Ctrl key, click each message header that indicates it is a part of the larger file. Next, choose News, Combine and Decode (or right-click the highlighted headers and choose Combine and Decode from the context menu). You will be asked to select the proper order in which to reassemble the individual messages back into the larger file. Once you have moved the message headers up and down to get the proper order, click OK, and a new window will open with the decoded file.

No unread messages

If you display both read and unread messages (View, All Messages), you'll notice that unread message headers appear in boldface, while the headers of read messages are displayed in a regular font. Many users choose the View, Unread Messages Only option in Internet News to reduce the amount of clutter in the message header pane.

Internet News sometimes has a problem keeping track of which messages are read and which are unread. If you have chosen View, Unread Messages Only, you won't see new message headers if they come in marked as read instead of unread, which is their actual status. (This happens all too often.) Outlook Express is supposed to have fixed this problem. We'll see.

Secret

To clear this problem, take the following steps:

STEPS

Unread Messages Marked As Read

Step 1. Exit Internet News.

Step 2. Use your Explorer to go to the \Program Files\Internet Mail and News*your username*\News folder. You'll notice the files have names that remind you of their news server and newsgroup names.

Step 3. Find the files with *sub* and *dat* extensions that start with the name of the news server whose newsgroups have the problem of unread messages marked as read. Delete these files.

Step 4. Restart Internet News. Choose News, Options, click the Server tab, and click the Add button. Fill in the information needed to connect to the news server.

Beware of cross posters

If you single-click a newsgroup message to view it in the preview pane, you won't be able to see which newsgroups it has been posted to. You might assume that it has only been posted to the newsgroup that you are currently reading it in. This may give you the feeling that you are part of a little community, and that you're only interacting with the people on this one newsgroup. This can be a false reading.

People can (and do) post messages to many different newsgroups at once. Sometimes this is legitimate; the person who posted the message is simply trying to get help wherever he or she can find it. Sometimes it's just SPAM. If you reply to a message that was posted in multiple newsgroups, your reply will by default get posted in all the newsgroups, not just the one you're currently participating in.

Undocumented

If you want to make sure that you're responding in just one newsgroup and not having your words spread all over the place, double-click the message header. If the message window shows multiple newsgroups in the Newsgroups field, click the newspaper icon to the left of the field, as shown in Figure 35-5, to display the Pick Newsgroups dialog box. Here, you can remove newsgroups and/or add others.

You can also click the newspaper icon when you're writing new messages if you want to send them off to other newsgroups.

Internet News always has a current news server. When you click a newsgroup on a different news server, the current news server changes.

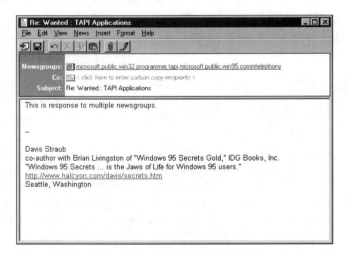

Figure 35-5: Click the newspaper icon on the left side of the Newsgroups field to tailor the list of newsgroups on which your message will be posted.

When you click the newspaper icon, the Pick Newsgroups dialog box only lists newsgroups available on the current news server.

Secret

If some of the newsgroups to which a message has been posted aren't present on the news server that you are currently logged onto, you'll get an error message stating that the newsgroup name can't be resolved. This is particularly true with the Microsoft's news server because it only lists its own newsgroups. If you see this error message, you know without even double-clicking the message header that a cross poster sent the message.

Reading the news offline

News readers (that is, human ones) who reside outside the United States often have to pay what appear to U.S. residents as exorbitant hourly rates to connect to the Internet. These readers, and the few remaining U.S. citizens who don't have nearby Internet service providers with fixed monthly fees, will find it much cheaper to take their reading offline. Microsoft Internet News gives you this option.

When you're offline, you can choose which messages to download based on their header information, or you can mark whole newsgroups to be downloaded (either just the headers, or the headers and the messages together). You can then go online to download all the new messages from your chosen newsgroups.

Internet News keeps a threaded list of message headers for each newsgroup on your computer. When you go online and browse each newsgroup, this threaded list is updated. If you have set Internet News to display unread messages only (View, Unread Messages Only), you'll see the headers of new messages scroll onto the screen as you stop at each newsgroup.

If you now go offline, you can still browse through the list of message headers (regardless of whether you view all message headers or just those that are unread). As you highlight various message headers (you can use Shift and Ctrl to choose multiple headers), you can choose options in the Offline menu (Tools, Offline in Outlook Express) to specify what you want to do with the messages when you go back online. Mark Message for Download (Mark for Retrieval in Outlook Express) marks the highlighted message to be downloaded; Mark Thread for Download (Mark Thread for Retrieval in Outlook Express) downloads the thread that contains the highlighted message; Mark All for Download downloads all the messages in the newsgroup associated with currently visible headers; and Unmark for Download (Unmark in Outlook Express) unmarks a message header you previously marked.

Once you have marked the messages you want to download, choose Offline, Post and Download (Tools, Synchronize, Synchronize All in Outlook Express). Internet News will download the messages from the news server. In addition, if you have created any new messages or replies, it will post those messages to their respective newsgroups.

You can bulk browse the newsgroups a bit more quickly when you're offline than you can if you went online and moved from newsgroup to newsgroup. While you're offline, choose Offline, Mark Newsgroups to display the Mark Newsgroups dialog box (see Figure 35-6). Choose just which newsgroups you want to browse offline and mark the Download headers only option button. If you want to set the freshness date on the downloaded headers, mark the check box at the bottom of the dialog box and type the number of days you want to use as a cut-off point. Internet News won't download any messages that are older than your cut-off. Click the Download Now button, and you'll soon have updated messages headers in all your selected newsgroups.

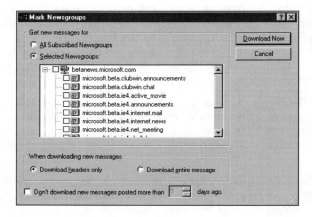

Figure 35-6: Mark newsgroups for downloading messages in bulk.

You can now go through the headers and mark those whose associated messages presumably merit downloading. Choose Offline, Post and Download to go online and get the marked messages.

With Outlook Express, highlight a newsgroup server in the left pane and Ctrl+click the newsgroups in the upper-right pane whose messages you wish to retrieve in bulk. Click Tools, Offline, and choose one of the following three options: Mark to Retrieve New Headers, Mark to Retrieve All Messages, or Mark to Retrieve New Messages. Finally, click Tools, Synchronize, Synchronize Selected Newsgroups.

If you choose to download both the headers and the messages at the same time, you obviously don't need to go back and download the messages later. Of course, the initial download takes a bit longer than if you just get the headers, and you'll get a lot of messages that aren't of interest to you.

When you use this bulk browse facility, Internet News only downloads new message headers. It knows which headers you already have stored on your computer, so it won't download any old ones. Even if you download both the headers and the messages at the same time, you don't have to worry about Internet News going out and downloading messages associated with headers you have previously stored.

If you do want to download messages associated with headers that you already have stored on your computer, you'll need to mark those headers for download individually.

Secret

Eric Miller points out that some users are having problems when download-ing a subset of their unread messages. If you run into this problem, he suggests that you first mark all headers in a newsgroup as read (Edit, Mark All as Read), and then choose View, All Messages, select the headers for the messages you want to download, mark them as unread (Edit, Mark as Unread), choose View, Unread Messages Only, and press the F5 key. Next, choose Offline, Mark All for Download to mark all the now marked as unread messages for download. Finally, choose Offline, Post and Download.

Another problem you might encounter is that all the message headers that you have just downloaded are marked as read. If you have View, Unread Messages Only checked, you won't even see that you have new message headers.

We have seen numerous suggested ways of dealing with this problem. Some of the more minor fixes described here may work for you, but if they don't, you're going to have to go in and start erasing some expendable newsgroup header files (files with the *nch* extension).

Secret

First, choose News, Options, and click the Read tab. Clear the check boxes labeled "Mark all messages as read when exiting a newsgroup" and "Mes-sage is read after being previewed for [   ] seconds."

If that is not enough, use your Explorer to navigate to the \Program Files\Internet Mail and News*yourusername*\News folder. Erase the *nch* files that correspond to the newsgroups that were displaying the problem. You'll have to download the headers from these newsgroups again.

If you are still having problems, delete all the *nch* files associated with the news server that delivers the offending newsgroups. Also delete the *sub* and *dat* files for that news server. Reconnect to the news server by choosing News, Options, clicking the Server tab, clicking the Add button, and entering the news server name. You'll have to re-subscribe to the newsgroups of interest to you.

Catching up with the news

Internet News doesn't give you a way to automatically "catch up" on a newsgroup by downloading all the previously unread messages in a newsgroup. You might want to do this to set the unread messages counter to zero and start fresh in the newsgroup, ignoring all the past (yesterday's) wisdom.

Undocumented

If you change a few settings in your Internet News configuration, you can accomplish the "catch up" task.

STEPS

Catching Up on Your Newsgroups with Internet News and Mail

Step 1. Open Internet News, choose News, Options, and click the Read tab.

Step 2. Clear the Download [ ] headers at a time check box. Click OK.

Step 3. Choose Offline, Mark Newsgroups. Choose the newsgroups that you want to "catch up" in. Clear the check box labeled "Don't download new messages posted more than [ ] days ago." Mark Download headers only. Click Download Now.

Step 4. When you have received all the headers on all your chosen newsgroups, you can decide whether to read the associated messages or mark all headers as read.

ROT 13 in the news

Some newsgroup messages come in ROT 13 format. If you find a message that looks scrambled, choose Edit, Unscramble (ROT13). This command makes messages formatted with ROT 13 readable by rotating the letters and numbers. It rotates the letters by 13 characters and the numbers by 5. For more information, check out http://www.microsoft.com/kb/articles/Q153/9/31.htm.

Windows 95 newsgroups

The following is a list of newsgroups pertaining to Windows 95. The first newsgroups are hosted on the Microsoft support news server at msnews.microsoft.com. The others are Usenet newsgroups, and you should be able to find them on your Internet service provider's local news server.

You might be able to subscribe to some of the Microsoft newsgroups on your local Internet service provider's news server. Your service provider decides which newsgroups it will carry.

Be sure to configure Internet News to access a news server before you try to subscribe to its newsgroups.

http://www.microsoft.com/support/news/

news:microsoft.public.internet.mail

news:microsoft.public.internet.news

news:microsoft.public.internet.netmeeting

news:microsoft.public.internet.netmeeting.beta

news:microsoft.public.internet.personalwebserv

news:microsoft.public.internetexplorer

news:microsoft.public.internetexplorer.beta.win95

news:microsoft.public.internetexplorer.ieak

news:microsoft.public.internetexplorer.java

news:microsoft.public.internetexplorer.java.cabdevkit

news:microsoft.public.internetexplorer.win95microsoft.public.win95.anniversary

news:microsoft.public.win95.coffeehouse.chat

news:microsoft.public.win95.commtelephony

news:microsoft.public.win95.dialupnetworking

news:microsoft.public.win95.exchangefax

news:microsoft.public.win95.filediskmanagement

news:microsoft.public.win95.msdosapps

news:microsoft.public.win95.multimedia

news:microsoft.public.win95.networking

news:microsoft.public.win95.printingfontsvideo

news:microsoft.public.win95.setup

news:microsoft.public.win95.shellui

news:microsoft.public.win95.win95applets

news:comp.os.ms-windows.networking.win95

news:comp.os.ms-windows.setup.win95

news:comp.os.ms-windows.apps.compatibility.win95

news:comp.os.ms-windows.apps.utilities.win95

news:comp.os.ms-windows.win95.misc

news:comp.os.ms-windows.win95.setup

news:comp.os.ms-windows.networking.windows

news:comp.os.ms-windows.networking.tcp-ip

news:comp.os.ms-windows.apps.misc

news:comp.os.ms-windows.apps.utilities

news:comp.os.ms-windows.apps.winsock.misc

news:comp.os.ms-windows.apps.winsock.news

news:comp.os.ms-windows.apps.winsock.mail

news:comp.os.ms-windows.apps.comm

news:comp.os.ms-windows.networking.ras

news:comp.os.ms-windows.misc

Access to public news servers

If your Internet service provider does have a news server, check out these locations for other news servers:

Site	Address
Deja News	http://www.dejanews.com
Public Access Usenet Sites	http://www.yahoo.com/News/Usenet/ Public_Access_Usenet_Sites/
JWA's Open NNTP Sites	http://www.nbs.nau.edu/~jwa
One list	http://www.ts.umu.se/~maxell/Newsgroups/ servers.html
Other sites	http://www.shout.net/~slim/smut/sitelist.html

Summary

Internet Mail and Internet News are useful programs that let you quickly get up to speed using Internet mail and reading newsgroups.

- ▶ We show you how to make Internet Mail and Internet News a lot easier to use and more powerful by making a few quick changes to their configuration.
- ▶ You'll find out where to turn to on the web for additional help using these programs.
- ▶ You can create highly formatted messages using Internet Mail and Internet News' built-in HTML capability.
- ▶ You can import your address books from Windows Messaging and other e-mail programs.
- ▶ We tell you where Microsoft and others are providing newsgroup support for their products.

Chapter 36

Networking

In This Chapter

Microsoft has made Windows 95 a very strong networking client as well as a peer server. We discuss:

- Connecting to Microsoft and Novell NetWare networks
- Working with 16-bit networks
- Setting up a $60 network
- Dealing with interrupts and I/O addresses in pre-plug and play network adapters
- Turning your Windows 95 computer into a NetWare file and print server
- Setting up a peer server on a share- or user-level network
- Connecting to multiple networks simultaneously
- Understanding network security so you can use the resources you need
- Connecting to folders and printers with the universal naming convention
- Cleaning up network problems with Net Watcher, System Monitor, System Policy Editor, Registry editor, and Password List Editor
- Using Windows networking applications

Basic Network Support

Windows 95 comes with all of the necessary networking software required to set up a 32-bit protected-mode Microsoft Windows network of computers running Windows 95, or to connect to a network with computers running Windows NT, LAN Manager, and Windows for Workgroups 3.11. Additionally, Windows 95 includes a 32-bit protected-mode client for Novell NetWare networks, so your Windows 95 computer can be a compatible client on this type of network as well.

Microsoft has finally agreed that, for the time being at least, Novell has almost as strong a monopoly in the networking operating system market as Microsoft has in the Desktop operating system market. To honor that market position (as well as to undermine it), Microsoft has written a very strong 32-bit protected-mode product called Client for NetWare Networks and an IPX/SPX-compatible protocol.

You can configure a Windows 95 computer as a NetWare print and file server on a NetWare network. Windows 95 provides three networking protocols: NetBEUI, IPX/SPX, and TCP/IP. Windows 95 workstations can directly access Windows NT and NetWare servers. Multiple (up to 10) 32-bit network clients can be running on your computer at the same time, allowing your computer to access multiple networks and network services simultaneously. For example, your computer could use TCP/IP to access a Unix server using the Internet Explorer while using Client for NetWare Networks to access a NetWare server. Because these network clients run in protected mode, they don't take up conventional memory.

All the networking components developed by Microsoft are 32-bit protected-mode Virtual Device Drivers (VxDs). Because Windows 95 uses protected-mode network components, it doesn't have to switch your processor (386, 486 or Pentium) from protected mode to real mode (a process that wastes too many processor cycles). As a result, networking speeds get much faster (50–200 percent).

Real-mode drivers, especially for NetWare, have a nasty habit of causing some programs to lock up your computer — the dreaded "black screen of death." There isn't any way to completely eliminate this problem without using protected-mode drivers. The real-mode drivers create memory conflicts and have unresolved disputes over control of interrupts.

Real-mode network drivers are loaded in conventional memory, although memory managers allow you to partially load these drivers between the 640K and 1MB memory addresses. Network components are particularly large, and if they run in real mode, they reduce the memory resources available to DOS programs to the point that some DOS programs can't run on networked computers. The new protected-mode network components are loaded above the lower 640K area, leaving this memory available for Doom and other mission-critical DOS programs.

Apart from its 32-bit network drivers, Windows 95 can still be a good client for the 16-bit real-mode versions of all of the major networks that are available for PCs. These include:

- Artisoft LANtastic version 5.0 or later
- Banyan VINES version 5.52 or later
- Beame and Whiteside Network File System 3.0c or later
- DEC Pathworks version 5.0 or later
- IBM OS/2 LAN Server
- Microsoft Windows Network version 3.11
- MS-Net compatibles
- Novell NetWare 3.11 or later
- Sunselect PC-NFS version 5.0 or later
- TCS 10Net version 4.1 or later

In addition to reading the material in this chapter, you should turn to the Windows 95 Networking FAQ for the latest updates regarding networking issues. You'll find it at http://www-leland.stanford.edu/~llurch/win95netbugs/faq.html.

What Windows 95 Networking Buys You

The whole point of networking is to be able to access resources that are beyond your computer. These resources are shared because they are too expensive to be given exclusively to one user, or because they are a managed resource (for example, a corporate transaction-processing database) that needs to be available to many different users simultaneously.

Windows 95 is designed to be a particularly good networking client (and peer-to-peer server). Microsoft put more programmer resources into this aspect of Windows 95 than any other.

Windows 95 supports:

- User profiles and system policies that make it possible (with appropriate network administration) for users to log onto any networked Windows 95 computer and have their own Desktop and applications available to them

- Protected-mode networking clients, protocols, and adapter drivers that don't take any conventional memory

- User-level security that is enforced by either Windows NT or NetWare servers and is centrally administered

- A single logon dialog box that allows users to log onto their Windows 95 computer (and bring up their user-specific Desktop) as well as onto all the network resources and servers available to them

- Backup agents, so backup software running on Windows NT or NetWare servers can back up Windows 95 computers

- Direct Cable Connection (DCC) and Dial-Up Networking (DUN)

- Diskless (or floppy disk-only) workstations connected to shared copies of Windows 95 on Windows NT or NetWare servers

- Browsing of shared network resources or resources on network servers through the Explorer, folder windows, the new common dialog boxes, or the Network Neighborhood

- Remote printing and printer administration

- Network management through Simple Network Management Protocols (SNMP) using third-party software and a supplied agent

- Simultaneous access to multiple networks and multiple networking protocols

- Multiple 32-bit protected-mode networking protocols: NetBEUI, IPX/SPX, and TCP/IP

- Remote administration and network resource monitoring

Quick and Dirty Networking

If you want to hook up a couple of computers to share resources (such as a printer and some folders), here's what you need to do:

STEPS

Setting Up a Quick and Dirty Network

Step 1. Buy (at about $25.95 each) two NE2000-compatible network cards. These don't need to be plug and play compatible (which will cost you a little more, most likely), but they should be software configurable (using a DOS-based configuration program that comes on a diskette from the card manufacturer).

Step 2. Get 25 feet or so of RG58 Thinnet Ethernet cable with BNC connectors on each end for less than $10.

Step 3. Install the cards in available slots in both of the computers. If one or both of the computers are portables, this is going to get a lot more expensive because you will need either a parallel port adapter or a docking station. (Too bad most portables don't have built-in Ethernet ports.)

Step 4. T-connectors and terminators come with the cards; use them to connect the cable to the T-connectors, the T-connectors to the cards, and the terminators to the other end of the T-connectors.

Step 5. If the cards aren't plug and play-compatible, run the DOS-based configuration software first to set up their interrupts and I/O addresses. The default values for the cards may be okay, depending on what hardware you have installed in your computers.

To find out which interrupts and I/O addresses are available on your computers, you can boot them, double-click the System icon in the Control Panel, click the Device Manager tab, and then highlight Computer and click the Properties button. Click the Input/output (I/O) option button to see what addresses are already used; used interrupts are shown first.

Reboot your computers and go to the DOS prompt by pressing the F8 key at bootup time and then run the DOS-based configuration software, or just open up a windowed DOS box and run the configuration software in it.

Setting Up a Quick and Dirty Network

Step 6. Double-click the Add New Hardware icon in the Control Panel on both computers. You can have the Add New Hardware Wizard search for your new adapters or you can specify what you have. The Wizard will load and configure the 32-bit protected-mode NDIS 3.1 driver for your adapters.

Step 7. Double-click the Network icon in the Control Panel. Highlight your adapter in the list of networking components. To see which networking protocols were bound to the adapter (in step 6), click the Properties button, and then click the Bindings tab. For a small computer network, you'll most likely want to bind either NetBEUI or IPX/SPX. If you need to bind a protocol, click the Add button in the Network dialog box, highlight Protocol, click the next Add button, and select the protocol in the Select Network Protocol dialog box.

Step 8. Make sure to allow sharing of your resources so either or both of the computers can be peer servers to the other. Make sure that Client for Microsoft Networks and file and printer sharing for Microsoft Networks are implemented in the Network dialog box. Add them if they aren't. (To add Client for Microsoft Networks, click Add, click Client, and click Add again. In the Select Network Client dialog box, highlight Microsoft on the left, and click Client for Microsoft Networks on the right. To add file and printer sharing for Microsoft Networks, click Add, click Service, and click Add again. In the Select Network Service dialog box, highlight Microsoft on the left, and click File and printer sharing for Microsoft Networks on the right.)

Step 9. Click the Identification tab in the Network dialog box. Make sure that both of the computers have different names, but the same workgroup name. Click OK.

Step 10. Click the OK button in the Network dialog box, and then reboot your computers for all of this to take effect.

Step 11. Open Explorer or folder windows on the Desktops of both computers. Right-click resources (disk drives and/or folders) that you want to share, click Sharing in the context menu, and configure the Sharing properties sheets. Do the same in the Printers folder for printers that you are going to share.

Step 12. Double-click the Network Neighborhood icon on the Desktop of one of the computers. You should see the name of the workgroup in the Network Neighborhood folder window. Double-click the workgroup name to see the name of the other computer. Double-click its name to see the shared resources.

If you need further elaboration and hand-holding for these steps, see the next section.

Network Installation

Windows 95 Setup can install Microsoft Networks or Microsoft's NetWare client software. It can also install the Windows 95 client software to work with other networks, but you should install the 16-bit real-mode network software from these other vendors before starting the Windows 95 setup process.

If you are at this moment setting up Windows 95 and you haven't yet installed the 16-bit network software from your other networking vendor (if you have one), click Cancel when you reach the network configuration dialog box, and restart the Windows 95 setup process after you install this software. Otherwise, you will have to configure the Windows 95 network components yourself, in addition to installing this third-party software.

If you do a Custom setup when you are setting up Windows 95 (this is what we recommend), you'll see the network configuration dialog box, as shown in Figure 36-1. This dialog box allows you to choose which network client to install, which network adapter to support, which networking protocol to bind to the adapter, and which networking services (for example, peer file and printer sharing) to offer.

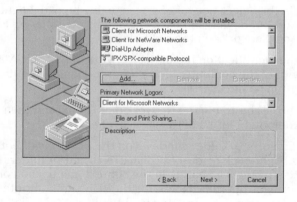

Figure 36-1: The network configuration dialog box. Click the Add button to install additional networking components.

If Windows 95 Setup has successfully detected your existing hardware and software network components, you don't need to make any changes in the network configuration dialog box. This is true even if the only network adapter you have installed is a serial or parallel port to use for Direct Cable Connection (DCC) or a modem to use for Dial-Up Networking (DUN). There are exceptions to this, however, as we discuss throughout this chapter.

If you add a network card or install networking software for networks other than Microsoft Networks or NetWare after you have installed Windows 95, you need to use the Network dialog box to install networking support. To display this dialog box, double-click the Network icon in the Control Panel. The Configuration tab of the Network dialog box looks a lot like the network configuration dialog box you see during Windows 95 Setup.

A network configuration consists of networking client software, software drivers for a given network adapter, a networking protocol, and networking services. To install any of these components, click the Add button in the Configuration tab of the Network dialog box to display the Select Network Component Type dialog box, as shown in Figure 36-2.

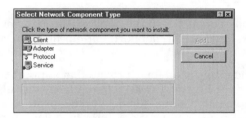

Figure 36-2: The Select Network Component Type dialog box.

Choosing a client

Highlight Client in the list box and click the Add button to display the Select Network Client dialog box, as shown in Figure 36-3. The 32-bit protected-mode clients for Microsoft Networks and NetWare Networks are provided by Microsoft on the Windows 95 source CD-ROM.

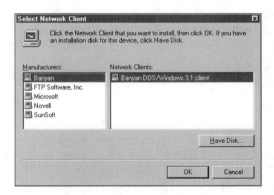

Figure 36-3: The Select Network Client dialog box. You can select a networking client from those provided on the Windows 95 source CD-ROM or find a client on another network vendor's diskette.

You can install one 16-bit real-mode networking client and up to 10 protected-mode clients. Only two 32-bit protected-mode clients are available from Microsoft — Client for Microsoft Networks and Client for NetWare Networks. If you install LANtastic, you can't install a protected-mode client.

If you install a 16-bit networking client only, you won't need to deal with the other networking components in this dialog box, because you will use the client software to specify how these items are configured.

If you install the Client for Microsoft Networks or NetWare Networks, you can add or change the network adapter, protocol, and network services.

Choosing an adapter

Your computer is physically connected to the network through your network adapter (card), your serial or parallel port, or your modem. Windows 95 installs adapter driver software that is specific to your network adapter.

Microsoft provides a broad range of adapter drivers that support the Network Device Interface Specification (NDIS) 3.1 standard. It is this standard that allows for multiple protected-mode networking protocols. Microsoft worked with all the major network adapter manufacturers to include adapter drivers for their cards.

The NDIS 3.1 specification supports Ethernet, Token Ring, and ArcNet networking cards and hot docking with plug and play adapters.

You can also use real-mode NDIS 2.*xx* and ODI (Open Datalink Interface) drivers that come (on diskettes) with pre-plug and play adapters if Microsoft hasn't provided a new NDIS 3.1 driver for your specific adapter.

The Windows 95 Setup hardware detection routines should have correctly determined which network adapter card is installed in your computer and its range of possible interrupt and I/O address settings. If you install a card after running Setup, or Setup didn't get it right, you can configure the adapter driver settings yourself. If you install a card after you install Windows 95, you may need to double-click the Add New Hardware icon in the Control Panel first to make Windows 95 find your network card. If you need to add an adapter driver, first take the following steps:

STEPS

Adding an Adapter Driver

Step 1.   Click the Add button in the Network dialog box or, during Windows 95 Setup, in the network configuration dialog box.

Step 2.   In the Select Network Component Type dialog box, highlight Adapter and click Add.

Adding an Adapter Driver

Step 3. In the Select Network Adapter dialog box, select an adapter manufacturer in the left-hand list and an adapter model in the right-hand list. Click OK twice.

If you use Direct Cable Connection (DCC) or Dial-Up Networking (DUN), you should add Microsoft's Dial-Up Adapter driver. The Dial-Up Adapter is the NDIS 3.1 driver for your serial or parallel port, or modem. DCC and DUN are real networking options and require full network configuration based on the Dial-Up Adapter.

See Chapters 28 and 29 for more details about these networking options.

Configuring resources for the adapter driver

Once you have told Windows 95 which network adapter you have physically installed, it will load the correct driver and determine the current hardware settings for your card. This is where it gets sticky, because Windows 95 may not correctly determine your network adapter's interrupt and I/O address settings. To determine which values Windows 95 has chosen, take the following steps:

STEPS

Determining Network Adapter Resource Values

Step 1. Highlight the network adapter in the Network dialog box or, during Windows 95 Setup, in the network configuration dialog box.

Step 2. Click the Properties button to display the Properties dialog box for your network adapter, and then click the Resources tab (see Figure 36-4).

Step 3. Compare the values in the Resources tab with the known values for the adapter card. If you don't know what those values are, you are going to have to accept the values in the dialog box for now.

(continued)

Determining Network Adapter Resource Values

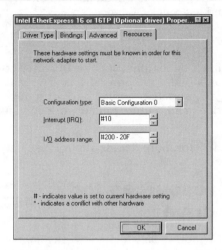

Figure 36-4: The Resources tab in a network adapter's Properties dialog box. During Windows 95 Setup, you can't change these values.

If you are going install Windows 95 over Windows for Workgroups 3.11, you can find the previous values for your network card by double-clicking the Network Setup icon in the Windows 3.*x* Program Manager. Windows 95 Setup will find these values (in the file Protocol.ini) and correctly configure the adapter driver to conform to the current card settings.

If you have a plug and play adapter, Windows 95 will configure it correctly. If you have a pre-plug and play adapter, you can change your adapter's settings either by changing jumpers on the adapter or by running configuration software provided by the manufacturer. The Resources tab for these pre-plug and play adapters (except for the Intel EtherExpress adapters) displays only possible settings for this adapter, not necessarily the actual current settings for the card. It is up to you to get the possible and the actual settings to match.

Windows 95 chooses possible adapter resource settings that don't conflict with other devices — if this is possible given the set of possible settings for the given adapter. If Windows 95 determines that a conflict exists (because all the possible settings of the adapter card conflict with other devices in your computer), it places an asterisk in the appropriate field in the Resources tab.

Secret

You can't change the resource settings during Windows 95 Setup, and this can be a source of some difficulty — especially if you are setting up Windows 95 over a network and through the adapter to which Windows 95 has now assigned the incorrect address or interrupt. Your CD-ROM drive might be connected to another computer on the network, for example. In this case, to complete the setup, Windows 95 will need to copy files over the network after the computer upon which you are installing Windows 95 has been rebooted and is running under Windows 95. But the network will no longer be available to this computer because the network adapter has been incorrectly configured — a little Catch-22.

The source files that may no longer be available include files Windows 95 needs to configure your modem, printer, and Windows Messaging. You will have to go back after you have correctly configured your network adapter and install these items separately, using the Printers folder, and the Modems icon and Add/Remove Programs icon (to configure Windows Messaging) in the Control Panel.

To get the adapter's settings to match the settings specified in the Resources tab of the Properties dialog box for your network adapter, you need to first complete as much of the Windows 95 setup process as you can, and then go back and change either the adapter or the settings in the Resources tab.

To change an adapter that uses jumpers: Turn off your computer, pull the card, move the jumpers to match the settings given in the Resources tab, reinstall the card, and restart Windows 95.

To change an adapter using the manufacturer's configuration software: Open a DOS window when Windows 95 restarts after Setup, and run the manufacturer's configuration software for the adapter. You'll need to restart Windows 95 after making these changes.

To change the resource settings to match the adapter's current settings, restart Windows 95, follow the steps earlier in this chapter entitled Determining Network Adapter Resource Values, and change the values to match your adapter's values. Then restart Windows 95 again.

Choosing a networking protocol

Individual computers have to speak the same language if you want them to talk to each other. The language they speak is the *networking protocol*. Microsoft provides 32-bit protected-mode implementations for three networking protocols: NetBEUI, IPX/SPX, and TCP/IP. You have to bind a networking protocol to the network adapter (or to multiple adapters) for the adapter and the protocol to work together to get the messages across the wire.

- NetBEUI (*NetBIOS extended user interface*) is Microsoft's fast, efficient, workgroup (non-routeable) protocol. It works great between Windows 95 computers and Windows for Workgroup 3.11, LAN Manager, and Windows NT workstations and servers.

- IPX/SPX *(Internetwork Packet Exchange)* is Novell NetWare's protocol, and therefore a standard for small- to medium-sized businesses and department-level networks. You can use this protocol to access both NetWare and Windows NT 3.5 servers (as well as Windows 95 computers). You can configure Windows 95 computers as NetWare file and print servers and address them through IPX/SPX. Microsoft's IPX/SPX-compatible protocol is the default for Windows 95.

- TCP/IP *(Transmission Control Protocol/Internet Protocol)* is the Unix and Internet standard protocol. It provides networking support to a broad range of computer operating systems — indeed, to all computers that can communicate over the Internet. Windows 95 includes a set of TCP/IP utilities, as described in Chapter 33. Internet addresses (which are assigned to each computer on the network) can be dynamically allocated because you can configure this version of TCP/IP to use the Dynamic Host Configuration Protocol (DHCP) or Windows Internet Naming Service (WINS). Microsoft also supplies a Winsock version 1.1 DLL, so Winsock-compliant Internet programs such as FTP Explorer, Netscape Navigator, and Internet mailers can work with TCP/IP.

Windows 95 supports protocols from other manufacturers in addition to the three provided by Microsoft.

To choose a protocol, take the following steps:

STEPS

Choosing a Protocol

Step 1.   Click the Add button in the Network dialog box or, during Windows 95 Setup, in the network configuration dialog box.

Step 2.   In the Select Network Component Type dialog box, highlight Protocol and click Add.

Step 3.   In the Select Network Protocol dialog box, select a manufacturer in the left-hand list and a protocol in the right-hand list. Click OK.

Choosing network services

Most network services — such as the ability to connect to remote computers and browse their disk drives — are available once you've configured your client, adapter, and protocol. Microsoft and other manufacturers provide additional network services. If you use Microsoft's clients for Microsoft or NetWare Networks, you can configure your computer to share its folders, drives, and/or printers with other users on the network. You can use tape-backup software running on a Windows NT or NetWare server to back up your files, and you can administer HP printers running on NetWare networks.

To add one or more of these services, take the following steps:

STEPS
Adding Network Services

Step 1. Click the Add button in the Network dialog box or, during Windows 95 Setup, in the network configuration dialog box.

Step 2. In the Select Network Component Type dialog box, highlight Service and click Add.

Step 3. In the Select Network Service dialog box, select a manufacturer in the left-hand list and the service in the right-hand list. Click OK.

Sharing your resources

You make your hard disk drives, folders, and printers available to others on the network by sharing them. Although sharing isn't always easy, in this case it is.

To share your folders or disk drives and printers using the network services provided on the Windows 95 source CD-ROM, you need to install either Client for Microsoft Networks or Client for NetWare Networks. In addition, you need to choose Microsoft as the manufacturer in step 3 of the Adding Network Services steps in the previous section, and either file and printer sharing for Microsoft Networks or file and printer sharing for NetWare Networks as the network service. For details on sharing a printer, turn to the *Sharing a Printer* section in Chapter 23.

You have three options for how you want to share your disk drives (or folders): Read-Only, Full, or Depends on Password (if your computer is set for share-level security). Full access allows users at other computers on the network to create files and folders on your drive. They can also delete or edit new or existing files and folders on your drive (or within a specific folder). If you are using user-level security, you can name the users who have access to your resources. (If you are a network administrator with remote administration privileges, you can determine who has access to which resources on a client computer.) We discuss user-level and share-level security in the *Network Security* section later in this chapter.

Read-Only access allows other users to view, but not change your files or folders. Depends on Passwords gives them either Full or Read-Only access depending on which privilege you or the network administrator has assigned to them.

If you share your disk drives or folders with only read-only access, other non-administrative users cannot delete your files and folders. If you don't share disk drives and folders at all, other users cannot see what you have on your computer.

Once you have chosen to turn on the ability to share, you still need to specify which resources you are going to share. Chapter 23 provides details on making your printer available across your network.

To share a folder or disk drive, take the following steps:

STEPS

Sharing a Folder or Drive

Step 1. In an Explorer window, right-click the icon for the drive or folder that you want to share.

Step 2. Click Sharing in the context menu to display the Sharing tab of the Properties dialog box for your drive or folder, as shown in Figure 36-5. (The Sharing option appears in the context menu only if you are on a network, have DCC configured, or have Dial-Up Networking (DUN), which lets you create connectoids to the Internet, MSN, and so on.)

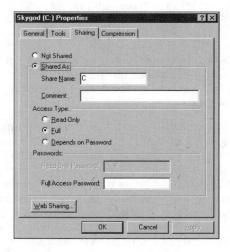

Figure 36-5: The Sharing tab in the Properties dialog box lets you set up share-level security. Choose Not Shared or Shared As. If you have configured your computer for user-level security, you will be able to specify which users can access your computer.

Step 3. To share your drive or folder, click Shared As.

Step 4. You can enter a new name for the resource as well as a comment to help other users understand what resource you're sharing.

Sharing a Folder or Drive

If you add a dollar sign to the end of the resource's share name, it is hidden from users who are using Network Neighborhood for network browsing. You might want to do this for your Microsoft Mail postoffice, which needs to be shared but not browsed.

Step 5. If your computer is configured for share-level security (most likely on a peer-to-peer network), you can set the access type (Read-Only or Full) and the password required to access your resource.

If your computer is configured for user-level security (you have a Windows NT or NetWare server on your network), you can specify who has access to your resources.

Step 6. Click OK.

If you've installed Internet Explorer 4.0 and Personal Web Server (http://www.microsoft.com/msdownload/personalweb.htm), you can click the Web Sharing button to specify what resources you are going to share via HTTP or FTP.

Primary Network Logon

If you display the Primary Network Logon drop-down list (either in the network configuration dialog box during a custom Windows 95 setup or in the Network dialog box accessed from the Control Panel), you'll see the following choices:

- Windows Logon
- Client for Microsoft Networks
- Client for NetWare Networks

Choose Windows Logon if you are not logging onto a network or are logging onto a peer-to-peer network. Choose one of the two clients if you are logging onto a network with either a Windows NT server or a NetWare server and have installed one or both of these clients.

File and Print Sharing

You can decide if you are going to share your printer(s), your folders and drives, or both. Click the File and Print Sharing button in the network configuration dialog box (during Windows 95 Setup) or the Network dialog box to make this choice.

Name that computer

During the Windows 95 setup process, you will be asked to give your computer a name. You will also need to enter the name of your local workgroup, as shown in Figure 36-6. The *workgroup name* is a name that a group of computers will share, and it defines them as an entity. Your computer name must be unique on your LAN.

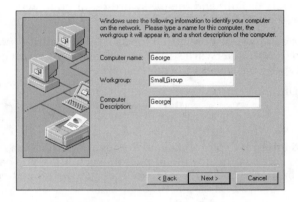

Figure 36-6: The identification dialog box you see during Setup. To display a similar properties sheet after you've installed Windows 95, double-click the Network icon in the Control Panel, and then click the Identification tab.

You must give your computer a name and specify a workgroup, no matter which networking software you are using. Your computer name can be as long as 15 characters, must contain no spaces, and can include only alpha-numeric characters and these special characters:

!@#$%^&()-_'{}.~

You also can enter a description of your computer up to 48 characters in length (no commas) to help other users on your network identify your computer.

You can change all of these values by double-clicking the Network icon in the Control Panel, and then clicking the Identification tab.

Microsoft Networks

You can install Client for Microsoft Networks to connect your Windows 95 computer with computers running Windows 95, Windows NT (versions 3.1 and 3.5*x*), LAN Manager, Windows for Workgroups 3.11, Workgroup Add-On for MS-DOS, as well as other Microsoft Networks-compatible networks. If you configure it as the Primary Network Logon client, you have the option to:

- Use a Windows NT server as a password server, which lets you configure user-level security (as opposed to share-level security, which is standard on peer-to-peer networks) and control it from the server

- Share your files and printer(s) with other network users

- Create user profiles, which you can use to set up different network connections and configurations for individual users

- Allow remote administration of the Registry on your computer

If you are installing Windows 95 on a computer that is running Windows for Workgroups 3.11 networking, Windows 95 Setup will automatically install Client for Microsoft Networks. Otherwise, you can install Client for Microsoft Networks using the procedure detailed in the *Network Installation* section earlier in this chapter, choosing Microsoft as the manufacturer in the Select Network Client dialog box.

If you install DCC and/or DUN (either during Windows 95 Setup or later using the Add/Remove Programs icon in the Control Panel), Client for Microsoft Networks and the Dial-Up Adapter are automatically installed.

Configuring your computer as Client for Microsoft Networks

If you are connecting your Windows 95 computer to other computers using Windows 95, Windows for Workgroups 3.11, or Workgroup Add-On for MS-DOS, you don't need to worry about logging onto a Windows NT domain for user-level security. This peer-to-peer networking scheme handles all security by assigning passwords to resources (share-level security). You can choose to reconnect to the resources that are shared on your network at startup time, or later when you actually browse the shared folders on another computer or print to a printer connected to another computer.

If you have a Windows NT computer on your Microsoft network, you may need to log onto it if you want to have access to network resources. If the Windows NT server has been configured to provide user-level security, shared resources on other peer servers (Windows 95 computers that are running file and printer sharing for Microsoft Networks) are available to you after you enter your user password.

To configure your Windows 95 computer to Client for Microsoft Networks (either during or after Windows 95 Setup), take the following steps:

STEPS

Configuring Client for Microsoft Networks

Step 1. Highlight Client for Microsoft Networks, either in the network configuration dialog box during Windows 95 Setup or in the Configuration tab of the Network dialog box. Click the Properties button to display the General tab of the Client for Microsoft Networks Properties dialog box, as shown in Figure 36-7.

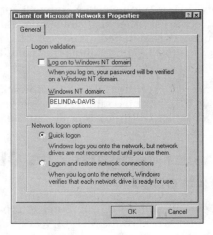

Figure 36-7: The General tab of the Client for Microsoft Networks Properties dialog box.

Step 2. To use a networked Windows NT server for logon validation, mark the Log on to Windows NT domain checkbox.

Step 3. To log onto your Microsoft network and delay connecting to network resources until you need them (if you have previously established a persistent network connection), mark the Quick logon option button.

You can establish a persistent network connection for shared folders and disk drives by checking the Reconnect at Logon check box in the Map Network Drive dialog box (choose Tools, Map Network Drive in the Explorer). For printers, check Reconnect at Logon in the Capture Printer Port dialog box (right-click a printer icon, choose Properties, click Details, and click the Capture Printer Port button).

Step 4. To establish a connection at startup with all the shared network resources with which you have previously specified a persistent connection, click Logon and restore network connections.

Step 5. Click OK.

Configuring a Microsoft Networking protocol

Client for Microsoft Networks can work with any of the three protocols provided by Microsoft. NetBEUI is the default protocol for communication among computers running Windows 95, Windows for Workgroups 3.11, Windows NT, LAN Manager, and Microsoft Workgroup Add-On for MS-DOS. However, you can also use IPX/SPX and TCP/IP to communicate with other Windows 95 and Windows NT computers.

Intranets are based on the TCP/IP protocol. If you are setting up Windows NT and Windows 95 web servers, then you should use TCP/IP as your networking protocol. You can use multiple protocols over your network, but it will run faster if you stick to one.

Undocumented

For Microsoft Networking, you only need NetBEUI. NetBEUI and IPX/SPX are the only protocols that route through the Windows 95 DUN server and allow you to see LAN resources beyond it. TCP/IP works between the DUN server and the dial-up client, but it doesn't allow access to any TCP/IP resources on the LAN beyond the server.

Highlight the protocol (or any of the protocols you've selected to work with your network adapter) in the Network dialog box and then click the Properties button. Click the Bindings tab, and then check Client for Microsoft Networks to bind it to the chosen protocol, as shown in Figure 36-8.

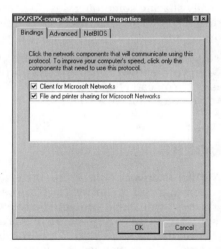

Figure 36-8: The Bindings tab in the Properties dialog box for a protocol. Mark the check boxes for the network components that you want to bind to this protocol.

Diagnosing Microsoft Networking problems

If you are having problems communicating from or to a Windows 95 computer that is attached to a Microsoft network, you might check in a couple of different areas:

1. Make sure that file and printer sharing for Microsoft Networks is part of your network configuration by double-clicking the Network icon in the Control Panel. Click the File and Print Sharing button, and make sure that you have enabled sharing by marking one or both of the File and Print Sharing check boxes).

2. Highlight File and printer sharing for Microsoft Networks in the Network dialog box, and click the Properties button. Set Browse Master to Enable, and LM Announce to Yes.

3. If you are using the IPX/SPX protocol, highlight that network component in the Network dialog box, click Properties, click the Advanced tab, click Frame, and be sure that the frame type value is set to the frame type that is used on your network. If you are communicating with WFWG 3.11 computers, you may want to set it to 802.3, for example.

4. Click the Identification tab in the Network dialog box, and carefully check your computer name to make sure that it is unique. Also verify that the workgroup name is the same as the workgroup name for the other computers in your workgroup, and confirm that there are no spaces in the names.

5. Make sure that you are actually sharing something. Just because you've enabled the ability to share, doesn't mean you have. Right-click a folder or drive icon in your Explorer, and click Sharing.

6. Check your network card setup in the Device Manager. There may be an unrecognized conflict between your network card and I/O port COM2. Disable COM2 to check this out. You can change the resources used by the network card later, if you do indeed have a conflict.

Novell NetWare Networks

Microsoft doesn't supply the NetWare network operating system software. That is, it doesn't provide the operating system for the NetWare server. That's Novell's job. Microsoft does provide 32-bit protected-mode versions of NetWare-compatible client software, the IPX/SPX-compatible protocol, and NDIS 3.1 adapter drivers. These drivers allow your Windows 95 computer to connect to a NetWare server. The server can be running Novell NetWare versions 2.15 or later, 3.x, or 4.x. You won't need to run any of the real-mode software from Novell to turn your computer into a NetWare-compatible client (or NetWare-compatible file and print server).

Novell offers two NetWare clients — NETX (for NetWare 3.x) and VLM (for NetWare 4.x). Windows 95 supports these two 16-bit real-mode clients, and you can use them instead of the Microsoft Client for NetWare Networks. There is no benefit to using the NETX client. VLM (Virtual Load Module) provides access to NetWare Directory Services (NDS), an enterprise-wide naming service that makes it simpler for you to manage user access to a wide range of network resources. Microsoft provides NDS access in an updated version of Client for NetWare Networks, which is included in Windows 95 beginning with Service Pack 1. If you have a pre-Service Pack 1 version of Windows 95, you can download the updated Client for NetWare Networks from Microsoft's web site at http://www.microsoft.com/windows/software.html.

Client for NetWare Networks goes naturally with Microsoft's 32-bit protected-mode IPX/SPX-compatible protocol and NDIS 3.1 adapter driver. If you choose to install it, these components are automatically configured and installed with it. You can use your existing real-mode ODI adapter drivers and Novell-supplied IPX/SPX protocol stack with Client for NetWare Networks if you want to run TSRs that absolutely require Novell's implementation of IPX/SPX.

Because Windows 95 computers can connect to NetWare networks using so many different configurations, you can try different combinations to see what difference the combinations make. It is very easy to go from one to the other, so you don't need to worry about causing problems if you start with something and change it later.

To install Client for NetWare Networks, use the procedure detailed in the *Network Installation* section earlier in this chapter. Choose Microsoft as the manufacturer in the Select Network Client dialog box, and select Client for NetWare Networks in the Network Clients list box.

Configuring your computer as Client for NetWare Networks

Client for NetWare Networks is automatically installed and configured if you install Windows 95 in the Windows directory of a computer configured correctly as a Novell NetWare client. Log onto a NetWare server before you install Windows 95 to make sure that everything gets configured correctly.

To configure your Windows 95 computer to Client for NetWare Networks (either during or after Windows 95 Setup), take the following steps:

STEPS

Configuring Client for NetWare Networks

Step 1.   Highlight Client for NetWare Networks, either in the network configuration dialog box during Windows 95 Setup, or in the Configuration tab of the Network dialog box. Click the Properties button. The General tab of the Client for NetWare Networks Properties dialog box will be displayed, as shown in Figure 36-9.

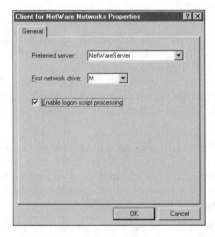

Figure 36-9: The General tab of the Client for NetWare Networks Properties dialog box. Type the UNC name of the NetWare server that you will log onto first.

Step 2.   Enter the UNC name of your preferred NetWare server. (See the section *The Universal Naming Convention (UNC)* later in this chapter for information on the UNC naming convention.)

Step 3.   Enter the volume designation letter for your first network connection.

Step 4.   If you want to process a NetWare logon script, click Enable logon script processing.

Step 5.   Click OK.

Using a Windows 95 computer as a NetWare file and print server

The Microsoft file and printer sharing for NetWare Networks software allows your Windows 95 computer to become a NetWare file and print server on a NetWare network. If you use this software, a Windows 95 computer can perform file and print services as if it were a NetWare server, and you can add Windows 95 peer servers to your network without purchasing additional NetWare licenses. For a Windows 95 computer to be a NetWare file and print server, you have at least one NetWare server on your NetWare network.

Configuring the IPX/SPX-compatible protocol

If you are using Microsoft's IPX/SPX-compatible protocol, you can configure it (or any of the Microsoft-supplied networking protocols) using the Network dialog box or the network configuration dialog box. Just highlight the protocol and click the Properties button.

Configuring the adapter driver

Highlight your network adapter in the network configuration dialog box (during Windows 95 Setup) or the Network dialog box and click the Properties button. You have the choice of three adapter driver types:

- Enhanced-mode (32-bit and 16-bit) NDIS driver (NDIS 3.1)
- Real-mode (16-bit) NDIS driver (NDIS 2.x)
- Real-mode (16-bit) ODI driver

The default adapter driver selected automatically when you choose Client for NetWare Networks or Client for Microsoft Networks is the NDIS 3.1 driver. The IPX/SPX-compatible networking protocol will be bound to this adapter. Click the Bindings tab to see which protocols are bound to your adapter.

The adapter's interrupt and I/O address are listed in the Resources tab of the network adapter's Properties dialog box (highlight the adapter in the Network dialog box and click the Properties button). For additional information, see the section earlier in this chapter entitled *Configuring resources for the adapter driver*.

The properties displayed in the Advanced tab of the Properties dialog box for the adapter depend on the specific adapter.

Logging onto the Network

If you are connected to a network using a 16-bit real-mode driver, a network logon prompt appears on your screen in text mode before the Windows 95 Desktop is displayed. You need to log on before Windows 95 starts.

If you have installed Client for Microsoft Networks or Client for NetWare Networks, separate logon dialog boxes appear the first time that you restart Windows 95. You will also see a logon dialog box for logging onto your own computer — pretty rude, actually.

If you use the same password in all the logon dialog boxes, the next time you start Windows 95, you will be presented with one "unified" logon dialog box. The only way this is going to work is if you have the same password for your logon to your primary NetWare server, to your Windows NT server, and to your own computer.

If you are logging onto a Microsoft network without a Windows NT server (for example, connecting to other Windows 95 and WFWG 3.11 computers), you won't be faced with a Microsoft Networks logon dialog box. Resources on peer-to-peer networks are protected with passwords that are unique to the resources, not to the users (if the resources are protected at all). You need to configure your logon correctly using the steps outlined earlier in this chapter in the section entitled *Configuring your computer as Client for Microsoft Networks*.

Passwords for resources that are protected by share-level (peer-to peer) security are encrypted and remembered in the *password cache*, a file stored on your Windows 95 computer. They are retrieved from the password cache after the first time you successfully log onto a shared network resource, so you don't have to enter the password for a resource again. You (or your network administrator) can configure your computer so passwords aren't cached and you have to enter them anew each time you access a resource or server that requires a password.

If you have the original version of Windows 95, you should download at least the Service Pack 1 upgrade that fixes problems with lax password security. You'll find the specific password upgrade as well as the entire Service Pack 1 at http://www.microsoft.com/windows/software/servpak1/sphome.htm.

If you have configured your Windows 95 computer to enable user profiles, you will always have to (at least) negotiate with the Windows 95 logon dialog box. To enable user profiles, double-click the Passwords icon in the Control Panel, click the User Profiles tab, and then click "Users can customize their preferences and desktop settings." Your password can be blank.

You can log onto the network without seeing a logon dialog box if you disable user profiles, select Windows Logon as the primary network logon in the Network dialog box, use a blank password, and your passwords for logging onto your NetWare or Windows NT server are also blank. This is also the case if you are logging onto a Microsoft peer-to-peer network under these conditions.

The great Windows 95 innovation is to cache your various passwords, so that you only need one logon dialog box to log onto a network (if you do it right), no matter whether it is a peer-to-peer network, a NetWare network, or a Microsoft network with a Windows NT server.

Your passwords are stored in an encrypted file, Share.pwl, referred to as a *password cache*. If you delete this file, you lose access to password-protected resources and servers.

You can change some passwords by double-clicking the Passwords icon in the Control Panel. You can also use the Password List Editor, a utility that comes with Windows 95, to manage your passwords. This utility doesn't let you change passwords, but it does let you delete passwords from your password cache. You might use the Password List Editor to get rid of passwords that you aren't using anymore, or, if you are a network administrator, to disallow access to some resources or servers whose passwords were previously cached.

You'll find the Password List Editor on the Windows 95 source CD-ROM in the \Admin\Apptools\Pwledit folder. You can use the Add/Remove Programs icon in the Control Panel to install it. Click the Windows Setup tab, click the Have Disk button, and type the pathname in the Install From Disk dialog box.

If you like, you can also set the minimum length required for a password to be valid. You'll need to edit the Registry to do this.

STEPS

Setting the Minimum Password Length

Step 1.   Double-click Regedit.exe in the \Windows folder.

Step 2.   Navigate to HKEY_LOCAL_MACHINE\SOFTWARE\Microsoft\Windows\CurrentVersion\Policies\Network.

Step 3.   With the Network key highlighted, right-click the right pane of the Registry editor, and choose New, Binary Value. Name the binary value **MinPwdLen**.

Step 4.   Double-click MinPwdLen. Give it a value that you want for your minimum password length. Click OK.

The Network Neighborhood

The servers and shared resources on the network are made visible through the Network Neighborhood. You can display the Network Neighborhood folder window by double-clicking this icon on the Desktop or by clicking it in an Explorer window. You'll also find the Network Neighborhood icon in common dialog boxes (such as the File Open dialog box) used by 32-bit Windows 95-aware applications such as WordPad and MS Paint.

You can click the Map Network Drive button in the Explorer or folder window toolbar (or choose Tools, Map Network Drive in the Explorer) to give a volume drive-letter designation to a server, a shared folder, or a shared drive. You can likewise map a network printer to an LPT port using the Capture Printer Port dialog box, which you access through the Details tab of the Properties dialog box for a network printer. (Right-click a printer icon in the Printers folder, click Properties, click the Details tab, and then click the Capture Printer Port button.)

The Network Neighborhood bridges the chasm between your computer and the network. You browse the network in the same manner that you browse your own computer. There isn't a different interface.

Microsoft hasn't written extensions to the Explorer that allow it to display file listings from Unix computers (which are prevalent on the Internet) in a manner consistent with the display of file listings on Windows 95 computers. Spry, the company that wrote Internet-in-a-Box, wrote a File Manager-like Internet (Winsock-compatible client) application that let you display files on other systems in a manner that mimicked the Windows 3.*x* File Manager.

Windows 95 integrates your computer and the network by making files and printers on other computers look and feel the same as local resources.

In Windows 95, unlike in Windows 3.*x*, you do not have to map a network drive to be able to see and use the files on that drive. As long as the file is displayed in your Explorer or folder window, it is available to you. You can run programs (you may need to make other adjustments in the program's configuration) and edit documents that reside on another computer without mapping that computer's disk drive to a logical drive letter.

The Universal Naming Convention (UNC)

Every computer and server on your network has a name. You provided a name for your computer when you installed Windows 95.

You refer to other computers and resources on the network by their names. For example, \\Billscomputer\Cdrive\Mystuff refers to another computer (Billscomputer) that is sharing a resource, the hard disk drive named Cdrive (most likely the C:\ drive on Bill's computer), and a folder found on that drive.

This way of referring to servers or computers that are sharing their resources is called the *universal naming convention* (UNC). You use two backslashes before the computer's name, a single backslash between the name of the computer and the name of the shared resource (a hard disk drive, in this example), and a single backslash between the name of the shared resource and the folder.

You can also use this convention to refer to networked printers. (You assign a name to each networked printer.) To see how to assign a name to a printer, turn to the *Installing a Printer Driver* section of Chapter 23.

Resource Sharing

The resources on your computer — printers, folders, drives, CD-ROMs — are accessible to other users over your network if you enable file and printer sharing through the Network dialog box or the network configuration dialog box (during Windows 95 Setup). This peer-to-peer resource sharing requires that you use Client for Microsoft Networks, Client for NetWare Networks, or both. Other users on your network who want to access your resources must be running the matching client as well as the same network protocol.

You don't have to share resources that are connected to individual computers with other computers on the network. You could set up the network so that your network servers are the only computers that have resources available to other users.

If your network is a peer-to-peer network — one without a server — then the only way individual users can access network resources is to share them. Not every computer needs to share its resources, and every computer that does becomes a peer server.

Network Security

Security issues affect all aspects of life on a computer network. As a user, you don't want others — whatever authority they hold over you — messing about with your files and programs. If you are a network administrator, you want to be able to allow people to use resources that are available on the network, no matter whose computer they are connected to. You also want to be able to install software on client computers from your computer. Users and administrators alike want to make sure that someone calling in from outside the network can't download private information from their computers or from the network.

You maintain network security by restricting access to network resources. You can restrict access by assigning passwords to resources or by maintaining lists of authorized users (who are assigned passwords). Your computer is quite secure if you:

- Don't share any resources
- Don't enable remote administration
- Don't enable the Windows 95 Dial-Up Server (a component of Microsoft Plus! and ISDN Accelerator Pack 1.1)
- Require a logon password to your computer
- Don't allow others physical access to your computer

If you allow any form of access to your computer, you need to provide some security measures to restrict that access.

Windows 95 computers are not completely secure. Even if you require a password to access Windows 95, anyone can press F8 at bootup time to boot your computer in Safe mode, and then make a choice from the menu that appears.

You can disallow the use of F8 by putting the statement BootKeys=0 in your Msdos.sys file.

Choosing between two kinds of security

Windows 95 provides two different kinds of security. The first is *share-level security,* which is used on peer-to-peer networks, for example, when you network Windows 95 computers together. Share-level security is also available in Windows for Workgroups 3.1*x* and other peer-to-peer Microsoft Networks-compatible networks. The second is *user-level security,* which requires a Windows NT or NetWare server.

You enforce share-level security by attaching passwords to each shared folder, disk drive, and printer. You enforce user-level security by maintaining lists of users on a Windows NT or NetWare server. You can mix both types of security on the same network, as long as you have a Windows NT or NetWare server to maintain user-level security.

Each Windows 95 peer server stores a list of shared resources on that computer, along with the accompanying passwords. The list of users allowed access to shared resources on a particular Windows 95 computer on the network is stored on the Windows NT or NetWare server.

A network administrator with the remote administration password can set up the list of users and passwords for shared resources on any of the client Windows 95 computers on the network, as long as they are configured for remote administration.

Share-level security

Armed with a remote administration password for each computer and for each shared resource, a network administrator in a share-level security system (for example, a peer-to-peer Microsoft Network with no Windows NT server) has some administrative control over the computers on the network. In this type of setup, the network administrator maintains security by managing the peer servers (that is, the Windows 95 computers with shared resources).

In a share-level security system, a remote administration password protects your computer. If someone (an officially designated network administrator or not) has that password, he or she can create, add, or delete shared resources on your computer. If you change the remote administration password, that person loses administrative access until you provide the new password. As a network administrator, you would normally store all the remote administration passwords for the computers you administer in a cached file on your computer.

If your network does not have a Windows NT or NetWare server, your security options are simple — you use share-level security. Share-level security is not available on computers running file and printer sharing for NetWare Networks.

User-level security

A network administrator who has been given remote administration authority can grant access to the resources on your computer to other users and administrative access to other system administrators. The names of the users and administrators are kept on the Windows NT or NetWare server.

Administrators who have remote administration authority over your computer can carry out any of the administrative-access actions detailed later in this chapter in the section entitled *Network Administration*. They can edit your Registry, customize your computer's configuration and Desktop, edit your password list, and monitor system performance. They can also add or remove other remote administrators.

User-level security is required in order to use the network management tools (other than Net Watcher) that come with Windows 95, and those available from third parties. The tools that come with Windows 95 are described in the *Network Administration* section later in this chapter.

Setting the type of security

It is not a good idea to switch back and forth between share-level and user-level security. Choose one, or follow the guidelines of your network administrator, and stay with it.

STEPS

Setting the Type of Security

Step 1. Double-click the Network icon in the Control Panel. Click the Access Control tab in the Network dialog box, as shown in Figure 36-10.

Step 2. Click either Share-level access control or User-level access control.

Step 3. If you choose User-level access control, enter the name of the server or the domain that stores the list of users who have access to your resources.

(continued)

Setting the Type of Security

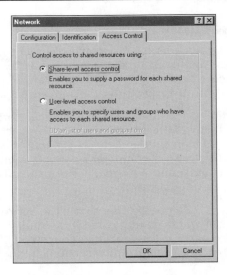

Figure 36-10: The Access Control tab of the Network dialog box.

Step 4. Ignore messages about being unable to find the security provider. If you are asked for Authenticator type, enter Server or Domain, depending on which one you are using.

Step 5. Click OK. Restart your computer.

Network Administration

Windows 95 comes with four network management tools: System Policy Editor, Registry editor, System Monitor, and Net Watcher. Only Net Watcher can be used on a peer-to-peer network to remotely administer shared resources on a peer server. The other tools require a Windows NT or NetWare server, the designation of user-level security on the computers to be administered, and the installation of Microsoft Remote Registry Service on Windows 95 client computers as well as on the network administrator's computer.

Using Net Watcher, a network administrator can:

■ Determine which clients are connected to any peer server on the network

■ Disconnect any clients from any peer server

- View which resources any peer server is sharing
- Change the share attributes of any resource on a peer server
- Start/stop sharing any peer server resource
- Determine which files are open on a peer server
- Close open files on a peer server

Because a network administrator can use Net Watcher to create, add, or change the properties of a shared resource, he or she can edit and delete files, as well as create new ones on any disk drive on your computer, even on drives that you have specified as read-only. The network administrator can install new software on your computer while sitting at his or her computer.

You have the ability to determine which disk drives, folders, and printers are shared on your computer; a network administrator with the remote administration password has the same ability.

A network administrator can use System Policy Editor to change many Registry settings and customize the Desktops of remote Windows 95 computers. Of course, you can also use System Policy Editor locally to customize your own Windows 95 computer without having to go through the network.

You can use the Registry editor locally to edit your own Registry, or remotely to edit other people's Registries. It is covered in detail in Chapter 15. If you want to connect to (and possibly edit) a Registry on a remote Windows 95 computer, choose Registry, Connect Network Registry in the Registry editor. Many of the changes you can make to a computer's Registry don't take effect until that computer is rebooted.

You can use the System Monitor both locally and remotely to get information about computer performance.

Enable remote administration

You can enable remote administration on a computer with either user-level or share-level security. If you have implemented user-level security on your Windows 95 computer as described in the *Setting the type of security* section, remote administration is automatically enabled.

To enable remote administration of a Windows 95 computer, take the following steps:

STEPS

Configuring Your Computer for Remote Administration

Step 1.   Double-click the Passwords icon in the Control Panel. Click the Remote Administration tab in the Passwords Properties dialog box, as shown in Figure 36-11.

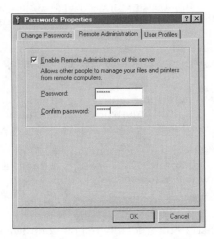

Figure 36-11: The Remote Administration tab of the Passwords Properties dialog box. Mark the Enable Remote Administration of this server check box and type a password to allow a network administrator to remotely administer your computer.

Step 2.   Click Enable Remote Administration of this server.

Step 3.   If the computer is configured for share-level security, enter a password.

If, instead, the computer is configured for user-level security, click the Add button and enter the names of the administrators. (The Add button isn't shown in Figure 36-11. If you have enabled user-level security, it will be displayed.)

Step 4.   Click OK.

You can enable remote administration as part of the Windows 95 setup process by editing the MSBatch.inf file. Refer to Bob Cerelli's Windows 95 home page at http://www.halcyon.com/cerelli/admin.htm for more details.

Install Remote Registry services

If you are going to allow a network administrator to edit your Registry using System Policy Editor and/or the Registry editor, or allow him or her to monitor the performance of your computer with System Monitor, you need to install Microsoft Remote Registry Service. Of course, if the administrator has your remote administration password, he or she can take these steps for you. You don't need to install Remote Registry Service unless you have enabled user-level security on your computer, because none of these network management tools work with share-level security. To install Remote Registry Service, take the following steps:

STEPS

Installing Microsoft Remote Registry Service

Step 1. Double-click the Network icon in the Control Panel. Click the Add button, and in the Select Network Component Type dialog box, click Service, and then click the Add button.

Step 2. Click the Have Disk button.

Step 3. Click the Browse button, and browse to the \Admin\Nettools\Remotreg folder on the Windows 95 source CD-ROM. Regsrv.inf will be highlighted. Click OK.

Step 4. Highlight Microsoft Remote Registry and click OK. Restart your computer.

Install Remote Registry Service on the network administrator's computer also. And keep in mind that the administrator's computer and the client computer must share a common networking protocol — and it must be one of the three from Microsoft.

Net Watcher

If you have multiple peer servers on the network, you can run multiple copies of Net Watcher to continuously keep track of them all. You can use Net Watcher to administer all peer servers that have been configured for remote administration, and you can use it to administer your own computer if it is a peer server (that is, if you are running file and printer sharing for Microsoft or NetWare Networks).

If your computer is using share-level security and file and printer sharing for Microsoft Networks, you can use Net Watcher to administer only other computers of the same configuration. If your computer is configured for user-level security and file and printer sharing for Microsoft Networks, you can use Net Watcher to administer other computers running file and printer sharing for Microsoft Networks irrespective of their security scheme. If you are running file and printer sharing for NetWare Networks, you can only administer peer servers that are also running it.

Net Watcher provides three different views of a peer server. The default view is Connections view, which displays the user connections to the peer server. Shared Folders view displays the resources that are shared on the server, and Open Files view displays the files that are open on the server.

You can install Net Watcher during Windows 95 Setup if you do a Custom setup and click the Net Watcher check box under Accessories in the Select Components dialog box. You can also install it later using the Windows Setup tab in the Add/Remove Programs Properties dialog box (double-click the Add/Remove Programs icon in the Control Panel).

To run Net Watcher after it is installed, click Net Watcher in the Programs, Accessories, System Tools menu. When Net Watcher first starts, it is focused on your computer. To administer another peer server, click the Select Server button at the left end of the Net Watcher toolbar (see Figure 36-12).

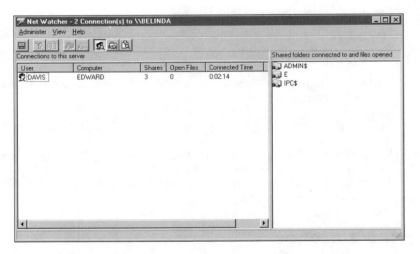

Figure 36-12: The Net Watcher with the default Connections and details views turned on.

Disconnecting users from a peer server

To disconnect a user from a peer server, highlight the user and click the Disconnect User button (the second button from the left) on the Net Watcher toolbar.

Changing or adding sharing on a peer server

You can share resources that aren't currently being shared on a peer server, change the share properties of an existing shared resource, or quit sharing.

STEPS

Changing Sharing on a Peer Server

Step 1. Click the Show Shared Folders button (the second from the right) in the Net Watcher toolbar to switch to the Shared Folders view. This view displays both shared printers and folders, as shown in Figure 36-13, despite its name.

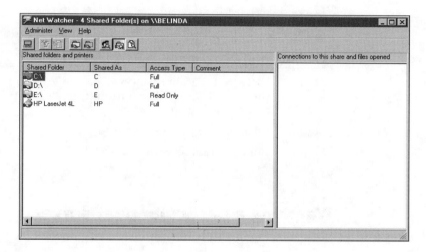

Figure 36-13: Net Watcher in Shared Folders view.

Step 2. Highlight the name of the resource whose sharing properties you want to modify.

Step 3. Press Alt+Enter. The Properties dialog box for this resource appears on your Desktop. You can choose Not Shared to quit sharing the resource, change sharing to Full, Read-Only, or Depends on Password, and change the passwords required to access the resources.

If the peer server uses user-level security, you can change the names of the users who can access that resource.

Step 4. Click OK.

You can also stop sharing a resource by highlighting it in the Shared Folders view, and choosing Administer, Stop Sharing Folder.

To turn the peer server into a shared resource, choose Administer, Add Shared Folder. Click the Browse button in the Enter path dialog box to display the resources on the peer server.

Dealing with open files

You can determine which files are open and close them if you need to. You might want to do this if a client computer is hung with an open file on the peer server.

STEPS

Closing an Open File on a Peer Server

Step 1.   In the Net Watcher window, choose View, by Open Files, or click the Show Files toolbar button (it looks like two pieces of paper and a magnifying glass).

Step 2.   Click the file that you want to close.

Step 3.   Choose Administrator, Close File.

Watching a particular peer server

You can set up multiple Net Watcher icons, one for each server.

STEPS

Watching Multiple Peer Servers

Step 1.   In an Explorer window, click Network Neighborhood.

Step 2.   Click the Entire Network icon, one of your workgroups, or the icon for the computer that you want to administer.

Step 3.   Right-click the computer icon for the peer server that you want to track with Net Watcher. Click Properties in the context menu. Click the Tools tab (see Figure 36-14).

Watching Multiple Peer Servers

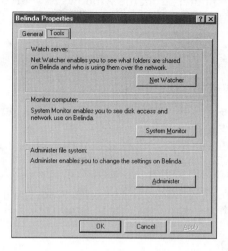

Figure 36-14: The Tools tab of the Properties dialog box for a peer server.

Step 4. Click the Net Watcher button.

Step 5. Continue doing this for as many peer servers as you want to track.

You can also browse for a peer server in Net Watcher by choosing Administer, Select Server.

System Policy Editor

System Policy Editor is a friendly front end to a number of user and computer configuration values stored in the Registry. You can use it to remove the Shut Down, Settings, and Run commands from the users' Start menus; get the Network Neighborhood icon off of the Desktop; remove a number of Control Panel icons, including System, Display, and Network; require validation from a network server for access to the local computer; disable password caching; disable dial-in from Dial-Up Networking; disallow print and/or file sharing; and so on.

You can define system policies for a given user and computer, or for similar groups of users. You can store these policies on a Windows NT or NetWare server, download them at logon time to an individual computer, and use them to modify the Registry settings. Storing the system policies on a server protects them from tampering.

You install System Policy Editor (on your computer or on the network administrator's computer) from the Windows 95 source CD-ROM. Take the following steps:

STEPS

Installing System Policy Editor

Step 1. Double-click the Add/Remove Programs icon in the Control Panel and then click the Windows Setup tab.

Step 2. Click the Have Disk button, and then click Browse. In the Open dialog box, browse to the folder \Admin\Apptools\Poledit on your Windows 95 source CD-ROM, and click OK.

Step 3. Click the OK button in the Install From File dialog box, and then click the check boxes next to Group policies and System Policy Editor in the Have Disk dialog box. Click the Install button.

Step 4. Click OK.

System Policy Editor is installed and its shortcut is now in the System Tools menu (under Start, Programs, Accessories).

To allow System Policy Editor to create group policies, each client Windows 95 computer needs to have the Grouppol.dll file in its \Windows\System folder. Take the steps above on each client computer, but only install Group policies.

Registry editor

To edit the Registry resident on another Windows 95 computer, choose Registry, Connect Network Registry in the Registry editor. You can then browse to find the computer whose Registry you wish to edit. The Registry editor is discussed in detail in Chapter 15.

System Monitor

The source files for the System Monitor are not stuck in some obscure folder on the Windows 95 CD-ROM, but you do need to click its check box in the Accessories dialog box during Windows 95 Setup if you want it installed (assuming you specified a Custom setup). You can also add it later using the the Windows Setup tab in the Add/Remove Programs Properties dialog box (double-click the Add/Remove Programs icon in the Control Panel).

You'll find the System Monitor in the Start, Programs, Accessories, System Tools menu. To connect System Monitor to another computer (or to connect multiple copies of System Monitor to monitor multiple computers) choose File, Connect in the System Monitor.

Network Applications

Microsoft still supplies network applications that let you do more than just share resources and administer the network. Windows Messaging (see Chapter 32) lets you send e-mail (and attachments) to anyone on your network. You can also share a fax modem over a network using Windows Messaging.

You can install WinPopup — a utility that broadcasts or sends messages and pops up when a job that you have sent to the network printer is complete — during Windows 95 Setup. (If you want to install it later, double-click Add/Remove Programs in the Control Panel, click the Windows Setup tab, highlight Accessories, click Details, mark the WinPopup check box, and click OK twice.)

WinChat, a precursor of NetMeeting, enables you to connect to other computers on the Internet and send chat messages back and forth. It is stored in the \Other\Chat folder on the Windows 95 CD-ROM. Clipbook (for network sharing of the Clipboard) is also in the \Other folder.

If you want to install and use WinChat, take the following steps:

STEPS

Installing and Using WinChat

Step 1.   Open in your Explorer the \Other\Chat folder on your Windows 95 CD-ROM. Right-click Winchat.inf and click Install.

Step 2.   Drag Netdde.exe from your \Windows folder to your \Windows\Start Menu\Programs\Startup folder. Double-click the shortcut to Netdde.exe in your Startup folder. You only need this shortcut in your Startup folder if you are going to configure your computer to allow others to call you with WinChat. You can call others without running Netdde.exe first.

Step 3.   Double-click Winchat.exe (or make a shortcut to it on your Desktop and double-click that). Type the UNC name of the computer to which you are networked.

To use WinChat over the Internet as though the Internet were a network (which it is), you need to know the IP address of the computer you are going to be chatting with, and that computer has to be running WinChat. If the remote computer has a dynamically assigned IP address, you'll need to have your chatee send you an e-mail message with the computer's current (that is, right this minute) address. If your computer's IP address is dynamically assigned by your service provider when you log in, you need to find out what your current IP address is and send it off to your chatee. To do this, log onto your service provider, click the Start button, click Run, and then type **nbtstat -n**. Your IP address is the first one listed.

You'll also have to edit your Lmhosts file to add the IP address if you don't already have it in there. If you are logging onto a WINS server over the Internet (not the normal course of things) and your chatee has a static IP address that is in the WINS table, you'll be able to connect to your chatee's computer.

To connect to the other computer, just type the remote computer's NetBIOS name (you'll see the list of NetBIOS names once you're connected) preceded by two backslashes (\\), and press Enter. You can connect to multiple remote computers at the same time by repeating this process for each computer. Once you're connected, two-way communication can take place.

Summary

We show you how to turn your Windows 95 computer into a networking client or peer server so that it can share resources with other computer users on your network.

▶ You can build a great little two-computer network for $60.

▶ Windows 95 will work with your existing 16-bit real-mode network.

▶ Windows 95 comes with 32-bit protected-mode networking clients, protocols, and adapter drivers, which reduces the load on conventional memory.

▶ It is a lot easier to configure pre-plug and play network adapters using built-in Windows 95 hardware detection and the Device Manager.

▶ You can turn a Windows 95 computer into a full- or part-time (shared) NetWare file and print server.

▶ You can configure Windows 95 as a protected-mode peer server on either a Microsoft network (with or without a Windows NT server) or a NetWare network.

▶ You can use different networking protocols to connect to multiple networks simultaneously.

▶ Windows 95 comes with a raft of network management tools and the ability to interact with third-party network management SNMP tools.

▶ You can configure your computer to allow remote administration.

▶ You don't have to map networked printers or drives to local logical ports or drive letters to access them using the universal naming convention.

Part VI

Windows 95 Shareware

Chapter 37: The Best in Windows Shareware

Chapter 37

The Best in Windows Shareware

The *Windows 95 Secrets, 4th Edition* CD-ROM contains hundreds of freeware and shareware programs — more software than we have ever been able to feature in previous *Windows Secrets* CD-ROMs. We are pleased to offer you this huge sampling of the best Windows shareware programs.

What Is Shareware?

Shareware refers to "try before you buy" software that is distributed electronically or on disks by software authors. You get a trial period to use the software — usually 30 days. After this period, you are required to register with the software author if you continue to use the software. Each program has its own accompanying file that explains how to register. Note that you do not receive a license to the software with the *Windows 95 Secrets, 4th Edition* CD-ROM. In this regard, the *Windows 95 Secrets, 4th Edition* CD-ROM is like a trial shareware diskette from a shareware catalog. If you plan to use a shareware program after the trial period, you should register it with the author.

Shareware is copyrighted software that is owned by the software author. We, the authors of *Windows 95 Secrets,* are authorized vendors of the Association of Shareware Professionals (ASP), and have permission from the ASP and from individual shareware authors to distribute their shareware to the public.

The two of us, as co-authors, have registered scores of shareware programs over the years, paying whatever registration fees were required. The benefits of registration have far outweighed the small registration fees. The upgraded versions, free additional software, and other offers continue to amaze us. Shareware programs are truly the biggest bargain in the software industry today.

What Is Freeware?

Freeware refers to programs that require no registration fee. Some freeware programs are also called *public domain* software. This means the software author has released the copyright to the program, and anyone may use the software for any purpose. Most freeware, however, is not in the public domain, and you should not assume you can use a freeware program for a commercial purpose (bundling it with retail software, for example) without contacting the software author for permission.

Freeware programs come with no technical support. If certain programs do not work on your system, try other similar programs on the CD-ROM.

The CD-ROM and Software Are Copyrighted

The software on the *Windows 95 Secrets, 4th Edition* CD-ROM is copyrighted by the various shareware authors, and the CD-ROM and its installation routines are copyrighted by the co-authors of *Windows 95 Secrets*. You may copy the contents of the CD-ROM to your personal computer system, but you may not distribute or sell the contents of the CD-ROM or bundle it with any product that is for sale without permission from the copyright holders.

How Do I Get Technical Support?

All Windows programs have bugs. This includes all retail Windows software and all shareware featured on the *Windows 95 Secrets, 4th Edition* CD-ROM. Every program, no matter how simple, has some unexpected behavior. This is the nature of software, and bugs are usually fixed with the release of a newer version.

Most shareware authors, but not all, provide technical support to users after they register. Some shareware authors provide limited technical support to unregistered users if they have problems installing the software. In either case, the best way to get technical support is to look in the text file or help file that accompanies each program and send electronic mail to the e-mail address listed there. Some shareware authors also provide technical support by fax or by U.S. mail. Shareware authors do not usually have a technical support telephone line, although some do for registered users.

Many shareware authors maintain web sites for registration and technical support purposes. The best way to contact shareware authors is through their web site, if they have one. A shareware developer's web site may contain updated versions of a program, entirely new programs, and information about accessory or related products. You may also be able to leave e-mail at the site for the author. Most shareware authors check and respond to their electronic messages once or more each business day.

If a program is freeware, it probably has no technical support. In this case, if a program does not work on your particular PC configuration, you probably will not be able to obtain technical support for it.

The co-authors of this book, and IDG Books Worldwide, Inc., are not familiar with the details of every program and do not provide any technical support for the programs on the *Windows 95 Secrets, 4th Edition* CD-ROM. The programs are supplied as is. Brian Livingston, Davis Straub, and IDG Books Worldwide individually and together disclaim all warranties, expressed or implied, including, without limitation, the warranties of merchantability and of fitness for any particular purpose; and assume no liability for damages, direct or consequential, which may result from the use of the programs or reliance on the documentation.

See the *IDG Books Worldwide License Agreement* at the back of the book for a complete description of the uses and limitations of the CD-ROM and the programs it contains.

What Do I Get if I Register?

We strongly encourage you to register any shareware you use past the initial "try before you buy" free evaluation period. Registration brings you a variety of benefits. Each program has its own set of registration benefits which are described in the accompanying text or help files. Depending on the specific program, you may receive one or more of the following:

■ At the very least, you receive a permanent license to use the program on your PC.

■ In most cases, you receive the capability to upgrade to a future version of the program with features that may significantly enhance the version you have.

■ In most cases, you are entitled to receive technical support to configure the software for optimum performance on your particular type of PC. This technical support is usually provided by electronic mail, in which case you receive a response directly from the software authors in a matter of hours. In other cases, technical support is also provided by fax, by mail, or by telephone.

■ Sometimes you receive a printed manual with more detail or better illustrations than can be provided in the shareware version. If you register multiple copies for a company installation, you may be able to receive a copy of the printed materials for each of the users in your company.

■ In a few cases, you may receive a diskette that contains "bonus" shareware programs along with the registered version of the program you licensed. Some shareware authors include a whole mini-library of shareware programs along with your registered diskette.

■ In *all* cases, when you register shareware, you help finance the development of new Windows shareware programs. This helps to bring new "killer apps" to the shareware marketplace — which you can, again, try out in advance, like all shareware.

Shareware Registration from Outside the U.S.

Most of the shareware authors in the U.S. require payment "in U.S. funds, drawn on a U.S. bank." The reason for this requirement is that U.S. banks charge large fees — sometimes more than the entire registration fee for a shareware package — to accept non-U.S. checks.

If you want to register a shareware package with a shareware author who lives in a different country, you can send payment in the form of a Postal International Money Order with a U.S. dollar amount. These money orders are available at most post offices around the world and are accepted without a fee by all U.S. post offices and by many U.S. banks. If you are in Europe, do not send Eurochecks to U.S. shareware authors because Eurochecks are not accepted by U.S. banks.

Why Have Shareware Registration Notices?

All shareware programs have some kind of popup window that lets you know how to contact the author and register the program. Some programs display this window after you click Help About or another menu choice, while others display it automatically when you start or exit the program.

The ASP specifically allows this type of reminder notice. It does not cripple a program in any way, but provides the user with the address of the shareware author and an incentive to register.

We view these incentives like the membership appeals you sometimes hear on listener-supported radio stations. The appeals are slightly annoying, but the stations could not continue to broadcast without the memberships they receive. Similarly, the shareware authors cannot continue to distribute their programs without the registrations they receive. Reminder notices — which disappear totally after you register a package — are a slight irritation but are well justified by the full functionality (no crippling) you get in a true shareware package.

What Is the Association of Shareware Professionals?

Shareware has become an accepted means of distributing serious software. In the mid-1980s shareware authors began to feel a need for a nonprofit organization to promote this new form of distribution. As a result, they formed the Association of Shareware Professionals (ASP) in 1987 to "strengthen the future of 'shareware' (user-supported software) as an alternative to software distributed under normal retail marketing methods."

The ASP certifies programs as meeting its criteria for shareware and also sponsors events at computer industry shows. If you are a software author, the ASP may help you find distribution channels for your programs. For more information, visit the ASP web site at http://www.asp-shareware.org.

The ASP Ombudsman program

To resolve any questions about the role of shareware — registrations, licenses, and so on — the ASP established an ombudsman program to hear all parties.

Not every shareware author represented on the *Windows 95 Secrets, 4th Edition* CD-ROM is a member of the ASP, but a good number of shareware authors *are* members. ASP members usually list this fact in the text or help files that accompany their programs.

If you have a problem with a software author who is an ASP member, and you have tried unsuccessfully to resolve the problem directly with that author, the ASP ombudsman may find a remedy. Remember that you cannot expect technical support from the author of a program unless you are a registered user of that program.

As the ASP's literature describes it, "The ASP wants to make sure that the shareware concept works for you. If you are unable to resolve a shareware-related problem with an ASP member by contacting the member directly, the ASP may be able to help. The ASP Ombudsman can help you resolve a dispute or problem with an ASP member, but does not provide technical support for members' products."

You can write to the ASP Ombudsman at 545 Grover Road, Muskegon, MI, 49442, or send e-mail to 70007.3536@compuserve.com.

General ASP license agreement

Each of the shareware programs on the accompanying disk has its own license agreement and terms. These may be found in a text or help file accompanying each program. In general, you should assume that any shareware program adheres to at least the following license terms suggested by the ASP, where *Program* is the specific shareware program, and *Company* is the program's author or publisher:

The Program is supplied as is. The author disclaims all warranties, expressed or implied, including, without limitation, the warranties of merchantability and of fitness for any purpose. The author assumes no liability for damages, direct or consequential, which may result from the use of the Program.

The Program is a "shareware program," and is provided at no charge to the user for evaluation. Feel free to share it with your friends, but please do not give it away altered or as part of another system. The essence of "user-supported" software is to provide personal computer users with quality software without high prices, and yet to provide incentives for programmers to continue to develop new products. If you find this Program useful, and find that you continue to use the Program after a reasonable trial period, you must make a registration payment to the Company. The registration fee will license one copy for one use on any one computer at any one time. You must treat this software just like a copyrighted book. An example is that this software may be used by any number of people and may be freely moved from one computer location to another as long as there is no possibility of it being used at one location while it's being used at another — just as a book cannot be read by two different persons at the same time.

Commercial users of the Program must register and pay for their copies of the Program within 30 days after first use or their license is withdrawn. Site-license arrangements may be made by contacting the Company.

Anyone distributing the Program for any kind of remuneration must first contact the Company at the address provided for authorization. This authorization will be automatically granted to distributors recognized by the ASP as adhering to its guidelines for shareware distributors, and such distributors may begin offering the Program immediately. (However, the Company must still be advised so that the distributor can be kept up-to-date with the latest version of the Program.)

You are encouraged to pass a copy of the Program along to your friends for evaluation. Please encourage them to register their copy if they find that they can use it. All registered users will receive a copy of the latest version of the Program.

Tips for New Windows Users

If you are a relatively new user of Windows, or PCs in general, the following tips can help you get the most out of your system.

How to add a program to a new directory or folder

Always install a new program into its own directory (or *folder*). Do not install a program into your Windows folder (such as C:\Windows) unless you are specifically instructed to do so by a program's documentation or installation instructions. Also, do not install a program into the root directory of your C drive (C:\) or into a folder that already contains another program. It would be a bad idea, for example, to create a folder called C:\Games and then install all game programs into that folder. Some files may have the same name, which would cause problems with other programs and would also make it hard to remove a particular program at a later date.

When you run a setup program and you are given a choice of which folder to install the program into, type a new folder name, such as **C:\Blue** for a program named Blue, or **C:\Red** for a program named Red.

How to add an application to your path

Windows programs do not need to be on the path (a listing of folders Windows will search in for programs) as much as they used to in the early days of Windows. However, if the documentation for a program asks that you "place it on the path," here's how to do it.

In Windows 95, click the Start button on the Taskbar, and then click Run. In the Run dialog box, type the command **Notepad C:\Autoexec.bat** and click OK. In the Autoexec.bat file, you should see a line that reads like the following:

```
path=c:\win95;c:\win95\command;c:\bat
```

This line indicates that three folders are on the path: the Windows 95 folder, the DOS 7 folder (called Win95\Command), and a folder containing batch files.

To add a folder, add a semicolon (;) to the end of the line, and then type the full name of the folder. If you added the folder C:\Calendar, for example, your path statement would look like this:

```
path=c:\win95;c:\win95\command;c:\bat;c:\calendar
```

You must save the file, exit Windows 95, and restart your PC for the change to take effect.

If you are at a plain DOS prompt, you can type **Edit C:\Autoexec.bat** to run a character-based editor to make changes in your Autoexec.bat file.

You must make sure that your path statement does not exceed 127 characters (including the word *path* and the equal sign). The characters after the 127th are ignored as part of the path, but they can cause strange behavior. If your path gets too long, you must take some folders out of the path or change their names to shorter alternatives.

How to make an application run when you start Windows 95

To make an application load automatically every time you run Windows 95, you must place a shortcut for that program in the Startup folder. One way to do this is with the Windows 95 Explorer. Find a copy of the program you want to start up every time. Use your *right* mouse button to drag the program's icon to the C:\Win95\Start Menu\Programs\Startup folder. Drop the icon on this folder, and click Create Shortcut(s) Here in the context menu that appears. (Do *not* click Copy Here or Move Here, which can create problems running your application.)

The Best Is Yet to Come

On the *Windows 95 Secrets, 4th Edition* CD-ROM, we have featured some of the best and most popular Windows shareware and freeware available today. Some of the software is specific for Windows 95 (with support for long filenames, for example), while some software is still available only in a Windows 3.1 version (supports only 8-character filenames). To the best of our knowledge, we have not included any programs that are not appropriate for Windows 95, such as utilities and shells that work poorly or not at all in the Windows 95 environment.

We hope you enjoy using the programs on the *Windows 95 Secrets, 4th Edition* CD-ROM.

Index

(continued)

(continued)

(continued)

If you liked this book...

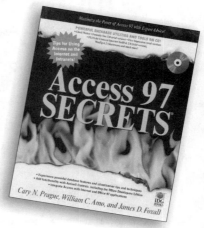

Bible Series

Comprehensive Tutorial/Reference Books with 100% of What You Need to Know

Bibles help readers reach higher skill levels by providing comprehensive information on a product or technology. Authors have extensive know-ledge of the topic through years of experience and provide numerous step-by-step examples, real-live uses, and much more.

Office 97 Bible
Ed Jones & Derek Sutton
0-7645-3037-2
$39.99 U.S./ $54.99 Canada
pp. 1200

Excel 97 Bible
John Walkenbach
0-7645-3036-4
$34.99 U.S./ $48.99 Canada
pp. 944

Word 97 Bible
Brent Heslop & David Angell
0-7645-3038-0
$34.99U.S./ $48.99 Canada
pp. 1008

Access 97 Bible
Cary N. Prague &
Michael R. Irwin
Updated Bestseller
0-7645-3035-6
$49.99 U.S.
$69.99 Canada
pp. 1128
Bonus CD-ROM

Intranet Bible
Ed Tittel & James Michael Stewart
0-7645-8013-2
$49.99 U.S.
$69.99 Canada
pp. 912
Bonus CD-ROM

To Order Call
800-762-2974

Notes